Microsoft

MCSE

Exam
70-270

Microsoft® Windows® XP Professional

Training Kit

PUBLISHED BY
Microsoft Press
A Division of Microsoft Corporation
One Microsoft Way
Redmond, Washington 98052-6399

Library of Congress Cataloging-in-Publication Data.
    MCSE Training Kit : Microsoft Windows XP Professional (Exam 70-270) / Microsoft Corporation
          p. cm.
       Includes index.
       ISBN 0-7356-1429-6
       1. Electronic data processing persnnel--Certification. 2. Microsoft Windows XP.   3.
    Operating Systems (Computers)

    QA76.3 .M3283   2001
    005.4'4769--dc21   2001055807

Printed and bound in the United States of America.

6 7 8 9   QWT   8 7 6 5 4

Distributed in Canada by H.B. Fenn and Company Ltd.

A CIP catalogue record for this book is available from the British Library.

Microsoft Press books are available through booksellers and distributors worldwide. For further information about international editions, contact your local Microsoft Corporation office or contact Microsoft Press International directly at fax (425) 936-7329. Visit our Web site at www.microsoft.com/mspress. Send comments to *tkinput@microsoft.com*.

Acquisitions Editor: Thomas Pohlmann
Project Editor: Karen Szall

Author: Rick Wallace

Body Part No. X08-06100

Contents

About This Book

Welcome to *MCSE Training Kit—Microsoft Windows XP Professional.* This kit introduces you to the Microsoft Windows XP Professional operating system and prepares you to install, configure, and support Windows XP Professional.

This kit prepares you to install Windows XP Professional from a CD-ROM or over the network, to perform unattended installations of Windows XP Professional, and to install Windows XP Professional using Remote Installation Services (RIS) and the System Preparation tool. It also prepares you to upgrade previous versions of Windows to Windows XP Professional, to perform postinstallation updates and product activation, to avoid problems during installation, and to troubleshoot problems you might encounter during installation.

This kit introduces the various tools for administering, configuring, and troubleshooting Windows XP Professional. These tools include Microsoft Management Console (MMC), Group Policy snap-in, Local Computer snap-in, Task Scheduler, Task Manager, Control Panel, Device Manager, Event Viewer, the registry, Help and Support Center, and the various troubleshooters included with Windows XP Professional.

You will also learn about the network protocols and services that ship with Windows XP Professional. This kit concentrates on Transmission Control Protocol/Internet Protocol (TCP/IP), the network protocol of choice for Windows XP Professional. It introduces you to the Domain Name System (DNS), which is an Internet and TCP/IP standard name service, and is required for Microsoft Windows 2000 domains and directory services based on Active Directory technology.

This training kit also covers setting up, configuring, administering, and troubleshooting common problems for network printers. It helps you understand NTFS permissions, special permissions, and shared folder permissions, and prepares you to assign and troubleshoot permissions. It covers auditing resources and events, configuring security settings and Internet options, managing data storage, and more.

Note For more information about becoming a Microsoft Certified Systems Engineer, see the section titled "The Microsoft Certified Professional Program" later in this chapter.

Each chapter in this book is divided into lessons. Most lessons include hands-on procedures that allow you to practice or demonstrate a particular concept or skill. Each lesson ends with a set of review questions to test your knowledge of the lesson material and a short summary of the major points covered in the lesson.

The "Getting Started" section of this chapter provides important setup instructions that describe the hardware and software requirements to complete the procedures in this course. It also provides information about the networking configuration necessary to complete some of the hands-on procedures. Read through this section thoroughly before you start the lessons.

Intended Audience

Anyone who wants to learn about Windows XP Professional will find this book useful. This book was developed for information technology (IT) professionals who need to design, plan, implement, and support Windows XP Professional or who plan to take the related Microsoft Certified Professional exam 70-270, *Installing, Configuring, and Administering Microsoft Windows XP Professional.*

Prerequisites

This course requires that students meet the following prerequisite: a knowledge of the fundamentals of current networking technology.

Reference Materials

You might find the *Microsoft Windows XP Professional Resource Kit* a useful reference for this training kit.

About the CD-ROM

The Supplemental Course Materials compact disc contains a variety of informational aids that can be used throughout this book. This includes demonstrations for many of the practices, multimedia presentations, electronic books (eBooks), and a sample of the test questions from the *MCSE Microsoft Windows XP Professional Readiness Review; Exam 70-270.* For more information regarding the contents of this CD-ROM, see the section titled "Getting Started" later in this introduction.

The Training Kit Demos supplement some of the key concepts covered in the book. You should view these demonstrations when suggested, and then use them as a review tool while you work through the material. In addition, demonstrations are provided from the Microsoft Official Curriculum (MOC) 2272: *Implementing and Supporting Microsoft Windows XP Professional.* For more information about viewing the demonstrations, see the section "About the Demos" later in this introduction.

Complete electronic versions of this book (eBook) and the *Microsoft Encyclopedia of Networking* are also available along with a variety of viewing options. For information about using the eBooks, see the section "About the eBooks" later in this introduction.

Features of This Book

Each chapter opens with a "Before You Begin" section, which prepares you for completing the chapter.

▶   The chapters are then divided into lessons. Whenever possible, lessons contain practices that give you an opportunity to use the skills being presented or explore the part of the application being described. All practices offer step-by-step procedures that are identified with a bullet symbol like the one to the left of this paragraph.

The "Review" section at the end of each lesson allows you to test what you have learned. The "Summary" section at the end of each lesson identifies the key concepts from the lesson.

Appendix A, "Questions and Answers," contains all of the questions asked in each chapter and the corresponding answers.

Notes

Several types of Notes appear throughout the lessons.

- Notes marked **Tip** contain explanations of possible results or alternative methods for performing tasks.

- Notes marked **Important** contain information that is essential to completing a task.

- Notes marked **Note** contain supplemental information.

- Notes marked **Caution** contain warnings about possible loss of data.

Conventions

The following conventions are used throughout this book.

Notational Conventions

- Characters or commands that you type appear in **bold** type.

- *Italic* in syntax statements indicates placeholders for variable information. *Italic* is also used for book titles.

- Names of files appear in full capital letters, except when you are to type them directly. Unless otherwise indicated, you can use all lowercase letters when you type a filename in a dialog box or at a command prompt.

- Filename extensions, when they appear without a filename, are in all lowercase letters.

- Acronyms appear in all uppercase letters.

- `Monospace` type represents code samples, examples of screen text, or entries that you might type at a command prompt or in initialization files.

- Square brackets [ ] are used in syntax statements to enclose optional items. For example, [*filename*] in command syntax indicates that you can choose to type a filename with the command. Type only the information within the brackets, not the brackets themselves.

- Braces { } are used in syntax statements to enclose required items. Type only the information within the braces, not the braces themselves.

- Icons represent specific sections in the book as follows:

Icon	Represents
	A multimedia presentation. You will find the applicable multimedia presentation on the course compact disc.
	A hands-on practice. You should perform the practice to give yourself an opportunity to use the skills being presented in the lesson.
	Lesson review questions. These questions at the end of each lesson allow you to test what you have learned in the lessons. You will find the answers to the review questions in the Questions and Answers appendix at the end of the book.

Keyboard Conventions

- A plus sign (+) between two key names means that you must press those keys at the same time. For example, "Press ALT+TAB" means that you hold down ALT while you press TAB.

- A comma (,) between two or more key names means that you must press each of the keys consecutively, not together. For example, "Press ALT, F, X" means that you press and release each key in sequence. "Press ALT+W, L" means that you first press ALT and W at the same time, and then release them and press L.

- You can choose menu commands with the keyboard. Press the ALT key to activate the menu bar, and then sequentially press the keys that correspond to the highlighted or underlined letter of the menu name and the command name. For some commands, you can also press a key combination listed in the menu.

- You can select or clear check boxes or option buttons in dialog boxes with the keyboard. Press the ALT key, and then press the key that corresponds to the underlined letter of the option name. Or you can press TAB until the option is highlighted, and then press SPACEBAR to select or clear the check box or option button.

- You can cancel the display of a dialog box by pressing the ESC key.

Chapter and Appendix Overview

This self-paced training course combines notes, hands-on procedures, demonstrations, multimedia presentations, sample test questions, and review questions to teach you how to install, configure, administer, and support Windows XP Professional. It is designed to be completed from beginning to end, but you can choose a customized track and complete only the sections that interest you. (See the next section, "Finding the Best Starting Point for You," for more information.) If you choose the customized track option, see the "Before You Begin" section in each chapter. Any hands-on procedures that require preliminary work from preceding chapters refer to the appropriate chapters.

The book is divided into the following chapters:

- The "About This Book" section contains a self-paced training overview and introduces the components of this training. Read this section thoroughly to get the greatest educational value from this self-paced training and to plan which lessons you will complete.

- Chapter 1, "Introduction to Windows XP Professional," introduces a number of the features and enhancements incorporated into Windows XP Professional since the release of Microsoft Windows 2000. It also presents the features available in Help and Support Center, introduces workgroups and domains, and explains logging on and off Windows XP Professional.

- Chapter 2, "Installing Windows XP Professional," prepares you to install Microsoft Windows XP Professional from a CD-ROM or over the network. It presents some preinstallation tasks that help ensure your installation will go smoothly and some tips on troubleshooting common errors you might encounter during setup. This chapter also covers upgrading earlier versions of Windows to Windows XP Professional. In the hands-on practices, you install Windows XP Professional from a CD-ROM onto your computer.

- Chapter 3, "Setting Up and Managing User Accounts," prepares you to plan, create, and manage Windows XP Professional local user accounts. It also presents the skills and knowledge necessary to set properties for these accounts. This chapter also prepares you to create, add users to, remove users from, and delete local groups, and it introduces you to built-in local groups and built-in system groups. In the hands-on practices, you create local user accounts using both the User Accounts tool and the Computer Management snap-in. You assign passwords to user accounts, test the user accounts, and delete a user account. You modify user account properties and test them. Finally, you create local groups, add members to the local groups, and then remove a member from a group.

- Chapter 4, "Installing, Configuring, and Troubleshooting Network Protocols," prepares you to install, configure, and troubleshoot TCP/IP and NWLink. It also discusses the process for configuring network bindings, which are links that enable communication among network adapter cards, protocols, and services. The hands-on practices allow you to verify your computer's configuration and then configure your computer to use a static Internet Protocol (IP) address. Next, you configure your computer to use a Dynamic Host Configuration Protocol (DHCP) server to automatically assign an IP address to your computer, and test the Automatic Private IP Addressing feature. Finally, you install and configure NWLink, change the binding order, unbind a protocol, bind a protocol, and then uninstall NWLink.

- Chapter 5, "Using the DNS Service and Active Directory Service," introduces Domain Name System (DNS), a distributed database that is used in TCP/IP networks to translate computer names to IP addresses. It also presents the skills and knowledge necessary to configure clients to use the DNS Service. In the hands-on practice you configure a computer running Windows XP Professional to be a DNS client. It also presents the Windows 2000 Active Directory service structure and replication. The Active Directory service provides a single point of network management, allowing you to add, remove, and relocate users and resources easily. Active Directory service is only available with the Windows 2000 Server products.

- Chapter 6, "Setting Up, Configuring, and Troubleshooting Common Setup and Configuration Problems for Network Printers," introduces you to Windows XP printing terminology and presents the skills and knowledge necessary to set up and share network printers. This chapter introduces the Network Setup Wizard, which you must run before you can share a printer or a folder on a computer running Windows XP Professional in a workgroup environment. In the hands-on practices, you run the Network Setup Wizard and then use the Add Printer Wizard to install and share a local printer.

- Chapter 7, "Administering and Troubleshooting Common Administrative Problems for Network Printers," presents the four major types of tasks involved with administering printers: managing printers, managing documents, troubleshooting common printer problems, and performing tasks that require the Manage Printers permission. This chapter shows you how to control printer usage and administration by assigning permissions. In the hands-on practices, you learn how to manage printers by assigning forms to paper trays and setting up a separator page. You also perform a task that requires the Manage Printers permission by taking ownership of a printer. Finally, you manage documents by printing a document, setting a notification for a document, changing the priority for a document, and then canceling a document.

- Chapter 8, "Securing Resources with NTFS Permissions," introduces the NTFS folder and file permissions and explains how to assign them to user accounts and groups. It explains how copying and moving files and folders affects NTFS file and folder permissions. It also covers how to troubleshoot common resource access problems. In the hands-on practices, you plan and apply NTFS permissions for folders and files based on business scenarios, and then test them. You also observe the effects of taking ownership of a file, and determine the effects of permission and ownership when you copy or move files.

- Chapter 9, "Administering Shared Folders," explains how to share folders so that the folders and their contents are accessible over the network. This chapter also explains how sharing folders provides another way to secure file resources, one that can be used on file allocation table (FAT), FAT32, and NTFS partitions. In the hands-on practices, you share a folder, determine the current permissions for the shared folder, assign shared folder permissions to groups, and stop sharing a folder. In the optional hands-on practices, you connect to a shared folder and test the combined effects of shared folder permissions and NTFS permissions.

- Chapter 10, "Configuring Windows XP Professional," explains how to use the Control Panel to configure and troubleshoot the display, including multiple displays; power management features, including System Power Management, Device Power Management, Processor Power Management, System Events, and Battery Management; and operating system settings. This chapter also explains how to configure and troubleshoot the Windows XP Professional desktop, including multiple languages and multiple locations and accessibility options. Finally, this chapter explains how to use the Add or Remove Programs tool in Control Panel to manage programs and Windows components on your computer. In the hands-on practices you configure power options and change operating system settings, including the default Remote Assistance setting and the paging file size. You add and test a new system environment variable, and configure multiple languages and multiple locations.

- Chapter 11, "Installing, Managing, and Troubleshooting Hardware Devices and Drivers," introduces Device Manager, a tool for implementing, managing, and troubleshooting hardware devices and drivers. This chapter explains how to install, configure, manage, and troubleshoot fax support and I/O devices. It also explains how to use Control Panel to view and configure hardware profiles. This chapter also explains how to use Device Manager to configure, monitor, and troubleshoot driver signing and upgrade your computer from a single-processor to multiprocessor system. In the hands-on practices you use Device Manager to review the devices on your system and their status, and to simulate troubleshooting an unterminated Small Computer System Interface (SCSI) chain. You also use File Signature Verification to monitor and troubleshoot driver signing on your system.

- Chapter 12, "Auditing Resources and Events," introduces Microsoft Windows XP Professional Group Policy. One of the features controlled by the Group Policy snap-in is auditing. This chapter explains audit policies, what you need to consider before you set one up, how to set up auditing on resources, and how to maintain security logs. This chapter also introduces Event Viewer, a tool used to perform a variety of tasks, including viewing the audit logs that are generated as a result of setting the audit policy and auditing events, and viewing the contents of application and security log files. In the hands-on practices you plan an audit policy, set up an audit policy by enabling auditing on certain events, and set up auditing of a file and a printer. Then you view the security log file and configure Event Viewer to overwrite events when the log file is filled.

- Chapter 13, "Configuring Security Settings and Internet Options," explains how to improve the security on your computer. It explains how to configure security settings that include Account Policies and Local Policies. This chapter also explains how to improve the security of your computer by configuring Internet Options to control and secure the way Microsoft Internet Explorer interacts with the Internet. In the hands-on practices, you configure Account Policy settings and then test them. You then configure the security settings and automatically rename the Guest account on your computer.

- Chapter 14, "Managing Data Storage," introduces data storage management on volumes formatted with NT file system (NTFS), including compression, disk quotas, and how you can increase the security of files and folders on your computer by using the Microsoft Encrypting File System (EFS). This chapter also introduces Disk Defragmenter, Check Disk, and Disk Cleanup, which are tools that help you organize your hard disks, recover readable information from damaged areas on your hard disk, and clean up any temporary files and unnecessary programs taking up space on your hard drive. In the hands-on practices you use NTFS compression to compress files and folders, uncompress a file, and test the effects that copying and moving files have on compression. You also create a compressed folder using the Compressed Folders feature. You configure default quota management settings, configure a custom quota setting, increase the amount of data a user can store on a drive, and turn off quota management.

- Chapter 15, "Monitoring, Managing, and Maintaining Network Resources," prepares you to use the Shared Folders snap-in to view and create shares, view sessions, open files, and disconnect users from your shared folders. This chapter also prepares you to use offline folders and files and to use Synchronization Manager to synchronize the cached files and folders on your local disk with those stored on the network. This chapter also covers Scheduled Tasks, used to schedule programs and batch files to run once, at regular intervals or at specific times. In the hands-on practices you use the Shared Folders snap-in to view the shared folders and open files on your server. You use the Computer Management snap-in to create a shared folder on your computer. You then use the Shared Folders snap-in to send a console message. You configure a computer running Windows XP Professional so that you can use offline folders and files. You configure a network share so users can access the files in the share and use them offline and then configure Synchronization Manager. Finally, you use Scheduled Tasks to start Address Book at a predetermined time and configure Task Scheduler options.

- Chapter 16, "Backing Up and Restoring Data," introduces the Backup Utility, which allows you to back up data and settings, restore data and settings, and perform an Automated System Recovery Backup. It prepares you to plan your backups and it introduces the five backup types—normal, copy, incremental, differential, and daily—and how these can be combined to meet your needs. In the hands-on practices, you use the Backup or Restore Wizard to back up some files to your hard disk, and you create a backup job to perform a backup operation later using Task Scheduler. You then restore some of the files you backed up.

- Chapter 17, "Configuring Network and Internet Connections," presents the New Connection Wizard, which guides you through creating network and Internet connections. It also introduces Internet Connection Firewall (ICF), which protects your network from attack; Internet Connection Sharing (ICS), which allows you to share one connection to the Internet with all computers on your network; and Network Bridge, which allows you to connect local area network (LAN) segments. Finally, it reviews the Network Setup Wizard, which helps you configure and set up your network. In the hands-on practices, you use the New Connection Wizard to configure an inbound connection and to configure an outbound connection to a private network. Finally, you enable and configure ICF and ICS.

- Chapter 18, "Modifying and Troubleshooting the Boot Process," introduces you to the Windows XP Professional boot process. You learn about the registry, a hierarchical database in which Windows XP Professional stores hardware and software settings, and how to use the Registry Editor to view and change the registry configuration. You also learn about some of the other tools and options that Windows XP Professional provides to help you troubleshoot problems with starting your computer and recovering from disasters. These tools include safe mode, LastKnownGood configuration, and the Recovery Console. In the hands-on practices, you use Registry Editor to view the information in the registry, use the Find Key command to search the registry, and modify the registry by adding a value to it. You also install the Recovery Console, review the commands available in it, use the Listsvc command to view all services, and then use the Disable command to disable the Alerter service.

- Chapter 19, "Deploying Windows XP Professional," prepares you to automate the installation of Windows XP Professional. It introduces you to the Windows Setup Manager so that you can easily create UNATTEND.TXT files for scripted installations. It introduces you to disk duplication, which is used to deploy Windows XP Professional, and to the most efficient method of deploying Windows XP Professional, remote installation. It also introduces the Files and Settings Transfer Wizard and reviews how Windows XP Professional allows you to apply a service pack at the same time that you install Windows XP. In the hands-on practices, you extract the Windows XP Professional Deployment Tools from the Windows XP Professional CD-ROM and use System Manager to create an unattended setup script. You also use the Windows System Preparation tool to prepare a master image for disk duplication and use that image to install Windows XP Professional. There are also some optional practices in which you install and configure Windows 2000 Remote Installation Services from a Windows 2000 Server CD-ROM. You learn about some tools that help with your Windows XP Professional deployment.

- Appendix A, "Questions and Answers," lists all of the review questions from the book, showing the page number on which the question appears and the suggested answer.

- The glossary provides definitions for many of the key words and concepts presented in the course. It also contains some additional basic networking terminology.

Finding the Best Starting Point for You

Because this book is self-paced, you can skip some lessons and revisit them later. But note that you must complete the procedures in Chapter 2, "Installing Windows XP Professional," before you can perform procedures in the other chapters. Use the following table to find the best starting point for you:

If you	Follow this learning path
Are preparing to take the Microsoft Certified Professional exam 70-270, *Installing, Configuring, and Administering Microsoft Windows XP Professional.*	Read the "Getting Started" section. Then work through Chapters 1 and 2. Work through the remaining chapters in any order.
Want to review information about specific topics from exam 70-270, *Installing, Configuring, and Administering Microsoft Windows XP Professional.*	Use the "Where to Find Specific Skills in This Book" section that follows this table.

Where to Find Specific Skills in This Book

The following tables provide a list of the skills measured on certification exam 70-270, *Installing, Configuring, and Administering Microsoft Windows XP Professional.* The table describes the skill and indicates where in this book you will find lessons relating to that skill.

Note   Exam skills are subject to change without prior notice and at the sole discretion of Microsoft.

Installing Windows XP Professional

Skill Being Measured	Location in Book
Performing an attended installation of Windows XP Professional	Chapter 2, Lessons 2 and 3
Performing an unattended installation of Windows XP Professional:	
■ Install Windows XP Professional using Remote Installation Services (RIS)	Chapter 19, Lesson 3
■ Install Windows XP Professional using the System Preparation Tool	Chapter 19, Lesson 2
■ Create unattended answer files by using Setup Manager to automate the installation of Windows XP Professional	Chapter 19, Lesson 1
Upgrading from a previous version of Windows to Windows XP Professional:	
■ Prepare a computer to meet upgrade requirements	Chapter 2, Lesson 4

Installing Windows XP Professional   *(continued)*

Skill Being Measured	Location in Book
■ Migrate existing user environments to a new installation	Chapter 19, Lesson 4
Performing postinstallation updates and product activation	Chapter 2, Lesson 2 and Chapter 10, Lesson 3
Troubleshooting failed installations	Chapter 2, Lesson 5

Implementing and Conducting Administration of Resources

Skill Being Measured	Location in Book
Monitoring, managing, and troubleshooting access to files and folders: ■ Configure, manage, and troubleshoot file compression	Chapter 14, Lesson 1
■ Control access to files and folders by using permissions	Chapter 8, Lessons 1, 2, and 3
■ Optimize access to files and folders	Chapter 8, Lessons 1, 2, and 3
Managing and troubleshooting access to shared folders: ■ Create and remove shared folders	Chapter 9, Lessons 1 and 2, and Chapter 15, Lessons 1 and 2
■ Control access to shared folders using permissions	Chapter 9, Lesson 3
■ Manage and troubleshoot Web server resources	Chapter 9, Lessons 2 and 3
Connecting to local and network print devices: ■ Manage printer and print jobs	Chapter 7, Lesson 1
■ Control access to printers by using permissions	Chapter 7, Lesson 1
■ Connect to an Internet printer	Chapter 6, Lesson 3
■ Connect to a local printer	Chapter 6, Lesson 2
Configuring and managing file systems: ■ Convert from one file system to another file system	Chapter 2, Lesson 1
■ Configure NTFS, FAT32, or FAT file systems	Chapter 2, Lesson 2 and Chapter 19, Lesson 4
Managing and troubleshooting access to and synchronization of offline files	Chapter 15, Lesson 4
Configuring and troubleshooting fax support	Chapter 11, Lesson 2

**Implementing, Managing, Monitoring, and Troubleshooting
Hardware Devices and Drivers**

Skill Being Measured	Location in Book
Implementing, managing, and troubleshooting disk devices: ■ Install, configure, and manage DVD and CD-ROM devices	Chapter 11, Lessons 1 and 2
■ Monitor and configure disks	Chapter 15, Lesson 6 and Chapter 19, Lesson 4
■ Monitor, configure, and troubleshoot volumes	Chapter 19, Lesson 4
■ Monitor and configure removable media, such as tape devices	Chapter 11, Lessons 1 and 2
Implementing, managing, and troubleshooting display devices: ■ Configure multiple-display support ■ Install, configure, and troubleshoot a video adapter	Chapter 10, Lesson 1
Configuring Advanced Configuration Power Interface (ACPI)	Chapter 10, Lesson 2
Implementing, managing, and troubleshooting input and output (I/O) devices: ■ Monitor, configure, and troubleshoot I/O devices, such as printers, scanners, multimedia devices, mouse and pointing devices, keyboard, and smart card readers	Chapter 6, Lessons 1–5, Chapter 7, Lessons 1–5, and Chapter 11, Lessons 1 and 2
■ Monitor, configure, and troubleshoot multimedia hardware, such as cameras	Chapter 11, Lessons 1 and 2
■ Install, configure, and manage modems	Chapter 11, Lessons 1 and 2
■ Install, configure, and manage Infrared Data Association (IrDA) devices	Chapter 11, Lessons 1 and 2
■ Install, configure, and manage wireless devices	Chapter 11, Lessons 1 and 2
■ Install, configure, and manage USB devices	Chapter 11, Lessons 1 and 2
■ Install, configure, and manage handheld devices	Chapter 11, Lessons 1 and 2
Managing and troubleshooting drivers and driver signing	Chapter 11, Lesson 4
Monitoring and configuring multiprocessor computers	Chapter 11, Lesson 5

Monitoring and Optimizing System Performance and Reliability

Skill Being Measured	Location in Book
Monitoring, optimizing, and troubleshooting performance of the Windows desktop:	
■ Optimize and troubleshoot memory performance	Chapter 10, Lesson 3
■ Optimize and troubleshoot processor utilization	Chapter 10, Lesson 3
■ Optimize and troubleshoot disk performance	Chapter 15, Lesson 6
■ Optimize and troubleshoot application performance	Chapter 10, Lesson 3
■ Configure, manage, and troubleshoot Scheduled Tasks	Chapter 15, Lesson 5
Managing, monitoring, and optimizing system performance for mobile users	Chapter 10, Lesson 3 and Chapter 15, Lesson 6
Restoring and backing up the operating system, system state data, and user data:	
■ Recover system state data and user data using Windows Backup	Chapter 16, Lessons 1, 2, and 3
■ Troubleshoot system restoration by starting in safe mode	Chapter 18, Lesson 3
■ Recover system state data and user data using the Recovery Console	Chapter 18, Lesson 3

Configuring and Troubleshooting the Desktop Environment

Skill Being Measured	Location in Book
Configuring and managing user profiles	Chapter 3, Lesson 4
Configuring support for multiple languages or multiple locations	Chapter 10, Lesson 4
■ Enable multiple-language support	
■ Configure multiple-language support for users	
■ Configure local settings	
■ Configure Windows XP Professional for multiple locations	
Managing applications using Windows Installer packages	Chapter 19, Lesson 4
Configuring and troubleshooting desktop settings	Chapter 10, Lessons 1–4
Configuring and troubleshooting accessibility services	Chapter 10, Lesson 4

Implementing, Managing, Monitoring, and Troubleshooting Network Protocols and Services

Skill Being Measured	Location in Book
Configuring and troubleshooting the TCP/IP protocol	Chapter 4, Lessons 1 and 2
Connecting to computers using dial-up networking:	
■ Connect to computers by using a virtual private network (VPN) connection	Chapter 17, Lessons 1 and 2
■ Create dial-up connection to connect to a remote access server	Chapter 17, Lesson 2
■ Connect to the Internet using dial-up networking	Chapter 17, Lesson 2
■ Configure and troubleshoot Internet Connection Sharing	Chapter 17, Lesson 3
Connecting to resources using Internet Explorer	Chapter 6, Lesson 3 and Chapter 9, Lesson 2
Configuring, managing, and implementing Internet Information Services (IIS)	Chapter 10, Lesson 5
Configuring, managing and troubleshooting Remote Desktop and Remote Assistance	Chapter 10, Lesson 3
Configuring, managing, and troubleshooting an Internet Connection Firewall	Chapter 17, Lesson 3

Configuring, Managing, and Troubleshooting Security

Skill Being Measured	Location in Book
Configuring, managing, and troubleshooting Encrypting File System (EFS)	Chapter 14, Lesson 3
Configuring, managing, and troubleshooting local security policy	Chapter 12, Lessons 1–3 and Chapter 13, Lessons 1–3
Configuring, managing, and troubleshooting local user and group accounts	
■ Configure, manage, and troubleshoot auditing	Chapter 12, Lessons 1–3
■ Configure, manage, and troubleshoot account settings	Chapter 3, Lesson 1–4
■ Configure, manage, and troubleshoot account policy	Chapter 13, Lesson 1
■ Configure and troubleshoot local users and groups	Chapter 3, Lesson 1–5
■ Configure, manage, and troubleshoot user and group rights	Chapter 13, Lesson 2
■ Troubleshoot cache credentials	Chapter 13, Lesson 3
Configuring, managing, and troubleshooting a security configuration	Chapter 13, Lessons 1–3
Configuring, managing, and troubleshooting Internet Explorer security settings	Chapter 13, Lesson 4

Getting Started

This self-paced training course contains hands-on procedures to help you learn about Windows XP Professional.

To complete the optional practices, you must have two networked computers or be connected to a larger network. One computer must be capable of running Windows XP Professional and the other must be capable of running Windows 2000 Server.

Caution   Several exercises might require you to make changes to your computers, such as changing your TCP/IP address. This could have undesirable results if you are connected to a larger network. Check with your network administrator before attempting these exercises.

Hardware Requirements

Each computer must have the following minimum configuration. All hardware should be on the Microsoft Windows XP Professional Hardware Compatibility List.

- 233 megahertz (MHz) or equivalent Intel Pentium-compatible CPU
- 64 megabytes (MB) minimum memory (128 MB recommended)
- 1.5 GB hard disk space on a 2 GB hard disk minimum
- Network adapter card, related cable (hub or connection to an existing network is required for the optional practices)
- Video display adapter and monitor with Video Graphics Adapter (VGA) resolution or higher
- CD-ROM drive, 12× or faster recommended (not required for installing Windows XP Professional over a network) or DVD drive
- Keyboard
- Microsoft Mouse or compatible pointing device

Software Requirements

The following software is required to complete the procedures in this course:

- Microsoft Windows XP Professional on either a CD-ROM or a network share
- For the optional exercises, a computer running Windows 2000 Server and configured as a domain controller

Setup Instructions

Set up your computer according to the manufacturer's instructions. You can create a partition for installing Windows XP Professional before or during the installation process. If you create the installation partition before the install, it must be at least 1.5 GB in size, though a larger partition is recommended, and be on a hard disk that is at least 2 GB. This is the only computer required to complete this course and is the computer on which you will install Windows XP Professional.

For the optional exercises, which require networked computers, you need to make sure the computers can communicate with each other. The additional computer will be running Windows 2000 Server, configured as a primary domain controller (PDC), and assigned the computer account name Server1 and the domain name Domain1. This computer acts as a domain controller and a DNS server, and it can also function as the DHCP server in Domain1.

Caution   If your computers are part of a larger network, you *must* verify with your network administrator that the computer names, TCP/IP addresses, domain name, and other information used in setting up Windows XP Professional as described in Chapter 2, "Installing Windows XP Professional," do not conflict with network operations. If they do conflict, ask your network administrator to provide alternative values and use those values throughout all of the exercises in this book.

About the Demos

The Supplemental Course Materials CD-ROM contains two sets of audiovisual demonstration files that you can view by running the files from the CD-ROM. For the Training Kit Demos, you will find a prompt within the book indicating when the demonstration should be run. You do not need any additional software to view these files.

The Microsoft Official Curriculum (MOC) Demos provide simulations from MOC course 2272: *Implementing and Supporting Microsoft Windows XP Professional*. These demos help explain the installation and implementation of Windows XP Professional. You can find more information about available training and training providers at: *www.microsoft.com/trainingandservices/*

▶   **To view the demonstrations**

1. Insert the Supplemental Course Materials CD-ROM into your CD-ROM drive.

Note   If AutoRun is disabled on your machine, refer to the README.TXT file on the CD-ROM.

2. Click Training Kit Demos or MOC Demos on the user interface menu and then select the demonstration you want to view.

For additional information about the MOC Demos, see the README.TXT file on the CD-ROM.

About the eBooks

The CD-ROM also includes an eBook for this training kit and one for the *Microsoft Encyclopedia of Networking*.

► **To use the eBooks**

1. Insert the Supplemental Course Materials CD-ROM into your CD-ROM drive.

Note If AutoRun is disabled on your machine, refer to the README.TXT file on the CD-ROM.

2. To install the eBook for this training kit, click Training Kit eBook on the user interface menu and follow the prompts.
3. To install the eBook for the *Microsoft Encyclopedia of Networking*, click Encyclopedia eBook and follow the prompts.

Note You must have the Supplemental Course Materials CD-ROM inserted in your CD-ROM drive to run the eBook.

About the Sample Exam Questions

The CD-ROM contains a sample of the exam questions from the *MCSE Microsoft Windows XP Professional Readiness Review; Exam 70-270*. This sample provides you with a demonstration of the exam questions and a sample of the format that is provided with the Readiness Review. For more information about this book, go to: *www.microsoft.com/mspress/*

The Microsoft Certified Professional Program

The Microsoft Certified Professional (MCP) program provides the best method to demonstrate your command of current Microsoft products and technologies. Microsoft, an industry leader in certification, is on the forefront of testing methodology. Our exams and corresponding certifications are developed to validate your mastery of critical competencies as you design and develop, or implement and support, solutions with Microsoft products and technologies. Computer professionals who become Microsoft certified are recognized as experts and are sought after industry-wide.

The Microsoft Certified Professional program offers multiple certifications, based on specific areas of technical expertise:

- *Microsoft Certified Professional (MCP).* Demonstrated in-depth knowledge of at least one Microsoft certification area. Candidates may pass additional Microsoft certification exams to further qualify their skills with Microsoft BackOffice products, development tools, or desktop programs.

- *Microsoft Certified Systems Engineer (MCSE)*. Qualified to effectively plan, implement, maintain, and support information systems in a wide range of computing environments with Microsoft Windows NT Server and the Microsoft BackOffice integrated family of server software.
- *Microsoft Certified Database Administrator (MCDBA)*. Individuals who derive physical database designs, develop logical data models, create physical databases, create data services by using Transact-SQL, manage and maintain databases, configure and manage security, monitor and optimize databases, and install and configure Microsoft SQL Server.
- *Microsoft Certified Solution Developer (MCSD)*. Qualified to design and develop custom business solutions with Microsoft development tools, technologies, and platforms, including Microsoft Office and Microsoft BackOffice.
- *Microsoft Certified Trainer (MCT)*. Instructionally and technically qualified to deliver Microsoft Official Curriculum through a Microsoft Certified Technical Education Center (CTEC).

Microsoft Certification Benefits

Microsoft certification, one of the most comprehensive certification programs available for assessing and maintaining software-related skills, is a valuable measure of an individual's knowledge and expertise. Microsoft certification is awarded to individuals who have successfully demonstrated their ability to perform specific tasks and implement solutions with Microsoft products. Not only does this provide an objective measure for employers to consider; it also provides guidance for what an individual should know to be proficient. As with any skills-assessment and benchmarking measure, certification brings a variety of benefits to the individual and to employers and organizations.

Microsoft Certification Benefits for Individuals

As an MCP, you receive many benefits:

- Industry recognition of your knowledge and proficiency with Microsoft products and technologies.
- Access to technical and product information direct from Microsoft through a secured area of the MCP Web site (go to *www.microsoft.com/ trainingandservices/* then expand the Certification node from the tree directory in the left margin, and then select the For MCPs Only link).
- Access to exclusive discounts on products and services from selected companies. Individuals who are currently certified can learn more about exclusive discounts by visiting the MCP secured Web site (go to *www.microsoft.com/ trainingandservices/*, then expand the Certification node from the tree directory in the left margin, and then select the For MCPs Only link) and select the Other Benefits link.

- MCSE logo, certificate, transcript, wallet card, and lapel pin to identify you as an MCP to colleagues and clients. Electronic files of logos and transcripts may be downloaded from the MCP secured Web site (go to *www.microsoft.com/ trainingandservices/*, then expand the Certification node from the tree directory in the left margin, and then select the For MCPs Only link) upon certification.

- Invitations to Microsoft conferences, technical training sessions, and special events.

- Free access to *Microsoft Certified Professional Magazine Online,* a career and professional development magazine. Secured content on the *Microsoft Certified Professional Magazine Online* Web site includes the current issue (available only to MCPs), additional online-only content and columns, an MCP-only database, and regular chats with Microsoft and other technical experts.

An additional benefit is received by MCSEs:

- A 50 percent rebate or discount off the estimated retail price of a one-year subscription to *TechNet* or *TechNet Plus* during the first year of certification. (Fulfillment details will vary, depending on your location. Please see your Welcome Kit.) In addition, about 95 percent of the CD-ROM content is available free online at the *TechNet* Web site (*www.microsoft.com/technet/*).

Microsoft Certification Benefits for Employers and Organizations

Through certification, computer professionals can maximize the return on their investment in Microsoft technology. Research shows that Microsoft certification provides organizations with the following:

- Excellent return on training and certification investments by providing a standard method of determining training needs and measuring results.

- Increased customer satisfaction and decreased support costs through improved service, increased productivity, and greater technical self-sufficiency.

- Reliable benchmark for hiring, promoting, and career planning.

- Recognition and rewards for productive employees by validating their expertise.

- Retraining options for existing employees so they can work effectively with new technologies.

- Assurance of quality when outsourcing computer services.

To learn more about how certification can help your company, see the backgrounders, white papers, and case studies available at *www.microsoft.com/ trainingandservices/* (expand the Certification node from the tree directory in the left margin, and then select the Case Studies link):

- A white paper, MCSE Criterion Validity Study White Paper, Oct. 1998, which evaluates the MCSE certification

- IDC Case Study

- Compaq Case Study
- CrossTier.com Case Study
- Extreme Logic Case Study
- Financial Benefits to Supporters of Microsoft Professional Certification, IDC white paper
- Lyondel Case Study
- Prudential Case Study
- Stellcom Case Study
- Unisys Case Study

Requirements for Becoming a Microsoft Certified Professional

The certification requirements differ for each certification and are specific to the products and job functions addressed by the certification.

To become a Microsoft Certified Professional, you must pass rigorous certification exams that provide a valid and reliable measure of technical proficiency and expertise. These exams are designed to test your expertise and ability to perform a role or task with a product, and are developed with the input of industry professionals. Questions in the exams reflect how Microsoft products are used in actual organizations, giving them real-world relevance.

Microsoft Certified Product Specialists are required to pass one current exam. Candidates may pass additional Microsoft certification exams to further qualify their skills with Microsoft BackOffice products, development tools, or desktop applications.

Microsoft Certified Systems Engineers are required to pass a series of core Microsoft Windows operating system and networking exams, demonstrating a technical proficiency and expertise in solution design and implementation.

Microsoft Certified Database Administrators are required to pass three core exams and one elective exam that provide a valid and reliable measure of technical proficiency and expertise.

Microsoft Certified Solution Developers are required to pass three core Microsoft Windows operating system technology exams and one BackOffice technology elective exam.

Microsoft Certified Trainers are required to meet instructional and technical requirements specific to each Microsoft Official Curriculum course they are certified to deliver. For more information about becoming an MCT, visit *www.microsoft.com/trainingandservices/* (expand the Certification node from the tree directory in the left margin, and then select the MCT link) or contact a regional service center near you.

Technical Training for Computer Professionals

Technical training is available in a variety of ways, with instructor-led classes, online instruction, or self-paced training available at thousands of locations worldwide.

Self-Paced Training

For motivated learners who are ready for the challenge, self-paced instruction is the most flexible, cost-effective way to increase your knowledge and skills.

A full line of self-paced print and computer-based training materials is available direct from the source—Microsoft Press. Microsoft Official Curriculum courseware kits designed for advanced computer system professionals are available from Microsoft Press and the Microsoft Developer Division. Self-paced training kits from Microsoft Press feature print-based instructional materials, along with CD-ROM–based product software, multimedia presentations, lab exercises, and practice files. The Mastering Series provides in-depth, interactive training on CD-ROM for experienced developers. They're both great ways to prepare for MCP exams.

Online Training

For a more flexible alternative to instructor-led classes, turn to online instruction. It's as near as the Internet and it's ready whenever you are. Learn at your own pace and on your own schedule in a virtual classroom, often with easy access to an online instructor. Without ever leaving your desk, you can gain the expertise you need. Online instruction covers a variety of Microsoft products and technologies. It includes options ranging from Microsoft Official Curriculum to choices available nowhere else. It's training on demand, with access to learning resources 24 hours a day. Online training is available through Microsoft Certified Technical Education Centers.

Microsoft Certified Technical Education Centers

Microsoft Certified Technical Education Centers (CTECs) are the best source for instructor-led training that can help you prepare to become a Microsoft Certified Professional (MCP). The Microsoft CTEC program is a worldwide network of qualified technical training organizations that provide authorized delivery of Microsoft Official Curriculum courses by Microsoft Certified Trainers to computer professionals.

For a listing of CTEC locations in the United States and Canada, visit *http://www.microsoft.com/CTEC/*.

Technical Support

Every effort has been made to ensure the accuracy of this book and the contents of the companion disc. If you have comments, questions, or ideas regarding this book or the companion disc, please send them to Microsoft Press using either of the following methods:

E-mail
TKINPUT@MICROSOFT.COM

Postal Mail
Microsoft Press
Attn: *MCSE Training Kit—Microsoft Windows XP Professional* Editor
One Microsoft Way
Redmond, WA 98052-6399

Microsoft Press provides corrections for books through the World Wide Web at the following address:

www.microsoft.com/mspress/support/

Please note that product support is not offered through the above mail addresses. For further information regarding Microsoft software support options, please connect to *www.microsoft.com/support/* or call Microsoft Support Network Sales at (800) 936-3500.

For information about ordering the full version of any Microsoft software, please call Microsoft Sales at (800) 426-9400 or visit *www.microsoft.com*.

CHAPTER 1

Introduction to Windows XP Professional

About This Chapter

This book is written to prepare you to install, configure, and support Windows XP Professional. This chapter introduces you to some of the areas in which Microsoft has improved Microsoft Windows XP Professional over earlier versions of Microsoft Windows. It also describes the features available in Windows XP Professional Help and Support Center, introduces the concepts of workgroups and domains, and explains how to log on and off Windows XP Professional.

Before You Begin

There are no special requirements to complete this chapter.

Lesson 1: Exploring New Features and Improvements

This lesson introduces a number of the features and enhancements incorporated into Windows XP Professional since the release of Microsoft Windows 2000.

After this lesson, you will be able to

- Identify the key new features of Windows XP Professional

Estimated lesson time: 45 minutes

Automatic Updates

Windows XP Professional includes an Automatic Updates (AU) feature. AU is a proactive service that allows users with administrative privileges to automatically download and install critical operating system updates, such as security fixes and patches. Because the installation might require you to restart your computer, you are notified before the installation takes place and given the opportunity to postpone the download operation. Updates are downloaded in the background so that you can continue to work during downloading.

AU uses the Windows Update control to scan the system and decide which updates apply to a particular computer. AU uses its innovative bandwidth-throttling technology for downloads. Bandwidth throttling uses only idle bandwidth so that downloads do not interfere with or slow down other network activity, such as Internet browsing. Only one administrative user at a time can run the AU client.

Note   For more information about the Automatic Updates feature, see Chapter 10, "Configuring Windows XP Professional."

Copying Files and Folders to a CD

Windows XP Professional enables users to save information such as photos and software to a compact disc (CD) without using third-party software. Because CD-recordable (CD-R) and CD-rewritable (CD-RW) drives are now inexpensive options on computers, this feature enhances the standard conveniences that Windows offers to users.

Users can select a folder of images from a digital camera, drag it to the CD-R icon, and then create a CD. They can also transfer files more easily to a CD instead of copying them to a smaller capacity floppy disk.

This feature also provides options for original equipment manufacturers (OEMs) and independent software vendors (ISVs). OEMs can create branded applications that generate emergency boot CDs instead of emergency boot floppy disks, and ISVs can offer a "burn to CD" option on their Windows versions.

To copy files or folders to a CD follow these steps:

1. Insert a blank, writable CD into the CD recorder.

   You must have a blank, writable CD and a CD-ROM drive that has the capability of writing CDs to use this feature.

2. Click Start, right-click My Computer, then click Explore, and then select the files and folders you want to write to the CD.

3. Under File And Folder Tasks, click Copy This File, Copy This Folder, or Copy The Selected Items.

4. In the Copy Items dialog box, click the CD recording drive and then click Copy.

5. In My Computer, click the CD recording drive and then under CD Writing Tasks, click Write These Files To The CD.

Note Standard CDs hold 650 MB of information. High-density CDs hold at least 700 MB of information. You must have enough space on your hard drive to temporarily hold the files you want to copy to the CD or the operation will fail.

ClearType Support

Windows XP Professional supports ClearType, a new text display technology. ClearType triples the horizontal resolution available for rendering text through software, which provides a clearer text display on a liquid crystal display (LCD) screen with digital interface.

To specify ClearType follow these steps:

1. Click Start and then click Control Panel.

2. Click Appearance And Themes, and then click Display.

3. In the Appearance And Themes dialog box, click Appearance.

4. In the Appearance tab, click Effects.

5. Select the Use The Following Method To Smooth Edges Of Screen Fonts check box, and then select ClearType from the drop-down list (see Figure 1.1).

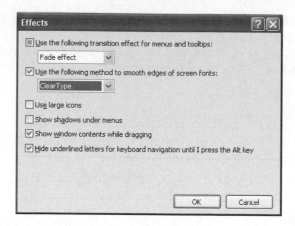

Figure 1.1   The Effects dialog box

6. Click OK to close the Effects dialog box.
7. Click OK to close the Display Properties dialog box.

Compressed Folders

The Compressed Folders feature provides the ability to create ZIP folders and view their contents. Compressed folders allow you to compress large files so that you can store more files on a floppy disk or hard drive.

To create a compressed folder follow these steps:

1. Click Start, right-click My Computer, and then click Explore.
2. Select a local drive letter, such as C:.
3. On the File menu, click New, and then click Compressed Folder.

Note   If you drag and drop files and folders into a compressed folder, they will be compressed. You cannot save a file to a compressed folder.

Desktop Cleanup Wizard

The Desktop Cleanup Wizard helps keep your desktop uncluttered by periodically checking for unused shortcuts and removing them without harming the installed program. By default, the Desktop Cleanup Wizard checks for unused shortcuts every 60 days and offers to move them to a folder on the desktop called Unused Desktop Shortcuts.

To run the Desktop Cleanup Wizard follow these steps:

1. Click Start, and then click Control Panel.
2. Click Appearance And Themes, and then click Display.
3. Click Desktop and then click Customize Desktop.

Windows XP Professional displays the Desktop Items dialog box, as shown in Figure 1.2.

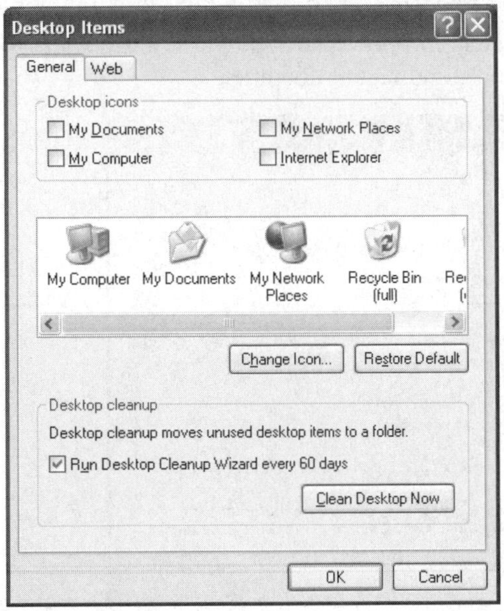

Figure 1.2   The Desktop Items dialog box

4. Under Desktop Cleanup, click Clean Desktop Now to run the Desktop Cleanup Wizard now.

Start Menu

The Start menu has been redesigned for easier access to important and frequently used tasks. In addition to prominent Internet and e-mail links, the new Start menu lists the programs that you use most frequently. Windows XP Professional continually updates this list based on your usage of programs. It adds programs that you are using and removes programs from the list that you have not been using. Windows XP Professional does not remove the programs from your computer, just from this list. The Start menu also lists important user folders such as My Documents, My Pictures, and My Music.

To customize the Start menu follow these steps:

1. Right-click Start, and then click Properties.

2. Click the Start Menu tab.

   The Start Menu tab lets you choose between the Windows XP Professional Start menu and the Classic Start menu used in earlier versions of Windows.

3. Click Customize.

   The Customize Start Menu dialog box has two tabs: General and Advanced.

The General tab allows you to select an icon size for programs, configure the amount of frequently used programs you want displayed on the Start menu, and select the Internet and e-mail items shown on the Start menu.

The Advanced tab, shown in Figure 1.3, allows you to configure Start menu settings, items, and recent documents.

Figure 1.3   The Advanced tab of the Customize Start Menu dialog box

Fax Support

Windows XP Professional provides fax support that enables you to send faxes over a network from a computer with an attached fax modem or fax board or with a local area network (LAN) connection. You can print to fax from any application, send cover fax pages, and track and monitor faxes. New wizards enable simpler configuration of this feature and fax sending.

IT administrators can use the Component Object Model (COM) application programming interface (API) to control fax capabilities and the Microsoft Management Console (MMC) to set up the fax service within their infrastructure. Developers can use COM to send faxes programmatically. In addition, they can use the fax APIs to write applications to automatically send faxes.

To send or manage faxes follow these steps:

1. Click Start, point to All Programs, and point to Accessories.
2. Point to Communications and point to Fax.

Note   For more information about fax support, see Chapter 11, "Installing, Managing, and Troubleshooting Hardware Devices and Drivers."

Fast User Switching for Multiple Users of a Computer

The Fast User Switching feature allows multiple users to simultaneously share a computer without closing all of their applications first. For example, if you are creating a Microsoft Word document and leave your computer for a short time, Fast User Switching permits another person to use your computer to access another computer account—perhaps to find a customer's account balance—while leaving your Word session open. All of this is done without either of you logging off the computer.

Note   For more information about Fast User Switching, see Chapter 3, "Setting Up and Managing User Accounts."

Locale Support Additions and Regional Options Enhancements

A locale is a set of cultural and regional preferences that correspond to a user's language and sublanguage (for example, Canadian French and U.K. English). Compared with Windows 2000 Professional, this feature adds support for the following locales: Galician, Gujarati, Kannada, Kyrgyz, Mongolian (Cyrillic), Punjabi, Divehi, Syriac, and Telugu. The feature also includes enhancements to the Regional and Language Options control panel.

Note   For more information about Locale Support and the Regional and Language Options enhancements, see Chapter 10, "Configuring Windows XP Professional."

Auto-Configuration for Multiple Network Connectivity

The Auto-Configuration for Multiple Network Connectivity feature provides easy access to network devices and the Internet. It also allows a mobile computer user to seamlessly operate both office and home networks without manually reconfiguring Transmission Control Protocol/Internet Protocol (TCP/IP) settings.

You can use this feature to specify an alternate configuration for TCP/IP if a Dynamic Host Configuration Protocol (DHCP) server is not found. The alternate configuration is useful when a computer is used on multiple networks, one of which does not have a DHCP server and does not use an automatic private Internet Protocol (IP) addressing configuration.

Note   For more information on specifying an alternate configuration for TCP/IP for multiple network connectivity, see Chapter 4, "Installing, Configuring, and Troubleshooting Network Protocols."

Microsoft Internet Explorer 6.0

Microsoft Internet Explorer 6.0 provides visual refresh and enhanced support for Document Object Model (DOM) Level 1 and Cascading Style Sheets (CSS) Level 1. Internet Explorer 6.0 also provides the following features:

- Media acquisition enhancements, which include a shortcut menu to make saving images more discoverable and support for My Videos and My Music folders as defaults for those media types.
- Native support for Macromedia Flash and Macromedia Shockwave Player files.
- Automatic Image Resize, which allows you to automatically resize an image to fit entirely within the current browser frame. This feature works only when you have directly navigated to an image; it does not resize images embedded within Hypertext Markup Language (HTML) pages.

Networking has also been enhanced to include changes to cookie handling for improved privacy, and changes to Passport and other authentication dialogs to allow a more integrated password and credential management.

Note   For more information about configuring Internet Explorer, see Chapter 13, "Configuring Security Settings and Internet Options."

Instant Messaging

Instant Messaging allows users to quickly communicate with one another over the Internet. Internet Explorer 6.0 includes the ability to show MSN Messenger, Outlook Express, and Outlook contacts in a side panel. The Windows Messenger in Windows XP Professional offers multimedia audio, video, and data real-time communication over the Internet. All you need is a .NET passport, which you can create using your Microsoft Hotmail account or using MSN Messenger, and a dial-in connection to the Internet. If you want real-time audio and video, you will need a microphone and a Web cam.

To access Instant Messaging follow these steps:

1. Click Start, point to All Programs, and then click Windows Messenger.
2. Double-click the contact name for the person you want to talk to that shows up under Online.

Note   If you are using a Web cam, you will have to click Start for the camera and both you and your friend will need to be using Windows Messenger and have audio/video enabled on your computers.

Internet Connection Firewall (ICF)

Microsoft designed the Internet Connection Firewall (ICF) for use in the home and by small businesses. It provides protection on computers directly connected to the Internet. It is available for LAN or dial-up networking, virtual private networking (VPN), and Point-to-Point Protocol over Ethernet (PPPoE) connections. It also prevents scanning of ports and resources (file and printer shares) from external resources.

Note For more information about Internet Connection Firewall, see Chapter 17, "Configuring Network and Internet Connections."

Terminal Services: Remote Desktop and Remote Desktop Connection

Windows XP Professional includes two Terminal Services features: Remote Desktop and Remote Desktop Connection. Remote Desktop provides access to a desktop from any Terminal Services client. It also allows you to access the following:

- The full set of installed applications, work in progress, and all connectivity usually found on a workstation or server
- Sessions on a computer running Windows 2000 Server products that can be used for computer administration or server-based computing

In addition, Remote Desktop enables Remote Console access, allowing the primary screen output to be redirected to a Terminal Server client.

The Remote Desktop Connection feature is the end-user tool for establishing connections to computers running Terminal Services. Corporate employees who work at home, using a line-of-business application that is hosted on a Terminal Server, can use the Remote Access Service (RAS) to dial in and the Remote Desktop Connection to use the application. Remote Desktop Connection has many features that allow optimization for almost any network speed.

To access the Remote Desktop Connection follow these steps:

1. Click Start, and then point to All Programs.
2. Point to Accessories, point to Communications, then click Remote Desktop Connection, and then click Options.

   Windows XP Professional displays the Remote Desktop Connection dialog box, as shown in Figure 1.4.

Figure 1.4   The Remote Desktop Connection dialog box

WebDAV Redirector

The Web Distributed Authoring and Versioning (WebDAV) redirector is a new mini-redirector that supports the WebDAV protocol for remote document sharing over Hypertext Transfer Protocol (HTTP). The WebDAV redirector supports the use of existing applications and allows file sharing across the Internet (through firewalls and routers) to HTTP servers. For example, the WebDAV redirector allows users at different locations to share and collaborate on a file. A user can also use WebDAV redirectors to publish Web data, or make use of Internet repositories for storing data or sharing information with family and friends.

To use the WebDAV redirector follow these steps:

1. Click Start, and then click My Computer. Click My Network Places.
2. Under Network Tasks, click Add A Network Place.

   Windows XP Professional starts the Add Network Place Wizard.
3. Click Next in the Welcome screen.

   The Add Network Place Wizard displays the Where Do You Want To Create This Network Place dialog box (see Figure 1.5).
4. Follow the instructions for adding a shortcut to a Web site that supports Web folders (WebDAV).

Note   The Web server must support Web folders (the WebDAV protocol) and Microsoft Internet Information Services (IIS) or the Web Extender Client (WEC) protocol and FrontPage extensions.

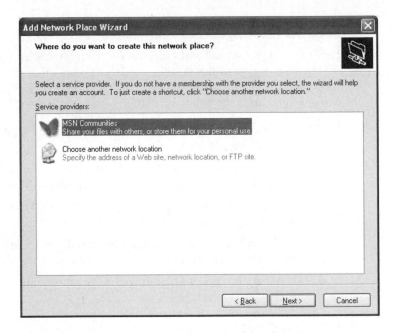

Figure 1.5   The Where Do You Want To Create This Network Place dialog box

Web Publishing

The Web Publishing feature enables users to publish files to a Web-hosting service. This feature uses the .NET Passport Wizard to sign up for passports so a user does not need to enter a password at the Web site.

Note   To publish files, click Start, click My Documents, and select the files you want to publish. Under File And Folder Tasks, click Publish This File To The Web. In the Web Publishing Wizard page, click Next. In the Destination Web Site page, select a destination location for your files, and then follow the wizard prompts to complete publishing the files.

Welcome Screen

The Welcome screen provides the ability to set up multiple user accounts on one computer. You create these accounts during Setup or from the Control Panel. The separate accounts establish profiles that separate each user's data. By default, the accounts are not password protected, but users can set passwords on their specific accounts if they want.

Note   For more information about configuring the Welcome screen, see Chapter 3, "Setting Up and Managing User Accounts."

Lesson Review

The following questions will help you determine whether you have learned enough to move on to the next lesson. If you have difficulty answering these questions, review the material in this lesson before beginning the next lesson. The answers are in Appendix A, "Questions and Answers."

1. Which of the following statements about Automatic Updates (AU) are correct? (Choose all that apply.)

   a. AU is a proactive service that runs in the background and automatically detects, downloads, and installs Windows updates on a computer.

   b. AU allows multiple administrative users to run the AU client concurrently.

   c. AU allows users with administrative privileges to automatically download and install Windows updates on a computer.

   d. AU uses only idle bandwidth so that downloads do not interrupt or slow down other network activity.

2. What is ClearType support?

3. The Desktop Cleanup Wizard helps you keep your desktop free of _____ that you don't use regularly. By default, it runs every _____ days.

4. What does the Fast User Switching for Multiple Users of a Computer feature provide on computers running Windows XP Professional?

5. Internet Explorer version _____ comes included with Windows XP Professional.

Lesson Summary

- AU is a proactive service that allows users with administrative privileges to automatically download and install Windows updates, such as security fixes and patches, on a computer.

- The CD Burning feature enables users to save information to a CD as easily as to a floppy or hard disk.

- Windows XP Professional supports ClearType, a new text display technology that triples the horizontal resolution available for rendering text through software. This feature provides a clearer text display on an LCD screen with digital interface.

- The Compressed Folders feature allows you to drag and drop files and folders into a compressed folder to compress large files. This enables you to store more files on a floppy or hard drive and to easily send large files as an attachment in e-mail.

- Windows XP Professional fax support enables users to send faxes using their network.

- Fast User Switching allows multiple users to share a computer without forcing each user to close all running applications and log off before another user can log on to the computer.

- Instant Messaging allows users to quickly communicate with one another using multimedia audio, video, and data real-time communication over the Internet.

- Internet Connection Firewall (ICF) protects computers in the home and small businesses environment.

- The Web Distributed Authoring and Versioning (WebDAV) redirector is a new mini-redirector that supports the WebDAV protocol for remote document sharing over HTTP.

Lesson 2: Troubleshooting Using Help and Support Center

Microsoft has greatly enhanced and improved the Help and Support Center in Windows XP Professional. This lesson acquaints you with the features available in Help and Support Center.

After this lesson you will be able to

- Identify the features in and use the Windows XP Professional Help and Support Center

Estimated lesson time: 15 minutes

Assisted Support

Windows XP Professional now includes two Assisted Support services— Microsoft Incident Submission and Management and Windows Newsgroups— which help users resolve computer support issues.

Microsoft Incident Submission and Management

The Microsoft Incident Submission and Management feature allows you to submit electronic support incidents to Microsoft, collaborate with support engineers, and manage submitted incidents. For example, if you are having problems installing drivers for new hardware on your computer, you can launch Help and Support to submit an electronic incident report to Microsoft.

To access Help and Support follow these steps:

1. Click Start.
2. Click Help And Support.

   Windows XP Professional displays the Help And Support Center window, as shown in Figure 1.6.

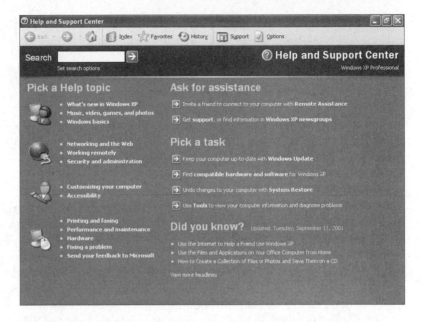

Figure 1.6   Help And Support Center window

Windows Newsgroups

Windows Newsgroups provide valuable information to help you resolve computer support issues in a free, online setting. You can use the connectionless message boards and the real-time chat rooms to get answers quickly without submitting incident reports to a Microsoft or OEM support organization. The goal of this feature is to promote Windows and MSN Community offerings in Windows XP Professional Help and Support, as well as to encourage users to add or extend this service in their own communities.

To access the Windows Newsgroups follow these steps:

1. Click Start, and then click Help And Support.
2. In the Help And Support Center window, under Get Assistance, click Get Support Or Find Information In Windows XP Newsgroups.

Compatible Hardware and Software

The Compatible Hardware and Software feature provides up-to-date, comprehensive, user-friendly hardware and software compatibility information to aid users in upgrading equipment, making purchasing decisions, and troubleshooting problems. For example, if you purchase an application that requires a 3-D accelerator card, you might not know which cards are compatible with your computer. You can use Help and Support to run a comprehensive query and find compatible 3-D accelerator cards. You can run queries based on manufacturer, product type, software, or hardware. The Microsoft compatibility teams use data from user interactions, independent hardware vendors (IHVs), and ISVs to improve their products.

To access the Compatible Hardware and Software feature follow these steps:

1. Click Start, and then click Help And Support.
2. In the Help And Support Center window, under Pick A Task, click Find Compatible Hardware And Software For Windows XP.

Full-Text Search

The Windows Help system uses HTML to format and display information. If you have an Internet connection, you can search for every occurrence of a word or phrase across all Windows compiled HTML Help files. Because the Windows Help System is also extensible, multiple search engines can plug into the Help and Support Center application using a set of standard interfaces. Users can search for content across multiple remote and online providers. For example, you can search for information resident on your computer or located remotely in the Microsoft Knowledge Base or in a participating OEM's knowledge base.

Note   The Microsoft Knowledge Base is a comprehensive database containing detailed articles with technical information about Microsoft products, fix lists, documentation errors, and answers to commonly asked technical support questions. To access Knowledge Base, connect to the following address: *http:// search.support.microsoft.com/kb/c.asp*

To access Full Text Search follow these steps:

1. Click Start, and then click Help And Support.

2. In the Help And Support Center window, in the Search box, type in the text you want to find.

3. To control how the search will be performed, click Set Search Options (see Figure 1.7).

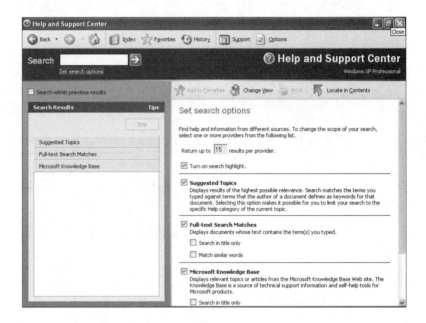

Figure 1.7   Help And Support Center Set Search Options window

My Computer Information

My Computer Information provides an easily understood, highly accessible view of personalized software and hardware information about your computer or another computer for which you have administrative permissions.

To access My Computer Information follow these steps:

1. Click Start, and then click Help And Support.

2. In the Help And Support Center window, under Pick A Task, click Use Tools To View Your Computer Information And Diagnose Problems.

3. Under Tools, click My Computer Information.

You can view information in five categories, as described in the following sections.

View General System Information about This Computer

The My Computer Information – General category allows you to view information about your computer such as the computer manufacturer, model, basic input/output system (BIOS) version, processor version and speed, operating system, amount of memory, and amount of available disk space.

View the Status of My System Hardware and Software

The My Computer Information – Status category allows you to examine diagnostic information about your computer, including the following:

- Obsolete applications and device drivers
- System software
- Hardware: video card, network card, sound card, and universal serial bus (USB) controller
- Hard disks
- Random access memory (RAM)

Find Information about the Hardware Installed on This Computer

The Computer Information – Hardware category allows you to examine descriptive information about your computer's hardware including the local disk, display, video card, modem, sound card, USB controller, network cards, CD-ROM drives, floppy drives, memory, and printers.

View a List of Microsoft Software Installed on This Computer

The Software category allows you to view a list of Microsoft products that are installed and registered by a product identification (PID) number on your computer, including products that run automatically from Startup. It also shows you Windows Watson Crash Information about any software that crashed while running on your computer.

View Advanced System Information

Advanced System Information allows you to choose from the following options:

- View Detailed System Information (MSINFO32.EXE). This option allows you to view detailed information on hardware resources, components (multimedia, input, network, ports, and storage), software environment, and Internet settings, as shown in Figure 1.8.

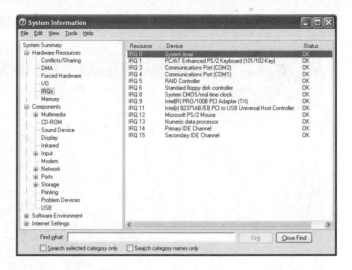

Figure 1.8   The System Information window

- View Running Services.
- View Group Policy Settings Applied.
- View The Error Log.
- View Information For Another Computer. If you have administrative permissions on a remote computer, you can view My Computer Information on that remote computer. If you click View Computer Information On Another Computer, the Web Page dialog box appears prompting you to enter the name of the remote computer you want to view. Enter the remote computer name and then click Open to view the remote computer information.

Multiple Instances

You can open two sessions of the Help and Support Center application at the same time. Running concurrent sessions enables you to submit incident reports while looking at Help or System Information.

Printing

The Help and Support Center application allows you to print an entire chapter of Help content with one print command; that is, it can iteratively print all available topics in a specified node. If some topics are not available because of network connection problems, Windows XP Professional prints only the available content. After you have located the information you want to print, click Print (see Figure 1.9).

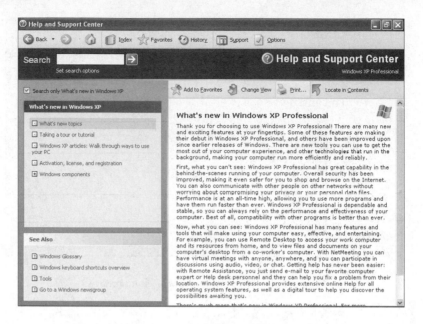

Figure 1.9   The Help And Support Center Print option

Remote Assistance

The Remote Assistance feature allows you to remotely view and control a computer for any support task. It also enables chat and file transfers. If you have a computer problem, you can invite another person (a remote assistant) to help you over the Internet. The remote assistant can accept your invitation, chat with you about the problem, and view your desktop. The remote assistant can also transfer any files required to fix the problem. With your permission, the remote assistant can also get full control of your computer to perform any complex steps needed to fix the problem.

Note   For more information about the Remote Assistance feature, see Chapter 10, "Configuring Windows XP Professional."

Lesson Review

The following questions will help you determine whether you have learned enough to move on to the next lesson. If you have difficulty answering these questions, review the material in this lesson before beginning the next lesson. The answers for these questions are in Appendix A, "Questions and Answers."

1. How can Windows XP Professional help you in making a recommendation about how to upgrade the equipment in your office?

2. If you are talking with a support engineer about a problem you are having with your computer and the engineer asks you for the BIOS level on your computer, how can you use Help and Support Center to find this information?

3. If you have administrative responsibility for your company's workgroup and have administrative control over all computers in the workgroup, how can you easily determine the model and driver for each network adapter in the workgroup?

Lesson Summary

- Assisted Support allows you to submit electronic support incidents to Microsoft, collaborate with support engineers, and manage submitted incidents.

- Windows Newsgroups are valuable facilities available to you to get information and resolve computer-related support issues in a free, online setting.

- The Compatible Hardware and Software feature provides up-to-date, comprehensive, user-friendly hardware and software compatibility information to aid users in upgrading, making purchasing decisions, and troubleshooting support issues.

- My Computer Information provides you with an easy-to-comprehend, accessible view of personalized software and hardware information specific to your computer or to remote computers on your network.

Lesson 3: Understanding Workgroups and Domains

Windows XP Professional supports two secure network environments in which users are able to share common resources, regardless of network size: workgroups and domains.

After this lesson, you will be able to

- Identify the key characteristics of workgroups and domains and explain how they work

Estimated lesson time: 15 minutes

Workgroups

A Windows XP Professional *workgroup* is a logical grouping of networked computers that share resources, such as files and printers. A workgroup is also called a *peer-to-peer network* because all computers in the workgroup can share resources as equals (peers) without a dedicated server.

Each computer in the workgroup maintains a *local security database*, which is a list of user accounts and resource security information for the computer on which it resides. Therefore, using a local security database decentralizes the administration of user accounts and resource security in a workgroup. Figure 1.10 shows a local security database.

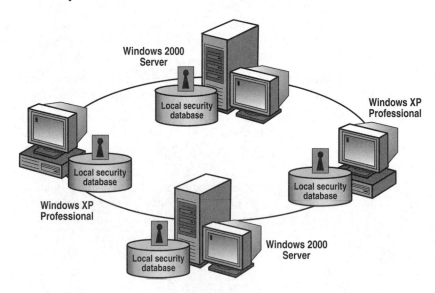

Figure 1.10   An example of a Windows XP Professional workgroup

---

Note A workgroup can contain computers running one of the Microsoft Windows NT and Windows 2000 Server products as long as the server is not configured as a domain controller. (Domain controllers are explained later in this lesson.) In a workgroup, a computer running Windows NT or Windows 2000 Server is called a *stand-alone server*.

Because workgroups have decentralized administration and security, the following are true:

- A user must have a user account on *each* computer to which he or she wants to gain access.

- Any changes to user accounts, such as changing a user's password or adding a new user account, must be made on each computer in the workgroup. If you forget to add a new user account to one of the computers in your workgroup, the new user will not be able to log on to that computer and will be unable to access resources on it.

A workgroup provides the following advantages:

- It does not require inclusion of a domain controller in the configuration to hold centralized security information.

- It is simple to design and implement. It does not require the extensive planning and administration that a domain requires.

- It is a convenient networking environment for a limited number of computers in close proximity. However, a workgroup becomes impractical in environments with more than 10 computers.

Domains

A *domain* is a logical grouping of network computers that share a central directory database (see Figure 1.11). A *directory database* contains user accounts and security information for the domain. This database is known as the directory and is the database portion of Active Directory service, the Windows 2000 directory service.

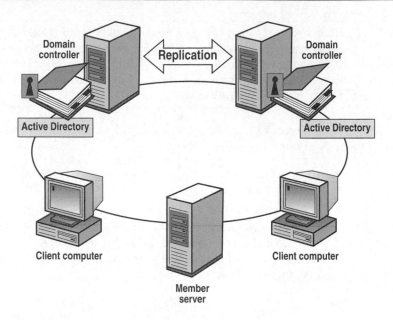

Figure 1.11   A Windows 2000 domain

In a domain, the directory resides on computers that are configured as domain controllers. A *domain controller* is a server that manages all security-related aspects of user and domain interactions, centralizing security and administration.

Note   You can designate only a computer running one of the Microsoft Windows 2000 Server products as a domain controller. If all computers on the network are running Windows XP Professional, the only type of network available is a workgroup.

A domain does not refer to a single location or specific type of network configuration. The computers in a domain can share physical proximity on a small LAN, or they can be located in different corners of the world. They can communicate over any number of physical connections, including dial-up lines, Integrated Services Digital Network (ISDN) lines, fiber lines, Ethernet lines, token ring connections, frame relay connections, satellite connections, and leased lines.

The benefits of a domain include the following:

- Centralized administration, because all user information is stored centrally.
- A single logon process for users to gain access to network resources (such as file, print, and application resources) for which they have permissions. In other words, you can log on to one computer and use resources on another computer in the network as long as you have appropriate permissions to access the resource.
- Scalability, so that you can create very large networks.

A typical Windows 2000 domain includes the following types of computers:

- **Domain controllers running Windows 2000 Server.**   Each domain controller stores and maintains a copy of the directory. In a domain, you create a user account once, which Windows 2000 records in the directory. When a user logs on to a computer in the domain, a domain controller authenticates the user by checking the directory for the user name, password, and logon restrictions. When there are multiple domain controllers in a domain, they periodically replicate their directory information.

- **Member servers running Windows 2000 Server.**   A *member server* is a server that is not configured as a domain controller. A member server does not store directory information and cannot authenticate users. Member servers provide shared resources such as shared folders or printers.

- **Client computers running Windows XP Professional, Windows 2000 Professional, or one of the other Microsoft Windows client operating systems.**   Client computers run a user's desktop environment and allow the user to gain access to resources in the domain.

Lesson Review

The following questions will help you determine whether you have learned enough to move on to the next lesson. If you have difficulty answering these questions, review the material in this lesson before beginning the next lesson. The answers for these questions are in Appendix A, "Questions and Answers."

1. Which of the following statements about a Windows XP Professional workgroup are correct? (Choose all that apply.)

    a. A workgroup is also called a peer-to-peer network.

    b. A workgroup is a logical grouping of network computers that share a central directory database.

    c. A workgroup becomes impractical in environments with more than 100 computers.

    d. A workgroup can contain computers running Microsoft Windows 2000 Server as long as the server is not configured as a domain controller.

2. What is a domain controller?

3. A directory database contains user accounts and security information for the domain and is known as the _____. This directory database is the database portion of _____, which is the Windows 2000 directory service.

4. A _____ provides a single logon for users to gain access to network resources that they have permissions to access, such as file, print, and application resources.

Lesson Summary

- A Windows XP Professional workgroup is a logical grouping of networked computers that share resources such as files and printers.

- A workgroup is referred to as a peer-to-peer network because all computers in the workgroup can share resources as equals (peers) without a dedicated server.

- Each computer in the workgroup maintains a local security database, which is a list of user accounts and resource security information for the computer on which it resides.

- A domain is a logical grouping of network computers that share a central directory database containing user accounts and security information for the domain.

- This central directory database is known as the directory and is the database portion of Active Directory service, which is the Windows 2000 directory service.

- The computers in a domain can share physical proximity on a small LAN or can be distributed worldwide, communicating over any number of physical connections.

- A computer running Windows 2000 Server can be designated as a domain controller. If all computers on the network are running Windows XP Professional, the only type of network available is a workgroup.

Lesson 4: Logging On and Off Windows XP Professional

This lesson explains the Welcome screen and the Enter Password dialog box, the two options that you use to log on to Windows XP Professional. It also explains how Windows XP Professional authenticates a user during the logon process. This mandatory authentication process ensures that only valid users can gain access to resources and data on a computer or the network.

After this lesson, you will be able to

- Explain how to use the Welcome screen to log on to Windows XP Professional
- Explain how to configure Windows XP Professional to use the Log On To Windows dialog box
- Identify the features of the Log On To Windows dialog box
- Identify how Windows XP Professional authenticates a user when the user logs on to a local computer or to a domain
- Explain how to log off or turn off a computer that is running Windows XP Professional
- Identify the features of the Windows Security dialog box

Estimated lesson time: 20 minutes

Logging On Locally to the Computer

Windows XP Professional offers two options for logging on locally: the Welcome screen and the Log On To Windows dialog box.

The Welcome Screen

By default, Windows XP Professional uses the Welcome screen to allow users to log on locally. To log on, click the icon for the user account you want to use. If the account requires a password, you are prompted to enter it. If the account is not password protected, you are logged on to the computer. You can also use CTRL+ALT+DELETE at the Welcome screen to get the Log On To Windows dialog box. This enables you to log on to the Administrator account, which is not displayed on the Welcome screen when other user accounts have been created. To use CTRL+ALT+DELETE, you must enter the sequence twice to get the logon prompt.

Note   For more information about creating user accounts during installation, see Chapter 2, "Installing Windows XP Professional." For more information about creating user accounts after installation, see Chapter 3, "Setting Up and Managing User Accounts."

A user can log on locally to either of the following:

- A computer that is a member of a workgroup
- A computer that is a member of a domain but is not a domain controller

Note   Because domain controllers do not maintain a local security database, local user accounts are not available on domain controllers. Therefore, a user cannot log on locally to a domain controller.

The User Accounts program in the Control Panel includes a Change The Way Users Log On Or Off task, which allows you to configure Windows XP Professional to use the Log On To Windows dialog box instead of the Welcome screen.

The Log On To Windows Dialog Box

To use the Log On To Windows dialog box to log on locally to a computer running Windows XP Professional, you must supply a valid user name; if the user name is password protected, you must also supply the password. Windows XP Professional authenticates the user's identity during the logon process. Only valid users can access resources and data on a computer or a network. Windows XP Professional authenticates users who log on locally to the computer at which they are seated and one of the domain controllers in a Windows 2000 domain authenticates users who log on to a domain.

When a user starts a computer running Windows XP Professional that is configured to use the Log On To Windows dialog box, an Options button also appears. Table 1.1 describes the options in the Log On To Windows dialog box for a computer that is part of a domain.

Table 1.1   Log On To Windows Dialog Box Options

Option	Description
User Name	A unique user logon name that is assigned by an administrator. To log on to a domain with the user name, the user must have an account that resides in the directory.
Password	The password that is assigned to the user account. Users must enter a password to prove their identity. Passwords are case sensitive. For security purposes, the password appears on the screen as asterisks (*). To prevent unauthorized access to resources and data, users must keep passwords secret.
Log On To	Allows the user to choose to log on to the local computer or to log on to the domain.
Log On Using Dial-Up Connection	Permits a user to connect to a domain server by using dial-up networking. Dial-up networking allows a user to log on and perform work from a remote location.

Table 1.1   *(continued)*

Option	Description
Shutdown	Closes all files, saves all operating system data, and prepares the computer so that a user can safely turn it off.
Options	Toggles on and off between the Log On To option and the Log On Using Dial-Up Connection option. The Options button appears only if the computer is a member of a domain.

Note   If your computer is not part of a domain, you will not get the Log On To option.

Windows XP Professional Authentication Process

To gain access to a computer running Windows XP Professional or to any resource on that computer, whether the computer is configured to use the Welcome screen or the Log On To Windows dialog box, you must provide a user name and possibly a password.

How Windows XP Professional authenticates a user depends on whether the user is logging on to a domain or logging on locally to a computer (see Figure 1.12).

- ■ **Access token**
  - • Provides user identity and security settings
  - • Enables a user to gain access to resources and perform system tasks

Figure 1.12   Windows XP Professional authentication process at logon

The steps in the authentication process are as follows:

1. The user logs on by providing logon information, such as user name and password, and Windows XP Professional forwards this information to the security subsystem of that local computer.

2. Windows XP Professional compares the logon information with the user information in the local security database, which resides in the security subsystem of the local computer.

3. If the information matches and the user account is valid, Windows XP Professional creates an access token for the user. An *access token* is the user's identification for that local computer. It contains the user's security settings, which allow the user to gain access to the appropriate resources on that computer and to perform specific system tasks.

> **Note** In addition to the logon process, any time a user makes a connection to a computer, that computer authenticates the user and returns an access token. This authentication process is invisible to the user.

If a user logs on to a domain, Windows XP Professional contacts an available domain controller in the domain. The domain controller compares the logon information with the user information that is in the directory for the domain. If the information matches and the user account is valid, the domain controller creates an access token for the user. The security settings contained in the access token allow the user to gain access to the appropriate resources in the domain.

Logging Off Windows XP Professional

To log off a computer running Windows XP Professional, click Start and then click Log Off. Notice that the Start menu, shown in Figure 1.13, also provides a method to turn off the computer.

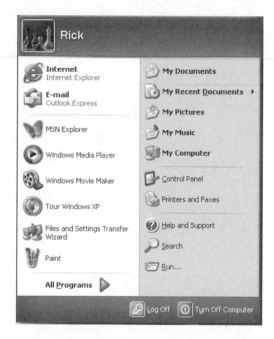

Figure 1.13 The Start menu provides a way to log off Windows XP Professional

The Windows Security Dialog Box

The Windows Security dialog box provides information such as the user account currently logged on and the domain or computer to which the user is logged on. This information is important for users with multiple user accounts, such as a user who has a regular user account as well as a user account with administrative privileges.

You access the Windows Security dialog box by pressing CTRL+ALT+DELETE if the computer is joined to a domain or the Welcome screen is disabled. Otherwise, the Task Manager will be activated. Figure 1.14 shows the Windows Security dialog box and Table 1.2 describes the Windows Security dialog box options.

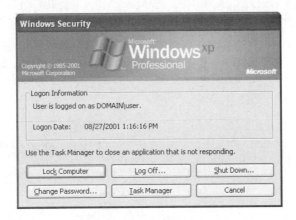

Figure 1.14   Windows Security dialog box

Table 1.2   The Windows Security Dialog Box Options

Option	Description
Lock Computer	Allows users to secure the computer without logging off. All programs remain running. Users should lock their computers when they leave for a short time. The user who locks the computer can unlock it by pressing CTRL+ALT+DELETE and entering the valid password. An administrator can also unlock a locked computer. This process logs off the current user.
Log Off	Allows a user to log off as the current user and close all running programs, but leaves Windows XP Professional running.
Shut Down	Allows a user to close all files, save all operating system data, and prepare the computer so that it can be safely turned off.
Change Password	Allows a user to change his or her user account password. The user must know the current password to create a new one. This is the only way users can change their own passwords. Administrators can also change the password.
Task Manager	Provides a list of the programs that are running and a summary of overall CPU and memory usage, as well as a quick view of how each program, program component, or system process is using the CPU and memory resources. Users can also use Task Manager to switch between programs and to stop a program that is not responding.
Cancel	Closes the Windows Security dialog box.

Lesson Review

The following questions will help you determine whether you have learned enough to move on to the next chapter. If you have difficulty answering these questions, go back and review the material in this lesson before proceeding to the next chapter. The answers for these questions are in Appendix A, "Questions and Answers."

1. What can you do when you log on locally to a computer, and what determines what you can do when you log on locally to a computer?

2. What is the main difference in the authentication process for logging on locally to a computer and logging on to a domain?

3. How can you configure Windows XP Professional to use the Log On To Windows dialog box instead of the Welcome screen to allow users to log on locally to the computer?

4. Which of the following computers can a user log on to locally? (Choose all that apply.)

   a. A computer running Windows XP Professional that is in a workgroup

   b. A computer running Windows XP Professional that is in a domain

   c. A computer running Windows 2000 Server that is configured as a domain controller

   d. A computer running Windows 2000 Server that is a member server in a domain

5. Which of the following statements about the Windows Security dialog box are correct? (Choose all that apply.)

   a. It is accessed by pressing CTRL+ALT+DELETE.

   b. It tells how long the current user has been logged on.

   c. It allows you to log off the computer or domain.

   d. It allows a user with administrative permissions to change other users' passwords.

Lesson Summary

- By default, Windows XP Professional uses the Welcome screen to allow users to log on locally to the computer.

- You can configure Windows XP Professional to use the Log On To Windows dialog box instead of the Welcome screen.

- When a user logs on, he or she can log on to the local computer or, if the computer is a member of a domain, the user can log on to the domain.

- When a user logs on locally, the local computer does the authentication.

- When a user logs on to a domain, a domain controller must do the authentication.

- In a workgroup environment, an access token is the user's identification for that local computer, and it contains the user's security settings. These security settings allow the user to gain access to the appropriate resources on that computer and to perform specific system tasks.

- The Windows Security dialog box, which is accessed by pressing CTRL+ALT+DELETE, provides information such as the user account that is currently logged on and the domain or computer to which the user is logged on.

- The Windows Security dialog box allows you to lock your computer, change your password, log off your computer, shut down your computer, and access Task Manager.

C H A P T E R   2

Installing Windows XP Professional

About This Chapter

This chapter prepares you to install Microsoft Windows XP Professional. You will learn some preinstallation tasks that help ensure your installation of Windows XP Professional will go smoothly. These tasks include verifying that your hardware and any software installed on the computer are compatible with Windows XP Professional, determining which file system to use, and deciding if your computer is going to join a workgroup or a domain. You will learn about installing Windows XP Professional from a CD-ROM and over the network. Finally, you will learn how to modify the installation using switches and how to troubleshoot Setup.

Before You Begin

To complete this chapter, you must have

- A computer that meets or exceeds the minimum hardware requirements listed in the preface, "About This Book"
- A Windows XP Professional CD-ROM

Lesson 1: Getting Started

When you install Windows XP Professional, the Windows XP Professional Setup program asks you to specify how to install and configure the operating system. Preparing in advance helps you avoid problems during and after installation.

After this lesson, you will be able to

- Identify the hardware and installation information required to install Windows XP Professional successfully

Estimated lesson time: 30 minutes

Preinstallation Tasks

Before you start the installation, complete the following tasks:

- Ensure that your hardware meets the requirements for installing Windows XP Professional.
- Determine whether your hardware is on the Hardware Compatibility List (HCL).
- Decide how you will partition the hard disk on which you will install Windows XP Professional.
- Choose a file system for the installation partition.
- Determine whether your computer will join a domain or a workgroup.
- Complete a preinstallation checklist.

Hardware Requirements

You must determine whether your hardware meets or exceeds the minimum requirements for installing and operating Windows XP Professional, as shown in Table 2.1.

Table 2.1   Windows XP Professional Hardware Requirements

Component	Requirements
Central processing unit (CPU)	Pentium 233 megahertz (MHz) or equivalent
Memory	64 megabytes (MB) minimum; 128 MB recommended 4 gigabytes (GB) of random access memory (RAM) maximum
Hard disk space	1.5 GB on a 2-GB hard disk minimum The minimum amount of hard disk space allows for auto-updates over the Internet, additional Windows components, applications that you will be installing, and users' data
Networking	Network adapter card and related cable
Display	Video display adapter and monitor with Video Graphics Adapter (VGA) resolution or higher
Other drives	CD-ROM drive, 12X or faster recommended (not required for installing Windows XP Professional over a network), or DVD drive A high-density 3.5-inch disk drive as drive A, unless the computer supports starting the Setup program from a CD-ROM or DVD drive
Accessories	Keyboard and mouse or other pointing device

Hardware Compatibility List

Although the Windows XP Professional Setup Wizard automatically checks your hardware and software for potential conflicts, before you install Windows XP Professional, you should verify that your hardware is on the Windows XP Professional HCL. Microsoft provides tested drivers for the listed devices only. Using hardware not listed on the HCL could cause problems during and after installation. The most recent versions of the HCL for released operating systems are on the Microsoft Web site at *http://www.microsoft.com/hcl/*.

Tip   If your hardware is not on the HCL, the hardware manufacturer might be able to provide you with a Windows XP Professional driver for the component.

Disk Partitions

The Windows XP Professional Setup program examines the hard disk to determine its existing configuration. Setup then allows you to install Windows XP Professional on an existing partition or to create a new partition on which to install it.

New Partition or Existing Partition

Depending on the hard disk configuration, do one of the following during installation:

- If the hard disk is unpartitioned, create and size the Windows XP Professional partition.

- If the hard disk is partitioned and contains enough unpartitioned disk space, use the unpartitioned space to create the Windows XP Professional partition.

- If the existing partition is large enough, install Windows XP Professional on that partition. Installing on an existing partition overwrites any existing data.

- If the existing partition is not large enough, delete it to provide more unpartitioned disk space for creating the Windows XP Professional partition.

Remaining Free Hard Disk Space

Although you can use Setup to create other partitions, you should create and size only the partition on which you will install Windows XP Professional. After you install Windows XP Professional, use the Disk Management administrative tool to partition any remaining unpartitioned space on the hard disk.

Installation Partition Size

Microsoft recommends installing Windows XP Professional on a 1.5-GB or larger partition. Although Windows XP Professional requires less disk space for installation, using a larger installation partition provides the flexibility to install Windows XP Professional updates, operating system tools, or other necessary files in the future.

File Systems

After you create the installation partition, Setup prompts you to select the file system with which to format the partition. Like Microsoft Windows NT 4 and Microsoft Windows 2000 Professional, Windows XP Professional supports the NT file system (NTFS) and file allocation table (FAT). Both Windows 2000 Professional and Windows XP Professional support FAT32. Figure 2.1 summarizes some of the features of these file systems.

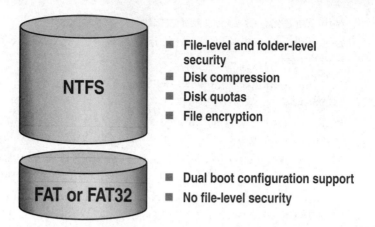

Figure 2.1   NTFS and FAT/FAT32 file system features

Use NTFS when the partition on which Windows XP Professional will reside requires any of the following features:

- **File- and folder-level security.**   NTFS allows you to control access to files and folders. For additional information, see Chapter 8, "Securing Resources with NTFS Permissions."

- **Disk compression.**   NTFS compresses files to store more data on the partition. For additional information, see Chapter 14, "Managing Data Storage."

- **Disk quotas.**   NTFS allows you to control disk usage on a per-user basis. For additional information, see Chapter 14, "Managing Data Storage."

- **Encryption.**   NTFS allows you to encrypt file data on the physical hard disk, using the Microsoft Encrypting File System (EFS). For additional information, see Chapter 14, "Managing Data Storage."

The version of NTFS in Windows XP Professional supports remote storage, dynamic volumes, and mounting volumes to folders. Windows XP Professional, Windows 2000, and Windows NT are the only operating systems that can access data on a local hard disk formatted with NTFS.

FAT and FAT32

FAT and FAT32 offer compatibility with other operating systems. You must format the system partition with either FAT or FAT32 if you will dual boot Windows XP Professional and another operating system that requires FAT or FAT32.

FAT and FAT32 do not offer many of the features (for example, file-level security) that NTFS supports. Therefore, in most situations, you should format the hard disk with NTFS. The only reason to use FAT or FAT32 is for dual booting with another operating system that does not support NTFS. If you are setting up a computer for dual booting, you need to format only the system partition as FAT or FAT32. For example, if drive C is the system partition, you could format drive C as FAT or FAT32 and format drive D as NTFS.

Converting a FAT or FAT32 Volume to NTFS

Windows XP Professional provides the Convert command for converting a partition to NTFS without reformatting the partition and losing all the information on the partition. To use the Convert command, click Start, click Run, type **cmd** in the Open text box, and then click OK. This opens a command prompt, which you use to request the Convert command. The following example shows how you might use switches with the Convert command.

```
Convert volume /FS:NTFS [/V] [/CvtArea:filename] [/Nosecurity] [/X]
```

Table 2.2 lists the switches available in the Convert command and describes their functions.

Table 2.2   Convert Command Switches

Switch	Function	Required
Volume	Specifies the drive letter (followed by a colon), volume mount point, or volume name that you want to convert	Yes
/FS:NTFS	Specifies converting the volume to NTFS	Yes
/V	Runs the Convert command in verbose mode	No
/CvtArea:*filename*	Specifies a contiguous file in the root directory to be the placeholder for NTFS system files	No
/NoSecurity	Sets the security settings to make converted files and directories accessible by everyone	No
/X	Forces the volume to dismount first if necessary, and all open handles to the volume are then not valid	No

For help with any command-line program, at the command prompt type the command followed by /? and then press ENTER. For example, to receive help on the Convert command, type **Convert /?** and then press ENTER.

Domain or Workgroup Membership

During installation, you must choose the type of network security group that the computer will join: a domain or a workgroup. Figure 2.2 shows the requirements for joining a domain or workgroup.

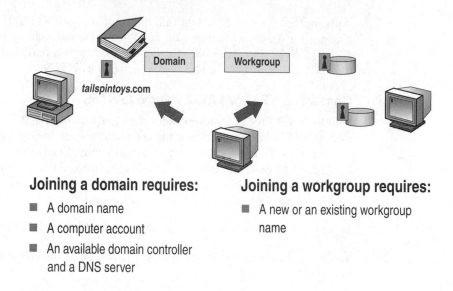

Joining a domain requires:

- A domain name
- A computer account
- An available domain controller and a DNS server

Joining a workgroup requires:

- A new or an existing workgroup name

Figure 2.2   Domain or workgroup membership requirements

Joining a Domain

When you install Windows XP Professional on a computer, you can add that computer to an existing domain. Adding a computer to a domain is referred to as *joining a domain.*

Note   A computer can join a domain during or after installation.

Joining a domain during installation requires the following:

- **A domain name.**   Ask the domain administrator for the Domain Name System (DNS) name for the domain that the computer will join. An example of a DNS-compatible domain name is *microsoft.com*, in which *microsoft* is the name of the organization's DNS identity.

- **A computer account.**   Before a computer can join a domain, you must create a computer account in the domain. You can ask a domain administrator to create the computer account before installation or, if you have administrative privileges for the domain, you can create the computer account during installation. If you create the computer account during installation, Setup prompts you for the name and password of a user account with authority to add domain computer accounts.

- **An available domain controller and a server running the DNS service (called the *DNS server*).**   At least one domain controller in the domain that you are joining and one DNS server must be online when you install a computer in the domain.

Joining a Workgroup

When you install Windows XP Professional on a computer, you can add that computer to an existing workgroup. This process is referred to as *joining a workgroup*.

If you join a computer to a workgroup during installation, you must assign a workgroup name to the computer. The workgroup name you assign can be the name of an existing workgroup or the name of a new workgroup that you create during installation.

Preinstallation Checklist

Use the following preinstallation checklist to ensure that you have all the necessary information available before you begin installing Windows XP Professional.

Task	Done
Verify that your components meet the minimum hardware requirements.	❏
Verify that all of your hardware is listed on the HCL.	❏
Verify that the hard disk on which you will install Windows XP Professional has a minimum of 1.5 GB of free disk space.	❏
Select the file system for the Windows XP Professional partition. Format this partition with NTFS unless you need to dual boot operating systems with an operating system that requires a FAT partition.	❏
Determine the name of the domain or workgroup that each computer will join. If the computer joins a domain, write down the domain name in the DNS format: *server.subdomain.domain*. If the computer joins a workgroup, use the 15-character NetBIOS naming convention: *Server_name*.	❏
Determine the name of the computer before installation.	❏
If the computer will join a domain, create a computer account in that domain. You can create a computer account during installation if you have administrative privileges in the domain.	❏
Determine a password for the Administrator account.	❏

Lesson Review

The following questions will help you determine whether you have learned enough to move on to the next lesson. If you have difficulty answering these questions, review the material in this lesson before beginning the next lesson. The answers are in Appendix A, "Questions and Answers."

1. What are the minimum and recommended memory requirements for installing Windows XP Professional?

2. The minimum hard disk space required for installing Windows XP Professional is

   a. 1.5 GB on a 2-GB hard disk

   b. 1 GB on a 2-GB hard disk

   c. 500 MB on a 1-GB hard disk

   d. 750 MB on a 2-GB hard disk

3. Where can you find the most recent versions of the HCL for released operating systems?

4. Joining a domain during Windows XP Professional installation requires which of the following? (Choose all that apply.)

   a. You must know the DNS name for the domain the computer will join.

   b. You must have a user account in the domain.

   c. At least one domain controller in the domain must be online when you install a computer in the domain.

   d. At least one DNS server must be online when you install a computer in the domain.

5. Which of the following statements about file systems are correct? (Choose all that apply.)

   a. File- and folder-level security are available only with NTFS.

   b. Disk compression is available with FAT, FAT32, and NTFS.

   c. Dual booting between Microsoft Windows 98 and Windows XP Professional is available only with NTFS.

   d. Encryption is available only with NTFS.

Lesson Summary

- The first preinstallation task is to ensure that your hardware meets the hardware requirements for installing Windows XP Professional.

- The next preinstallation task is to ensure that your hardware is on the Windows XP Professional HCL.

- Additional preinstallation tasks include determining how to partition the hard disk on which you will install Windows XP Professional and deciding whether to format the partition as NTFS, FAT, or FAT32.

- Your computer can join a domain or a workgroup during or after installation.

Lesson 2: Installing Windows XP Professional from a CD-ROM

This lesson covers the four-stage process of installing Windows XP Professional from a CD-ROM. After you learn about these four stages, you will install Windows XP Professional on your computer.

After this lesson, you will be able to

- Install Windows XP Professional from a CD-ROM

Estimated lesson time: 70 minutes

The Windows XP Professional Setup Program

The installation process for Windows XP Professional combines the Setup program with wizards and informational screens. Installing Windows XP Professional from a CD-ROM to a clean hard disk consists of these four stages:

1. **Running the Setup program.**

   Setup prepares the hard disk for the later installation stages and copies the files necessary to run the Setup Wizard.

2. **Running the Setup Wizard.**

   The Setup Wizard requests setup information about the computer, such as names, and passwords.

3. **Installing Windows XP Professional networking components.**

   After gathering information about the computer, the Setup Wizard prompts you for networking information and then installs the networking components that allow the computer to communicate with other computers on the network.

4. **Completing the installation.**

   Setup copies files to the hard disk and configures the computer. The system restarts after installation is complete.

   The following sections cover the four steps in more detail.

Running the Setup Program

To start the Setup program, insert the Windows XP Professional installation CD-ROM in your CD-ROM drive, and start your computer.

Figure 2.3 shows the six steps involved in running the Setup program.

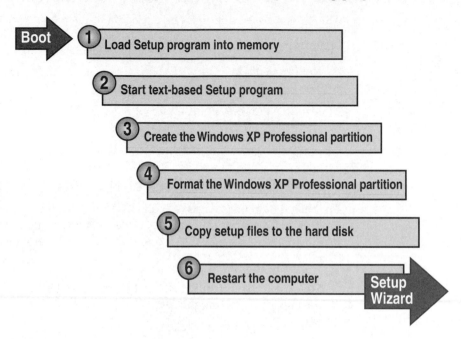

Figure 2.3   Steps in the Setup program

Running the Setup program involves the following steps:

1. After the computer starts, a minimal version of Windows XP Professional is copied into memory. This version of Windows XP Professional starts the Setup program.

2. Setup restarts the computer and then starts the text-mode portion of Setup, which prompts you to read and accept a licensing agreement.

3. Setup prompts you to select the partition on which to install Windows XP Professional. You can select an existing partition or create a new partition by using unpartitioned space on the hard disk.

4. Setup prompts you to select a file system for the new partition. Next, Setup formats the partition with the selected file system.

5. Setup copies files to the hard disk and saves configuration information.

6. Setup restarts the computer and then starts the Windows XP Professional Setup Wizard, the graphical user interface (GUI) portion of Setup. By default, the Setup Wizard installs the Windows XP Professional operating system files in the C:\Windows folder.

Running the Setup Wizard

The GUI-based Windows XP Professional Setup Wizard leads you through the next stage of the installation process. It gathers information about you, your organization, and your computer, including the following information:

- **Regional settings.**   Customize language, locale, and keyboard settings. You can configure Windows XP Professional to use multiple languages and regional settings.

> **Note**   You can add another language or change the locale and keyboard settings after installation is complete. For more information, see Chapter 10, "Configuring Windows XP Professional."

- **Name and organization.**   Enter the name of the person and the organization to which this copy of Windows XP Professional is licensed.

- **Computer name.**   Enter a computer name of up to 15 characters. The computer name must be different from other computer, workgroup, or domain names on the network. The Setup Wizard displays a default name (the organization name you entered earlier in the process). If Transmission Control Protocol/Internet Protocol (TCP/IP) is installed on your computer, the computer name can be up to 63 characters but should contain only alphanumeric characters (A–Z, a–z, 0–9) and hyphens.

> **Note**   To change the computer name after installation is complete, click Start, click My Computer, and then click View System Information. In the System Properties dialog box, click the Computer Name tab, and then click Change.

- **Password for Administrator account.**   Specify a password for the Administrator user account, which the Setup Wizard creates during installation. The Administrator account provides the administrative privileges required to manage the computer.

- **Time and date.**   Select the time zone, adjust the date and time settings if necessary, and determine whether you want Windows XP Professional to automatically adjust for daylight savings time.

After you complete this step, the Setup Wizard starts to install the Windows networking components.

Installing Windows XP Professional Networking Components

After gathering information about your computer, the Setup Wizard guides you through installing the Windows XP Professional networking components (see Figure 2.4).

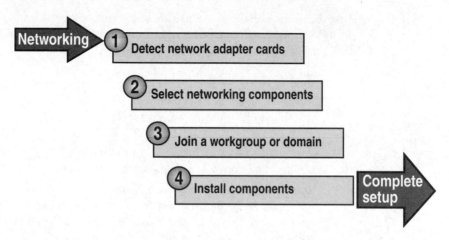

Figure 2.4   Installing Windows networking components

Installing Windows XP Professional networking components involves the following steps:

1. **Detect network adapter cards.**

    The Windows XP Professional Setup Wizard detects and configures any network adapter cards installed on the computer. After configuring network adapters, it attempts to locate a server running the Dynamic Host Configuration Protocol (DHCP) service (called the *DHCP server)* on the network.

2. **Select networking components.**

    The Setup Wizard prompts you to choose typical or customized settings for the networking components it installs. The typical installation includes the following options:

    ■ **Client For Microsoft Networks.**   Allows your computer to access network resources.

    ■ **File And Printer Sharing For Microsoft Networks.**   Allows other computers to access file and print resources on your computer.

    ■ **QoS Packet Scheduler.**   Helps provide a guaranteed delivery system for network traffic, such as Internet Protocol (TCP/IP) packets.

    ■ **Internet Protocol (TCP/IP).**   Allows your computer to communicate over local area networks (LANs) and wide area networks (WANs). TCP/IP is the default networking protocol.

Note   You can install other clients, services, and network protocols during the Windows XP Professional installation, or you can wait until after the installation has completed.

3. **Join a workgroup or domain.**

   If you choose to join a domain for which you have administrative privileges, you can create the computer account during installation. The Setup Wizard prompts you for the name and password of a user account with authority to add domain computer accounts.

Note   To change the domain or workgroup for your computer after you've installed Windows XP Professional, click Start, click My Computer, click View System Information, click the Computer Name tab, and then click Change.

4. **Install components.**

   The Setup Wizard installs and configures the Windows networking components you selected.

Completing the Installation

After installing the networking components, the Setup Wizard automatically starts the final step in the installation process (see Figure 2.5).

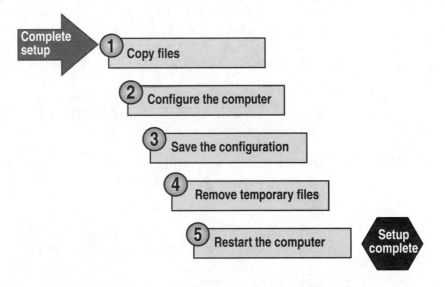

Figure 2.5   The final steps in completing the installation

To complete the installation, the Setup Wizard performs the following tasks:

1. **Installs Start menu items.**

   The Setup Wizard sets up shortcuts that will appear on the Start menu.

2. **Registers components.**

   The Setup Wizard applies the configuration settings that you specified earlier.

3. **Saves the configuration.**

   The Setup Wizard saves your configuration settings to the local hard disk. The next time you start Windows XP Professional, the computer uses this configuration automatically.

4. **Removes temporary files.**

   To save hard disk space, the Setup Wizard deletes any files used for installation only.

5. **Restarts the computer.**

   The Setup Wizard restarts the computer. This finishes the installation.

Practice 1: Installing Windows XP Professional from a CD-ROM

In this practice, you install Windows XP Professional from a CD-ROM on to a computer that contains no partitions or operating systems. If your computer will not boot from a CD-ROM or if there is already an operating system loaded on your computer, go to Practice 2 to install Windows XP Professional from a CD-ROM without having to boot from the Windows XP Professional installation CD-ROM.

▶ **To run the Setup program**

1. Insert the Windows XP Professional CD-ROM into the CD-ROM drive and turn on the computer.

   Note   Some computers will require you to press a key to boot from the CD-ROM drive. If you are prompted to press any key to boot from the CD, press the spacebar.

   Setup displays the Windows Setup screen while it is loading files, and then displays the Windows XP Professional Setup screen.

   Note   If you are loading an Evaluation Edition of Windows XP Professional, press ENTER to continue (or F3 to quit Setup). Setup displays the Welcome To Setup screen.

Important   You can also use Windows XP Professional Setup to repair or recover a damaged Windows XP Professional installation.

---

2. Read the Welcome To Setup screen and press ENTER to continue.

   Setup displays the Windows XP Licensing Agreement screen.

3. Read the licensing agreement, and press F8 to agree with the licensing terms.

   Setup displays another screen, which prompts you to create a partition in which to install Windows XP Professional.

Note   If you want to use only a portion of the available space, enter the amount of space you want to use and then press ENTER.

Important   You must create a space of at least 2000 MB in size.

---

4. Select an area of unpartitioned space, at least 2000 MB in size, and press C.

   Setup prompts you to enter a size for the partition.

5. If you want to use all the available space to create the partition, press ENTER.

Note   If you already have partitions created, you can also delete partitions at this time. If you have a C partition, you might not be able to delete it because Setup has already loaded some files onto it.

Setup displays the list of existing partitions for you to select a partition for the installation.

6. Press ENTER to install Windows XP Professional on the partition you created.

   Because you are installing into a newly created, unformatted partition, Windows XP Professional Setup prompts you to format the partition.

Caution   If you are planning on dual booting your computer with an operating system that does not support NTFS, your C drive cannot be formatted with NTFS. You might want to install Windows XP Professional in a different drive and format that drive with NTFS.

---

7. When prompted, format the partition with NTFS.

Note   If you format the partition with the FAT file system, Windows XP Professional provides the Convert command, which you can use to convert a partition to NTFS after installation is complete without reformatting the partition and losing all the information contained on the partition.

Setup formats the hard drive, examines it, and then copies files to the Windows XP Professional installation folders.

8. When Setup prompts you to restart the computer, remove all the disks from the drives, and then press ENTER.

Important   Ensure that you remove the Windows XP Professional CD-ROM from the CD-ROM drive. If you don't and your computer supports booting from the CD-ROM drive, the computer can attempt to reboot from the CD-ROM. If this happens, remove the CD-ROM and then restart the computer.

The computer restarts. A message box appears, prompting you to insert the Windows XP Professional CD-ROM into your CD-ROM drive.

▶   **To run the Setup Wizard**

1. Insert the Windows XP Professional CD-ROM into your CD-ROM drive, and then click OK.

   The Setup Wizard displays a Files Needed dialog box prompting you to verify the path to the Windows XP Professional installation files.

2. Ensure the path to the Windows XP Professional installation files is correct and then click OK.

   Windows installs the files. This might take several minutes.

   The Setup Wizard prompts you to customize Windows XP Professional for different regions and languages.

3. Select the appropriate system locale, user locale, and keyboard layout or ensure that they are correct for your language and location, and then click Next.

   The Setup Wizard displays the Personalize Your Software page, prompting you for your name and organization name. Setup uses your organization name to generate the default computer name. Many applications that you install later will use this information for product registration and document identification.

4. In the Name box, type your name. In the Organization box, type the name of your organization, and then click Next.

   The Setup Wizard displays the Your Product Key page.

5. Enter your 25-character product key located on the back of the Windows XP Professional CD-ROM case, and then click Next.

   The Setup Wizard displays the Computer Name And Administrator Password page.

6. Type **Pro1** in the Computer Name box.

Note   Windows XP Professional displays the computer name in all uppercase letters, no matter how you type it.

If your computer is on a network, check with the network administrator before assigning a name to your computer. The practice sessions in this training kit refer to Pro1. If you do not name your computer Pro1, you must substitute the name of your computer in each practice.

7. In the Administrator Password box and in the Confirm Password box, type **password**, and then click Next.

Important For the practice sections in this training kit, you will use *password* for the Administrator account. You should always use a complex password for the Administrator account (one that others cannot easily guess). Microsoft recommends mixing uppercase and lowercase letters, numbers, and symbols (for example, Lp6*g9f2).

The Setup Wizard displays the Modem Dialing Information page.

Note If the Setup Wizard does not display the Modem Dialing Information page, it is probably because there is not a modem installed on your computer. Skip to step 12.

---

8. Ensure that the correct country or region is selected.

9. Type the correct area code or city code.

10. If you dial a number to get an outside line, type the number.

11. Ensure that the correct type of phone system is selected, and then click Next.

    The Setup Wizard displays the Date And Time Settings page.

12. If necessary, adjust the date and time.

13. If necessary, select the time zone for your location from the Time Zone drop-down list.

14. Ensure that the Automatically Adjust Clock For Daylight Saving Changes check box is selected if you want Windows XP Professional to automatically adjust the time on your computer for daylight savings, and then click Next.

Note If you have configured your computer for dual booting with another operating system that can also adjust your clock for daylight savings, enable this feature for the operating system you use most frequently so that the daylight savings adjustment will occur only once.

The Setup Wizard installs some networking files and then displays the Networking Settings page.

▶ **To install Windows Networking**

1. Ensure that Typical Settings is selected, and then click Next.

   The Setup Wizard displays the Workgroup Or Computer Domain page.

2. Ensure that No, This Computer Is Not On A Network, Or Is On A Network Without A Domain is selected and that the workgroup name is WORKGROUP, and then click Next.

   The Setup Wizard copies files. This process takes several minutes.

▶ **To complete the installation**

The Setup Wizard finishes the configuration, copies files, and completes the networking portion of the installation. Then the Setup Wizard installs Start menu items, registers components, saves settings, and removes temporary files. This process takes several minutes.

The computer restarts, and the Setup Wizard displays the Welcome To Microsoft Windows page.

Important If your computer attempts to reboot from the CD-ROM, remove the CD-ROM and then restart the computer.

---

1. Click Next to continue.

   The Setup Wizard displays the Will This Computer Connect To The Internet Directly, Or Through A Network page.

2. If you would like to connect to the Internet at this time, select the appropriate connection method, and then click Next.

   The Setup Wizard displays the Ready To Activate Windows page.

Important At some point you will have to activate Windows XP Professional. However, it is not necessary to activate it while you complete this training kit.

---

3. Click Yes, Activate Windows Over The Internet Now, and then click Next.

   The Setup Wizard displays The Ready To Register With Microsoft page.

4. Click Yes, I'd Like To Register With Microsoft Now, and then click Next.

   The Setup Wizard displays the Collecting Registration Information page.

5. Fill in the appropriate text boxes.

   The Setup Wizard displays the Ready To Send Information page.

6. Click Next.

   The Setup Wizard displays the Do You Want To Set Up Internet Access Now page.

> **Note**   Internet access is not required for this training kit. If you want to con-
> nect to the Internet at this time, click Yes Help Me Connect To The Internet,
> click Next and follow the instructions on your screen.

7. Click No, Not At This Time, and then click Next.

   The Setup Wizard displays the Who Will Use This Computer page. Your name
   should already be entered.

8. Type **Fred** for the second user, and then click Next.

   The Setup Wizard displays the Thank You page.

9. Read the page and then click Finish.

10. To log on, select Fred (or the account name created for you during setup).

   You have completed your installation of Windows XP Professional and
   logged on as an administrator.

Practice 2: Installing Windows XP Professional without Booting from the CD-ROM

If your computer will not boot from a CD-ROM or if there is already an operating system loaded on your computer, you can install Windows XP Professional
from a CD-ROM without having to boot from the Windows XP Professional
installation CD-ROM. If you have completed Practice 1, do not do this practice.

> **Note**   If your computer is configured with an El-Torito compatible CD-ROM
> drive, you can install Windows XP Professional without using Setup disks. Run
> the Setup program by restarting the computer with the CD-ROM inserted in the
> CD-ROM drive.

▶   **To run the Setup program**

This begins the Collecting Information portion of Setup.

1. If there is an operating system currently installed on your computer, start the
   computer, log on, and then insert the Windows XP Professional CD-ROM
   into the CD-ROM drive.

2. When the Welcome To Microsoft Windows XP screen appears, click Install
   Windows XP.

3. If you get a Windows Setup message box indicating that the version of the
   operating system cannot be upgraded and that option to upgrade will not be
   available, click OK.

   Setup displays the Welcome To Setup screen.

4. In the Installation Type box, select New Installation (Advanced) and then click Next. Setup displays the License Agreement screen.

5. Read the license agreement, select I Accept This Agreement, and then click Next.

Setup displays the Your Product Key screen.

6. Type in your 25-character product key, and then click Next.

Setup displays the Setup Options screen that allows you to configure the following three options:

- Advanced Options, which allows you to control where the installation files are obtained, where the installation files are copied to, whether or not to copy all installation files to the hard disk, and whether or not you want to specify the drive letter and partition during Setup.

- Accessibility Options, which gives you the option of using the Microsoft Magnifier during setup to display an enlarged portion of the screen in a separate window for users with limited vision and the option of using the Microsoft Narrator to read the contents of the screen for users who are blind.

- Select The Primary Language And Region You Want To Use, which allows you to specify the primary language and region you use.

7. After you have configured any required Setup options, click Next.

Setup displays the Get Updated Setup Files dialog box.

Note   If your computer has access to the Internet, you might want to ensure that the Yes, Download The Updated Setup Files (Recommended) checkbox is selected and click Next.

---

8. Select No, Skip This Step And Continue Installing Windows, and then click Next.

If your partition is not currently formatted with Windows XP Professional NTFS, the Setup Wizard displays the Upgrade To The Windows NTFS File System screen.

Caution   If you are planning on dual booting your computer with an operating system that does not support NTFS, your C drive cannot be formatted NTFS. You might want to install Windows XP Professional in a different drive and format that drive with NTFS. If you install Windows XP Professional on a drive other than the C drive, for the rest of the practices in the training kit you must be sure you are using the correct drive.

---

9. If you get the Upgrade To The Windows NTFS File System screen, ensure Yes, Upgrade My Drive is selected, and then click Next.

If you are installing an Evaluation Edition of Microsoft Windows XP Professional, the Setup Wizard displays the Setup Notification screen informing you that this is an evaluation version.

10. If Setup displays the Setup Notification screen, press ENTER to continue.

Setup displays the Welcome To Setup screen.

Note   You can also use this method to access the Recovery Console to repair an existing Windows XP Professional installation by pressing R. You can quit the installation by pressing F3.

▶   **To run the Setup Wizard**

1. On the Welcome To Setup Screen, press ENTER to install Windows XP Professional.

The Setup Wizard prompts you to select an area of free space or an existing partition to install Windows XP Professional.

Note   You can also delete partitions at this time. If you have a C partition, you might not be able to delete it because Setup has already loaded some files onto it. The partition you choose to use must be at least 2000 MB in size. If you cannot use the C partition to install Windows XP Professional, you must replace the C partition in all following practices in this training kit with the appropriate partition, the one on which you install Windows XP Professional.

---

2. Select the C partition.

The Setup Wizard displays the following message: You chose to Install Windows XP on a partition that contains another operating system. Installing Windows XP Professional on this partition might cause the other operating system to function improperly.

3. Press C to have Setup continue and use this partition.

Caution   Depending on the operating system currently installed on the C partition, Setup might display the following message: A \WINDOWS folder already exists that may contain a Windows installation. If you continue the existing Windows installation will be overwritten. If you want to keep both operating systems, press Esc and specify a different folder to use.

---

4. If you get a warning about a \WINDOWS folder already existing, press L to use the folder and delete the installation in it.

If your partition was not formatted with NTFS and you choose to have the partition formatted as NTFS, then Setup formats it as NTFS and then copies files. Otherwise Setup examines the partition and then copies files.

The Setup Wizard reboots the computer and continues to copy files in GUI mode.

The Setup Wizard displays the Regional And Language Options page.

5. Select the appropriate system locale, user locale, and keyboard layout or ensure that they are correct for your language and location, and then click Next.

   Setup displays the Personalize Your Software page, prompting you for your name and your organization name. The Setup Wizard uses your organization name to generate the default computer name. Many applications that you install later will use this information for product registration and document identification.

6. In the Name text box, type your name. In the Organization text box, type the name of your organization, and then click Next.

   The Setup Wizard displays the Computer Name And Administrator Password page.

7. Type **Pro1** in the Computer Name text box.

   Windows XP Professional displays the computer name in all uppercase letters, no matter how you type it.

Caution   If your computer is on a network, check with the network administrator before assigning a name to your computer. The practice sessions here refer to Pro1. If you do not name your computer Pro1, substitute the name of your computer.

---

8. In the Administrator Password text box and in the Confirm Password text box, type **password**, and then click Next.

Important   For the practice sections in this self-paced training kit, you will use *password* for the Administrator account. You should always use a complex password for the Administrator account (one that others cannot easily guess). Microsoft recommends mixing uppercase and lowercase letters, numbers, and symbols (for example, Lp6*g9f2).

Depending on your computer configuration, the Setup Wizard might display the Modem Dialing Information page.

Note   If the Setup Wizard does not display the Modem Dialing Information page, skip to step 13.

---

9. Ensure that the correct country or region is selected.

10. Type the correct area code or city code.

11. If you dial a number to get an outside line, type the number.

12. Ensure that the correct dialing tone is selected, and then click Next.

    The Setup Wizard displays the Date And Time Settings page.

13. If necessary, select the time zone for your location from the Time Zone drop-down list and adjust the date and the time.

14. Ensure that the Automatically Adjust Clock For Daylight Saving Changes check box is selected if you want Windows XP Professional to automatically adjust the time on your computer for daylight savings time, and then click Next.

Note   If you have configured your computer for dual booting with another operating system that can also adjust your clock for daylight savings time, enable this feature for the operating system you use most frequently so that the daylight savings adjustment occurs only once.

The Setup Wizard displays the Networking Settings page.

▶   **To install Windows Networking**

1. Ensure that Typical Settings is selected, and then click Next.

   The Setup Wizard displays the Workgroup Or Computer Domain page.

2. Ensure that No, This Computer Is Not On A Network, Or Is On A Network Without A Domain is selected and that the workgroup name is Workgroup, and then click Next.

   The Setup Wizard configures the networking components and then copies files. This process takes several minutes.

▶   **To complete the installation**

The Setup Wizard installs Start menu items, registers components, saves settings, and removes temporary files. This process takes several minutes.

The computer restarts, and the Welcome To Microsoft Windows page appears.

Important   Ensure that you remove the Windows XP Professional CD-ROM from the CD-ROM drive. If you don't and your computer supports booting from the CD-ROM drive, the computer might attempt to reboot from the CD-ROM. If this happens, remove the CD-ROM and then restart the computer.

---

1. Click Next to continue.

   The Will This Computer Connect To The Internet Directly, Or Through A Network page appears.

2. If you would like to connect to the Internet at this time, select the appropriate connection method, and then click Next.

Note   If you do not want to connect to the Internet at this time, click Skip.

The Setup Wizard displays The Ready To Activate Windows page.

3. Click Yes, Activate Windows Over The Internet Now, and then click Next.

The Setup Wizard displays The Ready To Register With Microsoft page.

4. Click Yes, I'd Like To Register With Microsoft Now, and then click Next.

The Sctup Wizard displays the Collecting Registration Information page.

5. Fill in the appropriate text boxes.

The Setup Wizard displays the Ready To Send Information page.

6. Click Next.

The Setup Wizard displays Do You Want To Set Up Internet Access Now page.

Note   Internet access is not required for this training kit. If you want to connect to the Internet at this time, click Yes Help Me Connect To The Internet, and then click Next and follow the instructions on your screen.

7. Click No, Not At This Time, and then click Next.

The Setup Wizard displays the Who Will Use This Computer page. Your name should already be entered.

8. Type **Fred** in the Second User text box, and then click Next.

The Setup Wizard displays the Thank You page.

9. Read the page, and then click Finish.

10. To log on, select Fred (or the account name created for you during setup).

You have completed your installation of Windows XP Professional and logged on as an administrator.

Lesson Review

The following questions will help you determine whether you have learned enough to move on to the next lesson. If you have difficulty answering these questions, review the material in this lesson before beginning the next lesson. The answers are in Appendix A, "Questions and Answers."

1. If TCP/IP is installed on your computer, what is the maximum length for the computer name you specify during installation?

2. Can you change the computer name after installation without having to reinstall Windows XP Professional? If you can change the name, how do you do it? If you cannot change the name, why not?

3. Which of the following statements about joining a workgroup or a domain are correct? (Choose all that apply.)

    a. You can add your computer to a workgroup or a domain only during installation.

    b. If you add your computer to a workgroup during installation, you can join the computer to a domain later.

    c. If you add your computer to a domain during installation, you can join the computer to a workgroup later.

    d. You cannot add your computer to a workgroup or a domain during installation.

4. Which of the following configurations can you change after installing Windows XP Professional? (Choose all that apply.)

    a. Language

    b. Locale

    c. Keyboard settings

    d. Network protocol

5. When you install networking components with typical settings, what components are installed? What does each component do?

Lesson Summary

- If your computer does not support booting from a CD-ROM, you can install Windows XP Professional by booting another operating system first and then accessing the Windows XP Professional installation CD-ROM.

- The Setup Wizard asks you to provide regional settings, your name and your organization's name, a computer name, and a password for the Administrator account. It also asks you to specify the time zone, time, and date and to decide whether you want Windows XP Professional to automatically adjust for daylight savings time.

- Choosing to install networking components using typical settings installs the Client for Microsoft Networks, File and Printer Sharing for Microsoft Networks, and TCP/IP.

- You can customize the networking components during installation or any time after installation.

Lesson 3: Installing Windows XP Professional over the Network

You can install Windows XP Professional over the network. This lesson discusses the similarities and differences between installing from a CD-ROM and installing over the network. The major difference is the location of the source files needed for installation. This lesson also lists the requirements for an over-the-network installation.

After this lesson, you will be able to

- Complete a network installation of Windows XP Professional

Estimated lesson time: 30 minutes

Preparing for a Network Installation

In a network installation, the Windows XP Professional installation files are located in a shared location on a network file server, which is called a *distribution server*. From the computer on which you want to install Windows XP Professional (the target computer), you connect to the distribution server and then run the Setup program.

Figure 2.6 shows the requirements for a network installation.

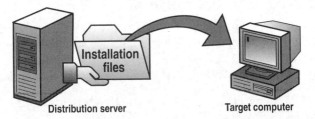

Requirements for a network installation:

- Distribution server
- FAT partition on the target computer
- Network client

Figure 2.6   Requirements for a network installation

Installing Windows XP Professional requires you to do the following:

- **Locate a distribution server.**   The distribution server contains the installation files from the I386 folder on the Windows XP Professional CD-ROM. These files reside in a common network location in a shared folder that allows computers on the network to access the installation files. Contact a network administrator to obtain the path to the installation files on the distribution server.

> **Note**   After you have created or located a distribution server, you can use the over-the-network installation method to concurrently install Windows XP Professional on multiple computers.

- **Create a FAT partition on the target computer.**   The target computer requires a formatted partition to which to copy the installation files. Create a partition containing at least 1.5 GB of disk space or more and format it with the FAT file system.
- **Install a network client.**   A *network client* is software that allows the target computer to connect to the distribution server. On a computer without an operating system, you must boot from a client disk that includes a network client that enables the target computer to connect to the distribution server.

Installing over the Network

The Setup program copies the installation files to the target computer and creates the Setup boot disks. After Setup copies the installation files, you start the installation on the target computer by booting from the Setup boot disks. From this point, you install Windows XP Professional as you would from a CD-ROM.

Figure 2.7 shows the process for installing Windows XP Professional over the network.

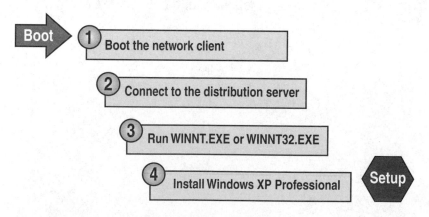

Figure 2.7   Installing Windows XP Professional over the network

Installing Windows XP Professional over the network involves the following steps:

1. **Boot the network client.**

   On the target computer, boot from a floppy disk that includes a network client or start another operating system that can be used to connect to the distribution server.

2. **Connect to the distribution server.**

   After you start the network client on the target computer, connect to the shared folder on the distribution server that contains the Windows XP Professional installation files.

3. **Run WINNT.EXE or WINNT32.EXE to start the Setup program.**

   WINNT.EXE and WINNT32.EXE reside in the shared folder on the distribution server.

   - Use WINNT.EXE for an installation using MS-DOS or Windows 3.0 or later versions on the source system.
   - Use WINNT32.EXE for an installation using Microsoft Windows 95, Windows 98, Microsoft Windows Me, Windows NT 4, or Windows 2000 Professional.

   Running WINNT.EXE or WINNT32.EXE from the shared folder does the following:

   - Creates the Win_nt.~ls temporary folder on the target computer
   - Copies the Windows XP Professional installation files from the shared folder on the distribution server to the Win_nt.~ls folder on the target computer

4. **Install Windows XP Professional.**

   Setup restarts the local computer and begins installing Windows XP Professional.

Modifying the Setup Process Using WINNT.EXE

You can modify an over-the-network installation by changing how WINNT.EXE runs Setup. Table 2.3 lists the switches you can use with WINNT.EXE and describes their functions.

Table 2.3   WINNT.EXE Switches

Switch	Function
/a	Enables accessibility options.
/r[:*folder*]	Specifies an optional folder to be copied and saved. The folder remains after Setup finishes.
/rx[:*folder*]	Specifies the optional folder to be copied. The folder is deleted after Setup finishes.
/s[:*sourcepath*]	Specifies the source location of Windows XP Professional files. This must be a full path of the form x:\[*path*] or \\server\share\[*path*]. The default is the current folder location

(continued)

Table 2.3   *(continued)*

Switch	Function
/t[:*tempdrive*]	Specifies a drive to contain temporary setup files and directs Setup to install Windows XP Professional on that drive. If you do not specify a drive, Setup attempts to locate the drive with the most available space.
/u[:*script_file*]	Performs an unattended installation by using an optional script file. Unattended installations also require using the /s switch. The answer file provides answers to some or all of the prompts that the end user normally responds to during Setup.
/udf:id[,*UDF_file*]	Indicates an identifier (id) that Setup uses to specify how a Uniqueness Database File (UDF) modifies an answer file. The /udf parameter overrides values in the answer file, and the identifier determines which values in the UDF file are used. If you do not specify a *UDF_file*, Setup prompts you to insert a disk that contains the $UNIQUE$.UDB file.

Modifying the Setup Process Using WINNT32.EXE

You can modify an over-the-network installation by changing how WINNT32.EXE runs Setup. Table 2.4 lists the switches you can use with WINNT32.EXE and describes their functions.

Table 2.4   WINNT32.EXE Switches

Switch	Function
/checkupgradeonly	Checks your computer for upgrade compatibility for Windows XP Professional. If you use this option with unattend, no user input is required. Otherwise the results are displayed on the screen and you can save them under the filename you specify. ■ For Windows 98 or Windows Me upgrades, the default filename is UPGRADE.TXT in the *%systemroot%* folder (the folder that contains the Windows XP Professional system files). ■ For Windows NT 4 or Windows 2000 upgrades, the default filename is NTCOMPAT.TXT in the *%systemroot%* folder. For more information about generating a compatibility report, see Lesson 4, "Upgrading Earlier Versions of Windows to WindowsXP Professional."
/cmd:command_line	Specifies a specific command that Setup is to run. This command is run after the computer restarts and after Setup collects the necessary configuration information.

Table 2.4   *(continued)*

Switch	Function
/cmdcons	Copies to the hard disk the additional files necessary to load a command-line interface, the Recovery Console, which is used for repair and recovery. The Recovery Console is installed as a Startup option. You can use the Recovery Console to stop and start services and to access the local drive, including drives formatted with NTFS. You can use this option only after you install Windows XP Professional.
/copydir:*foldername*	Creates an additional folder within the *%systemroot%* folder, which contains the Windows XP Professional system files. For example, if your source folder contains a folder called My_drivers, type **/copydir:My_drivers** to copy the My_drivers folder to your system folder. You can use the /copydir switch to create as many additional folders as you want.
/copysource:*foldername*	Creates an additional folder within the *%systemroot%* folder. Setup deletes folders created with /copysource after installation is complete.
/debug[*level*] [:file_name]	Creates a debug log at the specified level. By default, the debug log file is C:\WINNT32.LOG and the default level is 2. Includes the following levels: ■ 0 (severe errors) ■ 1 (errors) ■ 2 (warnings) ■ 3 (information) ■ 4 (detailed information for debugging) Each level includes the level below it.
/dudisable	Prevents Dynamic Update from running. Without Dynamic Updates, Setup runs only with the original Setup files. This option disables Dynamic Update even if you use an answer file and specify Dynamic Update options in that file.
/dushare: *pathname*	Specifies a share on which you previously downloaded Dynamic Update files (updated files for use with Setup) from the Windows Update Web site. When run from your installation share and used with /duprepare, it prepares the updated files for use in network-based client installations. When used without /duprepare and run on a client, it specifies that the client installation will use the updated files on the share specified in *pathname*.
/duprepare: *pathname*	Prepares an installation share for use with Dynamic Update files that you downloaded from the Windows Update Web site. You can use this share for installing Windows XP Professional for multiple clients (used only with /dushare).

(continued)

Table 2.4 *(continued)*

Switch	Function
/m:*foldername*	Instructs Setup to copy replacement files from an alternate location. Directs Setup to look in the alternate location first and, if files are present, to use them instead of the files from the default location.
/makelocalsource	Instructs Setup to copy all installation source files to the local hard disk. Use this switch when installing from a CD-ROM to provide installation files when the CD-ROM is not available later in the installation.
/noreboot	Prevents Setup from restarting the computer after completing the file-copy phase. This allows you to execute another command.
/s:sourcepath	Specifies the source location of Windows XP Professional installation files. To simultaneously copy files from multiple paths, use a separate /s switch for each source path. If you type multiple /s switches, the first location specified must be available or the installation will fail. You can use a maximum of eight /s switches.
/syspart:[*drive_letter*]	Copies Setup startup files to a hard disk and marks the drive as active. You can then install the drive in another computer. When you start that computer, Setup starts at the next phase. Using /syspart requires the /tempdrive switch. You can use /syspart on computers running Windows NT 4, Windows 2000, Windows XP Professional, or Windows 2000 Server. You cannot use it on computers running Windows 95, Windows 98, or Windows Me.
/tempdrive:*drive_letter*	Places temporary files on the specified drive and installs Windows XP Professional on that drive.
/unattend [number]: [answer_file]	Performs an unattended installation. The answer file provides your custom specifications to Setup. If you don't specify an answer file, all user settings are taken from the previous installation. You can specify the number of seconds between the time that Setup finishes copying the files and when it restarts with number. You can specify the number of seconds only on computers running Windows 98, Windows Me, Windows NT 4, or Windows 2000 that are upgrading to a newer version of Windows XP Professional.
/udf:id[,udb_file]	Indicates an identifier (id) that Setup uses to specify how a UDB modifies an answer file. The UDB file overrides values in the answer file, and the identifier determines which values in the UDB file are used. For example, /udf:RAS_user, OUR_COMPANY.UDB overrides settings that are specified for the RAS_user identifier in the OUR_COMPANY.UDB file. If you do not specify a UDB file, Setup prompts you to insert a disk that contains the $UNIQUE$.UDB file.

Lesson Review

The following questions will help you determine whether you have learned enough to move on to the next lesson. If you have difficulty answering these questions, review the material in this lesson before beginning the next lesson. The answers are in Appendix A, "Questions and Answers."

1. On which of the following operating systems running on the client computer do you use WINNT32.EXE to install Windows XP Professional? (Choose all that apply.)

   a. Windows 3.0 or later

   b. Windows 95

   c. Windows 98

   d. Windows NT 4

2. On which of the following operating systems running on the client computer do you use WINNT.EXE to install Windows XP Professional? (Choose all that apply.)

   a. Windows 3.0 or later

   b. Windows 95

   c. Windows Me

   d. Windows NT 4

3. What Windows XP Professional command allows you to verify that your computer is compatible with Windows XP Professional before you begin installing it?

4. You use the _____ switch with WINNT32.EXE to prevent Setup from restarting the computer after completing the file-copy phase.

5. You use the _____ switch with WINNT32.EXE to tell Setup to copy all installation source files to your local hard disk.

Lesson Summary

- When you install Windows XP Professional, the main difference between an over-the-network installation and an installation from CD-ROM is the location of the source files.

- After you connect to the shared folder containing the source files and start WINNT.EXE or WINNT32.EXE, the installation proceeds as an installation from CD-ROM.

- Several switches for WINNT.EXE and WINNT32.EXE allow you to modify the installation process.

- The /checkupgradeonly switch specifies that WINNT32.EXE should check your computer only for upgrade compatibility with Windows XP Professional.

Lesson 4: Upgrading Earlier Versions of Windows to Windows XP Professional

You can upgrade many earlier versions of Windows operating systems directly to Windows XP Professional. Before upgrading, however, you must do the following:

- Ensure that the computer hardware meets the minimum Windows XP Professional hardware requirements.
- Check the HCL or test the computer for hardware compatibility using the Windows XP Professional Compatibility tool. Using compatible hardware prevents problems when you start the upgrade on a large number of client computers.

You can upgrade computers directly to Windows XP Professional if they are running earlier versions of Windows that use compatible hardware. If your Windows 95 and Windows 98 client systems are using incompatible or insufficient hardware, you can still take advantage of the Active Directory service functionality provided by a Windows 2000 Server domain by installing the Windows 2000 Server Directory Services Client on these systems.

After this lesson, you will be able to

- Upgrade earlier Windows client operating systems to Windows XP Professional

Estimated lesson time: 25 minutes

Identifying Client Upgrade Paths

You can upgrade most client computers running earlier versions of Windows directly to Windows XP Professional. However, computers running some earlier versions of Windows (including Windows 95, Microsoft Windows NT 3.1, and Microsoft Windows NT 3.5) require an additional step. Table 2.5 lists the Windows XP Professional upgrade paths for various client operating systems.

Table 2.5   Windows XP Professional Upgrade Paths for Client Operating Systems

Upgrade from	Upgrade to
Windows 98	Windows XP Professional
Windows Me	Windows XP Professional
Windows NT Workstation 4.0	Windows XP Professional
Windows 2000 Professional	Windows XP Professional
Windows 95	Windows 98 first, and then upgrade to Windows XP Professional
Windows NT 3.1, 3.5, or 3.51	Windows NT 4 Workstation first, and then upgrade to Windows XP Professional

---

Note Windows XP Professional also upgrades all released service packs for Windows NT Workstation 4.0.

Generating a Hardware Compatibility Report

Before you upgrade a client computer to Windows XP Professional, ensure that it meets the minimum hardware requirements by using the Windows XP Compatibility tool to generate a hardware and software compatibility report. This tool runs automatically during system upgrades, but running it before beginning the upgrade should identify any hardware and software problems and allow you to fix compatibility problems ahead of time.

Generating the Report

To run the Windows XP Compatibility tool and generate a compatibility report, perform the following steps:

1. Insert the Windows XP Professional CD-ROM into the CD-ROM drive.
2. At a command prompt, type *d*:\i386\winnt32 /checkupgradeonly

---

Note *d*:\ represents the drive letter of the CD-ROM drive

---

3. Press ENTER.

Note Generating the upgrade report can take several minutes. The tool checks only for compatible hardware and software and generates a report that you can analyze to determine the system components that are compatible with Windows XP Professional.

Reviewing the Report

Winnt32 /checkupgradeonly generates a report that appears as a text document, which you can view in the tool or save as a text file. The report documents the system hardware and software that are incompatible with Windows XP Professional. It also specifies whether you need to obtain an upgrade pack for software installed on the system and recommends additional system changes or modifications to maintain functionality in Windows XP Professional.

Upgrading Compatible Windows 98 Computers

For client systems that test as compatible with Windows XP Professional, run WINNT32.EXE to complete the upgrade. To upgrade a Windows 98 computer, complete the following procedure.

To perform the upgrade follow these steps:

1. Insert the Windows XP Professional CD-ROM in the CD-ROM drive.

   The AUTORUN program on the Windows XP Professional CD-ROM displays the Welcome To Microsoft Windows XP screen.

Note If you do not want to use any switches with WINNT32.EXE, click Install Windows XP and follow the prompts on your screen. These steps are the same as Practice 2 in Lesson 2.

---

2. Run WINNT32.EXE with any appropriate switches.

3. Accept the license agreement.

4. If the computer is already a member of a domain, create a computer account in that domain. Windows 98 clients do not require a computer account, but Windows XP Professional clients do.

5. Provide *upgrade packs* for applications that need them. Upgrade packs update the software to work with Windows XP Professional. These packs are available from the software vendor.

6. Upgrade to NTFS when prompted. Select the upgrade if you do not plan to set up the client computer to dual boot.

7. Continue with the upgrade if the Windows XP Professional Compatibility tool generates a report showing that the computer is compatible with Windows XP Professional. The upgrade finishes without further intervention and adds your computer to a domain or workgroup.

   If the report shows that the computer is incompatible with Windows XP Professional, terminate the upgrade process, and then upgrade your hardware or software.

Upgrading a Windows NT 4 Client

The upgrade process for computers running Windows NT 4 is similar to the upgrade process for computers running Windows 98.

Verifying Compatibility

Before you perform the upgrade, use the Windows XP Professional Compatibility tool to verify that the systems are compatible with Windows XP Professional and to identify any potential problems.

Upgrading Compatible Systems

Windows NT 4 computers that meet the hardware compatibility requirements can upgrade directly to Windows XP Professional. To start the upgrade process, complete the following procedure.

To perform the upgrade follow these steps:

1. Insert the Windows XP Professional CD-ROM in the CD-ROM drive.

   The AUTORUN program on the Windows XP Professional CD-ROM displays the Welcome To Microsoft Windows XP screen.

   Note If you do not want to use any switches with WINNT32.EXE, click Install Windows XP and follow the prompts on your screen. These steps are the same as Practice 2 in Lesson 2.

   ---

2. Click Exit to close the Welcome To Microsoft Windows XP screen.

3. Click Start, and then click Run.

4. Type *d*:\i386\winnt32 */switch* (where *d* is the drive letter for your CD-ROM and */switch* represents one or more switches that you want to use with the WINNT32 command), and then press ENTER.

   The Welcome To Windows page appears.

5. In the Installation Type drop-down list, select Upgrade and then click Next.

   The License Agreement page is displayed.

6. Read the license agreement, click I Accept This Agreement, and then click Next.

   Setup displays the Product Key page.

7. Enter your 25-character product key, which is located on the back of the Windows XP Professional CD-ROM case.

   Setup displays the Upgrading To The Windows XP Professional NTFS File System page.

8. Click Yes, Upgrade My Drive and then click Next. The Copying Installation Files page appears.

9. The Restarting The Computer page appears, and the computer restarts. Then the upgrade finishes without further intervention.

Lesson Review

The following questions will help you determine whether you have learned enough to move on to the next lesson. If you have difficulty answering these questions, review the material in this lesson before beginning the next lesson. The answers are in Appendix A, "Questions and Answers."

1. Which of the following operating systems can be upgraded directly to Windows XP Professional? (Choose all that apply.)

   a. Windows NT Workstation 4.0

   b. Windows NT 3.51

   c. Windows 2000 Professional

   d. Windows NT Server 4.0

2. How can you upgrade a computer running Windows 95 to Windows XP Professional?

3. Before you upgrade a computer running Windows NT 4, which of the following actions should you perform? (Choose all that apply.)

   a. Create a 2-GB partition on which to install Windows XP Professional.

   b. Verify that the computer meets the minimum hardware requirements.

   c. Generate a hardware and software compatibility report.

   d. Format the partition containing Windows NT 4 so that you can install Windows XP Professional.

4. How can you verify that your computer is compatible with Windows XP Professional and therefore can be upgraded?

Lesson Summary

- Before you upgrade a client computer to Windows XP Professional, ensure that it meets the minimum hardware requirements.

- Use the Windows XP Professional Compatibility tool to generate a hardware and software compatibility report.

- For client systems that test as compatible with Windows XP Professional, run the Windows XP Professional Setup program (WINNT32.EXE) to complete the upgrade.

Lesson 5: Troubleshooting Windows XP Professional Setup

Your installation of Windows XP Professional should complete without any problems. However, this lesson covers some common issues you might encounter during installation.

After this lesson, you will be able to

- Troubleshoot Windows XP Professional installations

Estimated lesson time: 5 minutes

Resolving Common Problems

Table 2.6 lists some common installation problems and offers solutions.

Table 2.6   Troubleshooting Tips

Problem	Solution
Media errors occur	If you are installing from a CD-ROM, use a different CD-ROM. To request a replacement CD-ROM, contact Microsoft or your vendor. Try using a different computer and CD-ROM drive. If you can read the CD-ROM on a different computer, you can perform an over-the-network installation. If one of your Setup disks is not working, try using a different set of Setup disks.
CD-ROM drive is not supported	Replace the CD-ROM drive with a supported drive. If replacement is impossible, try another installation method such as installing over the network. After you complete the installation, add the adapter card driver for the CD-ROM drive if it is available.
Computer is unable to copy files from the CD-ROM	Test the CD-ROM on another computer. If you can copy the files using a different CD-ROM drive on a different computer, use the CD-ROM to copy the files to a network share or to the hard drive of the computer on which you want to install Windows XP Professional.
Insufficient disk space	Do one of the following: - Use the Setup program to create a partition by using existing free space on the hard disk. - Delete and create partitions as needed to create a partition that is large enough for installation. - Reformat an existing partition to create more space.

Table 2.6   *(continued)*

Problem	Solution
Dependency service fails to start	In the Windows XP Professional Setup Wizard, return to the Network Settings dialog box and verify that you installed the correct protocol and network adapter. Verify that the network adapter has the proper configuration settings, such as transceiver type, and that the local computer name is unique on the network.
Setup cannot connect to the domain controller	Verify the following: ■ The domain name is correct. ■ The server running the DNS service and the domain controller are both running and online. If you cannot locate a domain controller, install Windows XP Professional into a workgroup and then join the domain after installation. ■ The network adapter card and protocol settings are set correctly. If you are reinstalling Windows XP Professional and are using the same computer name, delete the computer account and recreate it.
Windows XP Professional fails to install or start	Verify the following: ■ Windows XP Professional is detecting all of the hardware. ■ All of the hardware is on the HCL. Try running Winnt32 /checkupgradeonly to verify that the hardware is compatible with Windows XP Professional.

Setup Logs

During Setup, Windows XP Professional generates a number of log files containing installation information that can help you resolve any problems that occur after setup is completed. The action log and the error log are especially useful for troubleshooting.

Action Log

The action log records in chronological order the actions that the Setup program performs. It includes actions such as copying files and creating Registry entries. It also contains entries that are written to the Setup error log. The action log is stored in SETUPACT.LOG.

Error Log

The error log describes errors that occur during setup and their severity. If errors occur, the log viewer displays the error log at the end of setup. The error log is stored in SETUPERR.LOG.

Additional Logs

Setup creates a number of additional logs, including the following:

- **% *windir%*\comsetup.log**   Outlines installation for Optional Component Manager and COM+ components.

- **% *windir%*\setupapi.log**   Receives an entry each time a line from an .inf file is implemented. If an error occurs, this log describes the failure.

- **% *windir%*\debug\NetSetup.log**   Logs activity when computers join domains or workgroups.

- **% *windir%*\repair\setup.log**   Provides information that is used by the Recovery Console. (In Windows NT 4, this was used by the Emergency Repair Process.) For more information about the Recovery Console, see Chapter 18, "Modifying and Troubleshooting the Boot Process."

Note   For additional information about troubleshooting installations, see Lesson 3, "Using Startup And Recovery Tools," in Chapter 18, "Modifying and Troubleshooting the Boot Process."

Lesson Review

The following questions will help you determine whether you have learned enough to move on to the next lesson. If you have difficulty answering these questions, review the material in this lesson before beginning the next chapter. The answers are in Appendix A, "Questions and Answers."

1. If you encounter an error during setup, which of the following log files should you check? (Choose all that apply.)

    a. SETUPERR.LOG

    b. NETSETUP.LOG

    c. SETUP.LOG

    d. SETUPACT.LOG

2. If your computer cannot connect to the domain controller during installation, what should you do?

3. If your computer cannot connect to read the CD-ROM during installation, what should you do?

Lesson Summary

- The action log, SETUPACT.LOG, records and describes in chronological order the actions that Setup performs.

- The error log, SETUPERR.LOG, describes errors that occur during setup and indicates the severity of each error.

- A number of additional logs are created during setup, including COMSETUP.LOG, SETUPAPI.LOG, NETSETUP.LOG, and SETUP.LOG.

C H A P T E R   3

Setting Up and Managing User Accounts

About This Chapter

This chapter explains how to plan, establish, and maintain Microsoft Windows XP Professional user accounts. It also presents the skills and knowledge necessary to create local user accounts and set properties for them.

Before You Begin

To complete this chapter, you must have

- A computer that meets the minimum hardware requirements listed in the preface, "About This Book"
- Windows XP Professional installed on the computer

Lesson 1: Understanding User Accounts

Windows XP Professional uses three types of user accounts: local user accounts, domain user accounts, and built-in user accounts.

- A *local user account* allows you to log on to a specific computer to access resources on that computer.

- A *domain user account* allows you to log on to the domain to access network resources.

- A *built-in user account* allows you to perform administrative tasks or access local or network resources.

After this lesson, you will be able to

- Explain how to create local user accounts and domain user accounts
- Describe how to create and disable built-in user accounts

Estimated lesson time: 30 minutes

Local User Accounts

Local user accounts allow users to log on only to the computer on which the local user account has been created and to access resources on only that computer. When you create a local user account, Windows XP Professional creates the account only in that computer's security database, called the *local security database,* shown in Figure 3.1. Windows XP Professional uses the local security database to authenticate the local user account, which allows the user to log on to that computer. Windows XP Professional does not replicate local user account information to any other computer.

Local user accounts

- Provide access to resources on the local computer
- Are created only on computers that are not in a domain
- Are created in the local security database

Figure 3.1   Characteristics of local user accounts

Microsoft recommends that you use local user accounts only on computers in workgroups. If you create a local user account in a workgroup of five computers running Windows XP Professional—for example, User1 on Computer1—you can only log on to Computer1 with the User1 account. If you need to be able to log on as User1 to all five computers in the workgroup, you must create a local user account, User1, on each of the five computers. Furthermore, if you decide to change the password for User1, you must change the password for User1 on each of the five computers because each computer maintains its own local security database.

Note A domain does not recognize local user accounts, so do not create local user accounts on computers running Windows XP Professional that are part of a domain. Doing so restricts users from accessing resources in the domain and prevents the domain administrator from administering the local user account properties or assigning access permissions for domain resources.

Domain User Accounts

Domain user accounts allow you to log on to the domain and access resources anywhere on the network. When you log on, you provide your logon information—your user name and password. Microsoft Windows 2000 Server uses this logon information to authenticate your identity and build an access token that contains your user information and security settings. The access token identifies you to the computers in the domain on which you try to access resources. The access token is valid throughout the logon session.

Note You can have domain user accounts only if you have a domain. You can have a domain only if you have at least one computer running one of the Windows 2000 Server products that is configured as a domain controller, which has the Active Directory directory service installed.

You create a domain user account in the copy of the Active Directory database (the *directory*) on a domain controller, as shown in Figure 3.2. The domain controller replicates the new user account information to all domain controllers in the domain. After Windows 2000 Server replicates the new user account information, all of the domain controllers in the domain tree can authenticate the user during the logon process.

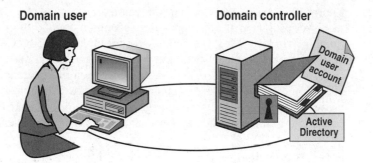

Domain user   **Domain controller**

Domain user accounts

- **Provide access to network resources**
- **Provide the access token for authentication**
- **Are created in Active Directory directory services on a domain controller**

Figure 3.2   Domain user accounts

Built-In User Accounts

Windows XP Professional automatically creates *built-in accounts*. Two commonly used built-in accounts are Administrator and Guest.

Administrator

Use the built-in Administrator account to manage the overall computer. You can perform tasks to create and modify user accounts and groups, manage security policies, create printer resources, and assign the permissions and rights that allow user accounts to access resources.

Note   If you want to log on as Administrator and are using the Welcome screen, you can press CTRL+ALT+DELETE twice. Windows XP Professional displays a logon prompt and you can log on as Administrator. The Administrator account will not appear on the Welcome screen if you are running in a workgroup environment, the Welcome screen is enabled, and you created a user account during Setup. See Chapter 2, "Installing Windows XP Professional," for information about creating a user account during Setup. Lesson 3 in this chapter explains how to configure the computer to use the logon prompt instead of the Welcome screen.

As the administrator, you should create a user account for performing nonadministrative tasks and use your Administrator account only for administrative tasks.

Note   You cannot delete the Administrator account. As a best practice, you should always rename the built-in Administrator account to provide greater security. Use a name that does not identify it as the Administrator account, making it more difficult for unauthorized users to use it to break into your computer.

The Administrator account is enabled by default, but you can configure the Account: Administrator Account Status Security Option to disable it. For more information, see Chapter 13, "Configuring Security Settings and Internet Options."

Guest

Use the built-in Guest account to allow occasional users to log on and access resources. For example, an employee who needs access to resources for a short time can use the Guest account.

Note   Allow Guest access only in low-security networks, and always assign a password to the Guest account. You can rename the Guest account, but you cannot delete it.

Enabling the Guest Account

Log on with a user account that is a member of the Administrators group and use the User Accounts tool in the Control Panel (shown in Figure 3.3) to give access to the Guest account on the computer.

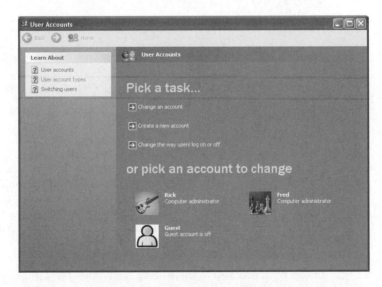

Figure 3.3   The User Accounts tool in a workgroup environment

Note   To access the User Accounts program, click Start, click Control Panel, and then click User Accounts.

The User Accounts program displays the user accounts that can log on to the computer. The User Accounts program in Figure 3.3 indicates that Guest access is off, meaning that the Guest account is disabled.

To enable the Guest account, complete the following steps:

1. Click Start, click Control Panel, and then click User Accounts.

2. In the User Accounts window, click the Guest icon to access the Do You Want To Turn On The Guest Account window (see Figure 3.4).

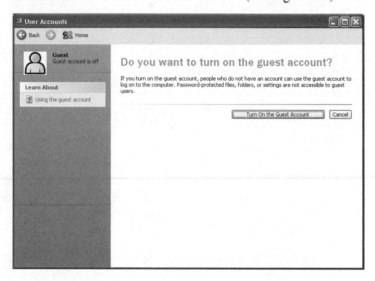

Figure 3.4   The Do You Want To Turn On The Guest Account window

3. Click Turn On The Guest Account. The Guest account is now enabled.

4. Close the User Accounts window and the Control Panel.

Disabling the Guest Account

You can also use the User Accounts program to disable Guest account access. If the Guest account is active, the User Accounts program indicates that Guest Access Is On.

To prevent Guest account access to the computer, complete the following steps:

1. In the User Accounts window, click the Guest icon.

2. In the What Do You Want To Change About The Guest Account window, click Turn Off The Guest Account.

   The Guest account is now disabled.

3. Close the User Accounts window and Control Panel.

Lesson Review

The following questions will help you determine whether you have learned enough to move on to the next lesson. If you have difficulty answering these questions, review the material in this lesson before beginning the next lesson. The answers are in Appendix A, "Questions and Answers."

1. Where do local user accounts allow users to log on and gain access to resources?

2. Where should you create user accounts for computers running Windows XP Professional that are part of a domain?

3. Which of the following statements about domain user accounts are correct? (Choose all that apply.)

   a. Domain user accounts allow users to log on to the domain and gain access to resources anywhere on the network, as long as the users have the required access permissions.

   b. If at least one computer running one of the Windows 2000 Server products is configured as a domain controller, you should use domain user accounts only.

   c. The domain controller replicates the new user account information to all other computers in the domain.

   d. A new domain user account is established in the local security database on the domain controller on which you created the account.

4. Which of the following statements about built-in accounts are correct? (Choose all that apply.)

   a. You can delete the Guest account.

   b. You cannot delete the Administrator account.

   c. You cannot rename the Guest account.

   d. You can rename the Administrator account.

5. How do you disable the Guest account?

Lesson Summary

- Windows XP Professional uses local user accounts, domain user accounts, and built-in user accounts.

- Local user accounts allow users to log on at and access resources on only the computer on which you create the local user account.

- When you create a local user account, Windows XP Professional creates the account only in that computer's security database, which is called the local security database.

- Do not create local user accounts on computers running Windows XP Professional that are part of a domain because the domain does not recognize local user accounts.

- Domain user accounts allow users to log on to the domain and access resources anywhere on the network.

- You create a domain user account in the copy of the Active Directory database (the *directory*) on a domain controller.

- You can only have domain user accounts if at least one computer is running one of the Windows 2000 Server products configured as a domain controller.

- Windows XP Professional automatically creates two commonly used built-in accounts: Administrator and Guest.

- Rename the Administrator account to provide greater security. The Administrator account is enabled by default.

- You can rename the Guest account, and you can use the User Accounts tool to enable or disable it.

- You cannot delete built-in accounts.

Lesson 2: Planning New User Accounts

You can streamline the process of creating user accounts by planning and organizing user account information such as:

- Naming conventions
- Password requirements

After this lesson, you will be able to

- Establish an effective naming convention for your organization
- Describe the password guidelines for protecting access to computers running Windows XP Professional

Estimated lesson time: 10 minutes

Naming Conventions

A *naming convention* is an organization's established standard for identifying users in the domain. Following a consistent naming convention helps administrators and users remember logon names. It also makes it easier for administrators to locate specific user accounts to add them to groups or perform account administration. Table 3.1 summarizes some guidelines for determining an effective naming convention for your organization.

Table 3.1   Naming Convention Guidelines

Guideline	Explanation
Create unique user logon names.	Local user account names must be unique on the computer on which you create the local user account. User logon names for domain user accounts must be unique to the directory.
Use a maximum of 20 characters.	User account names can contain up to 20 uppercase or lowercase characters. The field accepts more than 20 characters, but Windows XP Professional recognizes only the first 20.
Remember that user logon names are not case sensitive.	You can use a combination of special and alphanumeric characters to establish unique user accounts. User logon names are not case sensitive, but Windows XP Professional preserves the case for display purposes.
Avoid characters that are not valid.	The following characters are not valid: " / \ [ ] : ;	= , + * ? < >
Accommodate employees with duplicate names.	If two users have the same name, you could create a user logon name consisting of the first name, the last initial, and additional letters from the last name to differentiate the users. For example, if two users are named John Evans, you could create one user account logon as johne and the other as johnev. You could also number each user logon name—for example, johne1 and johne2.

(continued)

Table 3.1   *(continued)*

Guideline	Explanation
Identify the type of employee.	Some organizations prefer to identify temporary employees in their user accounts. You could add a T and a dash in front of the user's logon name (T-johne) or use parentheses at the end—for example, johne(Temp).
Rename the Administrator and Guest built-in user accounts.	You should rename the Administrator and Guest accounts to provide greater security.

Password Requirements

To protect access to the computer, every user account should have a password. Consider the following guidelines for passwords:

- Always assign a password to the Administrator account to prevent unauthorized access to the account.

- Determine whether the Administrator or the users will control passwords. You can assign unique passwords to user accounts and prevent users from changing them, or you can allow users to enter their own passwords the first time they log on. In most cases, users should control their passwords.

- Use passwords that are hard to guess. For example, avoid using passwords with an obvious association, such as a family member's name.

- Passwords can contain up to 128 characters; a minimum length of 8 characters is recommended.

- Include both uppercase and lowercase letters (unlike user names, user passwords are case sensitive), numerals, and the valid nonalphanumeric characters.

Lesson Review

The following questions will help you determine whether you have learned enough to move on to the next lesson. If you have difficulty answering these questions, review the material in this lesson before beginning the next lesson. The answers are in Appendix A, "Questions and Answers."

1. The maximum number of characters that Windows XP Professional recognizes in a local user account name is _____.

2. When are duplicate local user accounts valid in a network of computers running Windows XP Professional?

3. Passwords can be up to _____ characters long with a minimum length of _____ characters recommended.

4. Which of the following sets of characters are valid to use in a local user account name on a computer running Windows XP Professional? (Choose all that apply.)

   a. 0 ( ) 9

   b. - + = >

   c. A through Z; a through z

   d. [ ] _ |

5. When users create their own passwords, which of the following guidelines should they observe? (Choose all that apply.)

   a. Use the maximum number of characters allowed in a password.

   b. Use a password that is hard for others to guess.

   c. Use at least one uppercase letter, one lowercase letter, one numeral, and one valid nonalphanumeric character.

   d. Use the name of your spouse, child, cat, or dog so that you can easily remember it.

Lesson Summary

- Local user account names must be unique on the computer on which you create the account, and domain user accounts must be unique to the directory.

- User logon names can contain up to 20 uppercase or lowercase characters. The User Name text box in the Log On To Windows dialog box accepts more than 20 characters, but Windows XP Professional recognizes only the first 20.

- The following characters are not valid: " / \ [ ] : ; | = , + * ? < >

- User logon names are not case sensitive, but Windows XP Professional preserves the case for display purposes.

- Passwords can be up to 128 characters long; a minimum of 8 characters is recommended.

- Use uppercase and lowercase letters, numerals, and valid nonalphanumeric characters in creating passwords.

Lesson 3: Creating, Modifying, and Deleting User Accounts

Windows XP Professional provides two ways to create, modify, and delete user accounts: the User Accounts tool in the Control Panel and the Computer Management snap-in.

After this lesson, you will be able to

- Modify existing user accounts
- Create local user accounts
- Delete user accounts

Estimated lesson time: 50 minutes

User Accounts Tool

The User Accounts tool in the Control Panel (shown in Figure 3.5) is one of the tools you use to create, modify, and delete local user accounts.

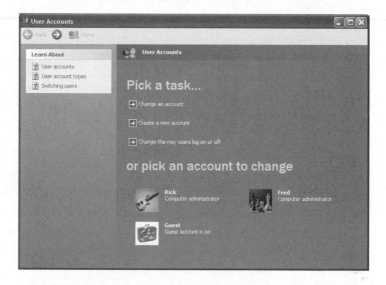

Figure 3.5   The User Accounts tool

If you are logged on with an account that is a member of the Administrators group, the Pick A Task portion of the User Accounts tool allows you to perform the following tasks:

- Change an account (which includes deleting the account)
- Create a new user account
- Change the way users log on or log off

Changing an Account

If you are an administrator, the Change An Account task allows you to make changes to any user account on the computer. If you are logged on with a limited user account, you do not see the same Pick A Task screen as an administrator; you see only a Pick A Task screen that contains some of the following options that an administrator can perform:

- **Change My/The Name.** Changes the user account name of an account on the computer. You only see this option if you are logged on as an administrator because only an administrator can perform this task.

- **Create A Password.** Creates a password for your account. You only see this option if your user account does not have a password. Only an administrator can create passwords for other user accounts.

- **Change My/The Password.** Changes the password for your account. You only see this option if your user account already has a password assigned to it; you see this option instead of the Create A Password option. Only an administrator can change passwords for other user accounts.

- **Remove My/The Password.** Removes the password for your account or any other account on the computer. You only see this option if your user account already has a password assigned to it. Only an administrator can remove passwords for other user accounts.

- **Change My/The Picture.** Changes the picture that appears on the Welcome screen. Only an administrator can change the pictures for other user accounts.

- **Change My/The Account Type.** Changes the account type for a specified account. Only an administrator can change the account type for a user account.

- **Set Up My Account To Use A .NET Passport.** Starts the Add A .NET Passport To Your Windows XP Professional Account Wizard. A passport allows you to have online conversations with family and friends, create your own personal Web pages, and sign in instantly to all .NET-enabled sites and services. You can set up only your own account to use a .NET passport.

- **Delete The Account.** Deletes a specified user account. You only see this option if you are logged on as an administrator because only an administrator can perform this task.

Note   When you delete a user account, Windows XP Professional displays the Do You Want To Keep *local_user_account's* Files window. If you click Keep Files, Windows XP Professional saves the contents of the *local_user_account's* desktop and My Documents folder to a new folder called *local_user_account* on your desktop. However, it cannot save *local_user_account's* e-mail messages, Internet Favorites, or other settings.

To change your account while logged on with a limited user account, complete the following steps:

1. Click Start, click Control Panel, and then click User Accounts.

   The Pick A Task window appears.

2. Click the appropriate option for the modification that you want to make and then follow the prompts on the screen.

To change an account while logged on as an administrator, complete the following steps:

1. Click Start, click Control Panel, and then click User Accounts.

2. In the User Accounts window, click Change An Account.

   The Pick An Account To Change window appears.

3. Click the account you want to change.

   The What Do You Want To Change About *account_name* Account window appears.

4. Click the appropriate option for the modification that you want to make and then follow the prompts on the screen.

Creating a New User Account

Only administrators can create new user accounts. This option is only available on the Pick A Task screen if you are logged on with a user account that is a member of the Administrators group.

To create a new user account, complete the following steps:

1. Click Start, click Control Panel, and then click User Accounts.

2. In the User Accounts window, click Create A New Account.

   The Name The New Account window appears.

3. In the Type A Name For The New Account box, type a user logon name (up to 20 characters), and then click Next.

Note   The user's logon name appears in the Welcome screen and on the Start menu. For information about valid characters for creating user accounts, see Table 3.1.

The Pick An Account Type window appears. Windows XP Professional provides two account types: Computer Administrator and Limited. Table 3.2 lists the capabilities of each account type.

4. Select the appropriate account type, and then click Create Account.

Table 3.2   User Account Types and Capabilities

Capability	Computer Administrator	Limited
Change your own picture	X	X
Create, change, or remove your password	X	X
Change your own account type	X	
Change your own account name	X	
Change other users' pictures, passwords, account types, and account names	X	
Have full access to other user accounts	X	
Create user accounts on this computer	X	
Access and read all files on this computer	X	
Install programs and hardware	X	
Make systemwide changes to the computer	X	

Changing the Way Users Log On or Log Off

Only administrators can change the way users log on or log off the computer. This option is only available on the Pick A Task screen if you are logged on with a user account that is a member of the Administrators group.

These two options control how all users log on and log off the computer:

- **Use The Welcome Screen.** This check box, enabled by default, allows you to click your user account on the Welcome screen to log on to the computer. If you clear this check box, you must type your user name and password at a logon prompt to log on.

- **Use Fast User Switching.** This check box, enabled by default, allows you to quickly switch to another user account without first logging off and closing all programs. When you are finished, you can switch to the first user account.

To change the way users log on or log off, complete the following steps:

1. Click Start, click Control Panel, and then click User Accounts.

2. In the User Accounts window, click Change The Way Users Log On Or Off. The Select Logon And Logoff Options window appears.

3. Select or clear the appropriate check boxes.

Picking an Account to Change

The Pick An Account To Change portion of the User Accounts tool is only available if you are logged on with a user account that is a member of the Administrators group. It allows you to select a user account to modify. The account modifications you can make depend on the account type and how it is configured. The account characteristics that you can change are the same as those discussed earlier in this lesson in the section entitled, "Changing an Account."

The Computer Management Snap-In

One of the tools for managing Microsoft Windows XP Professional is the Microsoft Management Console (MMC). The MMC provides a standardized method for creating, saving, and opening administrative tools. The MMC doesn't provide management functions itself, but it hosts management applications called *snap-ins* that you use to perform one or more administrative tasks.

The MMC allows you to do the following:

- **Administer tasks and troubleshoot problems locally.**   You can perform most of your administrative tasks and troubleshoot many problems using only the MMC.

- **Administer tasks and troubleshoot problems remotely.**   You can use most snap-ins for remote administration and troubleshooting. Windows XP Professional prompts you with a dialog box when you can use a snap-in remotely.

- **Centralize administration.**   You can use consoles to perform most of your administrative tasks from one computer. Each console can contain one or more snap-ins, including third-party snap-ins, so you can create one console that contains all the tools you need to perform your administrative tasks.

When you add snap-ins to an empty console, you create a customized console. One of the snap-ins that you can add is the Computer Management snap-in, shown in Figure 3.6. The Computer Management snap-in is another Windows XP Professional tool for creating, deleting, modifying, and disabling local user accounts and changing passwords.

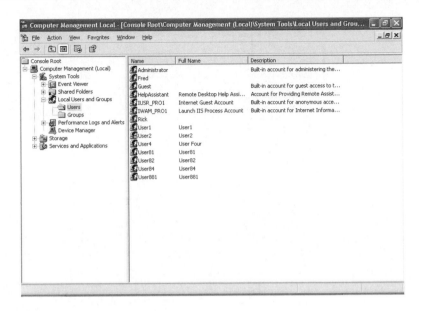

Figure 3.6   The Computer Management snap-in

Creating a Customized MMC Console

To create a customized MMC console containing Computer Management, complete the following steps:

1. Click Start, and then click Run.

2. In the Open text box, type **mmc** and then click OK.

   MMC starts and displays an empty console.

3. Maximize the Console1 window.

4. Maximize the Console Root window.

5. On the File menu, click Add/Remove Snap-In.

   MMC displays the Add/Remove Snap-In dialog box.

6. In the Standalone tab, click Add.

   MMC displays the Add Standalone Snap-In dialog box shown in Figure 3.7.

Figure 3.7 The Add Standalone Snap-In dialog box

7. In the Available Standalone Snap-Ins list, select Computer Management, and then click Add.

MMC displays the Computer Management dialog box (shown in Figure 3.8), which allows you to specify which computer you want to administer. The Local Computer: (The Computer This Console Is Running On) option is selected by default.

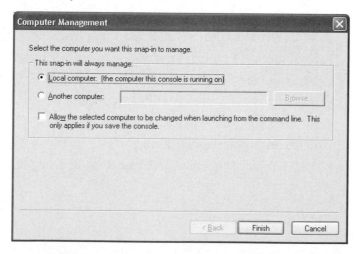

Figure 3.8 The Computer Management dialog box

Note   You can add Computer Management for the local computer on which you are working or, if your local computer is part of a network, you can add Computer Management and point to a remote computer. To add Computer Management for a remote computer, in the Computer Management Snap-In dialog box, select Another Computer and then click Browse. In the Select Computer dialog box, in the Enter The Object Name To Select text box, type the name of the remote computer that you want to administer with Computer Management and then click OK. There is also a check box that allows you to change the selected computer when you launch the MMC console from the command line.

8. In the Computer Management dialog box, click Finish.

9. In the Add Standalone Snap-In dialog box (see Figure 3.7), click Close.

10. In the Add/Remove dialog box, click OK to place the Computer Management snap-in in an MMC console.

Note   The MMC console you created is named Console1. To save this console to use again, go to the File menu and click Save As. In the File Name text box, type **Computer Management Local**, and then click Save.

Creating a Local User Account Using the Computer Management Snap-In

To create local user accounts using the Computer Management snap-in complete the following steps:

1. Expand the MMC console containing the Computer Management snap-in.

2. In the console pane of the Computer Management window, click the Computer Management plus sign (+) icon to expand the tree. Computer Management contains three folders: System Tools, Storage, and Services And Applications.

3. In the console pane, double-click System Tools, and then click Local Users And Groups.

4. In the details pane, right-click Users, and then click New User.

5. Fill in the appropriate text boxes in the New User dialog box (Figure 3.9), click Create, and then click Close.

Figure 3.9   New User dialog box

Table 3.3 describes the local user account options shown in Figure 3.9.

Table 3.3   Local User Account Options

Option	Action
User Name	Type the user's logon name. This field is required.
Full Name	Type the user's full name. You can include the user's first and last names, but you can also include the middle name or initial. This field is optional.
Description	Type descriptive text about the user account or the user. This field is optional.
Password	Type the account password that is used to authenticate the user. For greater security, always assign a password. As an additional security measure, the password appears as a string of asterisks as you type it.
Confirm Password	Confirm the password by typing it a second time. This field is required if you assign a password.
User Must Change Password At Next Logon	Select this check box if you want the user to change his or her password the first time that he or she logs on. This ensures that only the user knows the password. This option is selected by default.
User Cannot Change Password	Select this check box if more than one person uses the same user account (such as Guest), or if you want only administrators to control passwords. If you have selected the User Must Change Password At Next Logon check box, this option is not available.

Table 3.3   *(continued)*

Option	Action
Password Never Expires	Select this check box if you never want the password to change—for example, for a domain user account that a program or a Windows XP Professional service uses. The User Must Change Password At Next Logon option overrides this option, so if you have selected the User Must Change Password At Next Logon check box, this option is not available.
Account Is Disabled	Select this check box to prevent use of this account—for example, for a new employee who has not yet started working for your organization.

Note   Always require new users to change their passwords the first time they log on. This forces them to use passwords that only they know.

Tip   For added network security, use a combination of letters and numbers to create unique initial passwords for all new user accounts.

Practice: Creating, Modifying, and Deleting Local User Accounts

In this practice, you create a new local user account and assign it a password using the User Accounts tool. You then create a custom MMC console that contains the Computer Management snap-in and then use the snap-in to create two more new user accounts. Then you test one of the newly created local user accounts. You complete the practice by using the User Accounts tool to delete a local user account.

After completing this practice, you will be able to

- Use the User Accounts program to create a new local user account
- Create a customized MMC console containing the Computer Management snap-in
- Use the Computer Management snap-in to create a new local user account

Run the **LocalUserAccounts** file in the Demos folder on the CD-ROM accompanying this book for a demonstration of creating, modifying, and deleting local user accounts.

Exercise 1: Creating a New Local User Account Using the User Accounts Tool

In this exercise, you use the User Accounts tool to create a new user account.

▶ **To create a local user account**

1. Log on as Fred or with a user account that is a member of the Administrators group.

2. Click Start, click Control Panel, and then click User Accounts.

3. In the User Accounts window, under Pick A Task, click Create A New Account.

   Windows XP Professional displays the Name The New Account window.

4. In the Type A Name For The New User text box, type **User1**, and then click Next.

   Windows XP Professional displays the Pick An Account Type dialog box.

5. Click Limited.

Note   If your account is a limited account type, you can change or remove your password, change the picture displayed with your account, and change your theme and other desktop settings. You can also view files you created and files in the shared documents folder.

---

6. Click Create Account.

   Windows XP Professional displays the User Accounts window; User1 appears in the list of accounts.

7. Create an account for User2 using steps 3 through 6.

   Leave the User Accounts window open for the next exercise.

Exercise 2: Assigning a Password to a Local User Account Using the User Accounts Tool

In this exercise, you use the User Accounts tool to assign a password to a local user account.

▶ **To assign a password to a local user account using the User Accounts tool**

1. In the User Accounts window, click User1.

2. Click Create A Password.

3. Type **password** in both the Type A New Password text box and the Type The New Password Again To Confirm text box.

4. Type **the most commonly used password** in the Type A Word Or Phrase To Use As A Password Hint text box.

5. Click Create Password.

   The What Do You Want To Change About User1's Account window appears. Notice that the list of changes you can make now includes two new options: Change The Password and Remove The Password. The Create A Password option is gone.

6. Click the Home icon to return to the User Accounts window.

7. Assign User2 the password User2.

8. Close the User Accounts window and Control Panel.

Exercise 3: Creating a Customized MMC Console That Contains the Computer Management Snap-In

In this exercise, you create a customized MMC console that contains the Computer Management snap-in.

▶ **To create a custom MMC containing Computer Management**

1. Click Start and then click Run.

2. In the Open text box, type **mmc** and then click OK.

   MMC starts and displays an empty console.

3. Maximize the Console1 window by clicking Maximize.

4. Maximize the Console Root window by clicking Maximize.

5. On the File menu, click Add/Remove Snap-In.

   MMC displays the Add/Remove Snap-In dialog box.

6. Click Add.

   MMC displays the Add Standalone Snap-In dialog box.

7. In the Available Standalone Snap-Ins list, click Computer Management and then click Add.

   MMC displays the Computer Management dialog box, which allows you to specify the computer that you want to administer. The Local Computer option is selected by default.

8. In the Computer Management dialog box, click Finish.

   The MMC creates the console that contains the Computer Management snap-in for managing the local computer.

9. In the Add Standalone Snap-In dialog box, click Close.

10. In the Add/Remove Snap-In dialog box, click OK to place the Computer Management snap-in in your customized MMC console.

    Computer Management (Local) now appears in the console tree.

11. On the File menu, click Save As.

    MMC displays the Save As dialog box.

12. In the File Name text box, type **Computer Management Local**, and then click Save.

    The title bar is now Computer Management Local. You have just created a customized MMC console containing the Computer Management snap-in and have named it Computer Management Local.

Exercise 4: Creating a New Local User Account Using the Computer Management Snap-In

In this exercise, you use the Computer Management snap-in to create two new local user accounts.

▶ **To create a local user account using the Computer Management snap-in**

1. In the Computer Management window, in the console pane, click the plus sign in front of Computer Management (Local) to expand it.

   Computer Management contains three folders: System Tools, Storage, and Services And Applications.

2. In the console pane, double-click System Tools, and then click Local Users And Groups.

3. In the details pane, right-click Users, and then select New User.

   The New User dialog box appears.

4. In the User Name text box, type **User3**.

5. In the Full Name text box, type **User Three**.

   Do not assign a password to the user account.

6. Confirm that the User Must Change Password At Next Logon check box is selected.

7. Click Create to create the new user, and then click Close.

8. Click Start, click Control Panel, and then click User Accounts.

   The User Accounts window appears.

   What type of account is User3?

   Notice that User3 is a password-protected account. The password for User3 is a blank password.

9. Close the User Accounts window and then close Control Panel.

10. In the Computer Management details pane, right-click Users, and then click New User.

11. In the User Name text box, type **User4**.

12. In the Full Name text box, type **User Four**.

13. In the Password and Confirm Password text boxes, type **User4**.

    How does the password appear on the screen? Why?

Note In high-security environments, assign initial passwords to user accounts and then require users to change their passwords the next time they log on. This accomplishes two goals: it prevents a user account from existing without a password and ensures that only the user knows the password. The password assigned in this exercise was for ease of use in the exercise. The passwords you assign should be difficult to guess and should include both uppercase and lowercase letters, numerals, and valid nonalphanumeric characters.

14. Confirm that the User Must Change Password At Next Logon check box is selected and then click Create.

15. Close the New User dialog box.

16. In the Computer Management console, on the File menu, click Exit to close the Computer Management custom MMC console.

    The Microsoft Management Console dialog box appears, in which you indicate whether you want to save Console settings to Computer Management.

Note If you click Yes, the next time you open the Computer Management console, it appears as it does now. If you click No, Windows XP Professional does not save the settings.

17. Click Yes to save the Console settings.

Exercise 5: Testing a New Local User Account

In this exercise, you test one of the new local user accounts to verify that it works as expected.

▶ **To test a local user account**

1. Click Start and then click Log Off.

    Windows XP Professional displays a Log Off Windows dialog box telling you to click Switch User if you want to leave programs running and switch to another user. Your other options are to click Log Off or Cancel.

2. In the Log Off Windows dialog box, click Log Off.

3. On the Welcome screen, click User3.

    What happens?

4. Click OK. The Change Password dialog box appears.

5. Leave the Old Password text box blank, and in the New Password and Confirm New Password text boxes, type **User3**, and then click OK.

    Windows XP Professional displays a Change Password dialog box indicating that the password has been changed.

6. Click OK to close the Change Password dialog box.

The user account, User3, that you created using the Computer Management snap-in allowed you to log on. Because you left the default check box, User Must Change Password At Next Logon, selected when you created the account, you were prompted to change passwords when you logged on as User3. You confirmed that the User3 user account was created with a blank password when you left the Old Password box blank and successfully changed the password to User3.

7. Log off the computer.

Exercise 6: Deleting a Local User Account

In this exercise, you use the User Accounts tool to delete the User3 local user account.

▶ **To delete a local user account**

1. Log on as Fred or with a user account that is a member of the Administrators group.

2. In the Control Panel, click User Accounts.

3. Click User3.

Windows XP Professional displays the What Do You Want To Change About User Three's Account window.

4. Click Delete The Account.

Windows XP Professional displays the Do You Want To Keep User Three's Files window.

Note   Windows XP Professional can automatically save the contents of User Three's desktop and My Documents folder to a new folder called User Three on your desktop. However, it cannot save User Three's e-mail messages, Internet Favorites, and other settings.

---

5. Click Delete Files.

Windows XP Professional displays the Are You Sure You Want To Delete User Three's Account window.

6. Click Delete Account.

Windows XP Professional displays the User Accounts window. Notice that the User3 account is no longer listed under Or Pick An Account To Change.

7. Close the User Accounts tool and then close the Control Panel.

8. Log off the computer.

Lesson Review

The following questions will help you determine whether you have learned enough to move on to the next lesson. If you have difficulty answering these questions, review the material in this lesson before beginning the next lesson. The answers are in Appendix A, "Questions and Answers."

1. Which of the following statements about the Windows XP Professional User Accounts tool are correct? (Choose all that apply.)

   a. The User Accounts tool allows you to remotely create, modify, and delete user accounts on all computers in the network running Windows XP Professional.

   b. The User Accounts tool allows you to view and modify all accounts on the computer.

   c. The tasks you can perform with the User Accounts tool depend on the type of account you use to log on to the local computer.

   d. The User Accounts tool allows users to delete, create, or remove their individual passwords.

2. Which of the following tasks can both account types perform? (Choose all that apply.)

   a. Change your picture

   b. Change your account type

   c. Create, change, or remove your password

   d. Change your account name

3. Which of the following statements about logging on or logging off a computer running Windows XP Professional are true? (Choose all that apply.)

   a. When you use the Welcome screen to log on the local computer, you can quickly switch to another user account without logging off and closing all programs that you are running.

   b. The User Accounts tool allows you to disable a local user account to prevent users from using the disabled account to log on.

   c. When you use the Welcome screen to log on the local computer, you can only log on using one of the accounts displayed on the Welcome screen.

   d. The User Accounts tool allows you to replace the Welcome screen with a logon prompt that requires users to type their individual user names and passwords.

4. When you use the Computer Management snap-in to create a new user account, which check box do you select to prevent a new employee from using the new account until the employee starts working for the company?

Lesson Summary

- The User Accounts tool allows administrators to create a new user account, change an existing account, and change the way a user logs on or logs off.

- The two check boxes that control the way users log on and log off the computer, Use The Welcome Screen and Use Fast User Switching, are for all users. You cannot set them for individual local user accounts.

- The Computer Management snap-in allows you to create, modify, and delete user accounts for the local computer on which you are working. If your computer is part of a network, you can use the Computer Management snap-in on a remote computer.

- The Computer Management snap-in provides all the functionality of the User Accounts tool and additional functionality, including the ability to view all accounts in the local security database and to disable accounts.

- Always require new users to change their passwords the first time they log on to force them to use passwords that only they know.

- If you select the Use The Welcome Screen and the Use Fast User Switching check boxes, when you log off the computer, a dialog box appears allowing you to leave programs running and switch to another user without logging off and closing all programs.

Lesson 4: Setting Properties for User Accounts

Windows XP Professional creates a set of default account properties for each local user account. After you create a local user account, you can configure the account properties using the Computer Management snap-in. The account properties are grouped under three tabs in a user *account-name* Properties dialog box: General, Member Of, and Profile.

After this lesson, you will be able to

■ Set properties for user accounts

Estimated lesson time: 30 minutes

The General Tab

The General tab in the *account-name* Properties dialog box (see Figure 3.10) allows you to set or edit all the fields from the New User dialog box, except User Name, Password, and Confirm Password. In addition, it provides an Account Is Locked Out check box.

Figure 3.10   The General tab of the Properties dialog box for a user account

If the account is active and is not locked out of the system, the Account Is Locked Out check box is unavailable. The system locks out a user who exceeds the limit for the number of failed logon attempts. This security feature makes it more difficult for an unauthorized user to break into the system. If the system locks out an account, the Account Is Locked Out check box becomes available, and an administrator can clear the check box to allow user access.

The Member Of Tab

The Member Of tab in the *account-name* Properties dialog box allows you to add the user account to or remove the user account from a group. For information about groups, see Lesson 5, "Implementing Groups."

The Profile Tab

The Profile tab in the Properties dialog box allows you to set a path for the user profile, logon script, and home folder (see Figure 3.11).

Figure 3.11   The Profile tab of the Properties dialog box for a user account

User Profile

A *user profile* is a collection of folders and data that stores your current desktop environment, application settings, and personal data. It also contains all the network connections that are established when you log on to a computer, such as Start menu items and drives mapped to network servers. The user profile maintains consistency by providing the same desktop environment every time you log on to the computer.

Windows XP Professional creates a user profile the first time you log on to a computer and stores it on that computer. This user profile is also known as a *local user profile*.

User profiles operate in the following way on client computers running Windows XP Professional:

- When you log on the client computer, you always receive your desktop settings and connections, regardless of how many users share the same client computer.

- The first time you log on to the client computer, Windows XP Professional creates a default user profile for you. The default user profile is stored in the *system_partition_root*\Documents and Settings*user_logon_name* folder (typically C:\Documents and Settings*user_logon_name*), where *user_logon_name* is the name you enter when logging on to the system.

- The user profile contains the My Documents folder, which provides a place to store personal files. My Documents is the default location for the File Open and Save As commands. My Documents appears on the Start menu, which makes it easier to locate personal documents.

Important   Users can store their documents in My Documents or in home folders, such as a home directory located on a network server. Home folders are covered later in this lesson. Windows XP Professional automatically sets up My Documents as the default location for storing data for Microsoft applications. If there is adequate room on the C drive or the drive where Windows XP Professional was installed, users can store their documents in My Documents. However, using My Documents to store personal data greatly increases the amount of space required on a hard disk for installing Windows XP Professional well beyond the minimum.

- You can change your user profile by changing desktop settings. For example, if you make a new network connection or add a file to My Documents, Windows XP Professional incorporates the changes into your user profile when you log off. The next time you log on, the new network connection and the file are present.

Note   For information about creating, modifying, and managing user profiles, see Chapter 10, "Configuring Windows XP Professional."

Logon Script

A logon script is a file you can create and assign to a user account to configure the user's working environment. For example, you can use a logon script to establish network connections or start applications. Each time a user logs on, the assigned logon script is run.

Home Folder

In addition to the My Documents folder, Windows XP Professional allows you to create home folders for users to store their personal documents. You can store a home folder on a client computer, in a shared folder on a file server, or in a central location on a network server.

Storing all home folders on a file server provides the following advantages:

- Users can access their home folders from any client computer on the network.
- You can centralize backing up and administering user documents by moving the responsibility for backing up and managing the documents out of the hands of the users and into the hands of one of the network backup operators or network administrators.

Note   The home folders are accessible from a client computer running any Microsoft operating system, including MS-DOS, Microsoft Windows 95, Microsoft Windows 98, Windows 2000 Professional, and Windows XP Professional.

Important   Store home folders on an NT File System (NTFS) volume so that you can use NTFS permissions to secure user documents. If you store home folders on a file allocation table (FAT) volume, you can restrict home folder access only by using shared folder permissions.

To create a home folder on a network file server, complete the following steps:

1. Create and share a folder for storing all users' home folders on a network server.

   The home folder for each user will reside in this shared folder.

2. For the shared folder, remove the default Full Control permission from the Everyone group and assign Full Control to the Users group.

   This ensures that only users with domain user accounts can access the shared folder.

3. In the *account-name* Properties dialog box, in the Profile tab, click Connect and select or type a drive letter with which to connect to the user account home folder on the network.

4. In the To text box, type a Universal Naming Convention (UNC) name (for example, *\\server_name\shared_folder_name\user_logon_name*).

   Type the *username* variable as the user's logon name to automatically give each user's home folder the user logon name (for example, *\\server_name\Users\%username%*). Naming a folder on an NTFS volume with the *username* variable assigns the NTFS Full Control permission to the user and removes all other permissions for the folder, including those for the Administrator account.

To set User Account properties, complete the following steps:

1. Click Start, point to All Programs, point to Administrative Tools, and click Computer Management.

2. Under System Tools, double-click Local Users And Groups, and then click Users.

3. In the details pane, right-click the appropriate user account, and then click Properties.

4. Click the appropriate tab for the properties that you want to configure or modify, and then enter values for each property.

Practice: Modifying User Account Properties

This practice presents exercises that allow you to modify user account properties and test them.

Run the **UserAccountProperties** file in the Demos folder on the CD-ROM accompanying this book for a demonstration of modifying user account properties.

Exercise 1: Setting User Account Properties

In this exercise you set and then test the User Cannot Change Password property.

▶ **To set the User Cannot Change Password property and the Account Is Disabled property**

1. Log on as Fred or with a user account that is a member of the Administrators group.

2. Click Start, click Run, type **mmc,** and then click OK.

   MMC starts and displays an empty console.

3. On the File menu, click Computer Management Local.

4. Expand Local Users And Groups and then click Users.

   MMC displays the user accounts in the details pane.

5. Right-click User1 and then click Properties.

6. In the User1 Properties dialog box, in the General tab, select User Cannot Change Password, and then clear all other check boxes.

Tip   When you select the User Cannot Change Password check box, the User Must Change Password At Next Logon option is unavailable.

---

7. Click OK to close the User1 Properties dialog box.

8. Right-click User2 and then click Properties.

9. In the User2 Properties dialog box, in the General tab, select the Account Is Disabled check box and clear all other check boxes.

10. Click OK to close the User2 Properties dialog box.

11. Close the Computer Management window, and if you are prompted about saving the console settings, click No.

12. Log off the computer.

Exercise 2: Testing User Account Properties

In this exercise you test the properties for a user account.

▶ **To test User Account properties**

1. On the Welcome screen, click User1.

2. In the Type Your Password dialog box, click the question mark icon for your password hint.

   Windows XP Professional displays the password hint you entered.

3. In the Type Your Password text box, type **password,** and then press ENTER.

4. In the Control Panel, click User Accounts.

   Windows XP Professional starts the User Accounts tool.

5. Click Change My Password.

6. In the Type Your Current Password text box, type **password**.

7. In the Type A New Password and Type The New Password Again To Confirm text boxes, Type **User1**.

8. Click Change Password.

   What happens? Why?

9. Log off as User1.

   Notice that disabled accounts such as User2 don't appear on the Welcome screen.

Lesson Review

The following questions will help you determine whether you have learned enough to move on to the next lesson. If you have difficulty answering these questions, review the material in this lesson before beginning the next lesson. The answers are in Appendix A, "Questions and Answers."

1. When can you select the Account Is Locked Out check box for a user and why?

2. Which of the following statements about local user account properties are correct? (Choose all that apply.)

   a. You can configure all of the default properties associated with each local user account using the User Accounts tool located in the Control Panel.

   b. In Computer Management, the General tab in the *account-name* Properties dialog box for a user account allows you to disable the account.

   c. In Computer Management, the General tab in the *account-name* Properties dialog box for a user account allows you to select the Account Is Locked Out check box to prevent the user from logging on to the computer.

   d. You can use the Computer Management snap-in to configure all of the default properties associated with each local user account.

3. Which of the following statements about user profiles are correct? (Choose all that apply.)

   a. A user profile is a collection of folders and data that stores the user's current desktop environment, application settings, and personal data.

   b. A user profile contains all the network connections that are established when a user logs on to a computer.

   c. Windows XP Professional creates a user profile when you create a new local user account.

   d. You must create each user profile by copying and modifying an existing user profile.

4. Which of the following statements about user profiles are correct? (Choose all that apply.)

   a. Users should store their documents in home directories rather than in their My Documents folders.

   b. The Profile tab in the *account-name* Properties dialog box for a user account allows you to set a path for the user profile, logon script, and home folder.

   c. A user profile contains the My Documents folder, which provides a place for users to store personal files.

   d. When users change their desktop settings, the changes are reflected in their user profiles.

5. What three tasks must you perform to create a home folder on a network server?

Lesson Summary

- Each local user account that you create has an associated set of default properties.

- The Computer Management snap-in allows you to easily configure or modify the local user account properties.

- The General tab in the *account-name* Properties dialog box allows you to set or edit all the fields from the New User dialog box, except for User Name, Password, and Confirm Password. In addition, it provides an Account Is Locked Out check box.

- The Member Of tab in the *account-name* Properties dialog box allows you to add the user account to or remove the user account from a group.

- The Profile tab in the *account-name* Properties dialog box for a user account allows you to set a path for the user profile, logon script, and home folder.

Lesson 5: Implementing Groups

In this lesson, you will learn what groups are and how you can use them to simplify user account administration. You will also learn about built-in groups, which have a predetermined set of user rights and group membership. Windows XP Professional has two categories of built-in groups, local and system, which it creates for you to simplify the process of assigning rights and permissions for commonly used functions.

After this lesson, you will be able to

- Describe the key features of local groups and Windows XP Professional built-in groups
- Create and delete local groups
- Add members to and remove them from local groups

Estimated lesson time: 40 minutes

Understanding Groups

A *group* is a collection of user accounts. Groups simplify administration by allowing you to assign permissions and rights to a group of users rather than to each user account individually (see Figure 3.12).

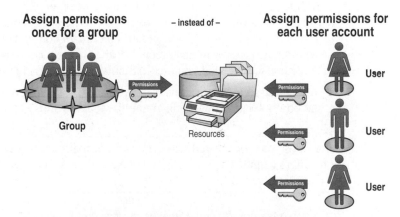

- Groups are collections of user accounts.
- Members receive permissions given to groups.
- Users can be members of multiple groups.
- Groups can be members of other groups.

Figure 3.12   Groups simplify administration

Permissions control what users can do with a resource such as a folder, file, or printer. When you assign permissions, you allow users to gain access to a resource and you define the type of access that they have. For example, if several users need to read the same file, you can add their user accounts to a group and then give the group permission to read the file. *Rights* allow users to perform system tasks, such as changing the time on a computer and backing up or restoring files.

Note   For more information about permissions, see Chapter 8, "Securing Resources with NTFS." For more information about rights, see Chapter 13, "Configuring Security Settings and Internet Options."

Understanding Local Groups

A *local group* is a collection of user accounts on a computer. Use local groups to assign permissions to resources residing on the computer on which the local group is created. Windows XP Professional creates local groups in the local security database.

Preparing to Use Local Groups

Guidelines for using local groups include the following:

- Use local groups on computers that do not belong to a domain.

  You can use local groups only on the computer on which you create them. Although local groups are available on member servers and domain computers running Windows 2000 Server, do not use local groups on computers that are part of a domain. Using local groups on domain computers prevents you from centralizing group administration. Local groups do not appear in the Active Directory service, and you must administer them separately for each computer.

- You can assign permissions to local groups to access only the resources on the computer on which you create the local groups.

Note   You cannot create local groups on domain controllers because domain controllers cannot have a security database that is independent of the database in Active Directory.

Membership rules for local groups include the following:

- Local groups can contain local user accounts from the computer on which you create the local groups.
- Local groups cannot belong to any other group.

Creating Local Groups

Use the Computer Management snap-in (shown in Figure 3.13) to create local groups in the Groups folder.

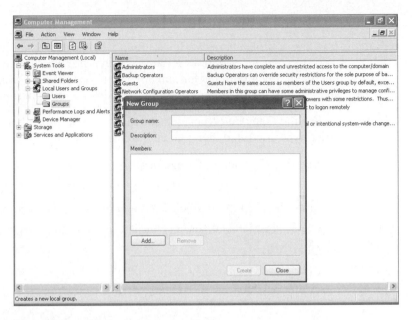

Figure 3.13   The New Group dialog box

To create a local group, complete the following steps:

1. In Computer Management, expand Local Users And Groups.

2. Right-click Groups and then click New Group.

   MMC displays the New Group dialog box. Table 3.4 describes the available options.

Table 3.4   New Local Group Options

Option	Description
Group Name	Requires a unique name for the local group. This is the only required entry. Use any character except for the backslash (\ ). The name can contain up to 256 characters, but very long names might not display in some windows.
Description	Describes the group.
Members	Lists the user accounts belonging to the group.
Add	Adds a user to the list of members.
Remove	Removes a user from the list of members.
Create	Creates the group.
Close	Closes the New Group dialog box.

3. Enter the appropriate information, and then click Create.

Adding Members to a Group

You can add members to a local group when you create the group by clicking Add. In addition, Windows XP Professional provides two methods for adding members to a group that has already been created: the Computer Management snap-in and the Member Of tab in the *user-name* Properties dialog box.

To use the Computer Management snap-in to add members to a group that has already been created, complete the following steps:

1. Start the Computer Management snap-in.
2. Expand Local Users And Groups and then click Groups.
3. In the details pane, right-click the appropriate group, and then click Properties.

   Computer Management displays the *group-name* Properties dialog box.
4. Click Add.

   Computer Management displays the Select Users dialog box, as shown in Figure 3.14.

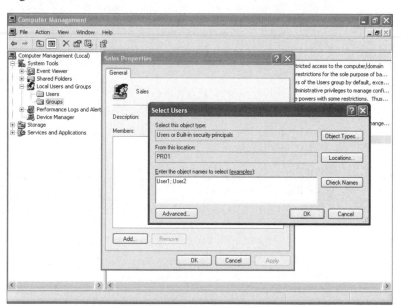

Figure 3.14   The Select Users dialog box

5. In the From This Location text box, ensure that the computer on which you created the group is selected.
6. In the Select Users dialog box, in the Enter The Object Names To Select text box, type the user account names that you want to add to the group, separated by semicolons, and then click OK.

Tip   The Member Of tab in the *user-name* Properties dialog box of a user account allows you to add a user account to multiple groups. Use this method to quickly add the same user account to multiple groups. To review how to use the Member Of tab, see the section in Lesson 4 entitled "The Member Of Tab."

Deleting Local Groups

Use the Computer Management snap-in to delete local groups. Each group that you create has a unique identifier that cannot be used again. Windows XP Professional uses this value to identify the group and its assigned permissions. When you delete a group, Windows XP Professional does not use the identifier again, even if you create a new group with the same name as the group that you deleted. Therefore, you cannot restore access to resources by recreating the group.

When you delete a group, you remove only the group and its associated permissions and rights. Deleting a group does not delete the user accounts that are members of the group. To delete a group, right-click the group name in the Computer Management snap-in and then click Delete.

Practice: Creating and Managing Local Groups

In this practice, you create two local groups, add members to the local groups when you create them, and then add a member to one of the groups after it has been created. You delete a member from one of the groups, and then delete one of the local groups that you created.

Run the **LocalGroups** file in the Demos folder on the CD-ROM accompanying this book for a demonstration of creating and managing local groups.

Exercise 1: Creating Local Groups and Adding and Removing Members

In this exercise, you create two local groups, Accounting and Marketing, and add members to both groups. You add a member to the existing Marketing group, and then remove a member from the Marketing group.

▶   **To create the Accounting and Marketing local groups**

1. Log on as Fred or with a user account that is a member of the Administrators group.

2. Click Start, point to All Programs, point to Administrative Tools, and then click Computer Management.

   Windows XP Professional starts Computer Management.

3. Under System Tools, if necessary, expand Local Users And Groups, right-click Groups, and then click New Group.

   MMC displays the New Group dialog box.

4. In the Group Name text box, type **Accounting**.

5. In the Description text box, type **Access to Accounts Receivable Files**.

6. Click Add.

   MMC displays the Select Users dialog box.

7. In the Name text box, type **User1; User2; User4** and then click OK.

   User1, User2, and User4 appear in the Members list in the New Group dialog box.

8. Click Create.

   Windows XP Professional creates the group and adds it to the list of groups in the details pane. Note that the New Group dialog box is still open and might block your view of the list of groups.

9. Repeat steps 4 through 9 to create a group named Marketing with a description of Access to Mailing Lists and User2 and User4 as group members.

10. When you finish creating both the Accounting and the Marketing groups, click Close to close the New Group dialog box.

    The Accounting and the Marketing groups now appear in the details pane.

▶ **To add members to and remove members from the Marketing local group**

1. In the details pane of the Computer Management window, double-click Marketing.

   The Marketing Properties dialog box displays the properties of the group. Notice that User2 and User4 are in the Members list.

2. To add a member to the group, click Add.

   Computer Management displays the Select Users dialog box.

3. In the Name text box, type **User1**, and then click OK.

   The Marketing Properties dialog box now displays User1, User2, and User4 in the Members list.

4. Select User4 and then click Remove.

   Notice that User4 is no longer in the Members list. User4 still exists as a local user account, but it is no longer a member of the Marketing group.

5. Click OK.

Exercise 2: Deleting a Local Group

In this exercise, you delete the Marketing local group.

▶ **To delete the Marketing local group**

1. In the details pane of the Computer Management window, right-click Marketing, and then click Delete.

   Computer Management displays a Local Users And Groups dialog box asking if you are sure that you want to delete the group.

2. Click Yes.

Marketing is no longer listed in the details pane indicating that the Marketing group was successfully deleted.

3. In the console pane of the Computer Management window, click Users.

User1 and User2 are still listed in the details pane indicating that the group was deleted, but the members of the group were not deleted from the Users folder.

4. Close Computer Management.

Understanding Built-In Local Groups

All stand-alone servers, member servers, and computers running Windows XP Professional have *built-in local groups*. These groups give rights to perform system tasks on a single computer, such as backing up and restoring files, changing the system time, and administering system resources. Windows XP Professional places the built-in local groups in the Groups folder in Computer Management.

Table 3.5 lists the most commonly used built-in local groups and describes their capabilities. Except where noted, these groups do not include initial members.

Table 3.5   Built-In Local Group Capabilities

Local group	Description
Administrators	Members can perform all administrative tasks on the computer. By default, the built-in Administrator account is a member. When a member server or a computer running Windows XP Professional joins a domain, Windows 2000 Server adds the Domain Admins group to the local Administrators group.
Backup Operators	Members can use Windows Backup to back up and restore the computer.
Guests	Members can do the following: ■ Perform only the tasks for which they have been specifically granted rights ■ Access only those resources for which they have assigned permissions Members cannot make permanent changes to their desktop environment. By default, the built-in Guest account is a member. When a member server or a computer running Windows XP Professional joins a domain, Windows 2000 Server adds the Domain Guests group to the local Guests group.
Power Users	Members can create and modify local user accounts on the computer and share resources.
Replicator	Supports file replication in a domain.

(continued)

Table   3.5   *(continued)*

Local group	Description
Users	Members can do the following: ■ Perform only the tasks for which they have been specifically granted rights ■ Access only those resources for which they have assigned permissions By default, Windows XP Professional adds to the Users group all local user accounts that an administrator creates on the computer. When a member server or a computer running Windows XP Professional joins a domain, Windows 2000 Server adds the Domain Users group to the local Users group.

Understanding Built-In System Groups

Built-in system groups exist on all computers running Windows XP Professional. System groups do not have specific memberships that you can modify, but they can represent different users at different times, depending on how a user gains access to a computer or resource. You do not see system groups when you administer groups, but they are available when you assign rights and permissions to resources. Windows XP Professional bases system group membership on how the computer is accessed, not on who uses the computer. Table 3.6 lists the most commonly used built-in system groups and describes their capabilities.

Table 3.6   Built-In System Group Capabilities

System group	Description
Everyone	All users who access the computer. By default, when you format a volume with NTFS, the Full Control permission is assigned to the Everyone group. This presented a problem in earlier versions of Windows, including Microsoft Windows 2000. In Windows XP Professional, the Anonymous Logon is no longer included in the Everyone group. When a Windows 2000 Professional system is upgraded to a Windows XP Professional system, resources with permission entries for the Everyone group and not explicitly for the Anonymous Logon group are no longer available to the Anonymous Logon group.
Authenticated Users	All users with valid user accounts on the computer. (If your computer is part of a domain, it includes all users in Active Directory.)
Creator Owner	The user account for the user who created or took ownership of a resource. If a member of the Administrators group creates a resource, the Administrators group owns the resource.
Network	Any user with a current connection from another computer on the network to a shared resource on the computer.

Table 3.6 *(continued)*

System group	Description
Interactive	The user account for the user who is logged on at the computer. Members of the Interactive group can access resources on the computer at which they are physically located. They log on and access resources by "interacting" with the computer.
Anonymous Logon	Any user account that Windows XP Professional cannot authenticate.
Dialup	Any user who currently has a dial-up connection.

Lesson Review

The following questions will help you determine whether you have learned enough to move on to the next lesson. If you have difficulty answering these questions, review the material in this lesson before beginning the next chapter. The answers are in Appendix A, "Questions and Answers."

1. What are groups, and why do you use them?

2. An administrator or owner of a resource uses _____ to control what users can do with a resource such as a folder, file, or printer.

3. You use local groups to assign permissions to resources residing

    _____ .

4. Which of the following statements about local groups are correct? (Choose all that apply.)

    a. If a computer running Windows XP Professional is part of a domain, the local groups for that computer are stored in the directory rather than in the local security database on that computer.

    b. Local groups allow you to grant permission to the group to perform system tasks, such as changing the time on a computer and backing up or restoring files.

    c. A local group is a collection of user accounts on a computer that you can use to control access to resources residing on that computer.

    d. You can use the Computer Management snap-in to create groups, to add members to existing groups, and to delete groups from a computer running Windows XP Professional.

5. Which of the following statements about local groups are correct? (Choose all that apply.)

    a. You can use local groups only on the computer on which you create them.

    b. Local groups are available on member servers and domain computers running Windows 2000 Server.

    c. Local groups appear in Active Directory so you can administer them centrally.

    d. You must create each user profile by copying and modifying an existing user profile.

6. Which of the following statements about deleting local groups are correct? (Choose all that apply.)

    a. Each group that you create has a unique identifier that cannot be reused.

    b. You can restore access to resources by recreating the group.

    c. When you delete a group, you also remove the permissions and rights associated with it.

    d. Deleting a group deletes the user accounts that are members of the group.

7. What is the difference between built-in system groups and built-in local groups found on computers running Windows XP Professional? Give at least two examples of each type of group.

Lesson Summary

- Groups simplify administration by allowing you to assign permissions and rights to a group of users rather than to individual user accounts.

- Permissions control what users can do with a resource such as a folder, file, or printer.

- Rights allow users to perform system tasks, such as changing the time on a computer and backing up or restoring files.

- Windows XP Professional creates local groups in the local security database, so you can use local groups only on the computer on which you create them. You cannot use local groups on computers that are part of a domain.

- You can use the Computer Management snap-in to create, add members to, and delete local groups.

- All stand-alone servers, member servers, and computers running Windows XP Professional have built-in local groups that give rights to perform system tasks on a single computer.

CHAPTER 4

Installing, Configuring, and Troubleshooting Network Protocols

About This Chapter

A *protocol* is a set of rules and conventions for sending information over a network. Microsoft Windows XP Professional relies on the Transmission Control Protocol/ Internet Protocol (TCP/IP) for logon, file and print services, replication of information between domain controllers, and other common functions.

This chapter presents the skills and knowledge necessary to install, configure, and troubleshoot TCP/IP and NWLink. The chapter also discusses the process for configuring network bindings, which are links that enable communication among network adapter cards, protocols, and services.

Before You Begin

To complete this chapter, you must have

- A computer that meets the minimum hardware requirements listed in the preface, "About This Book"
- Windows XP Professional software installed on the computer with TCP/IP installed as the only network protocol

Lesson 1: Understanding the TCP/IP Protocol Suite

TCP/IP provides communication across networks of computers with various hardware architectures and operating systems. Microsoft's implementation of TCP/IP enables enterprise networking and connectivity on computers running Windows XP Professional.

After this lesson, you will be able to

- Describe the TCP/IP protocol suite and the TCP/IP tools that ship with Windows XP Professional

Estimated lesson time: 25 minutes

The TCP/IP Protocol Suite

TCP/IP is an industry-standard suite of protocols that enables enterprise networking and connectivity on Windows XP Professional–based computers. Adding TCP/IP to a Windows XP Professional configuration offers the following advantages:

- A routable networking protocol supported by most operating systems. Most large networks rely on TCP/IP.

- A technology for connecting dissimilar systems. You can use many standard connectivity tools to access and transfer data across dissimilar systems. Windows XP Professional includes several of these standard tools.

- A robust, scalable, cross-platform client/server framework. TCP/IP supports the Microsoft Windows Sockets (Winsock) interface, which is ideal for developing client/server applications for Winsock-compliant stacks.

- A method of gaining access to Internet resources.

The TCP/IP suite of protocols provides a set of standards for how computers communicate and how networks are interconnected. The TCP/IP suite of protocols maps to a four-layer conceptual model: network interface, Internet, transport, and application. These layers can be seen in Figure 4.1.

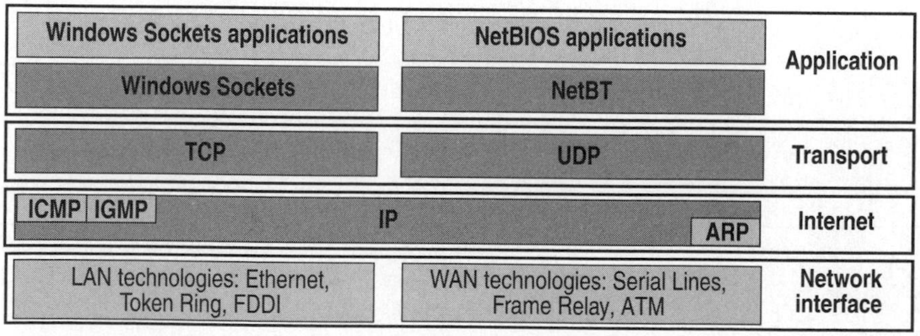

Figure 4.1   The TCP/IP suite of protocols within four layers

Network Interface Layer

At the base of the model is the network interface layer, which puts frames on the wire and pulls frames off the wire.

Internet Layer

Internet layer protocols encapsulate packets into Internet datagrams and run all the necessary routing algorithms. The four Internet layer protocols are Internet Protocol (IP), Address Resolution Protocol (ARP), Internet Control Message Protocol (ICMP), and Internet Group Management Protocol (IGMP). Table 4.1 describes these four Internet layer protocols.

Table 4.1   Protocols Included in the Internet Layer

Protocol	Description
IP	Provides connectionless packet delivery for all other protocols in the suite. Does not guarantee packet arrival or correct packet sequence. Does not try to recover from errors such as lost packets, packets delivered out of sequence, duplicated packets, or delayed packets. Packet acknowledgment and the recovery of lost packets are the responsibility of a higher layer protocol, such as TCP. IP is primarily responsible for addressing and routing packets between hosts.
ARP	Provides IP address mapping to the media access control (MAC) sublayer address to acquire the physical MAC control address of the destination. IP address resolution is required when IP packets are sent on shared access, broadcast-based networking technology, such as Ethernet. IP broadcasts a special ARP inquiry packet containing the IP address of the destination system. The system that owns the IP address replies by sending its physical address to the requester. The MAC sublayer communicates directly with the network adapter card and is responsible for delivering error-free data between two computers on a network.
ICMP	Provides special communication between hosts, allowing them to share status and error information. Higher level protocols use this information to recover from transmission problems. Network administrators use this information to detect network trouble. The Ping tool uses ICMP packets to determine whether a particular IP device on a network is functional. One instance in which ICMP provides special communication between hosts occurs when IP is unable to deliver a packet to the destination host; ICMP sends a Destination Unreachable message to the source host.
IGMP	Provides multicasting, which is a limited form of broadcasting, to communicate and manage information between all member devices in an IP multicast group. An IP multicast group is a set of hosts that listen for IP traffic destined for a specific IP multicast address. IP multicast traffic is sent to a single MAC address but is processed by multiple hosts. IGMP informs neighboring multicast routers of the host group memberships present on a particular network. Windows XP Professional supports multicast capabilities that allow developers to create multicast programs, such as Microsoft Windows 2000 Server NetShow Services.

Transport Layer

Transport layer protocols provide communication sessions between computers. The desired method of data delivery determines the transport protocol. The two transport layer protocols, described in Table 4.2, are Transmission Control Protocol (TCP) and User Datagram Protocol (UDP).

Table 4.2   Protocols Included in the Transport Layer

Protocol	Description
TCP	Provides connection-oriented, reliable communications for applications that typically transfer large amounts of data at once or require an acknowledgment for data received. TCP is connection-oriented, so a connection must be established before hosts can exchange data. TCP provides reliable communication by assigning a sequence number to each segment of data that is transmitted so that the receiving host can send an acknowledgment (ACK) to verify that the data was received. If an ACK is not received, the data is retransmitted. TCP guarantees the delivery of packets, ensures proper sequencing of the data, and provides a checksum feature that validates both the packet header and its data for accuracy.
UDP	Provides connectionless communications but does not guarantee the delivery or the correct sequence of packets. Applications that use UDP typically transfer small amounts of data at once. Reliable delivery is the responsibility of the application.

Application Layer

At the top of the model is the application layer, in which applications gain access to the network. There are many standard TCP/IP tools and services in the application layer, such as File Transfer Protocol (FTP), Telnet, Simple Network Management Protocol (SNMP), Domain Name System (DNS), and so on.

TCP/IP provides two interfaces for network applications to use the services of the TCP/IP protocol stack: Winsock and the NetBIOS over TCP/IP (NetBT) interface. Table 4.3 describes these two interfaces.

Table 4.3   Interfaces Through Which Applications Use TCP/IP Services

Interface	Description
Winsock	Serves as the standard interface between socket-based applications and TCP/IP protocols. An application specifies the protocol, the IP address of the destination host, and the port of the destination application. Winsock provides services that allow the application to bind to a particular port and IP address on a host, initiate and accept a connection, send and receive data, and close the connection.
NetBT	Serves as the standard interface for NetBIOS services, including name, datagram, and session services. It also provides a standard interface between NetBIOS-based applications and TCP/IP protocols.

Lesson Review

Here are some questions to help you determine whether you have learned enough to move on to the next lesson. If you have difficulty answering these questions, review the material in this lesson before beginning the next lesson. The answers are in Appendix A, "Questions and Answers."

1. What are the four layers to which the TCP/IP suite of protocols maps? What are the functions of the protocols that map to each layer?

2. Which of the following statements correctly describes IP? (Choose all answers that are correct.)

   a. IP guarantees packet arrival and correct packet sequence.

   b. IP provides connection-oriented, reliable communications for applications that typically transfer large amounts of data at one time.

   c. IP is primarily responsible for addressing and routing packets between hosts.

   d. IP provides connectionless packet delivery for all other protocols in the suite.

3. Which of the following statements correctly describes TCP? (Choose all answers that are correct.)

   a. TCP provides connectionless communications but does not guarantee that packets will be delivered.

   b. TCP provides connection-oriented, reliable communications for applications that typically transfer large amounts of data at one time.

   c. TCP provides services that allow the application to bind to a particular port and IP address on a host.

   d. TCP provides and assigns a sequence number to each segment of data that is transmitted.

4. Which of the four layers to which the TCP/IP suite of protocols maps does IGMP map to and what is IGMP used for?

5. What is multicasting?

6. The two transport layer protocols are _____ and
_____.

7. Which of the following statements correctly describes ARP? (Choose all
   answers that are correct.)

   a. ARP is a protocol included in the Internet layer.

   b. ARP is a protocol included in the transport layer.

   c. ARP provides IP address mapping to the MAC sublayer address to acquire
   the physical MAC control address of the destination.

   d. ARP is primarily responsible for addressing and routing packets between
   hosts.

Lesson Summary

- Microsoft's implementation of TCP/IP provides a robust, scalable, cross-
platform client/server framework that is supported by most large networks,
including the Internet.

- Windows XP Professional includes many standard connectivity tools to
access and transfer data between dissimilar systems.

- The TCP/IP suite of protocols maps to a four-layer conceptual model: network interface, Internet, transport, and application.

- The four Internet layer protocols—IP, ARP, ICMP, and IGMP—encapsulate
packets into Internet datagrams and run all the necessary routing algorithms.

- IP provides connectionless, unreliable packet delivery for all other protocols
in the TCP/IP suite and is primarily responsible for addressing and routing
packets between hosts.

- The two transport layer protocols—TCP and UDP—provide communication
sessions between computers.

- TCP provides connection-oriented, reliable communications for applications
that typically transfer large amounts of data at once or require an acknowledgment for data received.

- There are many standard TCP/IP tools and services in the application layer,
such as FTP, Telnet, SNMP, DNS, and so on.

- TCP/IP provides two interfaces for network applications to use the services of
the TCP/IP protocol stack: Winsock and the NetBT interface.

Lesson 2: Configuring and Troubleshooting TCP/IP

Each TCP/IP host is identified by a logical IP address that identifies a computer's location on the network in much the same way as a street address identifies a house on a street. Microsoft's implementation of TCP/IP enables a TCP/IP host to use a static IP address or to obtain an IP address automatically from a Dynamic Host Configuration Protocol (DHCP) server. For simple network configurations based on local area networks (LANs), it supports automatic assignment of IP addresses. Windows XP Professional includes tools that you can use to troubleshoot TCP/IP and test connectivity.

After this lesson, you will be able to

- Configure TCP/IP to use a static IP address
- Configure TCP/IP to obtain an IP address automatically
- Explain Automatic Private IP Addressing
- Disable Automatic Private IP Addressing

Estimated lesson time: 60 minutes

Understanding IP Addresses

Each IP address consists of a network ID and a host ID. The network ID, also known as the network address, identifies the systems that are located on the same physical network. All computers in the same physical network must have the same network ID, and the network ID must be unique to the internetwork. The host ID, also known as the host address, identifies each TCP/IP host within a network.

IP addresses are logical 32-bit numbers that are broken down into four 8-bit fields known as octets. Microsoft TCP/IP supports class A, B, and C addresses. The class addresses define which bits are used for the network ID and which bits are used for the host ID. Table 4.4 summarizes class A, B, and C IP addresses.

Table 4.4   Class A, B, and C IP Addresses

Class	Description
A	The first network ID is 1.0.0.0 and the last is 126.0.0.0. This allows for 126 networks and 16,777,214 hosts per network. The class A address 127.*x.y.z* is reserved for loopback testing and interprocess communications on the local computer. For class A addresses, the network ID is always the first octet in the address and the host ID is the last three octets.

(continued)

Table 4.4   *(continued)*

Class	Description
B	The first network ID is 128.0.0.0 and the last is 191.255.0.0. This allows for 16,384 networks and 65,534 hosts per network. For class B addresses, the network ID is always the first two octets in the address and the host ID is the last two octets.
C	The first network ID is 192.0.0.0 and the last is 223.255.255.0. This allows for 2,097,152 networks and 254 hosts per network. For class C addresses, the network ID is always the first three octets in the address and the host ID is the last octet.

Using a Static IP Address

By default, client computers, for example those running Windows XP Professional, Windows 2000, Windows Me, Windows NT, Microsoft Windows 98, or Microsoft Windows 95, obtain TCP/IP configuration information automatically from the DHCP Service. However, even in a DHCP-enabled environment, you should assign a static IP address to selected network computers. For example, the computer running the DHCP Service cannot be a DHCP client, so it must have a static IP address. If the DHCP Service is not available, you can also configure TCP/IP to use a static IP address. For each network adapter card that uses TCP/IP in a computer, you can configure an IP address, subnet mask, and default gateway, as shown in Figure 4.2.

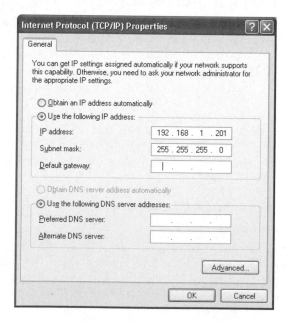

Figure 4.2   Configuring a static TCP/IP address

Table 4.5 describes the options used in configuring a static TCP/IP address.

Table 4.5   Options for Configuring a Static TCP/IP Address

Option	Description
IP address	A logical 32-bit address that identifies a TCP/IP host. Each network adapter card in a computer running TCP/IP requires a unique IP address, such as 192.168.0.108. Each address has two parts: a network ID, which identifies all hosts on the same physical network, and a host ID, which identifies a host on the network. In this example, the network ID is 192.168.0, and the host ID is 108.
Subnet mask	Subnets divide a large network into multiple physical networks connected with routers. A subnet mask blocks out part of the IP address so that TCP/IP can distinguish the network ID from the host ID. When TCP/IP hosts try to communicate, the subnet mask determines whether the destination host is on a local or remote network. To communicate on a local network, computers must have the same subnet mask.
Default gateway	The intermediate device on a local network that stores network IDs of other networks in the enterprise or Internet. To communicate with a host on another network, configure an IP address for the default gateway. TCP/IP sends packets for remote networks to the default gateway (if no other route is configured), which then forwards the packets to other gateways until the packet is delivered to a gateway connected to the specified destination.

To configure TCP/IP to use a static IP address, complete the following steps:

1. Click Start and then click Control Panel.

2. In the Control Panel window, click Network And Internet Connections.

3. In the Network And Internet Connections window, click Network Connections, double-click Local Area Connection, and then click Properties.

4. In the Local Area Connection Properties dialog box, click Internet Protocol (TCP/IP), verify that the check box to its left is selected, and then click Properties.

5. In the Internet Protocol (TCP/IP) Properties dialog box, in the General tab, click Use The Following IP Address, type the TCP/IP configuration parameters, and then click OK.

6. Click OK to close the Local Area Connection Properties dialog box and then close the Network And Dial-Up Connections window.

> **Caution**   IP communications can fail if duplicate IP addresses exist on a network. Therefore, you should always check with the network administrator to obtain a valid static IP address.

Obtaining an IP Address Automatically

If a server running the DHCP Service is available on the network, it can automatically assign TCP/IP configuration information to the DHCP client, as shown in Figure 4.3. You can then configure any clients running Windows XP Professional, Windows 95, and Windows 98 to obtain TCP/IP configuration information automatically from the DHCP Service. This can simplify administration and ensure correct configuration information.

> **Note**   Windows XP Professional does not include the DHCP Service. Only the Windows 2000 Server products provide the DHCP Service.

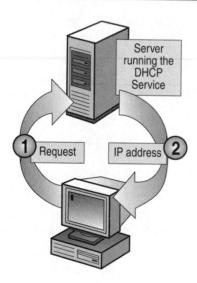

Figure 4.3   A server running the DHCP Service assigns TCP/IP addresses

> **Note**   Windows XP Professional also includes an Automatic Private IP Addressing feature that provides DHCP clients with limited network functionality if a DHCP server is unavailable during startup.

You can use the DHCP Service to provide clients with TCP/IP configuration information automatically. However, you must configure a computer as a DHCP client before it can interact with the DHCP Service.

To configure a DHCP client, complete the following steps:

1. Click Start and then click Control Panel.

2. In the Control Panel window, click Network And Internet Connections.

3. In the Network And Internet Connections window, click Network Connections, double-click Local Area Connection, and then click Properties.

4. In the Local Area Connection Properties dialog box, click Internet Protocol (TCP/IP), verify that the check box to its left is selected, and then click Properties.

5. In the Internet Protocol (TCP/IP) Properties dialog box, in the General tab, click Obtain An IP Address Automatically.

6. Click OK to close the Local Area Connection Properties dialog box and then close the Network And Dial-Up Connections window.

Using Automatic Private IP Addressing

The Windows XP Professional implementation of TCP/IP supports automatic assignment of IP addresses for simple LAN-based network configurations. This addressing mechanism is an extension of dynamic IP address assignment for LAN adapters, enabling configuration of IP addresses without using static IP address assignment or installing the DHCP Service. Automatic Private IP Addressing is enabled by default in Windows XP Professional so that home users and small business users can create a functioning, single-subnet, TCP/IP-based network without having to configure the TCP/IP protocol manually or set up a DHCP server.

The process for the Automatic Private IP Addressing feature, shown in Figure 4.4, is explained in the following steps:

1. Windows XP Professional TCP/IP attempts to find a DHCP server on the attached network to obtain a dynamically assigned IP address.

2. In the absence of a DHCP server during startup (for example, if the server is down for maintenance or repairs), the client cannot obtain an IP address.

3. Automatic Private IP Addressing generates an IP address in the form of 169.254.*x.y* (where *x.y* is the client's unique identifier) and a subnet mask of 255.255.0.0.

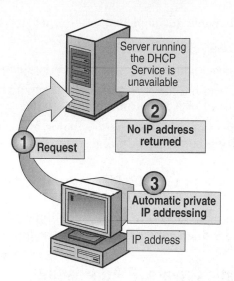

Figure 4.4 Automatic Private IP Addressing feature

Note The Internet Assigned Numbers Authority (IANA) has reserved 169.254.0.0 through169.254.255.255 for Automatic Private IP Addressing. As a result, Automatic Private IP Addressing provides an address that is guaranteed not to conflict with routable addresses.

After the computer generates the address, it broadcasts to this address and then assigns the address to itself if no other computer responds. The computer continues to use this address until it detects and receives configuration information from a DHCP server. This allows two computers to be plugged into a LAN hub to restart without any IP address configuration and to use TCP/IP for local network access.

If the computer is a DHCP client that has previously obtained a lease from a DHCP server and the lease has not expired at boot time, the sequence of events is slightly different. The client tries to renew its lease with the DHCP server. If the client cannot locate a DHCP server during the renewal attempt, it attempts to ping the default gateway listed in the lease.

If pinging the default gateway succeeds, the DHCP client assumes that it is still on the same network where it obtained its current lease, so it continues to use the lease. By default, the client attempts to renew its lease when 50 percent of its assigned lease time has expired. If pinging the default gateway fails, the client assumes that it has been moved to a network that has no DHCP services currently available and it autoconfigures itself as previously described. Once auto-configured, it continues to try to locate a DHCP server every 5 minutes.

Note   Windows 98, Microsoft Windows Millennium Edition, Microsoft Windows 2000, and Windows XP Home Edition also support Automatic Private IP Addressing.

Automatic Private IP Addressing can assign a TCP/IP address to DHCP clients automatically. However, Automatic Private IP Addressing does not generate all the information that typically is provided by DHCP, such as the address of a default gateway. Consequently, computers enabled with Automatic Private IP Addressing can communicate only with computers on the same subnet that also have addresses of the form 169.254.$x.y$.

Disabling Automatic Private IP Addressing

By default, the Automatic Private IP Addressing feature is enabled. However, you can disable it by specifying an alternate configuration to use if a DHCP server cannot be located (see Figure 4.5), as discussed in the next section.

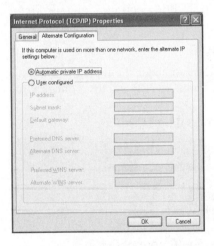

Figure 4.5   Specifying an alternate TCP/IP configuration

Specifying an Alternate Configuration for TCP/IP

Auto-Configuration for Multiple Networks Connectivity provides easy access to network devices and the Internet. It also allows a mobile computer user to seamlessly operate both office and home networks without having to manually reconfigure TCP/IP settings.

You specify an alternate configuration for TCP/IP if a DHCP server is not found. The alternate configuration is useful when a computer is used on multiple networks, one of which does not have a DHCP server and does not use an automatic private IP addressing configuration.

To configure Auto-Configuration for Multiple Networks Connectivity, do the following:

1. Click Start and then click Control Panel.
2. In the Control Panel window, click Network And Internet Connections.
3. In the Network And Internet Connections window, click Network Connections, and then click Local Area Connection.
4. Click Change Settings Of This Connection.

    Windows XP Professional displays the Local Area Connection Properties dialog box.

5. Click Internet Protocol (TCP/IP), and then click Properties.

    Windows XP Professional displays the Internet Protocol (TCP/IP) Properties dialog box with the General tab active.

6. Click Alternate Configuration.
7. Specify the alternate TCP/IP configuration (see Figure 4.5).

Using TCP/IP Tools

Windows XP Professional includes the tools diagrammed in Figure 4.6, which you can use to troubleshoot TCP/IP and test connectivity.

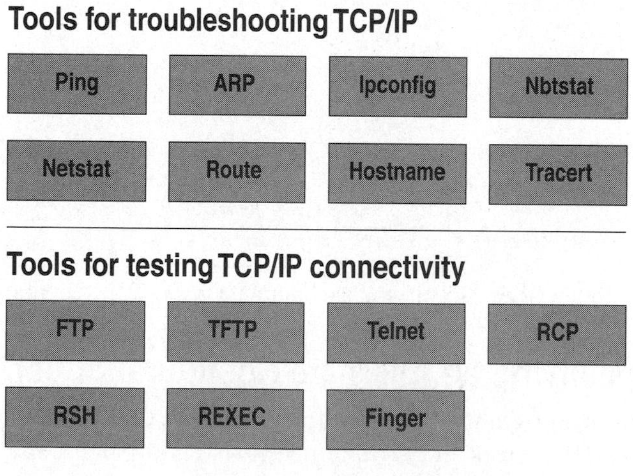

Tools for troubleshooting TCP/IP

Ping	ARP	Ipconfig	Nbtstat
Netstat	Route	Hostname	Tracert

Tools for testing TCP/IP connectivity

FTP	TFTP	Telnet	RCP
RSH	REXEC	Finger	

Figure 4.6   TCP/IP tools included with Windows XP Professional

Troubleshooting TCP/IP

Windows XP Professional offers several tools to assist you in troubleshooting TCP/IP, as described in Table 4.6.

Table 4.6   Tools Used to Troubleshoot TCP/IP

Option	Description
Ping	Verifies configurations and tests connections
ARP	Displays locally resolved IP addresses as physical addresses
Ipconfig	Displays the current TCP/IP configuration
Nbtstat	Displays statistics and connections using NetBT
Netstat	Displays TCP/IP protocol statistics and connections
Route	Displays or modifies the local routing table
Hostname	Returns the local computer's host name for authentication by the Remote Copy Protocol (RCP), Remote Shell (RSH), and Remote Execution (REXEC) tools
Tracert	Checks the route to a remote system
PathPing	Verifies that the routers on the way to a remote host are operating correctly by detecting packet loss over multiple-hop trips

These troubleshooting tools are all executed from within a command prompt. For information about how to use all of these commands, except Hostname and Tracert, open a command prompt, type the command followed by **/?**, and then press ENTER. For example, for information about the Ping tool, open a command prompt, type **ping /?**, and then press ENTER.

To use the Hostname tool, open a command prompt, type **hostname**, and then press ENTER. Hostname returns the name of the local computer.

For information about how to use the Tracert tool, open a command prompt, type **tracert**, and then press ENTER.

Testing TCP/IP Connectivity

Windows XP Professional also provides tools for testing TCP/IP connectivity, as described in Table 4.7.

Table 4.7   Tools Used to Test TCP/IP Connectivity

Option	Description
FTP	Provides bidirectional file transfer between a computer running Windows XP Professional and any TCP/IP host running FTP. Windows 2000 Server ships with the ability to serve as an FTP client or server.
Trivial File Transfer Protocol (TFTP)	Provides bidirectional file transfer between a computer running Windows XP Professional and a TCP/IP host running TFTP.
Telnet	Provides terminal emulation to a TCP/IP host running Telnet. Windows 2000 Server ships with a Telnet client as well as a Telnet Server (host).
RCP	Copies files between a client and a host that support RCP; for example, a computer running Windows XP Professional and a UNIX host.
RSH	Runs commands on a UNIX host.
REXEC	Runs a process on a remote computer.
Finger	Retrieves system information from a remote computer that supports TCP/IP and the Finger tool.

Testing a TCP/IP Configuration

After configuring TCP/IP and restarting the computer, you should use the Ipconfig and Ping command-prompt tools to test the configuration and connections to other TCP/IP hosts and networks. Such testing helps ensure that TCP/IP is functioning properly.

Using Ipconfig

You use the Ipconfig tool to verify the TCP/IP configuration parameters on a host. This helps to determine whether the configuration is initialized or if a duplicate IP address exists. Use the Ipconfig tool with the /all switch to verify configuration information.

Tip   Type **ipconfig /all | more** to prevent the Ipconfig output from scrolling off the screen; to scroll down and view additional output, press SPACEBAR.

The result of the Ipconfig /all command is as follows:

- If a configuration has initialized, the Ipconfig tool displays the IP address and subnet mask, and, if it is assigned, the default gateway.
- If a duplicate IP address exists, the Ipconfig tool indicates that the IP address is configured; however, the subnet mask is 0.0.0.0.
- If the computer is unable to obtain an IP address from a server running the DHCP Service on the network, the Ipconfig tool displays the IP address as the address provided by Automatic Private IP Addressing.

Using Ping

The Ping tool is a diagnostic tool that you can use to test TCP/IP configurations and diagnose connection failures. After you have verified the TCP/IP configuration, use the Ping tool to determine whether a particular TCP/IP host is available and functional. To test connectivity, use the Ping tool with the following syntax:

```
ping IP_address
```

Using Ipconfig and Ping

Figure 4.7 outlines the steps for verifying a computer's configuration and for testing router connections.

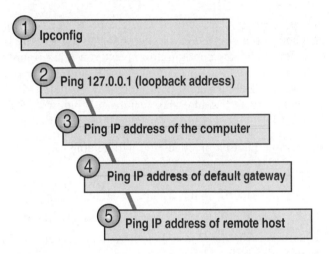

Figure 4.7   Using Ipconfig and Ping

The following list explains the steps outlined in Figure 4.7:

1. Use the Ipconfig tool to verify that the TCP/IP configuration has been initialized.

2. Use the Ping tool with the loopback address (ping 127.0.0.1) to verify that TCP/IP is correctly installed and bound to your network adapter card.

3. Use the Ping tool with the IP address of the computer to verify that your computer is not a duplicate of another IP address on the network.

4. Use the Ping tool with the IP address of the default gateway to verify that the default gateway is operational and that your computer can communicate with the local network.

5. Use the Ping tool with the IP address of a remote host to verify that the computer can communicate through a router.

Note   Typically, if you ping the remote host (step 5) and the ping is successful, steps 1 through 4 are successful by default. If the ping is not successful, ping the IP address of another remote host before completing the entire diagnostic process because the current host might be turned off.

By default, the following message appears four times in response to a successful Ping command:

```
Reply from IP_address
```

Practice: Configuring TCP/IP

In this practice, you'll use two TCP/IP tools to verify your computer's configuration. Then you'll configure your computer to use a static IP address and verify your computer's new configuration. Next you'll configure your computer to use a DHCP server to automatically assign an IP address to your computer, whether or not there is a DHCP server available on your network. Finally, you'll test the Automatic Private IPAddressing feature in Windows XP Professional by disabling the DHCP server, if there is one on your network.

After completing this practice, you will be able to

- Verify a computer's TCP/IP configuration
- Configure TCP/IP to use a static IP address using Automatic IP Addressing
- Configure TCP/IP to obtain an IP address automatically using DHCP
- Determine what happens when there is no server running the DHCP Service to provide an IP address

To complete this practice, you need

- TCP/IP as the only installed protocol.
- Optional: A server running the DHCP Service to provide IP addresses. If you are working on a computer that is not part of a network and there is no server running the DHCP Service, there are certain procedures in this practice that you will not be able to perform.

In the following table, record the IP address, subnet mask, and default gateway that your network administrator provides for you to use during this practice. Ask your network administrator if there is another computer that you can use to test your computer's connectivity, and record the IP address of that computer as well. If you are not on a network, you can use the suggested values.

Variable value	Suggested value	Your value
Static IP address	192.168.1.201	
Subnet mask	255.255.0.0	
Default gateway (if required)	None	
Computer to test connectivity	N/A	

Run the **ConfiguringTCP/IP** file in the Demos folder on the CD-ROM accompanying this book for a demonstration of configuring TCP/IP.

Exercise 1: Verifying a Computer's TCP/IP Configuration

In this exercise, you'll use two TCP/IP tools, Ipconfig and Ping, to verify your computer's configuration.

Note   As you complete the exercises in this practice, you will use the command prompt and Network Connections windows frequently. For the sake of efficiency, open the windows one time, and then minimize and restore them as necessary.

▶   **To verify a computer's configuration**

1. Click Start and then click Run.
2. In the Run dialog box, type **cmd** and then click OK to open a command prompt.
3. At the command prompt, type **ipconfig /all | more** and then press ENTER.

   The Windows XP Professional IP Configuration tool displays the TCP/IP configuration of the physical and logical adapters configured on your computer.
4. Press SPACEBAR as necessary to display the heading Local Area Connection. Use the information displayed in this section to complete as much of the following table as possible. Press SPACEBAR to display additional information as necessary and to return to the command prompt.

Local Area Connection setting	Value
Host name	
Primary DNS suffix	
Connection-specific DNS suffix description	
Physical address	
DHCP enabled	
Autoconfiguration enabled	
Autoconfiguration IP address	
Subnet mask	
Default gateway	

5. Press SPACEBAR as necessary to scroll through the configuration information and return to the command prompt.

6. To verify that the IP address is working and configured for your adapter, type **ping 127.0.0.1** and then press ENTER.

   A response similar to the following indicates a successful ping:

   ```
   Pinging 127.0.0.1 with 32 bytes of data:
   Reply from 127.0.0.1: bytes=32 time<10ms TTL=128
   Reply from 127.0.0.1: bytes=32 time<10ms TTL=128
   Reply from 127.0.0.1: bytes=32 time<10ms TTL=128
   Reply from 127.0.0.1: bytes=32 time<10ms TTL=128
   Ping statistics for 127.0.0.1:
   Packets: Sent = 4, Received = 4, Lost = 0 <0% loss>,
   Approximate round trip times in milliseconds:
   Minimum = 0ms, Maximum = 0ms, Average = 0ms
   ```

7. Minimize the command prompt.

Exercise 2: Configuring TCP/IP to Use a Static IP Address

In this exercise, you'll configure TCP/IP to use a static IP address.

▶ **To configure TCP/IP to use a static IP address**

1. Click Start and then click Control Panel.

2. In the Control Panel window, click Network And Internet Connections.

3. In the Network And Internet Connections window, click Network Connections, and then click Local Area Connection.

4. Under Network Tasks, click Change Settings Of This Connection.

   The Local Area Connection Properties dialog box appears, displaying the network adapter in use and the network components used in this connection.

5. Click Internet Protocol (TCP/IP), and then verify that the check box to the left of the entry is selected.

6. Click Properties.

   The Internet Protocol (TCP/IP) Properties dialog box appears.

7. Click Use The Following IP Address.

Important   In the next step, if the computer you are using is on a network, enter the IP address, subnet mask, and default gateway values you recorded in the table in Exercise 1. If you are on a stand-alone computer, complete the next step as it is written.

---

8. In the IP Address text box, type **198.168.1.201** and in the Subnet Mask text box type **255.255.255.0**.

Important   Be careful when entering IP configuration settings manually, especially numeric addresses. The most frequent cause of TCP/IP connection
problems is incorrectly entered IP address information.

9. Click OK to return to the Local Area Connection Properties dialog box.

10. Click OK to close the Local Area Connection Properties dialog box and return
    to the Network Connections window.

11. Minimize the Network Connections window.

▶ **To test the static TCP/IP configuration**

1. Restore the command prompt.

2. At the command prompt, type **ipconfig /all | more** and then press ENTER.

   The Windows XP Professional IP Configuration tool displays the physical and
   logical adapters configured on your computer.

3. Press SPACEBAR as needed to scroll through the configuration information and
   locate the local area connection information.

4. Record the current TCP/IP configuration settings for your local area connection in the following table.

Setting	Value
IP address	
Subnet mask	

5. Press SPACEBAR as necessary to scroll through the configuration information
   and return to the command prompt.

6. To verify that the IP address is working and configured for your adapter, type
   ping 127.0.0.1 and then press ENTER.

   If the address is working and configured, you receive the following result:

   ```
   Reply from 127.0.0.1: bytes=32 time<1ms TTL=128
   Reply from 127.0.0.1: bytes=32 time<1ms TTL=128
   Reply from 127.0.0.1: bytes=32 time<1ms TTL=128
   Reply from 127.0.0.1: bytes=32 time<1ms TTL=128
   ```

7. If you have a computer that you are using to test connectivity, type **ping**
   ip_address (where *ip_address* is the IP address of the computer you are using
   to test connectivity) and then press ENTER. Minimize the command prompt.

Exercise 3: Configuring TCP/IP to Automatically Obtain an IP Address

In this exercise, you'll configure TCP/IP to automatically obtain an IP address. You'll
then test the configuration to verify that the DHCP Service has provided the appropriate IP addressing information. Be sure to perform the first part of this exercise
even if you have no DHCP server because these settings are also used in Exercise 4.

▶ **To configure TCP/IP to automatically obtain an IP address**

1. Restore the Network Connections window, right-click Local Area Connection, and then click Properties.

   The Local Area Connection Properties dialog box appears.

2. Click Internet Protocol (TCP/IP) and verify that the checkbox to the left of the entry is selected.

3. Click Properties.

   The Internet Protocol (TCP/IP) Properties dialog box appears.

4. Click Obtain An IP Address Automatically.

5. Click OK to close the Internet Protocol (TCP/IP) Properties dialog box.

6. Click OK to close the Local Area Connection Properties dialog box.

7. Minimize the Network Connections window.

▶ **To test the TCP/IP configuration**

Note If there is not an available server running the DHCP Service to provide an IP address, skip this procedure and continue with Exercise 4.

1. Restore the command prompt, type **ipconfig /release** and then press ENTER.

2. At the command prompt, type **ipconfig /renew** and then press ENTER.

3. At the command prompt, type **ipconfig | more** and then press ENTER.

4. Pressing SPACEBAR as necessary, record the current TCP/IP configuration settings for your local area connection in the following table.

Setting	Value
IP address	
Subnet mask	
Default gateway	

   To test that TCP/IP is working and bound to your adapter, type **ping 127.0.0.1** and then press ENTER.

5. The internal loopback test displays four replies if TCP/IP is bound to the adapter.

Exercise 4: Obtaining an IP Address Using Automatic Private IP Addressing

In this exercise, if you have a server running the DHCP Service, you need to disable it on that server so that a DHCP server is not available to provide an IP address for your computer. Without a DHCP server available to provide an IP address, the Windows XP Professional Automatic Private IP Addressing feature provides unique IP addresses for your computer.

▶ **To obtain an IP address by using Automatic Private IP Addressing**

1. At the command prompt, type **ipconfig /release** and then press ENTER.

2. At the command prompt, type **ipconfig /renew** and then press ENTER.

   There is a pause while Windows XP Professional attempts to locate a DHCP server on the network.

   What message appears, and what does it indicate?

3. Click OK to close the dialog box.

▶ **To test the TCP/IP configuration**

1. At the command prompt, type **ipconfig | more** and then press ENTER.

2. Pressing SPACEBAR as necessary, record the current TCP/IP settings for your local area connection in the following table.

Setting	Value
IP address	
Subnet mask	
Default gateway	

   Is this the same IP address assigned to your computer in Exercise 3? Why or why not?

3. Press SPACEBAR to finish scrolling through the configuration information, as necessary.

4. To verify that TCP/IP is working and bound to your adapter, type **ping 127.0.0.1** and then press ENTER. The internal loopback test displays four replies if TCP/IP is bound to the adapter.

5. If you have a computer to test TCP/IP connectivity with your computer, type **ping *ip_address*** (where *ip_address* is the IP address of the computer that you are using to test connectivity) and then press ENTER. If you do not have a computer to test connectivity, skip this step and proceed to Exercise 5.

   Were you successful? Why or why not?

Exercise 5: Obtaining an IP Address Using DHCP

Before you begin this exercise, you'll need to enable the DHCP Service running on the computer that is acting as a DHCP server (or reconnect your network cable if you disconnected it in Exercise 4). In this exercise, your computer obtains IP addressing information from the DHCP server.

Note   If there is not an available server running the DHCP Service to provide an IP address, skip this exercise.

▶   **To obtain an IP address using DHCP**

1. At the command prompt, type **ipconfig /release** and then press ENTER.
2. At the command prompt, type **ipconfig /renew** and then press ENTER.

    After a short wait, a message box indicates that a new IP address was assigned.

3. Click OK to close the message box.
4. At the command prompt, type **ipconfig /all | more** and then press ENTER.
5. Verify that the DHCP server has assigned an IP address to your computer.
6. Close the command prompt.

Lesson Review

Here are some questions to help you determine whether you have learned enough to move on to the next lesson. If you have difficulty answering these questions, review the material in this lesson before beginning the next lesson. The answers are in Appendix A, "Questions and Answers."

1. Why would you assign a computer a static IP address?

2. Which of the following statements correctly describe IP addresses? (Choose all answers that are correct.)

    a. Logical 64-bit addresses that identify a TCP/IP host.

    b. Each network adapter card in a computer running TCP/IP requires a unique IP address.

    c. 192.168.0.108 is an example of a class C IP address.

    d. The host ID in an IP address is always the last two octets in the address.

3. What is the purpose of a subnet mask?

4. By default, client computers running Windows XP Professional, Windows 95, or Windows 98 obtain TCP/IP configuration information automatically from the DHCP Service: True or false?

5. Which of the following statements about obtaining an IP address automatically are true? (Choose all answers that are correct.)

    a. Windows XP Professional includes the DHCP Service.

    b. Windows XP Professional includes an Automatic Private IP Addressing feature, which provides DHCP clients with limited network functionality if a DHCP server is unavailable during startup.

    c. The Internet Assigned Numbers Authority (IANA) has reserved 169.254.0.0 through 169.254.255.255 for Automatic Private IP Addressing.

    d. You should always disable Automatic Private IP Addressing in small workgroups.

6. Your computer running Windows XP Professional was configured manually for TCP/IP. You can connect to any host on your own subnet, but you cannot connect to or even ping any host on a remote subnet. What is the likely cause of the problem and how would you fix it?

7. Your computer's Computer Name is Pro1 and you ping Pro1. The local address for Pro1 is returned as 169.254.$x.y$. What does this tell you?

Lesson Summary

- Each TCP/IP host is identified by a logical IP address that identifies a computer's location on the network.

- Microsoft's implementation of TCP/IP enables a TCP/IP host to use a static IP address, to obtain an IP address automatically from a DHCP server, or to use automatic assignment of IP addresses.

- Windows XP Professional does not include the DHCP Service; only the Windows 2000 Server products provide the DHCP Service.

- Computers enabled with Automatic Private IP Addressing can communicate only with computers on the same subnet that also have addresses of the form 169.254.$x.y$.

- You should use the Ipconfig and Ping command-prompt tools to test the configuration and connections to other TCP/IP hosts and networks.

Lesson 3: Installing, Configuring, and Troubleshooting NWLink

The NWLink IPX/SPX/NetBIOS Compatible Transport Protocol (usually referred to as NWLink) is Microsoft's implementation of Novell's NetWare Internetwork Packet Exchange/Sequenced Packet Exchange (IPX/SPX) protocol. NWLink is most commonly used in environments in which clients running Microsoft operating systems are used to access resources on NetWare servers, or in which clients running NetWare are used to access resources on computers running Microsoft operating systems.

After this lesson, you will be able to

- Install and configure NWLink

- Describe the tools Windows XP Professional provides for troubleshooting NWLink

Estimated lesson time: 40 minutes

Understanding NWLink Features

NWLink allows computers running Windows XP Professional to communicate with other network devices that are using IPX/SPX. NWLink also can be used in small network environments that use only clients running Windows XP Professional and other Microsoft operating systems.

NWLink supports the networking application programming interfaces (APIs) that provide the interprocess communication (IPC) services described in Table 4.8.

Table 4.8   Networking APIs Supported by NWLink

Networking API	Description
Winsock	Supports existing NetWare applications written to comply with the NetWare IPX/SPX Sockets interface
NetBIOS over IPX	Implemented as NWLink NetBIOS; supports communication between a NetWare client running NetBIOS and a computer running Windows XP Professional and NWLink NetBIOS

NWLink also provides NetWare clients with access to applications designed for Windows 2000 Server, such as Microsoft SQL Server and Microsoft SNA Server. To provide NetWare clients access to file and print resources on a computer running Windows 2000 Server, you should install File and Print Services for NetWare (FPNW).

In summary, the 32-bit Windows XP Professional implementation of NWLink provides the following features:

- Supports communications with NetWare networks

- Supports communications with NetWare networks
- Supports sockets and NetBIOS over IPX
- Provides NetWare clients with access to Windows 2000 servers

Installing NWLink

The procedure for installing NWLink is the same process used to install any network protocol in Windows XP Professional.

To install NWLink, complete the following steps:

1. Click Start and then click Control Panel.
2. In the Control Panel window, click Network And Internet Connections.
3. In the Network And Internet Connections window, click Network Connections, and then click Local Area Connection.
4. Under Network Tasks, click Change Settings Of This Connection. The Local Area Connection Properties dialog box appears, displaying the network adapter in use and the network components used in this connection.
5. Click Install.

   The Select Network Component Type dialog box appears.
6. In the Select Network Component Type dialog box, click Protocol, and then click Add.

   The Select Network Protocol dialog box appears.
7. In the Select Network Protocol dialog box, in the Network Protocol list, click NWLink IPX/SPX/NetBIOS Compatible Transport Protocol (see Figure 4.8), and then click OK.

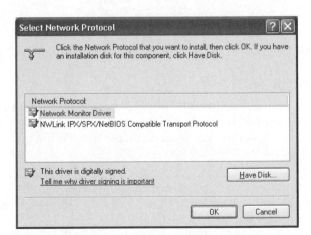

Figure 4.8 The Select Network Protocol dialog box

Configuring NWLink

NWLink configuration involves three components: frame type, network number, and internal network number. By default, Windows XP Professional detects a frame type and a network number automatically when you install NWLink. Windows XP Professional also provides a generic internal network number. However, you must specify an internal network number manually if you plan to run FPNW or IPX routing, as shown in Figure 4.9.

Note   Each network adapter card bound to NWLink in a computer requires a frame type and network number.

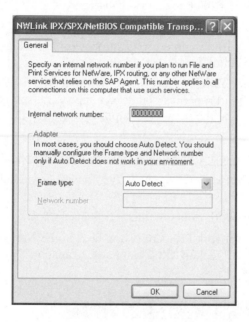

Figure 4.9   Configuring NWLink

Frame Type

A *frame type* defines the way the network adapter card formats data. To ensure proper communication between a computer running Windows XP Professional and a NetWare server, you must configure the NWLink frame type to match the frame type on the NetWare server.

Note   A connection between two computers that use different frame types is possible if the NetWare server is acting as a router. However, this is inefficient and can result in a slow connection.

Table 4.9 lists the topologies and frame types supported by NWLink.

Table 4.9   Topologies and Frame Types Supported by NWLink

Topology	Frame type
Ethernet	Ethernet II, 802.3, 802.2, and Subnetwork Access Protocol (SNAP), which defaults to 802.2
Token Ring	802.5 and SNAP
Fiber Distributed Data Interface (FDDI)	802.2 and SNAP

Note   On Ethernet networks, the standard frame type for NetWare 2.2 and NetWare 3.11 is 802.3. For NetWare 3.12 and later, the default is 802.2.

When you install NWLink, Windows XP Professional automatically determines which IPX frame type is in use on the network and sets the NWLink frame type accordingly. If Windows XP Professional detects frame types in addition to 802.2 during NWLink installation, the frame type for NWLink defaults to 802.2.

Network Number

Each frame type configured on a network adapter card requires a *network number,* which must be unique for each network segment. All computers on a segment using the same frame type must use the same network number to communicate with one another.

Note   On a computer running Windows XP Professional, type **ipxroute config** at a command prompt to display the network number, frame type, and device in use.

Although Windows XP Professional automatically detects a network number, you can also specify a network number manually by using the Registry Editor.

Setting a network number in the registry for a given frame type requires entering two corresponding entries, NetworkNumber and PktType, in the HKEY_LOCAL_ MACHINE\SYSTEM\CurrentControlSet\Services\ Nwlnkipx\Parameters\Adapters\Adapter subkey of the registry.

NetworkNumber specifies the network number (in hexadecimal) for the adapter. If the value for this entry is 0, NWLink gets the network number from the network while it is running. Network numbers are 4 bytes (eight hexadecimal characters). The NetworkNumber entry takes a REG_MULTI_SZ data type.

Note If an adapter uses multiple packet types, you can specify the network number for each packet type by adding corresponding values in the NetworkNumber entry.

PktType specifies the packet form to use. The PktType entry takes a *REG_MULTI_SZ* data type. Table 4.10 lists the values for the PktType entry and the packet forms supported by NWLink.

Table 4.10   Packet Types or Forms Supported by NWLink

Value	Packet form
0	Ethernet_II
1	Ethernet_802.3
2	Ethernet 802.2
3	Ethernet SNAP
FF (default)	Auto Detect

Note In most cases you should use Auto Detect. You should configure the frame type and network number manually only if Auto Detect does not work in your environment.

Internal Network Number

An *internal network number* uniquely identifies a computer on the network for internal routing. This eight-digit hexadecimal number, or virtual network number, is set to 00000000 by default.

The internal network number identifies a virtual network segment inside the computer. That is, it identifies another (virtual) segment on the network. Therefore, if an internal network number is configured for a computer running Windows XP Professional, a NetWare server or a router adds an extra hop in its route to the computer.

You must manually assign a unique, nonzero internal network number in the following situations:

- FPNW is installed and there are multiple frame types on a single adapter.
- FPNW is installed and NWLink is bound to multiple adapters in the computer.
- An application is using the NetWare Service Advertising Protocol (SAP). SQL Server and SNA Server are examples of applications that can use SAP.

Note   If a computer has multiple network adapter cards bound to NWLink, and if you want each to use a different frame type, configure each network adapter card to use the Manual Frame Type Detection option. You also must specify a frame type, network number, and internal network number for each network adapter card.

Troubleshooting NetWare Connectivity

Windows XP Professional provides several tools to help you resolve NetWare connectivity problems, including those listed in Table 4.11.

Table 4.11   Troubleshooting Tools for NetWare Connectivity Problems

Tool	Use
Ipxroute config	Type this command in a command prompt to determine information about the current state of the stack. It displays the current IPX status, including the network number, MAC address, interface name, and frame type.
Ipxroute ripout	Type **ipxroute ripout ####** (where #### is an eight-digit hexadecimal number, the network number) to determine whether there is a connection to a specific network.
Network Monitor	Allows you to detect and troubleshoot problems on LANs and on wide area networks (WANs). Network Monitor helps you identify network traffic patterns and problems.

Connection problems are usually caused by incorrect configuration settings for NWLink. The following sections include several common configuration problems that you should check when you are having problems connecting to a NetWare server from a client running Windows XP Professional.

Verify That NWLink and Client Services for NetWare Are Installed

For a client running Windows XP Professional to access a NetWare server, you must install NWLink and Client Services for NetWare on the client, and Client Services for NetWare must be running.

To verify that NWLink and Client Services for NetWare are installed, complete the following steps:

1. Click Start and then click Control Panel.
2. In the Control Panel window, Click Network And Internet Connections.
3. In the Network And Internet Connections window, click Network Connections, and then double-click Local Area Connection.

   The Local Area Connection Status dialog box appears.

4. Click Properties.

   The Local Area Connection Properties dialog box appears, displaying the network adapter in use and the network components used in this connection.

5. Verify that NWLink and Client Services for NetWare are listed.

To verify that Client Services for NetWare is running, complete the following steps:

1. Click Start and then click Control Panel.

2. In the Control Panel window, double-click Administrative Tools.

3. In the Status column, verify that Client Service for NetWare is listed as started.

Verify That the Frame Type Is Set to Auto Detect on the Client

For a client running Windows XP Professional to access a NetWare server, the frame type should be configured to Auto Detect.

To verify the frame type on the client is set to Auto Detect, complete the following steps:

1. Click Start and then click Control Panel.

2. In the Control Panel window, click Network And Internet Connections.

3. In the Network And Internet Connections window, click Network Connections, and then double-click Local Area Connection.

   The Local Area Connection Status dialog box appears.

4. Click Properties.

   The Local Area Connection Properties dialog box appears.

5. Double-click NWLink IPX/SPX/NetBIOS Compatible Transport Protocol.

6. In the General tab, verify that Auto Detect is selected in the Frame Type list.

Verify the Installed Network Number and Frame Type on the Client

For a client running Windows XP Professional to access a NetWare server, the frame type and network number must be configured to match the NetWare server.

To determine the installed network number and frame type on the client, complete the following steps:

1. Click Start and then click Run.

2. In the Run dialog box, type **cmd** and then click OK to open a command prompt.

3. At the command prompt, type **ipxroute config** and press ENTER.

4. Verify that the network number and frame type in the Network and Frame columns are correct for your installation.

Practice: Installing and Configuring NWLink

In this practice, you'll install and configure the NWLink IPX/SPX/NetBIOS Compatible Transport Protocol. Then you'll install and configure NWLink. With multiple protocols installed, you'll change the binding order of a protocol, unbind a protocol from a network adapter card, and remove NWLink from a computer.

After completing this practice, you will be able to

- Install NWLink
- Use Ipxroute config to determine the installed network number and frame type

To complete this practice, you need

- TCP/IP as the only installed protocol.

Note You can install any of the available protocols in Windows XP Professional using this procedure.

Run the **NWLink** file in the Demos folder on the CD-ROM accompanying this book for a demonstration of installing and configuring NWLink.

▶ **To install and configure NWLink**

1. Restore the Network Connections window.
2. Click Local Area Connection.
3. Under Network Tools, click Change Settings Of This Connection.

   Windows XP Professional displays the Local Area Connection Properties dialog box, which shows the network adapter card in use and the network components used in this connection.

4. Click Add.

   Windows XP Professional displays the Select Network Component Type dialog box.

5. Click Protocol, and then click Add.

   Windows XP Professional displays the Select Network Protocol dialog box.

   What protocols can you install?

6. Select NWLink IPX/SPX/NetBIOS Compatible Transport Protocol, and then click OK.

   Windows XP Professional displays the Local Area Connection Properties dialog box.

7. Select NWLink IPX/SPX/NetBIOS Compatible Transport Protocol, and then click Properties.

   What type of frame detection is selected by default?

   Notice that when the default frame type is selected, the Network Number option is not active.

8. Click the arrow to view the Frame Type drop-down menu selections.

   What other frame types are listed?

9. Select one of the frame types listed, other than Auto Detect.

   Why is the Network Number option now active?

10. Click Cancel to close the NWLink IPX/SPX/NetBIOS Compatible Transport Protocol Properties dialog box.

11. Click Close to close the Local Area Connection Properties dialog box.

▶ **To determine the installed network number and frame type on the client**

1. Click Start and then click Run.

2. In the Run dialog box, type **cmd** and then click OK to open a command prompt.

3. At the command prompt, type **ipxroute config** and press ENTER.

   What is the network number and frame type for the LAN?

4. Type **exit** and press ENTER to close the command prompt.

Lesson Review

Here are some questions to help you determine whether you have learned enough to move on to the next lesson. If you have difficulty answering these questions, review the material in this lesson before beginning the next lesson. The answers are in Appendix A, "Questions and Answers."

1. Your computer running Windows XP Professional can communicate with some but not all of the NetWare servers on your network. Some of the NetWare servers are running frame type 802.2 and some are running 802.3. What is the likely cause of the problem?

2. How can you verify that the network number and frame type are correct for your client computer running Windows XP Professional and attempting to access a NetWare server?

3. Which of the following statements about NWLink are true? (Choose all answers that are correct.)

   a. NWLink allows computers running Windows XP Professional to communicate with other network devices that are using IPX/SPX.

   b. NWLink provides NetWare clients with access to Microsoft SQL Server.

   c. NWLink provides NetWare clients access to file and print resources on a computer running Windows 2000 Server.

   d. NWLink provides NetWare clients with access to Microsoft SNA Server.

4. Which of the following commands or tools do you type in a command prompt to determine information about the stack, including the current IPX status, network number, MAC address, interface name, and frame type?

   a. Ipconfig

   b. Iproute config

   c. Ipxroute config

   d. Ipxroute ripout

Lesson Summary

- The NWLink IPX/SPX/NetBIOS Compatible Transport Protocol (NWLink) is Microsoft's implementation of Novell's NetWare IPX/SPX protocol.

- NWLink is most commonly used in environments in which clients running Microsoft operating systems are used to access resources on NetWare servers, or in which clients running NetWare are used to access resources on computers running Microsoft operating systems.

- NWLink provides NetWare clients with access to applications designed for Windows 2000 Server, such as Microsoft SQL Server and Microsoft SNA Server.

- To provide NetWare clients with access to file and print resources on a computer running Windows 2000 Server, you should install FPNW.

- NWLink configuration involves three components: frame type, network number, and internal network number.

- By default, Windows XP Professional detects a frame type and a network number automatically when you install NWLink.

- Windows XP Professional provides a generic internal network number, but you must specify an internal network number manually if you plan to run FPNW or IPX routing.

- For a client running Windows XP Professional to access a NetWare server, you must install NWLink and Client Services for NetWare on the client, and Client Services for NetWare must be running.

- Windows XP Professional provides Ipxroute config, Ipxroute ripout, and Network Monitor to help you resolve NetWare connectivity problems.

Lesson 4: Network Bindings

Network bindings enable communication among network adapter card drivers, protocols, and services. Figure 4.10 shows an example of network bindings. In this example, the workstation service is bound to each of three protocols, and each protocol is bound to at least one network adapter card. This lesson describes the function of bindings in a network and the process for configuring them.

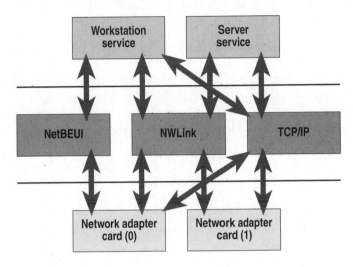

Figure 4.10   Network bindings

The Windows XP Professional network architecture uses a series of interdependent layers. The bottom layer of the network architecture ends at the network adapter card, which places information on the cable, allowing information to flow between computers.

After this lesson, you will be able to

■ Explain how to configure network bindings

Estimated lesson time: 20 minutes

Binding Between Architectural Levels

Binding is the process of linking network components on different levels to enable communication between those components. A network component can be bound to one or more network components above or below it. The services that each component provides can be shared by all other components that are bound to it. For example, in Figure 4.10, TCP/IP is bound to both the Workstation service and the Server service.

Combining Network Bindings

Many combinations of network bindings are possible. In the example shown in Figure 4.10, all three protocols are bound to the Workstation service, but only the routable protocols, NWLink and TCP/IP, are bound to the Server service. It is possible to select which protocols are bound to the network adapter cards if you are a member of the Administrators group. Network adapter card (0) is bound to all three protocols, and network adapter card (1) is bound only to the routable protocols.

When adding network software, Windows XP Professional automatically binds all dependent network components accordingly. Network Driver Interface Specification (NDIS) 5.1 provides the capability to bind multiple protocols to multiple network adapter card drivers.

Configuring Network Bindings

You can configure your network bindings using My Network Places.

To configure network bindings, complete the following steps:

1. Click Start and then click Control Panel.
2. In the Control Panel window, click Network And Internet Connections.
3. In the Network And Internet Connections window, click Network Connections.
4. In the Network Connections window, on the Advanced menu, click Advanced Settings.
5. In the Advanced Settings dialog box, under Client For Microsoft Networks, do one of the following:

   ▪ To bind the protocol to the selected adapter, select the check box to the left of the adapter.

      There should be a check mark in the check box.

   ▪ To unbind the protocol from the selected adapter, clear the check box to the left of the adapter.

      There should *not* be a check mark in the check box.

Note   Only an experienced network administrator familiar with the requirements of the network software should attempt to change binding settings.

Specifying Binding Order

You also can specify binding order to optimize network performance. For example, a computer running Windows XP Professional has NWLink IPX/SPX and TCP/IP installed. However, most of the servers to which this computer connects are running only TCP/IP. Verify that the Workstation binding to TCP/IP is listed before the Workstation bindings for the NWLink IPX/SPX protocol. In this way, when a user attempts to make a connection to a server, the Workstation service first attempts to establish the connection using TCP/IP.

To specify binding order, complete the following steps:

1. Click Start and then click Control Panel.
2. In the Control Panel window, click Network And Internet Connections.
3. In the Network And Internet Connections window, click Network Connections.
4. In the Network Connections window, on the Advanced menu, click Advanced Settings.
5. In the Advanced Settings dialog box, under Client For Microsoft Networks, click the protocol for which you want to change the binding order.
6. Use the arrow buttons to change the binding order for protocols that are bound to a specific adapter:

   ■ To move the protocol higher in the binding order, click the upward pointing arrow.

   ■ To move the protocol lower in the binding order, click the downward pointing arrow.

Practice: Working with Network Bindings

In this practice, you'll change the binding order of the protocols bound to your network adapter card. Then you'll unbind a protocol from your network adapter card and bind a protocol to your network adapter card. Finally, you'll uninstall a network protocol.

After completing this practice you will be able to

■ Change the binding order of protocols

■ Bind and unbind a protocol

■ Remove a protocol

To complete this practice, you need

■ TCP/IP installed as the first network protocol on the computer and NWLink installed as the only other installed protocol.

Run the **NetworkBindings** file in the Demos folder on the CD-ROM accompanying this book for a demonstration of changing the binding order for a protocol.

Exercise 1: Changing the Binding Order for a Protocol

In this exercise, you'll change the binding order of the protocols bound to your network adapter card.

▶ **To change the protocol binding order**

1. Click Start and then click Control Panel.
2. In the Control Panel window, click Network And Internet Connections.
3. In the Network And Internet Connections window, click Network Connections.
4. In the Network Connections window, on the Advanced menu, click Advanced Settings.

   The Advanced Settings dialog box appears.

   What is the order of the protocols listed under Client For Microsoft Networks?

5. Under Client For Microsoft Networks, click Internet Protocol (TCP/IP).

   There should still be a check mark in the check box in front of Internet Protocol (TCP/IP).
6. Click the upward pointing arrow.

   Notice that the order of the protocols listed under Client For Microsoft Networks has changed. Internet Protocol (TCP/IP) is now listed above NWLink IPX/SPX/NetBIOS Compatible Transport Protocol.
7. Leave the Advanced Settings window open.

Exercise 2: Unbinding a Protocol

In this exercise, you'll unbind TCP/IP from your network adapter card, leaving NWLink as the only protocol available to access other computers.

▶ **To unbind TCP/IP**

1. In the Advanced Settings dialog box, under Client For Microsoft Networks, unbind Internet Protocol (TCP/IP) by clearing the check box to the left of the entry.
2. Click OK.

   TCP/IP is no longer bound to your network adapter card.

Exercise 3: Binding a Protocol

In this exercise, you'll bind TCP/IP to your network adapter card.

▶ **To bind TCP/IP**

1. On the Advanced menu of the Network And Dial-Up Connections window, click Advanced Settings.

   The Advanced Settings dialog box appears.

2. Under Client For Microsoft Networks, select the check box to the left of Internet Protocol (TCP/IP).

   There should now be a check mark in the check box to the left of Internet Protocol (TCP/IP).

3. Click OK.

   TCP/IP is now bound to your network adapter card.

Exercise 4: Uninstalling NWLink

In this exercise, you'll uninstall the NWLink IPX/SPX/NetBIOS Compatible Transport Protocol.

▶ **To remove NWLink**

1. In the Network Connections window, double-click Local Area Connection, and then click Properties.

   The Local Area Connection Properties dialog box appears, displaying the adapter in use and the network components configured for this connection.

2. Click NWLink IPX/SPX/NetBIOS Compatible Transport Protocol, and then click Uninstall.

   The Uninstall NWLink IPX/SPX/NetBIOS Compatible Transport Protocol dialog box appears.

3. In the Uninstall NWLink IPX/SPX/NetBIOS Compatible Transport Protocol dialog box, click Yes to continue.

4. In the Local Network dialog box, click No.

   Notice that NWLink IPX/SPX/NetBIOS Compatible Transport Protocol is no longer listed as an installed protocol.

5. Click Close, and then click Yes.

Lesson Review

Here are some questions to help you determine whether you have learned enough to move on to the next chapter. If you have difficulty answering these questions, review the material in this lesson before beginning the next chapter. The answers are in Appendix A, "Questions and Answers."

1. What is binding?

2. What is the significance of the binding order of network protocols?

3. Can a network component bind to more than one component above or below it? Why is that important?

4. What function does NDIS provide and what version is in Windows XP Professional?

Lesson Summary

- Binding is the process of linking network components on different levels to enable communication between those components.

- A network component can be bound to one or more network components above or below it.

- The services that each component provides can be shared by all other components that are bound to it.

- To control which components are bound together, you must be a member of the Administrators group.

- You can specify binding order to optimize network performance.

CHAPTER 5

Using the DNS Service and Active Directory Service

About This Chapter

Domain Name System (DNS) is a naming system based on a distributed database used in Transmission Control Protocol/Internet Protocol (TCP/IP) networks to translate computer names to Internet Protocol (IP) addresses. It is the widely used default naming system for IP-based networks. DNS makes it easy to locate computers and other resources on these networks. The version of DNS that ships with Microsoft Windows 2000 Server products is compliant with standard DNS as described in the Request for Comments (RFC) documents of the Internet Engineering Task Force (IETF). This chapter presents an introduction to DNS and name resolution. It also presents the skills and knowledge necessary to configure clients to use the DNS Service.

A directory service uniquely defines users and resources on a network. Directory services based on Active Directory technology in Windows 2000 provide a single point of network management, allowing you to add, remove, and relocate users and resources easily. This chapter introduces you to the Active Directory service.

Note The DNS Service and Active Directory are not available with Microsoft Windows XP Professional. You must have a computer running one of the Windows 2000 Server products to use Microsoft's DNS Service and Active Directory.

Before You Begin

To complete this chapter, you must have

- A computer that meets the minimum hardware requirements listed in the preface, "About This Book"
- Installed the Windows XP Professional software on the computer
- Installed TCP/IP as the only protocol

Lesson 1: Understanding DNS

DNS is most commonly associated with the Internet. However, private networks use DNS extensively to resolve computer names and to locate computers within their local networks and the Internet. DNS provides the following benefits:

- DNS names are user-friendly, which means that they are easier to remember than IP addresses.

- DNS names remain more constant than IP addresses. An IP address for a server can change, but the server name remains the same.

- DNS allows users to connect to local servers using the same naming convention as the Internet.

Note For more information about DNS, see RFC 1034 and RFC 1035. To read the text of these RFCs, use your Web browser to search for "RFC 1034" and "RFC 1035."

After this lesson, you will be able to

- Explain the function of DNS and its components

Estimated lesson time: 20 minutes

Domain Namespace

The *domain namespace* is the naming scheme that provides the hierarchical structure for the DNS database. Each node, referred to as a *domain,* represents a partition of the DNS database.

The DNS database is indexed by name, so each domain must have a name. As you add domains to the hierarchy, the name of the parent domain is added to its child domain (called a *subdomain*). Consequently, a domain's name identifies its position in the hierarchy. For example, in Figure 5.1, the domain name sales.microsoft.com identifies the sales domain as a subdomain of the microsoft.com domain and microsoft as a subdomain of the com domain.

The hierarchical structure of the domain namespace consists of a root domain, top-level domains, second-level domains, and host names.

Note The term *domain*, in the context of DNS, is not related to the term as used in the Windows 2000 directory services. A Windows 2000 domain is a grouping of computers and devices that are administered as a unit.

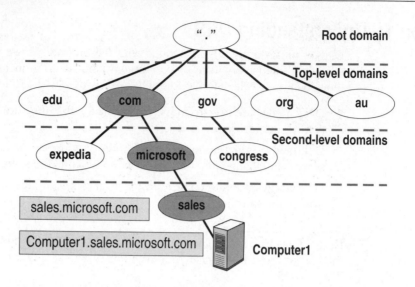

Figure 5.1 Hierarchical structure of a domain namespace

Root Domain

The root domain is at the top of the hierarchy and is represented as a period (.). The Internet root domain is managed by several organizations, including Network Solutions, Inc.

Top-Level Domains

Top-level domains are two- or three-character name codes. Top-level domains are grouped by organization type or geographic location. Table 5.1 provides some examples of top-level domain names.

Table 5.1   Top-Level Domains

Top-level domain	Description
gov	Government organizations
com	Commercial organizations
edu	Educational institutions
org	Noncommercial organizations
au	Country code of Australia

Top-level domains can contain second-level domains and host names.

Second-Level Domains

Organizations such as Network Solutions, Inc., assign and register second-level domains to individuals and organizations for the Internet. A second-level name has two name parts: a top-level name and a unique second-level name. Table 5.2 provides some examples of second-level domains.

Table 5.2   Second-Level Domains

Second-level domain	Description
ed.gov	United States Department of Education
Microsoft.com	Microsoft Corporation
Stanford.edu	Stanford University
w3.org	World Wide Web Consortium
pm.gov.au	Prime Minister of Australia

Host Names

Host names refer to specific computers on the Internet or a private network. For example, in Figure 5.1, Computer1 is a host name. A host name is the leftmost portion of a *fully qualified domain name* (FQDN), which describes the exact position of a host within the domain hierarchy. In Figure 5.1, Computer1.sales.microsoft.com. (including the end period, which represents the root domain) is an FQDN.

DNS uses a host's FQDN to resolve a name to an IP address.

Note   The host name does not have to be the same as the computer name. By default, TCP/IP setup uses the computer name for the host name, replacing illegal characters, such as the underscore (_), with a hyphen (-). For accepted domain naming conventions, see RFC 1035.

Domain Naming Guidelines

When you create a domain namespace, consider the following domain guidelines and standard naming conventions:

- Limit the number of domain levels. Typically, DNS host entries should be three or four levels down the DNS hierarchy and no more than five levels down the hierarchy. The numbers of levels increase the administrative tasks.
- Use unique names. Each subdomain must have a unique name within its parent domain to ensure that the name is unique throughout the DNS namespace.

- Use simple names. Simple and precise domain names are easier for users to remember and they enable users to search intuitively and locate Web sites or other computers on the Internet or an intranet.

- Avoid lengthy domain names. Domain names can be up to 63 characters, including periods. The total length of an FQDN cannot exceed 255 characters. Case-sensitive naming is not supported.

- Use standard DNS characters and Unicode characters.

- Windows 2000 supports the following standard DNS characters: A–Z, a–z, 0–9, and the hyphen (-), as defined in RFC 1035.

- The DNS Service also supports the Unicode character set. The Unicode character set includes additional characters not found in the American Standard Code for Information Interchange (ASCII) character set, which are required for languages such as French, German, and Spanish.

Note Use Unicode characters only if all servers running the DNS Service in your environment support Unicode. For more information about the Unicode character set, read RFC 2044 by searching for "RFC 2044" with your Web browser.

Zones

A zone represents a discrete portion of the domain namespace. Zones provide a way to partition the domain namespace into manageable sections and they provide the following functions:

- Multiple zones in a domain namespace are used to distribute administrative tasks to different groups. For example, Figure 5.2 depicts the microsoft.com domain namespace divided into two zones. These zones allow one administrator to manage the microsoft and sales domains and another administrator to manage the development domain.

- A zone must encompass a contiguous domain namespace. For example, in Figure 5.2, you could not create a zone that consists of only the sales.microsoft.com and development.microsoft.com domains, because these two domains are not contiguous.

Note For more information about contiguous namespaces, see Lesson 6, "Understanding Active Directory Concepts," later in this chapter.

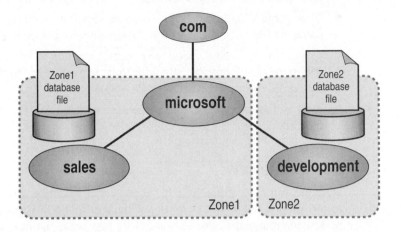

Figure 5.2   Domain namespace divided into zones

The name-to-IP address mappings for a zone are stored in the zone database file. Each zone is anchored to a specific domain, referred to as the zone's root domain. The zone database file does not necessarily contain information for all subdomains of the zone's root domain, only those subdomains within the zone.

In Figure 5.2, the root domain for Zone1 is microsoft.com, and its zone file contains the name-to-IP address mappings for the microsoft and sales domains. The root domain for Zone2 is development, and its zone file contains the name-to-IP address mappings only for the development domain. The zone file for Zone1 does not contain the name-to-IP address mappings for the development domain, although development is a subdomain of the microsoft domain.

Name Servers

A DNS name server stores the zone database file. Name servers can store data for one zone or multiple zones. A name server is said to have authority for the domain name space that the zone encompasses.

One name server contains the master zone database file, referred to as the *primary zone database file*, for the specified zone. As a result, there must be at least one name server for a zone. Changes to a zone, such as adding domains or hosts, are performed on the server that contains the primary zone database file.

Multiple name servers act as a backup to the name server containing the primary zone database file. Multiple name servers provide the following advantages:

- They perform zone transfers. The additional name servers obtain a copy of the zone database file from the name server that contains the primary database zone file. This process is called a zone transfer. These name servers periodically query the name server containing the primary zone database file for updated zone data.

- They provide redundancy. If the name server containing the primary zone database file fails, the additional name servers can provide service.

- They improve access speed for remote locations. If there are a number of clients in remote locations, use additional name servers to reduce query traffic across slow wide area network (WAN) links.

- They reduce the load on the name server containing the primary zone database file.

Lesson Review

Here are some questions to help you determine whether you have learned enough to move on to the next lesson. If you have difficulty answering these questions, review the material in this lesson before beginning the next lesson. The answers for these questions are in Appendix A, "Questions and Answers."

1. What is DNS and what is it used for?

2. Which of the following statements correctly describes DNS root domains? (Choose all answers that are correct.)

   a. The root domain is at the top of the hierarchy.

   b. The root domain is at the bottom of the hierarchy.

   c. The root domain is represented by a two- or three-character name code.

   d. The root domain is represented by a period (.).

3. Which of the following are second-level domain names? (Choose all answers that are correct.)

   a. gov

   b. Microsoft.com

   c. au

   d. ed.gov

4. _____ provide a way to partition the domain namespace into manageable sections and each _____ represents a discrete portion of the domain namespace.

Lesson Summary

- Domain Name System (DNS) is a distributed database that is the default naming system for IP-based networks.

- DNS is used to resolve computer names and to locate computers within local networks and on the Internet.

- Some of the benefits that DNS provides include user-friendly DNS names that are less likely to change than IP addresses, and allowing users to connect to local servers by using the same naming convention as the Internet.

- The DNS database is indexed by name, so each domain (node) must have a name. The hierarchical structure of the domain namespace consists of a root domain, top-level domains, second-level domains, and host names.

- Host names refer to specific computers on the Internet or a private network. A host name is the leftmost portion of a fully qualified domain name (FQDN), which describes the exact position of a host within the domain hierarchy.

- Zones provide a way to partition the domain namespace into smaller sections, so a zone represents a discrete portion of the domain namespace.

Lesson 2: Understanding Name Resolution

Name resolution is the process of resolving names to IP addresses. It is similar to looking up a name in a telephone book, in which the name is associated with a telephone number. For example, when you connect to the Microsoft Web site, you use the name www.microsoft.com. DNS resolves www.microsoft.com to its associated IP address. The mapping of names to IP addresses is stored in the DNS distributed database.

DNS name servers resolve forward and reverse lookup queries. A forward lookup query resolves a name to an IP address, and a reverse lookup query resolves an IP address to a name. A name server can only resolve a query for a zone for which it has authority. If a name server can't resolve the query, it passes the query to other name servers that can. The name server caches the query results to reduce the DNS traffic on the network.

After this lesson, you will be able to

- Explain the name resolution process

Estimated lesson time: 10 minutes

Forward Lookup Query

The DNS Service uses a client/server model for name resolution. To resolve a forward lookup query, which resolves a name to an IP address, a client passes a query to a local name server. The local name server either resolves the query and provides an IP address or queries another name server for resolution.

Figure 5.3 represents a client querying the name server for an IP address of www.microsoft.com.

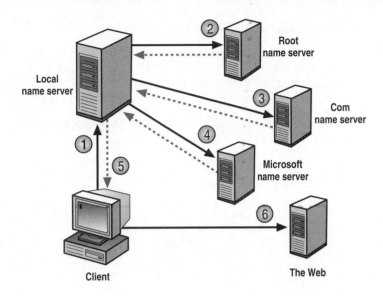

Figure 5.3   Resolving a forward lookup query

The numbers in Figure 5.3 depict the following activities:

1. The client passes a forward lookup query for www.microsoft.com to its local name server.

2. The local name server checks its zone database file to determine whether it contains the name-to-IP address mapping for the client query. The local name server does not have authority for the microsoft.com domain, so it passes the query to one of the DNS root servers, requesting resolution of the host name. The root name server sends back a referral to the com name servers.

3. The local name server sends a request to a com name server, which responds with a referral to the Microsoft name servers.

4. The local name server sends a request to the Microsoft name server. Because the Microsoft name server has authority for that portion of the domain namespace, when it receives the request, it returns the IP address for www.microsoft.com to the local name server.

5. The name server sends the IP address for www.microsoft.com to the client.

6. The name resolution is complete, and the client can access www.microsoft.com.

Name Server Caching

When a name server is processing a query, it might be required to send out several queries to find the answer. With each query, the name server discovers other name servers that have authority for a portion of the domain namespace. The name server caches these query results to reduce network traffic.

When a name server receives a query result, the following process takes place (see Figure 5.4):

1. The name server caches the query result for a specified amount of time, referred to as Time to Live (TTL).

Note   The zone that provided the query results specifies the TTL. The default value is 60 minutes.

2. After the name server caches the query result, TTL starts counting down from its original value.
3. When TTL expires, the name server deletes the query result from its cache.

Caching query results enables the name server to resolve other queries to the same portion of the domain namespace quickly.

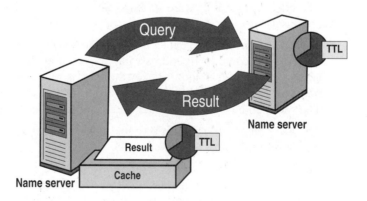

Figure 5.4   Caching query results

Note   Shorter TTL values ensure that data about the domain namespace is more current across the network. However, shorter TTL values cause the cached values to expire sooner and increase the DNS traffic. A longer TTL value causes the cached values to be retained longer, which decreases the DNS traffic but increases the risk of the entries becoming stale. If a change does occur, the client doesn't receive the updated information until the TTL expires and a new query to that portion of the domain namespace is resolved.

Reverse Lookup Query

A reverse lookup query maps an IP address to a name. Troubleshooting tools, such as the nslookup command-line tool, use reverse lookup queries to report back host names. Additionally, certain applications implement security based on the ability to connect to names, not IP addresses.

Because the DNS distributed database is indexed by name and not by IP address, a reverse lookup query would require an exhaustive search of every domain name. To solve this problem, in-addr.arpa was created. This special second-level domain follows the same hierarchical naming scheme as the rest of the domain namespace; however, it is based on IP addresses, not domain names, as follows:

- Subdomains are named after the numbers in the dotted-decimal representation of IP addresses.
- The order of the IP address octets is reversed.
- Companies administer subdomains of the in-addr.arpa domain based on their assigned IP addresses and subnet mask.

For example, Figure 5.5 shows a dotted-decimal representation of the IP address 192.168.16.200. A company that has an assigned IP address range of 192.168.16.0 to 192.168.16.255 with a subnet mask of 255.255.255.0 has authority over the 16.168.192.in-addr.arpa domain.

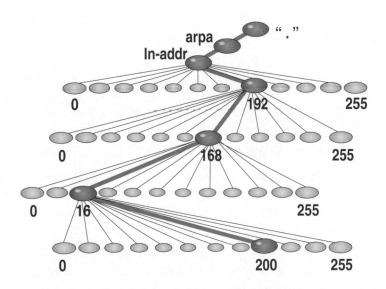

Figure 5.5   The in-addr.arpa domain

Lesson Review

Here are some questions to help you determine whether you have learned enough to move on to the next lesson. If you have difficulty answering these questions, review the material in this lesson before beginning the next lesson. The answers are in Appendix A, "Questions and Answers."

1. What is a forward lookup query and how is it resolved?

2. In DNS name resolution, which of the following statements about Time to Live (TTL) are correct? (Choose all answers that are correct.)

   a. TTL is the length of time a query can exist before it is resolved or discarded.

   b. Shorter TTL values help ensure that data about the domain namespace is more current across the network.

   c. Longer TTL values increase the amount of DNS traffic.

   d. Longer TTL values cause the cached values to be retained longer.

3. Which of the following statements about DNS name and address resolution are correct? (Choose all answers that are correct.)

   a. The DNS distributed database is indexed by both names and IP addresses.

   b. The top-level domain in-addr.arpa is used for both forward and reverse queries.

   c. In the in-addr.arpa domain the order of the IP address octets is reversed.

   d. Troubleshooting tools, such as the nslookup command-line tool, use reverse lookup queries to report back host names.

Lesson Summary

- Name resolution is the process of resolving names to IP addresses. The mapping of names to IP addresses is stored in the DNS distributed database.

- A forward lookup query resolves a name to an IP address, and a reverse lookup query resolves an IP address to a name.

- Name servers cache query results to reduce DNS traffic on the network.

- The DNS distributed database is indexed by name and not by IP address, so in-addr.arpa, a special second-level domain, was created. It is based on IP addresses instead of domain names.

Lesson 3: Configuring a DNS Client

There are several methods available for configuring TCP/IP name resolution on Windows XP Professional clients. The method covered in this lesson uses DNS to provide name resolution. A second method is to use a HOSTS file. For networks without access to a DNS name server, creating a HOSTS file, which is a manually maintained local file, can provide host-to-IP address and NetBIOS-to-IP name resolution for applications and services. HOSTS files can also be used in environments in which name servers are available, but not all hosts are registered, perhaps because some hosts are only available to a limited number of clients.

If there is a computer on your network that is running Windows 2000 Server and has the DNS Service installed and configured on it, you should use DNS for name resolution. This lesson shows you how to configure your computer as a DNS client.

After this lesson, you will be able to

- Configure a DNS client

Estimated lesson time: 25 minutes

Because DNS is a distributed database that is used in TCP/IP networks to translate computer names to IP addresses, you must first ensure that TCP/IP is installed on a client running Windows XP Professional. Internet Protocol (TCP/IP) is installed by default during Windows XP Professional installation. Once you have confirmed that TCP/IP is installed on your client, you are ready to configure your computer as a DNS client.

To configure your computer as a DNS client, you would do the following:

1. Click Start, and then click Control Panel.
2. In the Control Panel window, click Network And Internet Connections.
3. In the Network And Internet Connections window, click Network Connections.
4. Right-click Local Area Connection and then click Properties.

   Windows XP Professional displays the Local Area Connection Properties dialog box.
5. Click Internet Protocol (TCP/IP) and then click Properties.

   Windows XP Professional displays the Internet Protocol (TCP/IP) Properties dialog box (see Figure 5.6).

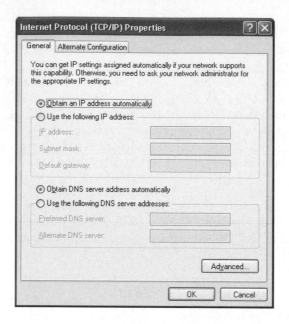

Figure 5.6   Internet Protocol (TCP/IP) Properties dialog box

Configuring DNS Server Addresses

You must select one of the two following options:

- **Obtain DNS Server Address Automatically.** If you select this option, you must have a Dynamic Host Configuration Protocol (DHCP) server available on your network to provide the IP address of a DNS server.

- **Use The Following DNS Server Addresses.** If you select this option, you must type in the IP addresses of the DNS servers you want this client to use. You can enter a Preferred DNS Server address and an Alternate DNS Server address.

If you click Advanced and then click the DNS tab, you can set additional configurations for DNS (see Figure 5.7).

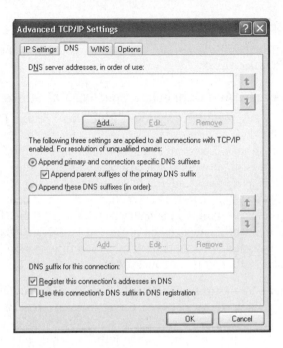

Figure 5.7   Advanced TCP/IP Settings dialog box

In the Advanced TCP/IP Settings dialog box, for the DNS Server Addresses, In Order Of Use box, you can do one of the following:

- Click Add to enter additional DNS server addresses to the list of servers that service this computer to resolve DNS domain names.

- Click Edit to modify the addresses listed (for example, to correct an error you made in entering an IP address).

- Click Remove to delete the address of a DNS server from the list.

- Click the up-pointing arrow or down-pointing arrow to change the order of the servers listed. These arrows work like the up-pointing and down-pointing arrows you use to change the binding order. The order that the addresses are listed is the order in which the servers are used. If you use the up-pointing arrow to move an address higher on the list, that server is used before all the servers listed after it. Conversely, using the down-pointing arrow to move a server lower on the list causes all servers that are listed above it to be used first to resolve DNS domain names.

Configuring DNS Query Settings

In the Advanced TCP/IP Settings dialog box, you can also configure how suffixes are added to queries.

Append Primary And Connection Specific DNS Suffixes

By default, the Append Primary And Connection Specific DNS Suffixes option is selected. This option causes the DNS resolver to append the client name to the primary domain name, as well as the domain name defined in the DNS Domain Name field of each network connection. The resolver then queries for that FQDN. If this query fails and you have specified a connection-specific DNS suffix in the DNS Suffix For This Connection text box, it causes the DNS resolver to append the client name to the name you specified there. If a DHCP server configures this connection and you do not specify a DNS suffix, a DNS suffix for the connection is assigned by an appropriately configured DHCP server. If you specify a DNS suffix, it is used instead of one assigned by a DHCP server.

The Append Parent Suffixes Of The Primary DNS Suffix check box is also selected by default. If it is selected, the DNS resolver strips off the leftmost portion of the primary DNS suffix and attempts the resulting domain name. If this fails, it continues stripping off the leftmost label and attempting the resulting domain name until only two labels remain.

Append These DNS Suffixes (In Order)

By default, the Append Primary And Connection Specific DNS Suffixes option is selected, so the Append These DNS Suffixes (In Order) option is not selected; only one of these two options can be selected at one time. This option allows you to specify a list of domains to try. The DNS resolver adds each one of these suffixes, one at a time and in the order you specified. Queries for unqualified names that are used on this computer are limited to the domains that you listed in Append These DNS Suffixes (In Order).

Register This Connection's Addresses In DNS

Selecting the Register This Connection's Addresses In DNS check box causes the computer to attempt to dynamically register the IP addresses (through DNS) of this computer with its full computer name. To view the computer name for this computer click Start, click My Computer, click View System Information, and click the Computer Name tab.

Use This Connection's DNS Suffix In DNS Registration

Selecting the Use This Connection's DNS Suffix In DNS Registration check box causes the computer to use DNS dynamic updates to register the IP addresses and the connection-specific domain name of the connection. The connection-specific name of this DNS connection is the computer name, which is the first label of the full computer name specified in the Computer Name tab located in View System Information, and the DNS suffix of this connection. If the Register This Connection's Addresses In DNS check box is selected, this registration is in addition to the DNS registration of the full computer name.

Practice: Configuring a DNS Client

After completing this practice, you will be able to configure computers running Windows XP Professional as DNS clients.

▶ **To configure a client to use the DNS Service**

1. Click Start and then click Control Panel.
2. In the Control Panel window, click Network And Internet Connections.
3. Click Network Connections.
4. Right-click Local Area Connection, and then click Properties.
5. Click Internet Protocol (TCP/IP), and then click Properties.
6. In the Internet Protocol (TCP/IP) Properties dialog box, select Use The Following DNS Server Addresses.
7. In the Preferred DNS Server text box, type the IP address of the primary name server for this client.

Note If you are on a network, ask your network administrator the IP address of a DNS server you can use and type that address in the Preferred DNS Server text box. If you are not on a network or if you do not have a DNS server on your network, you can type 192.168.1.203 as the Preferred DNS Server IP address.

8. If there is a second name server available for this client, in the Alternate DNS Server text box, type the IP address of the second name server for this client.

Note If you are on a network, ask your network administrator for the IP address of a second DNS server you can use and type that address in the Alternate DNS Server text box. If you are not on a network or if you do not have a DNS server on your network, you can type 192.168.1.205 as the Alternate DNS Server IP address.

A client attempts to send its query requests to the preferred name server. If that name server is not responding, the client sends the query request to the alternate name server.

Tip If you are going to configure several computers running Windows XP Professional as DNS clients, configure some of the clients to use the alternate name server as the preferred name server. This reduces the load on the primary server.

---

9. Click Advanced, and then in the Advanced TCP/IP Settings dialog box, click the DNS tab.

10. Under DNS Server Addresses, In Order Of Use, click Add.

11. If there is a third name server available for this client, in the TCP/IP DNS Server text box, type the IP address of the third available name server for this client.

Note If you are on a network, ask your network administrator for the IP address of a third DNS server you can use and type that address in the TCP/IP DNS Server text box. If you are not on a network or if you do not have a DNS server on your network, you can type 192.168.1.207 as an additional DNS Server IP address.

---

12. Click Add to add the third DNS server address and to close the TCP/IP DNS Server dialog box.

    There are now three addresses in the DNS Server Addresses, In Order Of Use list box.

13. Click OK to close the Advanced TCP/IP Settings dialog box.

14. Click OK to close the Internet Protocol (TCP/IP) Properties dialog box.

15. Click Close to close the Local Connection Properties dialog box.

16. Close the Network Connections window.

Lesson Review

Here are some questions to help you determine whether you have learned enough to move on to the next lesson. If you have difficulty answering these questions, review the material in this lesson before beginning the next lesson. The answers are in Appendix A, "Questions and Answers."

1. What is a HOSTS file and when would you create one?

2. Which of the following statements about configuring a DNS client are correct? (Choose all answers that are correct.)

   a. If you select the Obtain DNS Server Address Automatically option, at least one of the available DNS servers must be configured to broadcast its IP address.

   b. If you select the Use The Following DNS Server Addresses, you are limiting your DNS client to being able to use only two DNS servers, the preferred DNS server and the alternate DNS server.

   c. To use the Obtain DNS Server Address Automatically option, you must have a DHCP server available on your network.

   d. To configure a DNS client, you use Network and Internet Connections, which is located in Control Panel.

3. Which of the following functions do you perform using the Advanced TCP/IP Settings dialog box? (Choose all answers that are correct.)

   a. Edit the IP address of a DNS server.

   b. Delete the IP address of a DNS server.

   c. Enter additional IP addresses for other available DNS servers.

   d. Edit the IP addresses of the DHCP servers on the network.

4. What does selecting the Append These DNS Suffixes (In Order) option do?

Lesson Summary

- For networks without access to a DNS name server, you can manually create a HOSTS file, which provides host-to-IP address and NetBIOS-to-IP name resolution for applications and services.

- In configuring a DNS client in an environment where there are DNS name servers, you can configure the client to obtain the address of the DNS server automatically from a DHCP server or you can manually enter multiple addresses for DNS servers.

- In the Advanced TCP/IP Settings dialog box, you can configure how suffixes are added to queries.

Lesson 4: Understanding Active Directory

Most computers running Windows XP Professional will be clients in a Windows 2000 domain. One of the benefits of joining a Windows 2000 domain is the Active Directory service. It is important to understand the overall purpose of a directory service and the role that Active Directory plays in a Windows 2000 network. In addition, you should know about the key features of Active Directory, which have been designed to provide flexibility and ease of administration.

After this lesson, you will be able to
- Explain the purpose and function of Active Directory

Estimated lesson time: 15 minutes

What Is Active Directory?

Active Directory is the directory service included in the Windows 2000 Server products. A directory service is a network service that identifies all resources on a network and makes them accessible to users and applications.

Active Directory includes the directory or data store, which is a structured database that stores information about network resources, as well as all the services that make the information available and useful. The resources stored in the directory, such as user data, printers, servers, databases, groups, computers, and security policies, are known as objects.

Simplified Administration

Active Directory organizes resources hierarchically in *domains*, which are logical groupings of servers and other network resources under a single domain name. The domain is the basic unit of replication and security in a Windows 2000 network.

Each domain includes one or more domain controllers. A *domain controller* is a computer running one of the Windows 2000 Server products that stores a complete replica of the domain directory. To simplify administration, all domain controllers in the domain are peers. You can make changes to any domain controller, and the updates are replicated to all other domain controllers in the domain.

Active Directory further simplifies administration by providing a single point of administration for all objects on the network. Because Active Directory provides a single logon point for all network resources, an administrator can log on to one computer and administer objects on any computer in the network.

Scalability

In Active Directory, the directory stores information by organizing itself into sections that permit storage for a very large number of objects. As a result, the directory can expand as an organization grows, allowing you to scale from a small installation with a few hundred objects to a very large installation with millions of objects.

Note   You can distribute directory information across several computers in a network.

Open Standards Support

Active Directory integrates the Internet concept of a namespace with the Windows 2000 directory services. This allows you to unify and manage the multiple namespaces that now exist in the heterogeneous software and hardware environments of corporate networks. Active Directory uses DNS for its name system and can exchange information with any application or directory that uses Lightweight Directory Access Protocol (LDAP) or Hypertext Transfer Protocol (HTTP).

Important   Active Directory also shares information with other directory services that support LDAP version 2 and version 3, such as Novell Directory Services.

Domain Name System (DNS)

Because Active Directory uses DNS as its domain naming and location service, Windows 2000 domain names are also DNS names. Windows 2000 Server uses Dynamic DNS (DDNS), which enables clients with dynamically assigned addresses to register directly with a server running the DNS Service and update the DNS table dynamically. DDNS eliminates the need for other Internet naming services, such as Windows Internet Naming Service (WINS), in a homogeneous environment.

Important   For Active Directory and associated client software to function correctly, you must have installed and configured the DNS Service.

Support for LDAP and HTTP

Active Directory further embraces Internet standards by directly supporting LDAP and HTTP. LDAP is an Internet standard for accessing directory services, developed as a simpler alternative to the Directory Access Protocol (DAP). For more information about LDAP, use your Web browser to search for "RFC 1777" and retrieve the text of this RFC. Active Directory supports both LDAP version 2 and version 3. HTTP is the standard protocol for displaying pages on the World Wide Web. You can display every object in Active Directory as a Hypertext Markup Language (HTML) page in a Web browser. Thus, users receive the benefit of the familiar Web browsing model when querying and viewing objects in Active Directory.

Note   Active Directory uses LDAP to exchange information between directories and applications.

Support for Standard Name Formats

Active Directory supports several common name formats. Consequently, users and applications can access Active Directory by using the format with which they are most familiar. Table 5.3 describes some standard name formats supported by Active Directory.

Table 5.3   Standard Name Formats Supported by Active Directory

Format	Description
RFC 822	RFC 822 names are in the form *somename@domain* and are familiar to most users as Internet e-mail addresses.
HTTP URL	HTTP Uniform Resource Locators (URLs) are familiar to users with Web browsers and take the form http://*domain/path-to-page*.
UNC	Active Directory supports the Universal Naming Convention (UNC) used in Windows 2000 Server–based networks to refer to shared volumes, printers, and files. An example is \\microsoft.com\xl\budget.xls.
LDAP URL	An LDAP URL specifies the server on which the Active Directory service resides and the attributed name of the object. Active Directory supports a draft to RFC 1779 and uses the attributes in the following example: LDAP://someserver.microsoft.com/CN=FirstnameLastname,OU=sys, OU=product,OU=division,DC=devel where CN represents CommonName, OU represents OrganizationalUnitName, and DC represents DomainComponentName.

Lesson Review

Here are some questions to help you determine whether you have learned enough to move on to the next lesson. If you have difficulty answering these questions, review the material in this lesson before beginning the next lesson. The answers are in Appendix A, "Questions and Answers."

1. _____ is the directory service included in the Windows 2000 Server products.

2. What is a directory service?

3. What are two ways that Active Directory simplifies administration?

4. Active Directory uses _____ as its domain naming and location service.

Lesson Summary

- Active Directory is the directory service included in the Windows 2000 Server products.

- Active Directory is not included in Windows XP Professional, but if your Windows XP Professional clients are in a Windows 2000 domain, the features and benefits provided by Active Directory are also available on the clients.

- Active Directory includes the directory or data store, which stores information about network resources. The directory can scale from a small installation with a few hundred objects to a very large installation with millions of objects.

- Active Directory uses DNS as its domain naming and location service, so Windows 2000 domain names are also DNS names.

- Windows 2000 Server uses Dynamic DNS (DDNS), so clients with dynamically assigned addresses can register directly with a server running the DNS Service and dynamically update the DNS table.

Lesson 5: Understanding Active Directory Structure and Replication

Active Directory provides a method for designing a directory structure that meets the needs of your organization. As a result, before installing Active Directory, you should examine your organization's business structure and operations.

Many companies have a centralized structure. Typically, these companies have strong information technology (IT) departments that define and implement the network structure down to the smallest detail. Other organizations, especially large enterprises, are very decentralized. These companies have multiple businesses, each of which is very focused. They need decentralized approaches to managing their business relationships and networks.

With the flexibility of Active Directory, you can create the network structure that best fits your company's needs. Active Directory completely separates the logical structure of the domain hierarchy from the physical structure.

After this lesson, you will be able to

- Explain Active Directory structure and replication

Estimated lesson time: 30 minutes

Logical Structure

In Active Directory, you organize resources in a logical structure. This enables you to find a resource by its name rather than its physical location. Because you group resources logically, Active Directory makes the network's physical structure transparent to users.

Objects

An object is a distinct, named set of attributes that represents a network resource. Object attributes are characteristics of objects in the directory. For example, the attributes of a user account might include the user's first and last names, department, and e-mail address (see Figure 5.8).

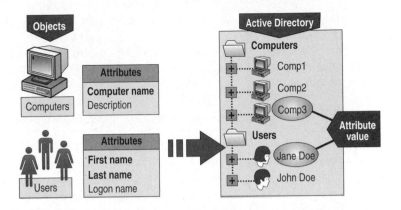

Figure 5.8   Active Directory objects and attributes

In Active Directory, you can organize objects in classes, which are logical group-ings of objects. For example, an object class might be user accounts, groups, computers, domains, or organizational units (OUs).

Note   Some objects, known as containers, can contain other objects. For example, a domain is a container object.

Organizational Units

An OU is a container used to organize objects within a domain into logical ad-ministrative groups. An OU can contain objects such as user accounts, groups, computers, printers, applications, file shares, and other OUs (see Figure 5.9).

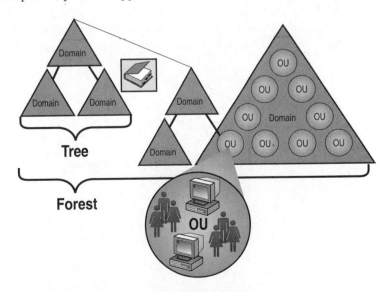

Figure 5.9   Resources organized in a logical hierarchical structure

The OU hierarchy within a domain is independent of the OU hierarchy structure of other domains—each domain can implement its own OU hierarchy. There are no restrictions on the depth of the OU hierarchy. However, a shallow hierarchy performs better than a deep one, so you should not create an OU hierarchy any deeper than necessary.

Note   You can delegate administrative tasks by assigning permissions to OUs.

Domains

The core unit of logical structure in Active Directory is the domain. Grouping objects into one or more domains allows your network to reflect your company's organization. Domains share the following characteristics:

- All network objects exist within a domain, and each domain stores information only about the objects that it contains. Theoretically, a domain directory can contain up to 10 million objects, but 1 million objects per domain is a more practical amount.

- A domain is a security boundary. *Access control lists* (ACLs) control access to domain objects. ACLs contain the permissions associated with objects that control which users can gain access to an object and what type of access users can gain. In Windows 2000, objects include files, folders, shares, printers, and Active Directory objects. All security policies and settings—such as administrative rights, security policies, and ACLs—do not cross from one domain to another. The domain administrator has absolute rights to set policies only within that domain.

Trees

A tree is a grouping or hierarchical arrangement of one or more Windows 2000 domains that share a contiguous namespace (see Figure 5.10).

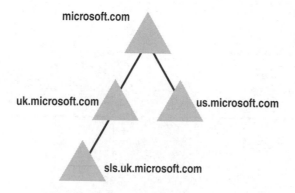

Figure 5.10   A domain tree

Trees have the following characteristics:

- Following DNS standards, the domain name of a child domain is the relative name of that child domain appended with the name of the parent domain.
- All domains within a single tree share a common schema, which is a formal definition of all object types that you can store in an Active Directory deployment.
- All domains within a single tree share a common Global Catalog, which is the central repository of information about objects in a tree.

Forests

A forest is a grouping or hierarchical arrangement of one or more domain trees that form a disjointed namespace (see Figure 5.11).

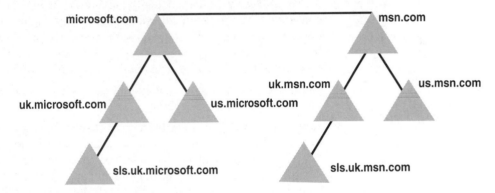

Figure 5.11   A forest of trees

Forests have the following characteristics:

- All trees in a forest share a common schema.
- Trees in a forest have different naming structures, according to their domains.
- All domains in a forest share a common Global Catalog.
- Domains in a forest operate independently, but the forest enables communication across the entire organization.

In Figure 5.11, microsoft.com and msn.com form a forest. The namespace is contiguous only within each tree.

Physical Structure

The physical components of Active Directory, domain controllers and sites, are used to mirror the physical structure of an organization.

Domain Controllers

A domain controller is a computer running Windows 2000 Server that stores a replica of the domain directory (local domain database). Because a domain can contain one or more domain controllers, each domain controller in a domain has a complete replica of the domain's portion of the directory.

The functions of domain controllers include the following:

- Each domain controller stores a complete copy of all Active Directory information for that domain, manages changes to that information, and replicates those changes to other domain controllers in the same domain.

- Domain controllers in a domain automatically replicate all objects in the domain to each other. When you perform an action that causes an update to Active Directory, you are actually making the change at one of the domain controllers. That domain controller then replicates the change to all other domain controllers within the domain. You can control replication of traffic between domain controllers in the network by specifying how often replication occurs and the amount of data that Windows 2000 replicates at one time.

- Domain controllers immediately replicate certain important updates, such as the disabling of a user account.

- Active Directory uses multimaster replication, in which no one domain controller is the master domain controller. Instead, all domain controllers within a domain are peers, and each domain controller contains a copy of the directory database that can be written to. Domain controllers can hold different information for short periods of time until all domain controllers have synchronized changes to Active Directory.

- Domain controllers detect collisions, which can occur when an attribute is modified on a domain controller before a change to the same attribute on another domain controller is completely propagated. Collisions are detected by comparing each attribute's property version number, a number specific to an attribute that is initialized on creation of the attribute. Active Directory resolves the collision by replicating the changed attribute with the higher property version number.

- Having more than one domain controller in a domain provides fault tolerance. If one domain controller is offline, another domain controller can provide all required functions, such as recording changes to Active Directory.

- Domain controllers manage all aspects of user domain interaction, such as locating Active Directory objects and validating user logon attempts.

In general there should be one domain controller for each domain in each site for authentication purposes. However, authentication requirements for your organization determine the number of domain controllers and their locations.

Sites

A site is a combination of one or more IP subnets connected by a highly reliable, fast link to localize as much network traffic as possible. Typically, a site has the same boundaries as a local area network (LAN). When you group subnets on your network, you should combine only those subnets that have fast, cheap, and reliable network connections with one another. Fast network connections are at least 512 kilobits per second (Kbps). An available bandwidth of 128 Kbps and higher is sufficient.

With Active Directory, sites are not part of the namespace. When you browse the logical namespace, you see computers and users grouped into domains and OUs, not sites. Sites contain only computer objects and connection objects used to configure replication between sites.

Note   A single domain can span multiple geographical sites, and a single site can include user accounts and computers belonging to multiple domains.

Replication Within a Site

Active Directory also includes a replication feature. Replication ensures that changes to a domain controller are reflected in all domain controllers within a domain. To understand replication, you must understand domain controllers. A domain controller is a computer running Windows 2000 Server that stores a replica of the domain directory. A domain can contain one or more domain controllers.

Within a site, Active Directory automatically generates a ring topology for replication among domain controllers in the same domain. The topology defines the path for directory updates to flow from one domain controller to another until all receive the directory updates (see Figure 5.12).

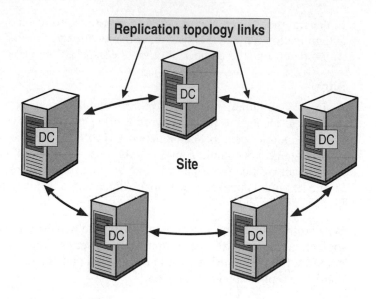

Figure 5.12   Replication topology

The ring structure ensures that there are at least two replication paths from one domain controller to another. Therefore, if one domain controller is down temporarily, replication still continues to all other domain controllers.

Active Directory periodically analyzes the replication topology within a site to ensure that it is still efficient. If you add or remove a domain controller from the network or a site, Active Directory reconfigures the topology to reflect the change.

Lesson Review

Here are some questions to help you determine whether you have learned enough to move on to the next lesson. If you have difficulty answering these questions, review the material in this lesson before beginning the next lesson. The answers are in Appendix A, "Questions and Answers."

1. In Active Directory, you organize resources in a logical structure. What advantage does this provide?

2. A(n) _____ is a distinct, named set of attributes that represents a network resource.

3. What component do you use to organize objects into logical administrative groups?

   a. Site

   b. Tree

   c. Domain

   d. OU

4. A(n) _____ is a grouping or hierarchical arrangement of one or more _____ that form a disjointed namespace.

5. A site is a combination of one or more IP subnets connected by a highly reliable and fast link to localize as much network traffic as possible. Fast network connections are at least _____ and an available bandwidth of _____ is sufficient.

   a. 256 Kbps, 128 Kbps and higher

   b. 512 Kbps, 128 Kbps and higher

   c. 512 Kbps, 256 Kbps and higher

   d. 1024 Kbps, 512 Kbps and higher

6. The physical components of Active Directory are _____ and _____.

Lesson Summary

- Active Directory completely separates the logical structure of the domain hierarchy from the physical structure.

- In Active Directory, grouping resources logically enables you to find a resource by its name rather than its physical location, making the network's physical structure transparent to users.

- The core unit of logical structure in Active Directory is the domain. All network objects exist within a domain, and each domain stores information only about the objects that it contains.

- An organizational unit (OU) is a container used to organize objects within a domain into logical administrative groups, and an OU can contain objects such as user accounts, groups, computers, printers, applications, file shares, and other OUs.

- A tree is a grouping or hierarchical arrangement of one or more Windows 2000 domains that share a contiguous namespace. A forest is a grouping or hierarchical arrangement of one or more trees that form a disjointed namespace.

- The physical structure of Active Directory is based on sites and domain controllers.

- A site is a combination of one or more IP subnets connected by a high-speed link.

- Within a site, Active Directory automatically generates a ring topology for replication among domain controllers in the same domain. The ring structure ensures that there are at least two replication paths from one domain controller to another; if one domain controller is down temporarily, replication continues to all other domain controllers.

Lesson 6: Understanding Active Directory Concepts

There are several new concepts introduced with Active Directory. It is important that you understand their meaning as applied to Active Directory.

After this lesson, you will be able to

- Explain concepts associated with Active Directory

Estimated lesson time: 30 minutes

Schema

The Active Directory schema defines objects that can be stored in Active Directory. The schema is a list of definitions that determines the kinds of objects and the type of information about those objects that can be stored in Active Directory, as shown earlier in Figure 5.8.

The schema contains two types of definition objects: schema class objects and schema attribute objects. Class objects and attribute objects are defined in separate lists within the schema (see Figure 5.13). Schema class and attribute objects are also referred to as schema objects.

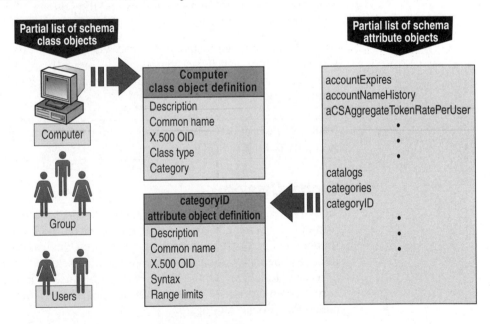

Figure 5.13   Schema class and attribute objects

Schema class objects describe the possible Active Directory objects that can be created. Each schema class is a collection of schema attribute objects. For each object class, the schema defines what attributes an instance of the class must have, what additional attributes it can have, and what object class can be a parent of the current object class. Every object in Active Directory is an instance of a schema class object.

Schema attribute objects define the schema class objects with which they are associated. Each schema attribute is defined only once and can be used in multiple schema classes. Because the schema definitions are themselves stored as objects in Active Directory, they can be administered in the same manner as the rest of the objects in Active Directory.

Installing Active Directory on the first domain controller in a network creates a default schema that contains a set of basic schema class attributes. The default schema also contains definitions of objects and properties that Active Directory uses internally to function.

The Active Directory schema is extensible, which means that you can define new directory object types and attributes and new attributes for existing objects. You can extend the schema by using the Schema Manager snap-in or the Active Directory Service Interfaces (ADSI). Only experienced developers or network administrators should dynamically extend the schema by defining new classes and attributes for existing classes.

The schema is implemented and stored within Active Directory itself (in the Global Catalog), and it can be updated dynamically. As a result, an application can extend the schema with new attributes and classes and use the extensions immediately.

Note   Write access to the schema is limited to members of the Schema Admins group by default.

Global Catalog

Active Directory allows users and administrators to find objects (such as files, printers, or users) in their own domain. However, finding objects outside of the domain and across the enterprise requires a mechanism that allows the domains to act as one entity. A catalog service contains selected information about every object in all domains in the directory, which is useful in performing searches across an enterprise. The catalog service provided by Active Directory services is called the Global Catalog.

The Global Catalog is the central repository of information about objects in a tree or forest, as shown in Figure 5.14. By default, a Global Catalog is created automatically on the first domain controller in the first domain in the forest, and the domain controller containing the Global Catalog is known as the Global Catalog server. Using Active Directory service's multimaster replication, the Global Catalog information is replicated between Global Catalog servers in other domains.

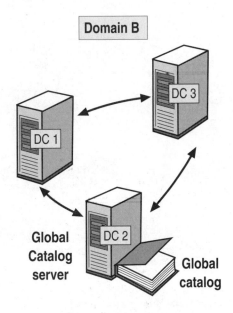

Figure 5.14   The Global Catalog

By default, the attributes stored in the Global Catalog are those most frequently used in search operations (such as a user's first and last names, logon name, and so forth) and those necessary to locate a full replica of the object. As a result, you can use the Global Catalog to locate objects anywhere in the network without replication of all domain information between domain controllers.

Note   You use the Schema Manager snap-in to define which attributes are included in the Global Catalog replication process.

You can designate additional domain controllers as Global Catalog servers using the Active Directory Sites and Services Management snap-in. When considering which domain controllers to designate as Global Catalog servers, base your decision on the ability of your network structure to handle replication and query traffic. The more Global Catalog servers you have, the greater the replication traffic is. However, the availability of additional servers can provide quicker responses to user inquiries. Every major site in your enterprise should have a Global Catalog server.

Namespace

Active Directory, like all directory services, is primarily a namespace. A namespace is any bounded area in which a name can be resolved. Name resolution is the process of translating a name into some object or information that the name represents. The Active Directory namespace is based on the DNS naming scheme, which allows for interoperability with Internet technologies. An example namespace is shown in Figure 5.15.

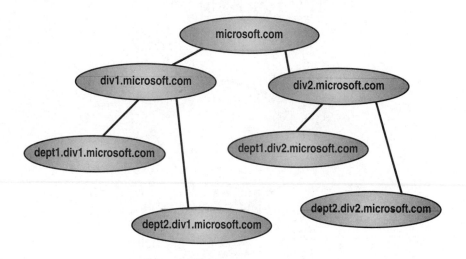

Figure 5.15   Namespace diagram

Using a common namespace allows you to unify and manage multiple hardware and software environments in your network. There are two types of namespaces:

- **Contiguous namespace.**   The name of the child object in an object hierarchy always contains the name of the parent domain. A tree is a contiguous namespace.

- **Disjointed namespace.**   The names of a parent object and a child of the same parent object are not directly related to one another. A forest is a disjointed namespace.

Naming Conventions

Every object in Active Directory is identified by a name. Active Directory uses a variety of naming conventions: distinguished names, relative distinguished names, globally unique identifiers, and user principal names.

Distinguished Name

Every object in Active Directory has a *distinguished name* (DN), which uniquely identifies an object and contains sufficient information for a client to retrieve the object from the directory. The DN includes the name of the domain that holds the object, as well as the complete path through the container hierarchy to the object.

For example, the following DN identifies the *Firstname Lastname* user object in the microsoft.com domain (where *Firstname* and *Lastname* represent the actual first and last names of a user account):

/DC=COM/DC=microsoft/OU=dev/CN=Users/CN=Firstname Lastname

Table 5.4 describes the attributes in the example.

Table 5.4   Distinguished Name Attributes

Attribute	Description
DC	DomainComponentName
OU	OrganizationalUnitName
CN	CommonName

DNs must be unique, because Active Directory does not allow duplicate DNs.

Relative Distinguished Name

Active Directory supports querying by attributes, so you can locate an object even if the exact DN is unknown or has changed. The *relative distinguished name* (RDN) of an object is the part of the name that is an attribute of the object itself. In the preceding example, the RDN of the Firstname Lastname user object is *Firstname Lastname*. The RDN of the parent object is Users.

You can have duplicate RDNs for Active Directory objects, but you cannot have two objects with the same RDN in the same OU. For example, if a user account is named Jane Doe, you cannot have another user account called Jane Doe in the same OU. However, objects with duplicate RDNs can exist in separate OUs because they have different DNs (see Figure 5.16).

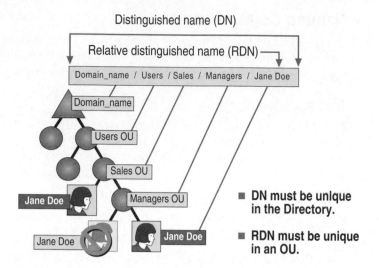

Figure 5.16   DNs and RDNs

Globally Unique Identifier

A *globally unique identifier* (GUID) is a 128-bit number that is guaranteed to be unique. GUIDs are assigned to objects when they are created. The GUID never changes, even if you move or rename the object. Applications can store the GUID of an object and use it to retrieve that object regardless of its current DN.

User Principal Name

User accounts have a "friendly" name, the user principal name (UPN). The UPN is composed of a "shorthand" name for the user account and the DNS name of the tree where the user account object resides. For example, user *Firstname Lastname* (substitute the first and last names of an actual user) in the microsoft.com tree might have a UPN of FirstnameL@microsoft.com (using the full first name and the first letter of the last name).

Lesson Review

Here are some questions to help you determine whether you have learned enough to move on to the next lesson. If you have difficulty answering these questions, review the material in this lesson before beginning the next chapter. The answers are in Appendix A, "Questions and Answers."

1. What is the Active Directory schema?

2. Which of the following statements are correct for Active Directory Global Catalogs?

   a. The Global Catalog is the central repository of information about objects in a tree or forest.

   b. By default, a Global Catalog is created automatically on the first domain controller in the first domain in the forest.

   c. The Global Catalog is a list of definitions that determines the kinds of objects and the type of information about those objects that can be stored in Active Directory.

   d. Only experienced developers or network administrators should dynamically extend the Global Catalog.

3. Every object in Active Directory has a _____ that uniquely identifies an object and contains sufficient information for a client to retrieve the object from the Directory.

4. A _____ is a 128-bit number that is assigned to an object when it is created and is guaranteed to be unique.

5. What is the difference between a contiguous namespace and a disjointed namespace? Give an example of each type of namespace.

Lesson Summary

- The schema contains a formal definition of the contents and structure of Active Directory, including all classes and attributes.

- Installing Active Directory on the first domain controller in a network creates a default schema.

- The Active Directory schema is extensible.

- The Global Catalog contains selected information about every object in all domains in the directory.

- In a contiguous namespace, the name of the child object in an object hierarchy always contains the name of the parent domain. A tree is an example of a contiguous namespace.

- In a disjointed namespace, the names of a parent object and of a child of the same parent object are not directly related to one another. A forest is an example of a disjointed namespace.

C H A P T E R   6

Setting Up, Configuring, and Troubleshooting Common Setup and Configuration Problems for Network Printers

About This Chapter

This chapter introduces you to setting up and configuring network printers so that users can print over the network. You will also learn how to troubleshoot common printing problems associated with setting up network printers.

Before You Begin

To complete this chapter, you must have

- A computer that meets the minimum hardware requirements listed in the preface, "About This Book"
- Installed the Microsoft Windows XP Professional software on the computer

Note You do not need a printer to complete the exercises in this chapter.

Lesson 1: Introduction to Windows XP Professional Printing

With Windows XP Professional printing, you can share printing resources across an entire network and administer printing from a central location. You can easily set up printing on client computers running Microsoft Windows XP, Microsoft Windows 2000 Professional, Microsoft Windows NT 4, Microsoft Windows Me, Microsoft Windows 98, and Microsoft Windows 95.

After this lesson, you will be able to

- Define Microsoft Windows XP Professional printing terms

Estimated lesson time: 15 minutes

Terminology

Before you set up printing, you should be familiar with Windows XP Professional printing terminology to understand how the different components fit together, as shown in Figure 6.1.

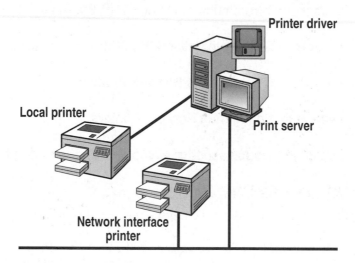

Figure 6.1   Printing terminology

The following list defines some Windows XP Professional printing terms:

- **Printer.**   A hardware device that puts text or images on paper or on other print media.

  Windows XP Professional supports the following print devices:

  - *Local printers*, which are connected to a physical port on the print server.

- *Network interface printers*, which are connected to a print server through the network instead of a physical port. Network interface printers require their own network interface cards and have their own network address or they are attached to an external network adapter.

- **Printer port.**   The software interface through which a computer communicates with a printer by means of a locally attached interface. Windows XP Professional supports the following interfaces: line printer (LPT), COM, universal serial bus (USB) 1.1, IEEE 1394 (FireWire), and network-attached devices such as the HP JetDirect and Intel NetPort.

Note   At this time, Windows XP Professional does not support USB 2.0. Windows XP Professional treats a FireWire card as a network and a peripheral connectivity device. FireWire is used to connect digital camcorders, scanners, and other high-bandwidth devices to computers.

- **Print server.**   The computer that manages one or more printers on a network. The print server receives and processes documents from client computers.

- **Printer driver.**   One file or a set of files containing information that Windows XP Professional requires to convert print commands into a specific printer language, such as Adobe PostScript. This conversion makes it possible for a printer to print a document. A printer driver is specific to each printer model.

Requirements for Network Printing

The requirements for setting up printing on a Windows 2000 network include the following:

- At least one computer to operate as the print server. If the print server is to manage many heavily used printers, Microsoft recommends a dedicated print server. The computer can run either of the following:

  - Windows 2000 Server, which can handle a large number of connections and supports Apple Macintosh and UNIX computers and Novell NetWare clients.

  - Windows XP Professional, which is limited to 10 concurrent connections from other computers for file and print services. It does not support Macintosh computers or NetWare clients but does support UNIX computers.

- Sufficient random access memory (RAM) to process documents. If a print server manages a large number of printers or many large documents, the server might require additional RAM beyond what Windows XP Professional or Windows 2000 Server requires for other tasks. If a print server does not have sufficient RAM for its workload, printing performance deteriorates.

- Sufficient disk space on the print server to ensure that the print server can store documents that are sent to it until it sends the documents to the print device. This is critical when documents are large or likely to accumulate. For example, if 10 users send large documents to print at the same time, the print server must have enough disk space to hold all of the documents until it can send them to the print device. If there is not enough space to hold all of the documents, users get error messages and are unable to print.

The requirements for network printing are as follows:

- A computer to operate as the print server running either Windows 2000 Server or, for networks with 10 or fewer concurrent client computers, Windows XP Professional
- Sufficient RAM to process documents
- Sufficient disk space on the print server to store documents until they print

Guidelines for a Network Printing Environment

Before you set up network printing, develop a network-wide printing strategy to meet users' printing needs without unnecessary duplication of resources or delays in printing. Table 6.1 provides some guidelines for developing such a strategy.

Table 6.1   Network Printing Environment Guidelines

Guideline	Explanation
Determine users' printing requirements	Determine the number of users who print and the printing workload. For example, 10 people in a billing department who print invoices continually will have a larger printing workload and might require more printers and possibly more print servers than 10 software developers who do all their work online.
Determine company's printing requirements	Determine the printing needs of your company. This includes the number and types of printers that are required. In addition, consider the type of workload that each printer will handle. Don't use a personal printer for network printing.
Determine the number of print servers required	Determine the number of print servers that your network requires to handle the number and types of printers that your network will contain.
Determine where to locate printers	Determine where to put the printers so that it's easy for users to pick up their printed documents.

Lesson Review

Here are some questions to help you determine whether you have learned enough to move on to the next lesson. If you have difficulty answering these questions, review the material in this lesson before beginning the next lesson. The answers for these questions are in Appendix A, "Questions and Answers."

1. _____ are connected to a physical port on the print server.

2. Do you have to have a computer running one of the Windows Server products to have a print server on your network? Why?

3. Windows XP Professional can provide _____ concurrent connections from other computers for file and print services.

   a. 20

   b. 10

   c. unlimited

   d. 30

4. A _____ is one file or a set of files containing information that Windows XP Professional requires to convert print commands into a specific printer language, such as PostScript.

5. Windows XP Professional printing supports which of the following software interfaces or printer ports? (Choose all answers that are correct.)

   a. LPT

   b. COM

   c. USB

   d. HP JetDirect

6. Windows XP Professional printing supports which of the following types of computers? (Choose all answers that are correct.)

   a. Macintosh computers

   b. UNIX computers

   c. NetWare clients

   d. Windows 98 computers

Lesson Summary

- A printer is a hardware device that puts text or images on paper or on other print media.

- Local printers are connected to a physical port on the print server, and network interface printers are connected to a print server through the network.

- Network interface printers require their own network interface cards and have their own network address, or they are attached to an external network adapter.

- Windows XP Professional supports the following printer ports (software interfaces): LPT, COM, USB, and network-attached devices such as the HP JetDirect and Intel NetPort.

- A printer driver is one file or a set of files containing information that Windows XP Professional requires to convert print commands into a specific printer language.

Lesson 2: Setting Up Network Printers

Setting up and sharing a network printer makes it possible for multiple users to utilize it. You can set up a local printer that is connected directly to the print server, or you can set up a network interface printer that is connected to the print server over the network. In larger organizations, most printers are network interface printers.

After this lesson, you will be able to

- Identify the requirements for setting up a network printer and network printing resources
- Add and share a new local or network interface printer
- Describe how to add a new printer port
- Set up client computers

Estimated lesson time: 30 minutes

Adding and Sharing a Local Printer

The steps for adding a local printer or a network interface printer are similar. You would use the following steps to add a local printer:

1. Log on as Administrator or with a user account that is a member of the Administrators group on the print server.
2. Click Start, click Control Panel, and then click Printers And Other Hardware.
3. Under Pick A Task, click Add A Printer to launch the Add Printer Wizard.

   The Add Printer Wizard starts with the Welcome To The Add Printer Wizard page displayed.

Note If you have a Plug and Play printer that connects through a USB port, an IEEE 1394 interface, or any other port that allows you to attach or remove devices without having to shut down and restart your computer, you do not need to use the Add Printer Wizard. Plug the printer's cable into your computer or point the printer toward your computer's infrared port and turn on the printer. Windows automatically installs the printer for you.

4. Click Next.

   The Add Printer Wizard displays the Local Or Network Printer page (see Figure 6.2).

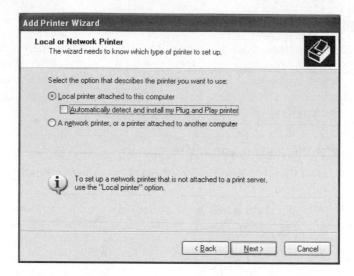

Figure 6.2   Local Or Network Printer page of the Add Printer Wizard

The Add Printer Wizard guides you through the steps to add a printer that is connected to the print server. The number of local printers that you can connect to a print server through physical ports depends on your hardware configuration.

Table 6.2 describes the Add Printer Wizard pages and options for adding a local printer.

Table 6.2   Add Printer Wizard Pages and Options for a Local Printer

Page	Option	Description
Local Or Network Printer	Local Printer Attached To This Computer	You are adding a printer to the computer at which you are sitting, which is the print server.
	Automatically Detect And Install My Plug and Play Printer	A check box that allows you to specify whether you want Windows XP Professional to automatically detect and install the Plug and Play printer.
Select A Printer Port	Use The Following Port	The port on the print server to which you attached the printer.
Install Printer Software	Manufacturer And Printers	Select the appropriate manufacturer and printer so that the correct printer driver for the local printer will be installed. If your printer is not in the list, you must provide a printer driver from the manufacturer or select a model that is similar enough that the printer can use it.

Table 6.2   *(continued)*

Page	Option	Description
Name Your Printer	Printer Name	A name that identifies the printer to the users. Some applications might not support more than 31 characters in the server and printer name combinations.
	Do You Want To Use This Printer As The Default Printer?	Select Yes to make this printer the default printer for all Windows-based applications and so that users do not have to set a printer for each application. The first time that you add a printer to the print server, this option does not appear because the printer is automatically set as the default printer.
Printer Sharing	Share Name	Users (with the appropriate permissions) can use the share name to connect to the printer over the network. This name appears when users browse for a printer or supply a path to a printer. The share name must be compatible with the naming conventions for all client computers on the network. By default, the share name is the printer name truncated to an 8.3 character filename.
Location And Comment	Location	Describe the location of the printer.
	Comment	Provide information that helps users determine whether the printer meets their needs. If your computer is in a domain, users can search the Active Directory service for the information that you enter here.
Print Test Page	Do You Want To Print A Test Page?	Select Yes to print a test page and verify that you have installed the printer correctly.
Completing The Add Printer Wizard	Finish	If the information about how you configured the printer to be installed is correct, click Finish.
	Back	If you need to correct some information, click Back.

Adding and Sharing a Network Interface Printer

In larger companies, most printers are network interface printers. These printers offer several advantages. First, you do not need to locate printers with the print server. In addition, network connections transfer data more quickly than printer cable connections.

To add a network interface printer, select Local Printer Attached To This Computer on the Local Or Network Printer page of the Add Printer Wizard. The main difference between adding a local printer and adding a network interface printer is that for a typical network interface printer, you provide additional port and network protocol information.

The default network protocol for Windows XP Professional is Transmission Control Protocol/Internet Protocol (TCP/IP), which many network interface printers use. For TCP/IP, you provide additional port information in the Add Standard TCP/IP Printer Port Wizard.

Figure 6.3 shows the Select A Printer Port page of the Add Printer Wizard, and Table 6.3 describes the options on this page that pertain to adding a network interface printer.

Figure 6.3   Select A Printer Port page of the Add Printer Wizard

Table 6.3   Options on the Select A Printer Port Page That Affect Adding a Network Interface Print Device

Option	Description
Create A New Port	This selection starts the process of creating a new port for the print server to which the network interface print device is connected. In this case, the new port points to the network connection of the print device.
Type Of Port	This selection determines the network protocol to use for the connection. If you select Standard TCP/IP it starts the Add Standard TCP/IP Printer Port Wizard.

Figure 6.4 shows the Add Port page of the Add Standard TCP/IP Printer Port Wizard, and Table 6.4 describes the options on this page.

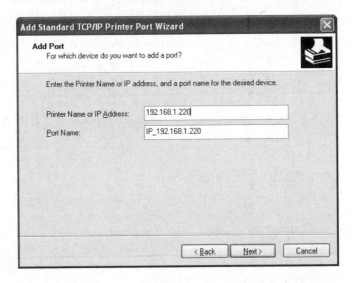

Figure 6.4   Add Port page of the Add Standard TCP/IP Printer Port Wizard

Table 6.4   Options on the Add Port Page That Affect Adding a Network Interface Printer

Option	Description
Printer Name Or IP Address	The network location of the printer. You must enter either the IP address or a Domain Name System (DNS) name of the network interface printer. If you provide an IP address, Windows XP Professional automatically supplies a suggested port name for the print device in the form IP_*Ipaddress*. If Windows XP Professional cannot connect to and identify the network interface printer, you must supply additional information about the type of printer. To enable automatic identification, make sure that the printer is powered on and connected to the network.
Port Name	The name that Windows XP Professional assigns to the port that you created and defined. You can enter a different name. After you create the port, Windows XP Professional displays it on the Select A Printer Port page of the Add Printer Wizard.

Note   If your printer uses a network protocol other than TCP/IP, you must install that network protocol before you can add additional ports that use it. The tasks and setup information required to configure a printer port depend on the network protocol.

Adding an LPR Port

The line printer remote (LPR) port is designed for computers that need to communicate with UNIX or VAX host computers in accordance with Request for Comments (RFC) 1179. For computers that need to submit print jobs to host computers, the standard TCP/IP port should be used in most cases. A network-connected printer must have a card that supports the line printer daemon (LPD) for TCP/IP printing to work properly.

If you want to add an LPR port, you must first install the optional networking component, Print Services for UNIX.

To install Print Services for UNIX complete the following steps:

1. Click Start, click Control Panel, and click Network And Internet Connections.
2. Click Network Connections.
3. On the Advanced menu, click Optional Networking Components.

4. In the Components list, click Other Network File And Print Services, and then click Details.

   Windows XP Professional displays the Other Network File And Print Services dialog box.

5. Select Print Services For UNIX, and then click OK.

6. Click Next to close the Other Network File And Print Services dialog box.

7. When the installation completes, close the Network Connections dialog box.

To add an LPR port complete the following steps:

1. Click Start, click Control Panel, and click Printers And Other Hardware.

2. Click Printers And Faxes.

3. Click Add A Printer.

   Windows XP Professional starts the Add Printer Wizard.

4. Click Next.

   The Add Printer Wizard displays the Local Or Network Printer page.

5. Ensure that Local Printer is selected and Automatically Detect And Install My Plug And Play Printer is cleared.

6. Click Next.

   The Select A Printer Port page appears.

7. Click Create A New Port, and on the Type Of Port drop-down list, select LPR Port.

Note If LPR Port is not available, make sure the optional networking component, Print Services for UNIX is installed. Click Cancel to exit the Add Printer Wizard.

---

8. Click Next.

9. In the Name Or Address Of Server Providing LPD text box, type the DNS name or Internet Protocol (IP) address of the host of the printer you are adding.

Note The host can be the direct-connect TCP/IP printing device or the UNIX computer to which the printer is connected. The DNS name can be the name specified for the host in the HOSTS file. LPD is a service on the print server that receives documents (print jobs) from the LPR utilities running on client systems.

---

10. Follow the directions on the screen to complete the installation of the TCP/IP printer.

You add and share a printer by using the Add Printer Wizard in the Printers folder.

Setting Up Client Computers

After you add and share a printer, you need to set up client computers so that users can print. Although the tasks to set up client computers vary depending on which operating systems are running on the client computers, all client computers require installation of a printer driver. The following points summarize the installation of printer drivers according to the computer's operating system:

- Windows XP Professional automatically downloads the printer drivers for client computers running Windows 2000, Windows NT versions 4 and earlier, Windows 95, or Windows 98.

- Client computers running other Microsoft operating systems require installation of printer drivers.

- Client computers running non-Microsoft operating systems require installation of both printer drivers and the print service on the print server.

Client Computers Running Windows 2000, Windows NT, Windows Me, Windows 95, or Windows 98

Users of client computers running Windows XP Professional, Windows XP Home Edition, Windows 2000, Windows NT, Windows Me, Windows 98, and Windows 95 only need to connect to the shared printer. The client computer automatically downloads the appropriate printer driver, as long as there is a copy of it on the print server.

If your client computer is running Windows XP Professional and you want to connect to the shared printer, start the Add Printer Wizard on the client computer. On the Local Or Network Printer page (see Figure 6.2), select A Network Printer, Or A Printer Attached To Another Computer, and then click Next. The Specify A Printer page appears, as shown in Figure 6.5.

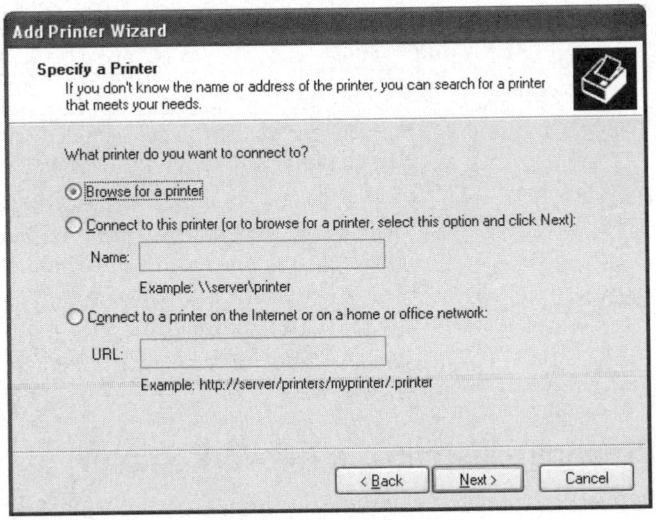

Figure 6.5   The Specify A Printer page of the Add Printer Wizard

If you are not sure what the name of the shared printer is, you can browse for it by selecting the Browse For A Printer option, and then clicking Next. After you have located the shared printer and selected it, click Next. You are then asked if it should be the default printer. If you want it to be the default printer, click Yes; otherwise select No and then click Next. The Completing The Add Printer Wizard page appears. Check over the information and then click Finish. You have successfully made a connection from your client computer to the shared printer.

Client Computers Running Other Microsoft Operating Systems

To enable client computers running other Microsoft operating systems (such as Windows 3.1 or MS-DOS) to print to a shared Windows XP Professional–based printer, you must manually install a printer driver on the client computer. You can get the appropriate printer driver for a Windows-based client computer from the installation disks for that client computer or from the printer manufacturer.

Client Computers Running Non-Microsoft Operating Systems

To enable users of client computers running non-Microsoft operating systems to print, the print server must have additional services installed on it. Table 6.5 lists services that are required for Macintosh and UNIX client computers or computers running a NetWare client.

Table 6.5   Services Required for Client Computers Running Non-Microsoft Operating Systems

Client computer	Required services
Macintosh	Services for Macintosh are included only with Windows 2000 Server, not Windows XP Professional.
UNIX	TCP/IP Printing, which is also called the LPD Service, is included with Windows 2000 Server but is not installed by default. It is not included with Windows XP Professional.
NetWare	File and Print Services for NetWare (FPNW), an optional add-on service for Windows 2000 Server, is not included with Windows XP Professional or Windows 2000 Server.

Practice: Installing a Network Printer

In this practice, you use the Add Printer Wizard to install and share a local printer. Sharing the printer makes it available to other users on the network. You also take the printer offline and then print a document, which loads the document into the print queue.

Before you can share a printer or a folder on a computer running Windows XP Professional in a workgroup environment, you must run the Network Setup Wizard.

Run the **NetworkSetupWizard** and **NetworkPrinter** files in the Demos folder on the CD-ROM accompanying this book for a demonstration of using the Network Setup Wizard and the Add Printer Wizard.

Exercise 1: Running the Network Setup Wizard

In this exercise you set up the network for your Windows XP Professional workgroup by running the Network Setup Wizard.

▶ **To run the Network Setup Wizard**

1. Log on as Fred or with a user account that is a member of the Administrators group.
2. Click Start, and then click Control Panel.
3. In Control Panel, click Network And Internet Connections.
4. Click Network Connections.
5. Under Network Tasks, click Set Up A Home Or Small Office Network.

   Windows XP Professional displays the Welcome To The Network Setup Wizard page.

6. Click Next to continue.

   Network Setup Wizard displays the Before You Continue page with the following steps that you should complete before running the wizard:

   ■ Install the network cards, modems, and cables.

   ■ Turn on all computers, printers, and external modems.

   ■ Connect to the Internet.

7. Ensure that you have completed the appropriate steps, and then click Next.

   The Network Setup Wizard displays the Select A Connection Method page with the following options:

   ■ This Computer Connects Directly To The Internet

   ■ This Computer Connects To The Internet Through Another Computer On My Network Or Through A Residential Gateway

   ■ Other

8. Select the appropriate option and then click Next.

   The Network Setup Wizard displays the Give This Computer A Description And Name page.

9. Enter a description. Ensure the computer name is already filled in and then click Next.

   The Network Setup Wizard displays the Name Your Network page.

10. Enter an appropriate name, and then click Next.

    The Network Setup Wizard displays the Ready To Apply Network Settings page.

11. Review the settings and then click Next to have the Network Setup Wizard set up your network.

    Setting up your network takes a few minutes and should not be interrupted.

    The Network Setup Wizard displays the You're Almost Done page with the following four options:

    ■ Create A Network Setup Disk

    ■ Use The Network Setup Disk I Already Have

    ■ Use My Windows XP CD

    ■ Just Finish The Wizard; I Don't Need To Run The Wizard On Other Computers

12. Ensure the default option, Create A Network Setup Disk, is selected and then click Next.

Note   If you do not have a floppy disk, select Use My Windows XP CD, click Next, and follow the directions on the screen to complete the wizard. Go to Exercise 2.

If you have more than one drive that can be used, The Network Setup Wizard displays the Select A Disk Drive page listing the drives you can use. This list of drives includes floppy drives and Zip drives.

13. Select the appropriate disk drive and then click Next.

    The Network Setup Wizard displays the Insert The Disk You Want To Use page.

14. Insert the disk you want to use to create a Network Setup Disk into the appropriate disk drive.

15. Click Format Disk.

    The Network Setup Wizard displays a Format dialog box, allowing you to configure how the format will be performed.

16. Ensure the appropriate options are selected and then click Start.

    The Format dialog box displays a warning message box indicating that formatting the disk will erase all information currently on the disk.

17. Click OK to continue.

    The Format dialog box formats the disk. This could take a few minutes.

    When the formatting is complete, the Format dialog box displays a Format Complete message box.

18. Click OK to close the Format Complete message box.

19. Click Close to close the Format dialog box.

20. In the Insert The Disk You Want To Use page, click Next to continue.

    The Network Setup Wizard displays a Copying message box.

    When the Network Setup Disk is completed, The Network Setup Wizard displays the To Run The Wizard With The Network Setup Disk page. This page tells you that you need to insert the Network Setup Disk in each computer on your network and run NETSETUP, located on the Network Setup Disk, on each computer in your network.

21. Click Next to continue.

22. Review the information on the page and then click Finish.

    Windows XP Professional displays a System Settings Change message box indicating that you must restart your computer for the changes to take effect.

23. Remove your Network Setup Disk and then click Yes to restart your computer.

Exercise 2: Adding and Sharing a Printer

In this exercise, you use the Add Printer Wizard to add a local printer to your computer and share it.

▶ **To add a local printer**

1. Log on as Administrator or with a user account that is a member of the Administrators group on the print server.

2. Click Start, click Control Panel, and then click Printers And Other Hardware.

3. Click Add A Printer to launch the Add Printer Wizard.

   Windows XP Professional starts the Add Printer Wizard.

4. Click Next in the Welcome To The Add Printer Wizard page to continue.

   The Add Printer Wizard displays the Local Or Network Printer page.

   The Add Printer Wizard prompts you for the location of the printer. Because you are adding a printer on the computer at which you are sitting, this printer is referred to as a local printer.

5. Click Local Printer.

6. Ensure that the Automatically Detect And Install My Plug And Play Printer check box is cleared, and then click Next.

   The Add Printer Wizard then displays the Select A Printer Port page. Which port types are available depends on the installed network protocols. For this exercise, assume that the print device that you are adding is directly attached to your computer using the LPT1 port.

Note If the print device is connected to a port that is not listed, click Create A New Port, and then enter the port type.

7. Scroll through the Use The Following Port drop-down list box and review the selection of ports.

Note You can select File to print to a file instead of a printer.

8. Verify that Use The Following Port is selected, and that LPT1 (Recommended Printer Port) is selected.

9. Click Next.

   The Add Printer Wizard prompts you for the printer manufacturer and model. You will add an HP Color LaserJet 4550 PS printer.

Tip The list of printers is sorted in alphabetical order. If you cannot find a printer name, make sure that you are looking in the correct location.

10. Under Manufacturer, select HP. Then, under Printers, select HP Color LaserJet 4550 PS.

Note   The selected driver is digitally signed to ensure reliability and to protect your system. Driver signing is covered in Chapter 11, "Implementing, Managing, and Troubleshooting Hardware Devices and Drivers."

---

11. Click Next.

    The Add Printer Wizard displays the Name Your Printer page. In the Printer Name list box, Windows XP Professional automatically defaults to the printer name HP Color LaserJet 4550 PS. For this exercise, do not change this name.

12. If other printers are already installed, the wizard also asks whether you want to make this the default printer. If the Add Printer Wizard displays the Do You Want To Use This Printer As The Default Printer message, click Yes.

13. To accept the default printer name, click Next.

    The Printer Sharing page appears, prompting you for printer sharing information.

▶ **To share a printer**

1. In the Add Printer Wizard, on the Printer Sharing page, select Share Name.

   You can assign a shared printer name, even though you already supplied a printer name. The shared printer name is used to identify a printer on the network and must conform to a naming convention. This shared name is different from the printer name that you entered previously. The printer name is a description that appears with the printer's icon in the Printers And Faxes folder and in Active Directory.

2. In the Share Name box, type **Printer1** and then click Next.

   The Add Printer Wizard displays the Location And Comment page.

Note   If your computer running Windows XP Professional is part of a domain, Windows 2000 displays the values that you enter for Location and Comment when a user searches Active Directory for a printer. Entering this information is optional, but it can help users locate the printer more easily.

---

3. In the Location text box type **second floor west** and in the Comment text box type **mail room – room 2624**.

4. Click Next.

The Add Printer Wizard displays the Print Test Page page.

You can print a test page to confirm that your printer is set up properly. In this exercise you do not need to have a printer, so you will not print a test page. When you are actually setting up a printer, you should print a test page to confirm that it is working properly.

5. Under Do You Want To Print A Test Page, ensure that No is selected and click Next.

The Add Printer Wizard displays the Completing The Add Printer Wizard page and provides a summary of your installation choices.

Note As you review the summary, you might notice an error in the information you entered. To modify these settings, click Back.

6. Confirm the summary of your installation choices, and then click Finish.

If necessary, Windows XP Professional displays the Files Needed dialog box, prompting you for the location of the Windows XP Professional distribution files.

7. If necessary, insert the Windows XP Professional CD-ROM and wait for about 10 seconds.

8. If Windows displays the Windows XP CD-ROM window, close it.

9. If prompted to insert the Windows XP Professional CD-ROM, click OK to close the Insert Disk dialog box.

If necessary, Windows XP Professional copies the printer files.

10. In the Printers And Other Hardware window, click Printers And Faxes.

Windows XP Professional created an icon for the shared HP Color LaserJet 4550 PS printer. Notice that Windows XP Professional displays an open hand on the printer icon, indicating that the printer is shared. The check mark just above the printer indicates that printer as the default printer.

Exercise 3: Taking a Printer Offline and Printing a Test Document

In this exercise, you take the printer that you created offline. Taking a printer offline causes documents that you send to this printer to be held on the computer while the print device is not available. This eliminates error messages about unavailable printers in later exercises. Windows XP Professional displays such error messages when it attempts to send documents to a printer that is not connected to the computer.

▶ **To take a printer offline**

1. In Control Panel, click Printers And Other Hardware.

2. In the Printers And Other Hardware window, click Printers And Faxes.

3. Right-click the HP Color LaserJet 4550 PS icon.

4. On the menu that appears, click Use Printer Offline.

   Windows XP Professional dims the icon and changes the status of the printer from Ready to Offline to reflect that the printer is not available.

▶ **To print a test document**

1. In the Printers And Faxes folder, double-click the HP Color LaserJet 4550 PS icon.

   The list of documents to be sent to the print device is empty.

2. Click Start, point to All Programs, point to Accessories, and then click Notepad.

3. In Notepad, type any text that you want.

4. Arrange Notepad and the HP Color LaserJet 4550 PS window so that you can see the contents of each.

5. In Notepad, on the File menu, click Print.

   Windows XP Professional displays the Print dialog box, allowing you to select the printer and print options.

Note   Many programs running under Windows XP Professional use the same Print dialog box.

The Print dialog box displays the location and comment information that you entered when you created the printer, and the Status for the printer shows that it is currently offline. You can also use this dialog box to search Active Directory for a printer.

Notice that HP Color LaserJet 4550 PS is selected as the printer.

6. Click Print.

   Notepad briefly displays a message on your computer stating that the document is printing. On a fast computer, you might not be able to see this message.

7. Close Notepad and click No when prompted to save changes to your document.

   In the HP Color LaserJet 4550 PS window, you will see the document waiting to be sent to the print device. Windows XP Professional holds the document because you took the printer offline. Otherwise, Windows XP Professional would have sent the document to the print device.

8. Close the HP Color LaserJet 4550 PS window.

9. Close all open windows.

Exercise 4: Adding an LPR Port

In this exercise, you install Print Services for UNIX and create an LPR port.

▶ **To install Print Services for UNIX**

1. In Control Panel, click Network And Internet Connections.

2. Click Network Connections.

3. On the Advanced menu, click Optional Networking Components.

4. In the Components list, click Other Network File And Print Services, and then click Details.

   The Other Network File And Print Services dialog box appears.

5. Select Print Services for UNIX, and then click OK.

   The Other Network And File Services dialog box appears.

6. Click Next and when the installation completes, close the Network Connections and Network And Internet Connections windows.

▶ **To add an LPR port**

1. In Control Panel, click Printers And Other Hardware, and then click Printers And Faxes.

2. Double-click Add Printer.

   The Add Printer Wizard starts.

3. Click Next.

   The Add Printer Wizard displays the Local Or Network Printer page.

4. Ensure that Local Printer is selected.

5. Ensure that the Automatically Detect And Install My Plug And Play Printer check box is not selected, and then click Next.

   The Select A Printer Port page appears.

6. Click Create A Printer Port.

7. On the Type Of Port drop-down menu, select LPR port and click Next.

8. In the Name Or Address Of Server Providing LPD text box, type the DNS name or IP address of the host of the printer you are adding.

Note The host can be the direct-connect TCP/IP printing device or the UNIX computer to which the printer is connected. The DNS name can be the name specified for the host in the HOSTS file. LPD is a service on the print server that receives documents (print jobs) from the LPR utilities running on client systems.

9. Follow the directions on the screen to complete the installation of the TCP/IP printer.

You add and share a printer by using the Add Printer Wizard in the Printers folder.

Lesson Review

Here are some questions to help you determine whether you have learned enough to move on to the next lesson. If you have difficulty answering these questions, review the material in this lesson before beginning the next lesson. The answers for these questions are in Appendix A, "Questions and Answers."

1. Which of the following tasks are done with the Add Printer Wizard? (Choose all answers that are correct.)

   a. Taking a local printer offline

   b. Printing multiple copies of a document

   c. Adding an LPR port

   d. Making a printer that is connected to your computer available to other network users

2. What is the default printer in Windows XP Professional?

3. After you get home from the store, you unpack your new computer and printer. You install Windows XP Professional, and you want to install your printer. You want to set up the printer as your default printer. During the installation you are not prompted to use the printer as your default printer for all Windows-based applications. You know you have seen this option at work when you install local printers. Why aren't you seeing it on your home computer?

4. Which of the following statements about adding and using an LPR port are correct? (Choose all answers that are correct.)

   a. The LPR port is designed for computers that need to communicate with Macintosh computers in accordance with RFC 1179.

   b. A network-connected printer must have a card that supports the LPD for TCP/IP printing to work properly.

   c. When you are trying to add an LPR port, if the LPR Port option is not available, install the optional networking component, Print Services for UNIX.

   d. LPD is a service on the client computer that sends documents (print jobs) out the LPR port.

5. After you add and share a printer on a computer running Windows XP Professional, the tasks to set up client computers vary depending on which operating systems are running on the client computers. Which of the following operating systems running on client computers would require additional software or services to be installed before users on these computers can connect to the shared printer? (Choose all answers that are correct.)

   a. Windows 98

   b. NetWare

   c. Windows 2000 Professional

   d. UNIX

Lesson Summary

- To set up and share a printer for a local print device or for a network interface print device, use the Add Printer Wizard.

- Sharing a local printer makes it possible for multiple users on the network to utilize it.

- Users of client computers running Windows XP Professional, Windows 2000, Windows Me, Windows NT, Windows 98, or Windows 95 only need to connect to the shared printer to be able to print.

- To enable users of client computers running non-Microsoft operating systems to print, the print server must have additional services installed.

Lesson 3: Connecting to Network Printers

After you have set up the print server with all required printer drivers for the shared printers, users on client computers running Windows XP Professional, Windows 2000, Windows Me, Windows NT, Windows 95, and Windows 98 can easily make a connection and start printing. For most Windows-based client computers, if the appropriate printer drivers are on the print server, the client computer automatically downloads the drivers when the user makes a connection to the printer. For information on how you can install additional drivers on a print server, see Lesson 4 later in this chapter.

When you add and share a printer, by default, all users can connect to that printer and print documents. The method used to connect to a printer depends on the client computer. Client computers running Windows XP Professional, Windows XP Home Edition, Windows 2000, Windows Me, Windows NT, Windows 98, or Windows 95 can use the Add Printer Wizard. Client computers running Windows XP Professional, Windows XP Home Edition, or Windows 2000 can also use a Web browser to connect to the printer.

After this lesson, you will be able to

- Connect to a network printer by using the Add Printer Wizard or a Web browser

Estimated lesson time: 15 minutes

Using the Add Printer Wizard

The Add Printer Wizard is one method that client computers running Windows XP Professional, Windows XP Home Edition, Windows 2000, Windows Me, Windows NT, Windows 98, or Windows 95 can use to connect to a printer. This is the same wizard that you use to add and share a printer. The options that are available in the Add Printer Wizard that allow you to locate and connect to a printer vary depending on the operating system that the client computer is running.

Client Computers Running Windows XP Professional or Windows 2000

By using the Add Printer Wizard on client computers running Windows XP Professional or Windows 2000, you can connect to a printer through the following methods:

- **Using the Universal Naming Convention (UNC) name.**   You can use the UNC name (*print_server**printer_name*) to make connections by selecting Type The Printer Name Or Click Next To Browse For A Printer on the Locate Your Printer page of the Add Printer Wizard. If you know the UNC name, this is a quick method.

- **Browsing the network.**   You can also browse the network for the printer by selecting Type The Printer Name Or Click Next To Browse For A Printer on the Locate Your Printer page of the Add Printer Wizard, leaving the Name text box blank and clicking Next.

- **Using the Uniform Resource Locator (URL) name.**   You can also connect to a printer on the Internet or your intranet by selecting Connect To A Printer On The Internet Or On Your Local Intranet on the Locate Your Printer page of the Add Printer Wizard.

- **Searching Active Directory.**   If your computer running Windows XP Professional or Windows 2000 is a member of a domain, you can find the printer by using Active Directory search capabilities. You can search either the entire Active Directory or just a portion of it. You can also narrow the search by providing features of the printer, such as color printing.

Client Computers Running Windows NT 4, Windows 95, or Windows 98

On client computers running Windows NT 4, Windows 95, or Windows 98, the Add Printer Wizard only allows you to enter a UNC name or to browse Network Neighborhood to locate the printer.

Note   You can also make a connection to a printer using the Run command on the Start menu. Type the UNC name of the printer in the Open text box and click OK.

Client Computers Running Other Microsoft Operating Systems

Users at client computers running early versions of Windows such as Windows 3.1, Windows 3.5, and Windows for Workgroups use Print Manager instead of the Add Printer Wizard to make a connection to a printer.

Users of any Windows-based client computer can connect to a network printer using the following command:

```
net use lptx: \\server_name\share_name
```

where x is the number of the printer port.

The Net Use command is also the only method available for making a connection to a network printer from client computers running MS-DOS or IBM OS/2 with Microsoft LAN Manager client software installed.

Using a Web Browser

If you are using a client computer running Windows XP Professional, Windows XP Home Edition, or Windows 2000, you can connect to a printer through your corporate intranet. You can type a URL in your Web browser, and you don't have to use the Add Printer Wizard. In Windows XP Professional you can use Microsoft Internet Explorer, the Printers And Faxes folder, My Computer, or any other window or folder that has an address bar. After you make a connection, Windows XP Professional copies the correct printer drivers to the client computer automatically.

A Web designer can customize this Web page, for example, to display a floor plan that shows the location of print devices to which users can connect. There are two ways to connect to a printer using a Web browser:

- If you don't know the printer's name, type **http://*server_name*/printers**.

  The Web page lists all of the shared printers on the print server that you have permission to use. The page provides information about the printers, including printer name, status of print jobs, location, model, and any comments that were entered when the printer was installed. This information helps you select the correct printer for your needs. Click the printer that you want to use.

- If you know the printer's name, type **http://*server_name*/ printer_share_name**.

  You provide the intranet path for a specific printer. You must have permission to use the printer.

Windows automatically copies the appropriate printer driver to your computer and the icon appears in Printers And Faxes. When you have connected to a shared printer from a Web browser, you can use the printer as if it were attached to your computer.

Note   For Internet printing, you must have Internet Information Services (IIS) installed on the print server. You must use Internet Explorer version 4.0 or higher to connect to a printer. For information about installing Windows Components, see Chapter 10, "Configuring Windows XP Professional."

Using Find Printer

In the Add Printer Wizard, the Find Printers feature allows you to search for printers in Active Directory when you are logged on to a Windows 2000 domain. When the Search Assistant has started, click Find Printers. When you have located a printer using Find Printers, you can double-click the printer or you can right-click it, and then click Connect to make a connection to the printer. The Find Printers dialog box has three tabs to help you locate a printer (see Figure 6.6).

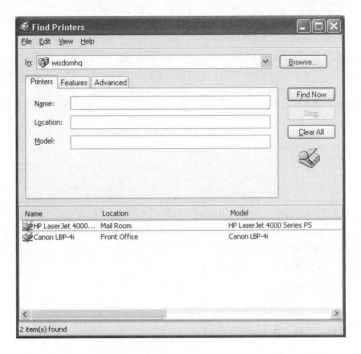

Figure 6.6   The Find Printers dialog box

The following list describes the three tabs of the Find Printers dialog box:

- **Printers tab.**   Allows you to enter and search for specific information, such as the name, location, and model of the printer.

- **Features tab.**   Allows you to select from a prepared list of additional search options, such as whether the printer can print double-sided copies or at a specific resolution.

- **Advanced tab.**   Allows you to use custom fields and Boolean operators to define complex searches, such as whether the printer supports collation and a specific printer language, such as PostScript.

If you want to search for all available printers, you can leave all search criteria blank and click Find Now. All of the printers in the domain will be listed.

Note   The Find Printers feature is not available in the Search Assistant unless you are logged on to a Windows 2000 domain. If you are using a stand-alone computer that is in a workgroup, the Find Printers feature is not available.

Lesson Review

Here are some questions to help you determine whether you have learned enough to move on to the next lesson. If you have difficulty answering these questions, review the material in this lesson before beginning the next lesson. The answers for these questions are in Appendix A, "Questions and Answers."

1. When you add and share a printer, by default, who can connect to that printer?

2. Which of the following operating systems running on a client computer allow you to use the Net Use command to connect to a network printer? (Choose all answers that are correct.)

    a. Windows 2000

    b. Windows Me

    c. Windows NT 4

    d. Windows XP Professional

3. Which of the following operating systems running on a client computer allow you to connect to a network printer by using Active Directory search capabilities? (Choose all answers that are correct.)

    a. Windows 2000

    b. Windows Me

    c. Windows NT 4

    d. Windows XP Professional

4. Which of the following operating systems running on a client computer allow you to use a Web browser to connect to a network printer? (Choose all answers that are correct.)

    a. Windows 2000

    b. Windows Me

    c. Windows NT 4

    d. Windows XP Professional

5. You have a small workgroup consisting of five computers running Windows XP Professional at your house. You are giving your friend, who has never seen Windows XP Professional, a tour around the new operating system. You are demonstrating how the Search Assistant works, but the Find Printers feature is missing. Why?

Lesson Summary

- Client computers running Windows XP Professional, Windows XP Home Edition, Windows 2000, Windows Me, Windows NT, Windows 98, or Windows 95 can use the Add Printer Wizard to connect to a printer.

- On client computers running Windows XP Professional, Windows XP Home Edition, or Windows 2000 that are part of a Windows 2000 domain, you can connect to a printer using Active Directory search capabilities.

- On client computers running Windows NT 4, Windows 95, or Windows 98, the Add Printer Wizard only allows you to enter a UNC name or to browse Network Neighborhood to locate the printer.

- Users on client computers running early versions of Windows (such as Windows 3.1, Windows 3.5, and Windows for Workgroups) use Print Manager to connect to a printer.

- Users on any Windows-based client computer can connect to a network printer using the Net Use command.

- The Find Printers feature of the Search Assistant allows you to search for printers in Active Directory when you are logged on to a Windows 2000 domain.

Lesson 4: Configuring Network Printers

After you have set up and shared network printers, user and company printing needs might require you to configure printer settings so that your printing resources better fit these needs.

Five common configuration changes you can make are as follows:

- You can share an existing nonshared printer if your printing load increases.
- You can download additional print drivers so that clients running other versions of Windows can use the shared printer.
- You can stop sharing an existing shared printer.
- You can create a printer pool so that the print jobs are automatically distributed to the first available printer. In this way, users do not have to search for an available printer.
- You can set priorities among printers so that critical documents always print before noncritical documents.

After this lesson, you will be able to

- Share an existing printer
- Download additional printer drivers
- Stop sharing a printer
- Create a printer pool
- Set priorities between printers

Estimated lesson time: 25 minutes

Sharing an Existing Printer

If the printing demands on your network increase and your network has an existing, nonshared printer for a print device, you can share it so that users can utilize the printer.

When you share a printer, you need to assign the printer a share name, which appears in My Network Places. Use an intuitive name to help users when they are browsing for a printer. You can also add printer drivers for all versions of Windows XP Professional, Windows XP Home Edition, Windows 2000, Windows NT, Windows 95, and Windows 98.

In the Properties dialog box for the printer, you can use the Sharing tab to share an existing printer (see Figure 6.7).

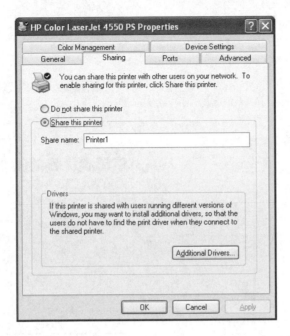

Figure 6.7   The Sharing Tab of the Properties dialog box for a printer

You would use the following steps to share an existing printer using the Sharing tab:

1. In Control Panel, click Printers And Other Hardware.
2. In Printers And Other Hardware, click Printers And Faxes.
3. In Printers And Faxes, right-click the icon for the printer that you want to share.
4. Click Sharing.
5. In the Sharing tab for the printer, click Share This Printer.
6. In the Share Name text box, type in a share name and then click OK.

After you have shared the printer, Windows XP Professional puts an open hand under the printer icon, indicating that the printer is shared.

Downloading Printer Drivers

If you are sharing the printer with users whose computers are running different versions of Windows, you need to install different drivers. To verify which printer drivers are downloaded or to download printer drivers to your print server, use the following steps:

1. On your print server, click Start, and then click Control Panel.
2. Click Printers And Other Hardware, and then click Printers And Faxes.
3. Right-click the printer for which you want to verify that the drivers are downloaded or for which you want to download additional printer drivers, and then click Properties.

4. In the Sharing tab, click Additional Drivers.

   In the Additional Drivers dialog box (Figure 6.8), if the check box is selected, the printer drivers are downloaded.

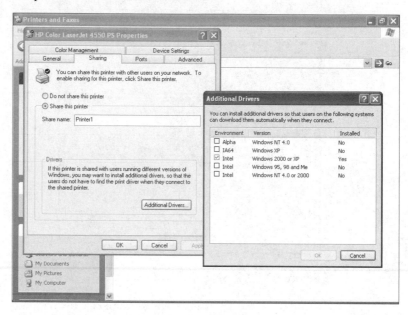

Figure 6.8   The Additional Drivers dialog box

5. Select the check box for any additional printer drivers you want to download, and then click OK.

   You are prompted to enter the path to the Windows XP Professional installation files.

6. Enter the path to the Windows XP Professional installation files, or insert the Windows XP Professional CD-ROM into the CD-ROM drive, and then click OK.

   The drivers are installed.

Stopping the Sharing of a Printer

If the printing demands on your network change, you can stop sharing an existing shared printer. Use the Sharing tab of the Properties dialog box for that printer to stop sharing it. The steps to stop sharing a printer are similar to those for sharing a printer. However, in the steps to stop sharing a printer, in the Properties dialog box for the printer, in the Sharing tab, click Not Shared (see Figure 6.7) and then click OK.

Setting Up a Printer Pool

A *printer pool* consists of two or more identical printers that are connected to one print server and act as a single printer. The printers can be local or network interface printers. Although the printers should be identical, you can use printers that are not identical but use the same printer driver. After you install a printer, you can create a printer pool using the Ports tab of the Properties dialog box for that printer. In the Ports tab, select the Enable Printer Pooling check box and select additional ports on the printer server (see Figure 6.9).

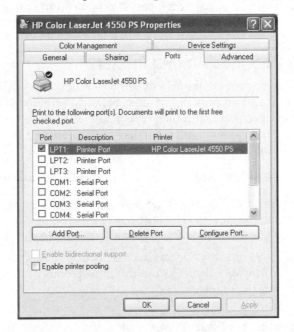

Figure 6.9   Enabling printer pooling

When you create a printer pool, users can print documents without checking which printer is available. The document prints on the first available printer in the printing pool.

Tip   When you set up a printer pool, you should place the printers in the same physical area so that users can easily locate their documents.

A printing pool has the following advantages:

- In a network with a high volume of printing, it decreases the time that documents wait on the print server.
- It simplifies administration because you can administer multiple printers simultaneously.

Before you create a printer pool, make sure that you connect the printers to the print server.

To create a printing pool complete the following steps:

1. Click Start, click Control Panel, and then click Printers And Other Hardware.
2. In the Printers And Other Hardware window, click Printers And Faxes.
3. Right-click the printer icon, and on the menu that appears, click Properties.
4. In the Properties dialog box for the printer, click the Ports tab.
5. In the Ports tab, select the Enable Printer Pooling check box.
6. Select the check box for each port to which a printer that you want to add to the pool is connected, and then click OK.

Setting Priorities Among Printers

Setting priorities among printers makes it possible to set priorities among groups of documents that all print on the same physical printer. Multiple virtual printers point to the same physical printer, which allows users to send critical documents to a high-priority printer and noncritical documents to a lower priority printer. The critical documents always print first.

There are two things that you must do to set priorities among printers:

- Add a printer and share it. Then add a second printer and point it to the same physical printer or port. The port can be either a physical port on the print server or a port that points to a network interface print device.

- Set a different priority for each of the printers that is pointing to the physical printer or hardware device. Have different groups of users print to different virtual printers, or have users send different types of documents to different virtual printers.

  For example, see Figure 6.10. User1 sends documents to a printer with the lowest priority of 1, and User2 sends documents to a printer with the highest priority of 99. In this example, User2's documents always print before User1's.

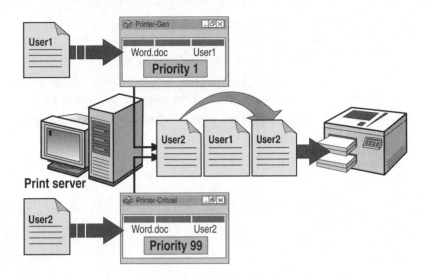

Figure 6.10   Printer pool with different priorities set

Use the following steps to set the priority for a printer:

1. Log on as Administrator or with a user account that is a member of the Administrators group on the print server.

2. Click Start, click Control Panel, and then click Printers And Other Hardware.

3. Right-click the icon for the printer, and then click Properties.

    The Properties dialog box for the printer appears.

4. Click the Advanced tab.

5. In the Advanced tab, adjust the Priority setting for the printer.

    This value for a printer can be set from 1 through 99—the higher the number, the higher the priority of the printer.

Lesson Review

Here are some questions to help you determine whether you have learned enough to move on to the next lesson. If you have difficulty answering these questions, review the material in this lesson before beginning the next lesson. The answers for these questions are in Appendix A, "Questions and Answers."

1. What are some advantages to sharing a printer?

2. How do you share a printer?

3. Which of the following statements about a printing pool in Windows XP Professional are correct? (Choose all answers that are correct.)

   a. All printers in a printing pool must be network interface printers.

   b. A printing pool consists of two or more identical printers that are connected to one print server and act as a single printer.

   c. If you use printers that are not identical, they must use the same printer driver.

   d. If you use printers that are not identical, you must install all the required printer drivers on the print server.

4. Why would you create virtual printers and vary the priorities on them?

Lesson Summary

- To share an existing printer, use the Sharing tab of the Properties dialog box for the printer and select Share This Printer.

- A printer pool consists of two or more identical printers that are connected to one print server and act as a single printer.

- Setting priorities on virtual printers makes it possible for users to send critical documents to a high-priority printer and noncritical documents to a lower priority printer, even when there is only one physical printer.

Lesson 5: Troubleshooting Setup and Configuration Problems

During setup and configuration of a printer, problems can occur. This lesson introduces you to a few common problems that you might encounter and provides some suggested solutions.

After this lesson, you will be able to

■ Troubleshoot network printing problems

Estimated lesson time: 5 minutes

Troubleshooters

Windows XP Professional helps you interactively troubleshoot problems you encounter. To troubleshoot problems with a printer, click Start, click Control Panel, and then click Printers And Other Hardware. In the Printers And Other Hardware window, under Troubleshooters, click Printing. The Help And Support Center window appears with the printing troubleshooter displayed, as shown in Figure 6.11.

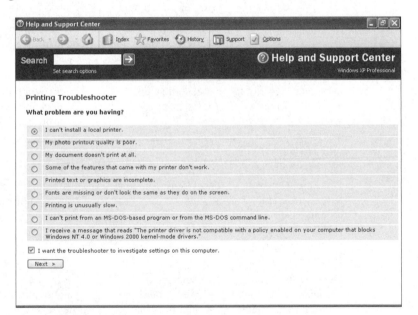

Figure 6.11   Printing troubleshooter

Notice the series of questions on the page. As you respond to these questions, the troubleshooter asks additional questions and makes suggestions to resolve your problem based on the answers you provide.

Common Troubleshooting Scenarios

Table 6.6 lists some of the common setup and configuration problems that you might encounter. It also gives probable causes of the problems and possible solutions.

Table 6.6   Common Printer Problems and Possible Solutions

Problem	Probable cause	Possible solution
Test page does not print. You have confirmed that the print device is connected and turned on.	The selected port is not correct.	Configure the printer for the correct port. For a printer that uses a network interface print device, make sure that the network address is correct.
Test page or documents print incorrectly as garbled text.	The installed printer driver is not correct.	Reinstall the printer with the correct printer driver.
Pages are only partially printing.	There might not be enough memory to print the document.	Consider adding memory to the print server.
	The printer might not have enough toner.	Try replacing the printer's toner cartridge.
Users report an error message that asks them to install a printer driver when they print to a print server running Windows XP Professional.	Printer drivers for the client computers are not installed on the print server.	On the print server, add the appropriate printer drivers for the client computers. Use the client computer operating system CD-ROM or a printer driver from the vendor.
Documents from one client computer do not print, but documents from other client computers do.	The client computer is connected to the wrong printer.	On the client computer, remove the printer, and then add the correct printer.
Documents print correctly on some printers in a printer pool but not all of them.	The printers in the printer pool are not identical.	Verify that all printers in the printer pool are identical or that they use the same printer driver. Remove inappropriate devices.

Table 6.6   *(continued)*

Problem	Probable cause	Possible solution
Printing is slow because the print server is taking a long time to render the job.	The print server's disk could be in need of defragmenting or could be getting close to capacity.	Try defragmenting the print server's disk and check that there is adequate space for temporary files on the hard disk.
Printing is slow and print jobs are taking a long time to reach the top of the queue.	If you are using a printing pool, you might not have enough printers in the pool.	Add printers to the printing pool.

Lesson Review

Here are some questions to help you determine whether you have learned enough to move on to the next lesson. If you have difficulty answering these questions, review the material in this lesson before beginning the next chapter. The answers for these questions are in Appendix A, "Questions and Answers."

1. How do you access and use the printing troubleshooter?

2. What should you check if documents print correctly on some printers in a printing pool but not all of them?

3. What should you check if printing is slow because the print server is taking a long time to render the job?

4. What should you check if pages are only partially printing?

Lesson Summary

- Windows XP Professional helps you interactively troubleshoot problems you encounter. To troubleshoot printing problems, use the printing troubleshooter.
- There are common setup and configuration problems that you learn how to handle as you encounter them.

CHAPTER 7

Administering and Troubleshooting Common Administrative Problems for Network Printers

About This Chapter

In this chapter, you will learn about setting up and administering network printers. You will learn how to manage printers and documents and how to troubleshoot common printing problems.

Before You Begin

To complete this chapter, you must have

- A computer that meets the minimum hardware requirements listed in the preface, "About This Book"
- Installed the Microsoft Windows XP Professional software on the computer
- Installed the software for an HP Color LaserJet 4550 PS printer as directed in Chapter 6, "Setting Up, Configuring, and Troubleshooting Common Setup and Configuration Problems for Network Printers"

Note You do *not* need a printer to complete the exercises in this chapter. You just need to have installed the software for the HP Color LaserJet 4550 PS printer.

Lesson 1: Understanding Printer Administration

After your printing network is set up, you will be responsible for administering it. You can administer network printers at the print server or remotely over the network. This lesson introduces you to the four major tasks involved in administering network printers: managing printers, managing documents, troubleshooting printers, and performing tasks that require the Manage Printers permission. In this lesson you will also learn that before you can administer printers, you must know how to access them and control access to them.

After this lesson, you will be able to

- Identify the tasks and requirements for administering a printer
- Gain access to printers for administration
- Assign printer permissions to user accounts and groups

Estimated lesson time: 30 minutes

Managing Printers

Managing printers is one of the most important aspects of printer administration, and it includes the following tasks:

- Assigning forms to paper trays
- Setting a separator page
- Pausing, resuming, and canceling documents on a printer
- Redirecting documents
- Taking ownership of a printer

Managing Documents

A second major aspect of printer administration is managing documents, which includes the following tasks:

- Pausing and resuming a document
- Setting notification, priority, and printing time
- Deleting a document

Troubleshooting Printers

Troubleshooting printers, which means identifying and resolving all printer problems, is a third major aspect of printer administration. The types of problems you need to troubleshoot include the following:

- Printers that are off or offline
- Printers that are out of paper or out of ink
- Users who cannot print or cannot print correctly
- Users who cannot access a printer

Performing Tasks That Require the Manage Printers Permission

The following tasks involved with administering printers require the Manage Printers permission:

- Adding and removing printers
- Sharing printers
- Taking ownership of a printer
- Changing printer properties or permissions

By default, members of the Administrators and Power Users groups have the Manage Printers permission for all printers.

Accessing Printers

You can access printers for administration using the Printers And Faxes window. Windows XP Professional has an improved user interface to make it easier for you to perform daily tasks. When you select a printer icon, many of the common printer management and document management tasks are listed for you, as shown in Figure 7.1.

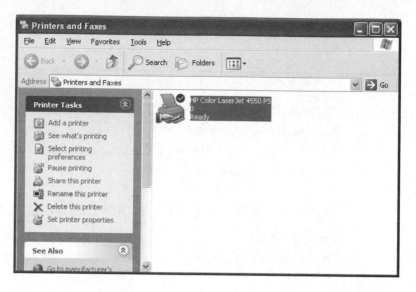

Figure 7.1   Managing printers and documents using the Printers And Faxes
window

Note   These tasks, as well as some additional printer management and document
management tasks, are covered in later lessons in this chapter.

To access printers using the Printers And Faxes window, complete the following
steps:

1. Click Start, and then click Control Panel.
2. In the Control Panel window, click Printers And Other Hardware, and then
click Printers And Faxes.
3. In the Printers And Faxes window, select the appropriate printer icon.
4. After you have selected a printer icon, you can also use the File menu to manage printers and documents.

   ■ Click Open to open the printer window to perform document management
   tasks.

   ■ Click Properties to open the Properties dialog box to perform printer management tasks such as changing printer permissions or editing Active
   Directory service information about the printer.

Setting Printer Permissions to Control Access

Windows XP Professional allows you to control printer usage and administration
by assigning permissions. With printer permissions, you can control who can use

a printer. You can also assign printer permissions to control who can administer a printer and the level of administration, which can include managing printers and managing documents.

For security reasons, you might need to limit user access to certain printers. You can also use printer permissions to delegate responsibilities for specific printers to users who are not administrators. Windows XP Professional provides three levels of printer permissions: Print, Manage Documents, and Manage Printers. Table 7.1 lists the capabilities of each level of permission.

Table 7.1   Printing Capabilities of Windows XP Professional Printer Permissions

	Permissions		
Capabilities	**Print**	**Manage documents**	**Manage printers**
Print documents	✔	✔	✔
Pause, resume, restart, and cancel the user's own document	✔	✔	✔
Connect to a printer	✔	✔	✔
Control job settings for all documents		✔	✔
Pause, resume, restart, and cancel all other users' documents		✔	✔
Cancel all documents			✔
Share a printer			✔
Change printer properties			✔
Delete a printer			✔
Change printer permissions			✔

You can allow or deny printer permissions. Denied permissions always override allowed permissions. For example, if you select the Deny check box next to Manage Documents for the Everyone group, no one can manage documents, even if you grant this permission to another user account or group. This is because all user accounts are members of the Everyone group.

Assigning Printer Permissions

By default, Windows XP Professional assigns the Print permission for each printer to the built-in Everyone group, allowing all users to send documents to the printer. You can also assign printer permissions to users or groups.

To assign printer permissions, complete the following steps:

1. Click Start, and then click Control Panel.

2. In the Control Panel window, click Printers And Other Hardware, and then click Printers And Faxes.

3. In the Printers And Faxes window, right-click the appropriate printer icon, and then click Properties.

4. Click the Security tab.

Note   If your computer running Windows XP Professional is in a workgroup environment and you do not have a Security tab in your printer's Properties dialog box, close the Properties dialog box. In Explorer, on the Tool menu, click Folder Options and click the View tab. Clear the Use Simple File Sharing (Recommended) check box, and then display your Printer's Properties dialog box.

---

5. In the Security tab, click Add.

6. In the Select Users, Groups, Or Computers dialog box, select the appropriate user account or group, and then click Add. Repeat this step for all users or groups that you are adding.

7. Click OK.

8. In the Security tab, shown in Figure 7.2, select a user account or group, and then do one of the following:

   ■ Click the permissions in the bottom part of the dialog box that you want to assign.

   ■ Click Advanced and assign additional printer permissions that do not fit into the predefined permissions in the Security tab, and then click OK.

   The bottom part of the dialog box shows the permissions granted to the user or group selected in the upper part.

9. Click OK to close the Properties dialog box.

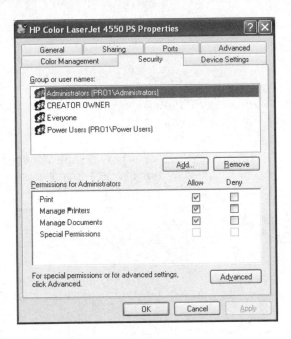

Figure 7.2   Assigning printer permissions

Modifying Printer Permissions

You can change the default printer permissions that Windows XP Professional assigned, or that you previously assigned for any user or group.

To modify printer permissions, complete the following steps:

1. In the Printers And Faxes window, right-click the appropriate printer icon, and then click Properties.

2. In the Security tab of the Properties dialog box for the printer, select the appropriate user account or group, and then do one of the following:

   - Click the permissions that you want to change for the user or group.

   - Click Advanced to modify additional printer permissions that do not fit into the predefined permissions in the Security tab.

3. Click OK.

Lesson Review

The following questions will help you determine whether you have learned enough to move on to the next lesson. If you have difficulty answering these questions, review the material in this lesson before beginning the next lesson. The answers for these questions are in Appendix A, "Questions and Answers."

1. What are the four major types of tasks involved with administering network printers?

2. Microsoft Windows XP Professional allows you to control printer usage and administration by assigning _____.

3. Which level of printer permissions provided by Windows XP Professional grants users the ability to perform the most printing tasks?

   a. Manage Printers

   b. Manage Documents

   c. Print

   d. Full Control

4. Which of the following tabs do you use to assign printer permissions to users and groups?

   a. Security tab of the Properties dialog box for the printer

   b. Security tab of the Properties dialog box for the user or group

   c. Permissions tab of the Properties dialog box for the printer

   d. Permissions tab of the Properties dialog box for the user or group

5. Which Windows XP Professional printer permission allows users to pause, resume, restart, and cancel all other users' documents? (Choose all answers that are correct.)

   a. Print

   b. Manage Printers

   c. Full Control

   d. Manage Documents

Lesson Summary

- There are four major types of tasks in administering printers: managing printers, managing documents, troubleshooting printers, and performing tasks that require the Manage Printers permission.

- You can gain access to printers for administration by using the Printers And Faxes window accessed through Control Panel.

- Windows XP Professional allows you to control printer usage and administration by assigning permissions.

Lesson 2: Managing Printers

Managing printers includes assigning forms to paper trays and setting a separator page. In addition, you can pause, resume, and cancel a document if a problem occurs on a printer. If a printer is faulty or you add printers to your network, you might need to redirect documents to a different printer. In addition, you might need to change which users have administrative responsibility for printers, which involves changing ownership.

After this lesson, you will be able to

- Assign forms to paper trays
- Set a separator page
- Pause, resume, and cancel documents on a printer
- Redirect documents to a different printer
- Take ownership of a printer

Estimated lesson time: 40 minutes

Assigning Forms to Paper Trays

If a printer has multiple trays that regularly hold different paper sizes, you can assign a form to a specific tray. A form defines a paper size. Users can then select the paper size from within their application. When the user prints, Windows XP Professional automatically routes the print job to the paper tray that holds the correct form. Examples of forms include the following: Legal, A4, Envelopes #10, and Letter Small.

To assign a form to a paper tray, complete the following steps:

1. Click Start, and then click Control Panel.
2. In the Control Panel window, click Printers And Other Hardware, and then click Printers And Faxes.
3. In the Printers And Faxes window, right-click the icon of the appropriate printer, and then click Properties.
4. In the printer's Properties dialog box, click the Device Settings tab.
5. In the box next to each paper tray, click the form for the paper type for the tray, as shown in Figure 7.3.
6. Click OK.

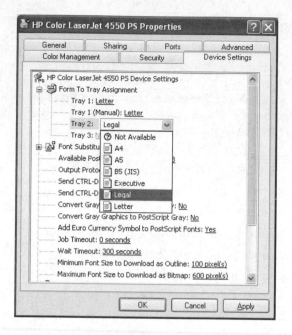

Figure 7.3   Setting forms for a printer

After you have set up a paper tray, users specify the paper size from within applications. Windows XP Professional knows in which paper tray the form is located.

Setting a Separator Page

A separator page is a file that contains print device commands. Separator pages have two functions:

- To identify and separate printed documents.
- To switch printers between print modes. Some printers can switch between print modes that take advantage of different device features. You can use separator pages to specify the correct page description language. For example, you can specify PostScript or Printer Control Language (PCL) for a print device that can switch between different print modes but cannot automatically detect which language a print job uses.

Windows XP Professional includes four separator page files, which are located in the *%systemroot%*\System32 folder. Table 7.2 lists the filename and describes the function for each of the included separator page files.

Table 7.2   Separator Page Files

Filename	Function
SYSPRINT.SEP	Prints a page before each document; compatible with PostScript print devices
PCL.SEP	Switches the print mode to PCL for HP-series print devices and prints a page before each document
PSCRIPT.SEP	Switches the print mode to PostScript for HP-series print devices but does not print a page before each document
SYSPRTJ.SEP	A version of SYSPRINT.SEP that uses Japanese characters

When you have decided to use a separator page and have chosen an appropriate one, use the Advanced tab in the printer's Properties dialog box to have the separator page printed at the beginning of each print job.

To set up a separator page, complete the following steps:

1. In the Advanced tab in the Properties dialog box for the printer (see Figure 7.4), click Separator Page.

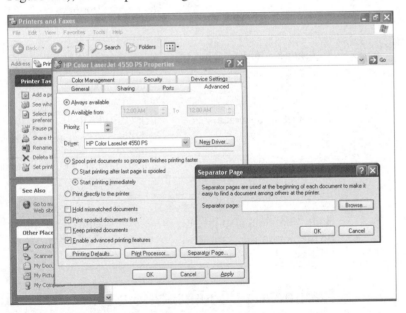

Figure 7.4   The Advanced tab for a printer's Properties dialog box

2. In the Separator Page dialog box, type the name of the separator page file.

Note   To browse for a separator file, click Browse.

3. Click OK to close the Separator Page box, and then click OK again to close the printer's Properties dialog box.

Pausing, Resuming, and Canceling Documents

Pausing and resuming a printer or canceling all documents on a printer might be necessary if there is a printing problem.

To pause or cancel all documents, right-click the icon for the printer in the Printers And Faxes window, and then click the appropriate command. To resume printing on a printer, right-click the printer and click Resume Printing.

Table 7.3 describes the tasks that you might perform when you manage printers, how to perform the tasks, and examples of situations in which you might perform these tasks.

Table 7.3   Managing Printers Tasks

Task	Action	Example
To pause printing	Click Pause Printing. The Pause Printing command changes to Resume Printing.	Pause the printer if there is a problem with the printer until you fix the problem.
To resume printing	Click Resume Printing. The Resume Printing command changes to Pause Printing.	Resume printing after you fix a problem with a printer.
To cancel all documents	Click Cancel All Documents. All documents are deleted from the printer.	Cancel all documents when you need to clear a print queue after old documents that no longer need to print have accumulated.

Note   You can also pause a printer by taking the printer offline. To take a printer offline, open the printer window, and on the Printer menu, click Use Printer Offline.

Redirecting Documents to a Different Printer

You can redirect documents to a different printer. For example, if a printer is not working, you should redirect the documents so that users do not need to resubmit them. You can redirect all print jobs for a printer, but you cannot redirect specific documents. The new printer must use the same printer driver as the current printer.

To redirect documents to a different printer, complete the following steps:

1. Open the Printers And Faxes window, right-click the printer, and then click Properties.

2. In the Properties dialog box, click the Ports tab.

3. Click Add Port.

4. In the Available Port Types list, click Local Port, and then click New Port.

5. In the Port Name dialog box, in the Enter A Port Name text box, type the Universal Naming Convention (UNC) name for the printer to which you are redirecting documents (for example, **\\prntsrv6\HPCLJ4550**), as shown in Figure 7.5.

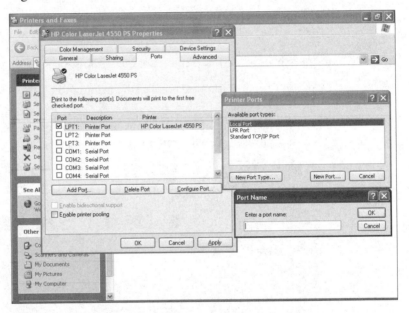

Figure 7.5   Redirecting documents to another printer

6. Click OK to accept the change and close the Port Name dialog box.

7. Click Close to close the Printer Ports dialog box.

8. Click OK to close the printer's Properties dialog box.

If another printer is available for the current print server, you can redirect the documents to that printer. To redirect documents to another local or network printer that uses the same printer driver, select the appropriate port on the print server and cancel the selection of the current port.

Taking Ownership of a Printer

There might be times when the owner of a printer can no longer manage that printer and you need to take ownership. Taking ownership of a printer enables you to change administrative responsibility for it. By default, the user who installed the printer owns it. If that user can no longer administer the printer, you should take ownership of it—for example, if the current owner leaves the company.

The following users can take ownership of a printer:

- A user or a member of a group who has the Manage Printers permission for the printer.

- Members of the Administrators and Power Users groups. By default these groups have the Manage Printers permission, which allows them to take ownership.

To take ownership of a printer, complete the following steps:

1. In the Properties dialog box for the printer, click the Security tab, and then click Advanced.

2. In the Advanced Security Settings dialog box, click the Owner tab, and then click your user account under Change Owner To, as shown in Figure 7.6.

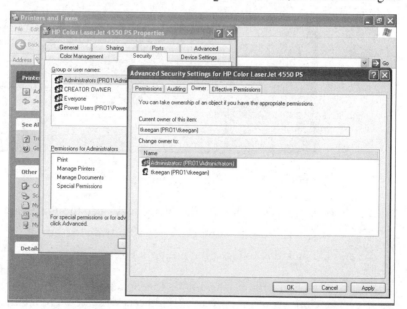

Figure 7.6   Taking ownership of a printer

3. Click OK to change ownership and to close the Advanced Security Settings dialog box.

4. Click OK to close the Properties dialog box for the printer.

Practice: Managing Printers

In this practice you perform three tasks that are part of managing printers. In the first exercise, you assign forms to paper trays. In the second exercise, you set up a separator page. In the third exercise you learn how to take ownership of a printer.

Exercise 1: Assigning Forms to Paper Trays

In this exercise, you assign a paper type (form) to a paper tray so that when users print to a specified form, the print job is automatically routed to and adjusted for the correct tray.

▶ **To assign forms to paper trays**

1. Log on as the user you created during installation or any user that is a member of the Administrators group.

2. Click Start, and then click Control Panel.

3. In the Control Panel window, click Printers And Other Hardware, and then click Printers And Faxes.

4. Right-click the icon of your printer, and then click Properties.

Note If you do not have a printer installed, see Exercise 1: Adding and Sharing a Printer in Chapter 6, "Setting Up, Configuring, and Troubleshooting Common Setup and Configuration Problems for Network Printers."

5. In the Properties dialog box, click the Device Settings tab.

   Some of the selections might be labeled Not Available because they depend on options that are not installed.

6. Click Tray 2, and then select Legal.

   Whenever a user prints on legal size paper, Windows XP Professional instructs the printer to use paper from Tray 2.

7. Click Apply and leave the Properties dialog box open for the next exercise.

Exercise 2: Setting Up Separator Pages

In this exercise, you set up a separator page to print between documents. You use the SYSPRINT.SEP separator page that ships with Windows XP Professional. This separator page includes the user's name and the date and time that the document was printed.

▶ **To set up a separator page**

1. Click the Advanced tab of the Properties dialog box.

2. In the Advanced tab, click Separator Page.

3. In the Separator Page dialog box, click Browse.

   Windows XP Professional displays a Separator Page dialog box that lists the contents of the System32 folder, which contains the separator pages that ship with Windows XP Professional. This dialog box also allows you to search in additional folders.

4. Select SYSPRINT.SEP, and then click Open.

   Windows XP Professional displays the Separator Page dialog box with the full path to the SYSPRINT.SEP separator page specified.

5. Click OK.

   Windows XP Professional is now set to print a separator page between print jobs.

6. Leave the Properties dialog box open for the next exercise.

Exercise 3: Taking Ownership of a Printer

In this exercise, you practice taking ownership of a printer.

▶ **To take ownership of a printer**

1. Click the Security tab of the Properties dialog box.

2. In the Security tab, click Advanced.

   The Advanced Security Settings For HP Color LaserJet 4550 dialog box is displayed.

3. Click the Owner tab.

4. To take ownership of the printer, select another user in the Name box.

5. If you actually wanted to take ownership you would click Apply, but for the purposes of this exercise, click Cancel and leave the ownership unchanged.

6. Click OK to close the Properties dialog box.

7. Click File and then click Close to close the Printers And Faxes window.

8. Log off Windows XP Professional.

Lesson Review

The following questions will help you determine whether you have learned enough to move on to the next lesson. If you have difficulty answering these questions, review the material in this lesson before beginning the next lesson. The answers for these questions are in Appendix A, "Questions and Answers."

1. If a printer has multiple trays that regularly hold different paper sizes, you can assign a form to a specific tray. How do you assign a form to a paper tray?

2. A _____ is a file that contains print device commands that identify and separate printed documents.

3. Which of the following tabs do you use to redirect documents to a different printer?

   a. Advanced tab of the Properties dialog box for the printer

   b. Security tab of the Properties dialog box for the printer

   c. Ports tab of the Properties dialog box for the printer

   d. Device Settings tab of the Properties dialog box for the printer

4. Which of the following tabs do you use to take ownership of a printer?

   a. Advanced tab of the Properties dialog box for the printer

   b. Security tab of the Properties dialog box for the printer

   c. Ports tab of the Properties dialog box for the printer

   d. Permissions tab of the Properties dialog box for the printer

5. Which of the following tabs do you use to set up a separator page?

   a. Advanced tab of the Properties dialog box for the printer

   b. Security tab of the Properties dialog box for the printer

   c. Ports tab of the Properties dialog box for the printer

   d. Permissions tab of the Properties dialog box for the printer

Lesson Summary

- If a printer has multiple trays that regularly hold different paper sizes, you can assign a form to a specific tray. A form defines a paper size.

- A separator page is a file that contains print device commands. Separator pages identify and separate printed documents, and they can be used to switch print devices between print modes.

- To pause a printer, cancel all documents, or resume printing, right-click the icon for the printer in the Printers And Faxes window and then click the appropriate command.

- You can redirect all print jobs for a printer, but you cannot redirect specific documents.

- To take ownership of a printer, a user must have or be a member of a group that has the Manage Printers permission for the printer. By default, members of the Administrators and Power Users groups have the Manage Printers permission.

Lesson 3: Managing Documents

In addition to managing printers, Windows XP Professional allows you to manage documents. Managing documents includes pausing, resuming, restarting, and canceling documents. In addition, you can set someone to be notified when a print job is finished, the priority to allow a critical document to print before other documents, and a specific time for a document to print.

After this lesson, you will be able to

- Pause, resume, restart, and cancel the printing of a document
- Set a notification, priority, and printing time
- Delete a document from the print queue

Estimated lesson time: 20 minutes

Pausing, Restarting, and Canceling a Document

If there is a printing problem with a specific document, you can pause and resume printing of that document. Additionally, you can restart or cancel a document. You must have the Manage Documents permission for the appropriate printer to perform these actions. Because the creator of a document has the default permissions to manage that document, users can perform any of these actions on their own documents.

To manage a document, right-click the icon representing the printer for the document in the Printers And Faxes window, and then click Open. Select the appropriate documents, click the Document menu, and then click the appropriate command to pause, resume, and restart from the beginning, or cancel a document, as shown in Figure 7.7.

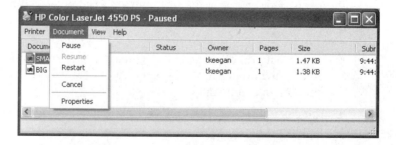

Figure 7.7 Managing documents

Table 7.4 describes the tasks that you might perform when you manage individual documents, how to perform the tasks, and examples of situations in which you might perform them.

Table 7.4   Managing Document Tasks

Task	Action	Example
To pause printing of a document	Select the documents for which you want to pause printing, and then click Pause. (The status changes to Paused.)	Pause printing of a document when there is a problem with the document.
To resume printing a document	Select the documents for which you want to resume printing, and then click Resume. (The status changes to Printing.)	Resume printing of the document after you fix the problem with the paused document.
To restart printing a document	Select the documents for which you want to restart printing, and then click Restart. Restart causes printing to start from the beginning of the document.	Restart printing of a partially printed document after you fix a problem with the document or the print device.
To cancel printing a document	Select the documents for which you want to cancel printing, and then click Cancel. You can also cancel a document by pressing the DELETE key.	When a document has the wrong printer settings or is no longer needed, you can cancel it so it is deleted before it prints.

Setting Notification, Priority, and Printing Time

You can control print jobs by setting the notification, priority, and printing time. To perform these document management tasks, you must have the Manage Documents permission for the appropriate printer.

You can set the notification, priority, and printing time for a document in the General tab of the Properties dialog box for the document, as shown in Figure 7.8. To open the Properties dialog box for one or more documents, first select the documents in the Printer window, click Document on the Printer window menu bar, and then click Properties.

Figure 7.8   Setting notification, priority, and printing time for a document

Table 7.5 describes the tasks that you might perform when you control print jobs, how to perform the tasks, and examples of situations in which you might perform them.

Table 7.5   Setting a Notification, Changing Priority, and Scheduling Print Times

Task	Action	Example
Set a notification	In the Notify text box, type the logon name of the user who should receive the notification. By default, Windows XP Professional enters the name of the user who printed the document.	Change the print notification when someone other than the user who printed the document needs to retrieve it.
Change a document priority	Move the Priority slider to the priority level that you want. The highest priority is 99 and the lowest is 1.	Change a priority so that a critical document prints before other documents.
Schedule print times	To restrict print times, select Only From in the Schedule section, and then set the hours between which you want the document to print.	Set the print time for a large document so that it prints during off hours, such as late at night.

Practice: Managing Documents

In this practice, you manage documents by printing a document, setting a notification for a document, changing the priority for a document, and then canceling a document.

▶ **To verify that a printer is offline**

1. Log on as the user you created during installation or any user that is a member of the Administrators group.

2. Click Start and then click Control Panel.

3. In the Control Panel window, click Printers And Other Hardware, and click Printers And Faxes.

4. In the Printers And Faxes window, click the printer icon.

5. Do one of the following to verify that the printer is offline:

   ■ On the File menu, verify that the Use Printer Online option is listed because that indicates that the printer is currently offline.

   ■ Right-click the printer icon and verify that the Use Printer Online command is listed because that indicates that the printer is currently offline.

   ■ If the Printers And Faxes window is displayed in Web view, verify that Use Printer Offline is displayed in the left portion of the window.

5. Verify that a check mark appears above the printer icon indicating that it is the default printer.

6. Minimize the Printers And Faxes window.

Note Keep the printer offline to keep it from trying to print. This eliminates error messages in later exercises when documents are spooled.

▶ **To print a document**

1. Click Start, point to All Programs, point to Accessories, and then click WordPad.

2. Type **How big is big?** and then, on the File menu, click Save.

3. In the File Name text box, type **BIG**, and then click Save.

4. Click File and then click Print.

   The Print dialog box appears. Notice that the file will be printed on the HP Color LaserJet 4550 PS printer.

5. Click Print, and then close WordPad.

▶ **To set a notification**

1. Restore the Printers And Faxes window.

2. Double-click HP Color LaserJet 4550 PS.

3. In the Printer window, select BIG, and then, on the Document menu, click Properties.

   Windows XP Professional displays the BIG Document Properties dialog box with the General tab active.

   Which user is specified in the Notify text box? Why?

4. In the Notify text box, type **Fred** and then click Apply.

   You set the notification to go to Fred.

▶ **To increase the priority of a document**

1. In the BIG Document Properties dialog box, in the General tab, notice the default priority.

   What is the current priority? Is it the lowest or highest priority?

2. In the Priority box, move the slider to the right to increase the priority of the document to 38, and then click OK.

   Nothing changes visibly in the HP Color LaserJet 4550 PS – Use Printer Offline window.

▶ **To cancel a document**

1. Select BIG in the Printer window document list.

2. On the Document menu, click Cancel.

   Notice that the Status column changes to Deleting. BIG is removed from the document list.

Tip   You can also cancel a document by pressing the DELETE key.

---

3. Close the Printer window, and then close the Printers And Faxes window.

Lesson Review

The following questions will help you determine whether you have learned enough to move on to the next lesson. If you have difficulty answering these questions, review the material in this lesson before beginning the next lesson. The answers for these questions are in Appendix A, "Questions and Answers."

1. What is the difference between resuming printing of a document and restarting printing of a document?

2. Which of the following statements about the range of priorities for a document to be printed is correct?

   a. Priorities for a document range from 1 to 10, with 1 being the highest priority.

   b. Priorities for a document range from 1 to 10, with 10 being the highest priority.

   c. Priorities for a document range from 1 to 99, with 1 being the highest priority.

   d. Priorities for a document range from 1 to 99, with 99 being the highest priority.

3. You set the notification, priority, and printing time for a document in the _____ tab of the Properties dialog box for the document.

4. By default, Windows XP Professional enters the _____ logon name in the Notify text box of a document.

   a. Administrator's

   b. Owner of the printer's

   c. Owner of the document's

   d. Person who printed the document's

Lesson Summary

- Managing documents includes pausing, resuming, restarting, and canceling documents.

- In the Notify text box for a document, you can set who is notified when the print job is finished.

- Setting the document priority allows a critical document to print before other documents.

- Setting a specific time for a document to print allows large documents to only print during off hours, such as late at night.

- You must have the Manage Documents permission for the appropriate printer to perform these document management tasks.

- The creator of a document has the default permissions to manage that document, so users can perform any of these actions on their own documents.

Lesson 4: Administering Printers Using a Web Browser

Windows XP Professional enables you to manage printers from any computer running a Web browser, regardless of whether the computer is running Windows XP Professional or has the correct printer driver installed. All management tasks that you perform with Windows XP Professional management tools are the same when you use a Web browser. The difference in administering with a Web browser is the interface, which is a Web-based interface. To access a printer using a Web browser, a print server running Windows 2000 Server or Windows XP Professional must have Microsoft Internet Information Services (IIS) installed.

Note   For information about installing IIS, see Chapter 10, "Configuring Windows XP Professional."

After this lesson, you will be able to

- Describe the advantages of administering printers using a Web browser
- Describe how to administer printers using a Web browser

Estimated lesson time: 10 minutes

Using a Web Browser to Manage Printers

The following are the advantages of using a Web browser, such as Microsoft Internet Explorer, to manage printers:

- It allows you to administer printers from any computer running a Web browser, regardless of whether the computer is running Windows XP Professional or has the correct printer driver installed.
- It allows you to customize the interface. For example, you can create your own Web page containing a floor plan with the locations of the printers and the links to the printers.
- It provides a summary page listing the status of all printers on a print server.
- It can report real-time print device data, such as whether the print device is in power-saving mode, if the printer driver makes such information available. This information is not available in the Printers And Faxes window.

Accessing Printers Using a Web Browser

You can access all printers on a print server by using a Web browser or you can use any of the windows or folders within the Windows XP Professional interface that has an address bar, such as the Printers And Faxes window or Internet Explorer (see Figure 7.9). In the Address text box, type **http://*print_server_name*/printers**. This command displays a page listing all the printers on the print server. Click the name of the printer that you want to use. When you are on that printer's page, under Printer Actions, click Connect to connect to the printer. Windows XP automatically copies the appropriate printer drivers to your computer and adds an icon for the printer to the Printers And Faxes window.

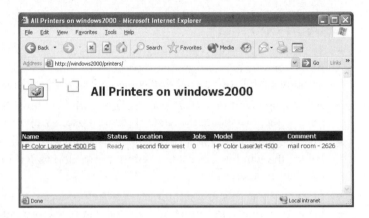

Figure 7.9   Using Internet Explorer to access all printers on a print server

If you want to gain access to a specific printer by using a Web browser, open the Web browser, and then in the Address text box, type ***http://server_name/printer_share_name***. You are directed to that printer's page. Under Printer Actions, click Connect to connect to the printer.

From the printer's URL page, you can view information about the printer, such as its model, its location, and the number of documents waiting to print. You can manage any document you have sent to the printer, and if you have the Manage Printers permission for the printer, you can also pause or resume operation of the printer.

Lesson Review

The following questions will help you determine whether you have learned enough to move on to the next lesson. If you have difficulty answering these questions, review the material in this lesson before beginning the next lesson. The answers for these questions are in Appendix A, "Questions and Answers."

1. If you are using a computer running Windows XP Professional as your print server, users can gain access to the printers on it by using a Web browser only if the print server has _____ installed.

2. How can you gain access to all printers on a print server?

3. Can you pause and resume operation of a printer that you have used Internet Explorer to connect to?

Lesson Summary

- Windows XP Professional enables you to manage printers from any computer running a Web browser, regardless of whether the computer is running Windows XP Professional or has the correct printer driver installed.

- All management tasks that you perform with Windows XP Professional management tools are the same when you use a Web browser.

- You can gain access to all printers on a print server by using a Web browser or any of the windows or folders within the Windows XP Professional interface that has an address bar.

- If you gain access to a printer using a Web browser and have the Manage Printers permission for the printer, you can pause or resume operation of the printer.

Lesson 5: Troubleshooting Common Printing Problems

In this lesson you will learn about some common printing problems and how to troubleshoot them. This chapter also introduces you to the built-in Printer Troubleshooter and some of the other troubleshooting features included in Windows XP Professional.

After this lesson, you will be able to

- Describe how to troubleshoot some common printing problems
- Describe the features included in Windows XP Professional to make it easier to resolve common printing problems

Estimated lesson time: 10 minutes

Examining the Problem

When you detect a printing problem, always verify that the printer is plugged in, turned on, and connected to the print server. For a network interface printer, verify that there is a network connection between the printer and the print server.

To determine the cause of a problem, first try printing from a different program to verify that the problem is with the printer and not with the program. If the problem is with the printer, ask the following questions:

- Can other users print normally? If so, the problem is most likely caused by insufficient permissions, no network connection, or client computer problems.
- Does the print server use the correct printer driver for the printer?
- Is the print server operational and is there enough disk space for spooling?
- Does the client computer have the correct printer driver?

Reviewing Common Printing Problems

There are some printing problems that are common to most network printing environments. Table 7.6 describes some of these common printing problems, as well as some possible causes and solutions.

Table 7.6   Common Printing Problems, Causes, and Solutions

Problem	Possible cause	Solution
A user receives an Access Denied message when trying to configure a printer from an application (for example, earlier versions of Microsoft Excel).	The user does not have the appropriate permission to change printer configurations.	Change the user's permission or configure the printer for the user.

(continued)

Table 7.6   *(continued)*

Problem	Possible cause	Solution
The document does not print completely or comes out garbled.	The printer driver is incorrect.	Install the correct printer driver.
The hard disk starts thrashing and the document does not reach the print server.	There is insufficient hard disk space for spooling.	Create more free space on the hard disk.

Windows XP Professional Printing Troubleshooter

Windows XP Professional has a built-in troubleshooter to help you resolve your printing problems. For example, in the Printers And Faxes window, you can click Troubleshoot Printing (see Figure 7.10).

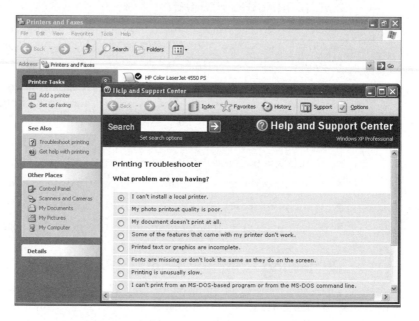

Figure 7.10   Printers And Faxes window built-in troubleshooter

When you click Troubleshoot Printing, Windows XP Professional presents you with a series of potential printing problems. After you make a selection from the list of potential problems and click Next, the troubleshooter takes you through a series of suggestions and questions to help you resolve the problem. You can also perform a search to help resolve your problem or you can select the I Want The Troubleshooter To Investigate Settings On This Computer option.

Additional Troubleshooting Options

If you experience a problem with your computer, Windows XP Professional provides a number of ways to help you resolve your problem. On the Start menu you can click Help And Support. If it is a printing problem, click Printing And Faxing (see Figure 7.11).

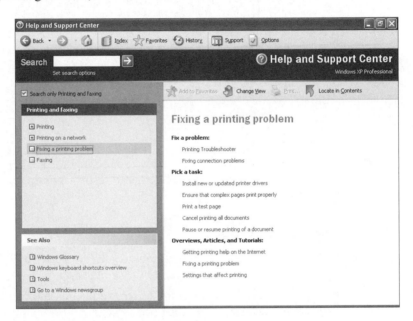

Figure 7.11   The Fixing A Printer Problem option in the Help And Support Center window

The Help and Support Center also allows you to use Remote Assistance to invite another person to help over the Internet. The expert can accept this invitation, chat with you, and view your desktop. He or she can also transfer any files required to fix the issue or perform any complex procedures that need to be performed. You can also visit the Windows XP newsgroups or try Microsoft Assisted Support.

Note   For more information about these support features, see Chapter 1, "Introduction to Windows XP Professional."

Lesson Review

The following questions will help you determine whether you have learned enough to move on to the next lesson. If you have difficulty answering these questions, review the material in this lesson before beginning the next chapter. The answers for these questions are in Appendix A, "Questions and Answers."

1. When you detect a printing problem, what three things should you always check before you start troubleshooting the problem?

2. If a user reports to you that he or she cannot print, what are some of the areas you should check?

3. The _____ feature included in Windows XP Professional allows you to invite an expert to take full control of your computer over the Internet to resolve printing problems on your computer.

Lesson Summary

- When you detect a printing problem, always verify that the printer is plugged in, turned on, and connected to the print server.

- For a network interface print device, verify that there is a network connection between the printer and the print server.

- You can access the Windows XP Professional built-in Printing Troubleshooter from the Printers And Faxes window by clicking Troubleshoot Printing.

- You can use Remote Assistance to invite another person to help over the Internet. This expert can chat with you and view your desktop. With your permission, the expert can get full control of your computer to help resolve problems.

C H A P T E R   8

Securing Resources with NTFS Permissions

About This Chapter

This chapter introduces you to NT file system (NTFS) folder and file permissions for Windows XP Professional. You will learn how to assign NTFS folder and file permissions to user accounts and groups, and you will see how moving or copying files and folders affects NTFS file and folder permissions. You will also learn how to troubleshoot common resource access problems.

Before You Begin

To complete this chapter, you must have

- A computer that meets the minimum hardware requirements listed in the preface, "About This Book"
- Microsoft Windows XP Professional installed on the computer

Lesson 1: Understanding and Applying NTFS Permissions

You use NTFS permissions to specify which users and groups can access files and folders and what they can do with the contents of the files or folders. NTFS permissions are available only on NTFS volumes. They are *not* available on volumes formatted with file allocation table (FAT) or FAT32 file systems. NTFS security is effective whether a user accesses the file or folder at the local computer or over the network.

The permissions you assign for folders are different from the permissions you assign for files. Administrators, the owners of files or folders, and users with Full Control permission can assign NTFS permissions to users and groups to control access to files and folders.

After this lesson, you will be able to

- Define the standard NTFS folder and file permissions
- Describe the result when you combine user account and group permissions
- Describe the result when folder permissions are different from those of the files in the folder

Estimated lesson time: 30 minutes

NTFS Folder Permissions

You assign folder permissions to control the access that users have to folders and to the files and subfolders that are contained within the folders.

Table 8.1 lists the standard NTFS folder permissions that you can assign and the type of access that each provides.

Table 8.1   NTFS Folder Permissions

NTFS folder permission	Allows the user to
Read	See files and subfolders in the folder and view folder ownership, permissions, and attributes (such as Read-Only, Hidden, Archive, and System)
Write	Create new files and subfolders within the folder, change folder attributes, and view folder ownership and permissions
List Folder Contents	See the names of files and subfolders in the folder
Read & Execute	Move through folders to reach other files and folders, even if the users don't have permission for those folders, and perform actions permitted by the Read permission and the List Folder Contents permission

Table 8.1 *(continued)*

NTFS folder permission	Allows the user to
Modify	Delete the folder plus perform actions permitted by the Write permission and the Read & Execute permission
Full Control	Change permissions, take ownership, and delete subfolders and files, plus perform actions permitted by all other NTFS folder permissions

You can deny permission to a user account or group. To deny all access to a user account or group for a folder, deny the Full Control permission.

NTFS File Permissions

You assign file permissions to control the access that users have to files. Table 8.2 lists the standard NTFS file permissions that you can assign and the type of access that each provides.

Table 8.2   NTFS File Permissions

NTFS file permission	Allows the user to
Read	Read the file, and view file attributes, ownership, and permissions
Write	Overwrite the file, change file attributes, and view file ownership and permissions
Read & Execute	Run applications, plus perform the actions permitted by the Read permission
Modify	Modify and delete the file, plus perform the actions permitted by the Write permission and the Read & Execute permission
Full Control	Change permissions and take ownership, plus perform the actions permitted by all other NTFS file permissions

Access Control List

NTFS stores an *access control list* (ACL) with every file and folder on an NTFS volume. The ACL contains a list of all user accounts and groups that have been assigned permissions for the file or folder, as well as the permissions that they have been assigned. When a user attempts to gain access to a resource, the ACL must contain an entry, called an *access control entry* (ACE), for the user account or a group to which the user belongs. The entry must allow the type of access that is requested (for example, Read access) for the user to gain access. If no ACE exists in the ACL, the user can't access the resource.

Multiple NTFS Permissions

You can assign multiple permissions to a user account and to each group of which the user is a member. To assign permissions, you must understand the rules and priorities by which NTFS assigns and combines multiple permissions and NTFS permissions inheritance.

Effective Permissions

A user's *effective permissions* for a resource are the sum of the NTFS permissions that you assign to the individual user account and to all of the groups to which the user belongs. If a user has Read permission for a folder and is a member of a group with Write permission for the same folder, the user has both Read and Write permissions for that folder.

Overriding Folder Permissions with File Permissions

NTFS file permissions take priority over NTFS folder permissions. If you have access to a file, you will be able to access the file if you have the Bypass Traverse Checking security permission, even if you don't have access to the folder containing the file. You can access the files for which you have permissions by using the full *Universal Naming Convention* (UNC) or local path to open the file from its respective application, even though the folder in which it resides is invisible if you have no corresponding folder permission. In other words, if you don't have permission to access the folder containing the file you want to access, you must have the Bypass Traverse Checking security permission and you have to know the full path to the file to access it. Without permission to access the folder, you can't see the folder, so you can't browse for the file.

Note   The Bypass Traverse Checking security permission is detailed further in Lesson 2 of this chapter.

Overriding Other Permissions with Deny

You can deny permission to a user account or group for a specific file, although this is not the recommended method of controlling access to resources. Denying permission overrides all instances in which that permission is allowed. Even if a user has permission to access a file or folder as a member of a group, denying permission to the user blocks any other permissions the user might have (see Figure 8.1).

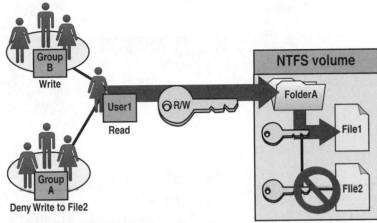

- NTFS permissions are cumulative.
- File permissions override folder permissions.
- Deny overrides other permissions.

Figure 8.1   Multiple NTFS permissions

In Figure 8.1, User1 has Read permission for FolderA and is a member of Group A and Group B. Group B has Write permission for FolderA. Group A has been denied Write permission for File2.

The user can read and write to File1. The user can also read File2 but cannot write to File2 because she is a member of Group A, which has been denied Write permission for File2.

NTFS Permissions Inheritance

By default, permissions that you assign to the parent folder are inherited by and propagated to the subfolders and files contained in the parent folder. However, you can prevent permissions inheritance, as shown in Figure 8.2.

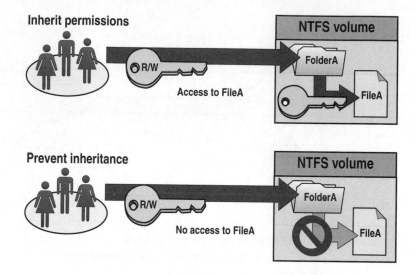

Figure 8.2   Inheritance

Understanding Permissions Inheritance

Whatever permissions you assign to the parent folder also apply to subfolders and files contained within the parent folder. When you assign NTFS permissions to give access to a folder, you assign permissions for the folder and for any existing files and subfolders, as well as for any new files and subfolders that are created in the folder.

Preventing Permissions Inheritance

You can prevent permissions that are assigned to a parent folder from being inherited by subfolders and files that are contained within the folder. That is, the subfolders and files will not inherit permissions that have been assigned to the parent folder containing them.

The folder for which you prevent permissions inheritance becomes the new parent folder. The subfolders and files contained within this new parent folder inherit the permissions assigned to it.

Lesson Review

The following questions will help you determine whether you have learned enough to move on to the next lesson. If you have difficulty answering these questions, review the material in this lesson before beginning the next lesson. The answers are in Appendix A, "Questions and Answers."

1. Which of the following statements correctly describe NTFS file and folder permissions? (Choose all answers that are correct.)

    a. NTFS security is effective only when a user gains access to the file or folder over the network.

    b. NTFS security is effective when a user gains access to the file or folder on the local computer.

    c. NTFS permissions specify which users and groups can gain access to files and folders and what they can do with the contents of the file or folder.

    d. NTFS permissions can be used on all file systems available with Windows XP Professional.

2. Which of the following NTFS folder permissions allow you to delete the folder?

    a. Read

    b. Read & Execute

    c. Modify

    d. Administer

3. Which of the NTFS file permissions should you assign to a file if you want to allow users to delete the file but do not want to allow users to take ownership of a file?

4. What is an access control list (ACL) and what is the difference between an ACL and an access control entry (ACE)?

5. What are a user's effective permissions for a resource?

6. By default, what inherits the permissions that you assign to the parent folder?

Lesson Summary

- NTFS permissions are available only on NTFS volumes and are used to specify which users and groups can access files and folders and what these users can do with the contents of those files or folders.

- NTFS folder permissions are Read, Write, List Folder Contents, Read & Execute, Modify, and Full Control.

- The NTFS file permissions are Read, Write, Read & Execute, Modify, and Full Control.

- Administrators, the owners of files or folders, and users with Full Control permission can assign NTFS permissions to users and groups to control access to files and folders.

- NTFS stores an ACL, which contains a list of all user accounts and groups that have been granted access to the file or folder, as well as the type of access that they have been granted, with every file and folder on an NTFS volume.

- A user attempting to gain access to a resource must have permission for the type of access that is requested to gain access.

- You can assign multiple permissions to a user account by assigning permissions to his or her individual user account and to each group of which the user is a member.

- NTFS file permissions take priority over NTFS folder permissions.

- A user's effective permissions for a resource are based on the NTFS permissions that you assign to the individual user account and to all of the groups to which the user belongs.

Lesson 2: Assigning NTFS Permissions and Special Permissions

You should follow certain guidelines for assigning NTFS permissions. Assign permissions according to group and user needs, which include allowing or preventing permissions to be inherited from parent folders to subfolders and files that are contained in the parent folder.

After this lesson, you will be able to

- Assign NTFS folder and file permissions to user accounts and groups
- Give users the ability to change permissions on files or folders
- Give users the ability to take ownership of files and folders

Estimated lesson time: 70 minutes

Planning NTFS Permissions

If you take the time to plan your NTFS permissions and follow a few guidelines, you will find that they are easy to manage. Use the following guidelines when you assign NTFS permissions:

- To simplify administration, group files into application, data, and home folders. Centralize home and public folders on a volume that is separate from applications and the operating system. Doing so provides the following benefits:

    - You assign permissions only to folders, not to individual files.

    - Backup is less complex because you don't need to back up application files, and all home and public folders are in one location.

- Allow users only the level of access that they require. If a user only needs to read a file, assign the Read permission to his or her user account for the file. This reduces the possibility of users accidentally modifying or deleting important documents and application files.

- Create groups according to the access that the group members require for resources, and then assign the appropriate permissions to the group. Assign permissions to individual user accounts only when necessary.

- When you assign permissions for working with data or application folders, assign the Read & Execute permission to the Users group and the Administrators group. This prevents application files from being accidentally deleted or damaged by users or viruses.

- When you assign permissions for public data folders, assign the Read & Execute permission and the Write permission to the Users group and the Full Control permission to the CREATOR OWNER. By default, the user who creates a file is also the owner of the file. The owner of a file can grant another user permission to take ownership of the file. The person who takes ownership would then become the owner of the file. If you assign the Read &

Execute permission and the Write permission to the Users group and the Full Control permission to the CREATOR OWNER, users have the ability to read and modify documents that other users create and the ability to read, modify, and delete the files and folders that they create.

- Deny permissions only when it is essential to deny specific access to a specific user account or group.

- Encourage users to assign permissions to the files and folders that they create and educate them about how to do so.

Setting NTFS Permissions

By default, when you format a volume with NTFS, the Full Control permission is assigned to the Everyone group. This presented a problem in earlier versions of Windows, including Microsoft Windows 2000. In Windows XP Professional, the Anonymous Logon is no longer included in the Everyone group.

Important When a Windows 2000 Professional system is upgraded to a Windows XP Professional system, resources with permission entries for the Everyone group and not explicitly for the Anonymous Logon group are no longer available to the Anonymous Logon group.

Assigning or Modifying Permissions

Administrators, users with the Full Control permission, and the owners of files and folders can assign permissions to user accounts and groups.

To assign or modify NTFS permissions for a file or a folder, in the Security tab of the Properties dialog box for the file or folder, configure the options that are shown in Figure 8.3 and described in Table 8.3.

Table 8.3   Security Tab Options

Option	Description
Group Or User Name	Allows you to select the user account or group for which you want to change permissions or that you want to remove from the list.
Permissions For *group or user name*	Allows and denies permissions. Select the Allow check box to allow a permission. Select the Deny check box to deny a permission.
Add	Opens the Select Users Or Groups dialog box, which you use to select user accounts and groups to add to the Group Or User Name list (see Figure 8.4).
Remove	Removes the selected user account or group and the associated permissions for the file or folder.
Advanced	Opens the Advanced Security Settings dialog box for the selected folder so that you can grant or deny special permissions (see Figure 8.5).

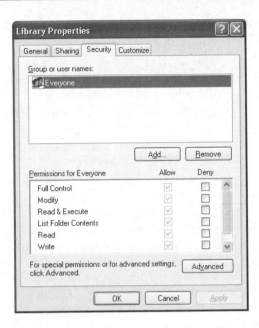

Figure 8.3   The Security tab of the Properties dialog box for a folder

Adding Users or Groups

Click Add to display the Select Users Or Groups dialog box (see Figure 8.4). Use this dialog box to add users or groups so that you can assign them permissions for accessing a folder or file. The options available in the Select Users Or Groups dialog box are described in Table 8.4.

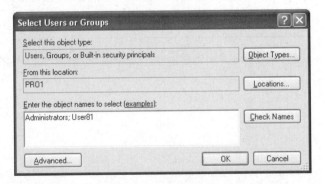

Figure 8.4   The Select Users or Groups dialog box for a folder

Table 8.4   Select Users Or Groups Dialog Box Options

Option	Description
Select The Object Type	Allows you to select the types of objects you want to look for, such as built-in security principals (users, groups, and computer accounts), user accounts, or groups.
From This Location	Indicates where you are currently looking, for example in the domain or on the local computer.
Locations	Allows you to select where you want to look, for example in the domain or on the local computer.
Enter The Object Names To Select	Allows you to type in a list of built-in security principals, users, or groups to be added.
Check Names	Verifies the selected list of built-in security principals, users, or groups to be added.
Advanced	Allows you access to advanced search features, including the ability to search for deleted accounts, accounts with passwords that do not expire, and accounts that have not logged on for a certain number of days.

Granting or Denying Special Permissions

Click Advanced to display the Advanced Security Settings dialog box (Figure 8.5), which lists the users and groups and the permissions they have on this object. The Permissions Entries box also shows where the permissions were inherited from and where they are applied.

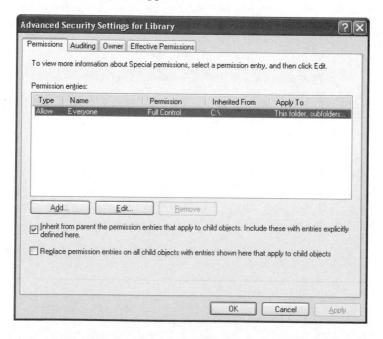

Figure 8.5   The Permissions tab of the Advanced Security Settings dialog box for a folder

You can use the Advanced Security Settings dialog box to change the permissions set for a user or group. To change the permissions set for a user or group, select a user and click Edit to display the Permission Entry For dialog box (see Figure 8.6). You can then select or clear the specific permissions, explained in Table 8.5, that you want to change.

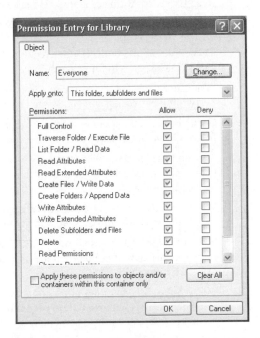

Figure 8.6   The Permission Entry dialog box for a folder

Table 8.5   Special Permissions

Permission	Description
Full Control	Full Control applies all permissions to the user or group.
Traverse Folder/ Execute File	Traverse Folder allows or denies moving through folders to access other files or folders, even when the user has no permissions for the traversed folder (the folder that the user is moving through). Traverse Folder is not applied if the user or group has the Bypass Traverse Checking user right granted in Group Policy. By default the Everyone group has Bypass Traverse Checking granted, so you must modify the Group Policy if you want to use Traverse Folder permission. Traverse Folder applies only to folders. Execute File allows or denies running executable files (application files). Execute File applies only to files.
List Folder/ Read Data	List Folder allows or denies viewing file names and subfolder names within the folder. List Folder applies only to folders.
	Read Data allows or denies viewing the contents of a file. Read Data applies only to files.

(continued)

Table 8.5   *(continued)*

Permission	Description
Read Attributes	Read Attributes allows or denies the viewing of the attributes of a file or folder. These attributes are defined by NTFS.
Read Extended Attributes	Read Extended Attributes allows or denies the viewing of extended attributes of a file or a folder. These attributes are defined by programs.
Create Files/ Write Data	Create Files allows or denies the creation of files within a folder. Create Files applies to folders only.
	Write Data allows or denies the making of changes to a file and the overwriting of existing content. Write Data applies to files only.
Create Folders/ Append Data	Create Folders allows or denies the creation of folders within the folder. Create Folders applies only to folders.
	Append Data allows or denies making changes to the end of the file, but not changing, deleting, or overwriting existing data. Append Data applies to files only.
Write Attributes	Write Attributes allows or denies the changing of the attributes of a file or folder. These attributes are defined by NTFS.
Write Extended Attributes	Write Extended Attributes allows or denies the changing of the extended attributes of a file or a folder. These attributes are defined by programs.
Delete Subfolders and Files	Delete Subfolders and Files allows or denies the deletion of subfolders or files within a folder, even if the Delete permission has not been granted on the particular subfolder or file.
Delete	Delete allows or denies the deletion of a file or folder. A user can delete a file or folder even without having the Delete permission granted on that file or folder, if the Delete Subfolder and Files permission has been granted to the user on the parent folder.
Read Permissions	Read Permissions allows or denies the reading of the permissions assigned to the file or folder.
Change Permissions	Change Permissions allows or denies the changing of the permissions assigned to the file or folder. You can give other administrators and users the ability to change permissions for a file or folder without giving them the Full Control permission over the file or folder. In this way, the administrator or user can't delete or write to the file or folder but can assign permissions to the file or folder.
Take Ownership	Take Ownership allows or denies taking ownership of the file or folder. The owner of a file can always change permissions on a file or folder, regardless of the permissions set to protect the file or folder.
Synchronize	Synchronize allows or denies different threads to wait on the handle for the file or folder and synchronize with another thread that may signal it. This permission applies only to multithreaded, multiprocess programs.

Taking Ownership

You can transfer ownership of files and folders from one user account or group to another. You can give someone the ability to take ownership and, as an administrator, you can take ownership of a file or folder.

The following rules apply for taking ownership of a file or folder:

- The current owner or any user with Full Control permission can assign the Full Control standard permission or the Take Ownership special access permission to another user account or group, allowing the user account or any member of the group to take ownership.

- An administrator can take ownership of a folder or file, regardless of assigned permissions. If an administrator takes ownership, the Administrators group becomes the owner and any member of the Administrators group can change the permissions for the file or folder and assign the Take Ownership permission to another user account or group.

For example, if an employee leaves the company, an administrator can take ownership of the employee's files and assign the Take Ownership permission to another employee, and then that employee can take ownership of the former employee's files.

Note   You cannot assign anyone ownership of a file or folder. The owner of a file, an administrator, or anyone with Full Control permission can assign Take Ownership permission to a user account or group, allowing them to take ownership. To become the owner of a file or folder, a user or group member with Take Ownership permission must explicitly take ownership of the file or folder.

To take ownership of a file or folder, the user or a group member with Take Ownership permission must explicitly take ownership of the file or folder, as follows:

1. In the Security tab of the Properties dialog box for the file or folder, click Advanced.

2. In the Advanced Security Settings dialog box, in the Owner tab, in the Change Owner To list, select your name.

3. Select the Replace Owner On Subcontainers And Objects check box to take ownership of all subfolders and files that are contained within the folder, and then click OK.

Preventing Permissions Inheritance

By default, subfolders and files inherit permissions that you assign to their parent folder. This is indicated in the Advanced Security Settings dialog box (Figure 8.5) when the Inherit From Parent The Permission Entries That Apply To Child Objects check box is selected. To prevent a subfolder or file from inheriting permissions from a parent folder, clear the check box. You are then prompted to select one of the options described in Table 8.6.

Table 8.6   Preventing Permissions Inheritance Options

Option	Description
Copy	Copy the permission entries that were previously applied from the parent to the child and then deny subsequent permissions inheritance from the parent folder.
Remove	Remove the permission entries that were previously applied from the parent to the child and retain only the permissions that you explicitly assign here.
Cancel	Cancel the dialog box.

Practice: Planning and Assigning NTFS Permissions

In this practice, you will plan NTFS permissions for folders and files based on a business scenario. Then you will apply NTFS permissions for folders and files on your computer running Windows XP Professional in a workgroup environment, based on a second scenario. Finally, you will test the NTFS permissions that you set up to make sure that they are working properly.

Before beginning the exercises that follow, log on with an account that is a member of the Administrators group and create the users listed in the following table:

User account	Type
User81	Limited
User82	Limited
User83	Limited
User84	Limited

Create the following folders:

- C:\Public
- C:\Public\Library

Run the **PlanningNTFSPermissions** file in the Demos folder on the CD-ROM accompanying this book for a demonstration of determining the default NTFS permissions applied to a folder. The demonstration also includes stopping a group from inheriting permissions from its parent object, deleting a group that has been assigned NTFS permissions, and adding a user and applying NTFS permissions to the user object for a folder.

Exercise 1: Determining the Default NTFS Permissions for a Folder

In this exercise, you determine the default NTFS permissions for the newly created Public folder located on a computer running Windows XP Professional in a workgroup environment.

▶ **To determine the default permissions on a folder**

1. Log on as Fred or with a user account that is a member of the Administrators group.

2. Right-click My Computer, and then click Explore.

3. Expand Local Disk (C:), right-click the Public folder, and then click Properties.

   Windows XP Professional displays the Public Properties dialog box with the General tab active.

4. Click the Security tab to display the permissions for the Public folder.

Tip If you do not have a Security tab, there are two things to check: Is your partition formatted as NTFS or FAT? Only NTFS partitions use NTFS permissions, so only NTFS partitions have a Security tab. Are you using Simple File Sharing? Click Cancel to close the Public Properties dialog box. On the Tools menu, click Folder Options. In the Folder Options dialog box, click View. Under Advanced Settings, clear the Use Simple File Sharing (Recommended) check box and click OK. Repeat steps 3 and 4 and continue with this practice.

If any of the users or groups have special permissions, click the user or group and then click Advanced to see which special permissions are set.

Windows XP Professional displays the Public Properties dialog box with the Security tab active.

What are the existing folder permissions?

5. Click OK to close the Public Properties dialog box.

6. Close Windows Explorer and log off.

▶ **To test the folder permissions for the Public folder**

1. Log on as User81, and then start Windows Explorer.

2. Expand the Public folder.

3. In the Public folder, create a text document named USER81 and type in the following text: **The first four letters in the alphabet are a, b, c, and d.**

Tip With the Public folder selected in the folder tree (the left pane), on the File menu, click New and then click Text Document to create the text document.

Were you successful? Why or why not?

4. Attempt to perform the following tasks for the file that you just created:

   ▪ Open the file

   ▪ Modify the file

   ▪ Delete the file

   Which tasks were you able to complete and why?

5. In the Public folder, recreate the text file named User81.

6. Log off Windows XP Professional.

7. Log on as User82.

8. Attempt to perform the following tasks on the USER81 text document.

   ▪ Open the file

   ▪ Modify the file

   ▪ Delete the file

   Which tasks were you able to perform and why?

Exercise 2: Assigning NTFS Permissions

In this exercise, you assign NTFS permissions for the Public folder.

The permissions that you assign are to be based on the following criteria:

- All users should be able to read documents and files in the Public folder.

- All users should be able to create documents in the Public folder.

- All users should be able to modify the contents, properties, and permissions of the documents that they create in the Public folder.

- User82 is responsible for maintaining the Public folder and should be able to modify and delete all files in the Public folder.

Based on what you learned in Exercise 1, what changes in permission assignments do you need to make to meet each of these four criteria? Why?

You are currently logged on as User82. Can you change the permissions assigned to User82 while logged on as User82? Why or why not?

▶ **To assign NTFS permissions for a folder**

1. Log on as Fred or with a user account that is a member of the Administrators group, and then start Windows Explorer.

2. Expand the Public folder.

3. Right-click the Public folder and then click Properties.

   Windows XP Professional displays the Properties dialog box for the folder with the General tab active.

4. In the Properties dialog box for the folder, click the Security tab.

5. In the Security tab, click Add.

   The Select Users Or Groups dialog box is displayed.

6. In the Enter The Object Names To Select text box, type **User82** and then click Check Names.

   PRO1\User82 should now appear in the Enter The Object Names To Select text box, indicating that Windows XP Professional located User82 on PRO1 and it is a valid user account.

7. Click OK to close the Select Users Or Groups dialog box.

   User82 now appears in the Group Or User Name box in the Public Properties dialog box.

   What permissions are assigned to User82?

8. Click Advanced.

   Windows XP Professional displays the Advanced Security Settings For Public dialog box with User82 (PRO1\User82) listed in the Permissions Entries text box.

9. Ensure User82 is selected and click Edit.

   Windows XP Professional displays the Permission Entry For Public dialog box with User82 (PRO1\User82) displayed in the Name text box.

10. In the Allow column, click Full Control.

    All the check boxes under Allow are now selected.

11. Click OK to close the Permission Entry For Public dialog box.

    Windows XP Professional displays the Advanced Security Settings For Public dialog box.

12. Click OK to close the Advanced Security Settings For Public dialog box.

13. Click OK to close the Public Properties dialog box.

14. Close Explorer and log off Windows XP Professional.

▶ **To test NTFS permissions for a folder**

1. Log on as User82 and type **password** when prompted for the password.

2. Start Windows Explorer.

3. Expand Local Disk (C:) and then expand the Public folder.

4. Attempt to perform the following tasks on the USER81 text document:

   ▪ Modify the file

   ▪ Delete the file

   Which tasks were you able to record and why?

5. Close Windows Explorer and then log off Windows XP Professional.

Exercise 3: Testing NTFS Permissions

In this exercise, you create a file in a subfolder and test how NTFS permissions are inherited through a folder hierarchy.

▶ **To test permissions for the Library folder**

1. Log on as User81, and then start Windows Explorer.

2. In Windows Explorer, expand the Public\Library folder.

3. Create a text document USER81 in the Library folder.

4. Log off Windows XP Professional.

▶ **To test permissions for the Library folder while logged on as User82**

1. Log on as User82, and then start Windows Explorer.

2. Expand the Public\Library folder.

3. Attempt to perform the following tasks on USER81:

   ▪ Open the file

   ▪ Modify the file

   ▪ Delete the file

   Which tasks were you able to record and why?

4. Log off Windows XP Professional.

Lesson Review

The following questions will help you determine whether you have learned enough to move on to the next lesson. If you have difficulty answering these questions, review the material in this lesson before beginning the next lesson. The answers are in Appendix A, "Questions and Answers."

1. By default, when you format a volume with NTFS, the _____ permission is assigned to the Everyone group.

2. When you assign permissions for public data folders, it is recommended that you assign the _____ permission and the _____ permission to the Users group and the _____ permission to the CREATOR OWNER user.

3. Which of the following users can assign permissions to user accounts and groups? (Choose all answers that are correct.)

   a. Administrators

   b. Power users

   c. Users with the Full Control permission

   d. Owners of files and folders

4. Which of the following tabs in the Properties dialog box for the file or folder do you use to assign or modify NTFS permissions for a file or a folder?

   a. Advanced

   b. Permissions

   c. Security

   d. General

5. What is the purpose of the Traverse Folder/Execute File special permission?

6. What is the difference between the Delete permission and Delete Subfolder and Files permission?

Lesson Summary

- By default, when you format a volume with NTFS, the Full Control permission is assigned to the Everyone group.

- To assign or modify NTFS permissions for a file or a folder, you use the Security tab of the Properties dialog box for the file or folder.

- By default, subfolders and files inherit permissions that you assign to their parent folder.

- To stop subfolders and files from inheriting permissions that you assign to their parent folder, clear the Inherit From Parent The Permission Entries That Apply To Child Objects check box in the Advanced Security Settings dialog box.

- The current owner or any user with Full Control permission can assign the Full Control standard permission or the Take Ownership special access permission to another user account or group, allowing the user account or a member of the group to take ownership.

- You cannot assign anyone ownership of a file or folder.

Lesson 3: Solving Permissions Problems

When you assign or modify NTFS permissions to files and folders, problems might arise. When you copy or move files and folders, the permissions you set on the files or folders might change. Specific rules control how and when permissions change. Understanding these rules helps you solve permissions problems. Troubleshooting these problems is important to keep resources available for the appropriate users and protected from unauthorized users.

After this lesson, you will be able to

- Describe the effect on NTFS file and folder permissions when files and folders are copied
- Describe the effect on NTFS file and folder permissions when files and folders are moved
- Troubleshoot resource access problems

Estimated lesson time: 50 minutes

Copying Files and Folders

When you copy files or folders from one folder to another or from one volume to another, permissions change, as shown in Figure 8.7.

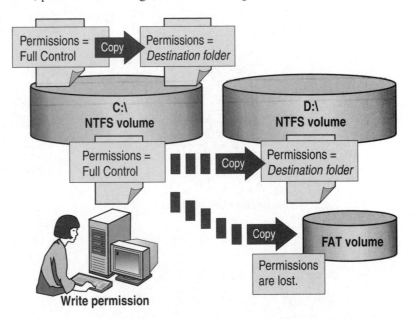

Figure 8.7   Copying files or folders between folders or volumes

When you copy a file within a single NTFS volume or between NTFS volumes, note the following:

- Windows XP Professional treats it as a new file. As a new file, it takes on the permissions of the destination folder.
- You must have Write permission for the destination folder to copy files and folders.
- You become the creator and owner.

Note   When you copy files or folders to FAT volumes, the folders and files lose their NTFS permissions because FAT volumes don't support NTFS permissions.

Moving Files and Folders

When you move a file or folder, permissions might or might not change, depending on where you move the file or folder (see Figure 8.8).

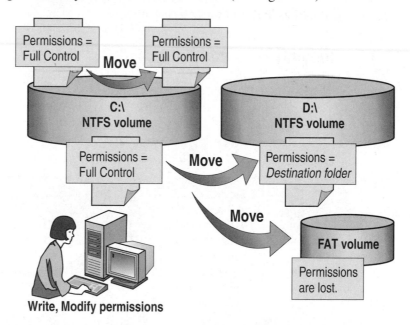

Figure 8.8   Moving files or folders between folders or volumes

Moving Within a Single NTFS Volume

When you move a file or folder within a single NTFS volume, note the following:

- The file or folder retains the original permissions.
- You must have the Write permission for the destination folder to move files and folders into it.

- You must have the Modify permission for the source file or folder. The Modify permission is required to move a file or folder because Windows XP Professional deletes the file or folder from the source folder after it is copied to the destination folder.

Moving Between NTFS Volumes

When you move a file or folder between NTFS volumes, note the following:

- The file or folder inherits the permissions of the destination folder.

- You must have the Write permission for the destination folder to move files and folders into it.

- You must have the Modify permission for the source file or folder. The Modify permission is required to move a file or folder because Windows XP Professional deletes the file or folder from the source folder after it is copied to the destination folder.

- You become the creator and owner.

Note When you move files or folders to FAT volumes, the folders and files lose their NTFS permissions because FAT volumes don't support NTFS permissions.

Troubleshooting Permissions Problems

Table 8.7 describes some common permissions problems that you might encounter and provides solutions that you can use to try to resolve these problems.

Table 8.7   Permissions Problems and Troubleshooting Solutions

Problem	Solution
A user can't gain access to a file or folder.	If the file or folder was copied or moved to another NTFS volume, the permissions might have changed.
	Check the permissions that are assigned to the user account and to groups to which the user belongs. The user might not have permission or might be denied access either individually or as a member of a group.
You add a user account to a group to give that user access to a file or folder, but the user still can't gain access.	For access permissions to be updated to include the new group to which you have added the user account, the user must either log off and then log on again or close all network connections to the computer on which the file or folder resides and then make new connections.

(continued)

Table 8.7   *(continued)*

Problem	Solution
A user with Full Control permission to a folder deletes a file in the folder, although that user doesn't have permission to delete the file itself. You want to stop the user from being able to delete more files.	You have to clear the special access permission, the Delete Subfolders And Files check box, for that folder to prevent users with Full Control of the folder from being able to delete files in it.

Note   Windows XP Professional supports Portable Operating System Interface for UNIX (POSIX) applications that are designed to run on UNIX. On UNIX systems, Full Control permission allows you to delete files in a folder. In Windows XP Professional, the Full Control permission includes the Delete Subfolders and Files special access permission, allowing you the same ability to delete files in that folder regardless of the permissions that you have for those files.

Avoiding Permissions Problems

The following list provides best practices for implementing NTFS permissions. These guidelines will help you avoid permission problems.

- Assign the most restrictive NTFS permissions that still enable users and groups to accomplish necessary tasks.

- Assign all permissions at the folder level, not at the file level. Group files in a separate folder for which you want to restrict user access, and then assign restricted access to that folder.

- For all application-executable files, assign Read & Execute and Change Permissions to the Administrators group, and assign Read & Execute to the Users group. Damage to application files is usually a result of accidents and viruses. By assigning Read & Execute to Users and Read & Execute and Change Permissions to Administrators, you can prevent users or viruses from modifying or deleting executable files. To update files, members of the Administrators group can assign Full Control to their user account to make changes and then reassign Read & Execute and Change Permissions.

- Assign Full Control to CREATOR OWNER for public data folders so that users can delete and modify files and folders that they create. Doing so gives the user who creates the file or folder full access to only the files or folders that he or she creates in the public data folder.

- For public folders, assign Full Control to CREATOR OWNER and Read and Write to the Everyone group. This gives users full access to the files that they

- Use long, descriptive names if the resource will be accessed only at the computer. If a folder will eventually be shared, use folder names and filenames that are accessible by all client computers.

- Allow permissions rather than denying permissions. If you don't want a user or group to access a particular folder or file, don't assign permissions. Denying permissions should be an exception, not a common practice.

Practice: Managing NTFS Permissions

In this practice, you will observe the effects of taking ownership of a file. Then you will determine the effects of permission and ownership when you copy or move files. Finally, you will determine what happens when a user with Full Control permission to a folder has been denied all access to a file in that folder but attempts to delete the file.

To successfully complete this practice, you must have completed "Practice: Planning and Assigning NTFS Permissions" in Lesson 2 of this chapter.

Exercise 1: Taking Ownership of a File

In this exercise, you observe the effects of taking ownership of a file. To do this, you must determine permissions for a file, assign the Take Ownership permission to a user account, and then take ownership as that user.

▶   **To determine the permissions for a file**

1. Log on as Fred or with a user account that is a member of the Administrators group, and then start Windows Explorer.

2. In the Public folder, create a text document named OWNER.

3. Right-click OWNER, and then click Properties.

   Microsoft Windows XP Professional displays the Owner Properties dialog box with the General tab active.

4. Click the Security tab to display the permissions for the OWNER file.

5. Click Advanced.

   Windows XP Professional displays the Advanced Security Settings For Owner dialog box with the Permissions tab active.

6. Click the Owner tab.

   Who is the current owner of the OWNER file?

▶   **To assign permission to a user to take ownership**

1. In the Advanced Security Settings For Owner dialog box, click the Permissions tab.

2. Click Add.

   Windows XP Professional displays the Select User Or Group dialog box.

3. In the From This Location text box at the top of the dialog box, ensure that your computer (PRO1) is selected.

4. In the Enter The Object Names To Select text box, type **User81**, and then click Check Name.

   PRO1\User81 should now appear in the Enter The Object Names To Select text box indicating that Windows XP Professional located User81 on PRO1 and it is a valid user account.

5. Click OK.

   Windows XP Professional displays the Permission Entry For Owner dialog box. Notice that all of the permission entries for User81 are blank.

6. Under Permissions, select the Allow check box next to Take Ownership.

7. Click OK.

   Windows XP Professional displays the Advanced Security Settings For Owner dialog box with the Permissions tab selected.

8. Click OK to return to the Owner Properties dialog box.

9. Click OK to apply your changes and close the Owner Properties dialog box.

10. Close Windows Explorer, and then log off Windows XP Professional.

▶ **To take ownership of a file**

1. Log on as User81, and then start Windows Explorer.

2. Expand the Public folder.

3. Right-click OWNER and then click Properties.

   Windows XP Professional displays the Owner Properties dialog box with the General tab active.

4. Click the Security tab to display the permissions for OWNER.

   Windows XP Professional displays the Owner Properties dialog box with the Security tab active.

5. Click Advanced to display the Advanced Security Settings For Owner dialog box, and then click the Owner tab.

6. Under Change Owner To, select User81, and then click Apply.

   Who is now the owner of the OWNER file?

7. Click OK to close the Advanced Security Settings For Owner dialog box.

8. Click OK to close the Owner Properties dialog box.

▶ **To test permissions for a file as the owner**

1. While you are logged on as User81, assign User81 the Full Control permission for the OWNER text document and click Apply.

2. Click Advanced and clear the Inherit From Parent The Permission Entries That Apply To Child Objects check box.

3. In the Security dialog box, click Remove.

4. Click OK to close the Advanced Security Settings For Owner dialog box.

5. Click OK to close the Owner Properties dialog box.

6. Delete the OWNER text document.

Exercise 2: Copying and Moving Folders

In this exercise, you see the effects of permissions and ownership when you copy and move folders.

▶ **To create a folder while logged on as a user**

1. While you are logged on as User81, in Windows Explorer, in the root folder of drive C, create a folder named Temp1.

   What are the permissions that are assigned to the folder?

User or group	Permissions

   Who is the owner? Why?

2. Close all applications, and then log off Windows XP Professional.

▶ **To create a folder while logged on as a member of the Administrators group**

1. Log on as Administrator, or as a user account that is a member of the Administrators group, and then start Windows Explorer.

2. In the root folder of drive C, create the folders Temp2 and Temp3.

What are the permissions for the Temp2 and Temp3 folders that you just created?

User or group	Permissions

Who is the owner of the Temp2 and Temp3 folders? Why?

3. Assign the following permissions to the Temp2 and Temp3 folders. Clear the Inherit From Parent The Permission Entries That Apply To Child Objects check box. When prompted, click Remove to remove all permissions except those explicitly set.

Folder	Assign these permissions
Temp2	Administrators: Full Control Users: Read & Execute
Temp3	Administrators: Full Control Backup Operators: Read & Execute Users: Full Control

▶ **To copy a folder to another folder within a Windows XP Professional NTFS volume**

1. While logged on with an account that is a member of the Administrators group, in Windows Explorer, copy C:\Temp2 to C:\Temp1 by selecting C:\Temp2, holding down Ctrl, and then dragging C:\Temp2 to C:\Temp1.

Because this is a copy, C:\Temp2 and C:\Temp1\Temp2 should both exist.

2. Select C:\Temp1\Temp2, and then compare the permissions and ownership with C:\Temp2.

Who is the owner of C:\Temp1\Temp2 and what are the permissions? Why?

▶ **To move a folder within the same NTFS volume**

1. Log on as User81.

2. In Windows Explorer, select C:\Temp3, and then move it to C:\Temp1.

   What happens to the permissions and ownership for C:\Temp1\Temp3? Why?

3. Close all windows and log off.

Exercise 3: Deleting a File with All Permissions Denied

In this exercise, you use the Temp3 folder for which the Users group has been given Full Control permission. You create a file in the Temp3 folder but deny all permissions to that file. You then observe what happens when a user attempts to delete that file.

▶ **To create a file and deny access to it**

1. Log on with a user account that is a member of the Administrators group.

2. In the C:\Temp1\Temp3 folder, create a text document named NOACCESS.

3. Deny the Users group the Full Control permission for the NOACCESS text document.

   Windows XP Professional displays a Security dialog box with the following message:

   ```
   You are setting a deny permissions entry. Deny entries take
   precedence over allow entries. This means that if a user is a member
   of two groups, one that is allowed a permission, and another that is
   denied the same permission, the user is denied that permission. Do
   you want to continue?
   ```

4. Click Yes to apply your changes and close the Security dialog box.

5. Click OK to close the NoAccess Properties dialog box.

▶ **To view the result of the Full Control permission being denied for a folder**

1. In Windows Explorer, double-click the NOACCESS text document in the Temp3 folder to open it.

   Were you successful? Why or why not?

2. Click Start and then click Run.

   Windows XP Professional displays the Run dialog box.

3. Type **cmd** in the Open text box and click OK.

4. Change to C:\Temp1\Temp3.

5. Type **Del NOACCESS.TXT** and press ENTER.

Were you successful? Why or why not?

How would you prevent users with Full Control permission for a folder from deleting a file in that folder for which they have been denied the Full Control permission?

Lesson Review

The following questions will help you determine whether you have learned enough to move on to the next lesson. If you have difficulty answering these questions, review the material in this lesson before beginning the next chapter. The answers are in Appendix A, "Questions and Answers."

1. Which of the following statements about copying a file or folder are correct? (Choose all answers that are correct.)

    a. When you copy a file from one folder to another folder on the same volume, the permissions on the file do not change.

    b. When you copy a file from a folder on an NTFS volume to a folder on a FAT volume, the permissions on the file do not change.

    c. When you copy a file from a folder on an NTFS volume to a folder on another NTFS volume, the permissions on the file match those of the destination folder.

    d. When you copy a file from a folder on an NTFS volume to a folder on a FAT volume, the permissions are lost.

2. Which of the following statements about moving a file or folder are correct? (Choose all answers that are correct.)

    a. When you move a file from one folder to another folder on the same volume, the permissions on the file do not change.

    b. When you move a file from a folder on an NTFS volume to a folder on a FAT volume, the permissions on the file do not change.

    c. When you move a file from a folder on an NTFS volume to a folder on another NTFS volume, the permissions on the file match those of the destination folder.

    d. When you move a file from a folder on an NTFS volume to a folder on the same volume, the permissions on the file match those of the destination folder.

3. When you assign NTFS permissions you should assign the
_____ (least/most) restrictive permissions.

4. If you don't want a user or group to gain access to a particular folder or file, should you deny access permissions to that folder or file?

Lesson Summary

- When you copy or move files and folders, the permissions you set on the files or folders might change.

- When you copy files or folders from one folder to another or from one volume to another, Windows XP Professional treats the copied file or folder as a new file or folder. Therefore, it takes on the permissions of the destination folder.

- You must have Write permission for the destination folder to copy files and folders.

- When you copy a file, you become the creator and owner of the file.

- When you move a file or folder within a single NTFS volume, the file or folder retains its original permissions.

- When you move a file or folder between NTFS volumes, the file or folder inherits the permissions of the destination folder.

- You should assign the most restrictive NTFS permissions that still enable users and groups to accomplish necessary tasks.

- You should assign permissions at the folder level, not the file level.

- You should assign Full Control to CREATOR OWNER for public folders and Read and Write to the Everyone group.

- Allow permissions rather than deny permissions.

C H A P T E R   9

Administering Shared Folders

About This Chapter

In Chapter 8, "Securing Resources with NTFS Permissions," you learned about NT file system (NTFS) permissions for Microsoft Windows XP Professional. You use NTFS permissions to specify which users and groups can access files and folders and what these permissions allow users to do with the contents of the file or folder. NTFS permissions are available only on NTFS volumes. NTFS security is effective whether a user gains access to the file or folder at the local computer or over the network.

In this chapter, you will learn how to make folders accessible over the network. You can access a computer's folders and their contents only by physically sitting at the computer and logging on to it or by accessing a shared folder on a remote computer. Sharing folders is the only way to make folders and their contents available over the network. Shared folders also provide another way to secure file resources, one that can be used on file allocation table (FAT) or FAT32 partitions. In this chapter, you will also learn how to share file resources, secure them with permissions, and provide access to them.

Before You Begin

To complete this chapter, you must have

- A computer that meets the minimum hardware requirements listed in the preface, "About This Book"
- Microsoft Windows XP Professional installed on the computer

Lesson 1: Understanding Shared Folders

You use *shared folders* to provide network users with access to file resources. When a folder is shared, users can connect to the folder over the network and access the files it contains. However, to access the files, users must have permissions to access the shared folders.

After this lesson, you will be able to

- Use shared folders to provide access to network resources
- Describe how permissions affect access to shared folders

Estimated lesson time: 30 minutes

Shared Folder Permissions

A shared folder can contain applications, data, or a user's personal data, called a *home folder*. Each type of data requires different shared folder permissions.

The following are characteristics of shared folder permissions:

- Shared folder permissions apply to folders, not individual files. Because you can apply shared folder permissions only to the entire shared folder and not to individual files or subfolders in the shared folder, they provide less detailed security than NTFS permissions.

- Shared folder permissions don't restrict access to users who gain access to the folder at the computer where the folder is stored. They apply only to users who connect to the folder over the network.

- Shared folder permissions are the only way to secure network resources on a FAT volume. NTFS permissions aren't available on FAT volumes.

- The default shared folder permission is Read, and it is assigned to the Everyone group when you share the folder.

Note A shared folder appears in Windows Explorer as an icon of a hand, shown in Figure 9.1, holding the shared folder.

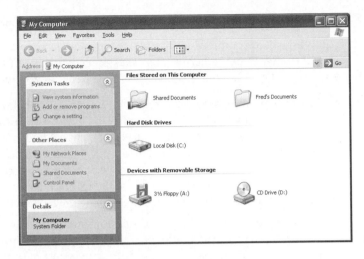

Figure 9.1   Shared folders in Windows Explorer

To control how users gain access to a shared folder, you assign shared folder permissions. Table 9.1 explains what each of the shared folder permissions allows a user to do, presented from most restrictive to least restrictive.

Table 9.1   Shared Folder Permissions

Shared folder permission	Allows the user to
Read	Display folder names, filenames, file data, and attributes; run program files; and change folders within the shared folder
Change	Create folders, add files to folders, change data in files, append data to files, change file attributes, delete folders and files; also allows the user to perform actions permitted by the Read permission
Full Control	Change file permissions, take ownership of files, and perform all tasks permitted by the Change permission

You can allow or deny shared folder permissions. Generally, it is best to allow permissions and to assign permissions to a group rather than to individual users. Deny permissions only when it is necessary to override permissions that are otherwise applied, for example, when it is necessary to deny permission to a specific user who belongs to a group to which you have given the permission. If you deny a shared folder permission to a user, the user won't have that permission. For example, to deny all access to a shared folder, deny the Full Control permission.

How Shared Folder Permissions Are Applied

Applying shared permissions to user accounts and groups affects access to a shared folder. Denying permission takes precedence over the permissions that you allow. The following list describes the effects of applying permissions:

- **Multiple permissions.**   A user can be a member of multiple groups, each with different permissions that provide different levels of access to a shared folder. When you assign permission to a user for a shared folder and that user is a member of a group to which you assigned a different permission, the user's effective permissions are the combination of the user and group permissions. For example, if a user has Read permission and is a member of a group with Change permission, the user's effective permission is Change, which includes Read.

- **Deny permissions.**   Denied permissions take precedence over any permissions that you otherwise allow for user accounts and groups. If you deny a shared folder permission to a user, the user won't have that permission, even if you allow the permission for a group of which the user is a member.

- **NTFS permissions.**   Shared folder permissions are sufficient to gain access to files and folders on a FAT volume but not on an NTFS volume. On a FAT volume, users can gain access to a shared folder for which they have permissions, as well as all of the folder's contents. When users gain access to a shared folder on an NTFS volume, they need the shared folder permission and also the appropriate NTFS permissions for each file and folder to which they gain access. A user's effective permission for a shared folder on a NTFS volume is the more restrictive of the shared and NTFS permissions.

Note   When you copy a shared folder, the original folder is still shared, but the copy is not. When you rename or move a shared folder, it is no longer shared.

Guidelines for Shared Folder Permissions

The following list provides some general guidelines for managing your shared folders and assigning shared folder permissions:

- Determine which groups need access to each resource and the level of access that they require. Document the groups and their permissions for each resource.

- Assign permissions to groups instead of user accounts to simplify access administration.

- Assign to a resource the most restrictive permissions that still allow users to perform required tasks. For example, if users only need to read information in a folder and they will never delete or create files, assign the Read permission.

- Organize resources so that folders with the same security requirements are located within a folder. For example, if users require Read permission for several application folders, store those folders within the same folder. Then share this folder instead of sharing each individual application folder.

- Use intuitive share names so that users can easily recognize and locate resources. For example, for the Application folder, use Apps for the share name. You should also use share names that all client operating systems can use.

Table 9.2 describes share and folder naming conventions for different client computer operating systems.

Table 9.2   Client Computer Operating Systems and Share Name Length

Operating system	Share name length
Windows XP and Microsoft Windows 2000	80 characters
Microsoft Windows NT, Microsoft Windows 98, and Microsoft Windows 95	12 characters
MS-DOS, Microsoft Windows 3.*x*, and Microsoft Windows for Workgroups	8.3 characters

Microsoft Windows XP Professional provides 8.3-character equivalent names, but the resulting names might not be intuitive to users. For example, a Windows XP Professional folder named Accountants Database would appear as Account~1 on client computers running MS-DOS, Windows 3.*x*, and Windows for Workgroups.

Practice: Applied Permissions

In the following practice, User101 has been assigned permissions to access resources as an individual and as a member of a group, as shown in Figure 9.2.

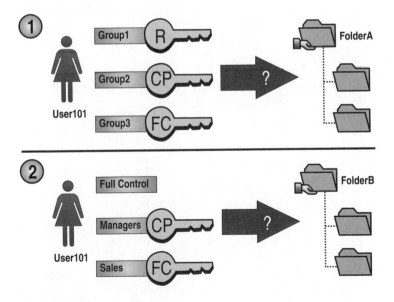

Figure 9.2   Applied permissions

Determine which effective permissions are assigned for User101 and User2.

1. User101 is a member of Group1, Group2, and Group3. Group1 has Read permission. Group2 has Full Control permission for FolderA, and Group3 has change permissions assigned for FolderA. What are User101's effective permissions for FolderA?

2. User102 has been granted the Full Control shared folder permission for FolderB as an individual user. User102 is a member of the Managers group, which has been granted Change permission for FolderB, and a member of the Sales group, which has been denied all access to FolderB. What are User102's effective permissions for FolderB?

Lesson Review

The following questions will help you determine whether you have learned enough to move on to the next lesson. If you have difficulty answering these questions, review the material in this lesson before beginning the next lesson. The answers are in Appendix A, "Questions and Answers."

1. Because you use NTFS permissions to specify which users and groups can access files and folders and what these permissions allow users to do with the contents of the file or folder, why do you need to share a folder or use shared folder permissions?

2. Which of the following permissions are shared folder permissions? (Choose all answers that are correct.)

   a. Read

   b. Write

   c. Modify

   d. Full Control

3. _____ (Denied /Allowed) permissions take precedence over _____ (denied /allowed) permissions on a shared folder.

4. When you copy a shared folder, the original folder is _____ (no longer shared /still shared) and the copy is _____ (not shared /shared).

5. When you move a shared folder, the folder is _____ (no longer shared /still shared).

6. When you rename a shared folder, the folder is _____ (no longer shared /still shared).

Lesson Summary

- You can make a folder and its contents available to other users over the network by sharing the folder.

- Using shared folder permissions is the only way to secure file resources on FAT volumes.

- Shared folder permissions apply to folders, not individual files.

- Shared folder permissions don't restrict access to users who gain access to the folder at the computer where the folder is stored. Shared folder permissions apply only to users who connect to the folder over the network.

- The three shared folder permissions are Read, Change, and Full Control.

- The default shared folder permission is Full Control, and it is assigned to the Everyone group when you share the folder.

Lesson 2: Planning, Sharing, and Connecting to Shared Folders

When you plan shared folders, you can reduce administrative overhead and ease user access by organizing resources that will be shared and putting them into folders according to common access requirements. You can also determine which resources you want shared, organize resources according to function and use, and decide how you will administer the resources.

Shared folders can contain applications and data. Use shared application folders to centralize administration and provide a central location for users to store and access common files. If all data files are centralized in one shared folder, users can find them easily. You will be able to back up data folders more easily if they are centralized, and you will be able to upgrade application software more easily if applications are centralized.

You can share resources with others by sharing folders containing those resources. To share a folder, you must be a member of one of several groups, depending on the role of the computer where the shared folder resides. When you share a folder, you can control access to the folder by limiting the number of users who can simultaneously gain access to it, and you can also control access to the folder and its contents by assigning permissions to selected users and groups. Once you have shared a folder, users must connect to the shared folder and must have the appropriate permissions to access it. After you have shared a folder, you might want to modify it. You can stop sharing it, change its share name, and change user and group permissions to gain access to it.

After this lesson, you will be able to

- Plan which shared folder permissions to assign to user accounts and groups for application and data folders
- Create and modify shared folders
- Make a connection to a shared folder

Estimated lesson time: 30 minutes

Shared Application Folders

Shared application folders are used for applications that are installed on a network server and can be used from client computers. The main advantage of shared applications is that you don't need to install and maintain most components of the applications on each computer. Although program files for applications can be stored on a server, configuration information for most network applications is often stored on each client computer. The exact way in which you share application folders will vary depending on the application and your particular network environment and company organization.

When you share application folders, consider the following points:

- Create one shared folder for applications and organize all of your applications under this folder. This designates one location for installing and upgrading software.

- Assign the Administrators group the Full Control permission for the applications folder so that members of this group can manage the application software and control user permissions.

- Remove the Full Control permission from the Everyone group and assign Read permission to the Users group.

- Assign the Change permission to groups that are responsible for upgrading and troubleshooting applications.

- Create a separate shared folder outside your application folder hierarchy for any application for which you need to assign different permissions. Then assign the appropriate permissions to that folder.

Shared Data Folders

Users on a network use data folders to exchange public and working data. Working data folders are used by members of a team who need access to shared files. Public data folders are used by larger groups of users who all need access to common data.

Create and share common data folders on a separate volume from the operating system and applications. Data files should be backed up frequently, and keeping data folders on a separate volume makes this convenient. If the operating system requires reinstallation, the volume containing the data folder remains intact.

Public Data

When you share a common public data folder, do the following:

- Use centralized data folders so that data can be easily backed up.

- Assign the Change permission to the Users group for the common data folder (see Figure 9.3). This provides users with a central, publicly accessible location for storing data files that they want to share with other users. Users will be able to access the folder and read, create, or change files in it.

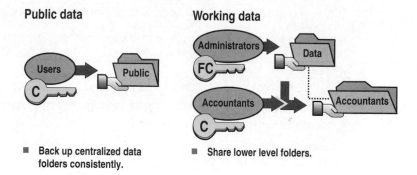

Figure 9.3   Public data and working data shared folders

Working Data

When you share a working data folder, do the following:

- Assign the Full Control permission to the Administrators group for a central data folder so that administrators can perform maintenance.
- Share lower level data folders below the central folder with the Change permission for the appropriate groups when you need to restrict access to those folders.

For an example, see Figure 9.3. To protect data in the Accountants folder, which is a subfolder of the Data folder, share the Accountants folder and assign the Change permission to the Accountants group so that only members of that group can access the Accountants folder.

Requirements for Sharing Folders

In Windows XP Professional, members of the built-in Administrators and Power Users groups are able to share folders. Which groups can share folders and on which machines they can share them depends on whether it is a workgroup or a domain and the type of computer on which the shared folders reside, as follows:

- In a Windows 2000 domain, the Domain Admins group can share folders residing on any machines in the domain. The Power Users group is a local group that can share folders residing only on the stand-alone server or computer running Windows XP Professional where the group is located.
- In a Windows workgroup, the Administrators and Power Users groups can share folders on the Windows 2000 stand-alone server or the computer running Windows XP Professional on which the group exists.

Tip   If the folder to be shared resides on an NTFS volume, users must also have at least the Read permission for that folder to be able to share it.

Administrative Shared Folders

Windows XP Professional automatically shares folders for administrative purposes. These shares are marked with a dollar sign ($), which hides them from users who browse the computer. The root of each volume, the system root folder, and the location of the printer drivers are hidden shared folders that you can access across the network.

Table 9.3 describes the purpose of the administrative shared folders that Windows XP Professional automatically provides.

Table 9.3   Windows XP Professional Administrative Shared Folders

Share	Purpose
C$, D$, E$, and so on	The root of each volume on a hard disk is automatically shared, and the share name is the drive letter with a dollar sign ($). When you connect to this folder, you have access to the entire volume. You use the administrative shares to remotely connect to the computer to perform administrative tasks. Windows XP Professional assigns the Full Control permission to the Administrators group.
Admin$	The system root folder, which is C:\Windows by default, is shared as Admin$. Administrators can access this shared folder to administer Windows XP Professional without knowing in which folder it is installed. Only members of the Administrators group have access to this share. Windows XP Professional assigns the Full Control permission to the Administrators group.
Print$	When you install the first shared printer, the *%systemroot%*System32\Spool\Drivers folder is shared as Print$. This folder provides access to printer driver files for clients. Only members of the Administrators and Power Users groups have the Full Control permission. The Everyone group has the Read permission.

Hidden shared folders aren't limited to those that the system automatically creates. You can share additional folders and add a dollar sign to the end of the share name. Only users who know the folder name can access it if they also possess the proper permissions.

Sharing a Folder

When you share a folder, you can give it a share name, provide comments to describe the folder and its content, control the number of users who have access to the folder, assign permissions, and share the same folder multiple times.

You can share a folder as follows:

1. Log on with a user account that is a member of a group that is able to share folders.

2. Right-click the folder that you want to share, and then click Properties.

3. In the Sharing tab of the Properties dialog box, click Share This Folder and configure the options shown in Figure 9.4 and described in Table 9.4.

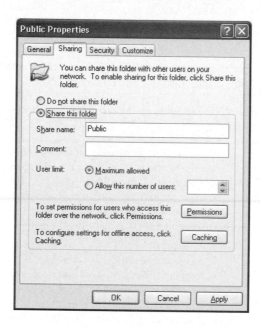

Figure 9.4   The Sharing tab of a folder's Properties dialog box

Table 9.4   Sharing Tab Options

Option	Description
Share Name	The name that users from remote locations use to connect to the shared folder. You must enter a share name. By default this is the same name as the folder. You can type in a different name up to 80 characters long.
Comment	An optional description for the share name. The comment appears in addition to the share name when users at client computers browse the server for shared folders. This comment can be used to identify contents of the shared folder.
User Limit	The number of users who can concurrently connect to the shared folder. If you click Maximum Allowed as the user limit, Windows XP Professional supports up to 10 connections. Windows 2000 Server can support an unlimited number of connections, but the number of client access licenses (CALs) that you purchase limits the connections.

Table 9.4   *(continued)*

Option	Description
Permissions	The shared folder permissions that apply only when the folder is accessed over the network. By default, the Everyone group is assigned Full Control for all new shared folders.
Caching	The settings to configure offline access to this shared folder.
New Share	The settings to configure more than one share name and set of permissions for this folder. This option appears only when the folder has already been shared.

Assigning Shared Folder Permissions

After you share a folder, the next step is to specify which users have access to the shared folder by assigning shared folder permissions to selected user accounts and groups. You can assign permissions to user accounts and groups for a shared folder as follows:

1. In the Sharing tab of the Properties dialog box of the shared folder, click Permissions.

2. In the Permissions dialog box, ensure that the Everyone group is selected and then click Remove.

3. In the Permissions dialog box, click Add.

4. In the Select Users Or Groups dialog box (see Figure 9.5), in the Enter The Object Names To Select text box, type the name of the user or group to which you want to assign permissions. Repeat this step for all user accounts and groups to which you want to assign permissions.

Tip   If you want to enter more than one user account or group at a time, separate the names by a semicolon. If you want to ensure the names are correct, click Check Names.

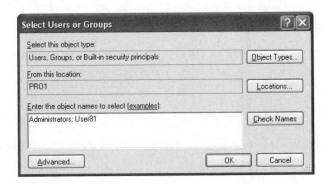

Figure 9.5   The Select Users Or Groups dialog box

5. Click OK.

6. In the Permissions dialog box for the shared folder, click the user account or group, and then, under Permissions, select the Allow check box or the Deny check box for the appropriate permissions for the user account or group.

Caching

To make shared folders available offline, copies of the files are stored in a reserved portion of disk space on your computer called a *cache*. Because the cache is on your hard disk, the computer can access it regardless of whether it is connected to the network. By default, the cache size is set to 10 percent of the available disk space. You can change the size of the cache in the Folder Options dialog box using the Offline Files tab. You can also see how much space the cache is using by opening the Offline Files folder and clicking Properties on the File menu.

Note   For more information about the cache, including how to change the cache size, see Chapter 15, "Monitoring, Managing, and Maintaining Network Resources."

When you share a folder, you can allow others to make the shared folder available offline by clicking Caching in the folder's Properties dialog box. In the Caching Settings dialog box (see Figure 9.6), use the Allow Caching Of Files In This Shared Folder check box to turn caching on and off.

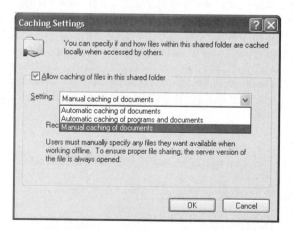

Figure 9.6   The Caching Settings dialog box

The Caching Settings dialog box contains three caching options:

- **Manual Caching Of Documents.**   Users must manually specify all files they want available when working offline. This caching option, the default, is recommended for a shared network folder containing files that are to be accessed and modified by several people. To ensure proper file sharing, the network version of the file is always opened.

- **Automatic Caching Of Documents.**   This option makes every file that a user opens from your shared folder available to that person offline. Files that aren't opened are not available offline. Each time a file is opened, the older copy of the file is automatically deleted. To ensure proper file sharing, the network version of the file is always opened.

- **Automatic Caching Of Programs And Documents.**   This option provides offline access to shared folders containing files that are read, referenced, or run, but that are not changed in the process. This setting reduces network traffic because offline files are opened directly without accessing the network versions in any way, and generally they start and run faster than the network versions. This option is recommended for folders containing read-only data or applications that are run from the network.

Creating Multiple Share Names

You might want to set different permissions on a shared folder. You can create multiple share names for the same folder and assign each a different one. To share a folder with multiple share names, click New Share in the folder's Properties dialog box. In the New Share dialog box (see Figure 9.7) you can assign a new share name, limit the number of connections to the share, and click Permissions to set the permissions for the shared folder.

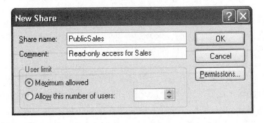

Figure 9.7   The New Share dialog box

Modifying Shared Folders

You can modify shared folders, stop sharing a folder, modify the share name, and modify shared folder permissions.

You can modify a shared folder as follows:

1. In the Properties dialog box of the shared folder, click the Sharing tab.

2. To complete the appropriate task, use the steps in Table 9.5.

Table 9.5   Steps to Modify a Shared Folder

To	Do this
Stop sharing a folder	Click Do Not Share This Folder.
Modify the share name	Click Do Not Share This Folder to stop sharing the folder and click Apply. Then click Share This Folder and type the new share name in the Share Name text box.
Modify shared folder permissions	Click Permissions. In the Permissions dialog box, click Add to add a user account or group so that you can specify permissions for a specific user or group, or click Remove to remove a user account or group. In the Select Users, Computers, Or Groups dialog box, click the user account or group whose permissions you want to modify and then select Allow or Deny for the appropriate permissions.

Caution   If you stop sharing a folder while a user has a file open, the user might lose data. If you click Do Not Share This Folder and a user has a connection to the shared folder, Windows XP Professional displays a dialog box notifying you of that fact.

Connecting to a Shared Folder

You can access a shared folder on another computer by using My Network Places, My Computer, the Add Network Place Wizard, or the Run command.

To connect to a shared folder using My Network Places, do the following:

1. Click Start.

Note   When you start using My Network Places, Windows XP Professional adds it to your Start menu. If My Network Places is listed on your Start menu, click it and go to step 4.

2. Click Control Panel and then click Network And Internet Connections.
3. In the Network And Internet Connections window, under See Also, click My Network Places.
4. Double-click the share you want to access.

Note   If the share you want to connect to is listed, when you double-click it, you are connected. If the share you want to connect to is not listed, go to step 5.

5. If the share you want to connect to is not listed, click Add A Network Place.
   The Welcome To The Add Network Place Wizard page is displayed.

6. Click Next.

7. In the Where Do You Want To Create This Network Place page, select Choose Another Network Location, and then click Next.

8. In the What Is The Address Of This Network Place page, you can type a Universal Naming Convention (UNC) path to the folder (for example, *computer_name**sharedfolder_name*; see Figure 9.8) and click Next.

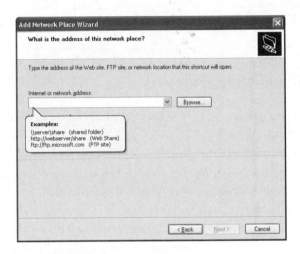

Figure 9.8   The What Is The Address Of This Network Place page

Tip   You can also use the Other Locations On Your Network page to make a network connection shortcut to a Web share (*http://Webserver\share*) or a File Transfer Protocol (FTP) site (*ftp://ftp.microsoft.com*).

To connect to a shared folder using My Computer, you can do the following:

1. Click Start and click My Computer.

2. On the Tools menu, click Map Network Drive.
   Windows XP Professional displays the Map Network Drive dialog box (Figure 9.9), which allows you to assign a drive letter to the connection. By default, the drive letter displayed is Z or the lowest letter of the alphabet that is currently unassigned.

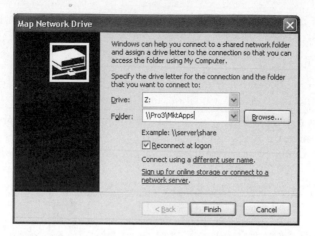

Figure 9.9   The Map Network Drive dialog box

3. In the Folder text box, type **\\server\sharename** or click Browse to browse for a share.

   By default, Reconnect At Logon is selected.

4. Clear the Reconnect At Logon check box unless you want to have Windows XP Professional create a connection to this share each time you log on to your computer.

5. Click Finish to establish the connection.

   On My Computer, under Network Drives, the connection to the shared folder is listed.

You can connect to a shared folder using the Run command, as follows:

1. Click Start, click Run, and then type ***computer_name*** in the Open text box.

   Windows XP Professional displays shared folders for the computer.

2. Double-click the shared folder to which you want to connect.

Lesson Review

The following questions will help you determine whether you have learned enough to move on to the next lesson. If you have difficulty answering these questions, review the material in this lesson before beginning the next lesson. The answers are in Appendix A, "Questions and Answers."

1. What is a shared application folder? What is the main advantage of using shared applications?

2. In a Windows workgroup, the _____ group and the _____ group can share folders on the Windows 2000 stand-alone server or the computer running Windows XP Professional on which the group exists.

3. Windows XP Professional automatically shares folders for administrative purposes. These shares are marked with a _____, which hides them from users who browse the computer.

4. The system root folder, which is C:\Windows by default, is shared as _____. Administrators can access this shared folder to administer Windows XP Professional without knowing in which folder it is installed. Only members of the Administrators group have access to this share. Windows XP Professional assigns the Full Control permission to the Administrators group.

5. To assign permissions to user accounts and groups for a shared folder, which of the following tabs do you use?

    a. The Permissions tab of the Properties dialog box of the shared folder

    b. The Sharing tab of the Properties dialog box of the shared folder

    c. The General tab of the Properties dialog box of the shared folder

    d. The Security tab of the Properties dialog box of the shared folder

6. Which of the following statements about size of the cache for making shared folders available offline is correct?

    a. By default, the cache size is set to 20 percent of the available disk space.

    b. By default, the cache size is set to 15 percent of the available disk space.

    c. By default, the cache size is set to 10 percent of the available disk space.

    d. By default, the cache size is set to 5 percent of the available disk space.

Lesson Summary

- When you use shared application folders, assign the Administrators group the Full Control permission for the applications folder so that members of this group can manage the application software and control user permissions.

- To access a shared folder, users must connect to it and have the appropriate permissions.

- Windows XP Professional automatically shares folders for administrative purposes. These shares are marked with a dollar sign ($), which hides them from users who browse the computer.

- In Windows XP Professional, members of the built-in Administrators and Power Users groups are able to share folders.

- To make shared folders available offline, copies of the files are stored in the cache on your hard disk. By default, the cache size is set to 10 percent of the available disk space.

- You can access a shared folder on another computer by using My Computer, the Add Network Place Wizard, the Run command, or My Network Places.

Lesson 3: Combining Shared Folder Permissions and NTFS Permissions

You share folders to provide network users with access to resources. If you are using a FAT volume, the shared folder permissions are the only resource available to provide security for the folders you have shared and the folders and files they contain. If you are using an NTFS volume, you can assign NTFS permissions to individual users and groups to better control access to the files and subfolders in the shared folders. When you combine shared folder permissions and NTFS permissions, the more restrictive permission is always the overriding permission.

After this lesson, you will be able to

- Combine shared folder permissions and NTFS permissions

Estimated lesson time: 45 minutes

Strategies for Combining Shared Folder Permissions and NTFS Permissions

One strategy for providing access to resources on an NTFS volume is to share folders with the default shared folder permissions and then control access by assigning NTFS permissions. When you share a folder on an NTFS volume, both shared folder permissions and NTFS permissions combine to secure file resources.

Shared folder permissions provide limited security for resources. You gain the greatest flexibility by using NTFS permissions to control access to shared folders. Also, NTFS permissions apply whether the resource is accessed locally or over the network.

When you use shared folder permissions on an NTFS volume, the following rules apply:

- You can apply NTFS permissions to files and subfolders in the shared folder. You can apply different NTFS permissions to each file and subfolder contained in a shared folder.

- In addition to shared folder permissions, users must have NTFS permissions for the files and subfolders contained in shared folders to access those files and subfolders. This is in contrast to FAT volumes, in which permissions for a shared folder are the only permissions protecting files and subfolders in the shared folder.

- When you combine shared folder permissions and NTFS permissions, the more restrictive permission is always the overriding permission.

In Figure 9.10, the Everyone group has the shared folder Full Control permission for the Public folder and the NTFS Read permission for FileA. The Everyone group's effective permission for FileA is the more restrictive Read permission. The effective permission for FileB is Full Control because both the shared folder permission and the NTFS permission allow this level of access.

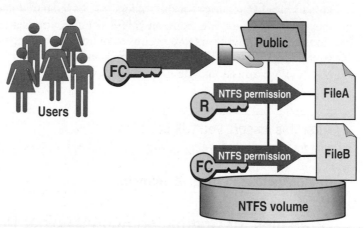

- Apply NTFS permissions to files and subfolders.
- The most restrictive permission is the effective permission.

Figure 9.10   Combining shared folder permissions and NTFS permissions

Practice: Managing Shared Folders

In this practice, you will determine users' effective permissions, plan shared folders, plan permissions, share a folder, assign shared folder permissions, connect to a shared folder, stop sharing a folder, and test the combined effects of shared folder permissions and NTFS permissions.

Important   To complete the optional exercises (5 and 8), you must have two networked computers. One computer must be running Windows XP Professional and the other must be running one of the following Windows products: Windows XP, Windows 2000 Professional, Windows 2000 Server, or Windows 2000 Advanced Server. Both computers must use *password* as the password for the Administrator account.

Exercise 1: Combining Permissions

Figure 9.11 shows examples of shared folders on NTFS volumes. These shared folders contain subfolders that have also been assigned NTFS permissions. Determine a user's effective permissions for each example.

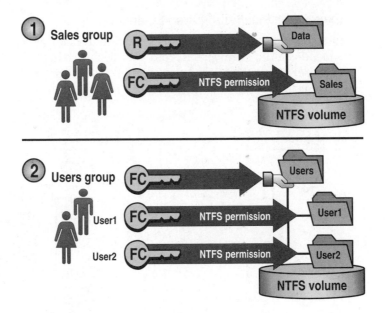

Figure 9.11   Combined permissions

1. In the first example, the Data folder is shared. The Sales group has the shared folder Read permission for the Data folder and the NTFS Full Control permission for the Sales subfolder.

   What are the Sales group's effective permissions for the Sales subfolder when they gain access to the Sales subfolder by making a connection to the Data shared folder?

2. In the second example, the Users folder contains user home folders. Each user home folder contains data accessible only to the user for whom the folder is named. The Users folder has been shared, and the Users group has the shared folder Full Control permission for the Users folder. User1 and User2 have the NTFS Full Control permission for their home folder only and no NTFS permissions for other folders. These users are all members of the Users group.

   What permissions does User1 have when he or she accesses the User1 subfolder by making a connection to the Users shared folder? What are User1's permissions for the User2 subfolder?

Exercise 2: Planning Shared Folders

In this exercise, you plan how to share resources on servers in the main office of a manufacturing company. Record your decisions in the table at the end of this exercise. Figure 9.12 illustrates a partial folder structure for the servers at the manufacturing company.

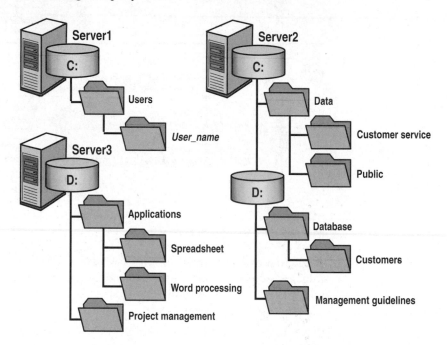

Figure 9.12   A partial folder structure for the servers at a manufacturing company

You need to make resources on these servers available to network users. To do this, determine which folders to share and which permissions to assign to groups, including the appropriate built-in groups. Base your planning decisions on the following criteria:

- Members of the Managers group need to read and revise documents in the Management Guidelines folder. Nobody else should have access to this folder.

- Administrators need complete access to all shared folders, except for Management Guidelines.

- The customer service department needs its own network location to store working files. All customer service representatives are members of the Customer Service group.

- All employees need a network location to share information with each other.

- All employees need to use the spreadsheet, database, and word processing software.

- Only members of the Managers group should have access to the project management software.

- Members of the CustomerDBFull group need to read and update the customer database.

- Members of the CustomerDBRead group need to read only the customer database.

- Each user needs a private network location to store files, which must be accessible only to that user.

- Share names must be accessible from Windows XP Professional, Windows 2000, Windows NT, Windows 98, Windows 95, and non–Windows-NT–based platforms.

Record your answers in this table.

Folder name and location	Shared name	Groups and permissions
Example: Management Guidelines	MgmtGd	Managers: Full Control

Exercise 3: Sharing Folders

In this exercise, you share a folder.

Run the **SharedFolders** file in the Demos folder on the CD-ROM accompanying this book for a demonstration of sharing a folder.

▶ **To share a folder**

1. Log on as Fred or with a user account that is a member of the Administrators group.

2. Start Windows Explorer, create a C:\MktApps folder, right-click MktApps, and then click Properties.

3. In the MktApps Properties dialog box, click the Sharing tab.

   Notice that the folder is currently not shared.

4. Click Share This Folder.

   The Share Name value defaults to the name of the folder. If you want the share name to be different from the folder's name, change it here.

5. In the Comment text box, type **Shared Marketing Applications** and then click OK.

   Windows Explorer changes the appearance of the Apps folder by placing a hand icon under it to indicate that it is a shared folder.

Exercise 4: Assigning Shared Folder Permissions

In this exercise, you determine the current permissions for a shared folder and assign shared folder permissions to groups in your domain.

▶ **To determine the current permissions for the MktApps shared folder**

1. In Windows Explorer, right-click C:\MktApps, and then click Sharing And Security.

   Windows XP Professional displays the MktApps Properties dialog box with the Sharing tab active.

2. Click Permissions.

   Windows XP Professional displays the Permissions For MktApps dialog box.

   The default permission for the MktApps shared folder is for the Everyone group to have Full Control permission.

▶ **To remove permissions for a group**

1. Verify that Everyone is selected.

2. Click Remove.

▶ **To assign permissions to a group**

1. Click Add.

   Windows XP Professional displays the Select Users Or Groups dialog box.

2. In the Name text box, type **administrators** and then click OK.

   Windows XP Professional adds Administrators to the list of names with permissions.

   Which type of access does Windows XP Professional assign to the Administrators group by default?

3. In the Permissions For Administrators dialog box, under Allow, select the Full Control check box.

Why did Windows Explorer also select the Change permission for you?

4. Click Add.

   Windows XP Professional displays the Select Users Or Groups dialog box.

5. In the Name text box, type **users** and then click OK.

   Windows XP Professional adds Users to the list of names with permissions and assigns Read as the default permission.

6. Click OK to close the Permissions For MktApps dialog box.

7. Click OK to close the MktApps Properties dialog box.

8. Close Windows Explorer.

Exercise 5 (Optional): Connecting to a Shared Folder

In this exercise, you use the Run command to connect to a shared folder.

Important   To complete this exercise, you must have two networked computers. One computer must be running Windows XP Professional and the other must be running Windows XP or Windows 2000. Both computers must use *password* as the password for the Administrator account.

▶ **To connect to a network drive using the Run command**

1. Log on as Administrator on your second computer.

2. Click Start and then click Run.

3. In the Open text box, type **\\PRO1.** (If you didn't use PRO1 as the name of your computer, use the appropriate name here and in the following steps.) Click OK.

   Your second computer displays the PRO1 window. Notice that only the folders that are shared appear to network users.

4. Double-click MktApps to confirm that you can gain access to its contents.

   MktApps contains no files or folders for you to access, but the system opens the folder and displays its contents.

5. Close the MktApps On PRO1 window.

Exercise 6: Stopping Folder Sharing

In this exercise, you stop sharing a folder.

▶ **To stop sharing a folder**

1. Log on as Administrator on the PRO1 computer (or the computer running Windows XP Professional with the name you specified), and then start Windows Explorer.

2. Right-click C:\MktApps, and then click Sharing And Security.

3. Click Do Not Share This Folder, and then click OK.

   A Sharing dialog box appears, indicating that a file is still open and asking if you want to continue.

4. Click Yes to continue.

   Windows XP Professional no longer displays the hand icon that identifies a shared folder under the MktApps folder. You might need to refresh the screen; if so, press F5.

5. Close Windows Explorer.

Exercise 7: Assigning NTFS Permissions and Sharing Folders

In this exercise, you assign NTFS permissions to the MktApps, Manuals, and Public folders. Then you will share MktApps.

▶ **To assign NTFS permissions**

1. Open Windows Explorer and create C:\MktApps.

2. In the Security tab of the MktApps Properties dialog box, add the Administrators group and assign it the Full Control NTFS permission.

3. Add the Users group and assign it the Read & Execute NTFS permission.

4. Remove the Everyone group.

Tip   Before you can remove the Everyone group, you must clear the Inherit From Parents The Permission Entries That Apply to Child Objects check box located in the Advanced Security Settings For MktApps dialog box. When prompted, remove the permission entries that were previously applied from the parent.

---

5. Click OK to close the Advanced Security Settings For MktApps dialog box and then click OK to close the MktApps Properties dialog box.

6. Use Windows Explorer to create the C:\MktApps\Manuals folder.

7. Clear the Inherit From Parents The Permission Entries That Apply to Child Objects check box, and when prompted, click Remove to remove the permission entries that were previously applied from the parent.

8. Click Add and add the Administrators group with the Full Control NTFS permission.

9. Click OK to close the Permission Entry For Manual dialog box.

10. Click OK to close the Advanced Security Settings For Manual dialog box.

11. Add the Users group with the Read & Execute NTFS permission.

12. Use Windows Explorer to create the C:\MktApps\Public folder.

13. Clear the Inherit From Parents The Permission Entries That Apply to Child Objects check box and, when prompted, click Remove to remove the permission entries that were previously applied from the parent.

14. Click Add and add the Administrators group with the Full Control NTFS permission.

15. Click OK to close the Permission Entry For Manual dialog box.

16. Click OK to close the Advanced Security Settings For Manual dialog box.

17. Add the Users group with the Read & Execute NTFS permission.

▶ **To share folders and assign shared folder permissions**

Share the MktApps folder and assign permissions to network user accounts based on the information in the following table. Remove all other shared folder permissions.

Path and shared folder name	Group or user account	Shared folder permissions
C:\MktApps shared as MktApps	Administrators	Full Control
	Users	Full Control

Exercise 8 (Optional): Testing NTFS and Shared Folder Permissions

In this exercise, you use different user accounts to test how NTFS permissions and shared folder permissions combine. To answer the questions in this exercise, refer to the tables in Exercise 7.

Important   To complete this exercise, you must have two networked computers. One computer must be running Windows XP Professional and the other must be running Windows XP or Windows 2000. Both computers must use *password* as the password for the Administrator account.

▶ **To test permissions for the Manuals folder when a user logs on locally**

1. Log on as User1 with a password of *password* on the PRO1 computer.

2. In Windows Explorer, expand C:\MktApps\Manuals.

3. In the Manuals folder, attempt to create a test document.

   Were you successful? Why or why not?

4. Close Windows Explorer.

▶ **To test permissions for the Manuals folder when a user makes a connection over the network**

1. Log on as Administrator with a password of *password* on your second computer.

2. Create a user account, User1, with a password of *User1* and clear the User Must Change Password At Next Logon check box, if necessary.

Note   In a workgroup, no centralized database of user accounts exists. Therefore, you must create the same user account with the same password on each computer in the workgroup. This applies to the Administrator account as well.

3. Log off and then log on as User1 at your second computer.

4. Click Start and then click Run.

5. In the Open text box, type **\\PRO1\MktApps** and then click OK.

6. In the MktApps On PRO1 window, double-click Manuals.

7. In the Manuals window, attempt to create a file.

   Were you successful? Why or why not?

8. Close all windows and log off Windows XP Professional.

▶ **To test permissions for the Manuals folder when a user logs on over the network as Administrator**

1. Log on as Administrator with a password of *password* at your second computer, not PRO1.

2. Make a connection to the shared folder C:\MktApps on PRO1.

3. In the MktApps On PRO1 window, double-click Manuals.

4. In the Manuals window, attempt to create a file.

   Were you successful? Why or why not?

5. Close all windows and log off Windows XP Professional.

▶ **To test permissions for the Public folder when a user makes a connection over the network**

1. Log on as User1 with a password of *User1* on your second computer.

2. Click Start and then click Run.

3. In the Open text box, type **\\PRO1\MktApps** and then click OK.

4. In the MktApps On PRO1 window, double-click Public.

5. In the Public window, attempt to create a file.

    Were you successful? Why or why not?

6. Close all windows and log off Windows XP Professional.

Lesson Review

The following questions will help you determine whether you have learned enough to move on to the next lesson. If you have difficulty answering these questions, review the material in this lesson before beginning the next chapter. The answers are in Appendix A, "Questions and Answers."

1. If you are using both shared folder and NTFS permissions, the _____ (least/most) restrictive permission is always the overriding permission.

2. Which of the following statements about combining shared folder permissions and NTFS permissions are true? (Choose all answers that are correct.)

    a. You can use shared folder permissions on all shared folders.

    b. The Change shared folder permission is more restrictive than the Read NTFS permission.

    c. You can use NTFS permissions on all shared folders.

    d. The Read NTFS permission is more restrictive than the Change shared folder permission.

3. Which of the following statements about shared folder permissions and NTFS permissions are true? (Choose all answers that are correct.)

    a. NTFS permissions apply only when the resource is accessed over the network.

    b. NTFS permissions apply whether the resource is accessed locally or over the network.

    c. Shared folder permissions apply only when the resource is accessed over the network.

    d. Shared folder permissions apply whether the resource is accessed locally or over the network.

4. If needed, you can apply different _____ permissions to each folder, file, and subfolder.

Lesson Summary

- On a FAT volume, the shared folder permissions are the only available way to provide security for the folders you have shared and for the folders and files they contain.

- On an NTFS volume, you can assign NTFS permissions to individual users and groups to better control access to the files and subfolders in the shared folders.

- On an NTFS volume, you can apply different NTFS permissions to each file and subfolder in a shared folder.

- When you combine shared folder permissions and NTFS permissions, the more restrictive permission is always the overriding permission.

C H A P T E R 1 0

Configuring Windows XP Professional

About This Chapter

Microsoft Windows XP Professional stores configuration information in two locations: the registry and the Active Directory service. Active Directory is only available in a domain environment and requires a computer running one of the Microsoft Windows 2000 server products configured as a domain controller. Modifications to the registry or Active Directory change the configuration of the Windows XP Professional environment. You use the following tools to modify the registry or Active Directory:

- Microsoft Management Console (MMC)
- Control Panel
- Registry Editor

Before You Begin

To complete this chapter, you must have

- A computer that meets the minimum hardware requirements listed in the preface, "About This Book"
- Installed the Windows XP Professional software on the computer

---

Note For information about the registry and the Registry Editor see Chapter 18, "Modifying and Troubleshooting the Boot Process."

Lesson 1: Configuring and Troubleshooting the Display

Users can configure and clean up the icons that appear on their computer's desktop. Users with permission to load and unload device drivers can also install and test video drivers. Windows XP Professional can change video resolutions dynamically without restarting the system and also supports multiple display configurations.

After this lesson, you will be able to

- Use Control Panel to configure, manage, and troubleshoot the display
- Use Control Panel to manage which icons appear on the desktop

Estimated lesson time: 30 minutes

Configuring Display and Desktop Properties

To view or modify the display or the Desktop properties, in Control Panel, click Appearance And Themes, and then click Display. The tabs in the Display Properties dialog box (see Figure 10.1) are described in Table 10.1.

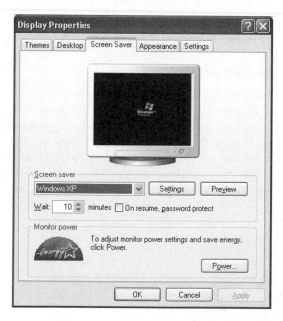

Figure 10.1   Screen Saver tab of the Display Properties dialog box

Table 10.1   Display Properties Dialog Box Tabs

Tab	Description
Themes	Allows you to chose a theme. A theme is a background, plus a set of sounds, icons, and other elements to help you personalize your computer.
Desktop	Allows you to choose a background and color for your desktop. The Customize Desktop button allows you to add or remove some Windows program icons and determine what icons represent those programs. You can also include Web content on your Desktop (see Figure 10.2).
Screen Saver	Allows you to choose a screen saver. A screen saver is a moving picture or pattern that appears on your screen after the keyboard or mouse has not been used for a specific period of time that you configure. The default is 15 minutes. Screen savers prevent damage to monitors by preventing an image from becoming burned into the monitor. You can use your own picture as a screen saver by uploading it from a digital camera or scanner, copying it from the Internet, or copying it from an e-mail attachment. You can also click Power to adjust monitor power settings and save energy. See Lesson 2, "Configuring Power Management."
Appearance	Allows you to configure the windows and buttons style, the color scheme, and font size. Click Effects to configure the following options: ▪ Use The Following Transition Effect For Menus And Tooltips ▪ Use The Following Method To Smooth Edges For Screen Fonts ▪ Use Large Icons ▪ Show Shadows Under Menus ▪ Show Windows Contents While Dragging ▪ Hide Underlined Letters For Keyboard Navigation Until I Press The Alt Key If you select Windows Classic as your theme, you can click Advanced to customize the look of windows, menus, fonts, and icons.
Settings	Allows you to configure display options including the number of colors, video resolution, font size, and refresh frequency, as shown in Figure 10.3 and explained in Table 10.2.

Important   You can enable Group Policy settings that restrict access to Display options. For example, you can remove the Appearance tab or the Settings tab from the Display Properties dialog box. For more information about Group Policy, see Chapter 12, "Auditing Resources and Events" and Chapter 13, "Configuring Security Settings and Internet Options."

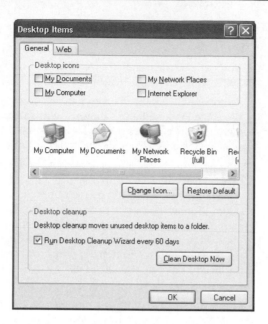

Figure 10.2   Desktop Items dialog box

To access the Desktop Items dialog box, on the Desktop tab, click Customize Desktop. The Desktop Items dialog box allows you to choose to include or exclude an icon for My Documents, My Computer, My Network Places, and the Internet Explorer on your Desktop, as well as to customize the icons used to represent these items. You can also configure the frequency with which the Desktop Cleanup Wizard is run from this dialog box. The default setting for running the Desktop Cleanup Wizard is every 60 days. Click Clean Desktop Now to run the Desktop Cleanup Wizard immediately. The Desktop Cleanup Wizard removes icons from the desktop that have not been used in the last 60 days, but it does not remove any programs from your computer.

To include Web content on your Desktop, in the Desktop Items dialog box, click the Web tab. Any Web page listed in the Web Pages text box can be included on your Desktop by selecting it. Click New to add a Web page and click Delete to remove a Web page from the list. Click Properties to view the Properties dialog box for the Web page. The Properties dialog box allows you to make the Web page available offline, synchronize immediately or schedule the synchronization of this offline Web page with the content on the Internet, and specify whether you want Internet Explorer to download more than just the top-level page of this Web site.

Note   If you want Internet Explorer to download more than just the top-level page, you can specify up to three levels deep, but specifying three levels deep downloads all the pages linked to the second-level pages.

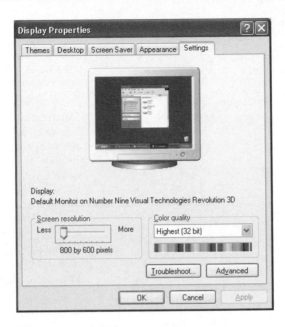

Figure 10.3   Settings tab of the Display Properties dialog box

Table 10.2 describes the options available in the Settings tab for configuring the display settings.

Table 10.2   Settings Tab Options for Configuring the Display

Option	Description
Color Quality	Displays the current color settings for the monitor attached to the video adapter listed under Display. This option allows you to change the color quality for the display adapter.
Screen Resolution	Displays the current screen resolution settings for the monitor attached to the video adapter listed under Display. This option allows you to set the resolution for the display adapter. As you increase the number of pixels, you display more information on the screen, but you decrease the size of the information.
Troubleshoot	Opens the Video Display Troubleshooter to aid you in diagnosing display problems.
Advanced	Opens the Properties dialog box for the display adapter, as described next.

To open the Properties dialog box for the display adapter, click Advanced. Table 10.3 describes the display adapter options.

Table 10.3   Display Adapter Advanced Options

Tab	Option	Description
General	Display	Provides small, large, or other display font option. The other option lets you choose any custom font size you want.
	Compatibility	Determines the action that the Windows XP operating systems should take when you make changes to display settings. After you change the color settings, you must choose one of the following options: ■ Restart The Computer Before Applying The New Display Settings ■ Apply The New Display Settings Without Restarting ■ Ask Me Before Applying The New Display Settings
Adapter	Adapter Type	Provides the manufacturer and model number of the installed adapter. Clicking Properties displays the Properties dialog box for your adapter. The General tab of the Properties dialog box provides additional information, including device status, resource settings, and any conflicting devices. The Driver tab of the Properties dialog box provides details about the driver and allows you to update the driver, roll back to the previously installed driver, and uninstall the driver. The Resources tab of the Properties dialog box indicates resources, such as areas of memory being used by the adapter.
	Adapter Information	Provides additional information about the display adapter, such as video chip type, digital-to-analog converter (DAC) type, memory size, and basic input/ output system (BIOS).
	List All Modes	Displays all compatible modes for your display adapter and lets you select resolution, color depth, and refresh frequency in one step.

Table 10.3   *(continued)*

Tab	Option	Description
Monitor	Monitor Type	Provides the manufacturer and model number of the monitor currently installed. The Properties button provides additional information and gives access to the Video Display Trouble-shooter to help resolve problems with this device.
	Monitor Settings	Configures the refresh rate frequency. This option applies only to high-resolution drivers. Do not select a refresh rate and screen resolution combination that is unsupported by the monitor. If you are unsure, refer to your monitor documentation or select the lowest refresh rate option.
Troubleshoot	Hardware Acceleration	Lets you progressively decrease your display hardware's acceleration features to help you isolate and eliminate display problems. Lets you select whether to use write combining, which improves video performance by speeding up the display of information to your screen. Increased speed can lead to screen corruption, however. If you experience trouble with your display, try clearing the Enable Write Combining check box.
Color Management		Chooses the color profile for your monitor.

Using Multiple Displays

Windows XP Professional supports multiple display configurations. Multiple displays allow you to extend your desktop across more than one monitor, as shown in Figure 10.4. Windows XP Professional supports the extension of your display across a maximum of 10 monitors.

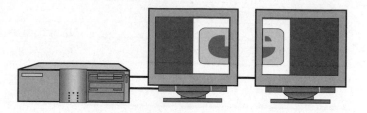

- Use of multiple displays extends the desktop across a maximum of 10 monitors.
- Multiple displays must use Peripheral Component Interconnect (PCI) or Accelerated Graphics Port (AGP) devices.
- Hardware requirements for primary (main) and secondary displays differ.

Figure 10.4   Multiple displays

Important   You must use Peripheral Component Interconnect (PCI) or Accelerated Graphics Port (AGP) video adapters when configuring multiple displays.

If one of the display adapters is built into the motherboard, note these additional considerations:

- The motherboard adapter always becomes the secondary adapter. It must be multiple-display compatible.

- You must set up Windows XP Professional before installing another adapter. Windows XP Professional Setup disables the motherboard adapter if it detects another adapter. Some systems completely disable the onboard adapter on detecting an add-in adapter. If you are unable to override this detection in the BIOS, you cannot use the motherboard adapter with multiple displays.

Typically, the system BIOS selects the primary display based on PCI slot order. However, on some computers, the BIOS allows the user to select the primary display device.

You cannot stop the primary display. This is an important consideration for laptop computers with docking stations. For example, some docking stations contain a display adapter; these often disable, or turn off, a laptop's built-in display. Multiple display support does not function on these configurations unless you attach multiple adapters to the docking station.

Configuring Multiple Displays

Before you can configure multiple displays, you must install them. When you configure multiple displays, you must configure each one in a multiple-display environment.

To install multiple monitors, complete the following steps:

1. Turn off your computer and insert one or more additional PCI or AGP video adapters into available slots on your computer.
2. Plug an additional monitor into each PCI or AGP video adapter that you installed.
3. Turn on your computer and allow Windows XP Professional to detect the new adapters and install the appropriate device drivers.
4. In Control Panel, click Appearance And Themes, and then click Display.
5. In the Settings tab, click the monitor icon that represents the monitor you want to use in addition to your primary monitor.
6. Select the Extend My Windows Desktop Onto This Monitor check box and then click OK.

To configure your display in a multiple-display environment, complete the following steps:

1. In Control Panel, click Appearance And Themes, and then click Display.
2. In the Display Properties dialog box, click the Settings tab.
3. Click the monitor icon for the primary display device.
4. Select the display adapter for the primary display, and then select the color depth and resolution.
5. Click the monitor icon for the secondary display device.
6. Select the display adapter for the secondary display, and then select the Extend My Windows Desktop Onto This Monitor check box.
7. Select the color depth and resolution for the secondary display.
8. Repeat steps 5 through 7 for each additional display.

Windows XP Professional uses the virtual desktop concept to determine the relationship of each display. The virtual desktop uses coordinates to track the position of each individual display desktop.

The coordinates of the top-left corner of the primary display always remain 0, 0. Windows XP Professional sets secondary display coordinates so that all the displays adjoin each other on the virtual desktop. This allows the system to maintain the illusion of a single, large desktop where users can cross from one monitor to another without losing track of the mouse.

To change the display positions on the virtual desktop, in the Settings tab click Identify and drag the display representations to the desired position. The positions of the icons dictate the coordinates and the relative positions of the displays to one another.

Troubleshooting Multiple Displays

If you encounter problems with multiple displays, use the troubleshooting guidelines in Table 10.4 to help resolve those problems.

Table 10.4   Troubleshooting Tips for Multiple Displays

Problem	Solution
You cannot see any output on the secondary displays.	Activate the device in the Display Properties dialog box. Confirm that you chose the correct video driver.
	Restart the computer to confirm that the secondary display initialized. If not, check the status of the video adapter inDevice Manager.
	Switch the order of the adapters in the slots. (The primary adapter must qualify as a secondary adapter.)
The Extend My Windows Desktop Onto This Monitor check box is unavailable.	Select the secondary display rather than the primary one in the Display Properties dialog box.
	Confirm that the secondary display adapter is supported.
	Confirm that Windows XP Professional can detect the secondary display.
An application fails to display on the secondary display.	Run the application on the primary display.
	Run the application in full-screen mode (Microsoft MS-DOS) or maximized (Microsoft Windows).
	Disable the secondary display to determine whether the problem is specific to multiple-display support.

Lesson Review

The following questions will help you determine whether you have learned enough to move on to the next lesson. If you have difficulty answering these questions, review the material in this lesson before beginning the next lesson. The answers are in Appendix A, "Questions and Answers."

1. You can enable _____ to restrict access to Display options.

2. Which of the following items does the Desktop Items dialog box allow you to choose to include or exclude an icon on your desktop? (Choose all answers that are correct.)

   a. My Documents

   b. Control Panel

   c. My Network Places

   d. Recycle Bin

3. Windows XP Professional supports extension of your display across a maximum of _____ monitors.

4. You must use _____ or _____ video adapters when configuring multiple displays.

5. If one of the display adapters is built into the motherboard, the motherboard adapter always becomes the _____ (primary/secondary) adapter.

Lesson Summary

- The Desktop Items dialog box allows you to choose to include or exclude an icon for My Documents, My Computer, My Network Places, and the Recycle Bin on your desktop.

- By default, the Desktop Cleanup Wizard runs every 60 days and removes any icons from the desktop that have not been used in the last 60 days.

- You must use Peripheral Component Interconnect (PCI) or Accelerated Graphics Port (AGP) video adapters when configuring multiple displays.

- Windows XP Professional supports the extension of your display across a maximum of 10 monitors.

Lesson 2: Configuring Power Management

Windows XP Professional contains a number of features that allow the operating system to manage the use of power by your computer and the hardware devices attached to it. Power management features included in Windows XP Professional include System Power Management, Device Power Management, Processor Power Management, System Events, and Battery Management.

After this lesson, you will be able to
- Use Control Panel to configure Power Options

Estimated lesson time: 40 minutes

Configuring Power Options

Power Options allows you to configure Windows XP Professional to turn off the power to your monitor and your hard disk or put the computer in hibernate mode. To configure Power Options, in Control Panel, click Performance And Maintenance, and then click Power Options. The Power Options Properties dialog box allows you to configure Power Options (see Figure 10.5).

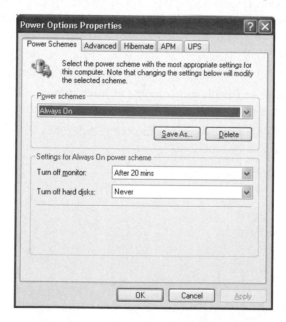

Figure 10.5   Power Schemes tab of the Power Options Properties dialog box

---

Note   Your hardware must support powering off the monitor and hard disk for you to configure power schemes.

Selecting a Power Scheme

Power schemes allow you to configure Windows XP Professional to turn off the power to your monitor and your hard disk, conserving energy. In the Power Options Properties dialog box, click the Power Schemes tab. Windows XP Professional provides the following six built-in power schemes:

- **Home/Office Desk.**   This power scheme is designed for a desktop computer. After 20 minutes of inactivity, the monitor is turned off, but the hard disks are never turned off.

- **Portable/Laptop.**   This power scheme is optimized for portable computers that will be running on batteries. After 15 minutes of inactivity the monitor is turned off, and after 30 minutes of inactivity the hard disks are turned off.

- **Presentation.**   This power scheme is designed for use with presentations for which the computer display is always to remain on. The monitor and the hard disks are never turned off.

- **Always On.**   This power scheme is designed for use with personal servers. After 20 minutes of inactivity, the monitor is turned off, but the hard disks are never turned off.

- **Minimal Power Management.**   This power scheme disables some power management features such as timed hibernation. After 15 minutes of inactivity, the monitor is turned off, but the hard disks are never turned off.

- **Max Battery.**   This power scheme is designed to conserve as much battery power as possible. After 15 minutes of inactivity, the monitor is turned off, but the hard disks are never turned off.

To select a power scheme, you can perform the following steps:

1. Ensure that you are logged on with a user account that is a member of the Administrators group.

2. Click Start, click Control Panel, and then click Performance And Maintenance.

3. Click Power Options.

   Windows XP Professional displays the Power Options Properties dialog box with the Power Schemes tab active.

4. Click the arrow at the end of the Power Schemes box to display the pull-down menu listing the available power schemes. Click the power scheme you want to use.

5. Click OK to close the Power Options Properties dialog box.

If none of these power schemes is appropriate for your computer environment, you can modify one of the built-in power schemes or configure a new power scheme. To modify a power scheme or to create a new power scheme, perform the following steps:

1. Ensure that you are logged on with a user account that is a member of the Administrators group.

2. Click Start, click Control Panel, and then click Performance And Maintenance.

3. Click Power Options.

   Windows XP Professional displays the Power Options Properties dialog box with the Power Schemes tab active.

4. Click the arrow at the end of the Power Schemes box to display the pull-down menu listing the available power schemes. Click the power scheme you want to use.

5. In the Settings For *Power_Scheme_Name* Power Scheme text box, modify the amount of inactive time before the monitor or hard drives are turned off.

6. Do one of the following:

   ▪ Click OK to modify the existing power scheme and close the Power Options Properties dialog box.

   ▪ Click Save As to create a new power scheme.

Configuring Advanced Power Options

To configure your computer to use advanced power options, use the Power Options Properties dialog box and click the Advanced tab. There are two options in the Advanced tab. If you want an icon for quick access to Power Management to appear on the taskbar, select the Always Show Icon On The Taskbar check box. The second check box in the Advanced tab is Prompt For Password When Computer Resumes From Standby. Selecting this check box causes you to be prompted for your Windows password when your computer comes out of standby mode.

Note On older systems, the Prompt For Password When Computer Resumes From Standby box might not be displayed unless the system is set to hibernate.

Enabling Hibernate Mode

When your computer hibernates, it saves the current system state to your hard disk, and then your computer shuts down. When you start the computer after it has been hibernating, it returns to its previous state. Restarting to the previous state includes automatically restarting any programs that were running when it went into hibernate mode, and it even restores any network connections that were active at the time. To configure your computer to use hibernate mode, use the

Power Options Properties dialog box. Click Hibernate and select the Enable Hibernation check box. If the Hibernate tab is unavailable, your computer does not support this mode.

Configuring Advanced Power Management

Windows XP Professional supports Advanced Power Management (APM), which helps reduce the power consumption of your system. To configure your computer to use APM, use the Power Options Properties dialog box. Click the APM tab and select the Enable Advanced Power Management Support check box. If the APM tab is unavailable, your computer is compliant with Advanced Configuration and Power Interface (ACPI), which automatically enables Advanced Power Management Support and disables the APM tab. You must be logged on as a member of the Administrators group to configure APM.

If your computer does not have an APM BIOS installed, Windows XP Professional does not install APM, so there will not be an APM tab in the Power Options Properties dialog box. However, your computer can still function as an ACPI computer if it has an ACPI-based BIOS, which takes over system configuration and power management from the Plug and Play BIOS.

Note   If your laptop has an ACPI-based BIOS, you can insert and remove PC cards on the fly and Windows XP Professional automatically detects and configures them without requiring you to restart your machine. This is known as *dynamic configuration of PC cards*. There are two other important features for mobile computers that rely on dynamic Plug and Play: hot and warm docking/undocking and hot swapping of Integrated Device Electronics (IDE) and floppy devices. Hot and warm docking/undocking means you can dock and undock from the Windows XP Professional Start menu without turning off your computer. Windows XP Professional automatically creates two hardware profiles for laptop computers: one for the docked state and one for the undocked state. (For more information about hardware profiles see Chapter 11, "Installing, Managing, and Troubleshooting Hardware Devices and Drivers.") Hot swapping of IDE and floppy devices means that you can remove and swap devices such as floppy drives, DVD/CD drives, and hard drives without shutting down your system or restarting your system; Windows XP Professional automatically detects and configures these devices.

Configuring an Uninterruptible Power Supply

An uninterruptible power supply (UPS) is a device connected between a computer or another piece of electronic equipment and a power source, such as an electrical outlet. The UPS ensures that the electrical flow to the computer is not interrupted because of a blackout and, in most cases, protects the computer against potentially damaging events such as power surges and brownouts.

Different UPS models offer different levels of protection. To configure your UPS, click the UPS tab in the Power Options Properties dialog box. The UPS tab shows the current power source, the estimated UPS run time, the estimated UPS capacity, and the battery condition. In the UPS tab, click Details to display the UPS Selection dialog box. It displays a list of manufacturers so that you can select the manufacturer of your UPS.

Note   Check the Windows XP Professional Hardware Compatibility List (HCL) to make sure the UPS you are considering is compatible with Windows XP Professional before you purchase it.

If you want to configure a custom simple-signaling UPS, in the Select Manufacturer list box select Generic. In the Select Model list box, click Generic and then click Next. You can configure the conditions that trigger the UPS device to send a signal in the UPS Interface Configuration dialog box (see Figure 10.6). These conditions include power failures, a low battery, and the UPS shutting down. You should select Positive if your UPS sends a signal with positive polarity when the power fails and the UPS is running on battery. Select Negative if your UPS sends a signal with negative polarity.

Caution   Be sure to check your UPS documentation before you configure signal polarity.

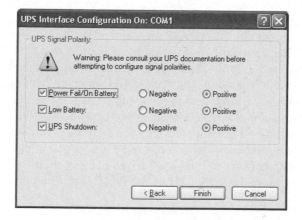

Figure 10.6   UPS Interface Configuration dialog box

After you have configured the UPS service for your computer, you should test the configuration to ensure that your computer is protected from power failures. Disconnect the main power supply to simulate a power failure. During your test the computer and the devices connected to the computer should remain operational. You should let the test run long enough for the UPS battery to reach a low level so that you can verify that an orderly shutdown occurs.

Caution   Do not test your UPS on a production computer. You could lose valuable data. Use a spare computer for the test.

Practice: Configuring Power Options

In this practice you use Control Panel to configure Power Options.

▶   **To configure Power Options**

1. Ensure that you are logged on as Fred or with a user account that is a member of the Administrators group.

2. Click Start, click Control Panel, and then click Performance And Maintenance.

3. Click Power Options.

   Windows XP Professional displays the Power Options Properties dialog box with the Power Schemes tab active.

4. In the Power Schemes list, select Portable/Laptop.

5. In the Turn Off Monitor box, select After 10 Minutes.

6. In the Turn Off Hard Disks box, select After 20 Minutes.

7. Click Save As, and then in the Save Scheme text box, type **Airplane**.

8. Click OK.

   You have just created a new power scheme. If you click the arrow at the end of the Power Scheme box, Airplane is now included in the list of available power schemes. If you want to use this power scheme, click Apply.

9. Click the Advanced tab and select the Always Show Icon In The Taskbar check box.

10. Click the Hibernate tab.

11. If the Enable Hibernate Support check box is not selected, select it and then click Apply.

12. Click the APM tab.

13. If the Enable Advanced Power Management Support check box is not selected, select it and then click Apply.

14. To apply these changes you would click OK; click Cancel.

    Windows XP Professional closes the Power Options Properties dialog box.

15. Close all open windows.

Lesson Review

The following questions will help you determine whether you have learned enough to move on to the next lesson. If you have difficulty answering these questions, review the material in this lesson before beginning the next lesson. The answers are in Appendix A, "Questions and Answers."

1. What is a power scheme and why would you use one?

2. Which of the following statements about Windows XP Professional power schemes are true? (Choose all answers that are correct.)

    a. Windows XP Professional ships with six built-in power schemes.

    b. Windows XP Professional allows you to create your own power schemes.

    c. Windows XP Professional allows you to modify existing power schemes, but you cannot create new ones.

    d. Windows XP Professional does not ship with any built-in power schemes.

3. A _____ is a device that connects between a computer and a power source to ensure that the electrical flow to the computer is not abruptly stopped because of a blackout.

4. What does hibernate mode do?

5. _____ means that you can remove or exchange devices such as floppy drives, DVD/CD drives, and hard drives without shutting down your system or restarting your system. Windows XP Professional automatically detects and configures these devices.

Lesson Summary

- Power Options allows you to configure Windows XP Professional to turn off the power to your monitor and your hard disk or put the computer in hibernate mode.

- To configure Power Options, in Control Panel, click Performance And Maintenance and then click Power Options.

- The advanced power management options allow you to add an icon for quick access to Power Management to the taskbar and choose to be prompted for your Windows password when your computer comes out of standby mode.

- When your computer hibernates, it saves the current system state to your hard disk, and then your computer shuts down. When you start the computer after it has been hibernating, it returns to its previous state.

- ACPI automatically enables Advanced Power Management Support and removes the APM tab.

- A UPS is a device that ensures that the electrical flow to a computer is not interrupted because of power loss.

Lesson 3: Configuring Operating System Settings

You use certain Control Panel programs to configure operating system settings. The System program that you use to configure the operating system settings affects the operating system environment regardless of which user is logged on to the computer.

After this lesson, you will be able to

- Configure the system's performance options
- Create, modify, and manage user profiles
- Configure the system's startup and recovery settings
- Configure the system's environment variables
- Configure the system's error reporting
- Configure the system's tracking and reversal of harmful changes
- Configure the system's Automatic Update feature
- Configure remote computers' access to your computer
- Join a domain or workgroup

Estimated lesson time: 70 minutes

Configuring Performance Options

To configure operating system settings, in Control Panel, click Performance And Maintenance. To view operating system performance configuration options, in the Performance And Maintenance window, click System, and then click the Advanced tab. The Advanced tab of the System Properties dialog box (see Figure 10.7) allows you to configure performance options, user profiles, startup and recovery settings, environment variables, and error reporting.

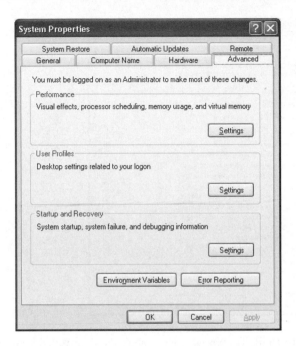

Figure 10.7   The Advanced tab of the System Properties dialog box

In the Advanced tab, in the Performance box, click Settings to display the Performance Options dialog box. There are two tabs on the Performance Options dialog box: the Visual Effects tab and the Advanced tab.

Visual Effects

The Visual Effects tab of the Performance Options dialog box is shown in Figure 10.8. There are a number of options that you can select to manually control the visual effects on your computer. Windows XP Professional provides four options to help you control the visual effects: Let Windows Choose What's Best For My Computer, Adjust For Best Appearance, Adjust For Best Performance, and Custom. If you want to manually indicate which visual effects to apply, select Custom.

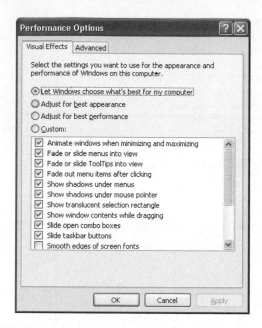

Figure 10.8   The Visual Effects tab of the Performance Options dialog box

Note   A second method for accessing the Performance Options dialog box is to click Adjust Visual Effects in the Performance And Maintenance window.

Advanced Performance Options

The Advanced tab of the Performance Options dialog box is shown in Figure 10.9. The options in this dialog box allow you to adjust the application response, which is the priority of foreground programs versus background programs, and virtual memory.

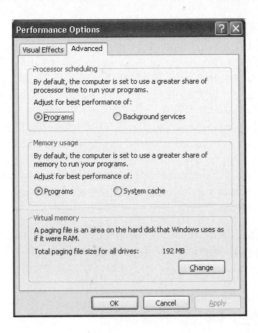

Figure 10.9 The Advanced tab of the Performance Options dialog box

Processor Scheduling

Windows XP Professional uses the Processor Scheduling settings to distribute microprocessor resources between running programs. Selecting Programs assigns more resources to the foreground program (the active program that is responding to user input). Windows XP Professional assigns more resources to the foreground program by allocating short, variable time slices, or quanta, to running programs. A time slice, or quantum, is a brief period of time during which a particular task is given control of the microprocessor. When you select Background Services, Windows assigns an equal number of resources to all programs by assigning long, fixed quanta instead.

Memory Usage

Windows XP Professional uses the Memory Usage settings to distribute memory resources between running programs. Select Programs if your computer is being used primarily as a workstation. With the Programs option, your programs will work faster and your system cache will be the default size for Windows XP Professional. Select System Cache if you are using your computer as a server or if the programs you are running require a large system cache.

Virtual Memory

For virtual memory, Windows XP Professional uses a process called demand paging to exchange data between random access memory (RAM) and paging files. When you install Windows XP Professional, Setup creates a virtual-memory paging file, PAGEFILE.SYS, on the partition where you installed Windows XP Professional. The default or recommended paging file size for Windows XP Professional is equal to 1.5 times the total amount of RAM. For best results, never set the value of the paging file size to less than the recommended amount. Typically, you can leave the size of the paging file set to the default value. In some circumstances, such as when you run a large number of applications simultaneously, you might find it advantageous to use a larger paging file or multiple paging files.

To configure the paging file, in the Performance Options dialog box, click Change. The Virtual Memory dialog box (see Figure 10.10) identifies the drives on which the paging files reside and allows you to modify the paging file size for the selected drive.

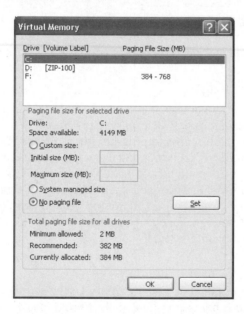

Figure 10.10   The Virtual Memory dialog box

Important   Only users with administrative rights can use the Performance Options dialog box to increase the paging file size.

Paging files never decrease below the value found in the Initial Size text box that was set during installation. Unused space in the paging file remains available to the internal Windows XP Professional Virtual Memory Manager (VMM). As needed, a paging file grows from its initial size to the maximum configured size, which is listed in the Maximum Size text box. When the paging file reaches the maximum size, system performance might degrade if you place additional demands on the system by running more applications.

When you restart a computer running Windows XP Professional, the system resizes all paging files to the initial size.

Enhancing Performance

You can enhance system performance in several ways. First, if your computer has multiple hard disks, create a paging file for each disk. Distributing information across multiple paging files improves performance because the hard disk controller can read from and write to multiple hard disks simultaneously. When attempting to write to the paging file, VMM tries to write the page data to the paging file on the disk that is the least busy.

Tip   When choosing the drives to contain paging files, don't use a paging file on heavily accessed drives, and don't put paging files on multiple partitions on the same physical drive.

Second, you can enhance performance by moving the paging file off the drive that contains the Windows XP Professional *%systemroot%* folder (by default, the Windows folder). This avoids competition between the various reading and writing requests. If you place a paging file on the Windows XP Professional system partition to facilitate the recovery feature, which is discussed in the section entitled "Recovery" later in this chapter, you can still increase performance by creating multiple paging files. Because the VMM alternates write operations between paging files, the paging file on the boot partition is accessed less frequently.

Third, you can enhance system performance by setting the initial size of the paging file to the value displayed in the Virtual Memory dialog box's Maximum Size box. This eliminates the time required to enlarge the file from the initial size to the maximum size.

Note   When applying new settings, be sure to click Set before clicking OK.

Configuring User Profiles

To view, create, delete, and change the type of user profiles, in Control Panel, click Performance And Maintenance, click System, and then click the Advanced tab (see Figure 10.7). In the User Profiles box, click Settings to display the User Profiles dialog box (see Figure 10.11).

Figure 10.11   The User Profiles dialog box

The User Profiles dialog box lists the profiles stored on the computer you are sitting at. You can perform the following tasks:

- **Change Type.**   Allows you to change the type of profile. There are two types of profiles:

    - **Local profile.**   Windows XP Professional creates a user profile the first time that a user logs on at a computer. After the user logs on for the first time, Windows XP Professional stores the local profile on that computer.

    - **Roaming profile.**   A roaming user profile is especially helpful in a domain environment because it follows the user around, setting up the same desktop environment for the user no matter which computer the user logs on to in the domain.

Note   A read-only roaming user profile is called a mandatory user profile. When the user logs off, Windows XP Professional does not save any changes made to the desktop environment during the session, so the next time the user logs on the profile is exactly the same as the last time the user logged on. See Chapter 3, "Setting Up and Managing User Accounts," for information about creating a mandatory user profile.

- **Delete.**   Allows you to delete user profiles.
- **Copy To.**   Allows you to create user profiles by copying an existing user profile and assigning it to another user.

The Copy Profile To text box allows you to specify a path for the location to which the user profile is to be copied. You can click Browse to locate the appropriate path.

The Permitted To Use box allows you to specify the user or users who can use the user profile.

Configuring Startup and Recovery Settings

The System Properties dialog box also controls the startup and recovery settings for a computer. Click Settings to display the Startup And Recovery dialog box, as shown in Figure 10.12. The System Startup options control the behavior of the Please Select The Operating System To Start menu. The Recovery options control the actions that Windows XP Professional performs in the event of a stop error, which is a severe error that causes Windows XP Professional to stop all processes. Stop errors are also known as fatal system errors or blue screen errors.

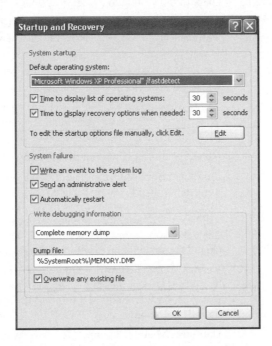

Figure 10.12   The Startup And Recovery dialog box

System Startup

When you first turn on the computer, the system displays the Please Select The Operating System To Start screen, which lists the available operating systems. By default, the system chooses one of the operating systems and displays a countdown timer. If you do not choose another operating system, the system starts the preselected operating system when the countdown timer reaches zero or when you press ENTER. Modify the options under System Startup to determine which operating system is preselected, how long the countdown timer runs, and whether to display the boot menu. You are also given the option of modifying the BOOT.INI file manually, but you should allow Windows XP Professional to modify the file rather than attempting to do so manually.

System Recovery

The four recovery options that Windows XP Professional provides to assist users in the event of a system failure are described in Table 10.5.

Important   You must be logged on as a member of the Administrators group to set the options in the Startup And Recovery dialog box.

Table 10.5   Recovery Options

Option	Additional information
Write An Event To The System Log	Select this check box to have Windows XP Professional write an event to the system log when a system stops unexpectedly.
Send An Administrative Alert	Select this check box to have Windows XP Professional send an administrative alert to administrators when the system stops unexpectedly.
Automatically Restart	Select this check box to have Windows XP Professional reboot whenever the system stops unexpectedly.
Write Debugging Information	The first option allows you to specify what information Windows XP Professional should write to the dump file, MEMORY.DMP. The following four choices are available:
	None. Nothing is written to the dump file.
	Small Memory Dump. The minimum amount of useful information will be dumped. This option requires a paging file of at least 2 MB on the boot volume of your computer. A new dump file will be created every time the system stops unexpectedly. The small dump directory stores a history of these dumps and can be set. By default the small dump directory is *%Systemroot%*\Minidump.
	Kernel Memory Dump. Only kernel memory is written to the dump file. Depending on the amount of RAM on your computer, you must have from 50 MB to 800 MB available in the paging file on the boot volume.
	Complete Memory Dump. Records the entire contents of system memory when the system stops unexpectedly. You must have a paging file on the boot volume large enough to hold all the RAM on your system plus 1 MB.
	There are also two additional options:
	Dump File. Specifies the name and location of the dump file. By default it is *%Systemroot%*\MEMORY.DMP
	Overwrite Any Existing File. By default, if you choose Complete Memory Dump or Kernel Memory Dump, Windows XP Professional always writes to the same dump file, MEMORY.DMP. Clear this check box to prevent Windows from overwriting MEMORY.DMP.

The following requirements must be met for the Write Debugging Information recovery option to work:

- A paging file must be on the system partition (the partition that contains the *%systemroot%* folder).
- The paging file must be at least 1 MB larger than the amount of physical RAM in your computer if you choose Complete Memory Dump.
- You must have enough disk space to write the file to the location you specify.

Configuring Environment Variables

Environment variables define the system and user environment information, and they contain information such as a drive, path, or filename. Environment variables provide information that Windows XP Professional uses to control various applications. For example, the TEMP environment variable specifies where an application places its temporary files.

In the Advanced tab of the System Properties dialog box, click Environment Variables to display the system and user environment variables that are currently in effect in the Environment Variables dialog box (see Figure 10.13).

Figure 10.13   The Environment Variables dialog box

System Environment Variables

System environment variables apply to the entire system. Consequently, these variables affect all system users. During installation, Setup configures the default system environment variables, including the path to the Windows XP Professional files. Only an administrator can add, modify, or remove a system environment variable.

User Environment Variables

The user environment variables differ for each user of a particular computer. The user environment variables include any user-defined settings (such as a desktop pattern) and any variables defined by applications (such as the path to the location of the application files). Users can add, modify, or remove their user environment variables in the System Properties dialog box.

How Windows XP Professional Sets Environment Variables

Windows XP Professional sets environment variables in the following order:

1. By default, Windows XP Professional searches the AUTOEXEC.BAT file, if it exists, and sets any environment variables.

2. Next the system environment variables are set. If any system environment variables conflict with environment variables set from the search of the AUTOEXEC.BAT file, the system environment variables override them.

3. Finally, the user environment variables are set. If any user environment variables conflict with environment variables set from the search of the AUTOEXEC.BAT file or from the system environment variables, the user environment variables override them.

For example, if you add the line SET TMP=C:\ in AUTOEXEC.BAT, and a TMP=X:\TEMP user variable is set, the user environment variable setting (X:\TEMP) overrides the prior setting C:\.

Note   You can prevent Windows XP Professional from searching the AUTOEXEC.BAT file by editing the registry and setting the value of the ParseAutoexec entry to 0. The ParseAutoexec entry is located in the registry under the following subkey:

\HKEY_CURRENT_USER\SOFTWARE\Microsoft\Windows NT\
    CurrentVersion\Winlogon

Configuring Error Reporting

Error reporting assists Microsoft in improving future products and in resolving any difficulties you might encounter with Windows XP Professional. To configure error reporting, in the Advanced tab of the System Properties dialog box, click Error Reporting. This displays the Error Reporting dialog box. Notice that Enable Error Reporting is selected. To turn off error reporting, click Disable Error Reporting.

If you do not want to turn off error checking, you can configure reporting to indicate which errors to report. Under Enable Error Reporting there are two check boxes selected by default. Clear the Windows Operating System check box if you do not want errors in the operating system to be reported. Clear the Programs check box if you do not want errors in any of the programs running on your system to be reported. If you want to specify the programs for which Windows XP Professional reports errors, click Select Programs.

Note   If a system or program error occurs and you have configured your system to report it, Windows XP Professional displays a dialog box that allows you to indicate whether you want to send the report to Microsoft.

Configuring System Restore

The Windows XP Professional System Restore feature allows you to track and reverse harmful changes made to your system. In the System Properties dialog box, click the System Restore tab (see Figure 10.14).

Figure 10.14   The System Restore tab of the System Properties dialog box

If you want to configure the status of System Restore on a drive, select the drive and then click Settings. The Settings dialog box for a drive allows you to turn off System Restore monitoring for the drive and to configure the amount of disk space reserved for System Restore. You cannot turn off System Restore on the drive on which Windows XP Professional is installed without turning off System Restore on all drives. System Restore monitors and restores only the partitions and drives that it is configured to monitor. It doesn't monitor partitions of drives that are redirected or excluded from System Restore monitoring. System Restore also doesn't monitor or restore the contents of redirected folders or any settings associated with roaming user profiles.

Note   For information about using the System Restore Wizard, see Chapter 16, "Backing Up and Restoring Data."

Configuring Automatic Updates

Automatic Updates (AU) is a proactive service that allows users with administrative privileges to automatically download and install critical operating system updates such as security fixes and patches. You are notified before the installation takes place and given the opportunity to postpone the download operation. Updates are downloaded in the background so that you can continue to work during downloading. To configure AU, click the Automatic Updates tab of the System Properties dialog box (see Figure 10.15).

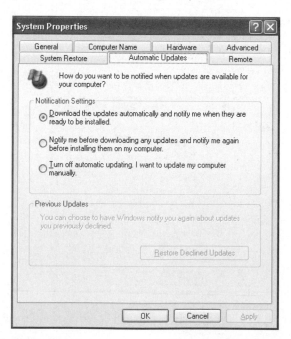

Figure 10.15   The Automatic Updates tab of the System Properties dialog box

Under Notification Settings, you can select one of the following three options:

- Download The Updates Automatically And Notify Me When They Are Ready To Be Installed.

- Notify Me Before Downloading Any Updates And Notify Me Again Before Installing Them On My Computer.

- Turn Off Automatic Updating. I Want To Update My Computer Manually.

AU uses the Windows Update control to scan the system and decide which updates apply to a particular computer. AU employs its innovative bandwidth-throttling technology, which uses only idle bandwidth for downloads so they do not interfere with or slow down other network activity, such as Internet browsing. Only one administrative user at a time can run the Automatic Updates feature.

If you choose not to install an update, Windows XP Professional deletes it from your computer. If you decide you want to install a previous update, in the Previous Updates box, click Restore Hidden Items. Any previous updates that are still applicable to your computer appear the next time Windows XP Professional notifies you that updates are available.

Note You can always go to the Windows Update Page at *www.microsoft.com* and manually install any update that is available.

Configuring Remote Access to Your Computer

If you have a computer problem, the Remote Assistance feature allows you to invite another person, a remote assistant, to help you over the Internet. The remote assistant can accept your invitation, chat with you about the problem, and view your desktop. He or she can also transfer any files required to fix the problem. To configure the Remote Assistance feature, click the Remote tab in the System Properties dialog box (see Figure 10.16).

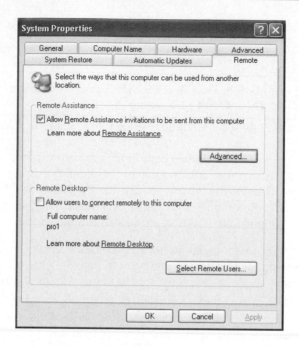

Figure 10.16   The Remote tab of the System Properties dialog box

Under Remote Assistance, you can configure your computer to allow or prevent remote assistance invitations to be sent from your computer. Click Advanced to display the Remote Assistance Settings dialog box. To allow the remote assistant full control of your computer, ensure that the default option, Allow This Computer To Be Controlled Remotely, is selected. To allow the assistant to view but not take control of your computer, clear the check box. You can also control the number of days, hours, or minutes before the invitation expires.

In the Remote tab of the System Properties dialog box, under Remote Desktop, you can configure your computer so that remote computers can make a connection to it. This allows you to leave an application running on your office computer, for example, and then connect to your computer from home. The Remote Desktop feature allows multiple users to have active sessions on a single computer.

You can also configure which users can have remote access to your computer. Click Select Remote Users to configure the users that can access your computer remotely in the Remote Desktop Users dialog box (see Figure 10.17). All users that are listed, as well as all users that are members of the Administrators group, have remote access. You can add other users to this list by clicking Add and supplying the complete user name when prompted.

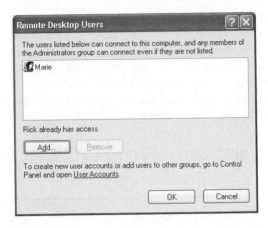

Figure 10.17   The Remote Desktop Users dialog box

Joining a Domain or Workgroup

You might need to install a computer when it is not attached to the network, the network is down, or a domain controller is not available. In those instances you can install Windows XP Professional and have your computer join a workgroup. When you add your computer to the network, or the network or a domain controller is available, you can join your computer to the domain. To join a domain or a workgroup, you use the Computer Name tab of the System Properties dialog box (see Figure 10.18).

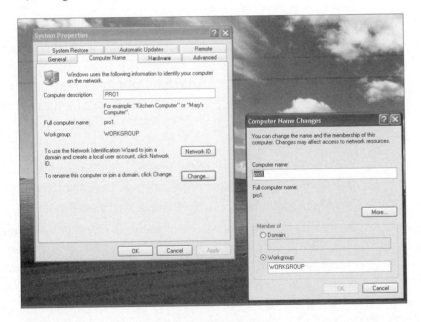

Figure 10.18   The Computer Name tab of the System Properties dialog box

The Computer Name tab shows you the full name of your computer and the domain or workgroup to which it currently belongs. You can add a description for your computer in the Computer Description text box, and you can click Change to change your computer's name or to join a domain or workgroup. To join a domain, there must be a computer account created for your computer in the domain or you must have the name and password of a user account that is a member of the Domain Admins group so that you can create the computer account as you join the domain.

Practice: Using Control Panel to Change Operating System Settings

In this practice, you use the System program to change some of the system settings. First you change the default Remote Assistance setting so that a remote assistant can only view your computer rather than take full control of your computer. Then you change the paging file size. Finally, you add and test a new system environment variable.

Run the **OSSettings** file in the Demos folder on the CD-ROM accompanying this book for a demonstration of changing system settings.

Exercise 1: Changing the Remote Assistance Access Permission

In this exercise, you change the access of a remote assistant from full control to being able to only view your computer. You also set the expiration time for the Remote Assistance invitation to six hours.

▶ **To decrease the Remote Assistance access permission**

1. Log on as Fred or a user account that is a member of the Administrators group.
2. In Control Panel, click Performance And Maintenance.

    Windows XP Professional displays the Performance And Maintenance window.
3. Click System.

    Windows XP Professional displays the System Properties dialog box.
4. In the System Properties dialog box, click the Remote tab.
5. In the Remote tab, in the Remote Assistance box, click Advanced.

    Windows XP Professional displays the Remote Assistance Settings dialog box.
6. Clear the Allow This Computer To Be Controlled Remotely check box.

    Clearing this check box allows the remote assistant to view but not take control of your computer.

7. In the Invitations box, change the Set The Maximum Amount Of Time Invitations Can Remain Open to six hours.

8. Click OK.

You are returned to the System Properties dialog box with the Remote tab active. Leave the System Properties dialog box open for the next exercise.

Exercise 2: Changing the Paging File Size

In this exercise, you use the System Properties dialog box to change the size of the Windows XP Professional paging file.

▶ **To change the paging file size**

1. In the System Properties dialog box, click the Advanced tab.

2. In the Performance box, click Settings.

   Windows XP Professional displays the Performance Options dialog box with the Visual Effects tab active.

3. Click the Advanced tab.

   By default, both Processor Scheduling and Memory Usage are optimized for applications.

4. In the Virtual Memory box, click Change.

   Windows XP Professional displays the Virtual Memory dialog box.

5. In the Drive list, click the drive that contains your paging file, if necessary.

6. In the Initial Size text box, increase the value by 10, and then click Set.

   You have just increased the initial size of the paging file.

7. Click OK to close the Virtual Memory dialog box.

8. Click OK to close the Performance Options dialog box.

Leave the System Properties dialog box open for the next exercise.

Exercise 3: Adding a System Environment Variable

In this exercise, you use the System Properties dialog box to add a new system environment variable. You then test the new variable by using it at the command prompt.

▶ **To add a system environment variable**

1. In the System Properties dialog box, in the Advanced tab, click Environment Variables.

   Windows XP Professional displays the Environment Variables dialog box.

2. Under System Variables, click New.

   Windows XP Professional displays the New System Variable dialog box.

3. In the Variable Name text box, type **WinXPdir**.

4. In the Variable Value text box, type the path to the folder containing the Windows XP Professional system files, for example, **C:\Windows**.

   If you are not sure of the path to the Windows XP Professional system files, use Windows Explorer to locate the Windows directory.

5. Click OK.

   You are returned to the Environment Variables dialog box.

6. Scroll through the System Environment Variables and verify that WinXPdir is listed.

7. Click OK to close the Environment Variables dialog box, and then click OK to close the System Properties dialog box.

8. Close the Performance And Maintenance window.

▶ **To test the new variable**

1. From the Start menu, click Run.

2. In the Open text box, type **cmd** and then click OK.

3. At the command prompt, type **set | more** and then press ENTER.

   The list of current environment variables is displayed and WinXPdir is listed. (Note you might need to press SPACEBAR to scroll down to see WinXPdir listed.)

4. If necessary, type **c:** and then press ENTER to switch to the drive on which you installed Windows XP Professional. (Adjust the drive letter if necessary.)

5. Type **cd** and then press ENTER to switch to the root directory.

6. Type **cd %WinXPdir%** and then press ENTER.

   You should now be in the Windows directory.

7. Type **exit** and press ENTER to close the command prompt.

Lesson Review

The following questions will help you determine whether you have learned enough to move on to the next lesson. If you have difficulty answering these questions, review the material in this lesson before beginning the next lesson. The answers are in Appendix A, "Questions and Answers."

1. What performance options can you control with the tabs of the Performance Options dialog box?

2. Which of the following statements about the use of virtual memory in Windows XP Professional are correct? (Choose all answers that are correct.)

   a. When you install Windows XP Professional, Setup creates a virtual memory paging file, PAGEFILE.SYS, on the partition where you installed Windows XP Professional.

   b. In some environments, you might find it advantageous to use multiple paging files.

   c. If the entire paging file is not in use, it can decrease below the initial size that was set during installation.

   d. Unused space in the paging file remains unavailable to all programs, even the internal Windows XP Professional VMM.

3. When you first turn on the computer, the system displays a Please Select The Operating System To Start screen, which lists the available operating systems. What happens if a user does not select an operating system before the countdown timer reaches zero?

4. What requirements must be met for the Write Debugging Information recovery option to work?

5. What is the Windows XP Professional Remote Assistance feature?

6. To join a domain, you use the _____ tab of the _____ dialog box.

Lesson Summary

- The System program that you use to configure the operating system settings affects the operating system environment regardless of which user is logged on to the computer.

- The Advanced tab of the System Properties dialog box allows you to configure performance options, user profiles, startup and recovery settings, environment variables, and error reporting.

- Windows XP Professional creates a local user profile the first time that a user logs on at a computer and stores the local profile on that computer.

- A roaming user profile follows the user around, setting up the same desktop environment for the user no matter which computer the user logs on to in the domain.

- The System program also controls the startup and recovery settings for a computer.

- Windows XP Professional first searches the AUTOEXEC.BAT file, if it exists, and sets any environment variables. Next the system environment variables are set, and if there are any conflicts with the environment variables, the system environment variables override them. Finally the user environment variables are set; the user environment variables override all other environment variables.

- The Windows XP Professional System Restore feature allows you to track and reverse harmful changes made to your system.

- AU is a proactive service that allows users with administrative privileges to automatically download and install critical operating system updates such as security fixes and patches.

- The Remote Assistance feature allows you to invite another person, a remote assistant, to help you over the Internet.

- To join a domain or a workgroup, use the Computer Name tab of the System Properties dialog box.

Lesson 4: Configuring and Troubleshooting the Desktop Environment

Windows XP Professional provides great flexibility in configuring the desktop. You can configure your computer for multiple languages and multiple locations. This is especially important for international companies that deal with customers in more than one country or users who live in a country where more than one language is spoken. Windows XP Professional also provides accessibility options that allow you to make the operating system easier to use. All of the desktop settings available through the Control Panel are as easy to configure as those discussed in detail.

After this lesson, you will be able to

- Configure and troubleshoot multiple languages
- Configure and troubleshoot accessibility options

Estimated lesson time: 40 minutes

Configuring Multiple Languages and Multiple Locations

To configure multiple languages and multiple locations, in Control Panel, click Date, Time, Language, and Regional Options. To configure multiple languages, in the Date, Time, Language, And Regional Options window, you can click Add Other Languages or Regional And Language Options. Both selections open the Regional And Language Options dialog box (see Figure 10.19).

The Regional Options tab allows you to configure standards and formats for each language. For example, you can configure the format for displaying numbers, currency, the time, and dates. If you have configured multiple locations, you can also choose your preferred location. In contrast to Microsoft Windows 2000 Professional, Windows XP Professional adds support for the following locales: Galician, Gujarati, Kannada, Kyrgyz, Mongolian (Cyrillic), Punjabi, Divehi, Syriac, and Telugu.

To configure multiple languages in the Languages tab of the Regional And Languages Options dialog box, click Details. Windows XP Professional displays the Text Services And Input Languages dialog box. There are two check boxes available in the Text Services And Input Languages dialog box. The first is Install Files For Complex Script And Right-To-Left Languages. These files are required for Arabic, Armenian, Georgian, Hebrew, Indic, Thai, and Vietnamese languages. The second is Install Files For East Asian Languages. These files are required for Chinese, Japanese, and Korean languages. In the Text Services dialog box, click Add to access the Add Input Language dialog box (see Figure 10.20).

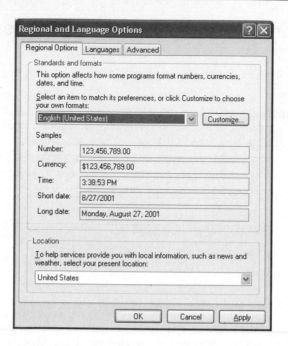

Figure 10.19   The Regional Options tab of the Regional And Language Options dialog box

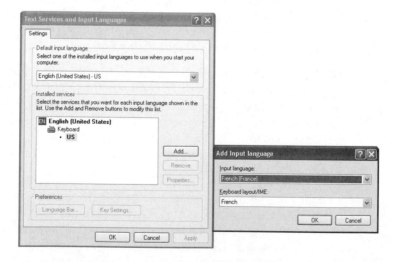

Figure 10.20   The Text Services And Input Languages and Add Input Language dialog boxes

To configure additional languages, scroll through the list of languages and select the one you want to add. If you added at least one language to the one already installed on your computer, your computer is now supporting multiple languages.

If there are any problems with the way your multiple languages or locales are working, you might want to double-check your settings. You can also try uninstalling the multiple language support or multiple locale support. Make sure that everything is working correctly with only one language or locale, and then reconfigure and reinstall the multiple language or multiple locale support.

Practice: Using Control Panel to Configure Multiple Languages

In this practice, you use the Regional And Language Options icon in Control Panel to configure multiple languages and multiple locations.

Run the **MultiLanguages** file in the Demos folder on the CD-ROM accompanying this book for a demonstration of configuring multiple languages.

▶ **To configure multiple languages**

1. Ensure that you are logged on as Fred or with a user account that is a member of the Administrators group.

2. In Control Panel, click the Date, Time, Language, And Regional Options icon.

3. Click Regional And Language Options.

   Windows XP Professional displays the Regional And Language Options dialog box with the Regional Options tab active.

4. Click the Languages tab.

5. In the Text Services And Input Languages box, click Details.

   Windows XP Professional displays the Text Services And Input Languages dialog box.

6. In the Installed Services box, click Add.

   Windows XP Professional displays the Add Input Language dialog box.

7. Click the down-pointing arrow at the end of the Input Languages box to scroll through the listed languages, and select French (France).

   The French Keyboard Layout/IME is selected automatically.

8. Click OK to close the Add Input Language dialog box.

   Windows XP Professional displays the Text Services And Input Languages dialog box. Notice that there are now two Installed Services.

9. Click OK to close the Text Services And Input Languages dialog box.

10. Click OK to close the Regional And Language Options dialog box.

11. Close all open programs.

Configuring and Troubleshooting Accessibility Options

Windows XP Professional provides the ability to configure accessibility options through the Accessibility Options icon in Control Panel.

Configuring Keyboard Options

To configure keyboard options, in Control Panel, click Accessibility Options. In the Accessibility Options window, click Accessibility Options to display the Accessibility Options dialog box. The Keyboard tab of the Accessibility Options dialog box, shown in Figure 10.21, allows you to configure the keyboard options StickyKeys, FilterKeys, and ToggleKeys.

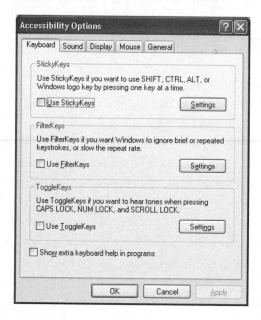

Figure 10.21   The Keyboard tab of the Accessibility Options dialog box

StickyKeys

Turning on StickyKeys allows you to press a multiple key combination, like CTRL+ALT+DELETE, one key at a time. This is useful for people who have difficulty pushing more than one key at a time. This is a check box selection, so it is either on or off. You can configure StickyKeys by clicking Settings to activate the Settings For StickyKeys dialog box (see Figure 10.22).

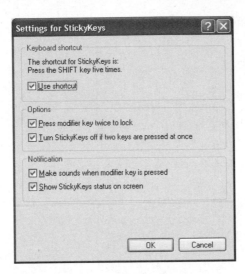

Figure 10.22   The Settings For StickyKeys dialog box

You can configure a shortcut key for StickyKeys. You can use the default shortcut key, pressing SHIFT five times, to turn on StickyKeys. This option is activated by default.

Two other options can also be configured for StickyKeys: Press Modifier Key Twice To Lock and Turn StickyKeys Off If Two Keys Are Pressed At Once. The modifier keys are CTRL, ALT, SHIFT, and the Windows Logo key. If you select the modifier key option, pressing one of the modifier keys twice will cause that key to remain active until you press it again. This is useful for people who have difficulty pressing key combinations. If you choose to use the second option, StickyKeys is disabled if two keys are pressed simultaneously.

Two Notification settings can be configured for StickyKeys: Make Sounds When Modifier Key Is Pressed and Show StickyKeys Status On Screen. The first notification setting causes a sound to be made when any of the modifier keys—CTRL, ALT, SHIFT, or the Windows Logo key—is pressed. The second notification setting causes a StickyKeys icon to be displayed in the taskbar when StickyKeys is turned on.

FilterKeys

The Keyboard tab also allows you to configure FilterKeys. Turning on FilterKeys causes the keyboard to ignore brief or repeated keystrokes. This option also allows you to configure the keyboard repeat rate, which is the rate at which a key continuously held down repeats the keystroke. This is a check box selection, so it is either on or off. You can configure FilterKeys by clicking Settings to activate the Settings For FilterKeys dialog box (see Figure 10.23).

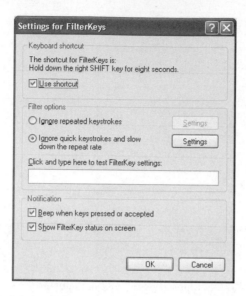

Figure 10.23   The Settings For FilterKeys dialog box

You can configure a shortcut key for FilterKeys. You can use the default shortcut key, holding down the RIGHT SHIFT key for eight seconds, to turn on FilterKeys. This setting is activated by default.

Two other Filter options can also be configured for FilterKeys: Ignore Repeated Keystrokes and Ignore Quick Keystrokes And Slow Down The Repeat Rate. Ignore Repeated Keystrokes is inactive by default, and Ignore Quick Keystrokes And Slow Down The Repeat Rate is active by default. Only one of these two filter options can be active at a time. Configure each of them by clicking Settings.

Two Notification settings can be configured for FilterKeys: Beep When Keys Pressed Or Accepted and Show FilterKey Status On Screen. The first notification setting causes a beep when you press a key and another beep when the keystroke is accepted. The second notification option causes a FilterKeys icon to be displayed in the taskbar when FilterKeys is turned on. These settings are check boxes, so one of the settings, both of the settings (the default), or neither of the settings can be selected.

ToggleKeys

You can also configure ToggleKeys in the Keyboard tab. Turning on ToggleKeys causes the computer to make a high-pitched sound each time the CAPS LOCK, NUM LOCK, or SCROLL LOCK keys are switched on. Turning on ToggleKeys also causes the computer to make a low-pitched sound each time these three keys are turned off.

You can configure a shortcut key for ToggleKeys by clicking Settings. You can use the shortcut key, holding down NUM LOCK for five seconds, to turn on ToggleKeys. This setting is activated by default.

> **Note**   There is one more check box on the Keyboard tab: Show Extra Keyboard Help In Programs. When activated, this causes other programs to display additional keyboard help if available.

Configuring Sound Options

The Sound tab provides the Use Sound Sentry check box, which allows you to configure Windows XP Professional to generate visual warnings when your computer makes a sound. The Sound tab also provides the Use ShowSounds check box, which allows you to configure Windows XP Professional programs to display captions for the speech and sounds they make.

Configuring Display Options

The Display tab of the Accessibility Options dialog box provides a High Contrast check box, which allows you to configure Windows XP Professional to use color and fonts designed for easy reading. You can click Settings to turn off or on the use of a shortcut, LEFT ALT+LEFT SHIFT+PRINT SCREEN, which is enabled by default. Clicking Settings also allows you to select the high-contrast appearance scheme that you want to use. The Display tab also provides cursor options that allow you to set the blink rate and the width of the cursor.

Configuring Mouse Options

The Mouse tab provides the Use MouseKeys check box, which allows you to configure Windows XP Professional to control the pointer with the numeric keypad on your keyboard. You can click Settings to configure MouseKeys in the Settings For MouseKeys dialog box (see Figure 10.24).

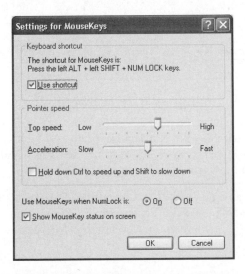

Figure 10.24   The Settings For MouseKeys dialog box

MouseKeys uses a shortcut, LEFT ALT+LEFT SHIFT+NUM LOCK, which is enabled by default. You can also configure the pointer speed and acceleration speed. There is even a check box, Hold Down Ctrl To Speed Up And Shift To Slow Down, that allows you to temporarily speed up or slow down the mouse pointer speed when you are using MouseKeys. To speed up the mouse pointer movement, hold down CTRL while you press the numeric keypad directional keys. To slow down the mouse pointer movement, hold down SHIFT while you press the numeric keypad directional keys.

Configuring General Tab Options

The General tab (see Figure 10.25) allows you to configure Automatic Reset. This feature turns off all the accessibility features, except the SerialKeys devices, after the computer has been idle for a specified amount of time.

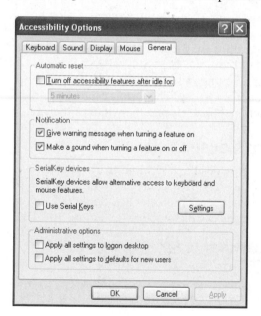

Figure 10.25   The General tab of the Accessibility Options dialog box

The General tab includes the Notification feature, which allows you to configure Windows XP Professional to give a warning message when a feature is activated and to make a sound when turning a feature on or off.

The General tab also allows you to activate the SerialKeys Devices feature, which configures Windows XP Professional to support an alternative input device (also called an augmentative communication device) to your computer's serial port.

The Administrative Options feature provides two check boxes, Apply All Settings To Logon Desktop and Apply All Settings To Defaults For New Users, that allow you to configure Windows XP Professional to apply all configured accessibility options to this user at logon and to apply all configured accessibility options to all new users.

Lesson Review

The following questions will help you determine whether you have learned enough to move on to the next lesson. If you have difficulty answering these questions, review the material in this lesson before beginning the next lesson. The answers are in Appendix A, "Questions and Answers."

1. How can you configure Windows XP Professional to use multiple languages?

2. Turning on _____ allows you to press a multiple key combination, like CTRL+ALT+DELETE, one key at a time. (Choose all answers that are correct.)

   a. FilterKeys

   b. StickyKeys

   c. ToggleKeys

   d. MultiKeys

3. Turning on _____ causes the keyboard to ignore brief or repeated keystrokes. This option also allows you to configure the keyboard repeat rate, which is the rate at which a key continuously held down repeats the keystroke.

4. When using MouseKeys, to speed up the mouse pointer movement, hold down the _____ key while you press the numeric keypad directional keys. To slow down the mouse pointer movement, hold down the _____ key while you press the numeric keypad directional keys.

5. The _____ tab in the Accessibility Options dialog box includes the Notification feature, which allows you to configure Windows XP Professional to give a warning message when a feature is activated and to make a sound when turning a feature on or off.

Lesson Summary

- In Control Panel, click Date, Time, Language, And Regional Options to configure Windows XP Professional for multiple languages and multiple locales.

- StickyKeys allows you to press a multiple key combination, like CTRL+ALT+DELETE, one key at a time.

- FilterKeys causes the keyboard to ignore brief or repeated keystrokes.

- ToggleKeys causes the computer to make a high-pitched sound each time the CAPS LOCK, NUM LOCK, or SCROLL LOCK keys are switched on.

- SoundSentry causes Windows XP Professional to generate visual warnings when your computer makes a sound.

- ShowSounds causes Windows XP Professional programs to display captions for the speech and sounds they make.

- The Display tab of the Accessibility Options dialog box provides a High Contrast check box that allows you to configure Windows XP Professional to use color and fonts designed for easy reading.

- MouseKeys allows you to configure Windows XP Professional to control the pointer with the numeric keypad on your keyboard.

Lesson 5: Managing Windows Components

Windows XP Professional provides the Add or Remove Programs tool in Control Panel to make it easy for you manage programs and Windows components on your computer. You use it to add applications, such as Microsoft Word from CD-ROM, floppy disk, or network shares. You also use it to add Windows components to a Windows XP Professional installation. Use the Add or Remove Programs tool to remove applications or Windows components as well. All the Windows components are installed in the same way. This lesson concentrates on Internet Information Services (IIS).

After this lesson, you will be able to

- Add and remove Windows components
- Install Microsoft Internet Information Services (IIS)

Estimated lesson time: 20 minutes

Installing and Removing Windows Components

To install or remove programs (such as Microsoft Word) on a computer running Windows XP Professional, in Control Panel, click Add Or Remove Programs. You also use the Add or Remove Programs tool to install or remove Windows components from a computer running Windows XP Professional. In the Add Or Remove Programs window, click Add/Remove Windows Components. Windows XP Professional starts the Windows Components Wizard (see Figure 10.26).

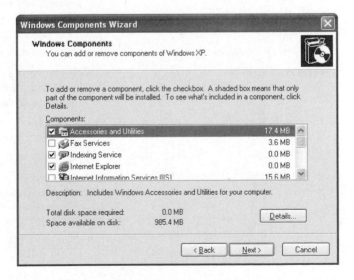

Figure 10.26 Windows Components Wizard

Installing Windows Components

You can install Windows components that you did not select when you installed Windows XP Professional on your computer. The components you can install include Fax Services, Internet Information Services (IIS), Management and Monitoring Tools, Message Queuing, and additional Network Services. If you want to install one of the Windows components, select it and then click Next.

To install IIS, you would do the following:

1. Click Start, click Control Panel, and then click Add Or Remove Programs.
2. In the Add Or Remove Programs window, click Add/Remove Windows Components.

   Windows XP Professional starts the Windows Components Wizard.
3. Select Internet Information Services (IIS).
4. Ensure that the checkbox to the left of Internet Information Services (IIS) is selected. Click Details.

   The Windows Components Wizard displays the Internet Information Services page, which shows the components included when you install Internet Information Services. Table 10.6 lists these components.

Table 10.6   Components Included with Internet Information Services (IIS)

Component	Selected by default	Description
Common Files	Yes	Installs the required IIS program files
Documentation	Yes	Installs documentation about publishing site content, and Web and FTP Server Administration
File Transfer Protocol (FTP) Service	No	Provides support to create FTP sites used to upload and download files
FrontPage 2000 Server Extensions	Yes	Enables authoring and administration of Web sites with Microsoft FrontPage and Microsoft Visual InterDev
Internet Information Services Snap-In	Yes	Installs the IIS Administrative interface into Microsoft Management Console
SMTP Service	Yes	Supports the transfer of electronic mail
World Wide Web Service	Yes	Uses the Hypertext Transfer Protocol (HTTP) to respond to Web client requests on a Transmission Control Protocol/ Internet Protocol (TCP/IP) network

5. Click OK to close the Internet Information Services (IIS) page.

6. In the Windows Components page, click Next to continue with the installation of IIS.

   The Windows Components Wizard displays the Configuring Components page while the appropriate files are copied and the components are configured. This might take a few minutes.

7. In the Completing The Windows Components Wizard page, click Finish.

8. Click Close to close the Add or Remove Programs tool.

Removing Windows Components

The Windows Components Wizard is also used to uninstall or remove Windows components from your computer. If you want to remove a Windows component, on the Windows Component page of the Windows Components Wizard, clear the check box for the component you want to remove and click Next. The Windows Components Wizard displays the Configuring Components page as the files are removed from your computer. When the component is removed, the Windows Components Wizard displays the Completing The Windows Components Wizard page; click Finish to close the wizard. Click Close to close the Add or Remove Programs tool and then close Control Panel.

Managing Internet Information Services

Internet Information Services (IIS) allows you to easily publish information on the Internet or on your or your company's intranet. You place your Web files in directories on your server and users establish HTTP connections and view your files with a Web browser. Internet Information Services for Windows XP Professional is designed for home or small business networks and only allows 10 simultaneous client connections. It also does not provide all of the features that the server version provides.

Use the Internet Information Services snap-in to manage IIS. The Internet Information Services snap-in helps you manage the content of and access to your Web and FTP sites. To access the Internet Information Services snap-in, click Start, point to All Programs, point to Administrative Tools, and then click Internet Information Services. The Internet Information Services snap-in lets you handle all aspects of administration for IIS. For example, every Web and FTP site must have a home directory. When you install IIS, a default home directory is created. When you create a new Web site, you can use the Internet Information Services snap-in to change your home directory.

To change your home directory, in the Internet Information Services snap-in, right-click a Web or FTP site and then click Properties. In the site's Properties dialog box, click the Home directory tab. You can specify a directory on this computer, a shared directory located on another computer, or a redirection to a Uniform Resource Locator (URL), and then type the path in the Local Path text box. Click OK and you have changed your home directory.

If your Web site contains files that are located in directories other than your home directory (for example, on another computer), you must create virtual directories to include these files on your Web site. You use the Internet Information Services snap-in to create these virtual directories. In the snap-in select the Web or FTP site to which you want to add a directory. On the Action menu, point to New, and click Virtual Directory. This starts the Virtual Directory Creation Wizard, which will guide you through creating the new directory.

Lesson Review

The following questions will help you determine whether you have learned enough to move on to the next lesson. If you have difficulty answering these questions, review the material in this lesson before beginning the next chapter. The answers are in Appendix A, "Questions and Answers."

1. How do you add Windows components to your Windows XP Professional installation?

2. What service does Internet Information Services (IIS) provide?

3. How many simultaneous client connections can you have using Internet Information Services for Windows XP Professional?

   a. 8

   b. 10

   c. 20

   d. 32

4. How do you administer Internet Information Services (IIS) for Windows XP Professional?

Lesson Summary

- You use the Add or Remove Programs tool in Control Panel to add and remove applications from CD-ROM, floppy disk, or network shares.

- You use the Add or Remove Programs tool to add or remove Windows components, such Internet Information Services (IIS).

- You click Add/Remove Windows Components in the Add or Remove Programs window to start the Windows Components Wizard.

- You use Internet Information Services (IIS) to publish information on the Internet or on your intranet.

- Internet Information Services for Windows XP Professional is designed for home or small business networks and only allows 10 simultaneous client connections.

- You use the Internet Information Services snap-in to manage IIS.

C H A P T E R   1 1

Installing, Managing, and Troubleshooting Hardware Devices and Drivers

About This Chapter

One of the primary tools for configuring hardware is the Control Panel. Another useful tool for implementing, managing, and troubleshooting hardware devices and drivers is the Device Manager, found in the Computer Management console.

Before You Begin

To complete this chapter, you must have

- A computer that meets the minimum hardware requirements listed in the preface, "About This Book"
- Installed the Microsoft Windows XP Professional software on the computer

Lesson 1: Understanding Automatic and Manual Hardware Installation

Windows XP Professional supports both Plug and Play and non–Plug and Play hardware. This lesson introduces you to the automatic hardware installation features of Windows XP Professional. Occasionally, Windows XP Professional fails to automatically detect a hardware device. When this occurs, you must install the hardware device manually. You might also have to do this if the device requires a specific hardware resource to ensure that it is installed properly.

After this lesson, you will be able to
- Describe how to install hardware automatically
- Describe how to install hardware manually

Estimated lesson time: 30 minutes

Installing Hardware Automatically

Windows XP Professional supports Plug and Play hardware. For most devices that are Plug and Play–compliant, as long as the appropriate driver is available and the basic input/output system (BIOS) on the computer is a Plug and Play BIOS or an Advanced Configuration and Power Interface (ACPI) BIOS, Windows XP Professional automatically detects, installs, and configures the device. When there is a new piece of hardware detected that cannot be installed automatically, Windows XP Professional displays the Found New Hardware Wizard (see Figure 11.1).

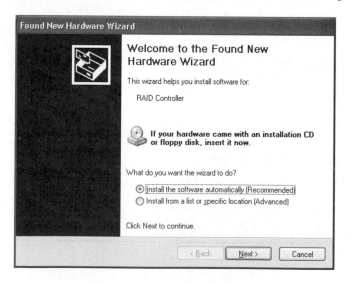

Figure 11.1   The Found New Hardware Wizard

However, you might occasionally need to initiate automatic installation for some Plug and Play hardware. You do this with the Add Hardware Wizard. For non–Plug and Play hardware, Windows XP Professional often identifies the hardware and automatically installs and configures it. For non–Plug and Play hardware that Windows XP Professional does not identify, install, and configure, you initiate the automatic installation of the hardware with the Add Hardware Wizard.

To automatically install hardware, complete the following steps:

1. Click Start, click Control Panel, and then click Printers And Other Hardware.

2. In the Printers And Other Hardware window, under See Also, click Add Hardware to start the Add Hardware Wizard.

   Windows XP Professional queries the hardware about the hardware resources that it requires and the settings for those resources. A hardware resource allows a hardware device to communicate directly with the operating system. Windows XP Professional can resolve conflicts between Plug and Play hardware for hardware resources.

3. Confirm the automatic hardware installation.

   After Windows XP Professional finishes the installation, you should verify correct installation and configure the hardware.

Using the Add Hardware Wizard

You can also use the Add Hardware Wizard to initiate automatic hardware installation for undetected hardware devices, both Plug and Play and non–Plug and Play, and to troubleshoot devices.

To start the Add Hardware Wizard, do the following:

1. In Control Panel, click Printers And Other Hardware.

2. Click Add Hardware.

   Windows XP Professional starts the Add Hardware Wizard, which is used to install software to support the hardware you add to your computer and to troubleshoot problems that you might be having with your hardware.

Note You can also click System in the Performance And Maintenance window accessed from Control Panel and start the Add Hardware Wizard from the Hardware tab of the System Properties dialog box.

---

3. Click Next to close the Welcome To The Add Hardware Wizard page.

   Windows XP Professional searches for new devices and one of the following three events occurs:

   - If Windows XP Professional detects any new Plug and Play hardware, it installs the new hardware.

- If Windows XP Professional detects new hardware, it starts the Found New Hardware Wizard.

- If the wizard cannot find a new device, it displays the Is The Hardware Connected page. If you have already connected the new device, click Yes, I Have Already Connected The Hardware and then click Next. The wizard displays the The Following Hardware Is Already Installed On Your Computer page, shown in Figure 11.2. To add hardware that is not in the list, click Add A New Hardware Device.

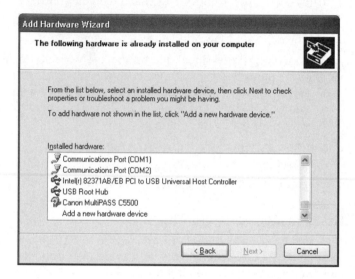

Figure 11.2   Adding hardware or troubleshooting with the Add Hardware Wizard

---

Note   To use the Add Hardware Wizard to troubleshoot a hardware device, click the device in the list of installed hardware devices and click Next. The Completing The Add Hardware Wizard page appears. Click Finish to launch a troubleshooter to help resolve any problems you might be having with that hardware device.

Confirming Hardware Installation

After installing hardware, you should confirm the installation using the Device Manager.

You can do the following to start Device Manager:

1. In Control Panel, click Performance And Maintenance.
2. Click System.
3. Click the Hardware tab, and then click Device Manager.

Note   Device Manager can also be launched from the Computer Management console. It is a snap-in located under System Tools.

This allows you to view the installed hardware, as shown in Figure 11.3.

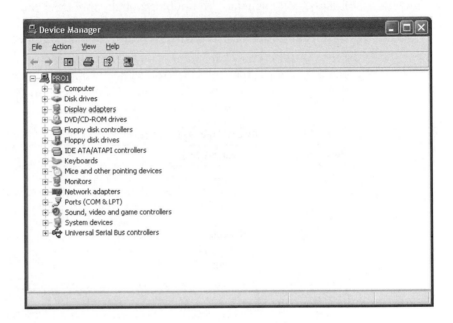

Figure 11.3   Device Manager showing devices listed by type

Windows XP Professional uses icons in the Device Manager window to identify each installed hardware device. If Windows XP Professional does not have an icon for the device type, it displays a question mark.

Expand the device tree to locate the newly installed hardware device. The device icon indicates whether the hardware device is operating properly. You can use the information in Table 11.1 to determine the hardware status.

Table 11.1   Device Manager Hardware Status

Icon	Hardware status
Normal icon	Hardware is operating properly.
Stop sign on icon	Windows XP Professional disabled the hardware device because of hardware conflicts. To correct this, right-click the device icon and then click Properties. Set the hardware resources manually according to what is available in the system.
Exclamation point on icon	The hardware device is incorrectly configured or its drivers are missing.

Installing Hardware Manually

To manually install hardware, first determine which hardware resource is required by the hardware device. Next, you must determine the available hardware resources. In some cases, you will have to change hardware resources. Finally, you might have to troubleshoot any problems you encounter.

Determining Which Hardware Resources Are Required

When installing new hardware, you need to know what resources the hardware can use. You can reference the product documentation to determine the resources that a hardware device requires. Table 11.2 describes the resources that hardware devices use to communicate with an operating system.

Table 11.2   Hardware Device Resources

Resource	Description
Interrupts	Hardware devices use interrupts to send messages. The microprocessor knows this as an interrupt request (IRQ). The microprocessor uses this information to determine which device needs its attention and the type of attention that it needs. Windows XP Professional provides 16 IRQs, numbered 0 to 15, that are assigned to devices. For example, Windows XP Professional assigns IRQ 1 to the keyboard.
Input/output (I/O) ports	I/O ports are a section of memory that a hardware device uses to communicate with the operating system. When a microprocessor receives an IRQ, the operating system checks the I/O port address to retrieve additional information about what the hardware device wants it to do. An I/O port is represented as a hexadecimal number.
Direct memory access (DMA)	DMAs are channels that allow a hardware device, such as a floppy disk drive, to access memory directly, without interrupting the microprocessor. DMA channels speed up access to memory. Windows XP Professional has eight DMA channels, numbered 0 through 7.
Memory	Many hardware devices, such as a network interface card (NIC), use onboard memory or reserve system memory. This reserved memory is unavailable for use by other devices or Windows XP Professional.

Determining Available Hardware Resources

After you determine which resources a hardware device requires, you can look for an available resource. Device Manager provides a list of all hardware resources and their availability, as shown in Figure 11.4.

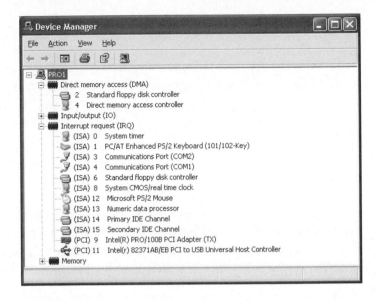

Figure 11.4   Device Manager showing resources listed by connection

You can do the following to view the hardware resource lists:

1. In the System Properties dialog box, click the Hardware tab, and then click Device Manager.

2. On the View menu, click Resources By Connection.

   The Device Manager displays the resources that are currently in use (for example, IRQs).

3. To view a list of resources for another type of hardware resource, click the type of hardware resource you want to see on the View menu.

When you know which hardware resources are available, you can install the hardware manually with the Add Hardware Wizard.

Note If you select a hardware resource during manual installation, you might need to configure the hardware device so that it can use the resource. For example, for a network adapter to use IRQ 5, you might have to set a jumper on the adapter and configure Windows XP Professional so that it recognizes that the adapter now uses IRQ 5.

Changing Hardware Resource Assignments

You might need to change hardware resource assignments. For example, a hardware device might require a specific resource presently in use by another device. You might also encounter two hardware devices requesting the same hardware resource, resulting in a conflict.

To change a resource setting, use the Resources tab in the device's Properties dialog box. You can use the following procedure to access the Resources tab:

1. In the Hardware tab of the System Properties dialog box, click Device Manager.

2. Expand the device list, right-click the specific device, and then click Properties.

3. In the Properties dialog box for the device, click the Resources tab.

Tip   When you change a hardware resource, print the content of Device Manager. This provides you with a record of the hardware configuration. If you encounter problems, you can use the printout to verify the hardware resource assignments.

From this point, follow the same procedures that you used to choose a hardware resource during a manual installation.

Note   Changing the resource assignments for non–Plug and Play devices in Device Manager does not change the resources used by that device. You only use Device Manager to instruct the operating system on device configuration. To change the resources used by a non–Plug and Play device, consult the device documentation to see whether switches or jumpers must be configured on the device.

Lesson Review

The following questions will help you determine whether you have learned enough to move on to the next lesson. If you have difficulty answering these questions, review the material in this lesson before beginning the next lesson. The answers are in Appendix A, "Questions and Answers."

1. When you initiate automatic hardware installation by starting the Add Hardware Wizard, what does Windows XP Professional query the hardware about?

2. _____ are channels that allow a hardware device, such as a floppy disk drive, to access memory directly, without interrupting the microprocessor.

3. Why would you install a hardware device manually?

Lesson Summary

- For most Plug and Play hardware, you connect the device to the computer, and Windows XP Professional automatically configures the new settings.

- For non–Plug and Play hardware, Windows XP Professional often identifies the hardware and automatically installs and configures it.

- For the occasional Plug and Play hardware device and for any non–Plug and Play hardware that Windows XP Professional does not identify, install, and configure, you initiate automatic hardware installation with the Add Hardware Wizard.

- When you manually install hardware, you must determine any resources required by that hardware device. Hardware resources include interrupts, I/O ports, and memory.

- The Device Manager snap-in provides a list of all hardware resources and their availability.

Lesson 2: Configuring and Troubleshooting Hardware Devices

Device Manager is one of the tools you use to manage and troubleshoot devices. This lesson also introduces the System Information snap-in, how to use it, and how it helps you manage your system.

After this lesson, you will be able to

- Use Device Manager to configure and troubleshoot devices
- Use System Information to manage devices

Estimated lesson time: 60 minutes

Using Device Manager

Device Manager provides you with a graphical view of the hardware installed on your computer and helps you manage and troubleshoot it. You can use Device Manager to disable, uninstall, and update device drivers. Device Manager also helps you determine if the hardware on your computer is working properly. It lists devices with problems, and each device that is flagged is displayed with the corresponding status information.

Tip   Windows XP Professional also provides the Hardware Troubleshooter to troubleshoot hardware problems. To access the Hardware Troubleshooter, on the Start menu, click Help And Support. In the Help And Support Center, under Pick A Help Topic, click Hardware. In the Hardware list, click Fixing A Hardware Problem. Under Fixing A Hardware Problem, click Hardware Troubleshooter.

Configuring and Troubleshooting Devices

When you change device configurations manually, Device Manager can help you avoid problems by allowing you to identify free resources and assign a device to that resource, disable devices to free resources, and reallocate resources used by devices to free a required resource. You must be logged on as a member of the Administrators group to change resource settings. Even if you are logged on as Administrator, if your computer is connected to a network, policy settings on the network might prevent you from changing resources.

Caution   Improperly changing resource settings on devices can disable your hardware and cause your computer to stop working.

Windows XP Professional automatically identifies Plug and Play devices and arbitrates their resource requests. However, the resource allocation among Plug and Play devices is not permanent. If another Plug and Play device requests a resource that has already been allocated, Windows XP Professional again arbitrates the requests to satisfy all of them.

You should not change resource settings for a Plug and Play device manually because Windows XP Professional will then be unable to arbitrate the assigned resources if requested by another Plug and Play device. In Device Manager, Plug and Play devices have a Resources tab in their Properties dialog box. To free the resource settings you manually assigned and allow Windows XP Professional to again arbitrate the resources, select the Use Automatic Settings check box in the Resources tab.

Note   Devices supported by Microsoft Windows NT 4 have fixed resource settings. These resource settings are usually defined during an upgrade from Windows NT 4 to Windows XP Professional, but you can also define them by using the Add New Hardware Wizard in Control Panel.

You can use the following procedure to configure or troubleshoot a device using Device Manager:

1. Click Start, right-click My Computer, and then click Manage.

   The Computer Management console opens, as shown in Figure 11.5.

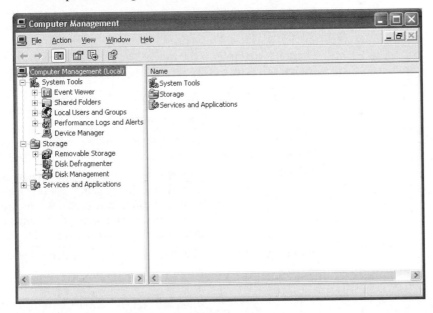

Figure 11.5   The Computer Management console

2. Under System Tools, click Device Manager.

3. In the Details pane, double-click the device type, and then double-click the device you want to configure.

   The *device* Properties dialog box appears (where *device* is a specific device; see Figure 11.6).

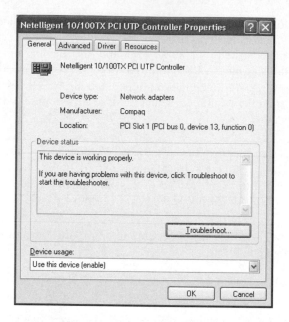

Figure 11.6   Netelligent 10/100TX PCI UTP Controller Properties dialog box

The tabs available in the *device* Properties dialog box vary depending on the device selected, but might include some of the ones listed in Table 11.3.

Table 11.3   **Device Properties Dialog Box Tabs**

Tab	Functionality
Advanced or Advanced Properties	The properties listed vary depending on the device selected.
General	Displays the device type, manufacturer, and location. It also displays the device status and provides a troubleshooter to help you troubleshoot any problems you are having with the device. The troubleshooter steps you through a series of questions to determine the problem and provide a solution.
Device Properties	The properties listed vary depending on the device selected.
Driver	Displays the driver provider, driver date, driver version, and digital signer. This tab also provides the following three additional buttons: Driver Details, Uninstall, and Driver Update. These buttons allow you to get additional information on the driver, uninstall the driver, or update the driver with a newer version, respectively.
Port Settings	In a communications port (COM1) Properties dialog box, displays and allows you to configure settings for bits per second, data bits, parity, stop bits, and flow control.

Table 11.3   *(continued)*

Tab	Functionality
Properties	Determines the way Windows uses the device. For example, on the CD-ROM, the properties could include volume and digital CD playback, which allows you to enable digital instead of analog playback. These settings determine how Windows uses the CD-ROM for playing CD music.
Resources	Displays the resource type and setting, whether there are any resource conflicts, and whether or not you can change the resource settings.

4. To configure a device, click the appropriate tab. To troubleshoot, in the General tab, click Troubleshooter.

Viewing Hidden Devices

By default, Device Manager does not display all devices. Some devices, like non–Plug and Play devices and devices that are not currently connected to the computer (phantom devices), are hidden.

To view any hidden non–Plug and Play devices, on the Device Manager View menu, click Show Hidden Devices.

To view phantom devices, follow these steps:

1. Click Start and then click Run. In the Open text box, type **cmd** and click OK.

2. At the command prompt, type **set DEVMGR_SHOW_NONPRESENT_DEVICES=1**

3. Press ENTER.

4. Start Device Manager.

5. At the command prompt, type **start devmgmt.msc**.

Note   To set Device Manager to always show phantom devices, add the following system environment variable:
set DEVMGR_SHOW_NONPRESENT_DEVICES=1
For information on adding system environment variables, see Chapter 10, "Configuring Windows XP Professional," Lesson 3, "Configuring Operating System Settings."

Practice: Using Device Manager

In this practice, you use Device Manager to review the devices on your system and their status. You also use Device Manager to simulate troubleshooting an unterminated Small Computer System Interface (SCSI) chain.

▶   **To use Device Manager**

1. Click Start, right-click My Computer, and then click Manage.

    The Computer Management console opens.

2. Under System Tools, click Device Manager.

3. In the details pane, double-click Disk Drives, and then double-click one of the drives listed.

    The Properties dialog box for that drive appears and in the General tab, the Device Status field indicates if there are any problems with the drive.

4. Click Troubleshoot. (Normally you would only do this if a problem was indicated with this device.)

    Windows XP Professional displays the Help And Support Center window with the Drives And Network Adapters Troubleshooter displayed. Troubleshooter steps you through a series of questions to help you resolve your problem.

5. Click I Am Having A Problem With A Hard Disk Drive Or Floppy Disk Drive, and then click Next.

6. Click Yes, I Am Having A Problem With A SCSI Device, and then click Next.

    You are asked, "Is Your Hardware On The HCL?"

7. Click Yes, My Hardware Is On The HCL.

    You are asked, "Does Your Drive Work When All The SCSI Components Have The Power They Need?"

8. Click No, My Drive Does Not Work, and then click Next.

    You are asked, "Does This Information Help You To Solve The Problem?"

9. Click No, My Device Still Does Not Work, and then click Next.

    You are asked, "Does Rolling Back To A Previous Driver Solve The Problem?"

10. Click No, I Still Have A Problem.

    You are asked, "Does Reinstalling Or Updating Your Driver Solve The Problem?"

11. Click No, I Still Have A Problem.

    You are asked, "Does Your Drive Work When You Replace Any Faulty Cables Or Adapters?"

12. Click No, My Drive Does Not Work.

    You are asked, "Does Your Drive Work When You Terminate The SCSI Chain?"

13. Click Yes, Terminating The SCSI Chain Solves The Problem, and then click Next.

    Had an unterminated SCSI chain been the problem you were trying to solve, you would have just fixed it.

14. Close Help And Support Center, close the Properties dialog box for the selected disk drive, and close Computer Management.

Installing, Configuring, Managing, and Troubleshooting Fax Support

Windows XP Professional can provide complete fax facilities from your computer. It provides you with the capability to send and receive faxes with a locally attached fax device, or with a remote fax device connected on your network. You can track and monitor fax activity as well. However, the Fax component of Windows XP Professional is not installed by default, so you must install it.

You can use the following procedure to install the Fax component:

1. Click Start, click Control Panel, and then click Add Or Remove Programs.

2. In the Add Or Remove Programs window, click Add/Remove Windows Components.

3. In the Windows Components Wizard, select Fax Services, and then click Next.

   The Configuring Components page appears while the Windows Components Wizard examines the components, copies the necessary files, and configures the Fax Service.

4. When the Completing The Windows Components Wizard page appears, read the page, and then click Finish.

5. Close the Add Or Remove Programs window.

6. In Control Panel, click Printers And Other Hardware.

7. In the Printers And Other Hardware window, click Printers And Faxes.

   Notice the Fax icon.

Note   If there is no Fax icon, click Install a Local Fax Printer to add one.

If you have a fax device, such as a fax modem, installed when you install the Fax Service, Control Panel has a Fax icon. The Fax icon is used to add, monitor, and troubleshoot fax devices, including fax modems and fax printers.

You can use the following procedure to configure the Fax component:

1. In the Printers And Faxes window, double-click the Fax icon.

   Windows XP Professional displays the Welcome To The Fax Configuration Wizard page. The Fax Configuration Wizard helps you configure your computer to send and receive faxes.

2. Click Next.

   The Fax Configuration Wizard displays the Sender Information page, which allows you to enter information in the following text boxes: Your Full Name, Fax Number, E-Mail Address, Title, Company, Office Location, Department, Home Phone, Work Phone, Address, and Billing Code.

3. Type the appropriate information in the text boxes and click Next.

4. On the Completing The Fax Configuration Wizard page, click Finish.

Windows XP Professional displays the Fax Console.

Tip To configure a fax, click Configure Fax on the Tools menu of the Fax Console. To open the Fax Console, click Start, point to All Programs, point to Accessories, point to Communications, point to Fax, and then click Fax Console.

Managing and Troubleshooting Fax Support

Windows XP Professional provides the Fax Console to help you manage and troubleshoot faxes.

To manage and troubleshoot faxes, complete the following steps:

1. Click Start, point to All Programs, and point to Accessories.

2. Point to Communications, point to Fax, and then click Fax Console.

Windows XP Professional displays the Fax Console (see Figure 11.7).

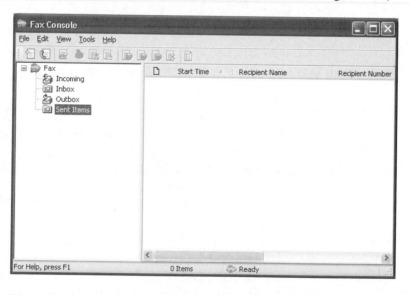

Figure 11.7 The Fax Console

The Outbox contains all faxes waiting to be sent, or in the process of being sent, whether the faxes were sent using a locally attached fax device or a network fax device. You can right-click any fax in the details pane, and then press DELETE or click Delete on the File menu to delete the fax. When you right-click a fax in the details pane, you can also click Pause to prevent it from being sent, or click Resume to place a fax that you paused back in the queue to be sent. If a fax fails, you can right-click the fax in the details pane and click Restart to attempt to resend the fax. Finally, when you right-click a fax in the details pane, you can click Save As to save a copy of the fax, Mail To to mail a copy of the fax to someone, or Print to print a copy of the fax.

The Incoming box allows you to manage incoming faxes in the same manner that the Outgoing box helps you manage outgoing faxes. You can click the Incoming box, and then right-click a fax in the details pane to delete, pause, resume, save, mail to someone, and print the fax. You can also click Properties to view the properties of an incoming fax.

Table 11.4 discusses some common troubleshooting scenarios.

Table 11.4   Common Troubleshooting Scenarios

Problem	Cause	Solution
When I click the Print button on my application's toolbar, my fax does not print to a fax printer.	The print button on the toolbar of some Windows applications does not use the Print dialog box, causing your document to be printed on the last printer used.	On the File menu of your Windows application, click Print to access the Print dialog box so that you can select your fax printer.
A fax I sent is pending in the Outbox.	There is a problem with the local fax device.	Either there is no local fax device configured to send faxes or there is a problem with the local fax device. Verify there is a local fax device and that it is configured for sending faxes. On the Tools menu of the Fax Console, click Fax Printer Status.
	The remote fax device is busy.	On the Tools menu of the Fax Console, click Fax Printer Status.
Someone sent me a fax, and my incoming fax device is not detecting the call.	There is a problem with your local fax device.	Verify that your local fax device is configured to receive faxes. If you have an external modem, turn it off and on. If you have an internal modem, shut down your computer and restart it.
I'm using dialing rules with calling cards, but the calling card information is not working.	Calling card information is defined on a per-user basis. Ensure the Fax Service is running using the same user account as the calling card information.	Right-click My Computer, click Manage, and then click Services And Applications. In the Services list, double-click Fax. Click Log On. Set the Fax Service to run under the calling card user account.

(continued)

Table 11.4 *(continued)*

Problem	Cause	Solution
I can't send faxes with Microsoft Outlook Express.	Outlook Express is not compliant with a Messaging Application Programming Interface (MAPI) client interface and cannot be used to send faxes.	Use Microsoft Outlook 2000.

Sending a Fax

Windows XP Professional makes it simple for you to use your computer to send faxes.

Note If you need to install a fax printer, the steps are the same as for installing a printer. For more information, see Chapter 6, "Setting Up, Configuring, and Troubleshooting Common Setup and Configuration Problems for Network Printers." To configure a fax printer or check the status of a fax printer, click Fax Printer Configuration or Fax Printer Status on the Tools menu of the Fax Console. To open the Fax Console, click Start, point to All Programs, point to Accessories, point to Communications, point to Fax, and then click Fax Console.

You can use the following procedure to send a fax:

1. Click Start, point to All Programs, and point to Accessories.
2. Point to Communications, point to Fax, and then click Send A Fax.

   Windows XP Professional displays the Welcome To The Send Fax Wizard page, which indicates that if you want to fax a document, you create or open the document in a Windows-based application and print it to a fax printer.
3. Click Next.

   The Send Fax Wizard displays the Recipient Information page, which allows you to enter the name and number of the person to whom you want to send a fax.

Tip To send the fax to multiple recipients, enter the first person's name and phone number and then click Add. Enter the information for each recipient and click Add until all recipients have been entered.

4. Enter the appropriate information, and then click Next.

   The Send Fax Wizard displays the Preparing The Cover Page page, which allows you to select a cover page template. You can also enter a subject line, a note, and sender information.

Note   Either the Subject Line or Note text boxes must be filled in to proceed.

5. Enter the appropriate information and then click Next.

   The Send Fax Wizard displays the Schedule page, which allows you to choose from the following options to send the fax: Now, When Discount Rates Apply, or A Specific Time In The Next 24 Hours. It also allows you to specify a priority of High, Normal, or Low.

6. Select the appropriate settings, and then click Next.

   The Send Fax Wizard displays the Completing The Send Fax Wizard page.

7. Review the information displayed on the Completing The Send Fax Wizard page and, if it is correct, click Finish to send the fax.

Managing and Troubleshooting I/O Devices

The list of devices that can be installed is too long to include here. The following paragraphs include some of the most common devices and how they are installed, configured, and managed.

Scanners and Cameras

Most digital cameras, scanners, and other imaging devices are Plug and Play devices and Windows XP Professional installs them automatically when you connect them to your computer. If your imaging device is not installed automatically when you connect it, or if it does not support Plug and Play, use the Scanner And Camera Installation Wizard. To open this wizard, in Control Panel, click Printers And Other Hardware, and then click Scanners And Cameras. In the Scanners And Cameras window, double-click Add An Imaging Device to start the Scanners And Camera Installation Wizard. Click Next and follow the on-screen instructions to install your digital camera, scanner, or other imaging device.

In Device Manager, select the appropriate device, and then click Properties. The standard color profile for Integrated Color Management (ICM 2.0) is RGB, but you can add, remove, or select an alternate color profile for a device. To change the color profile, click the Color Management tab on the *device* Properties dialog box. If you are having problems with your scanner or camera, click Troubleshoot in the Scanners And Cameras Properties dialog box.

Mouse Devices

Click the Mouse icon in the Printers And Other Hardware window of Control Panel to configure and troubleshoot your mouse. The Buttons tab (see Figure 11.8) allows you to configure your mouse for a left-handed or right-handed user. It also allows you to set a single mouse click as select or open and to control the double-click speed.

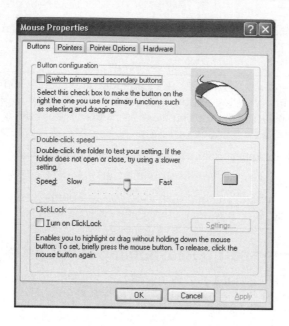

Figure 11.8 The Buttons tab of the Mouse Properties dialog box

The Pointers tab allows you to select or create a custom scheme for your pointer. The Pointer Options tab allows you to adjust the speed and acceleration of your pointer and to set the Snap To Default option, which moves the pointer automatically to the default button in dialog boxes. The last tab is the Hardware tab, which allows you to access the troubleshooter if you are having problems with your mouse. The Hardware tab also has a Properties button that allows you to do an advanced configuration for your mouse. This includes uninstalling or updating your driver, viewing or changing the resources allocated to your mouse, and increasing or decreasing the sensitivity of your mouse by varying the sample rate, which changes how often Windows XP Professional determines the position of your mouse.

Modems

Click Phone And Modem Options in the Printers And Other Hardware window of Control Panel to install, configure, or troubleshoot your modem. To install a new modem, in the Modems tab, click Add. The Add Hardware Wizard then starts to step you through the installation process. To configure an installed modem, click the Modems tab, select the modem from the list of installed modems, and click Properties. Click the appropriate tab for the configuration changes you wish to make; for example, click the Modem tab to set the maximum port speed and whether or not to wait for a dial tone before dialing. The Diagnostics tab allows you to query the modem and to view the modem log. If you need additional help in troubleshooting the modem, the General tab allows you to access the troubleshooter.

There are two other tabs on the Phone And Modem Options dialog box: the Dialing Rules tab and the Advanced tab. The Dialing Rules tab lists all the locations you have configured on the computer. Click Add on this tab to add a new location or click Edit to edit an existing location. The Advanced tab shows the telephony providers installed on this computer. It also allows you to add or remove telephony providers and to configure those already installed.

Game Controllers

Click Game Controllers in the Printers And Other Hardware window of Control Panel to install, configure, or troubleshoot your game controller. Attach the game controller to the computer (for example, if it is a universal serial bus [USB] game controller, attach it to a USB port). If it does not install properly, in Device Manager, look under Human Interface Devices. If the controller is not listed, then check to make sure that USB is enabled in the BIOS. When prompted during system startup, enter BIOS setup and enable USB. If USB is enabled in BIOS, contact the maker or vendor for your computer and obtain the current version of BIOS.

To configure the controller, select a device, then click Properties. To troubleshoot a device, select it and then click Troubleshoot.

IrDA and Wireless Devices

Most internal Infrared Data Association (IrDA) devices should be installed by Windows XP Professional Setup, or when you start Windows XP Professional after adding one of these devices. If you attach an IrDA transceiver to a serial port, you must install it using the Add Hardware Wizard. In Control Panel, click Printers And Other Hardware, and then click Add Hardware to start the Add Hardware Wizard. Click Next to close the Welcome To The Add Hardware Wizard page. Select Yes I Have Already Connected The Hardware, and then click Next. Select Add A New Hardware Device and then click Next, and follow the directions on your screen.

To configure an IrDA device, in Control Panel click Wireless Link. In the Hardware tab, click the device you want to configure and then click Properties. The Properties dialog box shows the status of the device, driver files, and any power management settings.

Note The Wireless Link icon appears in Control Panel only if you have already installed an infrared device on your computer.

Keyboards

Click Keyboard in the Printers And Other Hardware window of Control Panel to configure or troubleshoot a keyboard. In the Speed tab, you can configure the character repeat delay and the character repeat rate. You can also control the cursor blink rate. The Hardware tab shows you the device properties for the installed keyboard and allows you to access the troubleshooter if you are having problems with your keyboard. You can also install a device driver, roll back to a previous device driver, or uninstall a device driver.

Lesson Review

The following questions will help you determine whether you have learned enough to move on to the next lesson. If you have difficulty answering these questions, review the material in this lesson before beginning the next lesson. The answers are in Appendix A, "Questions and Answers."

1. Windows XP Professional automatically identifies Plug and Play devices and arbitrates their resource requests; the resource allocation among these devices is _____ (permanent/not permanent).

2. How can you free any resource settings that you manually assigned to a Plug and Play device?

3. Which of the following devices are not shown by default in Device Manager? (Choose all that apply.)

    a. Devices sharing an IRQ

    b. Phantom devices

    c. Plug and Play devices

    d. Non–Plug and Play devices

4. You get a call on the help desk from a user upset because he cannot send faxes from Outlook Express. What should you tell the user?

5. You get a call on the help desk from a user wondering why there is no Wireless Link icon in Control Panel on her desktop computer like the one on her laptop computer. What should you tell the user?

Lesson Summary

- Device Manager provides you with a graphical view of the hardware installed on your computer and helps you manage and troubleshoot it.

- Device Manager lists devices with problems, and each device that is flagged is displayed with the corresponding status information.

- By default, Device Manager does not display non–Plug and Play devices and devices that are not currently connected to the computer (phantom devices).

- Most imaging devices are installed automatically when you connect them, but if your device is not, Windows XP Professional provides the Scanner and Camera Installation Wizard to help you install it.

- Use the Mouse option in the Printers And Other Hardware window of Control Panel to configure and troubleshoot your mouse.

- Use the Phone And Modem Options option in the Printers And Other Hardware window of Control Panel to install, configure, or troubleshoot your modem.

- Use the Game Controllers option in the Printers And Other Hardware window of Control Panel to install, configure, or troubleshoot your game controller.

- Use the Add Hardware Wizard to install an IrDA transceiver you attach to a serial port.

- The Wireless Link icon that you use to configure an infrared device does not appear in Control Panel until you have installed an infrared device on your computer.

- Use the Keyboard option in the Printers And Other Hardware window of Control Panel to configure or troubleshoot a keyboard.

Lesson 3: Viewing and Configuring Hardware Profiles

Control Panel contains applications that you use to customize selected aspects of the hardware and software configuration for a computer. You configure hardware settings by creating and configuring hardware profiles. Windows XP Professional uses these hardware profiles to determine which drivers to load when system hardware changes.

After this lesson, you will be able to

- Manage hardware profiles

Estimated lesson time: 15 minutes

Understanding Hardware Profiles

A hardware profile stores configuration settings for a set of devices and services. Windows XP Professional can store different hardware profiles to meet the user's different needs. Hardware profiles are used primarily for portable computers. For example, a portable computer can use different hardware configurations depending on whether it is docked or undocked. A portable-computer user can create a hardware profile for each state (docked and undocked) and choose the appropriate profile when starting Windows XP Professional.

Creating or Modifying a Hardware Profile

To create or modify a hardware profile, in Control Panel, click Performance And Maintenance. In the Performance And Maintenance window, click System, and then in the System Properties dialog box, click the Hardware tab. Click Hardware Profiles to view the Available Hardware Profiles list (see Figure 11.9).

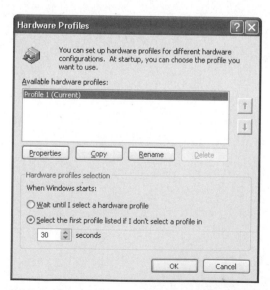

Figure 11.9   Available Hardware Profiles list in the Hardware Profiles dialog box

Windows XP Professional creates an initial profile during installation, listed as Profile 1 (Current). You can create a new profile with the same configuration as another profile. To create a new profile, in the Available Hardware Profiles list, select the profile that you want to copy, and then click Copy.

The order of the profiles in the Available Hardware Profiles list determines the default order at startup. The first profile in the list becomes the default profile. To change the order of the profiles, use the Up and Down arrow buttons.

Activating a Hardware Profile

If there are two or more profiles in the Available Hardware Profiles list, Windows XP Professional prompts the user to make a selection during startup. You can configure how long the computer waits before starting the default configuration. To adjust this time delay, click the Select The First Profile Listed If I Don't Select A Profile In option and then specify the number of seconds in the Seconds text box within the Hardware Profiles Selection group. You can configure Windows XP Professional to start the default profile by setting the number of seconds to 0. To override the default during startup, press SPACEBAR during the system prompt. You can also select the Wait Until I Select A Hardware Profile option to have Windows XP Professional wait for you to select a profile.

When using hardware profiles, be careful not to disable one of the boot devices with the Devices program in Control Panel. If you disable a required boot device, Windows XP Professional might not start. It is a good idea to make a copy of the default profile and then make changes to the new profile. This way, you can use the default profile again if a problem occurs.

Viewing Hardware Profile Properties

To view the properties for a hardware profile, in the Available Hardware Profiles list, select a profile, and then click Properties. This displays the Properties dialog box for the profile.

If Windows XP Professional identifies your computer as a portable unit, the This Is A Portable Computer check box is selected. If Windows XP Professional determines that your portable computer is docked, it automatically selects that option. You cannot change this docked option setting after Windows XP Professional selects it.

Lesson Review

The following questions will help you determine whether you have learned enough to move on to the next lesson. If you have difficulty answering these questions, review the material in this lesson before beginning the next lesson. The answers are in Appendix A, "Questions and Answers."

1. What is the minimum number of hardware profiles you can have on your computer?

2. Computer hardware profiles are an especially important feature for what type of computers?

    a. Computers in a network environment

    b. Computers in a domain

    c. Stand-alone computers

    d. Portable computers

3. Windows XP Professional creates an initial profile during installation and assigns it the name of _____ in the list of hardware profiles available on the computer.

4. Which of the following statements are true about hardware profiles in Windows XP Professional? (Choose all that apply.)

    a. Windows XP Professional only prompts the user to select a hardware profile during startup if there are two or more profiles in the Available Hardware Profiles list.

    b. It is a good idea to delete the default profile when you create a new profile to avoid confusion.

    c. You can configure Windows XP Professional to always start the default profile by selecting the Do Not Display The Select Hardware Profile check box.

    d. You can select the Wait Until I Select A Hardware Profile option to have Windows XP Professional wait for you to select a profile at startup.

Lesson Summary

- A hardware profile stores configuration settings for a set of devices and services.

- Windows XP Professional uses hardware profiles to determine which drivers to load when system hardware changes.

- The primary use of hardware profiles is for a portable computer that can use different hardware configurations depending on whether it is docked or undocked.

- To create or modify a hardware profile, in the System Properties dialog box, click the Hardware tab and then click Hardware Profiles to view the Available Hardware Profiles list.

- During installation, Windows XP Professional automatically creates an initial profile.

Lesson 4: Configuring, Monitoring, and Troubleshooting Driver Signing

Windows XP Professional drivers and operating system files have been digitally signed by Microsoft to ensure their quality. In Device Manager, you can look in the Driver tab of a *device* Properties dialog box to verify that the digital signer of the installed driver is correct. Some applications overwrite existing operating files as part of their installation process, which might cause system errors that are difficult to troubleshoot. Microsoft has greatly simplified the tracking and troubleshooting of altered files by signing the original operating system files and allowing you to easily verify these signatures.

After this lesson, you will be able to

- Configure driver signing
- Describe the System File Checker (SFC) tool and how to use it to verify and troubleshoot driver signing
- Use the Windows Signature Verification tool to monitor and troubleshoot driver signing

Estimated lesson time: 20 minutes

Configuring Driver Signing

You can configure how the system responds to unsigned files by clicking System in the Performance And Maintenance window in Control Panel and clicking the Hardware tab. In the Hardware tab, in the Device Manager box, click Driver Signing (see Figure 11.10).

Figure 11.10   Configuring driver signing in the Driver Signing Options dialog box

The following three settings are available to configure driver signing:

- **Ignore.**   This option allows any files to be installed regardless of their digital signature or the lack thereof.
- **Warn.**   This option, the default, displays a warning message before allowing the installation of an unsigned file.
- **Block.**   This option prevents the installation of unsigned files.

If you are logged on as Administrator or as a member of the Administrators group, you can select the Make This Action The System Default check box to apply the driver signing configuration you set up to all users who log on to the computer.

Monitoring and Troubleshooting Driver Signing

Windows XP Professional also provides System File Checker (SFC), a command-line tool that you can use to check the digital signature of files. The syntax of the SFC tool is as follows:

```
Sfc [/scannow] [/scanonce] [/scanboot] [/revert] [/purgecache]
[/cachesize=x]
```

Table 11.5 explains the SFC optional parameters.

Table 11.5   System File Checker Optional Parameters

Parameter	Description
/scannow	Causes the SFC tool to scan all protected system files immediately
/scanonce	Causes the SFC tool to scan all protected system files once at the next system restart
/scanboot	Causes the SFC tool to scan all protected system files every time the system restarts
/revert	Causes the SFC settings to be returned to the default settings
/purgecache	Purges the file cache
/cachesize=x	Sets the file cache size

Using the Windows File Signature Verification Tool

There is also a Windows File Signature Verification tool. To use it, click Start, click Run, type **sigverif**, and then press ENTER. Once the File Signature Verification tool begins, you can click Advanced to configure it (see Figure 11.11).

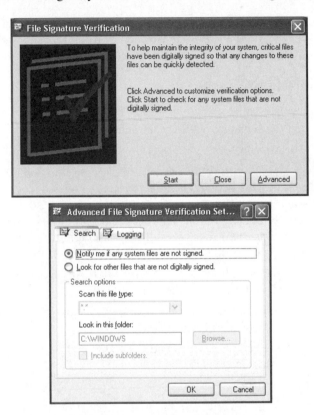

Figure 11.11   Configuring driver signing

The File Signature Verification tool allows you to view the file's name, location, modification date, file type, and version number.

Practice: Using the Windows File Signature Verification Tool

In this practice, you use File Signature Verification to monitor and troubleshoot driver signing on your system.

Run the **Signature Verification** file in the Demos folder on the CD-ROM accompanying this book for a demonstration of using the File Signature Verification tool to monitor and troubleshoot driver signing on your system.

▶ **To use sigverif**

1. Click Start, click Run, type **sigverif,** and then press ENTER.

   The File Signature Verification dialog box appears.

2. Click Advanced.

   The Advanced File Signature Verification Settings dialog box appears with the Search tab active. By default you are notified if any system files are not signed. Notice that you can select the Look For Other Files That Are Not Digitally Signed option. This setting has the File Signature Verification tool verify nonsystem files to see if they are digitally signed. If you select this option, you can specify the search parameters for the files you want checked.

3. Leave the default setting of Notify Me If Any System Files Are Not Signed selected, and then click the Logging tab.

   By default the Signature Verification tool saves the file signature verification to a log file named SIGVERIF.TXT.

4. Leave the default settings and click OK to close the Advanced File Signature Verification Settings dialog box.

5. Click Start.

   The Signature Verification tool builds a list of files to check and then scans the files. When the Signature Verification tool completes its check, a Signature Verification Results window appears if there are files that are not signed. Otherwise you see a Sigverif message box telling you that your files have been scanned and verified as being digitally signed.

6. If you get a Signature Verification Results window, review the results and then click Close to close the Signature Verification Results window. Otherwise, click OK to close the Sigverif message box.

7. Click Close to exit the File Signature Verification tool.

Lesson Review

The following questions will help you determine whether you have learned enough to move on to the next lesson. If you have difficulty answering these questions, review the material in this lesson before beginning the next lesson. The answers are in Appendix A, "Questions and Answers."

1. Why does Microsoft digitally sign the files in Windows XP Professional?

2. Which of the following tools would you use to block the installation of unsigned files?

   a. File Signature Verification

   b. Driver Signing Options in the System Control Panel

   c. System File Checker

   d. Sigverif

3. How can you view the file signature verification log file?

Lesson Summary

- Windows XP Professional provides two tools to verify the digital signatures of system files: SFC and File Signature Verification.

- SFC is a command-line tool. It has a number of optional parameters that let you control how and when it will run.

- File Signature Verification is a Windows tool. By default it saves the File Signature Verification to a SIGVERIF.TXT log file.

Lesson 5: Configuring Computers with Multiple Processors

This lesson explains how to use Device Manager to upgrade the device drivers on your computer. It covers scaling and upgrading your computer from a single processor to multiprocessor system.

After this lesson, you will be able to

- Use Device Manager to update drivers
- Use Device Manager to upgrade your computer from a single processor to a multiprocessor computer

Estimated lesson time: 10 minutes

Scaling

Adding processors to your system to improve performance is called *scaling*. This is more of an issue for Windows 2000 Server products than it is for Windows XP Professional because multiprocessor configurations are typically used for processor-intensive applications, such as those found on database servers or Web servers. However, any computer that runs applications that perform heavy computation, such as scientific or financial applications and complex graphic rendering (like computer-aided design programs), also benefit from multiprocessor systems.

Note   Upgrading to multiple processors can increase the load on other system resources. You might need to increase other resources such as disks, memory, and network components to get the maximum benefit from scaling.

Updating Drivers

You use Device Manager to update drivers. You update a driver whenever a newer version of the driver is released. You also update drivers to upgrade them, for example when you upgrade a driver to convert your computer from a single-processor system to one that supports multiple processors.

Caution   If your computer only has a single processor, upgrading the driver is not going to make it a multiple-processor computer. In fact, a computer with only one processor might no longer function if you upgrade the driver to one that supports multiple processors.

The following steps allow you to update the drivers loaded on a computer:

1. Open Device Manager and double-click Computer.
2. Right-click the appropriate model, and then click Properties.

3. In the Driver tab, click Update Driver.

   The Welcome To The Hardware Update Wizard page appears. The default option is Install The Software Automatically (Recommended), but you can also select the Install From A List Or Specific Location (Advanced) option.

4. Select Install From A List Or Specific Location (Advanced) and click Next.

   The Please Choose Your Search And Installation Options page appears.

5. Click Next to accept the default setting Search For The Best Driver In These Locations.

   Windows XP Professional searches for drivers. If it finds a better driver, you are given the chance to install it; otherwise you are prompted to click Finish to close the Hardware Update Wizard.

Note Windows XP Professional also includes an Automatic Updates feature. For more information about Automatic Updates, see Chapter 10, "Configuring Windows XP Professional."

Lesson Review

The following questions will help you determine whether you have learned enough to move on to the next lesson. If you have difficulty answering these questions, review the material in this lesson before beginning the next chapter. The answers are in Appendix A, "Questions and Answers."

1. Adding processors to your system to improve performance is called

   _____.

2. How can you manually update a driver on your computer?

Lesson Summary

- If your computer only has a single processor, upgrading the driver is not going to make it a multiple-processor computer.

- Scaling can increase the load on other system resources, so you might need to increase other system resources to maximize the benefits of using more than one processor.

- You use Device Manager to update drivers whenever a newer version of a driver is released or if you want to upgrade a driver, for example to convert your computer from a single-processor system to one that supports multiple processors.

CHAPTER 12

Auditing Resources and Events

About This Chapter

In this chapter, you will learn about auditing, one of the features controlled by the Microsoft Windows XP Professional Group Policy. *Auditing* is a tool for maintaining network security that allows you to track user activities and systemwide events. In addition, you will learn about audit policies and what you need to consider before you set one up. You will also learn how to set up auditing on resources and how to maintain security logs.

Before You Begin

To complete this chapter, you must have

- A computer that meets the minimum hardware requirements listed in the preface, "About This Book"
- Windows XP Professional installed on the computer
- Installed printer software (Hardware is not required. The software for an HP Color LaserJet 4500 PS printer was installed in Chapter 6, "Setting Up, Configuring, and Troubleshooting Common Setup and Configuration Problems for Network Printers.")
- User2 created in Chapter 3, "Setting Up and Managing User Accounts"

Lesson 1: Planning an Audit Policy

Auditing allows you to track both user activities and Windows XP Professional activities, which are called *events*, on a computer. Through auditing, you can specify that Windows XP Professional writes a record of an event to the *security log*, which maintains a record of valid and invalid logon attempts and events related to creating, opening, or deleting files or other objects. An audit entry in the security log contains the following information:

- The action that was performed
- The user who performed the action
- The success or failure of the event and when the event occurred

---

After this lesson, you will be able to

- Describe the purpose of auditing
- Plan an audit strategy and determine which events to audit

Estimated lesson time: 15 minutes

Understanding Audit Policies

An *audit policy* defines the types of security events that Windows XP Professional records in the security log on each computer. The security log allows you to track the events that you specify.

Windows XP Professional writes events to the security log on the computer on which the event occurs. For example, any time someone tries to log on and the logon attempt fails, Windows XP Professional writes an event to the security log on that computer.

You can set up an audit policy for a computer to do the following:

- Track the success and failure of events, such as logon attempts by users, an attempt by a particular user to read a specific file, changes to a user account or to group memberships, and changes to your security settings
- Eliminate or minimize the risk of unauthorized use of resources

You use Event Viewer to view events that Windows XP Professional has recorded in the security log. You can also archive log files to track trends over time—for example, to determine the use of printers or files or to verify attempts at unauthorized use of resources.

Determining What to Audit

When you plan an audit policy, you must determine what you want to audit and the computers on which to set up auditing. Auditing is turned off by default. As you determine which computers to audit, you must also plan what to audit on each one. Windows XP Professional records audited events on each computer separately.

The types of events that you can audit include the following:

- Accessing files and folders
- Logging on and off
- Shutting down a computer running Windows XP Professional
- Starting a computer running Windows XP Professional
- Changing user accounts and groups
- Attempting to make changes to Active Directory objects (only if your Windows XP Professional computer is part of a domain)

After you have determined the types of events to audit, you must also determine whether to audit the success of events, the failure of events, or both. Tracking successful events can tell you how often Windows XP Professional or users access specific files, printers, or other objects, and you can use this information for resource planning.

Tracking failed events can alert you to possible security breaches. For example, if you notice several failed logon attempts by a certain user account, especially if they are occurring outside normal business hours, you can assume that an unauthorized person is attempting to break into your system.

Other guidelines in determining your audit policy include the following:

- **Determine whether you need to track system usage trends.**   If so, plan to archive event logs. This will allow you to view how usage changes over time and will allow you to plan to increase system resources before they become a problem.
- **Review security logs frequently.**   You should set a schedule and regularly review security logs because configuring auditing alone doesn't alert you to security breaches.
- **Define an audit policy that is useful and manageable.**   Always audit sensitive and confidential data. Audit only those events that will provide you with meaningful information about your network environment. This minimizes usage of the computer's resources and makes essential information easier to locate. Auditing too many types of events can create excess overhead for Windows XP Professional.

Lesson Review

The following questions will help you determine whether you have learned enough to move on to the next lesson. If you have difficulty answering these questions, review the material in this lesson before beginning the next lesson. The answers are in Appendix A, "Questions and Answers."

1. What is auditing?

2. What is an audit policy?

3. On a computer running Windows XP Professional, auditing is turned _____ (on/off) by default.

4. When you are auditing events on a computer running Windows XP Professional, where are the audited events being recorded?

5. When you are auditing events on a computer running Windows XP Professional, why would you track failed events?

Lesson Summary

- On a computer running Windows XP Professional, auditing helps ensure that your network is secure by tracking user activities and systemwide events.
- You set up an audit policy to specify which events to record.
- Windows XP Professional records audited events in the security log.
- You use Event Viewer to view the security log.
- In planning an audit policy, you must determine on which computers to set up auditing and what to audit on each one.
- You can audit the success of events, the failure of events, or both.

Lesson 2: Implementing an Audit Policy

Auditing is a powerful tool for tracking events that occur on computers in your organization. To implement auditing, you need to consider auditing requirements and set the audit policy. After you set an audit policy on a computer, you can implement auditing on files, folders, and printers.

After this lesson, you will be able to

- Set up auditing on files and folders
- Set up auditing on printers

Estimated lesson time: 40 minutes

Configuring Auditing

For computers running Windows XP Professional, you set up an audit policy for each individual computer.

Auditing Requirements

The requirements to set up and administer auditing are as follows:

- You must have the Manage Auditing And Security Log user right for the computer on which you want to configure an audit policy or review an audit log. By default, Windows XP Professional grants these rights to the Administrators group.
- The files and folders to be audited must be on NT file system (NTFS) volumes.

Setting up Auditing

Setting up auditing is a two-part process:

1. **Set the audit policy.**   The audit policy enables auditing of objects but doesn't activate auditing of specific objects.
2. **Enable auditing of specific resources.**   You designate the specific events to audit for files, folders, printers, and Active Directory objects. Windows XP Professional then tracks and logs the specified events.

Setting an Audit Policy

The first step in implementing an audit policy is selecting the types of events for Windows XP Professional to audit. For each event that you can audit, the configuration settings indicate whether to track successful or failed attempts. You set audit policies for a local computer in the Group Policy snap-in, which can be accessed by using the Microsoft Management Console (MMC) console and adding the Group Policy snap-in.

Table 12.1 describes the types of events that Windows XP Professional can audit.

Table 12.1   Types of Events Audited by Windows XP Professional

Event	Description
Account Logon Events	A domain controller received a request to validate a user account. (This is applicable only if your computer running Windows XP Professional joins a Microsoft Windows 2000 domain.)
Account Management	An administrator created, changed, or deleted a user account or group. A user account was renamed, disabled, or enabled, or a password was set or changed.
Directory Service Access	A user gained access to an Active Directory object. You must configure specific Active Directory objects for auditing to log this type of event. (Active Directory is available only if your computer running Windows XP Professional joins a Windows 2000 domain.)
Logon Events	A user logged on or logged off, or a user made or canceled a network connection to the computer.
Object Access	A user gained access to a file, folder, or printer. You must configure specific files, folders, or printers for auditing. Object access is auditing a user's access to files, folders, and printers.
Policy Change	A change was made to the user security options, user rights, or audit policies.
Privilege Use	A user exercised a right, such as changing the system time. (This doesn't include rights that are related to logging on and logging off.)
Process Tracking	A program performed an action. This information is generally useful only for programmers who want to track details of program execution.
System Events	A user restarted or shut down the computer, or an event occurred that affected Windows XP Professional security or the security log. (For example, the audit log is full and Windows XP Professional starts discarding entries.)

To set an audit policy on a computer that is running Windows XP Professional, access the Group Policy snap-in, as follows:

1. Log on with an account that is a member of the Administrators group.

2. Click Start and click Run. In the Open text box, type **mmc** and then click OK.

3. In the Console 1 window, on the File menu, click Add/Remove Snap-In.

4. In the Add/Remove Snap-In dialog box, click Add.

5. In the Add Standalone Snap-In dialog box, select Group Policy and then click Add.

6. In the Select Group Policy Object dialog box, ensure that the Group Policy Object text box contains Local Computer, and then click Finish.

7. In the Add Standalone Snap-In dialog box, click Close.

   In the Add/Remove Snap-In dialog box, notice that it contains Local Computer Policy, even though you added Group Policy. Group Policy for the local computer is referred to as Local Computer Policy.

8. In the Add/Remove Snap-In dialog box, click OK.

9. In the console tree of the Local Computer Policy snap-in, double-click Local Computer Policy.

10. Double-click Computer Configuration, and then double-click Windows Settings.

11. Double-click Security Settings, and then double-click Local Policies.

12. Click Audit Policy.

   The console displays the current audit policy settings in the details pane of the Local Computer Policy window, as shown in Figure 12.1.

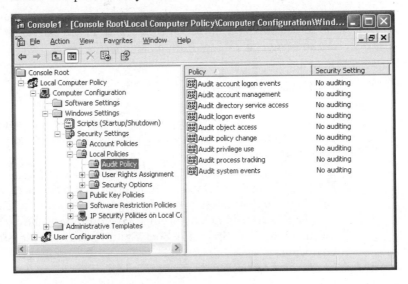

Figure 12.1   Events that Windows XP Professional can audit

13. Select the type of event to audit, and then, on the Action menu, click Properties.

   For example, if you select Audit Logon Events and on the Action menu you click Properties, the Audit Account Logon Events Properties dialog box appears, as shown in Figure 12.2.

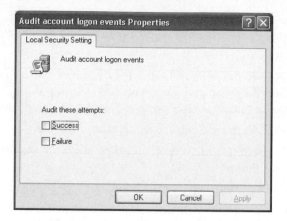

Figure 12.2   The Audit Account Logon Events Properties dialog box

14. Select the Success check box, the Failure check box, or both.

    A check mark in the Success check box indicates that auditing is in effect for successful attempts. A check mark in the Failure check box indicates that auditing is in effect for failed attempts.

15. Click OK.

16. Restart your computer.

Once you have set the audit policy, remember that the changes that you make to your computer's audit policy don't take effect immediately unless you restart your computer.

Tip   The Gpupdate command allows you to refresh local and Active Directory–based Group Policy settings, including Security settings. To update your local computer, start a command prompt, type **gpupdate** and press ENTER. For more information about Gpupdate, click Start, click Help And Support, and search for Gpupdate.

Auditing Access to Files and Folders

If security breaches are an issue for your organization, you can set up auditing for files and folders on NTFS partitions. To audit user access to files and folders, you must first set your audit policy to audit object access, which includes files and folders.

When you set your audit policy to audit object access, you enable auditing for specific files and folders and specify which types of access, by which users or groups, to audit.

You can enable auditing for specific files and folders as follows:

1. Click Start, right-click My Computer, and then click Explore.
2. Right-click the file or folder for which you want to enable auditing and click Properties.
3. In the Security tab of the Properties dialog box for a file or folder, click Advanced.

Tip If you do not have a Security tab on the Properties dialog box for your files and folders there are two things you should check:

Are your files and folders located on a partition formatted as NTFS?

If your computer is not a member of a domain, have you turned off Simple File Sharing? To stop using Simple File Sharing, click Start, right-click My Computer, and then click Explore. On the Tools menu, click Folder Options. Click the View tab, clear Use Simple File Sharing (Recommended), and click OK.

---

4. In the Auditing tab of the Advanced Security Settings For *folder_name* dialog box, click Add, select the users for whom you want to audit file and folder access, and then click OK.
5. In the Audit Entry For *folder_name* dialog box, select the Successful check box, the Failed check box, or both for the events that you want to audit.

   For a list of the events that can be audited for folders, see Figure 12.3.

   Table 12.2 describes the user activity that triggers these events so you can determine when you should audit these events.

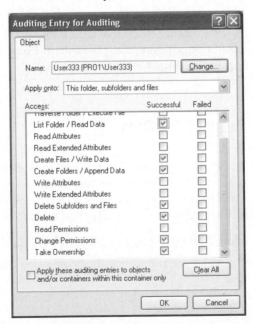

Figure 12.3 Events that can be audited for folders

Table 12.2   User Events and What Triggers Them

Event	User activity that triggers the event
Traverse Folder/Execute File	Running a program or gaining access to a folder to change directories
List Folder/Read Data	Displaying the contents of a file or a folder
Read Attributes Read Extended Attributes	Displaying the attributes of a file or folder
Create Files/Write Data	Changing the contents of a file or creating new files in a folder
Create Folders/Append Data	Creating folders in a folder
Write Attributes Write Extended Attributes	Changing attributes of a file or folder
Delete Subfolders And Files	Deleting a file or subfolder in a folder
Delete	Deleting a file or folder
Read Permissions	Viewing permissions for the file owner for a file or folder
Change Permissions	Changing permissions for a file or folder
Take Ownership	Taking ownership of a file or folder

6. Click OK to return to the Advanced Security Settings For *folder_name* dialog box.

   By default, any auditing changes that you make to a parent folder also apply to all child folders and all files in the parent and child folders.

7. To prevent changes that are made to a parent folder from applying to the currently selected file or folder, clear the Inherit From Parent The Auditing Entries That Apply To Child Objects check box.

8. Click OK.

Auditing Access to Printers

Audit access to printers to track access to sensitive printers. To audit access to printers, set your audit policy to audit object access, which includes printers. Enable auditing for specific printers and specify which types of access to audit and which users will have access. After you select the printer, you use the same steps that you use to set up auditing on files and folders, as follows:

1. Click Start, click Control Panel, and then click Printers And Other Hardware.

2. Click Printers And Faxes, right-click the printer you want to audit, and then click Properties.

3. In the Properties dialog box for the printer, click the Security tab, and then click Advanced.

    The Advanced Security Settings dialog box appears.

4. In the Auditing tab, click Add, select the appropriate users or groups for whom you want to audit printer access, and then click OK.

5. In the Apply Onto box in the Auditing Entry dialog box, select where the auditing setting applies.

    The options in the Apply Onto box for a printer are This Printer Only, Documents, and This Printer And Documents.

6. Under Access, select the Successful check box, the Failed check box, or both for the events that you want to audit (see Figure 12.4).

7. Click OK in the appropriate dialog boxes to exit.

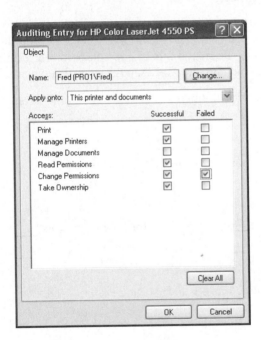

Figure 12.4   Printer events that can be audited

Table 12.3 describes audit events for printers and explains which user action triggers the event.

Table 12.3   Printer Events and What Triggers Them

Event	User activity that triggers the event
Print	Printing a file
Manage Printers	Changing printer settings, pausing a printer, sharing a printer, or removing a printer
Manage Documents	Changing job settings; pausing, restarting, moving, or deleting documents; sharing a printer; or changing printer properties
Read Permissions	Viewing printer permissions
Change Permissions	Changing printer permissions
Take Ownership	Taking printer ownership

Lesson Review

The following questions will help you determine whether you have learned enough to move on to the next lesson. If you have difficulty answering these questions, review the material in this lesson before beginning the next lesson. The answers are in Appendix A, "Questions and Answers."

1. What are the requirements to set up and administer auditing?

2. What are the two steps in setting up auditing?

3. How do you set audit policies for a local computer?

4. What are some reasons for auditing system events?

5. By default, any auditing changes that you make to a parent folder _____ (are inherited/are not inherited) by all child folders and all files in the parent and child folders.

Lesson Summary

- The first step in implementing an audit policy is selecting the types of events for Windows XP Professional to audit.

- You can select the events to audit for files and folders on NTFS volumes, and you can select the events you want to audit for printers.

- When you have set your audit policy to audit object access, you can enable auditing for specific files, folders, and printers and specify which types of access, by which users or groups, to audit.

- For each event that you can audit, the configuration settings indicate whether to track successful attempts, failed attempts, or both.

- You must have the Manage Auditing And Security Log user right for the computer on which you want to configure an audit policy or review an audit log. By default, Windows XP Professional grants these rights to the Administrators group.

- You use the Group Policy snap-in to set audit policies, and then you restart your computer if you want to immediately enable auditing.

Lesson 3: Using Event Viewer

You use Event Viewer to perform a variety of tasks, including viewing the audit logs that are generated as a result of setting the audit policy and auditing events. You can also use Event Viewer to view the contents of security log files and find specific events within log files.

After this lesson, you will be able to

- View a log
- Locate events in a log
- Filter events in a log
- Archive security logs
- Configure the size of audit logs

Estimated lesson time: 50 minutes

Understanding Windows XP Professional Logs

You use Event Viewer to view information contained in Windows XP Professional logs. By default, Event Viewer has three logs available to view, as described in Table 12.4.

Table 12.4   Logs Maintained by Windows XP Professional

Log	Description
Application log	Contains errors, warnings, or information that programs, such as a database program or an e-mail program, generate. The program developer presets which events to record.
Security log	Contains information about the success or failure of audited events. The events that Windows XP Professional records are a result of your audit policy.
System log	Contains errors, warnings, and information that Windows XP Professional generates. Windows XP Professional presets which events to record.

Note   If additional services are installed, they might add their own event logs.

Viewing Security Logs

The security log contains information about events that are monitored by an audit policy, such as failed and successful logon attempts. You can view the security log by performing the following steps:

1. Click Start, click Control Panel, click Performance And Maintenance, click Administrative Tools, and then double-click Event Viewer.

2. In the console tree, click Security.

   In the details pane, Event Viewer displays a list of log entries and summary information for each item, as shown in Figure 12.5.

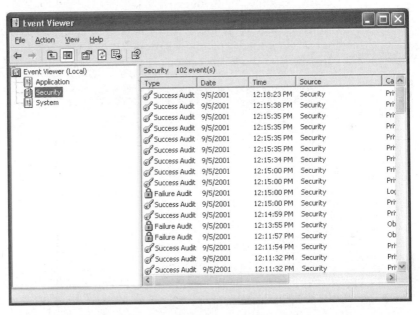

Figure 12.5   Event Viewer displaying a sample security log

Successful events are marked with a key icon and unsuccessful events are marked with a lock icon. Other important information includes the date and time that the event occurred, the category of the event, and the user who generated the event.

The category indicates the type of event, such as object access, account management, directory service access, or logon events.

3. To view additional information for any event, select the event, and then on the Action menu, click Properties.

Windows XP Professional records events in the security log on the computer on which the event occurred. You can view these events from any computer as long as you have administrative privileges for the computer where the events occurred. To view the security log on a remote computer, open the MMC console and point Event Viewer to a remote computer.

Locating Events

When you first start Event Viewer, it automatically displays all events that are recorded in the selected log. To change what appears in the log, you can locate selected events using the Filter command. You can also search for specific events using the Find command.

To filter or find events, start Event Viewer, and then on the View menu click Filter or click Find. The options provided by Filter and Find are almost identical. Figure 12.6 shows the options available in the Filter tab.

Figure 12.6   System Properties for Using Event Viewer with the Filter tab selected

Table 12.5 describes the options for using the Filter tab to filter events and the Find command to find events.

Table 12.5   Options for Filtering and Finding Events

Option	Description
Event Types	The types of events to view.
Event Source	The software or component driver that logged the event.

Table 12.5   *(continued)*

Option	Description
Category	The type of event, such as a logon or logoff attempt or a system event.
Event ID	An event number to identify the event. This number helps product support representatives track events.
User	A user logon name.
Computer	A computer name.
From and To	The date ranges for which to view events (Filter tab only).
Restore Defaults	Clears any changes in this tab and restores all defaults.
Description	The text that is in the description of the event (Find dialog box only).
Search Direction	The direction (up or down) in which to search the log (Find dialog box only).
Find Next	Finds and displays the next occurrence defined by the Find Settings.

Managing Audit Logs

You can track trends in Windows XP Professional by archiving event logs and comparing logs from different periods. Viewing trends helps you determine resource use and plan for growth. You can also use logs to determine if a pattern of unauthorized resource use is a concern. Windows XP Professional allows you to control the size of the logs and to specify the action that it takes when a log becomes full.

You can configure the properties of each individual audit log. To configure the settings for logs, select the log in Event Viewer, and then on the Action menu, click Properties to display the Properties dialog box for the log.

Use the Properties dialog box for each type of audit log to control the following:

- The maximum size of each log, which can be from 64 KB to 4,194,240 KB (4 GB). The default size is 512 KB.

- The action that Windows XP Professional takes when the log fills up. To control this action, click one of the options described in Table 12.6.

Table 12.6   **Options for Handling Full Audit Log Files**

Option	Description
Overwrite Events As Needed	You might lose information if the log becomes full before you archive it. However, this setting requires no maintenance.
Overwrite Events Older Than *X* Days	You might lose information if the log becomes full before you archive it, but Windows XP Professional will only lose information that is at least *x* days old. Enter the number of days for this option. The default is 7 days.

(continued)

Table 12.6   *(continued)*

Option	Description
Do Not Overwrite Events	This option requires you to clear the log manually. When the log becomes full, Windows XP Professional will stop, but no security log entries will be overwritten.

Archiving Logs

Archiving security logs allows you to maintain a history of security-related events. Many companies have policies on keeping archive logs for a specified period to track security-related information over time.

If you want to archive, clear, or view an archived log, select the log you want to configure in Event Viewer, click the Action menu, and then click one of the options described in Table 12.7.

Table 12.7   Options to Archive, Clear, or View a Log File

To	Do this
Archive the log	Click Save Log File As and then type a filename.
Clear the log	Click Clear All Events to clear the log. Windows XP Professional creates a security log entry stating that the log was cleared.
View an archived log	Click New Log View; add another view of the selected log.

Practice: Auditing Resources and Events

In this practice, you'll plan an audit policy for your computer. Then you'll set up an audit policy by enabling auditing on certain events. You'll also set up auditing of a file and a printer. Then you'll view the security log file and configure Event Viewer to overwrite events when the log file is filled.

Exercise 1: Planning an Audit Policy

In this exercise, you plan an audit policy for your computer. You need to determine the following:

- Which types of events to audit
- Whether to audit the success or failure of an event, or both

Use the following criteria to make your decisions:

- Record unsuccessful attempts to gain access to the computer.
- Record unauthorized access to the files that make up the customer database.
- For billing purposes, track color printer use.
- Track whenever someone tries to tamper with the computer's hardware.

- Keep a record of actions that an administrator performs to track unauthorized changes.
- Track backup procedures to prevent data theft.
- Track unauthorized access to sensitive Active Directory objects.

Record your decisions to audit successful events, failed events, or both for the actions listed in the following table:

Action to audit	Successful	Failed
Account Logon Events		
Account Management		
Directory Service Access		
Logon Events		
Object Access		
Policy Change		
Privilege Use		
Process Tracking		
System Events		

Exercise 2: Setting Up an Audit Policy

In this exercise, you open the MMC console, add the Group Policy snap-in pointing to the local machine, and then enable auditing for selected events.

▶ **To set up an audit policy**

1. Log on as Fred or with an account that is a member of the Administrators group.

2. Click Start, click Run, and in the Open text box, type **mmc** and then click OK.

3. In the Console 1 window, on the File menu, click Add/Remove Snap-In.

4. In the Add/Remove Snap-In dialog box, click Add.

5. In the Add Standalone Snap-In dialog box, select Group Policy and then click Add.

6. In the Select Group Policy Object dialog box, ensure that the Group Policy Object text box says Local Computer, and then click Finish.

7. In the Add Standalone Snap-In dialog box, click Close.

   In the Add/Remove Snap-In dialog box, notice that it says Local Computer Policy, even though you added Group Policy. Group Policy for the local computer is referred to as Local Computer Policy.

8. In the Add/Remove Snap-In dialog box, click OK.

9. In the console tree of the Local Computer Policy snap-in, double-click Local Computer Policy.

10. Double-click Computer Configuration, and then double-click Windows Settings.

11. Double-click Security Settings, and then double-click Local Policies.

12. Click Audit Policy.

The console displays the current audit policy settings in the details pane of the Local Computer Policy window.

13. To set the audit policy, in the details pane, double-click each type of event, and then select either the Audit Successful Attempts check box or the Audit Failed Attempts check box, as listed in the following table:

Event	Audit Successful Attempts	Audit Failed Attempts
Account Logon Events		
Account Management	X	
Directory Service Access		
Logon Events		X
Object Access	X	X
Policy Change	X	
Privilege Use	X	
Process Tracking		
System Events	X	X

14. Close the MMC console and save the Local Group Policy.

15. Restart your computer to make the changes take effect immediately.

Exercise 3: Setting Up Auditing of Files

In this exercise, you set up auditing for a file.

▶ **To set up auditing of files**

1. Log on as Fred or with an account that is a member of the Administrators group.

2. In Windows Explorer, create a folder named Audit in the root folder of your system disk (for example, C:\Audit).

3. Create a text file named AUDIT in the Audit folder (for example, C:\Audit\Audit).

4. Right-click the AUDIT file and then click Properties.

5. In the Properties dialog box, click the Security tab, and then click Advanced.

6. In the Access Control Settings dialog box, click the Auditing tab.

7. Click Add.

8. In the Select User Or Group dialog box, in the Name text box, type **Everyone** and click OK.

9. In the Audit Entry For Audit.txt dialog box, select the Successful check box and the Failed check box for each of the following events:

   ■ Create Files/Write Data

   ■ Delete

   ■ Change Permissions

   ■ Take Ownership

10. Click OK.

    Windows XP Professional displays the Everyone group in the Advanced Security Settings For dialog box.

11. Click OK to apply your changes.

    Leave the Audit Properties dialog box open for the next procedure.

▶ **To verify file permissions**

1. In the Audit Properties dialog box, click Users (PRO1\Users) and verify that the Allow permissions for the file are Read & Execute and Read.

2. Click OK to close the Properties dialog box, and then close Windows Explorer.

Exercise 4: Setting Up Auditing of a Printer

In this exercise, you set up auditing of a printer.

▶ **To set up auditing of a printer**

1. Click Start, click Control Panel, click Printers And Other Hardware, and click Printers And Faxes.

2. In the Printers window, right-click HP Color LaserJet 4500 PS and then click Properties. (Any installed printer will do. The procedure for installing a printer is covered in Chapter 6, "Setting Up, Configuring, and Troubleshooting Common Setup and Configuration Problems for Network Printers.")

3. Click the Security tab, and then click Advanced.

4. In the Advanced Security Settings For HP Color LaserJet 4500 PS dialog box, click the Auditing tab and then click Add.

5. In the Select User Or Group dialog box, in the Name text box type **Everyone** and then click OK.

6. In the Auditing Entry For HP Color LaserJet 4500 PS dialog box, select the Successful check box for all types of access.

7. Click OK.

   Windows XP Professional displays the Everyone group in the Access Control Settings For HP Color LaserJet 4500 PS dialog box.

8. Click OK to apply your changes.

9. Click OK to close the HP Color LaserJet 4500 PS Properties dialog box.

10. Close the Printers And Faxes window.

Exercise 5: Testing the Auditing Policy Set Up on the AUDIT File

In this exercise, you attempt to access and modify the AUDIT file to create entries in the security log for your computer.

▶ **To test the auditing policy**

1. Click Start, click Control Panel, and then click User Accounts.

2. Verify that User2 exists and is a Limited account.

3. Create a password of User2 for the User2 user account.

4. Close all open windows and log off the computer.

5. Log on to the computer as User2 with a password of User2.

6. Open Windows Explorer and then open the file C:\Audit\Audit.

   Notepad opens and displays the blank file AUDIT.

7. Type in the following text: **User2 has modified this file.**

8. Save the file.

   Were you able to save the file? Why or why not?

9. Close the file without saving it and log off as User2.

Exercise 6: Viewing the Security Log

In this exercise, you view the security log for your computer, and then you use Event Viewer to filter events and to search for potential security breaches.

▶ **To view and filter the security log for your computer**

1. Log on to your computer as Fred or with a user account that is a member of the Administrators group.

2. Click Start, click Control Panel, click Performance And Maintenance, click Administrative Tools, and then double-click the Event Viewer shortcut.

3. In the console tree, click the application log and view the contents. As you scroll through the logs, double-click a couple of events to view a description.

4. In the console tree, click the system log and view the contents. As you scroll through the logs, double-click a couple of events to view a description.

5. In the console tree, click the security log and view the contents. As you scroll through the logs, double-click each of the Failure Audit events until you can locate the one for User2 trying to access C:\Audit\Audit.

6. Click Filter on the View menu.

7. In the Security Properties dialog box, in the User text box, type **User2** and then click OK.

   Filtering reduces the number of events that you have to search through.

8. Double-click each of the events and notice that all of them have to do with User2.

Exercise 7: Managing the Security Log

In this exercise, you configure Event Viewer to overwrite events when the log file gets full. Then you clear the security log and view an archived security log.

▶ **To control the size and contents of a log file**

1. In the console tree, click System.

2. On the Action menu, click Properties.

3. In the System Properties dialog box, click Overwrite Events As Needed.

4. In the Maximum Log Size box, change the maximum log size to 2048 (KB) and then click OK.

   Windows XP Professional now allows the log to grow to 2048 KB and will then overwrite older events with new events as necessary.

5. Close Event Viewer, and then close Administrative Tools.

Lesson Review

The following questions will help you determine whether you have learned enough to move on to the next lesson. If you have difficulty answering these questions, review the material in this lesson before beginning the next chapter. The answers are in Appendix A, "Questions and Answers."

1. What are the three Windows XP Professional logs you can view with Event Viewer and what is the purpose of each log?

2. How can you view the security log on a remote computer?

3. The two ways that Event Viewer provides for locating specific events are the _____ command and the _____ command. What does each of the commands allow you to do?

4. The size of each log can be from ____ KB to ____ GB, and the default size is ____ KB.

5. If you select the Do Not Overwrite Events option, what happens when the log becomes full?

Lesson Summary

- Windows XP Professional has the following three logs by default: the application log, the security log, and the system log.
- You use Event Viewer to view the contents of the Windows XP Professional logs.
- You can use the Filter and Find commands in Event Viewer to easily locate specific events or types of events.
- You can view the security log on a remote computer by opening the MMC console and pointing Event Viewer to the remote computer.
- You can manage the Windows XP logs by archiving them to allow you to track trends over time and by controlling the size of the log files.

CHAPTER 13

Configuring Security Settings and Internet Options

About This Chapter

Group Policy administrators use Group Policy to define and control programs, network resources, and the operating system for users and computers. Typically Group Policy is set for the entire domain or network. It is used in an Active Directory environment and is applied to users or computers based on membership in sites, domains, or organizational units. The Group Policy snap-in is the tool used to configure Group Policy. As discussed in the previous chapter, when you add the Group Policy snap-in to a Microsoft Management Console (MMC) console and point it at the local computer, the snap-in that is added is the Local Computer Policy, which is Group Policy for the local computer.

In this chapter, you learn how to improve the security on your computer. You learn about configuring security settings that are part of the Local Computer Policy or Group Policy snap-in. The security settings include Account Policies and Local Policies. In Chapter 12, "Auditing Resources and Events," you learned about auditing, which is one of the three Local Policies found in the Local Computer Policy or Group Policy snap-in. In this chapter, you also learn how to improve the security of your computer by configuring Internet Options to control and secure the way Microsoft Internet Explorer interacts with the Internet.

Before You Begin

To complete this chapter, you must have

- A computer that meets the minimum hardware requirements listed in the preface, "About This Book"
- Microsoft Windows XP Professional software installed on the computer

Lesson 1: Configuring Account Policies

In Chapter 3, "Setting Up and Managing User Accounts," you learned about assigning user account passwords and how to unlock an account that was locked by the system. In this lesson, you learn how to improve the security of your user's passwords and how to control when the system locks out a user account.

After this lesson, you will be able to

- Configure Account Policies

Estimated lesson time: 40 minutes

Configuring Password Policy

Password Policy allows you to improve security on your computer by controlling how passwords are created and managed. You can specify the maximum length of time a password can be used before the user must change it. Changing passwords decreases the chances of an unauthorized person breaking into your computer. If an unauthorized user has discovered a user account and password combination for your computer, forcing users to change passwords regularly will cause the user account and password combination to eventually fail and lock the unauthorized user out of the system.

Other Password Policy options are available to improve a computer's security. For example, you can specify a minimum password length. The longer the password, the more difficult it is to discover. Another example is maintaining a history of the passwords used. This prevents a user from having two passwords and alternating between them.

You can configure Password Policy on a computer running Windows XP Professional by using the Group Policy snap-in. You use the Group Policy snap-in to configure Password Policy as follows:

1. Click Start, and then click Run.

2. Type **mmc** in the Open text box, and click OK to open an empty custom MMC console.

3. On the File menu, click Add/Remove Snap-In, and then click Add.

4. In the Add Standalone Snap-In dialog box, click Group Policy and then click Add.

   The Select Group Policy Object dialog box appears, allowing you to point the Group Policy snap-in at the local computer or at a remote computer. The Allow The Focus Of The Group Policy Snap-In To Be Changed When Launching From The Command Line check box allows you to configure the MMC so that you can decide which computer to use Group Policy on when you start the MMC.

5. Click Finish to leave Group Policy with its focus on the Local Computer, the default setting, and click Close to exit the Add Standalone Snap-In dialog box.

6. In the Add/Remove Snap-In dialog box, click OK, and save the console with Local Group Policy.

7. Expand Local Computer Policy, under Computer Configuration expand Windows Settings, expand Security Settings, expand Account Policies, and then click Password Policy.

8. Select the settings you want to configure, and then on the Action menu, click Properties.

The console displays the current Password Policy settings in the details pane, as shown in Figure 13.1.

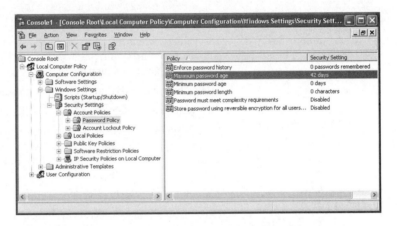

Figure 13.1   The Group Policy snap-in displaying Password Policy settings

Table 13.1 explains the available Password Policy settings.

Table 13.1   Password Policy Settings

Setting	Description
Enforce Password History	The value you enter for this setting indicates the number of passwords to be kept in a password history. The default value of 0 indicates that no password history is being kept. You can set the value from 0 to 24, indicating the number of passwords to be kept in password history. This value indicates the number of new passwords that a user must use before he or she can reuse an old password.
Maximum Password Age	The value you enter for this setting is the number of days a user can use a password before he or she is required to change it.
	A value of 0 indicates the password will not expire.
	The default value is 42 days and the range of values is 0 to 999 days.

(continued)

Table 13.1   *(continued)*

Setting	Description
Minimum Password Age	The value you enter for this setting is the number of days a user must keep a password before he or she can change it.
	The default value of 0 indicates that the password can be changed immediately. If you are enforcing password history, this value should not be set to 0.
	You can set the range of values from 0 to 999 days. This value indicates how long the user must wait before changing his or her password again. Use this value to prevent a user who was forced by the system to change his or her password from immediately changing it back to the old password.
	The minimum password age must be less than the maximum password age.
Minimum Password Length	The value you enter for this setting is the minimum number of characters required in a password. The value can range from 0 to 14 characters inclusive.
	The default value of 0 indicates that no password is required.
Passwords Must Meet Complexity Requirements	The options are Enabled or Disabled (the default).
	If enabled, all passwords must meet or exceed the specified minimum password length; must comply with the password history settings; must contain capitals, numerals, or punctuation; and cannot contain the user's account or full name.
Store Password Using Reversible Encryption For All Users In The Domain	The options are Enabled or Disabled (the default).
	This enables Windows XP Professional to store a reversibly encrypted password for all users in the domain—for example, to be used with the Challenge Handshake Authentication Protocol (CHAP). This option is only applicable if your computer running Windows XP Professional is in a domain.

The MMC Console displays the properties dialog box for the selected setting. Figure 13.2 shows the properties dialog box for the Maximum Password Age setting.

Figure 13.2   The Maximum Password Age Properties dialog box

By carefully planning and configuring your Password Policy settings you can improve the security of your computer by decreasing the chances of an unauthorized user gaining access to it.

Configuring Account Lockout Policy

The Account Lockout Policy settings also allow you to improve the security on your computer. If no account lockout policy is in place, an unauthorized user can repeatedly try to break into your computer. If, however, you have set an account lockout policy, the system locks out the user account under the conditions you specify in Account Lockout Policy.

You access the Account Lockout Policy settings using the Group Policy snap-in, just as you did to configure the Password Policy settings. The console displaying the current Account Lockout Policy settings in the details pane is shown in Figure 13.3.

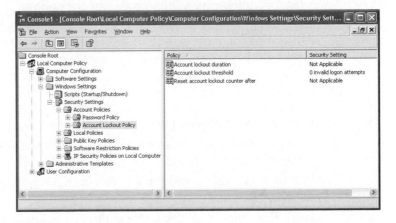

Figure 13.3   The Group Policy snap-in displaying the Account Lockout Policy settings

Table 13.2 explains the settings available in Account Lockout Policy.

Table 13.2   Account Lockout Policy Settings

Setting	Description
Account Lockout Duration	The value you enter for this setting indicates the number of minutes that the account is locked out. A value of 0 indicates that the user account is locked out indefinitely until an administrator unlocks the user account. You can set the value from 0 to 99,999 minutes. (The maximum value of 99,999 minutes is approximately 69.4 days.)
Account Lockout Threshold	The value you enter for this setting is the number of invalid logon attempts before the user account is locked out from logging on to the computer. A value of 0 indicates that the account will not be locked out, no matter how many invalid logon attempts are made. You can set the range of values from 0 to 999 attempts.
Reset Lockout Counter After	The value you enter for this setting is the number of minutes to wait before resetting the account lockout counter. You can set the range of values from 1 to 99,999 minutes.

Practice: Configuring Account Policy

In this practice you configure the Account Policy settings for your computer and then test them to make sure you set them correctly.

Run the **AccountPolicy** file in the Demos folder on the CD-ROM accompanying this book for a demonstration of configuring account policy.

Exercise 1: Configuring Minimum Password Length

In this exercise, you use the custom MMC console containing the Group Policy snap-in you created in Chapter 12, "Auditing Resources and Events," and saved with the name Local Group Policy. You use it to configure the minimum password length, one of the Account Policy settings for your computer. You then test the minimum password length to confirm it was correctly configured.

▶   **To configure the minimum password length**

1. Log on as Fred or with an account that is a member of the Administrators group.

2. Click Start, click Run, type **mmc** in the Open text box, and click OK to open the MMC console.

3. On the File menu, click Local Group Policy.

   The MMC console opens the Local Group Policy console you created in Chapter 12, "Auditing Resources and Events." If you have not created the

Local Group Policy console, see the first practice in that chapter for the steps to create it.

4. In the Local Group Policy console, expand Local Computer Policy\Computer Configuration\Windows Settings\Security Settings\and then Account Policies.

Account Policies has two nodes: Password Policy and Account Lockout Policy.

5. In the console tree, click Password Policy.

6. In the details pane, right-click Minimum Password Length and then click Properties.

Windows XP Professional displays the Minimum Password Length Properties dialog box.

7. In the Password Must Be At Least text box, type **8** to set the minimum password length to eight characters, and then click OK.

8. Click File and then click Exit to close the MMC console.

9. When prompted to Save Console Settings To Local Group Policy, click No.

▶ **To test minimum password length**

1. Click Start and then click Control Panel.

2. Click User Accounts and then click Create A New Account.

3. In the Type A Name For The New Account text box, type **User13** and then click Next.

4. Click Limited and then click Create Account.

5. Click User13 and then click Change The Password.

6. In the Type A New Password and the Type The New Password Again To Confirm text boxes, type **water**.

7. Click Change Password.

A User Accounts message box appears, indicating that your new password does not meet the password policy requirements. This test proves that you correctly configured the minimum password length account policy to eight characters.

8. Click OK to close the User Accounts message box.

9. Click Cancel to close the Change User13's Password window.

10. Close the What Do You Want To Change About User13's Account window, and then close Control Panel.

Exercise 2: Configuring and Testing Additional Account Policy Settings

In this exercise, you configure and test some additional Account Policy settings.

▶ **To configure Account Policy settings**

1. Use the Local Group Policy custom MMC console you created to configure the following Account Policy settings:

   ▪ A user should have at least five different passwords before using a previously used password.

   ▪ After changing a password, a user must wait 24 hours before he or she can change it again.

   ▪ A user should change his or her password every 3 weeks.

   What settings did you use for each of the three listed items?

2. Close the Local Group Policy custom MMC console.

▶ **To test Account Policy settings**

1. Log on as User13 with no password.

   Windows XP Professional displays a Logon Message message box indicating that you must change your password at first logon.

2. Click OK to close the message box.

3. Press TAB to move to the New Password text box and leave the Old Password text box blank.

4. In the New Password and Confirm New Password text boxes, type **hotwater** and then click OK.

   Windows XP Professional displays a Change Password message box indicating that your password was successfully changed.

5. Click OK to close the Change Password message box.

6. Click Start and then click Control Panel.

7. Click User Accounts and then click Change My Password.

8. In the Type Your Current Password text box, type **hotwater**.

9. In the Type A New Password and Type The New Password Again To Confirm text boxes, type **chocolate**.

10. Click Change Password.

    Were you successful? Why or why not?

11. Close any open message boxes and windows and log off.

Exercise 3: Configuring Account Lockout Policy

In this exercise, you configure Account Lockout Policy settings and then test them to make sure they are set up correctly.

▶ **To configure Account Lockout Policy settings**

1. Log on to your computer as Fred or with a user account that is a member of the Administrators group.

2. Click Start and click Run.

3. In the Open text box, type **mmc**, and then press ENTER.

4. Open the Local Group Policy custom MMC console you created.

5. In the Local Group Policy console tree, double-click Account Policies.

6. Click Account Lockout Policy.

7. Use Account Lockout Policy settings to do the following:

   ▪ Lock out a user account after four failed logon attempts.

   ▪ Lock out user accounts until an administrator unlocks the user account.

Note If a Suggested Value Changes dialog box appears, click OK and then verify that your settings are correct.

What Account Lockout Policy settings did you use for each of the two conditions?

8. Log off Windows XP Professional.

▶ **To test Account Lockout Policy settings**

1. Try to log on as User13 with a password of *chocolate* four times.

2. Try to log on as User13 with a password of *chocolate* again and a dialog box appears, indicating that the account is locked out.

3. Click OK and then log on as Fred or as a user that is a member of the Administrators group.

Lesson Review

The following questions will help you determine whether you have learned enough to move on to the next lesson. If you have difficulty answering these questions, review the material in this lesson before beginning the next lesson. The answers are in Appendix A, "Questions and Answers."

1. What tool does Microsoft Windows XP Professional provide for you to configure Password Policy?

2. What is the range of values Windows XP Professional allows you to set for the Enforce Password History setting and what do those values mean?

3. The range of values Windows XP Professional allows you to set for the Maximum Password Age setting is _____ to _____ days. The default value is _____ days.

4. Which of the following selections are requirements for a password if the Passwords Must Meet Complexity Requirements setting is enabled? (Choose all that apply.)

   a. All passwords must exceed the specified minimum password length.

   b. All passwords must comply with the password history settings.

   c. No passwords can contain capitals or punctuation.

   d. No passwords can contain the user's account or full name.

5. What is Account Lockout Duration and what is the range of values?

Lesson Summary

- The Group Policy snap-in allows you to improve the security on your computer by making it more difficult for an unauthorized user to gain access.

- Password Policy allows you to manage the passwords used on your computer. For example, you can force users to change passwords on a regular basis and you can control the minimum length of a password.

- The Enforce Password History setting allows you to set the number of passwords to be kept in a password history. The default value of 0 indicates that no password history is being kept.

- If the Passwords Must Meet Complexity Requirements setting is enabled, all passwords must meet or exceed the specified minimum password length; must comply with the password history settings; must contain capitals, numerals, or punctuation; and cannot contain the user's account or full name.

- Account Lockout Policy allows you determine the number of invalid logon attempts before a user account is locked out of the computer.

Lesson 2: Configuring User Rights

Under the Local Policies node, there are three nodes: Audit Policy, User Rights Assignment, and Security Options. Audit Policy was explained in Chapter 12, "Auditing Resources and Events." In this lesson you learn how use the Group Policy snap-in to assign user rights. Security options are covered in Lesson 3.

After this lesson, you will be able to

- Configure user rights

Estimated lesson time: 30 minutes

User Rights

You can assign specific rights to groups or individual user accounts. To simplify administration of user rights, Microsoft recommends that you assign user rights only to groups and not individual user accounts. Each user right allows the members of the group or the individual users assigned the right to perform a specific action, such as backing up files or changing the system time. If a user is a member of more than one group, the user rights applied to that user are cumulative, so the user has all the user rights assigned to all the groups of which he or she is a member.

You can configure user rights on a computer running Windows XP Professional by using the Group Policy snap-in as follows:

1. Click Start and click Run. Type **mmc** in the Open text box, and click OK to open an empty custom MMC console.

2. On the File menu, click Add/Remove Snap-In, and then click Add.

3. In the Add Standalone Snap-In dialog box, click Group Policy and then click Add.

   The Select Group Policy Object dialog box appears, allowing you to point the MMC console containing Group Policy at the local computer or at a remote computer. The Allow The Focus Of The Group Policy Snap-In To Be Changed When Launching From The Command Line check box allows you to configure the MMC so that you can decide which computer to use Group Policy on when you start the MMC.

4. Click Finish to leave Group Policy with its focus on the Local Computer, the default setting, and save the console with Local Group Policy.

5. Expand Local Computer Policy, Computer Configuration, Windows Settings, Security Settings, and Local Policies, and then click User Right Assignments.

6. In the details pane, select the user right you want to configure, and then on the Action menu, click Properties.

   The console displays the current groups and user accounts that have this user right assigned, as shown in Figure 13.4. To add groups or user accounts, click Add. To remove a group or user, select the group or user and click Remove.

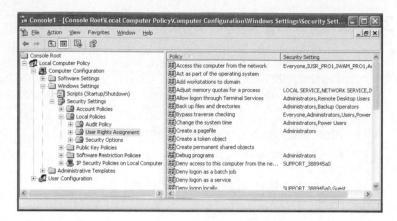

Figure 13.4   The Group Policy snap-in displaying User Rights Assignment

There are two types of user rights: privileges and logon rights.

Privileges

A *privilege* is a user right that allows the members of the group to which it is assigned to perform a specific task, usually one that affects an entire computer system rather than one object. Table 13.3 explains the privileges you can assign in Windows XP Professional.

Table 13.3   Privileges Available in Windows XP Professional

Privilege	Description
Act As Part Of The Operating System	Allows a process to authenticate like a user and thus gain access to the same resources as a user.
	Do not grant this privilege unless you are certain it is needed. Only low-level authentication services should require this privilege. Processes that require this privilege should use the LocalSystem account because it already has this privilege assigned.
	A separate user account with this privilege allows a user or process to build an access token, granting them more rights than they should have, and does not provide a primary identity for tracking events in the audit log.
Add Workstations To Domain	Allows a user to add a computer to a domain. The user specifies the domain being added on the computer, and an object is created in the Computer container of Active Directory in that domain.
	For this privilege to be effective, it must be assigned as part of the default domain controller policy for the domain.
Back Up Files And Directories	Allows a user to back up the system without being assigned permissions to access all files and folders on the system.
	By default, members of the Administrators and Backup Operators groups have this privilege on workstations, member servers, and domain controllers. On domain controllers, members of the Server Operators group have this privilege.

Table 13.3   *(continued)*

Privilege	Description
Bypass Traverse Checking	Allows a user to move through folders that he or she has no permission to access. This privilege does not allow the user to view the contents of a folder, just to move through the folder.
	By default, members of the Administrators, Backup Operators, Power Users, Users, and Everyone groups have this privilege on workstations and member servers.
Change The System Time	Allows a user to set the time for the internal clock of the computer.
	By default, members of the Administrators and Power Users groups, as well as the LocalSystem and NetworkService accounts, have this privilege on workstations and member servers. By default, members of the Administrators and Server Operators groups, as well as the LocalSystem and NetworkService accounts, have this privilege on domain controllers.
Create A Token Object	Allows a process to create a token that it can then use to access any local resource when the process uses a token-creating application programming interface (API).
	Microsoft recommends that processes requiring this privilege use the LocalSystem account because it already has this privilege.
Create Permanent Shared Objects	Allows a process to create a directory object in the Windows object manager. This privilege is useful to kernel-mode components that plan to extend the Windows object namespace. Components that run in kernel mode already have this privilege, so it is not necessary for you to assign it to them.
Create A Pagefile	Allows a user to create a pagefile and modify the size of existing pagefiles.
	By default, members of the Administrators group have this privilege on workstations, member servers, and domain controllers.
Debug Programs	Allows a user to attach a debugger on any process. This privilege provides powerful access to sensitive and critical system operating components.
	By default, members of the Administrators group have this privilege on workstations, member servers, and domain controllers.
Enable Computer And User Accounts To Be Trusted For Delegation	Allows the user to set the Trusted For Delegation setting on a user or computer object. A server process running on a computer that is trusted for delegation or run by a user who is trusted for delegation can access resources on another computer.
	Do not assign this privilege unless you understand that this privilege and the Trusted For Delegation setting can open your network to attacks from Trojan horse programs that impersonate incoming clients and use their credentials to access network resources.

(continued)

Table 13.3   *(continued)*

Privilege	Description
	This privilege is not assigned to anyone on workstations or member servers. On domain controllers it is assigned by default to the members of the Administrators group.
Force Shutdown From A Remote System	Allows a user to shut down a computer from a remote computer on the network.
	By default, members of the Administrators group have this privilege on workstations and member servers. By default, members of the Administrators and Server Operators groups have this privilege on domain controllers.
Generate Security Audits	Allows a process to make entries in the security log for object access auditing.
Adjust Memory Quotas For A Process	Allows a process to increase the processor quota assigned to another process. The process must have write access to the process for which it increases the processor quota.
Increase Scheduling Priority	Allows a process to increase the execution priority of another process. The process must have write access to the process for which it increases the execution priority.
	Allows users to change the scheduling priority of a process through Task Manager.
	By default, members of the Administrators group have this privilege on workstations, member servers, and domain controllers.
Load And Unload Device Drivers	Allows a user to install and uninstall Plug and Play device drivers. Non-Plug and Play device drivers are not affected by this privilege.
	By default, only Administrators have this privilege. Exercise caution in granting this privilege. Device drivers run as trusted programs and only device drivers with correct digital signatures should be installed.
	By default, members of the Administrators group have this privilege on workstations, member servers, and domain controllers.
Lock Pages In Memory	Allows a process to lock data in physical memory and prevent Windows XP Professional from paging the data to virtual memory (a pagefile) on disk.
	This privilege is not assigned to anyone by default. Some system processes have this privilege.
Manage Auditing And Security Log	Allows a user to specify object access auditing options for individual resources such as files, Active Directory objects, and registry keys.
	A user with this privilege can also view and clear the security log from the Event Viewer.
	By default, members of the Administrators group have this privilege on workstations, member servers, and domain controllers.

Table 13.3   *(continued)*

Privilege	Description
Modify Firmware Environment Values	Allows a user to use the System Properties program to modify system environment variables.
	Allows a process to use an API to modify the system environment variables.
Perform Volume Maintenance Tasks	Allows users to run disk tools, such as Disk Cleanup or Disk Defragmenter.
	By default, members of the Administrators group have this privilege on workstations, member servers, and domain controllers.
Profile A Single Process	Allows a user to use performance-monitoring tools to monitor the performance of nonsystem processes.
	By default, on workstations and member servers, Administrators and Power Users have this privilege. On domain controllers, only Administrators have this privilege.
Profile System Performance	Allows a user to use performance-monitoring tools to monitor the performance of system processes.
	By default, members of the Administrators group have this privilege on workstations, member servers, and domain controllers.
Remove Computer From Docking Station	Allows a user to undock a portable computer.
	By default, members of the Administrators, Power Users, and Users groups have this privilege on workstations and member servers.
Replace A Process-Level Token	Allows a parent process to replace the access token associated with a child process.
Restore Files And Directories	Allows a user to restore backed up files and directories without being assigned the appropriate file and folder permissions, and allows a user to set any valid security principal as the owner of the object.
	By default, members of the Administrators and Backup Operators groups have this privilege on workstations, member servers, and domain controllers. On domain controllers, members of the Server Operators group also have this privilege.
Shut Down The System	Allows a user to shut down the local computer.
	By default, members of the Administrators, Backup Operators, Power Users, and Users groups have this privilege on workstations.
	By default, members of the Administrators, Backup Operators, and Power Users groups have this privilege on member servers.
	By default, members of the Administrators, Account Operators, Backup Operators, Print Operators, and Server Operators groups have this privilege on domain controllers.

(continued)

Table 13.3 *(continued)*

Privilege	Description
Synchronize Directory Service Data	Allows a process to provide directory service synchronization services. This privilege is relevant only on domain controllers.
Take Ownership Of Files Or Other Objects	Allows a user to take ownership of objects in the system, including Active Directory objects, files and folders, printers, registry keys, processes, and threads. By default, members of the Administrators group have this privilege on workstations, member servers, and domain controllers.

Logon Rights

A *logon right* is a user right assigned to a group or an individual user account. Logon rights control the way users can log on to a system. Table 13.4 explains the logon rights you can assign in Windows XP Professional.

Table 13.4 **Logon Rights Available in Windows XP Professional**

Logon right	Description
Access This Computer From The Network	Allows a user to connect to the computer over the network. By default, members of the Administrators, Power Users, and Everyone groups are granted this logon right on workstations, member servers, and domain controllers.
Deny Access To This Computer From The Network	Prevents a user from connecting to the computer over the network. By default, this right is not granted to anyone.
Log On As A Batch Job	Allows a user to log on using a batch-queue facility. By default, members of the Administrators group are granted this logon right on workstations, member servers, and domain controllers. If Internet Information Services (IIS) is installed, the right is automatically assigned to the built-in account for anonymous access to IIS.
Deny Logon As A Batch Job	Prevents a user from logging on using a batch-queue facility. By default, this right is not granted to anyone.
Log On As A Service	Allows a security principal (an account holder such as a user, computer, or service) to log on as a service. Services can be configured to run under the LocalSystem, LocalService, or NetworkService accounts, which have the right to log on as a service. Any service that runs under a separate account must be granted this right. By default, this right is not granted to anyone.

Table 13.4   *(continued)*

Logon right	Description
Deny Logon As A Service	Prevents a security principal from logging on as a service.
	By default, this right is not granted to anyone.
Log On Locally	Allows a user to log on at the computer's keyboard.
	By default, members of the Administrators, Account Operators, Backup Operators, Print Operators, and Server Operators groups are granted this logon right.
Deny Logon Locally	Prevents a user from logging on at the computer's keyboard.
	By default, this right is not granted to anyone.
Allow Logon Through Terminal Services	Allows a user to log on using Terminal Services.
	By default, members of the Administrators and Remote Desktop Users groups are granted this logon right on workstations and member servers. On domain controllers, only Administrators are granted this logon right.
Deny Logon Through Terminal Services	Prevents a user from logging on using Terminal Services.
	By default, this right is not granted to anyone.

Lesson Review

The following questions will help you determine whether you have learned enough to move on to the next lesson. If you have difficulty answering these questions, review the material in this lesson before beginning the next lesson. The answers are in Appendix A, "Questions and Answers."

1. Which of the following statements about user rights are correct? (Choose all that apply.)

   a. Microsoft recommends that you assign user rights to individual user accounts.

   b. Microsoft recommends that you assign user rights to groups rather than individual user accounts.

   c. User rights allow users assigned the right to perform a specific action, such as backing up files and directories.

   d. There are two types of user rights: privileges and logon rights.

2. If your computer running Windows XP Professional is part of a Windows 2000 domain environment and you configure the Local Security Policies on your computer so that you assign yourself the Add Workstation To A Domain user right, can you add additional workstations to the domain? Why or why not?

3. What benefit does the Back Up Files And Directories user right provide?

4. What are logon rights and what do they do?

Lesson Summary

- User Rights Assignment is one of the three nodes located under the Local Policies node and it can be configured using the Group Policy snap-in.
- A privilege is a user right that allows users to perform a specific task, usually one that affects an entire computer system rather than one object.
- Bypass Traverse Tracking is a privilege that allows users to move through folders that they have no permission to access.
- Logon rights are user rights assigned to a group or an individual user account to control the way users can log on to a system.
- Logon rights control whether or not a user can connect to a computer over the network or sitting at the computer's keyboard.

Lesson 3: Configuring Security Options

Under the Local Policies node, there is a Security Options node. There are close to 60 additional security options grouped into the following categories: accounts, audit, devices, domain controller, domain member, interactive logon, Microsoft network client, network access, network security, recovery console, shutdown, system cryptography, and system objects. In this lesson, you learn about a few of these available options.

After this lesson, you will be able to

- Configure security options

Estimated lesson time: 15 minutes

Renaming the Administrator Account

You cannot delete the Administrator account, but you should rename the built-in Administrator account to provide a greater degree of security. You should use a name that does not identify it as the Administrator account to make it difficult for unauthorized users to break into the account. One of the account settings allows you to enter an account name to automatically rename the Administrator account.

To automatically rename the administrator account, access the security options using the Group Policy snap-in, expand Local Policies, and then select Security Options. Right-click Accounts: Rename The Administrator Account and then click Properties. Type in the new name you wish to use for the Administrator account and click OK.

Note   To automatically rename the Guest account, use Accounts: Rename Guest Account.

Tip   A security option that is important in securing your computer is the Interactive Logon: Number Of Previous Logons To Cache option. This allows you to determine the number of times users can log on to a Windows domain using cached account information. Logon information can be cached locally, so if a domain controller is not available, the user can still log on to the domain. This setting determines the number of times a user can log on using that cached information. The default is 10 times. Setting this value to 0 disables the local caching of this information. A second option is the Network Access: Do Not Allow Storage Of Credentials Or .NET Passwords For Network Authentication option. Enabling this option prevents the storing of credentials and .NET Passports.

Shutting Down the Computer Without Logging On

By default, Windows XP Professional does not require a user to be logged on to the computer to shut it down. One of the account settings allows you to force users to log on to the computer before it can be shut down. Access the security options using the Group Policy snap-in, just as you did to configure Account Policy. Once you start the Group Policy snap-in, expand Local Policies and then select Security Options.

Right-click Shutdown: Allow System To Be Shut Down Without Having To Log On, and then click Properties. Figure 13.5 shows the Properties dialog box for the Shutdown: Allow System To Be Shut Down Without Having To Log On setting. This setting is either enabled, which is the default, or disabled. To force users to have to log on to shut down the system, select Disabled.

Note Your computer must be a member of a domain or you must turn off the use of the Welcome screen to use this setting.

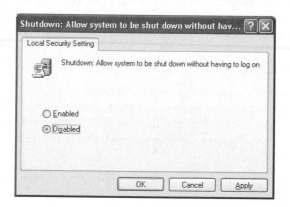

Figure 13.5   Setting the Allow System To Be Shut Down Without Having To Log On setting

Clearing the Virtual Memory Pagefile on Shutdown

By default, Windows XP Professional does not clear the virtual memory pagefile when the system is shut down. In some organizations this is considered a breach of security because the data in the pagefile might be accessible to users who are not authorized to view that information. To enable this feature and clear the pagefile each time the system is shut down, start the Group Policy snap-in, expand Local Policies, and then select Security Options. Right-click Shutdown: Clear Virtual Memory Pagefile and then click Properties. As shown in Figure 13.6, this feature is either enabled or disabled. By default, it is disabled. To force Windows XP Professional to clear the pagefile when the system is shut down, select Enabled.

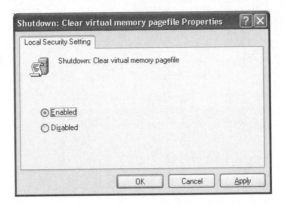

Figure 13.6   Setting the Clear Virtual Memory Pagefile option

Disabling CTRL+ALT+DELETE Requirement for Logon

Windows XP Professional allows you to configure your computer so that users are required to press CTRL+ALT+DELETE to log on to the computer. By forcing users to press CTRL+ALT+DELETE, you are using a key combination recognized only by Windows. This ensures that you are giving the password only to Windows and not to a Trojan horse program waiting to capture your password.

If you are in an environment where security is not a concern, you can leave the default setting of Not Defined or you can enable the Interactive Logon: Do Not Require CTRL+ALT+DEL option. With either of these settings, users will not have to use this key combination to log on to the computer. To require users to press this key combination to log on, start the Group Policy snap-in, expand Local Policies, and then select Security Options. Right-click Interactive Logon: Do Not Require CTRL+ALT+DEL and then click Properties and click Disabled. Disable this setting if security is a concern.

Note   Your computer must be a member of a domain or you must turn off the use of the Welcome screen to use this setting.

Preventing the Display of the Last User Name in Logon Screen

By default, Windows XP Professional displays the last user name to log on to the computer in the Windows Security dialog box. In some situations this is a security risk because an unauthorized user can see a valid user account name displayed on the screen. This makes it much easier to break into the computer.

Enable Interactive Logon: Do Not Display Last User Name to prevent the last user name from being displayed in the Windows Security dialog box. In the Group Policy snap-in, click the Local Policies node in the console pane, and then click Security Options. In the details pane, right-click Interactive Logon: Do Not Display Last User Name, click Properties, and then select Enabled to enable this feature, which is either enabled or disabled (see Figure 13.7).

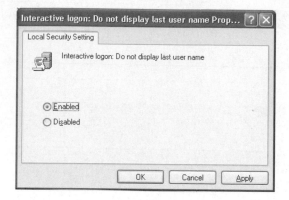

Figure 13.7   Disabling the Do Not Display Last User Name In Logon Screen option

Note   Your computer must be a member of a domain or you must turn off the use of the Welcome screen to use this setting.

Practice: Configuring Security Settings

In this practice, you configure the security setting that automatically renames the Guest account on your computer. Then you turn off the Welcome screen and configure some additional security settings on your computer.

Run the **SecuritySettings** file in the Demos folder on the CD-ROM accompanying this book for a demonstration of configuring security settings.

Exercise 1: Configuring the Accounts: Rename the Guest Account Security Setting

In this exercise, you use the custom MMC console containing the Group Policy snap-in you created and saved with the name Local Group Policy to automatically rename the Guest account.

▶   **To configure and test the Accounts: Rename The Guest Account security option**

1. Log on to your computer as Fred or with a user account that is a member of the Administrators group.

2. Click Start and click Run. In the Open text box, type **mmc**, and then click OK.

3. On the File menu, click Open and click the Local Group Policy MMC console you created in the first practice in this chapter.

4. In the Group Policy snap-in's console tree, click Local Computer Policy, Computer Configuration, Windows Settings, Security Settings, Local Policies, and Security Options.

5. Configure your computer so that the Guest account is automatically renamed Fox.

6. Start the User Accounts tool and verify that the Guest account is now named Fox.

Exercise 2: Turning off Use of the Welcome Screen

In this exercise, you turn off the use of the Welcome screen.

▶ **To turn off the Welcome screen**

1. Click Start and then click Control Panel.

2. Click User Accounts.

3. Click Change The Way Users Log On Or Off.

   Windows XP Professional displays the Select Logon And Logoff Options window.

4. Clear the Use The Welcome Screen check box.

   Windows XP Professional also clears the Use Fast User Switching check box.

5. Click Apply Options, close all open windows, and then log off Windows XP Professional.

   Notice that the Welcome Screen is not displayed and that the Welcome To Windows dialog box requiring you to press CTRL+ALT+DELETE is displayed.

Exercise 3: Configuring Additional Security Settings

In this exercise, you configure some additional security settings.

1. Press CTRL+ALT+DELETE.

   The Log On To Windows Screen is displayed and the name of the last user to log on to the computer is automatically filled in.

2. Click Options.

   Notice that Shut Down is available.

3. Log on as Fred or with a user account that is a member of the Administrators group.

4. Use the Group Policy snap-in and configure your computer so that the following conditions are true:

   ■ Windows XP Professional will not display the user account last logged on the computer in the Windows Security dialog box.

   ■ Users must log on to shut down the computer.

5. Log off Windows XP Professional.

6. Verify that the name of the user account last logged on is not displayed.

7. Verify that users must log on to shut down the computer; the Shut Down button is no longer available.

8. Log on to the computer and enable the use of the Welcome screen.

9. Log off Windows XP Professional.

Lesson Review

The following questions will help you determine whether you have learned enough to move on to the next lesson. If you have difficulty answering these questions, review the material in this lesson before beginning the next lesson. The answers are in Appendix A, "Questions and Answers."

1. How can you require a user to be logged on to the computer to shut it down? (Discuss using the Welcome screen and using CTRL+ALT+DELETE to log on.)

2. By default Windows XP Professional does not clear the virtual memory pagefile when the system is shut down. Why can this be considered a security breach and what can you do to resolve it?

3. Why does forcing users to press CTRL+ALT+DELETE improve security on your computer?

4. By default, Windows XP Professional displays the last user name to log on to the computer in the Windows Security dialog box. Why is this considered a security risk and what can you do to resolve it?

5. How can you disable the Welcome screen in Windows XP Professional?

Lesson Summary

- The security options in the Local Security Policy snap-in allow you to improve the effective security on any of your computers that require it.

- If you have disabled the Welcome screen, you can prevent an unauthorized user from shutting down your computer by forcing users to log on before they can shut down the computer.

- If you have disabled the Welcome screen, you can force users to press CTRL+ALT+DELETE before they can log on to prevent a Trojan horse application from stealing user passwords.

- The CTRL+ALT+DELETE key combination is recognized by Windows and ensures that only Windows picks up the keystrokes entered for user name and password.

- You can also increase security by not displaying a valid user name for the last user account that logged on in the Windows Security dialog box.

Lesson 4: Configuring Internet Explorer Security Options

Internet options allow you to configure Internet Explorer 6.0. You can specify the first Web page you see when you start Internet Explorer, delete temporary Internet files stored on your computer, use Content Advisor to block access to objectionable materials, and set your security level. This lesson introduces you to configuring Internet options.

After this lesson, you will be able to
- Configure Internet options

Estimated lesson time: 40 minutes

Using Internet Options

To access Internet options, you would do the following:

1. Click Start, and then click Control Panel.
2. Click Network And Internet Connections, and then click Internet Options.

   Windows XP Professional displays the Internet Properties dialog box, as shown in Figure 13.8.

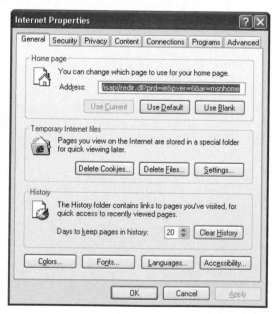

Figure 13.8   The General tab of the Internet Properties dialog box

Using the General Tab

The Home Page section in the General tab of the Internet Properties dialog box allows you to change the page you use for your *home page*, the page you see each time you start Internet Explorer. This is also the page you are returned to each time you click the Home icon on the toolbar.

The Temporary Internet Files section in the General tab allows you to delete all cookies and temporary Internet files stored on your computer. A *cookie* is a file created by a Web site that stores information about you on your computer. To delete all the cookies stored on your computer, click Delete Cookies. Windows XP Professional displays a Delete Cookies message box for you to confirm that you want to delete all the cookies stored on your computer. Click OK to delete all the cookies or click Cancel to leave the cookies stored on your computer. A *temporary Internet file* is a file downloaded from a Web site on the Internet to decrease your access time to the Web site the next time you view it. To delete all temporary Internet files on your computer, click Delete Files. A message box will be displayed for you to confirm that you want to delete all temporary Internet files on your computer. The Delete All Offline Content checkbox allows you to delete any sites you have configured to be available offline. Click OK to delete all the temporary Internet files on your computer. Click Settings to specify when your system should check for newer versions of stored files and the size and location of the folder that stores these temporary files.

The History section allows you to specify the length of time links to pages you have visited are kept and to clear all saved links. The General tab also allows you to configure the colors, fonts, languages, and accessibility options used.

Using the Security Tab

The Security tab of the Internet Properties dialog box allows you to assign Web sites into zones, so you can customize the security for each zone. The first zone is the Internet, which contains all Web sites not assigned to another zone (see Figure 13.9).

Figure 13.9   The Security tab of the Internet Properties dialog box

The second zone is for your local intranet. The third zone is for trusted sites, and the fourth zone is for restricted sites. To add Web sites to any of these zones, click the zone and then click Sites.

The Security Level For This Zone section allows you to customize the security settings for each zone. To customize a zone's security level, click the zone and then click Custom Level. Windows XP Professional displays the Security Settings dialog box (see Figure 13.10).

The Security Settings dialog box allows you to control what gets loaded onto your computer from the Internet. For example, for Download Signed ActiveX Controls you can choose one of the following three options:

- **Enable.**   Allows you to download signed ActiveX controls
- **Disable.**   Disables the downloading of ActiveX controls
- **Prompt.**   Prompts you so that you can determine whether or not you want to download ActiveX controls

Figure 13.10   The Security Settings dialog box

Other settings on the Security Settings dialog box include the following:

- File Download
- Font Download
- Access Data Sources Across Domains
- Allow META REFRESH
- Display Mixed Content
- Don't Prompt For Client Certificate Selection When No Certificates Or Only One Certificate Exists
- Drag And Drop Or Copy And Paste Files
- Installation Of Desktop Items
- Launching Programs And Files In An IFRAME
- Navigate Subframes Across Different Domains
- Submit Nonencrypted Form Data
- User Data Persistence
- Active Scripting
- Allow Paste Operations Via Script
- Scripting Of Java Applets
- User Authentication Logon

Note   Internet Explorer 6.0 and Windows XP Professional do not contain the Sun Microsystems Java Virtual Machine (JVM). The first time you connect to a Web site that requires JVM support, you must download JVM.

One other setting located in the Security Settings dialog box is Software Channel Permissions. The options you can set for it are as follows:

- **Low Safety.**   Allows software to be automatically downloaded and installed from software distribution channels without prompting
- **Medium Safety.**   Allows the automatic downloading of software from a software distribution channel without prompting, but does not allow automatic installation of the software
- **High Safety.**   Allows automatic notification, but not automatic downloading or installing of software from software distribution channels

Using the Privacy Tab

The Privacy tab allows you to determine how cookies are handled on your computer for all Web sites in the Internet zone. Table 13.5 explains the available privacy settings.

Table 13.5   Privacy Tab Settings

Setting	Description
Block All Cookies	Blocks cookies from all Web sites and makes existing cookies on your computer unreadable by Web sites.
High	Blocks cookies that do not have a compact privacy policy and those that use personally identifiable information without your explicit consent.
Medium High	Blocks third-party cookies that do not have a compact privacy policy and those that use personally identifiable information without your explicit consent. It also blocks first-party cookies that use personally identifiable information without your implicit consent.
Medium	Blocks third-party cookies that do not have a compact privacy policy and those that use personally identifiable information without your implicit consent. It also restricts first-party cookies that use personally identifiable information without your implicit consent.
Low	Restricts third-party cookies that do not have a compact privacy policy and those that use personally identifiable information without your implicit consent.
Accept All Cookies	Allows all cookies to be saved on the computer. Existing cookies on this computer can be read by the Web sites that created them.

Tip   You can also click Advanced to override automatic cookie handling and manually define whether to accept, block, or prompt first-party and third-party cookies.

Using the Content Tab

The Content tab gives you access to the Content Advisor, which allows you to control what can be viewed on the Internet. This is a valuable tool for parents who want to protect their children from areas of the Internet suitable only for adults. You can control access based on language, nudity, sex, and violence. You can also create a list of Web sites that are always viewable or never viewable, no matter how they are rated.

Note   The Connections tab helps you set up an Internet connection and the Programs tab allows you to specify which program Windows XP Professional automatically uses for each Internet service.

Using the Advanced Tab

The Advanced tab allows you to fine-tune accessibility, browsing, HTTP 1.1 settings, multimedia functionality, and security. Accessibility provides the following two check boxes:

- **Always Expand ALT Text For Images.**   Specifies whether the image size should expand to fit all of the alternate text when the Show Pictures text box is cleared.

- **Move System Caret With Focus/Selection Changes.**   Specifies whether to move the system caret whenever the focus or selection changes. Some accessibility aids, such as screen readers or screen magnifiers, use the system caret to determine which area of the screen to read or magnify.

Browsing provides many options that allow control browsing, including the following check boxes:

- **Always Send URLs As UTF-8.**   Specifies whether to use UTF-8, a standard that defines characters so they are readable in any language. This enables you to exchange Internet addresses (URLs) that contain characters from another language. This option is selected by default.

- **Enable Folder View For FTP Sites.**   Specifies that FTP sites be shown in folder view. This feature might not work with certain types of proxy connections. If you clear this check box, FTP sites will display their contents in a Hypertext Markup Language (HTML)–based layout. This option is selected by default.

- **Enable Install On Demand (Other).**   Specifies to automatically download and install Web components if a Web page needs them to display the page properly or perform a particular task. This option is selected by default.

The HTTP 1.1 settings allow you to specify whether you want to use HTTP 1.1. Many Web sites still use HTTP 1.0, so if you are having difficulties connecting to some Web sites, you might not want to use HTTP 1.1.

The Multimedia section provides many options including the following check boxes:

- **Play Animations In Web Pages.**   Specifies whether animations can play when pages are displayed. Pages that contain animations display very slowly. To display pages faster, clear this check box. You can still play an individual animation even when this check box is not selected if you right-click the icon that represents the animation and then click Show Picture. This option is selected by default.

- **Play Sounds In Web Pages.**   Specifies whether music and other sounds can play when pages are displayed. Some pages that contain sounds download very slowly. Clear this check box to speed up the downloading of these pages. If RealNetworks RealAudio is installed or if a video clip is playing, some sounds might play even though you cleared this check box. This option is selected by default.

- **Show Pictures.**   Specifies whether graphical images should be included when pages are displayed. Pages that contain several graphical images can display very slowly. Clear this check box to speed up the downloading of these pages. You can still view an individual image even when this check box is not selected if you right-click the icon that represents the graphic and then click Show Picture. This option is selected by default.

The Printing settings allow you to specify whether you want to print background colors and images.

The Security settings (see Figure 13.11) allow you to fine-tune your security settings.

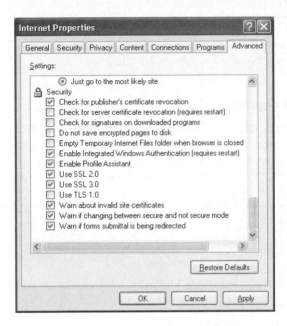

Figure 13.11   The Advanced tab of the Internet Properties dialog box

The Security section provides many options including the following check boxes:

- **Empty Temporary Internet Files Folder When Browser Is Closed.**
  Specifies whether you want to empty the Internet Temporary Files folder
  when the browser is closed. This option is not selected by default.

- **Use SSL 2.0.**   Controls whether you want to send and receive secured information through Secure Sockets Layer Level 2 (SSL 2.0), the standard protocol for secure transmissions. All Web sites support this protocol. This option
  is selected by default.

- **Use SSL 3.0.**   Specifies whether you want to send and receive secured information through Secure Sockets Layer Level 3 (SSL 3.0), which is designed to
  be more secure than SSL 2.0. Some Web sites might not support SSL 3.0.
  This option is selected by default.

- **Warn About Invalid Site Certificates.**   Specifies whether Internet Explorer
  should warn you if the address (URL) in a Web site's security certificate is not
  valid. This option is selected by default.

- **Warn If Changing Between Secure And Not Secure Mode.**   Specifies
  whether Internet Explorer should warn you if you are switching between
  Internet sites that are secure and sites that are not secure.

Note   For information about any of the other check boxes located in the Advanced tab of the Internet Properties dialog box, click on the question mark in the upper right corner of the dialog box and then click the check box.

Lesson Review

The following questions will help you determine whether you have learned enough to move on to the next lesson. If you have difficulty answering these questions, please go back and review the material in this lesson before beginning the next chapter. The answers are in Appendix A, "Questions and Answers."

1. What is a cookie? How can you delete all the cookies that are stored on your computer?

2. How can you control which cookies are stored on your computer?

3. As a concerned parent, how can you help protect your children from adult material found on the Internet?

4. How can you speed up the downloading of pages?

5. How can you have the Internet Temporary Files folder emptied each time you close your browser?

Lesson Summary

- To access the Internet Options dialog box, in Control Panel, click Network And Internet Connections, and then click Internet Options.

- The Home Page section in the General tab of the Internet Properties dialog box allows you to change the page you use for your home page.

- The Temporary Internet Files section in the General tab of the Internet Properties dialog box allows you to delete all cookies and temporary Internet files stored on your computer.

- The General tab also allows you to configure the colors, fonts, languages, and accessibility options used and to specify the length of time links to pages you have visited are stored.

- The Security tab of the Internet Properties dialog box allows you to assign Web sites into zones, so you can customize the security for each zone.

- Internet Explorer 6.0 and Windows XP Professional do not contain the Sun Microsystems Java Virtual Machine (JVM); the first time you connect to a Web site that requires JVM support, you must download JVM.

- The Privacy tab allows you to determine how cookies will be handled on your computer for all Web sites in the Internet zone.

- The Content tab gives you access to the Content Advisor, which allows parents to protect their children from areas of the Internet suitable only for adults.

- The Advanced tab allows you to fine-tune accessibility, browsing, HTTP 1.1 settings, multimedia functionality, and security.

CHAPTER 14

Managing Data Storage

About This Chapter

This chapter introduces data storage management on volumes formatted with NT file system (NTFS). You will learn about compression, which allows you to store more data on a disk, and you will learn about disk quotas, which allow you to control how much space a user can use on a disk. You will learn how you can increase the security of files and folders on your computer by using the Microsoft Encrypting File System (EFS). You will also learn about defragmenting a disk, which allows your system to access and save files and folders more efficiently.

Before You Begin

To complete this chapter, you must have

- A computer that meets the minimum hardware requirements listed in the preface, "About This Book"
- Microsoft Windows XP Professional installed on the computer

Lesson 1: Managing Compression

Windows XP Professional supports two types of compression: NTFS compression and Compressed Folders. NTFS compression enables you to compress files, folders, or an entire drive. NTFS compressed files and folders occupy less space on an NTFS-formatted volume, which enables you to store more data. Each file and folder on an NTFS volume has a *compression state*, which is either compressed or uncompressed. The Compressed Folders feature allows you to create a compressed folder so that all files you store in that folder are automatically compressed.

After this lesson, you will be able to

- Manage disk compression
- Compress and uncompress files, folders, and NTFS volumes

Estimated lesson time: 60 minutes

Using Compressed Folders

The Compressed Folders feature is new in Windows XP Professional and provides the ability to create compressed folders and view their contents. The Compressed Folders feature in Windows XP Professional allows you to compress large files so that you can store more files on a floppy disk or hard drive.

To create a compressed folder, start Windows Explorer, click File, click New, and then click Compressed Folder. This creates a compressed folder in the current folder. You can drag and drop files into the compressed folder and the files are automatically compressed. If you copy a file from the compressed folder to another that is not compressed, that file will no longer be compressed. A zipper icon is shown, marking compressed folders (see Figure 14.1), and these folders are labeled Compressed Folder.

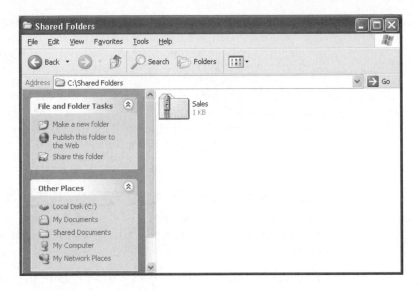

Figure 14.1 A compressed folder showing the zipper icon

Benefits of using compressed folders generated with the Compressed Folders feature include the following:

- You can create and use compressed files and folders on both file allocation table (FAT) and NTFS volumes.

- You can open files directly from the compressed folders and you can run some programs directly from compressed folders.

- You can move these compressed files and folders to any drive or folder on your computer, the Internet, or your network and they are compatible with other zip programs.

- You can encrypt compressed folders that you created using this feature.

- You can compress folders without decreasing performance.

- You can only compress individual files by storing them in a compressed folder. If you move or extract the files into an uncompressed folder, they will be uncompressed.

Using NTFS Compressed Files and Folders

NTFS compressed files can be read and written to by any Windows-based or MS-DOS–based application without first being uncompressed by another program. When an application, such as Microsoft Word 2000, or an operating system command, such as Copy, requests access to a compressed file, NTFS automatically uncompresses the file before making it available. When you close or explicitly save a file, NTFS compresses it again.

NTFS allocates disk space based on uncompressed file size. If you copy a compressed file to an NTFS volume with enough space for the compressed file, but not enough space for the uncompressed file, you might get an error message stating that there is not enough disk space for the file, and the file will not be copied to the volume.

Compressing Files and Folders Using NTFS Compression

You can set the compression state of folders and files and you can change the color that is used to display compressed files and folders in Microsoft Windows Explorer.

If you want to set the compression state of a folder or file, right-click the folder or file in Windows Explorer, click Properties, and then click Advanced. In the Advanced Attributes dialog box, shown in Figure 14.2, select the Compress Contents To Save Disk Space check box. Click OK, and then, in the Properties dialog box, click Apply.

Note   NTFS encryption and compression are mutually exclusive. For that reason, if you select the Encrypt Contents To Secure Data check box, you cannot compress the folder or file.

Figure 14.2   The Advanced Attributes dialog box

Important   To change the compression state for a file or folder, you must have Write permission for that file or folder.

The compression state for a folder does not reflect the compression state of the files and subfolders in that folder. A folder can be compressed, yet all of the files in that folder can be uncompressed. Alternatively, an uncompressed folder can contain compressed files. When you compress a folder that contains one or more files, folders, or both, Windows XP Professional displays the Confirm Attribute Changes dialog box, shown in Figure 14.3.

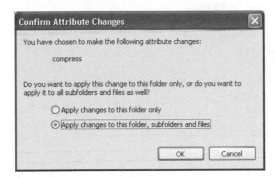

Figure 14.3   The Confirm Attribute Changes dialog box

The Confirm Attribute Changes dialog box has the two additional options explained in Table 14.1.

Table 14.1   Confirm Attribute Changes Dialog Box Options

Option	Description
Apply Changes To This Folder Only	Compresses only the folder that you have selected
Apply Changes To This Folder, Subfolders, And Files	Compresses the folder and all subfolders and files that are contained within it and subsequently added to it

Compressing a Drive or Volume Using NTFS Compression

You can set the compression state of an entire NTFS drive or volume. To do so, in Windows Explorer, right-click the drive or volume, and then click Properties. In the Properties dialog box, select the Compress Drive To Save Disk Space check box, as shown in Figure 14.4, and then click OK.

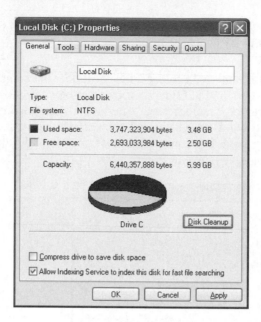

Figure 14.4   The Local Disk (C:) Properties dialog box

Displaying NTFS Compressed Files and Folders in a Different Color

Windows Explorer makes it easy for you to quickly determine if a file or folder is compressed. By default, it displays the names of compressed files and folders in a different color to distinguish them from those that are uncompressed.

You can control the display of compressed files and folders in a different color by doing the following:

1. In Windows Explorer, on the Tools menu, click Folder Options.
2. In the View tab, clear the Show Encrypted Or Compressed Files In Color check box to turn off the displaying of the names of compressed files and folders in a different color or select it to display the names in a different color.

Copying and Moving NTFS Compressed Files and Folders

There are rules that determine whether the compression state of files and folders is retained when you copy or move them within and between NTFS and FAT volumes. The following list describes how Windows XP Professional treats the compression state of a file or folder when you copy or move a compressed file or folder within or between NTFS volumes or between NTFS and FAT volumes.

- **Copying a file within an NTFS volume.** When you copy a file within an NTFS volume (shown as A in Figure 14.5), the file inherits the compression state of the target folder. For example, if you copy a compressed file to an uncompressed folder, the file is automatically uncompressed.

- **Moving a file or folder within an NTFS volume.** When you move a file or folder within an NTFS volume (shown as B in Figure 14.5), the file or folder retains its original compression state. For example, if you move a compressed file to an uncompressed folder, the file remains compressed.

- **Copying a file or folder between NTFS volumes.** When you copy a file or folder between NTFS volumes (shown as C in Figure 14.5), the file or folder inherits the compression state of the target folder.

- **Moving a file or folder between NTFS volumes.** When you move a file or folder between NTFS volumes (shown as C in Figure 14.5), the file or folder inherits the compression state of the target folder. Because Windows XP Professional treats a move as a copy and a delete, the files inherit the compression state of the target folder.

- **Moving or copying a file or folder to a FAT volume.** Windows XP Professional supports compression only for NTFS files, so when you move or copy a compressed NTFS file or folder to a FAT volume, Windows XP Professional automatically uncompresses the file or folder.

- **Moving or copying a compressed file or folder to a floppy disk.** When you move or copy a compressed NTFS file or folder to a floppy disk, Windows XP Professional automatically uncompresses the file or folder.

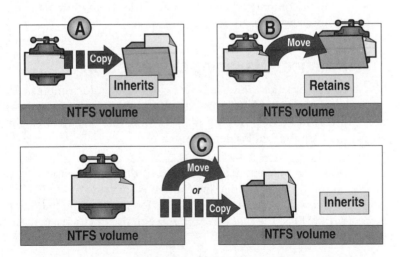

Figure 14.5 The effects of copying and moving compressed folders and files

> **Note**   When you copy a compressed NTFS file, Windows XP Professional uncompresses the file, copies the file, and then compresses the file again as a new file. This might cause performance degradation.

Using NTFS Compression Guidelines

The following list provides best practices for using compression on NTFS volumes:

- Because some file types compress more than others, select file types to compress based on the anticipated resulting file size. For example, because Windows bitmap files contain more redundant data than application executable files, this file type compresses to a smaller size. Bitmaps often compress to less than 50 percent of the original file size, whereas application files rarely compress to less than 75 percent of the original size.

- Do not store compressed files, such as PKZIP files, in a compressed folder. Windows XP Professional will attempt to compress the file, wasting system time and yielding no additional disk space.

- Compress static data rather than data that changes frequently. Compressing and uncompressing files incurs some system overhead. By choosing to compress files that are infrequently accessed, you minimize the amount of system time dedicated to compression and uncompression activities.

- NTFS compression can cause performance degradation when you copy and move files. When a compressed file is copied, it is uncompressed, copied, and then compressed again as a new file. Compress data that is not copied or moved frequently.

Practice: Managing Compression

In this practice, you use NTFS compression to compress files and folders. You uncompress a file and test the effects that copying and moving files have on compression. In the last portion of the practice, you create a compressed folder using the Compressed Folders feature.

> **Note**   In this practice, it is assumed that you installed Windows XP Professional on the C drive and that the C drive is formatted with NTFS. If you installed Windows XP Professional on a different partition and that partition is formatted with NTFS, use that drive letter when the practice refers to drive C.

Run the **Compression** file in the Demos folder on the CD-ROM accompanying this book for a demonstration of creating a compressed folder using the Compressed Folders feature and using NTFS compression to compress files and folders, and testing the effects that copying and moving files have on compression.

Exercise 1: Compressing Files in an NTFS Partition

In this exercise, you use Windows Explorer to compress files and folders to make more disk space available on your NTFS partition. You also configure Windows Explorer to display the compressed files and folders in a different color. Next, you uncompress a file. Finally, you view the effects that copying and moving files have on compressed files.

▶ **To view the capacity and free space for drive C**

1. Log on as Fred or with an account that is a member of the Administrators group.

2. Click Start, right-click My Computer, and then click Explore.

3. Right-click drive C, and then click Properties.

   Windows XP Professional displays the Local Disk (C:) Properties dialog box with the General tab active.

   What is the capacity of drive C?

   What is the free space on drive C?

4. Click Cancel to close the Local Disk (C:) Properties dialog box and return to Windows Explorer.

▶ **To create an NTFS compressed folder**

1. In Windows Explorer, expand Local Disk (C:).

2. Create a folder on drive C and name it Compressed.

Note   To create a folder on drive C, click Local Disk (C:). On the File menu, click New. Windows XP Professional creates a folder named New Folder in the root folder of the C drive. Right-click New Folder and then click Rename. Type **Compressed** and then press ENTER.

---

3. Click Compressed to select it.

4. Create a folder in Compressed and name it Compressed2.

5. Right-click the Compressed folder, and then click Properties.

   Windows XP Professional displays the Compressed Properties dialog box with the General tab active.

6. In the General tab, click Advanced.

   Windows XP Professional displays the Advanced Attributes dialog box.

7. Select the Compress Contents To Save Disk Space check box.

8. Select the Encrypt Contents To Secure Data check box.

    Notice that the system automatically removes the check from the Compress Contents To Save Disk Space check box.

9. Select the Compress Contents To Save Disk Space check box.

10. Click OK to return to the Compressed Properties dialog box.

11. Click Apply to apply your settings.

    Windows XP Professional displays the Confirm Attribute Changes dialog box, prompting you to specify whether to compress only this folder or this folder and all subfolders.

12. Select the Apply Changes To This Folder, Subfolders And Files check box, and then click OK.

    Windows XP Professional displays the Applying Attributes message box, indicating the progress of the operation and the paths and names of folders and files as they are compressed. Because there is little data on drive C, compression completes too quickly for you to view this dialog box.

13. Click OK to close the Properties dialog box.

►   **To uncompress a folder**

1. In Windows Explorer, expand the Compressed folder.

2. In the Compressed folder, right-click Compressed2, and then click Properties.

    Windows XP Professional displays the Compressed2 Properties dialog box with the General tab active.

3. In the General tab, click Advanced.

    Windows XP Professional displays the Advanced Attributes dialog box.

4. Clear the Compress Contents To Save Disk Space check box, and then click OK to apply your settings and return to the Compressed2 Properties dialog box.

5. Click OK to close the Compressed2 Properties dialog box.

    Because the Compressed2 folder is empty, Windows XP Professional does not display the Confirm Attributes Changes dialog box asking you to specify whether to uncompress only this folder or this folder and all subfolders.

    What indication do you have that the Compressed2 folder is no longer compressed?

Exercise 2: Copying and Moving Files

In this exercise, you see the effects that copying and moving files has on compressed files.

▶ **To create a compressed file**

1. In Windows Explorer, click the Compressed folder.

2. On the File menu, click New, and then click Text Document.

3. Type **Text1** and then press ENTER.

   How can you verify that Text1 is compressed?

▶ **To copy a compressed file to an uncompressed folder**

1. Copy (hold down CTRL and drag the file) Text1 to the Compressed\Compressed2 folder.

2. Examine the properties for Text1 in the Compressed2 folder.

   Is the Text1 file in the Compressed\Compressed2 folder compressed or uncompressed? Why?

▶ **To move a compressed file to an uncompressed folder**

1. Examine the properties of the Text1 file in the Compressed folder.

   Is Text1 compressed or uncompressed?

2. Move Text1 to the Compressed\Compressed2 folder. If the Confirm File Replace dialog box appears, asking whether you want to replace the file, click Yes.

3. Examine the properties of Text1 in the Compressed2 folder.

   Is Text1 compressed or uncompressed? Why?

▶ **To uncompress the NTFS Compressed folder**

1. In Windows Explorer, right-click the Compressed folder, and then click Properties.

   Windows XP Professional displays the Compressed Properties dialog box with the General tab active.

2. In the General tab, click Advanced.

   Windows XP Professional displays the Advanced Attributes dialog box.

3. Clear the Compress Contents To Save Disk Space check box, and then click OK to return to the Compressed Properties dialog box.

4. Click Apply.

   Windows XP Professional displays the Confirm Attributes Changes dialog box, prompting you to specify whether to uncompress only this folder or this folder and all subfolders.

5. Click Apply Changes To This Folder, Subfolders And All Files, and then click OK.

   Windows XP Professional briefly displays the Applying Attributes message box. This might happen so fast that you do not see it.

6. Click OK to close the Properties dialog box, and then close Windows Explorer.

Exercise 3: Creating Compressed Folders

In this exercise, you will create a compressed folder using the Compressed Folders feature.

▶ **To create a compressed folder using the Compressed Folders feature**

1. Start Windows Explorer.

2. Click File and then click New.

   Compressed Folder is an option on the New menu.

3. Click Compressed Folder.

   You have just created a compressed folder. Notice the zipper icon that identifies compressed folders. You can drag and drop files into the compressed folder and they will automatically be compressed. If you copy a file from the compressed folder to another that is not compressed, the file will no longer be compressed.

4. Close Windows Explorer.

Lesson Review

The following questions will help you determine whether you have learned enough to move on to the next lesson. If you have difficulty answering these questions, review the material in this lesson before beginning the next lesson. The answers are in Appendix A, "Questions and Answers."

1. When Bob tried to copy a compressed file from one NTFS volume to another, the file was not copied and he got an error message stating that there was not enough disk space for the file. Before he attempted to copy the file, Bob verified that there was enough room for the compressed bitmap on the destination volume. Why did he get the error message?

2. Which of the following will Windows XP Professional allow you to compress using NTFS compression? (Choose all answers that are correct.)

   a. A FAT volume

   b. An NTFS volume

   c. A bitmap stored on a floppy

   d. A folder on an NTFS volume

3. When you move a file between NTFS volumes, does the file retain the compression state of the source folder or does the file inherit the compression state of the target folder? Why?

4. What does Windows XP Professional do when you try to copy a compressed file to a floppy disk? Why?

5. Which of the following types of files or data are good candidates for NTFS compression? (Choose all statements that are correct.)

   a. Encrypted data

   b. Frequently updated data

   c. Bitmaps

   d. Static data

Lesson Summary

- In Windows XP Professional, NTFS compression allows you to compress files, folders, or an entire volume.

- Any Windows-based or MS-DOS–based application can read and write to compressed files without having the files uncompressed by another program.

- Use the View tab in the Folder Options dialog box in Windows Explorer to display NTFS compressed files and folders in a different color to distinguish them from uncompressed files and folders.

- NTFS encryption and compression are mutually exclusive.

- When you copy a file within an NTFS volume, the file inherits the compression state of the target folder.

- When you move a file or folder within an NTFS volume, the file or folder retains its original compression state.

- When you copy a file or folder between NTFS volumes, the file or folder inherits the compression state of the target folder.

- When you move or copy a compressed NTFS file or folder to a floppy disk or to a FAT volume, Windows XP Professional automatically uncompresses the file or folder.

- To create a compressed folder using the Compressed Folders feature, start Windows Explorer, click File, click New, and then click Compressed Folder.

- A compressed folder created by the Compressed Folders feature appears in Windows Explorer as an icon of a zipper across a folder.

- You can drag and drop files into a compressed folder created using the Compressed Folders feature and the files are automatically compressed.

Lesson 2: Managing Disk Quotas

You use disk quotas to manage storage growth in distributed environments. Disk quotas allow you to allocate disk space to users based on the files and folders that they own. You can set disk quotas, quota thresholds, and quota limits for all users and for individual users. You can also monitor the amount of hard disk space that users have used and the amount that they have left against their quota.

After this lesson, you will be able to

- Configure and manage disk quotas

Estimated lesson time: 20 minutes

Understanding Disk Quota Management

Windows XP Professional disk quotas track and control disk usage on a per-user, per-volume basis. Windows XP Professional tracks disk quotas for each volume, even if the volumes are on the same hard disk. Because quotas are tracked on a per-user basis, every user's disk space is tracked regardless of the folder in which the user stores files. Table 14.2 describes the characteristics of Windows XP Professional disk quotas.

Table 14.2   Disk Quota Characteristics and Descriptions

Characteristic	Description
Disk usage is based on file and folder ownership.	Windows XP Professional calculates disk space usage for users based on the files and folders that they own. When a user copies or saves a new file to an NTFS volume or takes ownership of a file on an NTFS volume, Windows XP Professional charges the disk space for the file against the user's quota limit.
Disk quotas do not use compression.	Windows XP Professional ignores compression when it calculates hard disk space usage. Users are charged for each uncompressed byte, regardless of how much hard disk space is actually used. This is done partially because file compression produces different degrees of compression for different types of files. Different uncompressed file types that are the same size might end up being very different sizes when they are compressed.
Free space for applications is based on quota limit.	When you enable disk quotas, the free space that Windows XP Professional reports to applications for the volume is the amount of space remaining within the user's disk quota limit.

Note   Disk quotas can only be applied to Windows XP Professional NTFS volumes.

You use disk quotas to monitor and control hard disk space usage. System administrators can do the following:

- Set a disk quota limit to specify the amount of disk space for each user.
- Set a disk quota warning to specify when Windows XP Professional should log an event, indicating that the user is nearing his or her limit.
- Enforce disk quota limits and deny users access if they exceed their limit, or allow them continued access.
- Log an event when a user exceeds a specified disk space threshold. The threshold could be when users exceed their quota limit or when they exceed their warning level.

After you enable disk quotas for a volume, Windows XP Professional collects disk usage data for all users who own files and folders on the volume. This allows you to monitor volume usage on a per-user basis. By default, only members of the Administrators group can view and change quota settings. However, you can allow users to view quota settings.

Setting Disk Quotas

You can enable disk quotas and enforce disk quota warnings and limits for all users or for individual users.

If you want to enable disk quotas, open the Properties dialog box for a disk, click the Quota tab, and configure the options that are described in Table 14.3 and displayed in Figure 14.6.

Table 14.3   Quota Tab Options

Option	Description
Enable Quota Management	Select this check box to enable disk quota management.
Deny Disk Space To Users Exceeding Quota Limit	Select this check box so that when users exceed their hard disk space allocation, they receive an "out of disk space" message and cannot write to the volume.
Do Not Limit Disk Usage	Click this option when you do not want to limit the amount of hard disk space for users.
Limit Disk Space To	Configure the amount of disk space that users can use.
Set Warning Level To	Configure the amount of disk space that users can fill before Windows XP Professional logs an event, indicating that a user is nearing his or her limit.

Table 14.3   *(continued)*

Option	Description
Log Event When A User Exceeds Their Quota Limit	Select this option if you want Windows XP Professional to log an event in the Security log every time a user exceeds his or her quota limit.
Log Event When A User Exceeds Their Warning Level	Select this option if you want Windows XP Professional to log an event in the Security log every time a user exceeds the warning level.
Quota Entries	Click this button to open the Quota Entries For dialog box, where you can add a new entry, delete an entry, and view the per-user quota information.

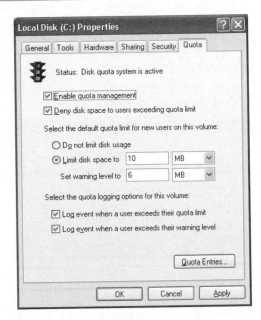

Figure 14.6   The Quota tab of the Properties dialog box for a disk

You can enforce identical quota limits for all users as follows:

1. In the Limit Disk Space To text box and the Set Warning Level To text box, enter the values for the limit and warning levels that you want to set.

2. Select the Deny Disk Space To Users Exceeding Quota Limit check box.

Windows XP Professional will monitor usage and will not allow users to create files or folders on the volume when they exceed the limit.

Determining the Status of Disk Quotas

You can determine the status of disk quotas in the Properties dialog box for a disk by checking the traffic light icon and reading the status message to its right (see Figure 14.6). The color shown on the traffic light icon indicates the status of disk quotas as follows:

- A red traffic light indicates that disk quotas are disabled.
- A yellow traffic light indicates that Windows XP Professional is rebuilding disk quota information.
- A green traffic light indicates that the disk quota system is active.

You can enforce different quota limits for one or more specific users, as follows:

1. Open the Properties dialog box for a disk, click the Quota tab, and then click Quota Entries.
2. In the Quota Entries For dialog box, shown in Figure 14.7, double-click the user account for which you want to set a disk quota limit or create an entry by clicking New Quota Entry on the Quota menu.

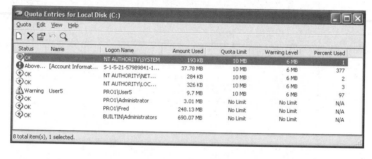

Figure 14.7   The Quota Entries For dialog box

3. Configure the disk space limit and the warning level for each individual user.

Monitoring Disk Quotas

You use the Quota Entries For dialog box (see Figure 14.7) to monitor usage for all users who have copied, saved, or taken ownership of files and folders on the volume. Windows XP Professional scans the volume and monitors the amount of disk space in use by each user. Use the Quota Entries For dialog box to view the following:

- The amount of hard disk space that each user uses
- Users who are over their quota warning threshold, signified by a yellow triangle
- Users who are over their quota limit, signified by a red circle
- The warning threshold and the disk quota limit for each user

Best Uses for Disk Quotas

Use the following guidelines for using disk quotas:

- If you enable disk quota settings on the volume where Windows XP Professional is installed and your user account has a disk quota limit, log on as Administrator to install additional Windows XP Professional components and applications. In this way, Windows XP Professional will not charge the disk space that you use to install applications against the disk quota allowance for your user account.

- You can monitor hard disk usage and generate hard disk usage information without preventing users from saving data. To do so, clear the Deny Disk Space To Users Exceeding Quota Limit check box when you enable disk quotas.

- Set more restrictive default limits for all user accounts and then modify the limits to allow more disk space to users who work with large files.

- If multiple users share computers running Windows XP Professional, set disk quota limits on computer volumes so that disk space is shared by all users who share the computer.

- Generally, you should set disk quotas on shared volumes to limit storage for users. Set disk quotas on public folders and network servers to ensure that users share hard disk space appropriately. When storage resources are scarce, you might want to set disk quotas on all shared hard disk space.

- Delete disk quota entries for users who no longer store files on a volume. You can delete quota entries for a user account only after all files that the user owns have been removed from the volume or another user has taken ownership of the files.

Practice: Enabling and Disabling Disk Quotas

In this practice you configure default quota management settings to limit the amount of data users can store on drive C (their hard disk drive). Next, you configure a custom quota setting for a user account. You increase the amount of data the user can store on drive C to 20 MB with a warning level set to 16 MB. Finally, you turn off quota management for drive C.

Note If you did not install Windows XP Professional on drive C, substitute the NTFS partition on which you did install Windows XP Professional whenever drive C is referred to in the practice.

Run the **DiskQuotas** file in the Demos folder on the CD-ROM accompanying this book for a demonstration of configuring disk management and disabling disk quotas.

Exercise 1: Configuring Quota Management Settings

In this exercise, you configure the quota management settings for drive C to limit the data that users can store on the volume. You then configure custom quota settings for a user account.

▶ **To configure default quota management settings**

1. Log on as Fred or with an account that is a member of the Administrators group.

2. Use the User Accounts tool in Control Panel to create a user account, User5, and assign it a Limited account type.

3. In Windows Explorer, right-click the drive C icon, and then click Properties.

   Windows XP Professional displays the Local Disk (C:) Properties dialog box with the General tab active.

4. Click the Quota tab.

   Notice that disk quotas are disabled by default.

5. In the Quota tab, select the Enable Quota Management check box.

   Notice that by default, the Do Not Limit Disk Usage option is selected.

6. Click Limit Disk Usage To.

   What is the default disk space limit for new users?

   If you wanted to place the same quota limit on all users of this computer, you would use the Limit Disk Usage To option.

7. Click Do Not Limit Disk Usage.

8. Select Deny Disk Space To Users Exceeding Quota Limit.

9. Select Log Event When A User Exceeds Their Quota Limit and Log Event When A User Exceeds Their Warning Limit, and then click Apply.

   Windows XP Professional displays the Disk Quota dialog box, telling you that you should enable the quota system only if you are going to use quotas on this disk volume and warning you that the volume will be rescanned to update disk usage statistics if you enable quotas.

10. Click OK to enable disk quotas.

▶ **To configure quota management settings for a user**

1. In the Quota tab of the Local Disk (C:) Properties dialog box, click Quota Entries.

   Windows XP Professional displays the Quota Entries For Local Disk (C:) dialog box.

Are any user accounts listed? Why or why not?

2. On the Quota menu, click New Quota Entry.

    Windows XP Professional displays the Select Users dialog box.

3. Ensure the Look In box says Pro1.

Note If you did not name your computer Pro1 or if your computer is part of a domain, select the appropriate computer or domain name.

---

4. In the Name text box, type **User5**, and then click OK.

    Windows XP Professional displays the Add New Quota Entry dialog box.

    What are the default settings for the user you just set a quota limit for?

5. Increase the amount of data that the user can store on drive C by changing the Limit Disk Space To setting to 10 MB and the Set Warning Level To setting to 6 MB.

6. Click OK to return to the Quota Entries For Local Disk (C:) dialog box.

7. Close the Quota Entries For Local Disk (C:) dialog box.

8. Click OK to close the Local Disk (C:) Properties dialog box.

9. Log off.

▶ **To test quota management settings**

1. Log on as User5 with no password.

2. Start Windows Explorer and create a User5 folder on drive C.

3. Insert the CD-ROM you used to install Windows XP Professional into your CD-ROM drive.

4. If a dialog box appears as a result of inserting the CD-ROM, close it.

5. Copy the i386 folder from your CD-ROM to the User5 folder.

    Windows XP Professional begins copying files from the i386 folder on the CD-ROM to a new i386 folder in the User5 folder on drive C. After copying some files, Windows XP Professional displays the Error Copying File Or Folder dialog box indicating that there is not enough room on the disk.

    Why did you get this error message?

6. Click OK to close the dialog box.

7. Right-click the User5 folder and then click Properties.

   Notice that the Size On Disk value is slightly less than your quota limit of 10 MB.

8. Close all open windows and log off.

Exercise 2: Disabling Quota Management

In this exercise, you disable quota management settings for drive C.

▶ **To disable quota management settings for drive C**

1. Log on as Fred or another account that is a member of the Administrators group.

2. Start Windows Explorer.

3. Delete the User5 folder.

4. Right-click the drive C icon, and then click Properties.

   Windows XP Professional displays the Local Disk (C:) Properties dialog box with the General tab active.

5. Click the Quota tab.

6. In the Quota tab, clear the Enable Quota Management check box.

   All quota settings for drive C are no longer available.

7. Click Apply.

   Windows XP Professional displays the Disk Quota dialog box, warning you that if you disable quotas, the volume will be rescanned if you enable them later.

8. Click OK to close the Disk Quota dialog box.

9. Click OK to close the Local Disk (C:) Properties dialog box.

10. Close all applications and log off Windows XP Professional.

Lesson Review

The following questions will help you determine whether you have learned enough to move on to the next lesson. If you have difficulty answering these questions, review the material in this lesson before beginning the next lesson. The answers are in Appendix A, "Questions and Answers."

1. What is the purpose of disk quotas?

2. Which of the following statements about disk quotas in Windows XP Professional is correct?

a. Disk quotas track and control disk usage on a per-user, per-disk basis.

b. Disk quotas track and control disk usage on a per-group, per-volume basis.

c. Disk quotas track and control disk usage on a per-user, per-volume basis.

d. Disk quotas track and control disk usage on a per-group, per-disk basis.

3. Which of the following statements about disk quotas in Windows XP Professional is correct? (Choose all answers that are correct.)

a. Disk quotas can only be applied to Windows XP Professional NTFS volumes.

b. Disk quotas can be applied to any Windows XP Professional volume.

c. You must be logged on with the Administrator user account to configure default quota management settings.

d. Members of the Administrators and Power Users groups can configure default quota management settings.

4. You get a call from an administrator who cannot delete a quota entry for a user account. What would you tell the administrator to check?

Lesson Summary

- Use Windows XP Professional disk quotas to allocate disk space usage to users.

- You can set disk quotas, quota thresholds, and quota limits for all users and for individual users.

- Windows XP Professional ignores compression when it calculates hard disk space usage.

- You can apply disk quotas only to Windows XP Professional NTFS volumes.

- Windows XP Professional disk quotas track and control disk usage on a per-user, per-volume basis.

- Windows XP Professional tracks disk quotas for each volume, even if the volumes are on the same hard disk.

- Windows XP Professional quotas track every user's disk space regardless of the folder in which the user stores files.

Lesson 3: Increasing Security with EFS

Encryption is the process of making information indecipherable to protect it from unauthorized viewing or use. A key is required to decode the information. The Microsoft Encrypting File System (EFS) provides encryption for data in NTFS files stored on disk. This encryption is public key–based and runs as an integrated system service, making it easy to manage, difficult to attack, and transparent to the file owner. If a user who attempts to access an encrypted NTFS file has the private key to that file, the file can be decrypted so that the user can open the file and work with it transparently as a normal document. A user without the private key is denied access.

Windows XP Professional also includes the Cipher command, which provides the ability to encrypt and decrypt files and folders from a command prompt. Windows XP Professional also provides a recovery agent. In the event that the owner loses the private key, the recovery agent can still recover the encrypted file.

After this lesson, you will be able to

- Encrypt folders and files
- Decrypt folders and files

Estimated lesson time: 40 minutes

Understanding EFS

EFS allows users to encrypt NTFS files by using a strong public key–based cryptographic scheme that encrypts all files in a folder. Users with roaming profiles can use the same key with trusted remote systems. No administrative effort is needed to begin, and most operations are transparent. Backups and copies of encrypted files are also encrypted if they are in NTFS volumes. Files remain encrypted if you move or rename them, and temporary files created during editing and left unencrypted in the paging file or in a temporary file do not defeat encryption.

You can set policies to recover EFS-encrypted data when necessary. The recovery policy is integrated with overall Windows XP Professional security policy. Control of this policy can be delegated to individuals with recovery authority, and different recovery policies can be configured for different parts of the enterprise. Data recovery discloses only the recovered data, not the key that was used to encrypt the file. Several protections ensure that data recovery is possible and that no data is lost in the case of total system failure.

EFS is implemented either from Windows Explorer or from the command line. It can be enabled or disabled for a computer, domain, or organizational unit (OU) by resetting recovery policy in the Group Policy console in Microsoft Management Console (MMC).

Note   To set Group Policy for the domain or for an OU, your computer must be part of a Microsoft Windows 2000 domain.

You can use EFS to encrypt and decrypt files on remote file servers but not to encrypt data that is transferred over the network. Windows XP Professional provides network protocols, such as Secure Sockets Layer (SSL) authentication, to encrypt data over the network.

Table 14.4 lists the key features provided by Windows XP Professional EFS.

Table 14.4   EFS Features

Feature	Description
Transparent encryption	In EFS, file encryption does not require the file owner to decrypt and re-encrypt the file on each use. Decryption and encryption happen transparently on file reads and writes to disk.
Strong protection of encryption keys	Public key encryption resists all but the most sophisticated methods of attack. Therefore, in EFS, the file encryption keys are encrypted using a public key from the user's certificate. (Note that Windows XP Professional and Windows 2000 use X.509 v3 certificates.) The list of encrypted file encryption keys is stored with the encrypted file and is unique to it. To decrypt the file encryption keys, the file owner supplies a private key, which only he or she has.
Integral data-recovery system	If the owner's private key is unavailable, the recovery agent can open the file using his or her own private key. There can be more than one recovery agent, each with a different public key, but at least one public recovery key must be present on the system to encrypt a file.
Secure temporary and paging files	Many applications create temporary files while you edit a document, and these temporary files can be left unencrypted on the disk. On computers running Windows XP Professional, EFS can be implemented at the folder level, so any temporary copies of an encrypted file are also encrypted, provided that all files are on NTFS volumes. EFS resides in the Windows operating system kernel and uses the nonpaged pool to store file encryption keys, ensuring that they are never copied to the paging file.

Encrypting

The recommended method to encrypt files is to create an NTFS folder and then encrypt the folder. To encrypt a folder, in the Properties dialog box for the folder, click the General tab. In the General tab, click Advanced, and then select the Encrypt Contents To Secure Data check box. All files placed in the folder are encrypted and the folder is now marked for encryption. Folders that are marked for encryption are not actually encrypted; only the files within the folder are encrypted.

Note   Compressed files cannot be encrypted, and encrypted files cannot be compressed with NTFS compression.

After you encrypt the folder, when you save a file in that folder, the file is encrypted using file encryption keys, which are fast symmetric keys designed for bulk encryption. The file is encrypted in blocks, with a different file encryption key for each block. All of the file encryption keys are stored and encrypted in the Data Decryption field (DDF) and the Data Recovery field (DRF) in the file header.

You use a file that you encrypted just like you would use any other file, as encryption is transparent. You do not need to decrypt a file you encrypted before you can use it. When you open an encrypted file, your private key is applied to the DDF to unlock the list of file encryption keys, allowing the file contents to appear normally. EFS automatically detects an encrypted file and locates a user certificate and associated private key. You open the file, make changes to it, and save it, as you would any other file. However, if someone else tries to open your encrypted file, he or she is unable to access the file and receives an access denied message.

Caution   If an administrator removes the password on a user account, the user account will lose all EFS-encrypted files, personal certificates, and stored passwords for Web sites or network resources. Each user should make a password reset disk to avoid this situation. To create a password floppy disk, open User Accounts and, under Related Tasks, click Prevent A Forgotten Password. The Forgotten Password Wizard steps you through creating the password reset disk.

Decrypting

Decrypting a folder or file refers to clearing the Encrypt Contents To Secure Data check box in a folder's or file's Advanced Attributes dialog box, which you access from the folder's or file's Properties dialog box. Once decrypted, the file remains so until you select the Encrypt Contents To Secure Data check box. The only reason you might want to decrypt a file would be if other people needed access to the folder or file—for example, if you want to share the folder or make the file available across the network.

Using the Cipher Command

The Cipher command provides the ability to encrypt and decrypt files and folders from a command prompt. The following example shows the available switches for the Cipher command, described in Table 14.5:

```
cipher [/e | /d] [/s:folder_name] [/a] [/i] [/f] [/q] [/h] [/k]
[file_name [...]]
```

Table 14.5   Cipher Command Switches

Switch	Description
/e	Encrypts the specified folders. Folders are marked so any files that are added later are encrypted.
/d	Decrypts the specified folders. Folders are marked so any files that are added later are not encrypted.
/s	Performs the specified operation on files in the given folder and all subfolders.
/a	Performs the specified operation on files as well as folders. Encrypted files could be decrypted when modified, if the parent folder is not encrypted. To avoid this, encrypt the file and the parent folder.
/i	Continues performing the specified operation even after errors have occurred. By default, Cipher stops when an error is encountered.
/f	Forces the encryption operation on all specified files, even those that are already encrypted. Files that are already encrypted are skipped by default.
/q	Reports only the most essential information.
/h	Displays files with the hidden or system attributes, which are not shown by default.
/k	Creates a new file encryption key for the user running the Cipher command. Using this option causes the Cipher command to ignore all other options.
file_name	Specifies a pattern, file, or folder.

If you run the Cipher command without parameters, it displays the encryption state of the current folder and any files that it contains. You can specify multiple filenames and use wildcards. You must put spaces between multiple parameters.

Using the Recovery Agent

If you lose your file encryption certificate and associated private key through disk failure or any other reason, a person designated as the recovery agent can open the file using his or her own certificate and associated private key. If the recovery agent is on another computer in the network, send the file to the recovery agent. The recovery agent can bring his or her private key to the owner's computer, but it is never a good security practice to copy a private key onto another computer.

Note   In a domain, the domain administrator is the default recovery agent. You can designate alternative EFS recovery accounts for computers grouped by OUs. Before you can designate accounts to alternate recovery agents in a Windows 2000 domain, you must deploy Windows 2000 Server and Certificate Services to issue recovery agent certificates. For more information about Certificate Services, see Chapter 16, "Windows 2000 Certificate Services and Public Key Infrastructure" in the *Microsoft Windows 2000 Server Resource Kit Distributed System Guide*.

It is a good security practice to rotate recovery agents. However, if the agent designation changes, access to the file is denied. For this reason, you should keep recovery certificates and private keys until all files that are encrypted with them have been updated.

The person designated as the recovery agent has a special certificate and associated private key that allow data recovery. To recover an encrypted file, the recovery agent does the following:

1. Use Backup or another backup tool to restore a user's backup version of the encrypted file or folder to the computer where his or her file recovery certificate is located.
2. In Windows Explorer, open the Properties dialog box for the file or folder, and in the General tab, click Advanced.
3. Clear the Encrypt Contents To Secure Data check box.
4. Make a backup version of the decrypted file or folder and return the backup version to the user.

Disabling EFS

You can disable EFS for a domain, OU, or computer by applying an empty Encrypted Data Recovery Agent policy setting. Until Encrypted Data Recovery Agent settings are configured and applied through Group Policy, there is no policy, so the default recovery agents are used by EFS. EFS must use the recovery agents that are listed in the Encrypted Data Recovery Agents Group Policy agent if the settings have been configured and applied. If the policy that is applied is empty, EFS does not operate.

Practice: Encrypting Files

In this practice, you log on as an administrator and encrypt a folder and its files. You then log on using a different user account and attempt to open an encrypted file and disable encryption on the encrypted file. Finally, you log on again with the same administrative account and decrypt the folder and its contents that you previously encrypted.

Run the **EncryptingFiles** file in the Demos folder on the CD-ROM accompanying this book for a demonstration of encrypting folders and files, accessing encrypting files, and decrypting encrypted files.

Exercise 1: Encrypting Files

In this exercise, you will encrypt a folder and its contents.

▶ **To encrypt a file**

1. In Windows Explorer, create C:\Secret\File1, and then right-click File1 and click Properties.

   Windows XP Professional displays the Properties dialog box with the General tab active.

2. Click Advanced.

   The Advanced Attributes dialog box appears.

3. Click the Encrypt Contents To Secure Data check box and then click OK.

4. Click OK to close the File1 Properties dialog box.

   An Encryption Warning dialog box informs you that you are about to encrypt a file that is not in an encrypted folder. The default is to encrypt the folder and file, but you can also choose to encrypt only the file.

5. Click Cancel to close the Encryption Warning dialog box, and then click Cancel again to close the File1 Properties dialog box without encrypting File1.

6. In Windows Explorer, right-click C:\Secret and then click Properties.

7. Click Advanced.

   The Advanced Attributes dialog box appears.

8. Select the Encrypt Contents To Secure Data check box and then click OK.

9. Click OK to close the Secret Properties dialog box.

   The Confirm Attribute Change dialog box informs you that you are about to encrypt a folder. You have two choices: you can encrypt only this folder, or you can encrypt the folder and all subfolders and files in the folder.

10. Select the Apply Changes To This Folder, Subfolders And Files option, and then click OK.

11. In the Secret folder, right-click File1 and then click Properties.

    The File1 Properties dialog box appears.

12. Click Advanced.

    The Advanced Attributes dialog box appears. Notice that the Encrypt Contents To Secure Data check box is selected.

13. Close the Advanced Attributes dialog box.

14. Close the Properties dialog box.

15. Close all windows and log off.

Exercise 2: Testing the Encrypted Files

In this exercise, you log on using the User5 account and then attempt to open an encrypted file. You then try to disable encryption on the encrypted files.

▶ **To test an encrypted file**

1. Log on as User5 with a password of *password*.

2. Start Windows Explorer and open C:\Secret\File1.

   What happens?

3. Close Notepad.

▶ **To attempt to disable the encryption**

1. Right-click C:\Secret\File1 and then click Properties.

2. Click Advanced.

3. Clear the Encrypt Contents To Secure Data check box and then click OK.

4. Click OK to close the File1 Properties dialog box.

   The Error Applying Attributes dialog box appears and informs you that access to the file is denied.

5. Click Cancel.

6. Close all open windows and dialog boxes.

7. Log off as User5 and log on as Administrator.

Exercise 3: Decrypting Folders and Files

In this exercise, you decrypt the folder and file that you previously encrypted.

▶ **To decrypt files**

1. Start Windows Explorer.

2. Right-click C:\Secret\File1, and then click Properties.

3. Click Advanced.

4. Clear the Encrypt Contents To Secure Data check box and then click OK.

5. Click OK to close the File1 Properties dialog box.

6. Close Windows Explorer and log off.

Lesson Review

The following questions will help you determine whether you have learned enough to move on to the next lesson. If you have difficulty answering these questions, review the material in this lesson before beginning the next lesson. The answers are in Appendix A, "Questions and Answers."

1. What is encryption and what is the Microsoft EFS?

2. Which of the following files and folders will Windows XP Professional allow you to encrypt? (Choose all answers that are correct.)

    a. A file on an NTFS volume

    b. A folder on a FAT volume

    c. A file stored on a floppy

    d. A folder on an NTFS volume

3. How do you encrypt a folder? Is the folder actually encrypted?

4. If the private key belonging to the owner of an encrypted file is not available, how can you decrypt the file?

5. By default, the recovery agent for a computer running Windows XP Professional in a workgroup is _____ and the recovery agent for a computer running Windows XP Professional in a domain environment is _____.

Lesson Summary

- EFS provides the core file encryption technology for storage of NTFS files on disk.
- EFS allows users to encrypt NTFS files by using a strong public key–based cryptographic scheme that encrypts all files in a folder.
- Users with roaming profiles can use the same key with trusted remote systems.
- Backups and copies of encrypted files are also encrypted if they are in NTFS volumes.

- Files remain encrypted if you move or rename them, and encryption is not defeated by leakage to paging files.

- Windows XP Professional also provides a recovery agent. In the event an owner loses the private key, the recovery agent can still recover the encrypted file.

- EFS is implemented either from Windows Explorer or from the command line using commands such as Cipher.

- EFS can be enabled or disabled for a computer, domain, or OU by resetting recovery policy in the Group Policy console in MMC.

- You can use EFS to encrypt and decrypt files on remote computers, but not to encrypt data that is transferred over the network. Windows XP Professional provides network protocols, such as SSL, to encrypt data over the network.

Lesson 4: Using Disk Defragmenter, Check Disk, and Disk Cleanup

Windows XP Professional saves files and folders in the first available space on a hard disk and not necessarily in an area of contiguous space. The parts of the files and folders are scattered over the hard disk rather than being in a contiguous area. This scattering of files and folders across a hard disk is known as fragmentation. When your hard disk contains numerous fragmented files and folders, your computer takes longer to access them because it requires several additional reads to collect the various pieces. Creating new files and folders also takes longer because the available free space on the hard disk is scattered. Your computer must save a new file or folder in various locations on the hard disk.

Temporary files, Internet cache files, and unnecessary programs also take up space on your computer's hard drive. Sometimes there are file system errors and sometimes sectors on your hard disk go bad, which can cause you to lose data you have stored on your hard disk. This lesson introduces three Windows XP Professional tools—Disk Defragmenter, Check Disk, and Disk Cleanup—that help you organize your hard disks, recover readable information from damaged areas on your hard disk, and clean up any temporary files and unnecessary programs taking up space on your hard drive.

After this lesson, you will be able to
- Describe fragmentation and defragmentation
- Use Disk Defragmenter to organize your hard disks
- Use Check Disk to search for and repair file system errors and recover readable information from bad sectors
- Use Disk Cleanup to clean up your hard disks

Estimated lesson time: 60 minutes

Defragmenting Disks

The process of finding and consolidating fragmented files and folders is called *defragmenting*. Disk Defragmenter locates fragmented files and folders and defragments them by moving the pieces of each file or folder to one location so that each occupies a single, contiguous space on the hard disk. Consequently, your system can access and save files and folders more efficiently. By consolidating files and folders, Disk Defragmenter also consolidates free space, making it less likely that new files will be fragmented. Disk Defragmenter can defragment FAT, FAT32, and NTFS volumes.

You access Disk Defragmenter by selecting Start, pointing to All Programs, pointing to Accessories, pointing to System Tools, and then clicking Disk Defragmenter. The Disk Defragmenter dialog box is split into three areas, as shown in Figure 14.8.

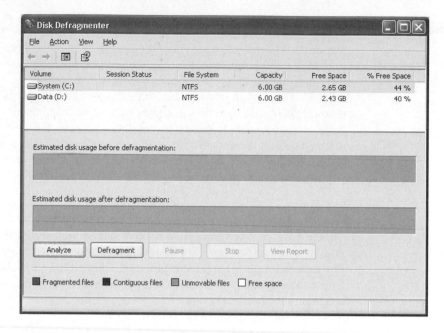

Figure 14.8 The Disk Defragmenter dialog box

The upper portion of the dialog box lists the volumes that you can analyze and defragment. The middle portion provides a graphic representation of how fragmented the selected volume is. The lower portion provides a dynamic representation of the volume that continuously updates during defragmentation. The display colors indicate the condition of the volume as follows:

- Red indicates fragmented files.
- Blue indicates contiguous (nonfragmented) files.
- Green indicates system files, which Disk Defragmenter cannot move.
- White indicates free space on the volume.

By comparing the Analysis Display band to the Defragmentation Display band during and after defragmentation, you can easily see the improvement in the volume.

You can also open Disk Defragmenter by selecting a drive you want to defragment in Windows Explorer or My Computer. On the File menu, click Properties, click the Tools tab, and click Defragment Now. Then select one of the options described in Table 14.6.

Table 14.6   Disk Defragmenter Options

Option	Description
Analyze	Click this button to analyze the disk for fragmentation. After the analysis, the Analysis Display band provides a graphic representation of how fragmented the volume is.
Defragment	Click this button to defragment the disk. After defragmentation, the Defragmentation Display band provides a graphic representation of the defragmented volume.

Figure 14.9 shows the Disk Defragmenter dialog box after you have analyzed the C drive. Windows XP Professional displays another Disk Defragmenter dialog box indicating that you need to defragment the volume. You can view a report showing more details about the fragmentation on your volume, close the dialog box and run the defragmenter at a later time, or defragment the volume now.

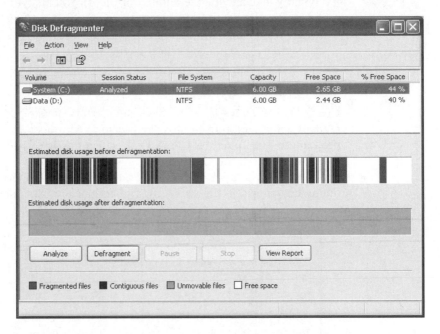

Figure 14.9   The Disk Defragmenter window showing a completed analysis

If there is not enough fragmentation to require you to defragment the volume, Windows XP Professional displays a Disk Defragmenter dialog box indicating that there is no need to defragment the volume at this time.

Using Disk Defragmenter Effectively

The following list provides some guidelines for using Disk Defragmenter:

- Run Disk Defragmenter when the computer will receive the least usage. During defragmentation, data is moved around on the hard disk and that process is microprocessor-intensive. The defragmentation process will adversely affect access time to other disk-based resources.

- Educate users to defragment their local hard disks at least once a month to prevent accumulation of fragmented files.

- Analyze the target volume before you install large applications and defragment the volume if necessary. Installations complete more quickly when the target media has adequate contiguous free space. Additionally, accessing the application after installation is faster.

- When you delete a large number of files or folders, your hard disk might become excessively fragmented, so be sure that you analyze it afterward. Generally, you should defragment hard disks on busy file servers more often than those on single-user client computers.

Using Check Disk

Check Disk attempts to repair file system errors, locate bad sectors, and recover readable information from those bad sectors. All files must be closed for this program to run. To access Check Disk, select the drive you want to check in Windows Explorer or My Computer. Click the File menu, click Properties, click the Tools tab, and click Check Now. Select one of the options on the Check Disk dialog box shown in Figure 14.10. The options are explained in Table 14.7.

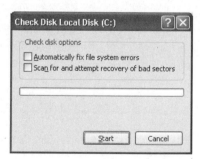

Figure 14.10   The Check Disk dialog box

Table 14.7   Check Disk Options

Check box	Description
Automatically Fix File System Errors	Select this check box to have Windows XP Professional attempt to repair file system errors found during disk checking. All files must be closed for this program to run. If the drive is currently in use, a message asks you if you would like to reschedule the disk checking for the next time you restart your computer. Your drive is not available to run other tasks while the disk is being checked.
Scan For And Attempt Recovery Of Bad Sectors	Select this check box to have Windows XP Professional attempt to repair file system errors found during disk checking, locate bad sectors, and recover any readable information located in those bad sectors. All files must be closed for this program to run. If the drive is currently in use, a message asks you if you would like to reschedule the disk checking for the next time you restart your computer. Your drive is not available to run other tasks while the disk is being checked. If you select this check box, you do not need to select Automatically Fix File System Errors because Windows XP Professional attempts to fix any errors on the disk.

Note   Check Disk runs in five phases: file verification, index verification, security descriptor verification, file data verification, and free space verification.

You can also use the command-line version of Check Disk. The command-line syntax for Chkdsk is as follows:

```
Chkdsk [volume[[path]filename]] [/f] [/v] [/r] [/x] [/i] [/c]
[/l[:size]]
```

The switches used by Chkdsk are explained in Table 14.8.

Table 14.8   Chkdsk Switches

Switch	Description
filename	Specifies the file or set of files to check. You can use the wildcards * and ?. This switch is only valid on volumes formatted with FAT or FAT32 file systems.
path	Specifies the location of a file or set of files within the folder structure of the volume. This switch is only valid on volumes formatted with FAT or FAT32 file systems.
size	Changes the log file size. You must use the /l switch with this switch. This switch is only valid on volumes formatted with NTFS.

(continued)

Table 14.8   *(continued)*

Switch	Description
volume	Specifies the drive letter (followed by a colon), mount point, or volume name. This switch is only valid on volumes formatted with FAT12, FAT16, and FAT32 file systems.
/c	Skips the checking of cycles within the folder structure. This switch is only valid on volumes formatted with NTFS.
/f	Fixes errors on the volume. If Chkdsk cannot lock the volume, you are prompted to have Chkdsk check it the next time the computer starts.
/i	Performs a less vigorous check of index entries. This switch is only valid on volumes formatted with NTFS.
/l	Displays the current size of the log file. This switch is only valid on volumes formatted with NTFS.
/r	Locates bad sectors and recovers readable information. If Chkdsk cannot lock the volume, you are prompted to have Chkdsk check it the next time the computer starts.
/v	On volumes formatted with FAT12, FAT16, or FAT32, displays the full path and name of every file on the volume. On volumes formatted with NTFS, displays any cleanup messages.
/x	Forces the volume to dismount first, if necessary. All opened handles to the volume would then be invalid (implies /f).
/?	Displays this list of switches.

Used without parameters, Chkdsk displays the status of the disk in the current volume.

Using Disk Cleanup

You can use Disk Cleanup to free up disk space by deleting temporary files and uninstalling programs. Disk Cleanup lists the temporary files, Internet cache files, and unnecessary programs that you can safely delete. To access Disk Cleanup, select the drive you want to check in Windows Explorer or My Computer. On the File menu, click Properties, and in the General tab, click Disk Cleanup. The Disk Cleanup dialog box is shown in Figure 14.11 and its options are explained in Table 14.9.

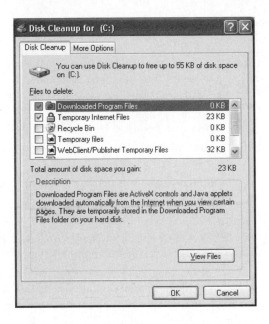

Figure 14.11   The Disk Cleanup dialog box

Table 14.9   Disk Cleanup Deletion Options

Check box	Description
Downloaded Program Files	Select this check box to have Windows XP Professional delete the ActiveX controls and Java applets that have been downloaded automatically from the Internet when users viewed certain pages.
	These files are temporarily stored in the Downloaded Program Files folder on the computer's hard disk.
Temporary Internet Files	Select this check box to have Windows XP Professional delete the files in the Temporary Internet Files folder on the computer's hard drive.
	These files are Web pages stored on the hard disk for quick viewing. Users' personalized settings for Web pages are not deleted.
Recycle Bin	Select this check box to have Windows XP Professional delete the files in the Recycle bin.
	When you delete a file from your computer, it is not permanently removed from the computer until the Recycle Bin is emptied (by deleting the files contained in the Recycle Bin).
Temporary Files	Select this check box to have Windows XP Professional delete any Temporary files on this volume.
	Programs sometimes store temporary information in a Temp folder. Before a program closes, it usually deletes this information. You can safely delete temporary files that have not been modified in more than a week.

(continued)

Table 14.9   *(continued)*

Check box	Description
WebClient/Publisher Temporary Files	Select this check box to have Windows XP Professional delete any temporary WebClient/Publisher files.
	The WebClient/Publisher service maintains a cache of accessed files on this disk. These files are kept locally for performance reasons only and can be deleted safely.
Compress Old Files	Select this check box to compress files that have not been accessed in a while.
	No files are deleted and all files are still accessible.
	Because files compress at different rates, the value displayed for the amount of space you will recover is an approximation.
Catalog Files For The Content Indexer	Select this check box to have Windows XP Professional delete any old catalog files left over from previous indexing operations.
	The Indexing Service speeds up and enriches file searches by maintaining an index of the files on this disk.

There are additional ways to free up space on your hard disk using Disk Cleanup. Click the More Options tab in the Disk Cleanup dialog box (see Figure 14.12). The available options are explained in Table 14.10.

Figure 14.12   The More Options tab of the Disk Cleanup dialog box

Table 14.10   Disk Cleanup More Options Tab Options

Option	Description
Windows Components	Click Clean Up under Windows Components to launch the Windows Components Wizard, which allows you to add and remove Windows components from your installation.
	The Windows Components include Accessories and Utilities, Fax Services, Indexing Services, Microsoft Internet Explorer, Internet Information Services (IIS), Management and Monitoring Tools, Message Queuing, MSN Explorer, Networking Services, Other Network File and Print Services, and Update Root Certificates.
Installed Programs	Click Clean Up under Installed Programs to launch Add Or Remove Programs, which allows you to install programs and to uninstall programs that are no longer in use.
	The list of programs available to be uninstalled depends on what programs are installed on your computer.
System Restore	Click Clean Up under System Restore to delete all but the most recent restore points.
	For more information about restore points and System Restore, see Chapter 18, "Modifying and Troubleshooting the Boot Process."

Practice: Using Disk Degragmenter

In this practice you use the Disk Defragmenter to determine if your hard disk is fragmented. If it is, you will defragment your hard disk. You then use Check Disk to examine your hard disk for file system errors, fix them, locate any bad sectors, and recover any readable information from those bad sectors. Finally, you use Disk Cleanup to free up disk space by deleting temporary files and uninstalling programs.

Note   If you started with a clean hard disk and installed Windows XP Professional in Chapter 2, "Installing Windows XP Professional," there should be little for any of these disk maintenance tools to clean up or repair.

Exercise 1: Defragmenting a Hard Drive

In Exercise 1, you use the Disk Defragmenter to determine if your hard disk is fragmented. If it is, you will defragment your hard disk.

▶   **To defragment a hard drive**

1. Log on as Fred or an account that is a member of the Administrators group.

2. Click Start, and then point to All Programs.

3. Point to Accessories, point to System Tools, and then click Disk Defragmenter.

    Windows XP Professional displays the Disk Defragmenter dialog box.

4. If there are multiple volumes on your computer, select C and then click Analyze.

5. If Windows XP Professional displays a dialog box indicating that there is no need to defragment your volume at this time, click Close and then read through steps 6 through 12.

6. If Windows XP Professional displays a Disk Defragmenter dialog box indicating that you need to defragment your volume now (see Figure 14.13), click View Report.

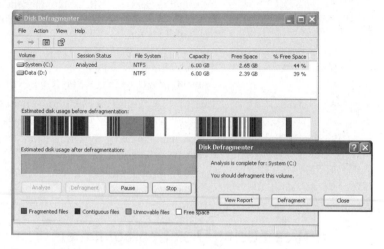

Figure 14.13   The Disk Defragmenter dialog box

7. In the Analysis Report dialog box, shown in Figure 14.14, scroll through the Volume Information box.

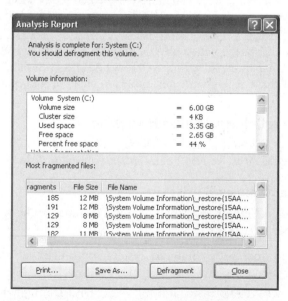

Figure 14.14   The Analysis Report dialog box

8. Scroll through the Most Fragmented Files box, and then click Save As.

   Windows XP Professional displays the Save Defragmentation Report dialog box. Notice that the default title for the report is VolumeC and the default location for the report is in the My Documents folder.

9. Click Save to save the report as VolumeC in the My Documents folder.

   You are returned to the Analysis Report dialog box.

10. Click Defragment.

    Disk Defragmenter defragments the volume. This could take a long time to complete, depending on the size of the volume and the amount of fragmentation.

11. Compare the Analysis Display with the Defragmentation Display (see Figure 14.15).

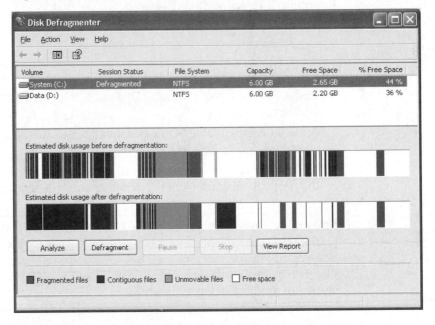

Figure 14.15   The Disk Defragmenter dialog box

12. Close Disk Defragmenter.

    Leave the Local Disk (C:) Properties dialog box open for the next exercise.

Exercise 2: Running Check Disk

In Exercise 2, you run Check Disk to examine your hard disk for file system errors. If any errors are found, you fix them. You also locate any bad sectors and recover any readable information from those bad sectors.

▶ **To use Check Disk on a hard drive**

1. In the Local Disk (C:) Properties dialog box, click the Tools tab.

2. In the Tools tab, click Check Now.

   Windows XP Professional displays the Check Disk Local Disk (C:) dialog box.

3. Select Scan For And Attempt Recovery Of Bad Sectors.

4. Click Start.

   It might take a few minutes to complete all five phases.

5. When prompted that the Disk Check is complete, click OK.

   Leave the Local Disk (C:) Properties dialog box open for the next exercise.

Exercise 3: Running Disk Cleanup

In Exercise 3, you run Disk Cleanup to free up disk space. Disk Cleanup allows you to delete temporary files and uninstall programs.

▶ **To use Disk Cleanup on a hard drive**

1. In the General tab of the Local Disk (C:) Properties dialog box, click Disk Cleanup.

   A Disk Cleanup dialog box appears, indicating that it is calculating how much space you will be able to free on the C drive.

2. In the Files To Delete list box in the Disk Cleanup For (C:) dialog box, review the files that Disk Cleanup is recommending you delete.

Note If you started with a clean hard disk and installed Windows XP Professional in Chapter 2, there might be few, if any, files that Disk Cleanup found to delete. If you wanted to delete any files that Disk Cleanup recommended you delete, make sure that the files you want to delete are selected (a check mark is in the check box in front of the files) and then click OK.

---

3. Click the More Options tab.

   When would you use the options available in the More Options tab?

4. Click Cancel.

5. Close Disk Cleanup and all open windows.

Lesson Review

The following questions will help you determine whether you have learned enough to move on to the next chapter. If you have difficulty answering these questions, review the material in this lesson before beginning the next chapter. The answers are in Appendix A, "Questions and Answers."

1. What is fragmentation and what problems does it cause?

2. The process of finding and consolidating fragmented files and folders is called _____. The Windows XP Professional system tool that locates fragmented files and folders and arranges them in contiguous space is

   _____.

3. Windows XP Professional provides a tool to locate fragmented files and folders and arrange them in contiguous space on volumes formatted with which file systems?

4. Which of the following functions does Check Disk perform? (Choose all answers that are correct.)

   a. Locate fragmented files and folders and arrange contiguously

   b. Locate and attempt to repair file system errors

   c. Locate bad sectors and recover readable information from those bad sectors

   d. Delete temporary files and offline files

5. Why do you need to empty the Recycle Bin?

Lesson Summary

- Windows XP Professional saves files and folders in the first available space on a hard disk and not necessarily in an area of contiguous space, which can lead to file and folder fragmentation.

- Windows XP Professional takes longer to access existing files and folders and to create new files and folders when the hard disk is fragmented.

- Disk Defragmenter, a Windows XP Professional system tool, locates fragmented files and folders and defragments them, enabling your system to access and save files and folders more efficiently.

- Disk Defragmenter not only consolidates files and folders, it also consolidates free space, making it less likely that new files will be fragmented.

- Disk Defragmenter can defragment FAT, FAT32, and NTFS volumes.

- Check Disk attempts to repair file system errors, locate bad sectors, and recover readable information from those bad sectors.

- Disk Cleanup frees up disk space by locating temporary files, Internet cache files, and unnecessary programs that you can safely delete, and it also deletes temporary files and uninstalling programs.

CHAPTER 15

Monitoring, Managing, and Maintaining Network Resources

About This Chapter

This chapter prepares you to monitor network resources. You learn about the Shared Folders snap-in and how to use it to view and create shares. You also learn how to use the Shared Folders snap-in to view sessions, open files, and disconnect users from your shared folders.

Before You Begin

To complete this chapter, you must have

- A computer that meets or exceeds the minimum hardware requirements listed in the preface, "About This Book"

- Microsoft Windows XP Professional installed on the computer

Lesson 1: Monitoring Access to Shared Folders

Windows XP Professional includes the Shared Folders snap-in, which allows you to easily monitor access to network resources and send administrative messages to users. You monitor access to network resources to assess and manage current usage on network servers. You monitor access to shared folders to determine how many users currently have a connection to each folder. You can also monitor open files to determine which users are accessing the files, and you can disconnect users from one open file or from all open files.

After this lesson, you will be able to

- Identify three reasons for monitoring access to network resources
- Identify who can monitor access to network resources
- View and monitor the shared folders on a computer
- View and modify the properties of a shared folder
- Monitor open files and disconnect users from one or all open files

Estimated lesson time: 30 minutes

Understanding Monitoring Network Resources

It is important that you understand why you should monitor the network resources in your computer environment. Some of the reasons it is important to assess and manage network resources are included in the following list:

- **Maintenance.**   You should determine which users are currently using a resource so that you can notify them before making the resource temporarily or permanently unavailable.
- **Security.**   You should monitor user access to resources that are confidential or need to be secure to verify that only authorized users are accessing them.
- **Planning.**   You should determine which resources are being used and how much they are being used so that you can plan for future system growth.

When you add the Shared Folders snap-in to the Microsoft Management Console (MMC) console, you specify whether you want to monitor the resources on the local computer or a remote computer.

Requirements to Monitor Network Resources

Not all users can monitor access to network resources. Table 15.1 lists the group membership requirements for monitoring access to network resources using the Shared Folders snap-in.

Table 15.1   Groups That Can Access Network Resources

A member of these groups	Can monitor
Administrators or Server Operators for the domain	All computers in the domain
Administrators or Power Users for a member server or a computer running Windows XP Professional	Local or remote computers in the workgroup

Monitoring Shared Folders

You use the Shares folder in the Shared Folders snap-in to view a list of all shared folders on the computer and to determine how many users have a connection to each folder. In Figure 15.1, the Shares folder has been selected in the Computer Management console tree and all the shared folders on that computer are shown in the details pane.

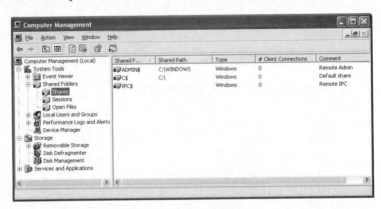

Figure 15.1   Shares folder of the Shared Folders snap-in

Table 15.2 explains the information provided in the details pane shown in Figure 15.1.

Table 15.2   Fields in the Details Pane for the Shares Folder

Column name	Description
Shared Folder	The shared folders on the computer. This is the name that was given to the folder when it was shared.
Shared Path	The path to the shared folder.
Type	The type of network connection: Microsoft Windows, Novell NetWare, or Apple Macintosh.
# Client Connections	The number of clients who have made a remote connection to the shared folder.
Comment	Descriptive text about the folder. This comment was provided when the folder was shared.

Note   Windows XP Professional does not update the list of shared folders, open files, and user sessions automatically. To update these lists, on the Action menu, click Refresh.

Determining How Many Users Can Access a Shared Folder Concurrently

You can use the Shared Folders snap-in to determine the maximum number of users that are permitted to access a folder. In the Shared Folders details pane, click the shared folder for which you want to determine the maximum number of concurrent users who can access the folder. On the Action menu, click Properties, displaying the Properties dialog box for the shared folder. The General tab shows you the user limit. In Windows XP Professional the maximum is 10, but you can set this to a lower value. You can also use the Shared Folders snap-in to determine if the maximum number of users that are permitted to access a folder has been reached.

Tip   There is a quick and easy way to troubleshoot connectivity problems when a user can't connect to a share. Determine the number of connections to the share and the maximum connections allowed. If the maximum number of connections has already been made, the user cannot connect to the shared resource.

Modifying Shared Folder Properties

You can modify existing shared folders, including shared folder permissions, from the Shares folder. To change a shared folder's properties, click the shared folder, and then on the Action menu, click Properties. The General tab of the Properties dialog box shows you the share name, the path to the shared folder, and any comment that has been entered. The General tab also allows you to view and set a user limit for accessing the shared folder. The Security tab allows you to view and change the shared folder permissions.

Monitoring Open Files

Use the Open Files folder in the Shared Folders snap-in to view a list of open files that are located in shared folders and the users who have a current connection to each file. You can use this information when you need to contact users to notify them that you are shutting down the system. Additionally, you can determine which users have a current connection and should be contacted when another user is trying to access a file that is in use.

Table 15.3 describes the information that is available in the Open Files folder.

Table 15.3   Information Available in the Open Files Folder

Column name	Description
Open File	The name of the open files on the computer.
Accessed By	The logon name of the user who has the file open.
Type	The operating system running on the computer where the user is logged on.
# Locks	The number of locks on the file. Programs can request the operating system to lock a file to gain exclusive access and prevent other programs from making changes to the file.
Open Mode	The type of access that the user's application requested when it opened the file, such as Read or Write.

Disconnecting Users from Open Files

You can disconnect users from one open file or from all open files. If you make changes to the NT file system (NTFS) permissions for a file that is currently opened by a user, the new permissions will not affect the user until he or she closes and then attempts to reopen the file.

You can force these changes to take place immediately by doing either of the following:

- **Disconnecting all users from all open files.**   To disconnect all users from all open files, in the Shared Folders snap-in console tree, click Open Files, and then on the Action menu, click Disconnect All Open Files.

- **Disconnecting all users from one open file.**   To disconnect users from one open file, in the Shared Folders snap-in console tree, click Open Files. In the details pane select the open file, and then on the Action menu, click Close Open File.

Caution   Disconnecting users from open files can result in data loss.

Practice: Managing Shared Folders

In this practice you use the Shared Folders snap-in to view the shared folders and open files on your server. If there are any open files on your server and you want to disconnect them, use the Disconnect All Open Files selection. This selection will disconnect all users from all open files.

▶   **To view the shared folders on your computer**

1. Log on as Fred or with a user account that is a member of the Administrators group.

2. Click Start, and point to All Programs.

3. Point to Administrative Tools and click Computer Management.

   Windows XP Professional displays Computer Management.

Note   You can also use Computer Management Local that you created in Chapter 3, "Setting Up and Managing User Accounts." It is also listed in Administrative Tools.

---

4. In the console tree (left pane) of Computer Management, expand System Tools, and then expand Shared Folders.

5. In the console tree, under Shared Folders, click Shares.

   Notice that the details pane shows a list of the existing shared folders on your computer.

▶   **To view the open files on your computer**

1. In the console tree, under Shared Folders, click Open Files.

   If you are working on a computer that is not connected to a network, there will not be any open files because the open files only show connections from a remote computer to a share on your computer.

2. If there are any open files and you want to disconnect them, on the Action menu, click Disconnect All Open Files.

3. Leave Computer Management open and remain logged on as Fred or a user account that is a member of the Administrators group for the next practice.

Lesson Review

The following questions will help you determine whether you have learned enough to move on to the next lesson. If you have difficulty answering these questions, review the material in this lesson before beginning the next lesson. The answers are in Appendix A, "Questions and Answers."

1. Why is it important to manage network resources?

2. On a computer running Windows XP Professional, members of the
_____ and _____ groups
can use the Shared Folders snap-in to monitor network resources.

3. How can you determine what files are open on a computer running
Windows XP Professional?

4. Which of the following statements about monitoring network resources are
correct? (Choose all answers that are correct.)

   a. You can use the Shared Folders snap-in to disconnect all users from all
   open files.

   b. You can use the Shared Folders snap-in to disconnect one user from one
   file.

   c. If you change the NTFS permissions for an open file, the changes affect
   all users who have the file open immediately.

   d. If you make changes to the NTFS permissions for an open file, the
   changes do not affect the user who has that file opened until he or she
   closes and reopens the file.

Lesson Summary

- Monitoring network resources helps you determine whether a network resource is
  still needed and if it is secure, and it helps you plan for future growth.

- Use the Shared Folders snap-in to monitor access to network resources on local or
  remote computers.

- Use the Shared Folders snap-in to send administrative messages to remote users.

- In a workgroup, only members of the Administrators group or the Power Users
  group can monitor resources.

- In a domain, only members of the Administrators group or the Server Operators
  group for the domain can monitor resources on all the computers in the domain.

- Use the Shares folder in the Shared Folders snap-in to manage shared folders
  and open files on a computer.

Lesson 2: Creating and Sharing Local and Remote Folders

You can use the Computer Management snap-in or the Shared Folders snap-in to share an existing folder or to create a new folder and share it on the local computer or on a remote computer. You can also modify the shared folder and NTFS permissions when you share the folder.

After this lesson, you will be able to

- Share a folder
- Stop sharing a folder

Estimated lesson time: 20 minutes

From either the Computer Management snap-in or the Shared Folders snap-in, you can run the Create Shared Folder Wizard to create a new folder and share it. When you use the Computer Management snap-in or Shared Folders snap-in to share an existing folder or to create a new shared folder and share it, Windows XP Professional assigns the Full Control shared folder permission to the Everyone group by default. If you select the Customize Share And Folder Permissions option, you can also assign NTFS permissions when you share the folder. Table 15.4 describes the basic share permissions you can assign to a newly created shared folder when you use the Create Shared Folder Wizard.

Table 15.4   Basic Share Permissions

Option	Description
All Users Have Full Control	The Create Shared Folder Wizard assigns the Full Control share permission to the Everyone group.
Administrators Have Full Control, Other Users Have Read-Only Access	The Create Shared Folder Wizard assigns the Full Control share permission to the Administrators group and the Read share permission to the Everyone group.
Administrators Have Full Control, Other Users Have No Access	The Create Shared Folder Wizard assigns the Full Control share permission to the Administrators group.
Customize Share And Folder Permissions	Select this option to create your own custom share permissions and NTFS permissions.

Note   Using either the Computer Management snap-in or the Shared Folders snap-in is the only way to create a shared folder on a remote computer. Otherwise, you need to be physically located at the computer where the folder resides to share it.

Practice: Creating a Shared Folder

In this practice, you use the Computer Management snap-in to create a new shared folder on your computer.

▶ **To create a new shared folder on your computer**

1. In the console tree, under Shared Folders, click Shares.

2. On the Action menu, click New File Share.

   The Create Shared Folder Wizard starts.

3. In the Create Shared Folder Wizard page, in the Folder To Share text box, type **C:\Library.**

4. In the Share Name text box, type **Library**.

5. Click Next.

   A message box appears asking you if you want to create C:\Library.

6. Click Yes.

   A message box appears informing you that C:\Library has been created.

7. Click OK.

   The Create Shared Folder Wizard displays a final page of three basic share permission options and a customizable permissions option, as described in Table 15.4. You can use one of the three basic permissions or you can choose Customize Share And Folder Permissions to create your own permissions.

8. Click Finish to accept the default permissions option, All Users Have Full Control.

   The Create Shared Folder Wizard displays a message box telling you that the folder has been successfully shared and asking if you want to create another shared folder.

9. Click No.

You can also use either the Computer Management snap-in or the Shared Folders snap-in to stop sharing a shared folder.

▶ **To stop sharing a folder**

1. In the console tree, under Shared Folders, click Shares.

2. Select the Library folder in the details pane.

3. On the Action menu, click Stop Sharing.

   Windows XP Professional displays a message box asking if you are sure you want to stop sharing Library.

4. Click Yes.

   The Library share disappears from the list of shared folders.

Caution   If you stop sharing a folder while a user has a file open, the user might lose data.

Sharing a Folder on a Remote Computer

If you want to share a folder on a remote computer, you run MMC and add the Computer Management snap-in or the Shared Folders snap-in to it. When you add either of these snap-ins, point it to the remote computer on which you want to create and manage shared folders.

▶ **To create a Shared Folder console to use on a remote computer**

1. On the Start menu, click Run. Type **mmc**, and then click OK.

   Windows XP Professional starts the Microsoft Management Console with a blank console displayed.

2. On the File menu, click Add/Remove Snap-In.

   The Microsoft Management Console displays the Add/Remove Snap-In dialog box.

3. In the Add/Remove Snap-In dialog box, click Add.

   The Microsoft Management Console displays the Add Standalone Snap-In dialog box.

4. Click Shared Folders and then click Add.

   The Shared Folders dialog box appears (see Figure 15.2).

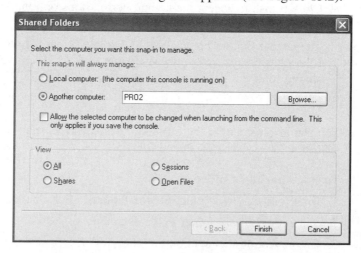

Figure 15.2   The Shared Folders dialog box that allows you to specify a remote computer

5. In the Shared Folders dialog box, select Another Computer and then type in the name of the remote computer.

Note If you select the Allow The Selected Computer To Be Changed When Launching From The Command Line check box, you can choose which remote computer on which you want to create and manage shares. If you do not select this check box, the console is always directed to the same remote computer.

6. Click Finish.
7. Close the Add/Remove Snap-In and Add Standalone Snap-In dialog boxes.

Note If you want to create and manage shared folders on remote computers and you are not in a domain, you must create the same user account with the same password on each computer. In workgroups, you do not have a central database that contains all user accounts. Instead, each computer in the workgroup has its own local security database. For more information on local security databases, see Chapter 3, "Setting Up and Managing User Accounts."

Lesson Review

The following questions will help you determine whether you have learned enough to move on to the next lesson. If you have difficulty answering these questions, review the material in this lesson before beginning the next lesson. The answers are in Appendix A, "Questions and Answers."

1. Which of the following tools can you use to create a shared folder on a remote computer? (Choose all answers that are correct.)

    a. Windows Explorer

    b. Computer Management snap-in

    c. Domain Management snap-in

    d. Shared Folders snap-in

2. How can you create and share a folder on a remote computer?

3. Can you create a custom tool that will allow you to administer more than one specific remote computer? How?

Lesson Summary

- You use the Computer Management snap-in or the Shared Folders snap-in to share an existing folder or to create and share a new folder on the local computer.

- You use only the Computer Management snap-in or Shared Folders snap-in to monitor access to network resources on local or remote computers.

- You create a custom MMC console for creating and managing shares on remote computers by specifying a remote computer when you add the Computer Management snap-in or Shared Folders snap-in to the MMC console.

- You can only create a shared folder on a remote computer using the Computer Management snap-in or Shared Folders snap-in.

- You can allow administrators to specify the remote computer that a custom MMC console points to when they launch it from the command line.

Lesson 3: Monitoring Network Users

You can also use the Computer Management snap-in or Shared Folders snap-in to monitor which users are currently accessing shared folder resources on a server from a remote computer, and you can view the resources to which the users have connections. You can disconnect users and send administrative messages to computers and users, including those not currently accessing network resources.

After this lesson, you will be able to

- Disconnect a specific user from his or her network connection
- Send administrative messages to users

Estimated lesson time: 20 minutes

Monitoring User Sessions

You can use the Computer Management snap-in or Shared Folders snap-in to view which users have a connection to open files on a server and the files to which they have a connection. This information enables you to determine which users you should contact when you need to stop sharing a folder or shut down the server on which the shared folder resides. You can disconnect one or more users to free idle connections to the shared folder, to prepare for a backup or restore operation, to shut down a server, or to change group membership and permissions for the shared folder.

You use the Sessions folder in the Computer Management snap-in or Shared Folders snap-in to view a list of the users with a current network connection to the computer that you are monitoring (see Figure 15.3).

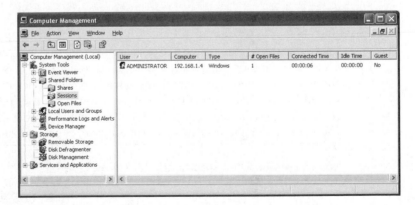

Figure 15.3   Sessions folder of the Shared Folders snap-in

Table 15.5 describes the information that is available in the Sessions folder.

Table 15.5   Information Available in the Sessions Folder

Column name	Description
User	The users with a current network connection to this computer
Computer	The name of the user's computer
Type	The operating system running on the user's computer
# Open Files	The number of files that the user has open on this computer
Connected Time	The time that has elapsed since the user established the current session
Idle Time	The time that has elapsed since the user last accessed a resource on this computer
Guest	Whether this computer authenticated the user as a member of the built-in Guest account

Disconnecting Users

You can disconnect one or all users with a network connection to a computer so that you can do any of the following:

- Have changes to shared folder and NTFS permissions take effect immediately. A user retains all permissions for a shared resource that Windows XP Professional assigned when the user connected to it. Windows XP Professional evaluates the permissions again the next time that a connection is made.

- Free idle connections on a computer so that other users can make a connection when the maximum number of connections has been reached. User connections to resources might remain active for several minutes after a user finishes accessing a resource.

- Shut down a server.

Note   After you disconnect a user, he or she can immediately make a new connection. If the user gains access to a shared folder from a Windows-based client computer, the client computer automatically reestablishes the connection with the shared folder. This connection is established without user intervention unless you change the permissions to prevent the user from accessing the shared folder or you stop sharing the folder to prevent all users from accessing it.

You can disconnect a specific user as follows:

1. In the Computer Management console tree, under Shared Folders, click Sessions.

2. In the list of users in the details pane, select the user that you want to disconnect, and then, on the Action menu, click Close Session.

Note If you want to disconnect all users, click Sessions in the console tree, and then, on the Action menu, click Disconnect All Sessions.

To prevent data loss, you should always notify users who are accessing shared folders or files that you are ready to stop sharing a folder or shut down the computer.

Sending Administrative Messages to Users

You can send administrative messages to one or more users or computers. Send them to users with a current connection to a computer on which network resources are shared to notify them when there will be a disruption to the computer or resource availability. Some common reasons for sending administrative messages are to notify users when you intend to do any of the following:

- Perform a backup or restore operation
- Disconnect users from a resource
- Upgrade software or hardware
- Shut down the computer

Use the Shared Folders snap-in to send administrative messages to users. By default, all currently connected computers to which you can send a message appear in the list of recipients. You can add other users or computers to this list even if they do not have a current connection to resources on the computer.

Practice: Sending Console Messages

In this practice, you use the Shared Folders snap-in to send a console message.

▶ **To send a console message**

1. In the console tree, under Shared Folders, select Shares.

2. On the Action menu, point to All Tasks, and then click Send Console Message.

3. In the Message box, type **Log Off Now — Pro1 is shutting down in 5 minutes**.

   If your computer is not connected to a network, you will notice that Send is unavailable and that the Recipients list box is empty.

4. Click Add.

   The Select Computer dialog box appears.

5. Type **Pro1** in the Enter The Object Name To Select (Examples) text box.

   Pro1 should be the name of your computer. If you did not name your computer Pro1, type the name of your computer in the Recipients text box.

6. Click OK.

   Notice that Send is now available.

7. Click Send.

A message box briefly appears, showing that the message is being sent, and then the Messenger Service dialog box appears, as shown in Figure 15.4. It confirms that a message was sent from Pro1 to Pro1, indicates the date and time the message was sent, and displays the message that was sent.

8. Click OK to close the Messenger Service dialog box.

Figure 15.4   Messenger Service dialog box

Lesson Review

The following questions will help you determine whether you have learned enough to move on to the next lesson. If you have difficulty answering these questions, review the material in this lesson before beginning the next lesson. The answers are in Appendix A, "Questions and Answers."

1. How can you determine which users have a connection to open files on a computer and the files to which they have a connection?

2. How can you disconnect a specific user from a file?

3. Why would you send an administrative message to users with current connections?

4. What can you do to prevent a user from reestablishing a network connection after you have disconnected that user from a shared folder?

Lesson Summary

- Use the Sessions folder in the Computer Management snap-in or Shared Folders snap-in to view which users have a connection to open files on a computer and the files to which they have a connection.

- Use the Sessions folder in the Computer Management snap-in or Shared Folders snap-in to disconnect a specific user or all users with a network connection to a computer.

- Use the Computer Management snap-in or Shared Folders snap-in to send administrative messages to one or more users or computers.

Lesson 4: Using Offline Folders and Files

When the network is unavailable or when you are on the road and your laptop is undocked, offline folders and files allow you to continue working on files that are stored on shared folders on the network. These network files are cached on your local disk so that they are available even if the network is not. When the network becomes available or when you dock your laptop, your connection to the network is reestablished. Offline files synchronize the cached files and folders on your local disk with those stored on the network.

After this lesson, you will be able to

- Configure and use offline folders and files

Estimated lesson time: 30 minutes

Configuring Your Computer to Use Offline Folders and Files

Before you can use offline folders and files, you must configure your computer to use them. You configure offline folders and files by using the Folder Options selection located on the Tools menu of My Computer. In the Offline Files tab of Folder Options, you must select the Enable Offline Files and the Synchronize All Offline Files Before Logging Off check boxes (see Figure 15.5).

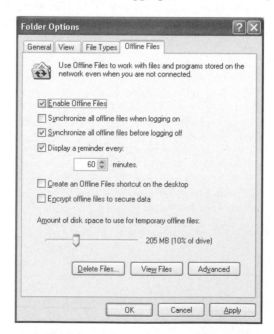

Figure 15.5   The Offline Files tab in the Folder Options dialog box

In the Offline Files tab, you can click Delete Files to delete the locally cached copy of a network file. Click View Files to view the files stored in the Offline Files folder; these are the locally cached files that you have stored on your system. Click Advanced to configure how your computer responds when a network connection is lost. For example, when a network connection is lost, you can configure your computer to notify you and allow you to begin working offline.

Practice: Configuring Offline Folders

In this practice you configure your computer running Windows XP Professional just as you would if it were a laptop computer running Windows XP Professional so that you can use offline folders and files. This allows you to work offline.

Run the **OfflineFolders** file in the Demos folder on the CD-ROM accompanying this book for a demonstration of configuring a computer so you can use offline files.

▶ **To configure Offline Folders and Files**

1. Log on as Fred or with a user account that is a member of the Administrators group.
2. Click Start, right-click My Computer, and then click Open.
3. On the Tools menu, click Folder Options.

   Windows XP Professional displays the Folder Options dialog box.
4. Click the Offline Files tab.

Note   If Fast User Switching is enabled, Offline Files cannot be enabled. Click Cancel to close the Folder Options dialog box. Open User Accounts in Control Panel, and select Change The Way Users Log On Or Off. Clear the Use Fast User Switching check box and click Apply Options. Close User Accounts. In My Computer, on the Tools menu, click Folder Options and then click the Offline Files tab. Go to step 5.

---

5. Select the Enable Offline Files check box.
6. Ensure that the Synchronize All Offline Files Before Logging Off check box is selected, and then click OK.

   Your computer is now configured so that you can use offline folders and files.
7. Close the My Computer window.

Configuring Your Computer to Share Offline Folders and Files

Before other users on the network can use offline folders and files on your computer, you must configure the resource to allow caching for offline use. You configure offline folders and files through Windows Explorer or My Computer. Figure 15.6 shows the Allow Caching Of Files In This Shared Folder check box in Windows Explorer.

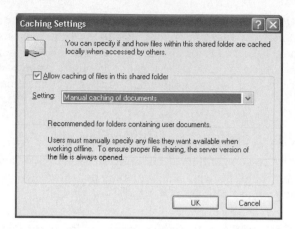

Figure 15.6   The Allow Caching Of Files In This Shared Folder check box

Windows XP Professional provides the following three settings for caching:

- **Manual Caching Of Documents.**   The default setting. Users must manually specify any files that they want available when they are working offline. To ensure proper file sharing, the server version of the file is always open.

- **Automatic Caching Of Documents.**   Every file a user opens is automatically downloaded and cached on the user's hard drive so that it will be available offline. If an earlier version of a file is already loaded on the user's hard drive, it is automatically replaced with the newer version. To ensure proper file sharing, the server version of the file is always opened.

- **Automatic Caching Of Programs and Documents.**   Opened files are automatically downloaded and cached on the user's hard drive so that it will be available offline. If an earlier version of a file is already loaded on the user's hard drive, it is automatically replaced with the newer version. File sharing is not ensured.

Practice: Configuring Offline Folders for Sharing

In this practice, you configure a network share on a computer running Windows XP Professional so that users can access the files in the share and use them offline.

▶ **To enable a network share to provide files to be used offline**

1. Ensure that you are still logged on as Administrator, and start Windows Explorer.

2. Create a folder C:\Offline.

3. Right-click Offline and then click Sharing And Security.

   Windows Explorer displays the Offline Properties dialog box with the Sharing tab active.

4. Click Share This Folder, and then click Caching.

   Windows Explorer displays the Caching Settings dialog box.

5. Click the down arrow at the end of the Setting dialog box.

6. Ensure Manual Caching Of Documents is selected and then click OK.

7. Click OK to close the Offline Properties dialog box.

   Leave Windows Explorer open.

Synchronizing Files

File synchronization is straightforward if the copy of the file on the network does not change while you are editing a cached version of the file. Your edits are incorporated into the copy on the network. However, it is possible that another user could edit the network version of the file while you are working offline. If both your cached offline copy of the file and the network copy of the file are edited, you must decide what to do. You are given a choice of retaining your edited version and not updating the network copy with your edits, of over-writing your cached version with the version on the network, or of keeping a copy of both versions of the file. In the last case, you must rename your version of the file, and both copies will exist on your hard disk and on the network.

Configuring the Synchronization Manager

To configure the synchronization manager, open Windows Explorer, click the Tools menu, and then click Synchronize. Notice that you can manually synchronize your offline files with those on the network by clicking Synchronize. You can also configure the Synchronization Manager by clicking Setup.

In configuring the Synchronization Manager, you have three sets of options for configuring synchronization. The first set of options is accessed through the Logon/ Logoff tab (see Figure 15.7). You can configure synchronization to occur when you log on, when you log off, or both. You can also specify that you want to be prompted before synchronization occurs. You can specify the items to be synchronized at log on or log off, or both, and you can specify the network connection.

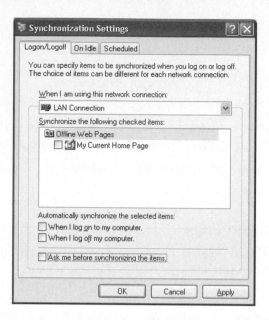

Figure 15.7 Logon/Logoff tab of the Synchronization Settings dialog box

The second set of options in configuring the Synchronization Manager is accessed through the On Idle tab. The items configurable are similar to those configurable through the Logon/Logoff tab. The following items are configurable through the On Idle tab:

- **When I Am Using This Network Connection.** This option allows you to specify the network connection and which items to synchronize.

- **Synchronize The Following Checked Items.** This option allows you to specify which items you want to synchronize.

- **Synchronize The Selected Items While My Computer Is Idle.** This option allows you to turn off or on synchronization during idle time.

Click Advanced on the On Idle tab to configure the following options: Automatically Synchronize The Specified Items After My Computer Has Been Idle For X Minutes; While My Computer Remains Idle, Repeat Synchronization Every X Minutes; and Prevent Synchronization When My Computer Is Running On Battery Power.

The third set of options for scheduling synchronization is accessed through the Scheduled tab. You can click Add to start the Scheduled Synchronization Wizard. The first page of the Scheduled Synchronization Wizard allows you to specify the connection, the items to synchronize and whether you want the computer to auto-matically connect if you are not connected when the scheduled time for synchroniza-tion arrives. The second page of the wizard is the Select The Time And Day You Want The Synchronization To Start page. It allows you to configure the starting time and date for the synchronization. You can also configure the frequency of the syn-chronization, which can be set for every day, every weekday, or at a specified interval measured in days. On the third page of the wizard you assign a name to this sched-uled synchronization and, on the final page, you review your settings.

Practice: Configuring Synchronization Manager

In this practice you configure the Synchronization Manager.

Run the **SynchronizationManager** file in the Demos folder on the CD-ROM accompanying this book for a demonstration of configuring Synchronization Manager.

▶ **To configure Synchronization Manager**

1. Ensure that you are still logged on as Administrator.

   Windows Explorer should be open from the last practice.

2. Click Tools and then click Synchronize.

   Windows XP Professional displays the Items To Synchronize dialog box, which allows you to specify which folders you want to synchronize.

3. If nothing is selected, click My Current Home Page, and then click Setup.

   Windows XP Professional displays the Synchronization Settings dialog box with the Logon/Logoff tab selected.

4. Review the options on the Logon/Logoff tab, and then review the options on the On-Idle tab and the Scheduled tab.

5. On the Logon/Logoff tab, select My Current Home Page.

6. Ensure that both the When I Log On To My Computer and When I Log Off My Computer check boxes are checked.

7. Select the Ask Me Before Synchronizing The Items check box, and then click OK.

8. Click Close to close the Items To Synchronize dialog box, and then close Windows Explorer.

Lesson Review

The following questions will help you determine whether you have learned enough to move on to the next lesson. If you have difficulty answering these questions, review the material in this lesson before beginning the next lesson. The answers are in Appendix A, "Questions and Answers."

1. How do you configure your computer to use offline folders and files?

2. What tools does Windows XP Professional provide for you to configure your computer to provide offline files? What must you do to allow others to access files on your computer?

3. What does Synchronization Manager do?

Lesson Summary

- Offline files are network files that are cached on your local disk so that they are available even if the network is not.

- Before you can use offline files, you must use the Folders Options selection on the Tools menu of My Computer or Windows Explorer to configure your computer to use offline files.

- You must use the User Accounts tool to disable Fast User Switching before you can enable Offline Files.

- You use Synchronization Manager to configure synchronization of the offline files you are using and the copies on the server.

- Synchronization Manager allows you to configure synchronization to occur when you log on, when you log off, or both, and you can specify that you want to be asked before synchronization occurs.

Lesson 5: Using Scheduled Tasks

Use Scheduled Tasks to identify programs and batch files you want to run once, at regular intervals, or at specific times. You can schedule any script, program, or document to start at a specified time and interval or when certain operating system events occur. This feature can complete many administrative tasks for you.

After this lesson, you will be able to

- Use Scheduled Tasks

Estimated lesson time: 25 minutes

Introducing Scheduled Tasks

Windows XP Professional saves scheduled tasks in the Scheduled Tasks folder, which can be accessed through the Control Panel under Performance And Maintenance. In addition, you can access Scheduled Tasks on another computer by browsing that computer's resources using My Network Places. This allows you to move tasks from one computer to another. For example, you can create task files for maintenance and then add them to a user's computer as needed.

Use Scheduled Tasks to perform the following tasks:

- Run maintenance programs at specific intervals
- Run programs when there is less demand for computer resources

Configuring Options

Use the Scheduled Task Wizard to schedule tasks. You access the wizard in the Scheduled Tasks folder by double-clicking Add Scheduled Task. Table 15.6 describes the options that you can configure in the Scheduled Task Wizard.

Table 15.6   Scheduled Task Wizard Options

Option	Description
Application	The applications to schedule. Select from a list of applications that are registered with Windows XP Professional, or click Browse to specify any program or batch file.
Name	A descriptive name for the task.
Perform This Task	How often Windows XP Professional will perform the task. You can select daily, weekly, monthly, one time only, when the computer starts, or when you log on.
Start Time	The start time for the task to occur.
Start Date	The start date for the task.

(cont

Table 15.6   *(continued)*

Option	Description
Name And Password	A user name and password. You can enter your user name and password or another user name and password to have the application run under the security settings for that user account. If the user account that you used to log on does not have the rights required by the scheduled task, you can use another user account that does have the required rights. For example, you can run a scheduled backup by using a user account that has the required rights to back up data but does not have other administrative privileges.
Advanced Properties	Select this check box if you want the wizard to display the Advanced Properties dialog box so that you can configure additional properties after you click Finish.

Setting Advanced Properties

In addition to the options that are available in the Scheduled Task Wizard, you can set several additional options for tasks. You can change options that you set with the Scheduled Task Wizard or set additional advanced options by configuring advanced properties for the task.

Table 15.7 describes the tabs in the Advanced Properties dialog box for the scheduled task.

Table 15.7   Scheduled Task Wizard Advanced Options

Tab	Description
Task	Change the scheduled task or change the user account that is used to run the task. You can also turn the task on and off.
Schedule	Set and display multiple schedules for the same task. You can set the date, time, and number of repeat occurrences for the task. For example, you can set up a task to run every Friday at 10:00 p.m.
Settings	Set options that affect when a task starts or stops, such as how long a backup can take, if the computer can be in use, or if the computer can be running on batteries when it runs the task.

Troubleshooting Scheduled Tasks

In general, troubleshooting the Scheduled Tasks involves checking the parameters that you have set up. However, the Advanced menu provides a few options to help you with troubleshooting. When you open Scheduled Tasks and click Advanced, the first option on the Advanced menu allows you to stop and start the Task Scheduler Service, and the selection is either Stop Using The Task Scheduler or Start Using The

Task Scheduler. If your scheduled tasks are not starting, you can check this option to be sure that the Task Scheduler Service is running and if it is not, you can start it. The second option is similar to the first, only it pauses and continues the service. If the service is paused, scheduled tasks do not start.

The third option on the Advanced menu is Notify Me Of Missed Tasks. This option causes the system to send you a message when a scheduled task does not occur. The next option on the Advanced menu is the AT Service Account, which allows you to change the account being used from the System account. The final option, View Log, allows you to view a log of when the Task Scheduler Service started, stopped, paused, and continued. It also logs the name of each scheduled task, the application or task that started, and the time and date the task was started.

Practice: Using Task Scheduler

In this practice, you schedule Address Book to start at a predetermined time. You can use this as a reminder to review address information. You also configure Task Scheduler options.

Run the **TaskScheduler** file in the Demos folder on the CD-ROM accompanying this book for a demonstration of using Task Scheduler.

▶ **To schedule a task to start automatically**

1. Click Start, click Control Panel, click Performance And Maintenance, and then click Scheduled Tasks.

    Windows XP Professional opens the Scheduled Tasks folder.

2. Double-click Add Scheduled Task.

    The Scheduled Task Wizard appears.

3. Click Next.

    Windows XP Professional displays a list of currently installed programs. To schedule a program that is not registered with Windows XP Professional, click Browse to locate the program.

4. Click Browse.

    Windows XP Professional displays the Select Program To Schedule page.

5. Double-click Program Files, and then double-click Windows NT.

6. Double-click Accessories, and then double-click WordPad.

7. Type **Launch WordPad** in the Type A Name For This Task text box.

    The Type A Name For This Task text box allows you to enter a description that is more intuitive than the program name. Windows XP Professional displays this name in the Scheduled Tasks folder when you finish the wizard.

8. Click One Time Only, and then click Next.

9. In the Start Time box, set the time to 4 minutes after the current system time and make a note of this time.

   To confirm the current system time, look at the Windows taskbar. Do not change the entry in the Start Date text box.

10. Click Next.

    The wizard requires you to enter the name and password of a user account. When Task Scheduler runs the scheduled task, the program receives all of the rights and permissions of the user account that you enter here. The program is also bound by any restrictions on the user account. Notice that the user name you are currently using is already filled in as the default. You must type the correct password for the user account in both password boxes before you can continue.

    You will schedule the console to run with your administrative privileges.

11. In both the Enter The Password text box and the Confirm Password text box, type **password.**

12. Click Next.

    Do not select the Open Advanced Properties For This Task When I Click Finish check box. You will review the Advanced properties in the next procedure.

13. Click Finish.

    Notice that the wizard added the task to the list of scheduled tasks.

14. To confirm that you scheduled the task successfully, wait for the time that you configured in step 9 and WordPad will start.

15. Close WordPad.

▶ **To configure advanced Task Scheduler options**

1. In the Scheduled Tasks folder, double-click Launch WordPad.

   Windows XP Professional displays the Launch WordPad dialog box. Notice the tabs and review the options in the tabs. These are the same options that are available if you select the check box for setting advanced options on the last page of the Scheduled Task Wizard. Do not change any of the settings.

2. Click the Settings tab.

3. Select the Delete The Task If It Is Not Scheduled To Run Again check box.

4. Click the Schedule tab, and then set the start time for 2 minutes after the current system time.

   Make a note of this time.

5. Click OK.

   To confirm that you scheduled the task successfully, wait for the time that you set in step 4 of this procedure. WordPad will start.

6. Close WordPad.

   Notice that the scheduled event is no longer in the Scheduled Tasks folder. The option of automatically deleting a task after it finishes is useful for cleaning up after tasks that only need to run once.

7. Close the Scheduled Tasks folder.

8. Log off Windows XP Professional.

Lesson Review

The following questions will help you determine whether you have learned enough to move on to the next lesson. If you have difficulty answering these questions, review the material in this lesson before beginning the next lesson. The answers are in Appendix A, "Questions and Answers."

1. How can Scheduled Tasks help you monitor, manage, and maintain network resources?

2. Which of the following are valid choices for the frequency with which Scheduled Tasks schedules programs to run? (Choose all answers that are correct.)

   a. Daily

   b. One time only

   c. When the computer shuts down

   d. When a user logs off

3. Why do you have to assign a user account and password for each task that you schedule using the Scheduled Task Wizard?

4. If none of your scheduled tasks are starting, what is one thing that you need to check?

Lesson Summary

- You can use Scheduled Tasks to schedule programs and batch files to run once, at regular intervals, at specific times, or when certain operating system events occur.

- Windows XP Professional saves scheduled tasks in the Scheduled Tasks folder, which can be accessed through Performance and Maintenance in Control Panel.

- After you have scheduled a task to run, you can still modify any of the options or advanced features for the task, including the program to be run.

- You can access Scheduled Tasks on another computer by browsing that computer's resources using My Network Places, so you can move tasks from one computer to another.

Lesson 6: Using Task Manager

Task Manager provides information about the programs and processes running on your computer and the performance of your computer. You can use Task Manager to start programs, to stop programs and processes, and to view a dynamic view of your computer's performance.

After this lesson, you will be able to

- Identify three methods for starting Task Manager
- Use Task Manager to monitor programs, processes, and system performance
- Add columns to the Processes tab display
- Use Task Manager to start and stop programs

Estimated lesson time: 25 minutes

Monitoring Programs

Task Manager allows you to monitor applications and processes currently running on your computer. It also provides information about the processes, including the memory usage of each one. It provides statistics about the memory and processor performance and network usage. You can start Task Manager in any of the following three ways:

- Press CTRL+SHIFT+ESC
- Right-click the Windows taskbar, and then click Task Manager
- Press CTRL+ALT+DELETE

Note Depending on whether your computer running Windows XP Professional is in a workgroup environment or a domain environment and, if it is in a workgroup environment, how the Logon and Logoff Options are configured, you start Task Manager by either pressing CTRL+ALT+DELETE or by selecting it.

The Task Manager dialog box shown in Figure 15.8 has four tabs: Applications, Processes, Performance, and Networking.

Figure 15.8   Task Manager dialog box with the Applications tab selected

You can use the options in the Applications tab of the Task Manager dialog box to stop a program from running (End Task), to switch to a program and bring the program into the foreground (Switch To), and to start a program (New Task). At the bottom of the display, Task Manager shows you the number of processes currently running, the CPU usage, and the memory usage.

Note   When the Task Manager is running, Windows XP Professional displays an accurate miniature CPU usage icon on the taskbar. If you point to the icon, Task Manager displays the percentage of processor usage in text format.

Monitoring Processes

The Processes tab in the Task Manager dialog box (see Figure 15.9) lists all processes currently running on your computer that run in their own address space, including all applications and system services. Task Manager also allows you to end processes.

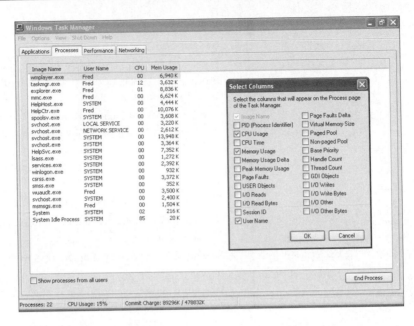

Figure 15.9   Task Manager dialog box showing the Select Columns option

By default, the Processes tab shows you the processes, the users running each process, and the CPU and memory usage for each process that is running. You can add additional performance measures to those shown by default in the Processes tab. To add performance measures, on the View menu, click Select Columns (see Figure 15.9). Table 15.8 describes the columns that are displayed in Task Manager by default and some of the columns that can be added to the Processes tab.

Table 15.8   Processes Tab Columns

Column	Description
Image Name	The name of the process, displayed by default.
PID (Process Identifier)	The numerical identifier assigned to the process while it is running.
User Name	The name of the user that the process is running under, displayed by default.
CPU Usage	The percentage of time the threads of the process used the processor since the last update, displayed by default.
CPU Time	The total processor time (in seconds) used by the process since it was started.
Memory Usage	The amount of memory (in kilobytes) used by the process, displayed by default.

(continued)

Table 15.8 *(continued)*

Column	Description
Base Priority	Determines the order in which threads are scheduled for the processor. The base priority is not set by the operating system; it is set by the code.
	You can use Task Manager to change the base priority of processes. To change the base priority of a process, right-click the process and click Set Priority.
I/O Read Bytes	The number of bytes transferred in input/output operations generated by a process.
I/O Reads	The number of read input/output operations generated by a process.
I/O Write Bytes	The number of bytes written in input/output operations generated by a process.
I/O Writes	The number of write input/output operations generated by a process.
Nonpaged Pool	The amount of memory (in kilobytes) that is used by a process; operating system memory that is never paged (moved from memory) to disk.
Paged Pool	The amount of system-allocated virtual memory (in kilobytes) used by a process; virtual memory that can be paged to disk. Paging is the moving of infrequently used data from RAM to the paging file on the hard disk.
Page Faults	The number of times that data had to be retrieved from the pagefile on the hard disk for this process because it had been paged out of physical memory.
Peak Memory Usage	The maximum amount of physical memory resident in a process since it started.
Thread Count	The number of threads running in the process.

Monitoring System Performance

You can use the Performance tab in the Task Manager dialog box (see Figure 15.10) to see a dynamic overview of system performance.

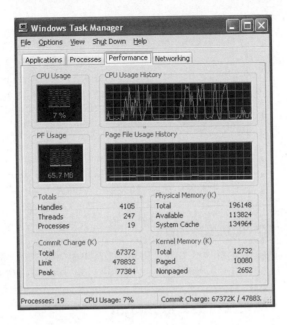

Figure 15.10   Task Manager dialog box with the Performance tab selected

Table 15.9 describes the fields that are displayed in Task Manager by default in the Performance tab.

Table 15.9   Performance Tab Fields

Field	Description
CPU Usage	The percentage of time that the processor is running a thread other than the idle thread
CPU Usage History	The percentage of time that the processor is running a thread other than the idle thread shown over time
PF Usage	The amount of virtual memory used (in MB)
Page File Usage History	The amount of virtual memory used (in kilobytes) shown over time
Total: Handles	The number of object handles in the tables of all processes
Threads	The number of running threads including one idle thread per processor
Processes	The number of active processes, including the idle process
Physical Memory (K): Total	The amount of physical RAM installed in the computer
Available	The amount of physical memory available to processes
System Cache	The amount of physical memory released to the file cache on demand

(continued)

Table 15.9   *(continued)*

Field	Description
Commit Charge:	
Total	The size of virtual memory in use by all processes
Limit	The amount of virtual memory that can be committed to all processes without enlarging the paging file
Peak	The maximum amount of virtual memory used in the session
Kernel	
Memory (K): Total	The sum of the paged and nonpaged memory
Paged	The size of the paged pool allocated to the operating system
Non paged	The size of the nonpaged pool allocated to the operating system

Monitoring Networking

The Networking tab in the Task Manager dialog box lists the adapter name, the network utilization, the link speed, and the state of the connection.

Practice: Using Task Manager

In this practice, you use Task Manager to monitor programs, processes, and system performance. You use Task Manager to start a program and to stop a program. Finally, you add new columns to the Processes tab.

Run the **TaskManager** file in the Demos folder on the CD-ROM accompanying this book for a demonstration of using Task Manager.

▶ **To monitor programs, processes, and system performance**

1. If necessary, log on as Fred or with a user account that is a member of the Administrators group.

2. Press CTRL+SHIFT+ESC to launch Task Manager.

   What programs are currently running on your system?

3. Click New Task.

   Windows XP Professional displays a Create New Task dialog box.

4. In the Open text box, type **wordpad** and click OK.

   WordPad should start and be listed as a running application.

5. Click the Processes tab.

   How many processes are running?

6. On the View menu, click Select Columns.

   The Select Columns dialog box appears.

7. Click Peak Memory Usage, and then click Page Faults. Click OK.

   Two new columns, Peak Memory Usage and Page Faults, are added to the Processes tab display. You might need to maximize Task Manager to see all columns.

8. Click the Performance tab.

   What percentage of your CPU's capacity is being used?

   Do you think that your CPU could be slowing down the performance on your system?

9. Click the Applications tab.

10. Click WordPad and then click End Task.

    WordPad closes and is removed from the list of running applications.

11. Close Task Manager.

Lesson Review

The following questions will help you determine whether you have learned enough to move on to the next lesson. If you have difficulty answering these questions, review the material in this lesson before beginning the next lesson. The answers are in Appendix A, "Questions and Answers."

1. Which of the following methods can you use to start Task Manager? (Choose all answers that are correct.)

   a. Press CTRL+ALT+ESC

   b. Right-click the Desktop and click Task Manager

   c. Press CTRL+SHIFT+ESC

   d. Press CTRL+ALT+DELETE and, if necessary, click Task Manager

2. Which of the following tabs can be found in Task Manager? (Choose all answers that are correct.)

   a. Networking tab

   b. Programs tab

   c. Processes tab

   d. General tab

3. What are page faults? Do you think a larger or smaller number of page faults indicate better system performance? Why?

4. What does CPU usage represent? In general, is system performance better with a high CPU usage value or a low value?

Lesson Summary

- You can use Task Manager to monitor applications and processes currently running on your computer, as well as to monitor memory and processor performance and network usage.

- You can use the Applications tab of Task Manager to stop a program, switch to a program, and start a program.

- After you have scheduled a task to run, you can still modify any of the options or advanced features for the task, including the program to be run.

- You can add additional columns to the Processes tab.

Lesson 7: Using Performance Console

Windows XP Professional provides two tools for monitoring resource usage: the System Monitor snap-in and the Performance Logs and Alerts snap-in. Both of these snap-ins are contained in the Performance console. You use the System Monitor snap-in to track resource use and network throughput. You use the Performance Logs and Alerts snap-in to collect performance data from the local or a remote computer.

After this lesson, you will be able to

- Use System Monitor to monitor resource usage
- Add objects and counters to System Monitor
- Change the output to view it in a graph, a histogram, or a report

Estimated lesson time: 30 minutes

Using System Monitor

To access the Performance console click Start, click Control Panel, click Performance And Maintenance, click Administrative Tools, and then double-click the Performance shortcut. The Performance console contains the System Monitor snap-in and the Performance Logs and Alerts snap-in (see Figure 15.11).

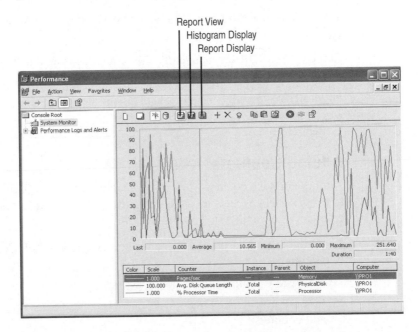

Figure 15.11 System Monitor snap-in displaying counter values in a graph

You use System Monitor to collect and view real-time data about memory, disk, processor, network, and other activity on your computer or on remote computers. You can view this data in a graph, a histogram, or a report. To change the display you can click the appropriate icon, as shown in Figure 15.11, or use the following key combinations: CTRL+G for the graph, CTRL+B for the histogram, and CTRL+R for the report.

Note   A *histogram* is a chart that consists of horizontal or vertical bars. The widths or heights of these bars represent the values of certain data.

Monitoring resources on your computer and overall system performance can help you to do the following:

- Evaluate how well your system is currently performing
- Detect and eliminate bottlenecks to improve performance
- Look for trends to plan for future growth and upgrades
- Evaluate the effects of tuning and configuration changes on your system

System Monitor helps you gauge a computer's efficiency and locate and resolve current or potential problems. You monitor resources on your computer by selecting objects in System Monitor. A set of counters exists for each object; Table 15.10 describes some of the available objects.

Table 15.10   Partial List of Available Objects in System Monitor

Object	Description
Cache	Used to monitor the file system cache used to buffer physical device data
Memory	Used to monitor the physical and virtual memory on the computer
PhysicalDisk	Used to monitor a hard disk as a whole
Processor	Used to monitor CPUs

Adding Counters

Adding counters, such as those described in Table 15.10, to an object allows you to track certain aspects of the object. The following steps allow you to add counters to an object in System Monitor:

1. At the bottom of the Performance console, right-click Counter and click Add Counters.

   The Add Counters dialog box appears.

2. In the Performance Object list box, select the object for which you want to add counters.

3. Ensure that Select Counters From List is selected.

   You can add all counters, but that usually provides more information than you need or can interpret.

4. Select a counter from the list and click Add.

For an explanation of a counter, select it and then click Explain.

Tip If you want to add several counters at the same time, you can hold down CTRL to select individual counters from the list. You can hold down SHIFT if you want to select several counters in a row, and click the first in the list you want and then click the last in the list that you want to select. All counters listed between the first and last you clicked are automatically selected.

---

5. When you have completed your selection of objects and counters, click Close to return to the Performance console.

Table 15.11 explains a few of the counters you might find useful in evaluating your system's performance.

Table 15.11 Partial List of Counters Available in System Monitor

Counter	Description
Under Processor, choose % Processor Time	Indicates the percentage of time that the processor spends executing a nonidle thread, which is the percentage of time that the processor is active. During some operations this might reach 100%. Periods of 100% activity should only occur occasionally.
Under Processor, choose Interrupts/Sec	Indicates the average number of hardware interrupts the processor is receiving and servicing in each second. It does not include deferred procedure calls (DPCs). This counter value is an indicator of the activity of devices that generate interrupts, such as the system clock, mouse, network adapter cards, and other peripheral devices. If the Processor Time value is more than 90 percent and the Interrupts/Sec value is greater than 15 percent, this processor is probably in need of assistance to handle the interrupt load.
Under Processor, choose % DPC Time	Indicates how much time the processor is spending processing DPCs. DPCs are software interrupts or tasks that require immediate processing, causing other tasks to be handled at a lower priority. DPCs represent further processing of client requests.
Under System, choose Processor Queue Length	Indicates the number of threads in the processor queue. There is a single queue for processor time, even on computers with multiple processors. A sustained processor queue of greater than two threads usually indicates that the processor is slowing down the overall system performance.

Using Performance Logs and Alerts

You use Performance Logs and Alerts to record performance data and system alerts. You can automatically collect performance data from the local computer or from remote computers. You can view the logged data from System Monitor or you can export it to a spreadsheet program or a database, such as structured query language (SQL). The details pane of the console window shows logs and alerts that you have created (see Figure 15.12).

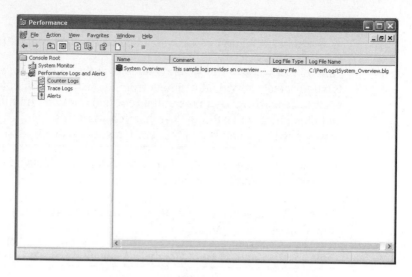

Figure 15.12 Performance Logs and Alerts snap-in

Table 15.12 explains the information provided by the columns in the details pane.

Table 15.12   Performance Logs and Alerts Columns

Column	Description
Name	The name of the log or alert. Note that a sample log file, System Overview, is provided.
Comment	Any descriptive information you want to include about the log or alert.
Log File Type	The log file format: For alerts it is always alerts. For trace logs it is always sequential. For logs it can be binary, binary circular, text-CSV for comma-delimited text, or text-TSV for tab-delimited text.
Log File Name	The path and filename you defined for the files generated by this log.

Establishing a Baseline

When you are ready to begin monitoring the resources on your system, the first thing you need to do is establish a baseline. A baseline is a measurement derived from collecting data over an extended period of time. The data should reflect typical types of workloads and user connections, but should also include any unusual activity that might occur. The baseline represents resource usage under normal conditions.

Once you have collected data on performance over an extended period of time, with data reflecting periods of low, average, and high usage, you can determine what is acceptable performance for your system, and that determination becomes your baseline. You use the baseline to determine when bottlenecks are developing or to watch for changes in usage patterns. Determining bottlenecks will help you in troubleshooting problems that might arise. Watching for changes in usage patterns will help you plan for the future.

Identifying and Resolving Bottlenecks

Deviations from your baseline are good indicators of performance problems. A bottleneck exists if a particular component's limitation is slowing the entire system performance. Even if one component in your system is heavily used, if the other components or the system as a whole are not slowed down, there is no bottleneck.

If you discover a bottleneck on your system, here are some basic suggestions to help you solve the problem:

- Verify that your hardware and software configurations meet or exceed Microsoft's recommendation for Windows XP Professional and the services you are running.

- Review the applications that you are running and ensure the resources that they require are available.

- Review network and disk utilization and other activities occurring at the times that you see increased resource utilization.

- Never make more than one change at a time when trying to resolve a bottleneck and always repeat monitoring to verify that the change you made actually improved the situation.

Practice: Using System Monitor

In this practice, you use System Monitor to monitor system resources. You add objects and counters to control what is being monitored, and you then view the three views—graph, histogram, and report—for output.

▶ **To monitor system resources**

1. If necessary, log on as Fred or with a user account that is a member of the Administrators group.

2. Click Start, click Control Panel, and then click Performance And Maintenance.

3. Click Administrative Tools, and then double-click the Performance shortcut.

   Windows XP Professional starts the Performance console with the System Monitor selected.

   What objects and counters are selected by default?

4. Under the graph, right-click Counter and then click Add Counters.

   Windows XP Professional displays the Add Counters dialog box.

   What performance object is selected by default?

5. In the Select Counters From list, select Interrupts/Sec and then click Explain.

   Windows XP Professional displays an Explain Text dialog box indicating that Interrupts/Sec is the average number of hardware interrupts the processor receives and services each second.

6. Close the Explain Text dialog box.

7. Click Add to add the Interrupts/Sec counter to the Processor object.

8. In the Performance Object list box, select Paging File.

9. Under Select Counters From List, ensure that %Usage is selected and then click Add to add the Paging File object with the %Usage counter.

10. Close the Add Counters dialog box.

11. Press CTRL+B to view a histogram.

12. Press CTRL+R to view a report.

13. Press CTRL+G to return to a graph.

14. Close the Performance console.

Lesson Review

The following questions will help you determine whether you have learned enough to move on to the next lesson. If you have difficulty answering these questions, review the material in this lesson before beginning the next lesson. The answers are in Appendix A, "Questions and Answers."

1. Which of the following monitoring tools are included in the Performance console? (Choose all answers that are correct.)

   a. System Monitor snap-in

   b. Task Manager snap-in

   c. Performance Logs and Alerts snap-in

   d. Task Scheduler

2. Why should you monitor resources and overall system performance?

3. What is a baseline and what is a bottleneck?

4. Why do you need to determine a baseline when you monitor system resources and system performance?

Lesson Summary

- The Performance console contains the System Monitor snap-in and the Performance Logs and Alerts snap-in.

- The System Monitor snap-in allows you to monitor the performance of your computer or other computers on the network.

- The System Monitor snap-in provides performance objects that consist of counters for collecting data.

- The Performance Logs and Alerts snap-in automatically records performance data and system alerts on your local computer or from remote computers.

- A baseline is a measurement derived from collecting data over an extended period of time that represents resource usage under normal conditions.

- A bottleneck is any component that slows down the entire system's performance.

CHAPTER 16

Backing Up and Restoring Data

About This Chapter

Now that you have learned to install Microsoft Windows XP Professional and set up a network, it is important that you are able to ensure that your data is not lost. Windows XP Professional provides the Backup or Restore Wizard to allow you to back up data. This chapter introduces you to backing up and restoring data, including Automated System Recovery Backup.

Before You Begin

To complete this chapter, you must have

- A computer that meets or exceeds the minimum hardware requirements listed in the preface, "About This Book"
- Windows XP Professional installed on the computer

Lesson 1: Using the Backup Utility

The efficient recovery of lost data is the goal of all backup jobs. A *backup job* is a single process of backing up data. Regularly backing up the data on server hard disks and client computer hard disks prevents data loss caused by disk drive failures, power outages, virus infections, and other such incidents. If data loss occurs, and you have carefully planned and performed regular backup jobs, you can restore the lost data, whether it is a single file or an entire hard disk.

After this lesson, you will be able to

- Identify the purpose of backing up and restoring data
- Identify the user rights and permissions that are necessary to back up and restore data
- Identify planning issues for backing up data
- Identify the different backup types
- Explain how to change the default options for the Backup Utility

Estimated lesson time: 30 minutes

Introducing the Backup Utility

Windows XP Professional provides the Backup or Restore Wizard, shown in Figure 16.1, which allows you to easily back up data. To access the Backup or Restore Wizard, on the Start menu, point to All Programs, point to Accessories, point to System Tools, and then click Backup. Alternatively, on the Start menu, you can click Run, type **ntbackup,** and then click OK. You can use the Backup or Restore Wizard to back up data manually or to schedule unattended backup jobs on a regular basis. You can back up data to a file or to a tape. Files can be stored on hard disks, removable disks (such as Iomega Zip and Jaz drives), and recordable compact discs and optical drives.

Figure 16.1   The Welcome To The Backup Or Restore Wizard page

On the Welcome To The Backup Or Restore Wizard page, click Next. The Backup Or Restore page allows you to specify whether you want to back up files and settings or restore files and settings.

To successfully back up and restore data on a computer running Windows XP Professional, you must have the appropriate permissions and user rights, as described in the following list:

- All users can back up their own files and folders. They can also back up files for which they have the Read, Read and Execute, Modify, or Full Control permission.

- All users can restore files and folders for which they have the Write, Modify, or Full Control permission.

- Members of the Administrators and Backup Operators groups can back up and restore all files (regardless of the assigned permissions). By default, members of these groups have the Backup Files and Directories and Restore Files and Directories user rights.

Planning Issues for Backups

You should plan your backup jobs to fit the needs of your company. The primary goal of backing up data is to be able to restore that data if necessary, so any backup plan that you develop should incorporate how you restore data. You should be able to quickly and successfully restore critical lost data. There is no single correct backup plan for all networks.

Consider the following issues in formulating your backup plan.

Determine Which Files and Folders to Back Up

Always back up critical files and folders that your company needs to operate, such as sales and financial records, the registry for each server, and if you are in a domain, the directory service files based on Microsoft Active Directory service.

Determine How Often to Back Up

If data is critical for company operations, back it up daily. If users create or modify reports once a week, backing up the reports weekly is sufficient. You only need to back up data as often as it changes. For example, there is no need to do daily backups on files that rarely change, such as monthly reports or the Windows XP Professional operating system files.

Determine Which Target Media to Use for Storing Backup Data

With the Backup Utility, you can back up to the following removable media:

- **Files.**   You can store the files on a removable media device, such as an Iomega Zip drive, or on a network location, such as a file server. The file that is created has a .bkf extension and contains the files and folders that you have selected to back up. Users can back up their personal data to a network server. Use this only for temporary backup jobs.

- **Tape.**   A less expensive medium than other removable media, a tape is more convenient for large backup jobs because of its high storage capacity. However, tapes have a limited life and can deteriorate. Be sure that you check the manufacturer's recommendations for usage.

Note   If you use a removable media device to back up and restore data, be sure that you verify that the device is supported on the Windows XP Professional Hardware Compatibility List (HCL).

Determine Whether to Perform Network or Local Backup Jobs

A network backup can contain data from multiple network computers. This allows you to consolidate backup data from multiple computers to a single removable backup medium. A network backup also allows one administrator to back up the entire network. Whether you perform a network or local backup job depends on the data that must be backed up. For example, you can only back up the registry and Active Directory at the computer where you are performing the backup.

If you decide to perform local backups, you must perform a local backup at each computer, including servers and client computers. There are several issues to consider for performing local backups. First of all, you must move from computer to computer so that you can perform a backup at each computer, or you must rely on users to back up their own computers. Most users fail to back up their data on a regular basis. A second consideration with local backups is the number of removable storage media devices. If you use removable storage media devices, such as tape drives, you must have one for each computer, or you must move the tape drive from computer to computer so that you can perform a local backup on each computer.

You might also choose to use a combination of network and local backup jobs. Do this when critical data resides on client computers and servers and you do not have a removable storage media device for each computer. In this situation, users should perform a local backup and store their backup files on a server. You then back up the server.

Selecting the Type of Backup Operation

The Backup Utility provides five types of backup operations that define what data is backed up, such as only those files that have changed since the last backup (see Figure 16.2).

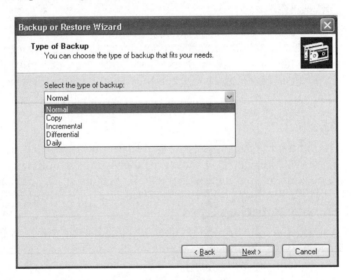

Figure 16.2   Available types of backup

Some backup types use backup *markers*, also known as archive attributes, which mark a file as having changed. When a file changes, an attribute is set on the file that indicates that the file has changed since the last backup. When you back up the file, this clears or resets the attribute.

Normal

During a *normal* backup, all selected files and folders are backed up. A normal backup does not rely on markers to determine which files to back up. During a normal backup any existing marks are cleared and each file is marked as having been backed up. Normal backups speed up the restore process because the backup files are the most current and you do not need to restore multiple backup jobs.

Copy

During a *copy* backup, all selected files and folders are backed up. It neither looks for nor clears markers. If you do not want to clear markers and affect other backup types, use a copy backup. For example, use a copy backup between a normal and an incremental backup to create an archival snapshot of network data.

Incremental

During an *incremental* backup, only selected files and folders that have a marker are backed up, and then the backup clears markers. Because an incremental backup clears markers, if you did two consecutive incremental backups on a file and nothing changed in the file, the file would not be backed up the second time.

Differential

During a *differential* backup, only selected files and folders that have a marker are backed up, but the backup does not clear markers. Because a differential backup does not clear markers, if you did two consecutive differential backups on a file and nothing changed in the file, the entire file would be backed up each time.

Daily

During a *daily* backup, all selected files and folders that have changed during the day are backed up. This backup neither looks for nor clears markers. If you want to back up all files and folders that change during the day, use a daily backup.

Combining Backup Types

An effective backup strategy is likely to combine different backup types. Some backup types require more time to back up data but less time to restore data. Conversely, other backup types require less time to back up data but more time to restore data. If you combine backup types, markers are critical. Incremental and differential backups check for and rely on the markers.

The following are some examples of combining different backup types:

- **Normal and differential backups.**   On Monday a normal backup is performed, and on Tuesday through Friday differential backups are performed. Differential backups do not clear markers, which means that each backup includes all changes since Monday. If data becomes corrupt on Friday, you only need to restore the normal backup from Monday and the differential backup from Thursday. This strategy takes more time to back up but less time to restore.

- **Normal and incremental backups.** On Monday a normal backup is performed, and on Tuesday through Friday incremental backups are performed. Incremental backups clear markers, which means that each backup includes only the files that changed since the previous backup. If data becomes corrupt on Friday, you need to restore the normal backup from Monday and all incremental backups, from Tuesday through Friday. This strategy takes less time to back up but more time to restore.

- **Normal, differential, and copy backups.** This strategy is the same as the first example that used normal and differential backups, except that on Wednesday you perform a copy backup. Copy backups include all selected files and do not clear markers or interrupt the usual backup schedule. Therefore, each differential backup includes all changes since Monday. The copy backup done on Wednesday is not part of the Friday restore. Copy backups are helpful when you need to create a snapshot of your data.

Changing Windows Default Backup Options

The Backup Utility allows you to change the default settings for all backup and restore jobs. These default settings are in the tabs in the Options dialog box. To access the Options dialog box, in the Welcome To The Backup Or Restore Wizard page, click Advanced Mode, then on the Tools menu, click Options.

The following list provides an overview of the settings for the Backup Utility:

- **General tab.** These settings affect data verification, the status information for backup and restore jobs, alert messages, and what is backed up. Figure 16.3 shows the default settings for the options in the General tab. You should select the Verify Data After The Backup Completes check box because it is critical that your backup data is not corrupt.

- **Restore tab.** These settings affect what happens when the file to restore is identical to an existing file. Figure 16.4 shows the available settings; the default setting is selected.

- **Backup Type tab.** These settings affect the default backup type when you perform a backup job. The settings you select depend on how often you back up, how quickly you want to restore, and how much storage space you have. The backup types are Normal (which is the default), Copy, Differential, Incremental, and Daily.

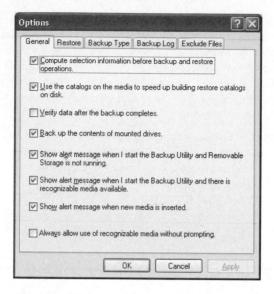

Figure 16.3   The General tab of the Backup Utility's Options dialog box

- **Backup Log tab.**   These settings affect the amount of information that is included in the backup log. The default setting is Summary, which logs key operations such as loading the tape, starting the backup, or failing to open a file. Two additional settings are available: Detailed, which logs all information, including the names of the files and folders; and None, which turns off logging.

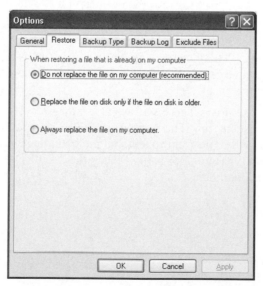

Figure 16.4   The Restore tab of the Backup Utility's Options dialog box

- **Exclude Files tab.**   These settings affect which files are excluded from backup jobs.

You can modify some default settings in the Backup or Restore Wizard for a specific backup job. For example, the default backup type is normal, but you can change it to another backup type in the Backup or Restore Wizard. However, the next time that you run the Backup or Restore Wizard, the default backup type (normal) is selected.

Lesson Review

The following questions will help you determine whether you have learned enough to move on to the next lesson. If you have difficulty answering these questions, review the material in this lesson before beginning the next lesson. The answers for these questions are in Appendix A, "Questions and Answers."

1. How do you access the Backup or Restore Wizard?

2. What two operations can you perform using the Backup or Restore Wizard?

3. What is the primary goal of backing up data?

4. If you want to perform a backup but do not want to clear markers or affect other backup types, you should perform a _____ backup.

5. During a _____ backup, only selected files and folders that have a marker are backed up, but the backup does not clear markers. If you performed two of these backups in a row on a file and nothing changed in the file, the entire file would be backed up each time.

6. How can you change the default settings for backup and restores for all backup and restore operations using the Backup Utility?

7. You performed a normal backup on Monday. For the remaining days of the week, you only want to back up files and folders that have changed since the previous day. What backup type do you select? Why?

Lesson Summary

- The efficient recovery (restoring) of lost data is the goal of all backup jobs.
- The Backup or Restore Wizard allows you to easily back up and restore data.
- The Backup or Restore Wizard allows you to back up data manually or to schedule unattended backup jobs on a regular basis.
- The Backup or Restore Wizard provides five types of backup: normal, copy, differential, incremental, and daily.
- The Backup Utility has default settings that apply to all backup and restore operations.
- The tabs in the Options dialog box for the Backup Utility allow you to change the default settings for the Backup Utility.

Lesson 2: Backing Up Data

After you have planned your backup, including planning the type of backup to use and when to perform backup jobs, the next step is to prepare to back up your data. There are certain preliminary tasks that must be completed before you can back up your data. After completing these tasks, you can perform a backup or schedule an unattended backup.

After this lesson, you will be able to

- Back up data at a computer and over the network
- Schedule a backup job
- Set backup options for the Backup Utility

Estimated lesson time: 50 minutes

Performing Preliminary Tasks

An important part of each backup job is performing the preliminary tasks, which includes ensuring that the files that you want to back up are closed. You should notify users to close files before you begin backing up data. You can use e-mail or the Send Console Message dialog box in the Computer Management snap-in to send administrative messages to users.

You can send a console message as follows:

1. On the Start menu, right-click My Computer, and then click Manage.
2. On the Action menu, click All Tasks, and then click Send Console Message.

   The Send Console Message dialog box appears (see Figure 16.5).

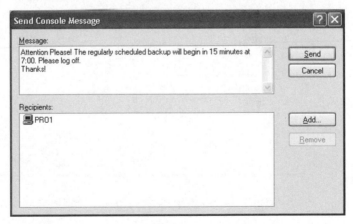

Figure 16.5   The Send Console Message dialog box

3. Type the desired message in the Message text box. Note the recipients in the Recipients box. You can add or remove recipients.

4. Click Send to send the message to the listed recipients.

If you use a removable media device, make sure that the following preliminary tasks are taken care of:

- The backup device is attached to a computer on the network and is turned on. If you are backing up to tape, you must attach the tape device to the computer on which you run the Backup Utility.

- The media device is listed on the Windows XP Professional HCL.

- The media is loaded in the media device. For example, if you are using a tape drive, ensure that a tape is loaded in the tape drive.

Selecting Files and Folders to Back Up

After you have completed the preliminary tasks, you are ready to perform the backup. You can use the Backup or Restore Wizard, shown in Figure 16.1. To start the Backup or Restore Wizard, click Start, point to All Programs, point to Accessories, point to System Tools, and then click Backup. Click Next to close the Welcome To The Backup Or Restore Wizard page. On the Backup Or Restore page, ensure that Back Up Files And Settings is selected, and click Next to display the What To Back Up page (see Figure 16.6).

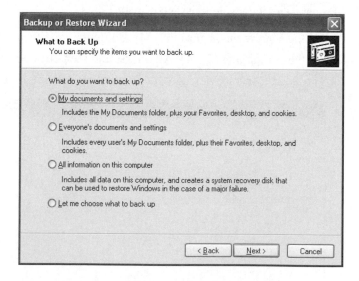

Figure 16.6   The What To Back Up page of the Backup or Restore Wizard

Specify what to back up by choosing one of the following options:

- **My Documents And Settings.**   Backs up the My Documents folder, along with the Favorites folder, desktop, and cookies of the current user. This is the default selection.

- **Everyone's Documents And Settings.**   Backs up the My Documents folder, along with the Favorites folders, desktop, and cookies of all users.

- **All Information On This Computer.**   Backs up all files on the computer on which you are running the Backup Utility, except those files that the Backup Utility excludes by default, such as certain power management files.

- **Let Me Choose What To Back Up.**   Backs up selected files and folders. This includes files and folders on the computer where you run the Backup Utility and any shared file or folder on the network. When you click this option, the Backup or Restore Wizard provides a hierarchical view of the computer and the network (through My Network Places).

Specifying Backup Destination, Media Settings, and Advanced Settings

After you select what you want to back up, you need to provide information about backup media. Table 16.1 describes the information that you must provide on the Backup Type, Destination, And Name page.

Table 16.1   Backup Type, Destination, And Name Page Options

Option	Description
Select The Backup Type	The target medium to use, such as a tape or file. A file can be located on any disk-based media, including a hard disk, a shared network folder, or a removable disk, such as an Iomega Zip drive.
Choose A Place To Save Your Backup	The location where the Backup Utility will store the data. For a tape, enter the tape name. For a file, enter the path for the backup file.
Type A Name For This Backup	The name of the backup. If it is a filename, the extension .bkf is appended automatically.

After you provide the media information, the Backup or Restore Wizard displays the Completing The Backup Or Restore Wizard page and you have the opportunity to do either of the following:

- **Start the backup.**   If you click Finish, during the backup process, the Backup or Restore Wizard displays status information about the backup job in the Backup Progress dialog box.

- **Specify advanced backup options.**   If you click Advanced, the Backup or Restore Wizard allows you to select the advanced backup settings listed in Table 16.2.

Table 16.2   Advanced Backup Settings

Advanced option	Description
Select The Type Of Backup	Allows you to choose the backup type that is used for this backup job. Select one of the following types: normal, copy, incremental, differential, or daily.
Verify Data After Backup	Confirms that files are correctly backed up. The Backup Utility compares the backup data and the source data to verify that they are the same. This option is recommended.
Use Hardware Compression, If Available	Enables hardware compression for tape devices that support it. If your tape device does not support hardware compression, this option is unavailable.
Disable Volume Shadow Copy	Allows files to be backed up even though they are in the process of being written to. By default, the Backup Utility will use volume shadow copies because this checkbox is cleared.
If The Archive Media Already Contains Backups:	
Append This Backup To The Existing Backups	Choose this option to store multiple backup jobs on a storage device.
or	
Replace The Existing Backups	Choose this option if you do not need to save previous backup jobs and you only want to save the most recent backup data.
Allow Only The Owner And The Administrator Access To The Backup Data And Any Backups Appended To This Medium	Allows you to restrict who can gain access to the completed backup file or tape. This option is only available if you choose to replace an existing backup on a backup medium, rather than appending to the backup medium. If you back up the registry or Active Directory services, click this option to prevent others from getting copies of the backup job.
When To Backup	Allows you to specify Now or Later. If you select Later, you specify the job name and the start date. You can also set the schedule.

When you specify advanced backup settings that cover the backup media and characteristics of the backup job, you are changing the default backup settings for only the current backup job.

Depending on whether you chose to back up now or later, the Backup or Restore Wizard provides you with the opportunity to do either of the following:

- If you chose to finish the backup process, the Backup or Restore Wizard displays the Completing The Backup Or Restore Wizard settings and then presents the option to finish and immediately start the backup. During the backup, the wizard displays status information about the backup job.

■ If you chose to back up later, you are shown additional dialog boxes to
   schedule the backup process to occur later, as described in the next section.

Note When the backup process is complete, you can choose to review the
backup log, a text file that records backup operations. The backup log is stored
on the hard disk of the computer on which you are running the Backup Utility.

Scheduling Backup Jobs

Scheduling a backup job means that you can have an unattended backup job
occur when users are not at work and files are closed. You can also schedule
backup jobs to occur at regular intervals. To enable this, Windows XP Professional
integrates the Backup Utility with the Task Scheduler service.

You can schedule a backup as follows:

1. Click Later on the When To Back Up page of the Backup or Restore Wizard.

    Task Scheduler presents the Set Account Information dialog box, prompting
    you for your password. The user account must have the appropriate user
    rights and permissions to perform backup jobs.

2. Enter your password in the Password text box and Confirm Password text
    box, and then click OK.

    Task Scheduler displays the When To Back Up page. You must provide a
    name for the backup job, and by default, the wizard displays the present date
    and time for the start date.

3. Type the appropriate name in the Job Name text box.

4. Click Set Schedule to set a different start date and time. This selection causes
    Task Scheduler to display the Schedule Job dialog box.

    In the Schedule Job dialog box, you can set the date, time, and number of
    occurrences for the backup job to repeat, such as every Friday at 10:00 P.M.
    You can also display all of the scheduled tasks for the computer by selecting
    the Show Multiple Schedules check box. This helps prevent you from
    scheduling multiple tasks on the same computer at the same time.

    You can also click Advanced to schedule how long the backup can last and for
    how many days, weeks, months, or years you want this schedule to continue.

After you schedule the backup job and complete the Backup or Restore Wizard,
the Backup Utility places the backup job on the calendar in the Schedule Jobs tab
in Windows Backup. The backup job automatically starts at the time that you
specified.

Practice: Backing Up Files

In this practice, you use the Backup or Restore Wizard to back up some files to your hard disk. You then create a backup job to perform a backup operation at a later time by using Task Scheduler.

Exercise 1: Starting a Backup Job

In this exercise, you use the Backup or Restore Wizard to back up files to your hard disk.

▶ **To back up files using the Backup or Restore Wizard**

1. Log on as Fred or with an account that is a member of the Administrators group.

2. Click Start, point to All Programs, point to Accessories, point to System Tools, and then click Backup.

3. In the Welcome To The Backup Or Restore Wizard page, click Next.

   The Backup or Restore Wizard displays the Backup Or Restore page.

4. Ensure that Back Up Files And Settings is selected and click Next.

   The Backup or Restore Wizard displays the What To Back Up page, prompting you to choose the scope of the backup job.

5. Click Let Me Choose What To Back Up, and then click Next to continue.

   The Backup or Restore Wizard displays the Items To Back Up page, prompting you to select the local and network drives, folders, and files to be backed up.

6. Click the plus sign in front of My Computer to expand it, expand drive C, and then click C.

   Do not select drive C. There should not be a check mark in the check box in front of drive C.

7. In the details pane, select AUTOEXEC.BAT.

   There should be a check mark in the check box in front of the filename AUTOEXEC.BAT.

8. Click Next to continue.

   The Backup or Restore Wizard displays the Backup Type, Destination, And Name page.

Note If there is no tape drive connected to your computer, Select The Backup Type is set to File and is unavailable for you to change.

---

9. Ensure Select The Backup Type is set to File.

   The Choose A Place To Save Your Backup box is set to 3½ Floppy (A:) by default. The Type A Name For This Backup box is set to Backup by default.

10. For the Choose A Place To Save Your Backup box, click Browse.

11. In the Save As dialog box, click the down-pointing arrow at the end of the Save In text box and click Local Disk (C:).

12. In the File Name text box, type **backup1** and click Save.

> **Note**   You would not normally back up files from a drive to a file on that same drive, as is done in this exercise. You would normally back up data to a tape or to a file stored on another hard disk, removable disks (such as Iomega Zip and Jaz drives), or recordable compact discs or optical drives.

13. Click Next to continue.

    The Backup or Restore Wizard displays the Completing The Backup Or Restore Wizard page, prompting you to finish the wizard and begin the backup job or to specify advanced options.

14. Click Advanced to specify additional backup options.

    The Backup or Restore Wizard displays the Type Of Backup page, prompting you to select a backup type for this backup job.

15. Ensure that Normal is selected in the Select The Type Of Backup list box and click Next.

    The Backup or Restore Wizard displays the How To Back Up page.

16. Select the Verify Data After Backup check box to confirm that the files are correctly backed up.

> **Note**   If the Use Hardware Compression, If Available check box is unavailable, either you do not have a tape drive or your tape device does not support hardware compression.

17. Click Next.

    The Backup or Restore Wizard displays the Backup Options page.

18. Click Replace The Existing Backups.

19. Ensure that the Allow Only The Owner And The Administrator Access To The Backup Data And To Any Backups Appended To This Media check box is cleared, and then click Next.

    The Backup or Restore Wizard displays the When To Backup page.

20. Make sure that Now is selected, and then click Next.

    The Backup or Restore Wizard displays the Completing The Backup Or Restore Wizard page.

21. Review the options and settings that you selected for this backup job and then click Finish to start the backup job.

    The Backup Utility briefly displays the Selection Information dialog box, indicating the estimated amount of data for, and the time to complete, the backup job. Because of the speed of your computer and the small number of files to back up, you might not see this dialog box.

In the Backup Progress dialog box, the Backup Utility displays the status of the backup operation, statistics on estimated and actual amount of data being processed, the time that has elapsed, and the estimated time that remains for the backup operation.

▶   **To view the backup report**

1. When the Backup Progress dialog box indicates that the backup is complete, click Report.

   Notepad starts, displaying the backup report. The backup report contains key details about the backup operation, such as the time that it started and how many files were backed up.

2. Examine the report, and when you are finished, quit Notepad.

3. In the Backup Progress dialog box, click Close.

Exercise 2: Creating and Running an Unattended Backup Job

In this exercise, you create a backup job to perform a backup operation at a later time by using Task Scheduler.

▶   **To create a scheduled backup job**

1. Click Start, point to All Programs, point to Accessories, point to System Tools, and then click Backup.

2. In the Welcome To The Backup Or Restore Wizard page, click Next.

3. In the Select An Operation page, ensure that Back Up Files And Settings is selected and click Next.

4. In the What To Back Up page, click Let Me Choose What To Back Up, and then click Next to continue.

5. In the Items To Back Up page, expand My Computer, expand drive C, and then select the System Volume Information check box.

6. Click Next to continue.

7. In the Backup Type, Destination, And Name page, in the Choose A Place To Save Your Backup list box, select C:\.

8. In the Type A Name For This Backup text box, type **backup2**, and then click Next.

9. In the Completing The Backup Or Restore Wizard page, click Advanced to specify additional backup options.

10. In the Type Of Backup page, ensure that Normal is selected in the Select The Type Of Backup list box, and then click Next.

11. In the How To Back Up page, select the Verify Data After Backup check box, and then click Next.

12. In the Backup Options page, click Replace The Existing Backups.

13. Ensure that the Allow Only The Owner And The Administrator Access To The Backup Data And To Any Backups Appended To This Media check box is not selected, and then click Next.

14. In the When To Backup page, click Later.

    The Backup or Restore Wizard makes the Schedule Entry box available.

15. In the Job Name text box, type **Pro1 SysVolInfo Backup** and then click Set Schedule.

    The Backup or Restore Wizard displays the Schedule Job dialog box, prompting you to select the start time and schedule options for the backup job.

16. In the Schedule Task box, ensure that Once is selected, and in the Start Time text box, enter a time three minutes from the present time, and then click OK.

17. In the When To Back Up dialog box, click Next to continue.

    The Backup or Restore Wizard displays the Set Account Information dialog box.

    For purposes of this exercise, use the Administrator account to run the scheduled backup job.

18. Make sure that Pro1\Administrator appears in the Run As box (or the name of your computer, if it is not Pro1), and then type **password** in the Password text box and the Confirm Password text box.

19. Click OK.

    The Backup or Restore Wizard displays the Account Information Warning dialog box.

20. Click OK to continue.

21. Review the information on the Completing The Backup Or Restore Wizard page and then click Finish to schedule the backup job.

    When the time for the backup job is reached, the Backup Utility starts and performs the requested backup operation.

▶ **To verify that the backup job was performed**

1. Start Microsoft Windows Explorer and click drive C.

2. Verify that BACKUP2.BKF was created and you have confirmed that the backup occurred.

3. Log off Windows XP Professional.

Lesson Review

The following questions will help you determine whether you have learned enough to move on to the next lesson. If you have difficulty answering these questions, review the material in this lesson before beginning the next lesson. The answers for these questions are in Appendix A, "Questions and Answers."

1. What are the four choices in the What To Back Up page of the Backup or Restore Wizard and what does each choice allow you to do?

2. When should you select the Allow Only The Owner And The Administrator Access To The Backup Data And Any Backups Appended To This Media check box?

3. If your boss wants daily backups to occur at 1:00 A.M., what could you do to save yourself the trouble of having to go to the office each morning at 1:00 A.M. to do the backups?

4. If you don't have a tape drive, can you still perform backups? How?

5. Why should you e-mail or send a console message to users before you begin a backup?

Lesson Summary

- The Backup Utility allows you to back up everything on the computer; to specify selected files, drives, or network data; or to back up only the system state data.

- The Backup Utility allows you to provide the target destination and the backup media or filename.

- The Backup or Restore Wizard Advanced backup settings include the following options: selecting the type of backup operation to perform, verifying data after backup, using hardware compression, and scheduling the backup to run at a later time or to run at regularly scheduled times.

Lesson 3: Restoring Data

In this lesson you learn about restoring data. The ability to restore corrupt or lost data is critical to all corporations and is the goal of all backup jobs. To ensure that you can successfully restore data, you should follow certain guidelines, such as keeping thorough documentation on all of your backup jobs.

After this lesson, you will be able to

■ Restore data, whether an entire volume or a single file

Estimated lesson time: 30 minutes

Preparing to Restore Data

To restore data, you must select the backup sets, files, and folders to restore. You can also specify additional settings based on your restore requirements. The Backup or Restore Wizard helps you restore data.

When critical data is lost, you need to restore it quickly. Use the following guidelines to help prepare for restoring data:

■ Base your restore strategy on the backup type that you used for the backup. If time is critical when you are restoring data, your restore strategy must ensure that the backup types that you choose for backups expedite the restore process. For example, use normal and differential backups so that you only need to restore the last normal backup and the last differential backup.

■ Perform a trial restore periodically to verify that the Backup Utility is functioning correctly. A trial restore can uncover hardware problems that do not show up with software verifications. Restore the data to an alternate location, and then compare the restored data to the data on the original hard disk.

■ Keep documentation for each backup job. Create and print a detailed backup log for each backup job, containing a record of all files and folders that were backed up. By using the backup log, you can quickly locate which piece of media contains the files that you need to restore without having to load the catalogs. A *catalog* is an index of the files and folders from a backup job that Windows XP Professional automatically creates and stores with the backup job and on the computer running the Backup Utility.

■ Keep a record of multiple backup jobs in a calendar format that shows the days on which you perform the backup jobs. For each job, note the backup type and identify the storage that is used, such as a tape number or the name of the Iomega Zip disk. Then, if you need to restore data, you can easily review several weeks' worth of backup jobs to select which tape or disk to use.

Selecting Backup Sets, Files, and Folders to Restore

The first step in restoring data is to select the data to restore. You can select individual files and folders, an entire backup job, or a backup set, which is a collection of files or folders from one volume that you back up during a backup job. If you back up two volumes on a hard disk during a backup job, the job has two backup sets. You select the data to restore in the catalog.

To restore data, use the Restore Wizard, which you access through the Backup Utility, as follows:

1. In the Backup or Restore Wizard, in the Backup Or Restore page, select Restore Files And Settings and then click Next.

2. In the What To Restore page, expand the media type that contains the data that you want to restore. This can be either tape or file media.

3. Expand the appropriate media set until the data that you want to restore is visible. You can restore a backup set or specific files and folders.

4. Select the data that you want to restore, and then click Next.

   The Backup or Restore Wizard displays the settings for the restore.

5. Do one of the following:

   ■ Finish the restore process. If you choose to finish the restore job, during the restore, the Backup or Restore Wizard requests verification for the source of the restore media and then performs the restore. During the restore, the Backup or Restore Wizard displays status information about the restore.

   ■ Specify advanced restore options.

Specifying Advanced Restore Settings

The advanced settings in the Backup or Restore Wizard vary, depending on the type of backup media from which you are restoring, such as a tape device or an Iomega Zip drive. Table 16.3 describes the advanced restore options.

Table 16.3   Advanced Restore Settings

Option	Description
Restore Files To	The target location for the data that you are restoring. The choices are as follows:
	Original Location. Replaces corrupted or lost data.
	Alternate Location. Restores an older version of a file or does a practice restore.
	Single Folder. Consolidates the files from a tree structure into a single folder. For example, use this option if you want copies of specific files but do not want to restore the hierarchical structure of the files.

Table 16.3 *(continued)*

Option	Description
	If you select either an alternate location or a single directory, you must provide the path.
When Restoring Files That Already Exist On Your Computer	Whether you want to overwrite existing files. The choices are as follows:
	Leave Existing Files (Recommended). Prevents accidental overwriting of existing data. This setting is the default.
	Replace Existing Files If They Are Older Than The Backup Files. Verifies that the most recent copy exists on the computer.
	Replace Existing Files. The Backup Utility does not provide a confirmation message if it encounters a duplicate filename during the restore operation.
Select The Options You Want To Use	Whether you want to restore security or special system files. The choices are as follows:
	Restore Security Settings. Applies the original permissions to files that you are restoring to a Windows NT file system (NTFS) volume. Security settings include access permissions, audit entries, and ownership. This option is only available if you have backed up data from an NTFS volume and are restoring to an NTFS volume.
	Restore Junction Points, But Not The Folders And File Data They Reference. Restores junction points on your hard disk as well as the data that the junction points refer to. If you have any mounted drives, and you want to restore the data that mounted drives point to, select this check box. If you do not select this check box, the junction point is restored but the data your junction point refers to might not be accessible.
	Preserve Existing Volume Mount Points. Prevents the operation from writing over any volume mount points you have created on the partition or volume to which you are restoring data. This option is primarily applicable when you are restoring data to an entire drive or partition.

After you have finished the Backup or Restore Wizard, the Backup Utility does the following:

- Prompts you to verify your selection of the source media to use to restore data. After the verification, the Backup Utility starts the restore process.

- Displays status information about the restore process. As with a backup process, you can choose to view the report (restore log) of the restore. It contains information about the restore, such as the number of files that have been restored and the duration of the restore process.

Practice: Restoring Files

In this practice, you restore a file that you backed up in Exercise 1 in Lesson 2 of this chapter.

Important   To complete this practice, you must have completed the practice in the previous lesson, or you must have some files you have backed up using the Backup Utility that you can restore.

▶ **To restore files from a previous backup job**

1. Log on as Fred or with an account that is a member of the Administrators group.

2. Click Start, point to All Programs, point to Accessories, point to System Tools, and then click Backup.

3. In the Welcome To The Backup Or Restore Wizard page, click Next.

4. In the Backup Or Restore page, click Restore Files And Settings and then click Next.

   The Backup or Restore Wizard displays the What To Restore page.

5. In the What To Restore box, expand the File node that you created.

   Notice that Backup1 is listed.

6. Expand Backup1.

   Notice that drive C appears under Backup1.

7. Expand drive C.

8. Select drive C and then click Next.

   The Backup or Restore Wizard displays the Completing The Backup Or Restore Wizard page. Notice that the file is being restored to its original location and that the existing files are not to be replaced.

9. Click Advanced.

   The Backup or Restore Wizard displays the Where To Restore page.

10. In the Restore Files To list, select Alternate Location.

    The Backup or Restore Wizard displays the Alternate Location box.

11. In the Alternate Location text box, type **C:\Restored data** and then click Next.

    The Backup or Restore Wizard displays the How To Restore page, prompting you to specify how to process duplicate files during the restore job.

12. Make sure that Leave Existing Files (Recommended) is selected, and then click Next.

13. In the Advanced Restore Options page, ensure that all check boxes are cleared and then click Next.

14. Review the options you specified in the Completing The Backup Or Restore Wizard page, and then click Finish to begin the restore process.

    The Backup Utility displays the Check Backup File Location dialog box, prompting you to supply or verify the name of the backup file that contains the folders and files to be restored.

15. Make sure that the file BACKUP1.BKF is entered in the Please Verify This Is The Correct Location For The Backup text box, and then click OK.

    The Backup Utility displays the Selection Information dialog box, indicating the estimated amount of data for, and the time to complete, the restore job. (This dialog box may appear very briefly, because you are restoring only a single file.)

    The Backup Utility displays the Restore Progress dialog box, providing the status of the restore operation, statistics on estimated and actual amount of data that is being processed, the time that has elapsed, and the estimated time that remains for the restore operation.

▶ **To view the restore report**

1. When the Restore Progress dialog box indicates that the restore is complete, click Report.

   Notepad starts, displaying the report. Notice that the details about the restore operation are appended to the previous backup log. This provides a centralized location for viewing all status information for backup and restore operations.

2. Examine the report, and then exit Notepad.

3. In the Restore Progress dialog box, click Close.

▶ **To verify that the data was restored**

1. Start Windows Explorer and expand drive C.

2. Open Windows Explorer and verify that the Restored data folder exists and contains AUTOEXEC.

3. Close Windows Explorer.

Lesson Review

The following questions will help you determine whether you have learned enough to move on to the next lesson. If you have difficulty answering these questions, review the material in this lesson before beginning the next lesson. The answers for these questions are in Appendix A, "Questions and Answers."

1. What is a trial restore and why is it important that you perform it?

2. A _____ is an index of the files and folders from a backup job that Windows XP Professional automatically creates and stores with the backup job and on the computer running the Backup Utility.

3. What is a backup set?

4. If you back up two volumes on a hard disk during a backup job, how many backup sets are created for the job?

5. What are the three Advanced restore settings that allow you to specify how to restore files that already exist?

6. When do you use the Advanced restore setting Restore Security and when is it available?

Lesson Summary

- The Backup or Restore Wizard helps you restore data as well as back up data.
- The Backup Utility allows you to restore individual files and folders, an entire backup job, or a backup set.
- The Backup Utility's advanced settings for restoring data vary depending on the type of backup media from which you are restoring.

Lesson 4: Using the Automated System Recovery Wizard

In this lesson you learn how to use the Automated System Recovery Wizard, which helps you back up your system partition so that you can restore it in case it is lost or damaged because of some type of disaster.

After this lesson, you will be able to

- Understand how to use the Automated System Recovery Wizard

Estimated lesson time: 15 minutes

Using the Automated System Recovery Wizard

The Backup Utility provides access to the Automated System Recovery Wizard. To access the Automated System Recovery Wizard, click Start, point to Accessories, point to System Tools, and then click Backup. In the Welcome To The Backup Or Restore Wizard page, click Advanced Mode. The Automated System Recovery Wizard is one of the three wizards provided by the Backup Utility (see Figure 16.7).

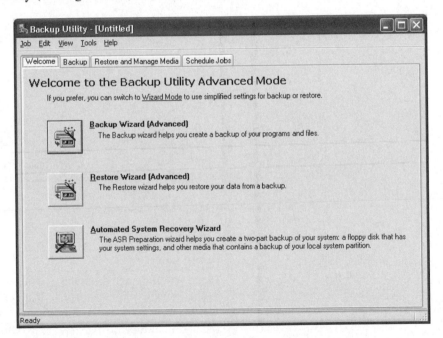

Figure 16.7   The Backup Utility Advanced Mode window

The Automated System Recovery Wizard creates a floppy disk, which contains your system settings, and a backup of your local system partition on tape or as a file located on a network server.

To back up your system partition, do the following:

1. In the Advanced Mode window of the Backup Utility, click Automated System Recovery Wizard.

   The Backup Utility displays the Welcome To The Automated System Recovery Preparation Wizard page.

2. Click Next to continue.

   The Automated System Recovery Wizard begins and displays the Backup Destination page (see Figure 16.8). The options on the Backup Destination page are explained in Table 16.4.

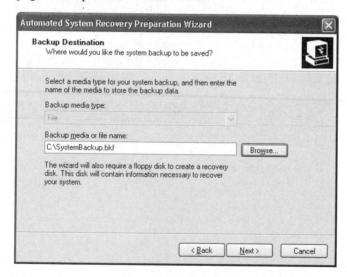

Figure 16.8   The Backup Destination page

Table 16.4   Backup Destination

Option	Description
Backup Media Type	The target medium to use, such as a tape or file. A file can be located on any disk-based media, including a hard disk, a shared network folder, or a removable disk, such as an Iomega Zip disk.
Backup Media Or File Name	The location where the Backup Utility will store the data. For a tape, enter the tape name. For a file, enter the path for the backup file.

3. Select the appropriate media type and backup media name or filename, and then click Next.

   The Automated System Recovery Wizard verifies the information you entered and displays the Completing The Automated System Recovery Preparation Wizard page.

4. Review the information on the Completing The Automated System Recovery Preparation Wizard page, and then click Next.

   The Automated System Recovery Wizard makes a backup of your system files. This could take an hour or more.

5. When prompted, insert a floppy disk in your floppy disk drive.

6. When the backup completes, click Report to read the report. When you finish reviewing the report, close Notepad.

7. Click Close to close the Backup Progress dialog box, and then close the Backup Utility.

If you need to restore your system partition, you can use the floppy disk created by the Automated System Recovery Wizard. The backup of your local system partition on tape or as a file must be available to be restored. You would then use the Backup or Restore Wizard to restore your data and applications.

Lesson Review

The following questions will help you determine whether you have learned enough to move on to the next lesson. If you have difficulty answering these questions, review the material in this lesson before beginning the next chapter. The answers for these questions are in Appendix A, "Questions and Answers."

1. What four wizards does the Backup Utility provide access to?

2. What two things does the Automated System Recovery Wizard create during a backup?

3. What two pieces of information do you have to supply to the Automated System Recovery Wizard?

Lesson Summary

- The Automated System Recovery Wizard helps you back up your system partition so that you can restore it in case of an emergency.

- The Automated System Recovery Wizard creates a floppy disk, which contains your system settings and a backup of your local system partition on tape or as a file.

- The target medium to use can be a tape or file located on any disk-based media, including a hard disk, a shared network folder, or a removable disk, such as an Iomega Zip disk.

CHAPTER 17

Configuring Network and Internet Connections

About This Chapter

Microsoft Windows XP Professional provides many new features to simplify the configuration of network and Internet connections for home and small business environments. In this chapter you learn about the New Connection Wizard, which guides you through creating network and Internet connections. You also learn about Internet Connection Firewall (ICF), which protects your network from attack; Internet Connection Sharing (ICS), which allows you to share one connection to the Internet with all computers on your network; and Network Bridge, which allows you to connect local area network (LAN) segments. Finally, you are introduced to the Network Setup Wizard, which helps you configure and set up your network.

Before You Begin

To complete this chapter, you must have

- A computer that meets the minimum hardware requirements listed in the preface, "About This Book"
- Windows XP Professional installed on the computer

Lesson 1: Configuring Inbound Connections

In Windows XP Professional, all of the processes for creating network connections are consolidated in the New Connection Wizard. Inbound connections are one of the types of network connections created using the New Connection Wizard.

After this lesson, you will be able to

- Configure inbound connections in Windows XP Professional
- Configure Remote Access to allow incoming virtual private network (VPN) connections

Estimated lesson time: 30 minutes

Allowing Incoming Dial-Up Connections

To configure and administer inbound connections on a computer running Windows XP Professional, you use the New Connection Wizard. To access the New Connection Wizard, click Start, click My Computer, click My Network Places, click View Network Connections, and then click Create A New Connection. Windows XP Professional displays the Welcome To The New Connection Wizard page. Click Next to continue, and Windows XP Professional displays the Network Connection Type page. To configure an inbound connection, click Set Up An Advanced Connection and then click Next. The New Connection Wizard displays the Advanced Connection Options page (see Figure 17.1).

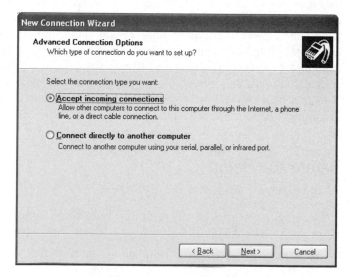

Figure 17.1   The Advanced Connection Options page

On the Advanced Connection Options page, click Accept Incoming Connections and then click Next to display the Devices For Incoming Connection page.

Configuring Devices for Incoming Connections

The Devices For Incoming Connections page allows you to choose one of the available devices on your computer to accept incoming calls. If the device you select is configurable, click Properties to configure it. For example, if you have selected a modem, possible options to configure in the device's Properties dialog box include port speed, error correction, use of compression, and the type flow control (see Figure 17.2). The Advanced tab contains additional configurable options, which might include the number of data bits, the parity, the number of stop bits, and the modulation type.

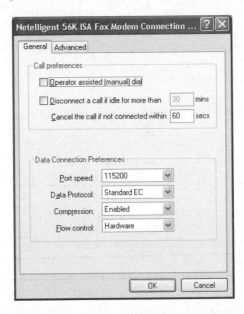

Figure 17.2   The General tab of the Properties dialog box for a modem

Allowing VPN Connections

When you are through configuring the device, click OK to close the Properties dialog box and then click Next in the Devices For Incoming Connection page. The New Connection Wizard displays the Incoming Virtual Private Network (VPN) Connection page. If you click Allow Virtual Private Connections, Windows XP Professional modifies the ICF so that your computer can send and receive VPN packets. Select the option either to allow or not allow VPN connections, and then click Next.

Note   For more information on ICF, see Lesson 3 of this chapter, "Enabling and Configuring Home and Small Business Components."

Specifying User Permissions and Callback Options

You must specify which users can use this inbound connection in the User Permissions page (see Figure 17.3).

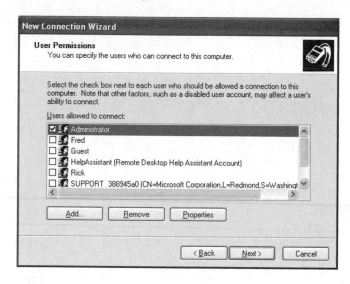

Figure 17.3   The User Permissions page

After you select a user, click Properties. In the *user-name* Properties dialog box, click the Callback tab to set the callback options. You can choose Do Not Allow Callback, Allow The Caller To Set The Callback Number, or Always Use The Following Callback Number. Enabling callback causes the remote server, in this case your computer, to disconnect from the client calling in, and then to call the client computer back. By using callback, you can have the bill for the phone call charged to the office phone number rather than to the phone number of the user who called in. Callback can also be used to increase security because if you specify the callback number you don't have to worry about someone trying to break in. Even if an unauthorized user calls in, the system calls back at the number you specified, not the number of the unauthorized user.

Selecting Networking Software

After you specify the callback options, click Next. The New Connection Wizard displays the Networking Software page. You can choose the networking software you want to enable for incoming connections. You can also install additional networking software by clicking Install. For example, to install NWLink IP/SPX/ NetBIOS Compatible Transport Protocol, click Install, select Protocol, and then click Add. On the Select Network Protocol page, select NWLink IP/SPX/ NetBIOS Compatible Transport Protocol, insert the Windows XP Professional CD-ROM in the CD-ROM drive, and then click OK. Windows XP Professional installs the protocol. After the protocol is installed, you are returned to the Networking Components page. When you click Next, you will be prompted to type a name for the connection, and then click Finish. If you would like a shortcut to appear on your desktop, select the Add A Shortcut To My Desktop check box. Click Finish to create the connection.

Practice: Configuring an Inbound Connection

In this practice, you use the New Connection Wizard to configure an inbound connection.

▶ **To configure an inbound connection**

1. Log on as Fred or with an account that is a member of the Administrators group.

2. On the Start menu, click My Computer, click My Network Places, and then click View Network Connections.

    Windows XP Professional displays the Network Connections window.

3. Click Create A New Connection.

    Windows XP Professional starts the New Connection Wizard.

4. In the Welcome To The New Connection Wizard page, click Next.

    The New Connection Wizard displays the Network Connection Type page.

5. Select Set Up An Advanced Connection, and then click Next.

    The New Connection Wizard displays the Advanced Connection Options page.

6. Ensure that Accept Incoming Connections is selected, and then click Next.

    The New Connection Wizard displays the Devices For Incoming Connections page.

7. Select the modem device option for your computer in the Connection Devices list, and then click Next.

Note If you do not have a modem, select Direct Parallel.

The New Connection Wizard displays the Incoming Virtual Private Network (VPN) Connection page.

8. Ensure that Allow Virtual Private Connections is selected, and then click Next.

    The New Connection Wizard displays the User Permissions page.

9. Select Administrator, and then click Properties.

    The New Connection Wizard displays the Administrator Properties dialog box with the General tab selected.

10. Click the Callback tab.

    The New Connection Wizard displays the Callback tab of the Administrator Properties dialog box.

11. Review the callback options, leave the default setting of Do Not Allow Callback, and then click OK.

12. In the User Permissions page, click Next.

    The New Connection Wizard displays the Networking Software page.

13. Review the available networking components, click Internet Protocol (TCP/IP), and then click Properties.

    The New Connection Wizard displays the Incoming TCP/IP dialog box.

14. Select Specify TCP/IP Addresses.

15. In the From text box, type **192.168.1.201**, and in the To text box, type **192.168.1.205**, and then click OK.

Note   If your computer is on a network and there is a valid address that you can use to test your inbound connection, use a range that includes that address.

---

16. In the Networking Software page, click Next.

    The New Connection Wizard displays the Completing The New Connection Wizard page. The name assigned to the connection is Incoming Connections.

17. Click Finish.

    Notice that Incoming Connections now appears in the Network Connections window.

Lesson Review

The following questions will help you determine whether you have learned enough to move on to the next lesson. If you have difficulty answering these questions, review the material in this lesson before beginning the next lesson. The answers are in Appendix A, "Questions and Answers."

1. The Network Connection Type page of the New Connection Wizard has four selections. What are the four selections and which selection do you use to allow inbound dial-up connections?

2. Other than allowing VPN connections, what does Windows XP Professional do when you configure a new connection to allow virtual private connections?

3. What is callback and why would you enable it?

Lesson Summary

- You configure inbound connections in Windows XP Professional with the New Connection Wizard.
- You can choose which of the available devices on your computer you will allow to accept incoming calls in the Devices For Incoming Connections page of the New Connection Wizard, and if the device you select is configurable, click Properties to configure it.
- You must specify which user accounts can use the inbound connections you configure using the New Connection Wizard.
- You can specify whether or not to allow callback for each user account.
- You can specify whether the caller should indicate the callback number or whether you want to set it.

Lesson 2: Configuring Outbound Connections

You can configure all outbound connections in Windows XP Professional with the New Connection Wizard. Much of the work of configuring protocols and services is automated when you use this process. Understanding the options found in this wizard will help you configure connections efficiently.

There are three outbound connection selections that you can configure using the New Connection Wizard:

- Connect To The Internet
- Connect To The Network At My Workplace
- Set Up An Advanced Connection

After this lesson, you will be able to

- Configure outbound connections in Windows XP Professional

Estimated lesson time: 30 minutes

Connect To The Internet

To connect to the Internet, use the New Connection Wizard. To access the New Connection Wizard, click Start, click My Computer, click My Network Places, click View Network Connections, and then click Create A New Connection. The Welcome To The New Connection Wizard appears. Click Next to continue and proceed to the Network Connection Type page (see Figure 17.4).

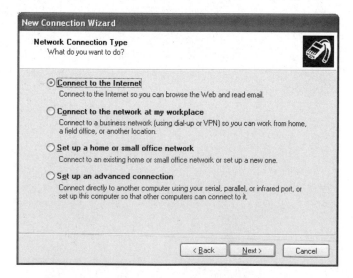

Figure 17.4   The Network Connection Type page

If you want to connect to the Internet, select Connect To The Internet on the Network Connection Type page and click Next. The New Connection Wizard displays the Getting Ready page, which has the following three options:

- Choose From A List Of Internet Service Providers (ISPs)
- Set Up My Connection Manually
- Use The CD I Got From An ISP

Choose From A List Of Internet Service Providers (ISPs)

If you select Choose From A List Of Internet Service Providers (ISPs) on the Getting Ready page, and then click Next, the New Connection Wizard displays the Completing The New Connection Wizard page. You can select Set Up Internet Access Using MSN Explorer (U.S. Only) or Select From A List Of Other ISPs. When you have made your selection, click Finish.

Set Up My Connection Manually

If you select Set Up My Connection Manually on the Getting Ready page, and then click Next, the New Connection Wizard displays the Internet Connection page. The following three options are available in the Internet Connection page:

- **Connect Using A Dial-Up Modem.**   Select this option if your connection uses a modem and a regular or Integrated Services Digital Network (ISDN) phone line. If you select Connect Using A Dial-Up Modem and click Next, you are prompted to enter the information in Table 17.1.

Table 17.1   Connect Using A Dial-Up Modem

New Connection Wizard page	Description
Connection Name	The name of your ISP is typically used as the connection name for dial-up connections to the Internet.
Phone Number To Dial	The phone number you use to connect to your ISP.
Internet Account Information	You will be prompted to enter the ISP account name and password. You can select or clear the following three check boxes: ■ Use The Account Name And Password When Anyone Connects To The Internet From This Computer ■ Make This The Default Internet Connection ■ Turn On Internet Connection Firewall For This Connection (for more information on ICF, see Lesson 3 later in this chapter, "Enabling and Configuring Home and Small Business Components")

When you have entered the information on each of the pages listed in Table 17.1, the New Connection Wizard displays the Completing The New Connection Wizard page, which displays a summary of the information you entered to manually create a connection to the Internet. If you would like a shortcut to appear on your desktop, select the Add A Shortcut To This Connection To My Desktop check box. Click Finish to create the connection.

- **Connect Using A Broadband Connection That Requires A User And Password.**   Select this option if your high-speed connection uses either a Digital Subscriber Line (DSL) or cable modem. This type of connection is also known as Point-to-Point Protocol over Ethernet (PPPoE). If you select Connect Using A Broadband Connection That Requires A User And Password and click Next, you are also prompted to enter the information in Table 17.1.

- **Connect Using A Broadband Connection That Is Always On.**   Select this option if your high-speed connection uses a cable modem, DSL, or LAN connection. If you select Connect Using A Broadband Connection That Is Always On, the New Connection Wizard displays the Completing The New Connection Wizard page because the connection should already be configured and working.

Use The CD I Got From An ISP

If you select Use The CD I Got From An ISP on the Getting Ready page, and then click Next, the New Connection Wizard displays the Completing The New Connection Wizard page. You are instructed to click Finish and then insert the CD-ROM you received from your ISP. The setup program on the CD-ROM should start automatically to assist you in connecting to the Internet.

Connect To The Network At My Workplace

If you want to connect to a private network, select Connect To The Network At My Workplace on the Network Connection Type page and click Next. The New Connection Wizard displays the Network Connection page, which has the following two options:

- Dial-Up Connection
- Virtual Private Network Connection

Dial-Up Connection

Select this option if you want to connect to the network at your office using a modem and phone line or an ISDN phone line. If you select Dial-Up Connection and click Next, you are prompted to enter the information in Table 17.2.

Table 17.2   Dial-Up Connection Information

New Connection Wizard page	Description
Connection Name	The name of your company or the name of the server to which you will be connecting is typically used as the connection name for dial-up connections when you are connecting to a private network.
Phone Number To Dial	The phone number used to make the connection.

When you have entered the information on each of the pages listed in Table 17.2, the New Connection Wizard displays the Completing The New Connection Wizard page, which displays a summary of the information you entered to create the connection. If you would like a shortcut to appear on your desktop, select the Add A Shortcut To The Connection To My Desktop check box. Click Finish to create the connection.

Virtual Private Network Connection

Select this option if you want to connect to the network at your office using a VPN connection over the Internet. If you select Virtual Private Network Connection and click Next, you are prompted to enter the information in Table 17.3.

Table 17.3   Virtual Private Network Connection Information

New Connection Wizard page	Description
Connection Name	The name of your company or the name of the server to which you will be connecting is typically used as the connection name.
VPN Server Selection	The host name or Internet Protocol (IP) address of the VPN server to which you are connecting.

When you have entered the information on each of the pages listed in Table 17.3, the New Connection Wizard displays the Completing The New Connection Wizard page, which displays a summary of the information you entered to create the connection. If you would like a shortcut to appear on your desktop, select the Add A Shortcut To The Connection To My Desktop check box. Click Finish to create the connection.

Set Up An Advanced Connection

Select this option to connect directly to another computer using a serial, parallel, or infrared port or to set up this computer so that other computers can connect to it. If you select Set Up An Advanced Connection, the New Connection Wizard displays the Advanced Connection Options page (see Figure 17.1). There are two options in the Advanced Connection Options page:

- **Accept Incoming Connections.** This option allows you to configure and administer inbound connections on a computer running Windows XP Professional. For more information about this option, see Lesson 1, "Configuring Inbound Connections," earlier in this chapter.

- **Connect Directly To Another Computer.** This option allows you to create a direct cable connection to another computer. If you select this option and click Next, you must provide the information in Table 17.4.

Table 17.4   Connect Directly To Another Computer

New Connection Wizard page	Description
Host Or Guest	Select Host if your computer contains information that other computers will access; select Guest if your computer will be accessing information on a computer configured as a host.
Connection Device	Select the device you want to use to make this connection. Possible choices include Direct Parallel (LPT1), Communications Port (COM1), and Communications Port (COM2).
User Permissions	Select the users who can connect to this computer.

When you have entered the information on each of the pages listed in Table 17.4, the New Connection Wizard displays the Completing The New Connection Wizard page, which displays a summary of the information you entered to create the connection. If you would like a shortcut to appear on your desktop, select the Add A Shortcut To The Connection To My Desktop check box. Click Finish to create the connection.

Practice: Configuring an Outbound Connection

In this practice, you use the New Connection Wizard to configure an outbound connection to a private network.

▶   **To configure an outbound connection**

1. Log on as Fred or with an account that is a member of the Administrators group.

2. On the Start menu, click My Computer, click My Network Places, click View Network Connections, and then click Create A New Connection.

   Windows XP Professional starts the New Connection Wizard.

3. In the Welcome To The New Connection Wizard page, click Next.

   The New Connection Wizard displays the Network Connection Type page.

4. Click Connect To The Network At My Workplace, and then click Next.

   The New Connection Wizard displays the Network Connection page.

5. Click Virtual Private Network Connection and then click Next.

   The New Connection Wizard displays the Connection Name page.

6. In the Company Name text box, type **Work** and then click Next.

   The New Connection Wizard displays the Public Network page.

7. Ensure that Do Not Dial The Initial Connection is selected, and then click Next.

   The New Connection Wizard displays the VPN Server Selection page.

8. In the Host Name Or IP Address text box, type **192.168.1.202** and then click Next.

Note   If your computer is on a network and there is a valid address that you can use to test your outbound connection, use that address instead of 192.168.1.202.

   The New Connection Wizard displays the Completing The New Connection Wizard page.

9. Review the information summary and then click Finish.

   Windows XP Professional displays the Connect Work dialog box.

10. In the User Name text box, type **Administrator** and type **password** for the password.

Note   If your computer is on a network and you entered a valid IP address in Step 8, enter a valid user name and password in Step 10.

---

11. Click Connect.

Note   If your computer is a stand-alone computer, this operation will fail. If your computer is on a network and you entered a valid address in Step 8 and a valid user name and password in Step 10, a message will be displayed indicating that a connection has been made.

---

12. If your connection failed, click Cancel. If you connected successfully to another computer, double-click the connection icon in the system tray, click Disconnect, and then click Yes.

13. Close all windows and log off.

Lesson Review

The following questions will help you determine whether you have learned enough to move on to the next lesson. If you have difficulty answering these questions, review the material in this lesson before beginning the next lesson. The answers are in Appendix A, "Questions and Answers."

1. What are the three outbound connection selections that you can configure using the New Connection Wizard, and what does each allow you to do?

2. How can you configure a direct connection to another computer?

3. Using the New Connection Wizard to create an outgoing connection to the network at your office, how can you have a shortcut appear on your desktop for easy access to the connection?

Lesson Summary

- You can configure all outbound connections in Windows XP Professional with the New Connection Wizard.

- You can choose from a list of ISPs, configure your connection to the Internet manually, or use a CD-ROM provided by your ISP when using the New Connection Wizard to connect to the Internet.

- You can manually configure a connection to the Internet using a modem and a regular or ISDN phone line by selecting Connect Using A Dial-Up Modem.

- You can configure a connection to a private network using a dial-up connection or a virtual private network (VPN) connection over the Internet.

- You can create a direct cable connection to another computer by selecting Set Up An Advanced Connection and then selecting Connect Directly To Another Computer.

- You can create a shortcut on your desktop for any connection you create using the New Connection Wizard by selecting the Add A Shortcut To The Connection To My Desktop check box in the Completing the New Connection Wizard page of the New Connection Wizard.

Lesson 3: Enabling and Configuring Home and Small Business Components

In this lesson you learn how to enable and configure some of the home and small business components in Windows XP Professional. These features include ICF, ICS, and Network Bridge.

After this lesson, you will be able to

- Enable and configure ICF
- Enable and configure ICS
- Enable and configure Network Bridge

Estimated lesson time: 45 minutes

Enabling and Configuring Internet Connection Firewall

A firewall protects a network against external threats from another network, including the Internet. Firewalls prevent an organization's networked computers from communicating directly with computers that are external to the network and prevent computers external to the network from communicating directly with the computers in the organization's network. All incoming and outgoing communication is routed through a proxy server outside the organization's network. Firewalls also audit network activity, recording the volume of traffic and information about attempts to gain unauthorized access. ICF is firewall software that is used to set restrictions on what information is communicated from your home or small business network to and from the Internet.

To enable and configure ICF, do the following:

1. On the Start menu, click My Computer, click My Network Places, and then click View Network Connections.

   Windows XP Professional displays the Network Connections window.

2. Click the dial-up, LAN, or high-speed Internet connection that you want to protect.

3. Under Network Tasks, click Change Settings Of This Connection.

4. In the Advanced tab, select the Protect My Computer And Network By Limiting Or Preventing Access To This Computer From The Internet check box.

Note   To disable ICF, clear the Protect My Computer And Network By Limiting Or Preventing Access To This Computer From The Internet check box.

---

5. To configure ICF, click Settings.

Tip   If you are not certain how to configure ICF, click Network Setup Wizard instead of Settings.

Windows XP Professional displays the Advanced Settings dialog box (see Figure 17.5).

Figure 17.5   The Services tab of the Advanced Settings dialog box

The Services tab allows you to specify the services running on your network that Internet users can access.

The Security Logging tab allows you to specify whether or not you want to log dropped packets and successful connections. It also allows you to set the size limit and location of the log file. By default, the log file is PFIREWALL.LOG and the size limit is 4096 KB.

To enable security logging, select one or both of the following options: Log Dropped Packets and Log Successful Connections. To view the security log file, in the Security tab, click Browse.

The ICMP tab allows you to select which requests for information from the Internet this computer will respond to (see Table 17.5). By default none of these check boxes are selected.

Note   Internet Control Message Protocol (ICMP) allows computers on a network to share error and status information.

Table 17.5   Configurable ICMP Options

Option	Description
Allow Incoming Echo Request	Messages sent to the computer will be repeated back to the sender. This option is commonly used for troubleshooting, such as pinging a computer.
Allow Incoming Timestamp Request	Data sent to this computer can be acknowledged with a confirmation message indicating the time that the data was received.
Allow Incoming Mask Request	This computer will listen for and respond to requests for more information about the public network to which it is attached.
Allow Incoming Router Request	This computer will respond to requests for information about the routes it recognizes.
Allow Outgoing Destination Unreachable	Data sent over the Internet that fails to reach this computer because of an error will be discarded and acknowledged with a "Destination Unreachable" message explaining the failure.
Allow Outgoing Source Quench	When this computer's ability to process incoming data cannot keep up with the rate of a transmission, data will be dropped and the sender will be asked to slow down.
Allow Outgoing Parameter Problem	When this computer discards data it has received because of a problematic header, it will reply to the sender with a "Bad Header" error message.
Allow Outgoing Time Exceeded	When this computer discards an incomplete data transmission because the entire transmission required more time than allowed, it will reply to the sender with a "Time Expired" message.
Allow Redirect	Data sent from this computer will be rerouted if the default path changes.

Caution   If you enable any of the ICMP options, your network can become visible to the Internet and vulnerable to attack.

The following are some important ICF considerations:

- ICF is available in the Windows XP Professional 32-bit edition and the Windows XP Home Edition, but it is not available in the Windows XP Professional 64-bit edition.

- ICF should be enabled on your shared Internet connection if your network is using ICS to provide Internet access to multiple computers.

- ICF also protects a single computer that is connected to the Internet with a cable modem, a DSL modem, or a dial-up modem.

- ICF should not be enabled on VPN connections or on client computers; it will interfere with file and printer sharing.

Enabling Internet Connection Sharing

ICS allows you to connect multiple computers on your home or small business network to the Internet using one connection. One of the computers on your network connects to the Internet using a cable modem, DSL modem, or dial-up modem. You enable ICS on the computer that has the Internet connection and it becomes the ICS host. The other computers on the network then connect to the Internet through this connection.

Note   ICS is available in the Windows XP Professional 32-bit edition and the Windows XP Home Edition, but it is not available in the Windows XP Professional 64-bit edition.

To enable ICS, do the following:

1. On the Start menu, click My Computer, click My Network Places, and then click View Network Connections.

   Windows XP Professional displays the Network Connections window.

2. Click the dial-up, LAN, PPPoE, or VPN Internet connection that you want to share.

3. Under Network Tasks, click Change Settings Of This Connection.

4. In the Advanced tab, select the Allow Other Network Users To Connect Through This Computer's Internet Connection check box.

   The following two additional check boxes are available when you enable ICS (see Figure 17.6):

   - **Establish A Dial-Up Connection Whenever A Computer On My Network Attempts To Access The Internet.**   This check box allows you to enable on-demand dialing for the shared connection.

   - **Allow Other Network Users To Control Or Disable The Shared Internet Connection.**   This check box allows you to enable client control for this shared Internet connection.

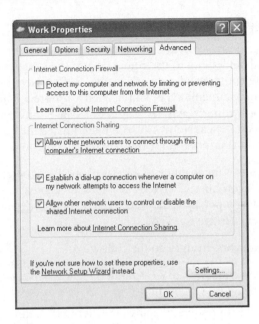

Figure 17.6　The Advanced tab of the Work Properties dialog box

5. To configure ICS and select the services running on your network that Internet users can access, click Settings.

The following are important ICS considerations:

- Do not use ICS on networks with Microsoft Windows 2000 Server domain controllers, Domain Name System (DNS) servers, gateways, Dynamic Host Configuration Protocol (DHCP) servers, or computers configured for static IP addresses.

- The ICS host computer needs two network connections. The LAN connection automatically created by installing a network adapter connects it to the other computers on the network. The second connection uses a dial-up modem, ISDN, DSL modem, or high-speed connection to connect to the Internet. Only enable ICS on the connection to the Internet.

- Enabling ICS automatically assigns a static IP address to the LAN connection to the network. Any TCP/IP connections will be lost and need to be reestablished.

Enabling and Configuring Network Bridge

Network Bridge allows you to connect LAN segments, groups of networked computers, without having to use routers or bridges. Network Bridge allows you to connect different types of network media. Before Network Bridge, if you were using more than one media type, you needed a different subnet for each media type. Packet forwarding would be required because different protocols are used on different media types. Network Bridge automates the configuration that is required to forward information from one media type to another.

Network Bridge uses the Institute of Electrical and Electronics Engineers (IEEE) Spanning Tree Algorithm (STA). STA provides an automated mechanism to ensure that the forwarding topology is loop free. You do not have to do any configuration to configure Network Bridge for STA.

To configure Network Bridge, do the following:

1. On the Start menu, click My Computer, click My Network Places, and then click View Network Connections.

   Windows XP Professional displays the Network Connections window.

2. Under LAN or High-Speed Internet, select each of the private network connections that you want to make part of the bridge.

3. Right-click one of the selected private network connections, and then click Bridge Connections.

The following are important Network Bridge considerations:

- Only Ethernet adapters, IEEE-1394 adapters, or Ethernet-compatible adapters, such as wireless or home phone network adapter (HPNA), can be part of the Network Bridge.

- Adapters that have ICF or ICS enabled cannot be included in the Network Bridge.

- You can add connections to the Network Bridge after it has been created, using the Add To Bridge menu command.

- Only one bridge can exist on a Windows XP Professional computer, but it can be used to connect as many different media types as the computer can physically accommodate.

- You cannot create a bridge connection on computers running Windows 2000 or an earlier version of Windows.

Note   Network Bridge is available in the Windows XP Professional 32-bit edition and the Windows XP Home Edition, but it is not available in the Windows XP Professional 64-bit edition.

Using the Network Setup Wizard

The Network Setup Wizard is another one of the home and small business components in Windows XP Professional. You first run the Network Setup Wizard on the computer that will be your ICS host computer. The Network Setup Wizard automatically enables and configures ICS and ICF for you. After you run the Network Setup Wizard on the ICS host computer, run it on each of the other computers in the network. All computers other than the ICS host computer are known as client computers. The wizard automatically configures all of the computers on the network so that they function properly in the network.

To run the Network Setup Wizard, do the following:

1. On the Start menu, click Control Panel.

2. In Control Panel, click Network And Internet Connections.

3. Click Network Connections and under Pick A Task, click Set Up Or Change Your Home Or Small Office Network.

Practice: Enabling and Configuring ICF and ICS

In this practice, you enable and configure ICF and ICS.

Run the **ICFandICS** file in the Demos folder on the CD-ROM accompanying this book for a demonstration of enabling and configuring ICF and ICS.

Exercise 1: Enabling and Configuring ICF

In this exercise, you enable ICF on your computer. You also configure it by increasing the maximum size of the Security Log file.

▶ **To enable and configure ICF**

1. Log on as Fred or with an account that is a member of the Administrators group.

2. On the Start menu, click My Computer, click My Network Places, and then click View Network Connections.

   Windows XP Professional displays the Network Connections window.

3. Click the Work connection that you created in Lesson 2.

4. Under Network Tasks, click Change Settings Of This Connection.

   Windows XP Professional displays the Work Properties dialog box with the General tab selected.

5. Click the Advanced tab.

   By default, the Protect My Computer And Network By Limiting Or Preventing Access To This Computer From The Internet check box is cleared, indicating that ICF is not enabled.

6. Click Protect My Computer And Network By Limiting Or Preventing Access To This Computer From The Internet.

There should be a check mark in the Protect My Computer And Network By Limiting Or Preventing Access To This Computer From The Internet check box, and the Settings button should now be available.

7. Click Settings to configure ICF.

   Windows XP Professional displays the Advanced Settings dialog box with the Services tab selected.

8. Click Security Logging.

9. Under Log File Options, increase the size of the Security Log file to 4500 KB. Click OK to close the Advanced Settings dialog box.

10. Click OK to close the Work Properties dialog box and to enable ICF.

    Leave the Network Connections window open for the next exercise.

Exercise 2: Enabling and Configuring ICS

In this exercise, you enable ICS on your computer. You also configure ICS by enabling on-demand dialing for the users sharing this connection to the Internet.

▶ **To enable and configure ICS**

1. In the Network Connections window, click Work.

Note   The Work connection is not a connection to the Internet, but for the purposes of this exercise you can enable ICS for it.

---

2. Under Network Tasks, click Change Settings Of This Connection.

   Windows XP Professional displays the Work Properties dialog box with the General tab selected.

3. Click the Advanced tab.

   There should not be a check mark in the Allow Other Network Users To Connect Through This Computer's Internet Connection check box, indicating that ICS is not enabled by default.

4. Click the Allow Other Network Users To Connect Through This Computer's Internet Connection check box.

   There should now be a check mark in the Allow Other Network Users To Connect Through This Computer's Internet Connection check box.

5. Click Establish A Dial-Up Connection Whenever A Computer On My Network Attempts To Access The Internet to configure ICS by enabling on-demand dialing for the shared connection.

   There should now be a check mark in the Establish A Dial-Up Connection Whenever A Computer On My Network Attempts To Access The Internet check box.

6. Click OK to close the Work Properties dialog box.

Lesson Review

The following questions will help you determine whether you have learned enough to move on to the next lesson. If you have difficulty answering these questions, review the material in this lesson before beginning the next chapter. The answers are in Appendix A, "Questions and Answers."

1. What is ICF?

2. What happens if you configure ICF and enable any one of the ICMP options?

3. By default, the ICF Security Log file is named _____ and has a size limit of _____.

4. Which of the following statements about ICF are correct? (Choose all answers that are correct.)

   a. ICF is available in the Windows XP Professional 64-bit edition.

   b. ICF should not be enabled on VPN connections.

   c. ICF should be enabled on your shared Internet connection.

   d. ICF must be purchased as an add-on package and is not included in Windows XP Professional.

5. When do you use ICS?

6. How do you enable on-demand dialing for a shared ICS connection?

7. What is Network Bridge and what algorithm does it use?

8. Which of the following types of adapters can you use in a Network Bridge? (Choose all answers that are correct.)

   a. Ethernet adapters

   b. IEEE-1394 adapters

   c. Token Ring adapters

   d. Adapters that have ICF or ICS enabled

Lesson Summary

- Internet Connection Firewall (ICF) is firewall software that you use to set restrictions on what information is communicated from your network to and from the Internet.

- ICF is enabled by selecting the Protect My Computer And Network By Limiting Or Preventing Access To This Computer From The Internet check box located in the Advanced tab of the connection's Properties dialog box.

- ICF, ICS, and Network Bridge are available in the Windows XP Professional 32-bit edition and the Windows XP Home Edition, but they are not available in the Windows XP Professional 64-bit edition.

- ICF should not be enabled on VPN connections or on client computers because it will interfere with file and printer sharing.

- ICS allows you to connect multiple computers on your home or small business network to the Internet using one connection.

- ICS is enabled by selecting the Allow Other Network Users To Connect Through This Computer's Internet Connection check box located in the Advanced tab of the connection's Properties dialog box.

- On-demand dialing for ICS is enabled by selecting Establish A Dial-Up Connection Whenever A Computer On My Network Attempts To Access The Internet.

- ICS should not be used on networks with Windows 2000 Server domain controllers, DNS servers, gateways, DHCP servers, or computers configured for static IP addresses.

- Network Bridge allows you to connect LAN segments, groups of networked computers, without having to use routers or bridges to connect them.

- Network Bridge uses the IEEE Spanning Tree Algorithm (STA).

CHAPTER 18

Modifying and Troubleshooting the Boot Process

About This Chapter

This chapter introduces you to the Microsoft Windows XP Professional boot process. You learn about the boot process, the BOOT.INI file, the Registry Editor, safe mode, the last known good configuration, and the Recovery Console.

Before You Begin

To complete this chapter, you must have

- A computer that meets the minimum hardware requirements listed in the preface, "About This Book"
- The Windows XP Professional software installed on your computer

Lesson 1: Understanding the Boot Process

In this lesson, you learn about the files used in the Windows XP Professional boot process. You also learn that the Windows XP Professional boot process occurs in five stages: the preboot sequence, boot sequence, kernel load, kernel initialization, and logon. You learn during which phase each of the boot processes are used and come to understand how to more effectively troubleshoot the Windows XP Professional boot process by learning about its files and phases.

After this lesson, you will be able to

- Explain the boot process
- Describe the files used in the boot process
- Explain the purpose and function of the BOOT.INI file

Estimated lesson time: 40 minutes

Files Used in the Boot Process

The boot sequence requires certain files. Table 18.1 lists the files used in the Windows XP Professional boot process, the appropriate location of each file, and the stages of the boot process associated with each file. *Systemroot* (typed as %systemroot%) represents the path to your Windows XP Professional installation directory, which will be C:\Windows if you've followed the installation instructions in Chapter 2, "Installing Windows XP Professional."

Note To view the files listed in Table 18.1, open Windows Explorer and click Folder Options on the Tools menu. In the View tab of the Folder Options dialog box, under Hidden Files And Folders, click Show Hidden Files And Folders. Clear the Hide Protected Operating System Files (Recommended) check box. A Warning message box appears, indicating that it is not a good idea to display the protected operating system files. Click Yes to display them. Click OK to close the Folder Options dialog box.

Table 18.1 Files Used in the Windows XP Professional Boot Process

File	Location	Boot stage
NTLDR	System partition root (C:\ )	Preboot and boot
BOOT.INI	System partition root	Boot
BOOTSECT.DOS	System partition root	Boot (optional)
NTDETECT.COM	System partition root	Boot
NTBOOTDD.SYS	System partition root	Boot (optional)
NTOSKRNL.EXE	systemroot\System32	Kernel load
HAL.DLL	systemroot\System32	Kernel load

Table 18.1   *(continued)*

File	Location	Boot stage
SYSTEM	systemroot\System32	Kernel initialization
Device drivers (.sys)	*systemroot*\System32\Drivers	Kernel initialization

The BOOT.INI File

When you install Windows XP Professional on a computer, Windows Setup saves the BOOT.INI file in the active partition. NTLDR uses information in the BOOT.INI file to display the boot loader screen, from which you select the operating system to start. In this lesson you learn how to modify the BOOT.INI file, including modifying Advanced RISC Computing (ARC) paths and using the optional BOOT.INI switches.

The BOOT.INI file includes two sections, [boot loader] and [operating systems], that contain information that NTLDR uses to create the Boot Loader Operating System Selection menu. A typical BOOT.INI might contain the following lines:

```
[boot loader]

timeout=30

default=multi(0)disk(0)rdisk(0)partition(2)\WINDOWS

[operating systems]

multi(0)disk(0)rdisk(0)partition(2)\WINDOWS="Microsoft Windows XP
Professional" /fastdetect

multi(0)disk(0)rdisk(0)partition(1)\WINNT="Windows NT Workstation
Version 4.00"

multi(0)disk(0)rdisk(1)partition(1)\ WINNT="Windows NT Server
4.00 [VGA mode]" /basevideo /sos

C:\CMDCONS\BOOTSECT.DAT="Microsoft Windows Recovery Console" /cmdcons
```

The [operating systems] section of a BOOT.INI file that is created during a default installation of Windows XP Professional contains a single entry for Windows XP Professional. If your computer is a Microsoft Windows 95–based or Microsoft Windows 98–based dual-boot system, the [operating systems] section also contains an entry for starting the system using the other operating system. If you installed Windows XP Professional on a computer and kept an installation of Microsoft Windows NT 4.0 on another partition of the same computer, the [operating systems] section also contains an entry for starting the system using this version of Windows NT.

ARC Paths

During installation, Windows XP Professional generates the BOOT.INI file, which contains Advanced RISC Computing (ARC) paths pointing to the computer's boot partition. (RISC stands for Reduced Instruction Set Computing, a microprocessor design that uses a small set of simple instructions for fast execution.) The following is an example of an ARC path:

```
multi(0)disk(0)rdisk(1)partition(2)
```

Table 18.2 describes the naming conventions for ARC paths.

Table 18.2   ARC Path Naming Conventions

Convention	Description
Multi (x) | scsi (x)	The adapter/disk controller. Use scsi to indicate a Small Computer System Interface (SCSI) controller on which SCSI basic input/output system (BIOS) is not enabled. For all other adapter/disk controllers, use multi, including SCSI disk controllers with the BIOS enabled. Here, x represents a number that indicates the load order of the hardware adapter. For example, if you have two SCSI adapters in a computer, the first to load and initialize receives number 0, and the next SCSI adapter receives number 1.
Disk(y)	The SCSI ID. For multi, this value is always 0.
Rdisk(z)	A number that identifies the disk (ignored for SCSI controllers).
Partition(a)	A number that identifies the partition.

In both multi and scsi conventions, multi, scsi, disk, and rdisk numbers are assigned starting with 0. Partition numbers start with 1. All nonextended partitions are assigned numbers first, followed by logical drives in extended partitions.

See Figure 18.1 for some examples of how to determine the ARC path name.

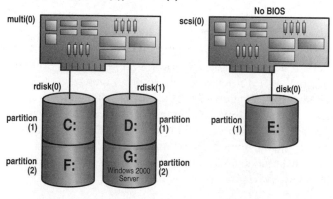

Figure 18.1   ARC paths

The scsi ARC naming convention varies the disk(y) parameter for successive disks on one controller, whereas the multi format varies the rdisk(z) parameter.

BOOT.INI Switches

You can add a variety of switches to the entries in the [operating systems] section of the BOOT.INI file to provide additional functionality. Table 18.3 describes some of these optional switches that you can use for entries in the BOOT.INI file.

Table 18.3   BOOT.INI Optional Switches

Switch	Description
/basevideo	Boots the computer using the standard Video Graphics Adapter (VGA) video driver. If a new video driver is not working correctly, use this switch to start Windows XP Professional, and then change to a different driver.
/fastdetect=[com$x$ | comx,y,z.]	Disables serial mouse detection. Without a port specification, this switch disables peripheral detection on all COM ports. This switch is included in every entry in the BOOT.INI file by default.
/maxmem:n	Specifies the amount of random access memory (RAM) that Windows XP Professional uses. Use this switch if you suspect that a memory chip is bad.
/noguiboot	Boots the computer without displaying the graphical boot status screen.
/sos	Displays the device driver names as they are loading. Use this switch when startup fails while loading drivers to determine which driver is triggering the failure.

Modifications to BOOT.INI

You can modify the time out and default parameter values in the BOOT.INI file using System Properties in Control Panel. In addition, you can manually edit these and other parameter values in the BOOT.INI file. For example, you might modify the BOOT.INI file to add more descriptive entries for the Boot Loader Operating System Selection menu or to include various switches to aid in troubleshooting the boot process.

During Windows XP Professional installation, Windows Setup sets the read-only and system attributes for the BOOT.INI file. Before editing the BOOT.INI file with a text editor, you must make the file visible and turn off the read-only attribute. You can change file attributes using My Computer, Windows Explorer, or the command prompt.

To change file attributes by using My Computer or Windows Explorer, complete the following steps:

1. Double-click the icon for the drive containing the BOOT.INI file.
2. On the View menu, click Folder Options.
3. In the Folder Options dialog box, click the View tab.
4. Under Hidden Files, click Show All Files, and then click OK.
5. Right-click BOOT, and then click Properties.
6. In the General tab, under Attributes, clear the Read-Only check box, and then click OK.

To change file attributes using the command prompt, switch to the directory containing the BOOT.INI file if necessary, and then type

```
attrib -s -r boot.ini
```

After you have changed the attributes of the BOOT.INI file, you can open and modify the file using a text editor.

Preboot Sequence

During startup, a computer running Windows XP Professional initializes and then locates the boot portion of the hard disk.

The following four steps occur during the preboot sequence:

1. The computer runs power-on self test (POST) routines to determine the amount of physical memory, whether the hardware components are present, and so on. If the computer has a Plug and Play BIOS, enumeration and configuration of hardware devices occurs at this stage.
2. The computer BIOS locates the boot device and loads and runs the master boot record (MBR).
3. The MBR scans the partition table to locate the active partition, loads the boot sector on the active partition into memory, and then executes it.
4. The computer loads and initializes the NTLDR file, which is the operating system loader.

Note   Windows XP Professional Setup modifies the boot sector during installation so that NTLDR loads during system startup.

Boot Sequence

After the computer loads NTLDR into memory, the boot sequence gathers information about hardware and drivers in preparation for the Windows XP Professional load phases. The boot sequence uses the following files: NTLDR, BOOT.INI, BOOTSECT.DOS (optional), NTDETECT.COM, and NTOSKRNL.EXE.

The boot sequence has four phases: initial boot loader phase, operating system selection, hardware detection, and configuration selection.

Initial Boot Loader Phase

During the initial boot loader phase, NTLDR switches the microprocessor from real mode to 32-bit flat memory mode, which NTLDR requires to carry out any additional functions. Next, NTLDR starts the appropriate minifile system drivers. The minifile system drivers are built into NTLDR so that NTLDR can find and load Windows XP Professional from partitions formatted with file allocation table (FAT), FAT32, or NT file system (NTFS).

Operating System Selection

During the boot sequence, NTLDR reads the BOOT.INI file. If more than one operating system selection is available in the BOOT.INI file, then the Please Select The Operating System To Start screen appears, listing the operating systems specified in the BOOT.INI file. If you do not select an entry before the timer reaches zero, NTLDR loads the operating system specified by the default parameter in the BOOT.INI file. Windows XP Professional Setup sets the default parameter to the most recent Windows XP Professional installation. If there is only one entry in the BOOT.INI file, the Please Select The Operating System To Start screen does not appear and the default operating system is automatically loaded.

Note If the BOOT.INI file is not present, NTLDR attempts to load Windows XP Professional from the first partition of the first disk, typically C:\.

Hardware Detection

NTDETECT.COM and NTOSKRNL.EXE perform hardware detection. NTDETECT.COM executes after you select Windows XP Professional on the Please Select The Operating System To Start screen (or after the timer times out).

Note If you select an operating system other than Windows XP Professional, such as Microsoft Windows 98, NTLDR loads and executes BOOTSECT.DOS, which is a copy of the boot sector that was on the system partition at the time that Windows XP Professional was installed. Passing execution to BOOTSECT.DOS starts the boot process for the selected operating system.

NTDETECT.COM collects a list of currently installed hardware components and returns this list to NTLDR for later inclusion in the registry under the HKEY_LOCAL_MACHINE\HARDWARE key.

NTDETECT.COM detects the following components:

- Bus/adapter type
- Communication ports
- Floating-point coprocessor
- Floppy disks
- Keyboard
- Mouse/pointing device
- Parallel ports
- SCSI adapters
- Video adapters

Configuration Selection

After NTLDR starts loading Windows XP Professional and collects hardware information, the operating system loader presents you with the Hardware Profile/Configuration Recovery menu, which contains a list of the hardware profiles that are set up on the computer. The first hardware profile is highlighted. You can press the down-pointing arrow key to select another profile. You also can press L to invoke the LastKnownGood configuration.

If there is only a single hardware profile, NTLDR does not display the Hardware Profile/Configuration Recovery menu and loads Windows XP Professional using the default hardware profile configuration.

Kernel Load

After configuration selection, the Windows XP Professional kernel (NTOSKRNL.EXE) loads and initializes. NTOSKRNL.EXE also loads and initializes device drivers and loads services. If you press ENTER when the Hardware Profile/Configuration Recovery menu appears, or if NTLDR makes the selection automatically, the computer enters the kernel load phase. The screen clears and a series of white rectangles appears across the bottom of the screen.

During the kernel load stage, NTLDR does the following:

- Loads NTOSKRNL.EXE but does not initialize it.
- Loads the hardware abstraction layer file (HAL.DLL).

- Loads the HKEY_LOCAL_MACHINE\SYSTEM registry key from *%systemroot%*\System32\Config\System.

- Selects the control set it will use to initialize the computer. A *control set* contains configuration data used to control the system, such as a list of the device drivers and services to load and start.

- Loads device drivers with a value of 0x0 for the Start entry. These typically are low-level hardware device drivers, such as those for a hard disk. The value for the List entry, which is specified in the HKEY_LOCAL_MACHINE\SYSTEM\CurrentControlSet\Control\ServiceGroupOrder subkey of the registry, defines the order in which NTLDR loads these device drivers.

Kernel Initialization

When the kernel load stage is complete, the kernel initializes, and then NTLDR passes control to the kernel. At this point, the system displays a graphical screen with a status bar indicating load status. Four tasks are accomplished during the kernel initialization stage:

1. **The Hardware key is created.**   On successful initialization, the kernel uses the data collected during hardware detection to create the registry key HKEY_LOCAL_MACHINE\HARDWARE. This key contains information about hardware components on the system board and the interrupts used by specific hardware devices.

2. **The Clone control set is created.**   The kernel creates the Clone control set by copying the control set referenced by the value of the Current entry in the HKEY_LOCAL_MACHINE\SYSTEM\Select subkey of the registry. The Clone control set is never modified, as it is intended to be an identical copy of the data used to configure the computer and should not reflect changes made during the startup process.

3. **Device drivers are loaded and initialized.**   After creating the Clone control set, the kernel initializes the low-level device drivers that were loaded during the kernel load phase. The kernel then scans the HKEY_LOCAL_MACHINE\SYSTEM\CurrentControlSet\Services subkey of the registry for device drivers with a value of 0x1 for the Start entry. As in the kernel load phase, a device driver's value for the Group entry specifies the order in which it loads. Device drivers initialize as soon as they load.

   If an error occurs while loading and initializing a device driver, the boot process proceeds based on the value specified in the ErrorControl entry for the driver.

   Table 18.4 describes the possible ErrorControl values and the resulting boot sequence actions.

Table 18.4   ErrorControl Values and Resulting Action

ErrorControl value	Action
0x0 (Ignore)	The boot sequence ignores the error and proceeds without displaying an error message.
0x1 (Normal)	The boot sequence displays an error message but ignores the error and proceeds.
0x2 (Severe)	The boot sequence fails and then restarts using the LastKnownGood control set. If the boot sequence is currently using the LastKnownGood control set, the boot sequence ignores the error and proceeds.
0x3 (Critical)	The boot sequence fails and then restarts using the LastKnownGood control set. However, if the LastKnownGood control set is causing the critical error, the boot sequence stops and displays an error message.

ErrorControl values appear in the registry under the subkey HKEY_LOCAL_MACHINE\SYSTEM\CurrentControlSet\ Services*name_of_service_or_driver*\ErrorControl.

4. **Services are started.**   After the kernel loads and initializes devices drivers, the Session Manager (SMSS.EXE) starts the higher order subsystems and services for Windows XP Professional. Session Manager executes the instructions in the BootExecute data item, and in the Memory Management, DOS Devices, and SubSystems keys.

Table 18.5 describes the function of each instruction set and the resulting Session Manager action.

Table 18.5   Session Manager Reads and Executes These Instruction Sets

Data item or key	Action
BootExecute data item	Session Manager executes the commands specified in this data item before it loads any services.
Memory Management key	Session Manager creates the paging file information required by the Virtual Memory Manager.
DOS Devices key	Session Manager creates symbolic links that direct certain classes of commands to the correct component in the file system.
SubSystems key	Session Manager starts the Win32 subsystem, which controls all input/output (I/O) and access to the video screen and starts the WinLogon process.

Logon

The logon process begins at the conclusion of the kernel initialization phase. The Win32 subsystem automatically starts WINLOGON.EXE, which starts the Local Security Authority (LSASS.EXE) and displays the Logon dialog box. You can log on at this time, even though Windows XP Professional might still be initializing network device drivers.

Next, the Service Controller executes and makes a final scan of the HKEY_LOCAL_MACHINE\SYSTEM\CurrentControlSet\Services subkey, looking for services with a value of 0x2 for the Start entry. These services, including the Workstation service and the Server service, are marked to load automatically.

The services that load during this phase do so based on their values for the DependOnGroup or DependOnService entries in the HKEY_LOCAL_MACHINE\SYSTEM\CurrentControlSet\ Services registry subkey.

A Windows XP Professional startup is not considered good until a user successfully logs on to the system. After a successful logon, the system copies the Clone control set to the LastKnownGood control set.

Note For more information on LastKnownGood configuration, see Lesson 3, "Using Startup and Recovery Tools," later in this chapter.

Lesson Review

The following questions will help you determine whether you have learned enough to move on to the next lesson. If you have difficulty answering these questions, review the material in this lesson before beginning the next lesson. The answers are in Appendix A, "Questions and Answers."

1. Windows XP Professional modifies the boot sector during installation so that _____ loads during system startup.

2. What is the purpose of the BOOT.INI file and what happens if it is not present?

3. What does the BOOTSECT.DOS file contain and when is it used?

4. A user calls you and tells you that Windows XP Professional does not appear to be loading correctly. The Hardware Profile/Configuration Recovery menu does not appear when the computer is restarted, but it does appear on the computer of the person sitting in the next cubicle when that computer is restarted. What would you tell the user?

Lesson Summary

- NTLDR and NTDETECT.COM are required files in the Windows XP Professional boot process.

- BOOTSECT.DOS is a copy of the boot sector that was on the system partition at the time that Windows XP Professional was installed. It is only used if you choose to load an operating system other than Windows XP Professional.

- When you install Windows XP Professional on a computer, Windows Setup saves the BOOT.INI file in the active partition.

- NTLDR uses information in the BOOT.INI file to display the boot loader screen, from which you select the operating system to start.

- You can edit the BOOT.INI file, including modifying ARC paths and using the optional BOOT.INI switches.

- The Windows XP Professional boot process occurs in five phases: preboot sequence, boot sequence, kernel load, kernel initialization, and logon.

Lesson 2: Editing the Registry

Microsoft Windows XP Professional stores hardware and software settings centrally in a hierarchical database called the *registry*. The registry replaces many of the .ini, .sys, and .com configuration files used in earlier versions of Microsoft Windows. The registry controls the Windows XP Professional operating system by providing the appropriate initialization information to boot Windows XP Professional, to start applications, and to load components, such as device drivers and network protocols.

Most users of Windows XP Professional never need to access the registry. However, management of the registry is an important part of the system administrator's job and includes viewing, editing, backing up, and restoring the registry. You use Registry Editor to view and change the registry configuration.

After this lesson, you will be able to

- Identify the purpose of the registry
- Define the hierarchical structure of the registry
- View and edit the registry with Registry Editor

Estimated lesson time: 60 minutes

Understanding the Registry

The registry contains a variety of different types of data, including the following:

- The hardware installed on the computer, including the central processing unit (CPU), bus type, pointing device or mouse, and keyboard.
- Installed device drivers.
- Installed applications.
- Installed network protocols.
- Network adapter card settings. Examples include the interrupt request (IRQ) number, memory base address, I/O port base address, I/O channel ready, and transceiver type.

The registry structure provides a secure set of records. The data in the registry is read, updated, or modified by many of the Windows XP Professional components.

Table 18.6 describes some of the components that access and store data in the registry.

Table 18.6   Components That Use the Registry

Component	Description
Windows XP Professional kernel	During startup, the Windows XP Professional kernel (NTOSKRNL.EXE) reads information from the registry, including the device drivers to load and the order in which they should be loaded. The kernel writes information about itself to the registry, such as the version number.
Device drivers	Device drivers receive configuration parameters from the registry. They also write information to the registry. A device driver informs the registry which system resources it is using, such as hardware interrupts or direct memory access (DMA) channels. Device drivers also report discovered configuration data.
User profiles	Windows XP Professional creates and maintains user work environment settings in a user profile. When a user logs on, the system caches the profile in the registry. Windows XP Professional first writes user configuration changes to the registry and then to the user profile.
Setup programs	During setup of a hardware device or application, a setup program can add new configuration data to the registry. It can also query the registry to determine whether required components have been installed.
Hardware profiles	Computers with two or more hardware configurations use hardware profiles. When Windows XP Professional starts, the user selects a hardware profile and Windows XP Professional configures the system accordingly.
NTDETECT.COM	During system startup, NTDETECT.COM performs hardware detection. This dynamic hardware configuration data is stored in the registry.

Reviewing the Hierarchical Structure of the Registry

The registry is organized in a hierarchical structure similar to the hierarchical structure of folders and files on a disk. Figure 18.2 shows the hierarchical structure of the registry as displayed by the Registry Editor.

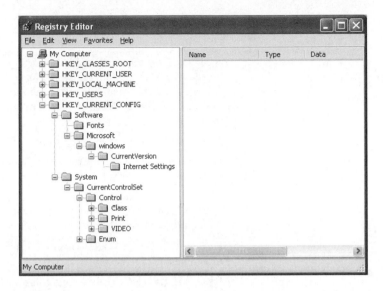

Figure 18.2   Registry Editor displays the hierarchical structure of the registry

Table 18.7 describes the components that make up the hierarchical structure of the registry.

Table 18.7   Components That Make Up the Registry

Component	Description
Subtree	A subtree (or subtree key) is analogous to the root folder of a disk. The Windows XP Professional registry has two subtrees: HKEY_LOCAL_MACHINE and HKEY_USERS. However, to make the information in the registry easier to find and view, there are five predefined subtrees that can be seen in the editor: HKEY_CLASSES_ROOT HKEY_CURRENT_USER HKEY_LOCAL_MACHINE HKEY_USERS HKEY_CURRENT_CONFIG
Keys	Keys are analogous to folders and subfolders. Keys correspond to hardware or software objects and groups of objects. Subkeys are keys within higher level keys.
Entries	Keys contain one or more entries. An entry has three parts: name, data type, and value (data or configuration parameter).

(continued)

Table 18.7   *(continued)*

Component	Description
Hive	A hive is a discrete body of keys, subkeys, and entries. Each hive has a corresponding registry file and .log file located in *%systemroot%* System32\Config. Windows XP Professional uses the .log file to record changes and ensure the integrity of the registry.
Data types	Each entry's value is expressed as one of these data types: **REG_SZ (String value).** One value; Windows XP Professional interprets it as a string to store. **REG_BINARY (Binary value).** One value; it must be a string of hexadecimal digits. Windows XP Professional interprets each pair as a byte value. **REG_DWORD (DWORD value).** One value; must be a string of 1–8 hexadecimal digits. **REG_MULTI_SZ (Multistring value).** Multiple values allowed; Windows XP Professional interprets each string as a component of MULTI_SZ separate entries. **REG_EXPAND_SZ (Expandable string value).** Similar to REG_SZ, except the text can contain a replaceable variable; for example, in the string *%systemroot%*\NTVDM.EXE, Windows XP Professional replaces the *systemroot* environmental variable with the path to the Windows XP Professional System32 folder. **REG_FULL_RESOURCE_DESCRIPTOR.** Stores a resource list for hardware components or drivers. You cannot add or modify an entry with this data type.

Registry Subtrees

Understanding the purpose of each subtree can help you locate specific keys and values in the registry. The following five subtrees or subtree keys are displayed in the Registry Editor (see Figure 18.2):

- **HKEY_LOCAL_MACHINE.**   Contains all configuration data for the local computer, including hardware and operating system data such as bus type, system memory, device drivers, and startup control data. Applications, device drivers, and the operating system use this data to set the computer configuration. The data in this subtree remains constant regardless of the user.

- **HKEY_USERS.**   Contains two subkeys:
  - **DEFAULT.**   Contains the system default settings (system default profile) used to display the CTRL+ALT+DELETE logon screen, and the security identifier (SID) of the current user.
  - **HKEY_CURRENT_USER.**   Is a child of HKEY_USERS.

- **HKEY_CURRENT_USER.**   Contains data about the current user. Retrieves a copy of each user account used to log on to the computer from the NTUSER.DAT file and stores it in the *%systemroot%*\Profiles*username* key. This subtree points to the same data contained in HKEY_USERS\ *SID_currently_logged_on_user*. This subtree takes precedence over HKEY_LOCAL_MACHINE for duplicated values.

- **HKEY_CLASSES_ROOT.**   Contains software configuration data: object linking and embedding (OLE) and file-class association data. This subtree points to the Classes subkey under HKEY_LOCAL_MACHINE\SOFTWARE.

- **HKEY_CURRENT_CONFIG.**   Contains data on the active hardware profile extracted from the SOFTWARE and SYSTEM hives. This information is used to configure settings such as the device drivers to load and the display resolution to use.

The HKEY_LOCAL_MACHINE Subtree

HKEY_LOCAL_MACHINE provides a good example of the subtrees in the registry for two reasons:

- The structure of all subtrees is similar.

- HKEY_LOCAL_MACHINE contains information specific to the local computer and is always the same, regardless of the user who is logged on.

The HKEY_LOCAL_MACHINE root key has five subkeys, which are explained in Table 18.8.

Table 18.8   HKEY_LOCAL_MACHINE Subkeys

Subkey	Description
HARDWARE	The type and state of physical devices attached to the computer. This subkey is volatile, meaning that Windows XP Professional builds it from information gathered during startup. Because the values for this subkey are volatile, it does not map to a file on the disk. Applications query this subkey to determine the type and state of physical devices attached to the computer.
SAM	The directory database for the computer. The SAM hive maps to the SAM and SAM.LOG files in the *%systemroot%*\ System32\Config directory. Applications that query SAM must use the appropriate application programming interfaces (APIs). This hive is a pointer to the same one accessible under HKEY_LOCAL_MACHINE\ SECURITY\SAM.
SECURITY	The security information for the local computer. The SECURITY hive maps to the Security and SECURITY.LOG files in the *%systemroot%*\System32\Config directory.

(continued)

Table 18.8 *(continued)*

Subkey	Description
	Applications cannot modify the keys contained in the SECURITY subkey. Instead, applications must query security information by using the security APIs.
SOFTWARE	Information about the local computer software that is independent of per-user configuration information. This hive maps to the Software and SOFTWARE.LOG files in the *%systemroot%*\System32\Config directory. It also contains file associations and OLE information.
SYSTEM	Information about system devices and services. When you install or configure device drivers or services, they add or modify information under this hive. The SYSTEM hive maps to the System and SYSTEM.LOG files in the *%systemroot%*\System32\Config directory. The registry keeps a backup of the data in the SYSTEM hive in the SYSTEM.ALT file.

Control Sets

A typical Windows XP Professional installation contains the following control set subkeys: Clone, ControlSet001, ControlSet002, and CurrentControlSet. Control sets are stored as subkeys of the registry key HKEY_LOCAL_MACHINE\ SYSTEM (see Figure 18.3). The registry might contain several control sets, depending on how often you change or have problems with system settings.

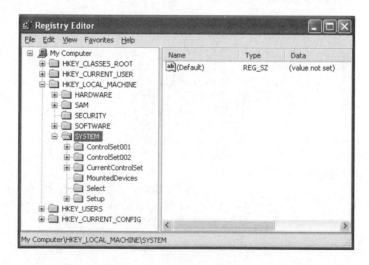

Figure 18.3 Registry Editor displaying the control sets

The CurrentControlSet subkey is a pointer to one of the ControlSet00*x* keys. The Clone control set is a clone of the control set used to initialize the computer (either Default or LastKnownGood), and is created by the kernel initialization process each time you start your computer. The Clone control set is not available after you log on.

To better understand control sets, you should know about the registry subkey HKEY_LOCAL_MACHINE\SYSTEM\Select. The entries contained in this subkey include the following:

- **Current.**   Identifies which control set is the CurrentControlSet. When you use Control Panel options or the Registry Editor to change the registry, you modify information in the CurrentControlSet.

- **Default.**   Identifies the control set to use the next time Windows XP Professional starts, unless you select the LastKnownGood configuration. Default and Current typically contain the same control set number.

- **Failed.**   Identifies the control set that was designated as failed the last time the computer was started using the LastKnownGood control set.

- **LastKnownGood.**   Identifies a copy of the control set that was used the last time the computer started Windows XP Professional successfully. After a successful logon, the Clone control set is copied to the LastKnownGood control set.

Each of these entries in HKEY_LOCAL_MACHINE\SYSTEM\Select takes a REG_DWORD data type, and the value for each entry refers to a specific control set. For example, if the value for the Current entry is set to 0x1, the CurrentControlSet points to ControlSet001. Similarly, if the value for the LastKnownGood entry is set to 0x2, the LastKnownGood control set points to ControlSet002.

Using the Registry Editor

Setup installs Registry Editor (REGEDT32.EXE) in the *%systemroot%*\System32 directory during installation. However, because most users do not need to use Registry Editor, it does not appear on the Start menu. You start Registry Editor by selecting Run on the Start menu.

Although Registry Editor allows you to perform manual edits on the registry, it is intended for troubleshooting and problem resolution. You should make most configuration changes through either Control Panel or Administrative Tools. However, some configuration settings can only be made directly through the registry.

> **Caution**   Using Registry Editor incorrectly can cause serious, system-wide problems that could require reinstallation of Windows XP Professional. When using Registry Editor to view or edit data, use a program such as Windows Backup to save a backup copy of the registry file before viewing. In Windows XP Professional, you can use Backup to back up the System State, which includes the registry, the COM class registration database, and the system boot files.

Registry Editor saves data automatically as you make entries or corrections. New registry data takes effect immediately.

You can select Find Key on the View menu to search the registry for a specific key. Key names appear in the left pane of Registry Editor. The search begins at the currently selected key and parses all descendant keys for the specified key name. The search is local to the subtree in which the search begins. For example, a search for a key in the HKEY_LOCAL_MACHINE subtree does not include keys under HKEY_CURRENT_USER.

Practice: Using the Registry Editor

In this practice, you use Registry Editor to view the information in the registry. You determine information such as the BIOS, the processor on your computer, and the version of the operating system. You use Registry Editor's Find Key command to search the registry for a specific word with key names. You then modify the registry by adding a value to it, and you save a subtree as a file so that you can use an editor, like Notepad, to search the file.

Exercise 1: Exploring the Registry

In this exercise, you use Registry Editor to view information in the registry.

▶ **To view information in the registry**

1. Ensure that you are logged on as Administrator.
2. Click Start and then click Run.
3. In the Open text box, type **Regedt32** and then click OK.
4. Maximize the Registry Editor window, and then expand HKEY_LOCAL_MACHINE.
5. Under HKEY_LOCAL_MACHINE, expand HARDWARE.
6. Expand DESCRIPTION and then double-click the System subkey.

   What are the SystemBIOSDate and SystemBIOSVersion of your computer?

What is the computer type of your local machine according to the Identifier entry?

7. Expand SOFTWARE\Microsoft\Windows NT.

8. Click CurrentVersion, and then fill in the following information.

Software configuration	Value and string
Current build number	
Current version	
Registered organization	
Registered owner	

Exercise 2: Using the Find Command

In this exercise, you use the Registry Editor's Find command to search the registry to find a specific word in the keys, values, and data in the registry.

▶   **To use the find command**

1. Click the HKEY_LOCAL_MACHINE subkey to ensure that the entire subtree is searched.

2. On the Edit menu, click Find.

   The Registry Editor displays the Find dialog box.

3. In the Find What text box, type **serial**, and clear Values and Data.

4. Click Find Next.

   The Registry Editor locates and highlights the first entry containing serial.

5. Press F3 to find the next entry containing serial.

6. Continue pressing F3 until a Registry Editor dialog box appears, indicating that Registry Editor has finished searching the registry.

   Notice that serial appears in many locations in the registry.

7. Click OK to close the Registry Editor dialog box.

Exercise 3: Modifying the Registry

In this exercise, you add a value to the registry.

▶   **To add a value to the registry**

1. Right-click HKEY_CURRENT_USER and then click Expand.

2. In the left pane of the Registry Editor window, click Environment.

The values in the Environment key appear in the right pane of the Registry Editor window.

3. On the Edit menu, click New, and then click String Value.

The Registry Editor adds A New Value #1 entry in the right pane of the Registry Editor window.

4. Type **Test** and then press ENTER.

5. Right-click Test and then click Modify.

The Registry Editor displays an Edit String dialog box.

6. In the Value Data text box, type **%windir%\system32** and then click OK.

Test REG_SZ %windir%\ system32 is now an entry in the right pane of the Registry Editor window.

7. Minimize the Registry Editor window.

▶ **To verify the new registry value**

1. Click Start, right-click My Computer, and then click Properties.

The System Properties dialog box appears.

2. Click the Advanced tab, and then click Environment Variables.

The Environment Variables dialog box appears.

Does the test variable appear in the User Variables For Administrator list?

3. Close the Environment Variables dialog box, and then close the System Properties dialog box.

Lesson Review

The following questions will help you determine whether you have learned enough to move on to the next lesson. If you have difficulty answering these questions, review the material in this lesson before beginning the next lesson. The answers are in Appendix A, "Questions and Answers."

1. What is the registry and what does it do?

2. What is the purpose of the BOOTSECT.DOS file and what happens if it is not present?

3. What are some of the Windows XP Professional components that use the registry?

4. How do you access the Registry Editor?

5. Why should you make most of your configuration changes through either Control Panel or Administrative Tools rather than by editing the registry directly with the Registry Editor?

Lesson Summary

- Windows XP Professional stores hardware and software settings in the registry, a hierarchical database that replaces many of the .ini, .sys, and .com configuration files used in earlier versions of Windows.

- The registry provides the appropriate initialization information to boot Windows XP Professional, to start applications, and to load components, such as device drivers and network protocols.

- The registry structure provides a secure set of records that can be read, updated, or modified by many of the Windows XP Professional components.

- The registry has two subtrees: HKEY_LOCAL_MACHINE and HKEY_USERS.

- The Registry Editor (REGEDT32.EXE) allows you to view and change the registry.

- The Registry Editor is primarily intended for troubleshooting. For most configuration changes, you should use either Control Panel or Administrative Tools, not Registry Editor.

Lesson 3: Using Startup and Recovery Tools

In this lesson, you learn about the tools and options Windows XP Professional provides to help you troubleshoot problems with starting your computer and recovering from disasters. These tools include safe mode, LastKnownGood configuration, the Recovery Console, and the Automated System Restore Wizard.

Note   The Automated System Restore Wizard is explained in Chapter 16, "Backing Up and Restoring Data."

After this lesson, you will be able to
- Describe how to use safe mode
- Describe how to use the LastKnownGood configuration
- Describe the advanced boot options
- Install and use the Windows XP Professional Recovery Console

Estimated lesson time: 60 minutes

Using Safe Mode

If your computer will not start, you might be able to start it by using the safe mode. Pressing F8 during the operating system selection phase displays a screen with advanced options for booting Windows XP Professional. If you select safe mode, Windows XP Professional starts with limited device drivers and system services. These basic device drivers and system services include the mouse, standard VGA monitor, keyboard, mass storage, default system services, and no network connections. Safe mode also ignores programs that automatically start up, user profiles, programs listed in the registry to automatically run, and all local group policies.

Safe mode provides access to Windows XP Professional configuration files, so you can make configuration changes. You can disable or delete a system service, a device driver, or an application that automatically starts that prevents the computer from starting normally.

If you choose to start your computer in safe mode, the background will be black and "Safe Mode" will appear in all four corners of the screen (see Figure 18.4). If your computer does not start using safe mode, you can try Windows XP Professional Automatic System Recovery.

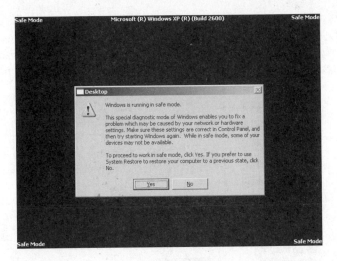

Figure 18.4   Running Windows XP Professional in safe mode

Safe Mode with Networking

There are a couple of variations of safe mode. You can select safe mode with networking, which is identical to safe mode except that it adds the drivers and services necessary to enable networking to function when you restart your computer. Safe mode with networking allows Group Policy to be implemented, including those implemented by the server during the logon process and those configured on the local computer.

Safe Mode with Command Prompt

A second variation of safe mode is safe mode with command prompt, which is similar to safe mode, but it loads the command interpreter as the user shell, so when the computer restarts it displays a command prompt.

Using the LastKnownGood Configuration

Selecting the LastKnownGood configuration advanced boot option starts Windows XP Professional using the registry information that Windows XP Professional saved at the last shutdown.

If you change the Windows XP Professional configuration to load a driver and have problems rebooting, you can use the last known good process to recover your working configuration. The last known good process uses the LastKnownGood configuration, stored in the registry, to boot Windows XP Professional.

Windows XP Professional provides two configurations for starting a computer, Default and LastKnownGood. Figure 18.5 shows the events that occur when you make configuration changes to your system. Any configuration changes (for example, adding or removing drivers) are saved in the Current control set.

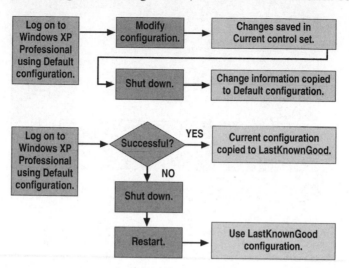

Figure 18.5   Using Default and LastKnownGood configurations

After you reboot the computer, the kernel copies the information in the Current control set to the Clone control set during the kernel initialization phase. When you successfully log on to Windows XP Professional, the information in the Clone control set is copied to the LastKnownGood control set, as shown in the lower part of Figure 18.5.

If you experience startup problems that you think might relate to Windows XP Professional configuration changes, shut down the computer without logging on, and then restart it. When you are prompted to select the operating system to start from a list of the operating systems specified in the BOOT.INI file, press F8 to open the Windows Advanced Options Menu screen. Then select the LastKnownGood Configuration option.

The next time you log on, the Current configuration is copied to the Default configuration. If your configuration changes work correctly, the next time you log on, the Current configuration is copied to the Default configuration. If your configuration changes do not work, you can restart and use the LastKnownGood Configuration option to log on.

Table 18.9 summarizes the purpose of the Default and LastKnownGood configurations.

Table 18.9   Default and LastKnownGood Configurations

Configuration	Description
Default	Contains information that the system saves when a computer shuts down. To start a computer using the default configuration, select Windows XP Professional on the Please Select The Operating System To Start menu.
LastKnownGood	Contains information that the system saves after a successful logon. The LastKnownGood configuration loads only if the system is recovering from a severe or critical device driver loading error or if it is selected during the boot process.

Table 18.10 lists situations in which you can use the LastKnownGood configuration and the related solutions.

Table 18.10   Situations in Which to Use the LastKnownGood Configuration

Situation	Solution
After a new device driver is installed, Windows XP Professional restarts, but the system stops responding.	Use the LastKnownGoodConfiguration option to start Windows XP Professional because the LastKnownGood configuration doesn't contain any reference to the new, and possibly faulty, driver.
You accidentally disable a critical device driver (such as the Scsiport driver).	Some critical drivers are written to keep users from making the mistake of disabling them. With these drivers, the system automatically reverts to the LastKnownGood control set if a user disables the driver. If the driver does not automatically cause the system to revert to the LastKnownGood control set, you must manually select the LastKnownGood Configuration option.

Using the LastKnownGood configuration does not help in the following situations:

- When the problem is not related to Windows XP Professional configuration changes. Such a problem might arise from incorrectly configured user profiles or incorrect file permissions.

- After you log on. The system updates the LastKnownGood control set with Windows XP Professional configuration changes after a successful logon.

- When startup failures relate to hardware failures or missing or corrupted files.

Important   Starting Windows XP Professional using the LastKnownGood configuration overwrites any changes made since the last successful boot of Windows XP Professional.

Using Other Advanced Boot Options

Pressing F8 during the operating system selection phase displays a screen with the Windows Advanced Options menu. This menu provides the following options:

- **Enable Boot Logging.**   Selecting the Enable Boot Logging advanced boot option logs the loading and initialization of drivers and services for trouble-shooting boot problems. All drivers and services that are loaded and initialized or that are not loaded in a file are logged. The log file, NTBTLOG.TXT, is located in the *%windir%* folder. All three versions of safe mode automatically create this boot log file.

- **Enable VGA Mode.**   Selecting the Enable VGA Mode advanced boot option starts Windows XP Professional with a basic VGA driver.

- **Directory Services Restore Mode.**   Selecting the Directory Services Restore Mode advanced boot option is only applicable to domain controllers, so it does not apply to computers running Windows XP Professional.

- **Debugging Mode.**   Selecting the Debugging Mode advanced boot option starts Windows XP Professional in kernel debug mode, which allows a debugger to break into the kernel for troubleshooting and system analysis.

Note   When using the advanced boot options in Windows XP, logging is enabled with every option except LastKnownGood Configuration. The system writes the log file (NTBTLOG.TXT) to the *%systemroot%* folder. In addition, each option except LastKnownGood Configuration loads the default VGA driver.

Using an advanced boot option to boot the system sets the environment variable *%SAFEBOOT_OPTION%* to indicate the mode used to boot the system.

Using the Recovery Console

The Windows XP Professional Recovery Console is a text-mode command interpreter that you can use to access NTFS, FAT, and FAT32 volumes without starting Windows XP Professional. The Recovery Console allows you to perform a variety of troubleshooting and recovery tasks, including the following:

- Starting and stopping services
- Reading and writing data on a local drive
- Formatting hard disks
- Repairing the MBR

Installing and Starting the Recovery Console

To install the Recovery Console, insert the Microsoft Windows XP Professional CD-ROM into your CD-ROM drive, and close the Microsoft Windows XP Professional CD dialog box, if it opens. Open a Run dialog box or a Command Prompt window in Windows XP Professional, change to the i386 folder on the Windows XP Professional CD, and then run the winnt32 command with the /cmdcons switch. After you install the Recovery Console, you can use the Windows XP Professional CD-ROM to start your computer, and then to access the Recovery Console, select the Recovery Console option when you are prompted to choose repair options.

After you start the Recovery Console, you must specify which installation of Window XP Professional you want to log on to (if you have a dual-boot or multiple-boot configuration), and then you must log on as the Administrator.

Using the Windows XP Professional Recovery Console

You can also run the Recovery Console from the Windows XP Professional CD-ROM. The Recovery Console provides a limited set of administrative commands that you can use to repair your Windows XP Professional installation. You can use the following steps to start the Recovery Console from the Windows XP Professional CD-ROM:

1. Insert the Windows XP Professional CD-ROM into the CD-ROM drive and restart the computer. If your computer or the workstation you want to repair does not have a bootable CD-ROM drive, you will need to insert your Windows XP Professional Setup Boot disk into your floppy disk drive. Insert the additional Windows XP Professional Setup disks when you are prompted to do so.

2. When Setup displays the Setup Notification message, read it, and then press ENTER to continue.

   Setup displays the Welcome To Setup screen. In addition to the initial installation of Windows XP Professional, you can use Windows Setup to repair or recover a damaged Windows XP Professional installation.

3. Press R to repair a Windows XP Professional installation.

   The Windows XP Recovery Console screen appears.

4. Press C to start the Recovery Console.

   If you have more than one installation of Windows XP Professional on the computer, you are prompted to select which installation you want to repair.

5. Type **1** and then press Enter.

   You are prompted to enter the Administrator's password.

6. Type the Administrator's password and then press ENTER.

   Setup displays a command prompt.

7. Type **help** and press ENTER for a list of the commands available.

8. When you have completed the repair process, type **exit** and press ENTER.

   The computer will restart.

Understanding the Recovery Console Commands

There are a number of commands available in the Recovery Console, some of which are described in Table 18.11.

Table 18.11   Recovery Console Commands

Command	Description
Attrib	Changes the attributes of a file or folder. – Clears an attribute + Sets an attribute **c** Compressed file attribute **h** Hidden file attribute **r** Read-only attribute **s** System file attribute
Chdir (cd)	Displays the name of the current folder or changes the current folder.
Chkdsk	Checks a disk and displays a status report.
Cls	Clears the screen.
Copy	Copies a single file to another location. You can't copy a file from a hard drive to a floppy disk, but you can copy a file from a floppy disk or a CD-ROM to a hard drive or from a hard drive to another hard drive.
Delete (Del)	Deletes one or more files.
Dir	Displays a list of files and subfolders in a folder. The wildcard characters * and ? are permitted.
Disable	Disables a system service or a device driver.
Diskpart	Creates, deletes, and manages partitions on your hard disk. **/add** Creates a new partition **/delete** Deletes an existing partition Do not modify the structure of dynamic disks with this command, because you might damage your partition table.
Enable	Starts or enables a system service or a device driver.
Exit	Exits the Recovery Console and restarts your computer.
Expand	Expands a compressed file stored on the Windows XP Professional CD-ROM or from within a .cab file and copies it to a specified destination.
Fdisk	Manages partitions on your hard disk.
Fixboot	Writes a new partition boot sector onto the system partition.

Table 18.11   *(continued)*

Command	Description
Fixmbr	Repairs the MBR of the partition boot sector. This command only overwrites the master boot code, leaving the existing partition table intact. If corruption in the MBR affects the partition table, running fixmbr might not resolve the problem.
Format	Formats a disk. If no file system is specified, NTFS is used by default.
Help	Lists the commands you can use in the Recovery Console.
Logon	Logs on to a Windows XP Professional installation.
Map	Displays the drive letter mappings.
Mkdir (md)	Creates a folder.
More	Displays a test file.
Rmdir (rd)	Deletes a folder.
Rename (ren)	Renames a single file.
Systemroot	Sets the current folder to the *%systemroot%* folder of the system you are currently logged on to.
Type	Displays a text file.

Practice: Using the Windows XP Professional Recovery Console

In this practice, you use the Windows XP Professional Recovery Console to troubleshoot a Windows XP Professional installation that will not boot. You also install and then start the Recovery Console, and you look at Help to determine what commands are available in the Recovery Console. You also use the Listsvc command to view the services and then use the Disable command to disable the Alerter service.

Caution   If your computer is not equipped with a CD-ROM drive that is capable of booting from a CD-ROM, do not do Exercise 1 or you might have to reinstall Windows XP Professional. Skip to Exercise 2.

Optional Exercise 1: Troubleshooting a Windows XP Professional Installation

In this exercise, you troubleshoot a Windows XP Professional installation and repair it using the Recovery Console.

▶   **To create a system boot failure**

1. Click Start, right-click My Computer, and then click Explore.
2. In the left pane of the Explorer window, click Local Disk (C:).

3. In the right pane of the Explorer window, right-click NTLDR and then click Rename.

4. Type **oldntldr** and then press ENTER.

   Windows XP Professional displays a Confirm File Rename dialog box asking if you are sure you want to rename the system file NTLDR to OLDNTLDR.

5. Click Yes.

6. Restart the computer.

   What error do you receive when attempting to restart the computer?

▶ **To use the Recovery Console to repair the installation**

1. Insert the Windows XP Professional installation CD into the CD-ROM drive and press CTRL+ALT+DELETE to restart the computer.

2. If your computer requires you to press a key to boot from the CD-ROM, press SPACEBAR when prompted.

3. When Setup displays the Setup Notification message, read it, and then press ENTER to continue.

   Setup displays the Welcome To Setup screen.

4. Press R to repair a Windows XP Professional installation.

   Setup starts the Recovery Console.

5. Type **1** and then press ENTER.

   You are prompted to enter the Administrator's password.

6. Type **password** and then press ENTER.

   Setup displays a C:\Windows command prompt.

7. Type **d:** and press ENTER.

Note   If your CD-ROM drive is not drive d, use the correct drive letter.

---

8. Type **cd i386** and press ENTER.

9. Type **dir** and press ENTER.

   Most of the files on the CD-ROM end with an _, for example, NTOSKRNL.EX_.

10. Press SPACEBAR to scroll through the files and locate NTLDR.

    NTLDR is not compressed so you can copy it directly to your computer.

11. Type **copy ntldr c:\ntldr** and then press ENTER.

    When the copy is complete, Setup displays a 1 file(s) copied message.

12. If there is a disk in your floppy drive, remove it. If your computer is capable of booting from the CD-ROM drive, remove the Windows XP Professional CD from your CD-ROM drive.

13. Type **exit** and press ENTER.

The computer reboots and should start normally.

Exercise 2: Installing the Windows XP Professional Recovery Console

In this exercise, you install the Recovery Console.

1. Log on as Administrator.

2. Insert the Windows XP Professional CD into the CD-ROM drive.

3. When the Microsoft Windows XP Professional CD window appears, close it.

4. Click Start, and then click Run.

5. In the Run dialog box, type **<cd-drive>:\i386\winnt32 /cmdcons** (where <cd-drive> represents the letter assigned to your CD-ROM drive), and then click OK.

A Windows Setup message box appears, indicating that you can install the Windows Recovery Console as a startup option.

6. Click Yes to install the Windows XP Professional Recovery Console.

Windows Setup attempts to contact Microsoft and confirm that you have the latest version of Setup and then it installs the Windows XP Recovery Console on your hard disk.

Windows XP Professional displays a Microsoft Windows XP Professional Setup message box indicating that the Windows Recovery Console has been successfully installed.

7. Click OK to close the Microsoft Windows XP Professional Setup dialog box.

Exercise 3: Using the Windows XP Professional Recovery Console

In this exercise you use the Help command to view the available commands. You then use the available Listsvc and Disable commands.

1. Restart your computer.

2. In the Please Select The Operating System To Start screen, select Microsoft Windows Recovery Console.

The Microsoft Windows XP Recovery Console starts and prompts you to select which Windows installation you would like to log on to. If you had more than one Windows XP Professional installation on this computer, all of them would be listed here.

3. Type **1** and then press ENTER.

4. Type **password** when prompted for the Administrator password, and then press ENTER.

5. Type **help** and then press ENTER to see the list of available commands.

6. Scroll through the list of commands.

   The Listsvc command allows you to view all the available services.

7. Type **listsvc** and press ENTER, and then scroll through the list of available services.

8. Press ESC to stop.

9. Type **disable** and then press ENTER.

   The Disable command allows you to disable a Windows system service or driver.

10. Type **disable alerter** and then press ENTER.

    Recovery Console displays several lines of text describing how the registry entry for the Alerter service has been changed from Service_Demand_Start to Service_Disabled. The Alerter service is now disabled.

11. Type **exit** and then press ENTER to restart your computer.

Exercise 4: Restarting the Alerter Service

In this exercise you confirm that the Alerter service is disabled and then restart it.

1. Log on as Administrator.

2. Click Start, click All Programs, click Administrative Tools, and then click Computer Management.

3. In the Computer Management window, expand Services And Applications.

4. Under Services And Applications, click Services.

5. Double-click Alerter.

6. In the Alerter Properties dialog box, change the Startup Type option to Automatic and then click OK.

7. Right-click Alerter, and then click Start.

8. Close the Computer Management window.

Lesson Review

The following questions will help you determine whether you have learned enough to move on to the next lesson. If you have difficulty answering these questions, review the material in this lesson before beginning the next chapter. The answers are in Appendix A, "Questions and Answers."

1. What is safe mode and why do you use it?

2. How do you start Windows XP Professional in safe mode?

3. When is the LastKnownGood configuration created?

4. When do you use the LastKnownGood configuration?

5. How can you install the Windows XP Professional Recovery Console on your computer?

Lesson Summary

- If your computer will not start, you might be able to start it by using the safe mode because Windows XP Professional starts with limited device drivers and system services.

- If you change the Windows XP Professional configuration to load a driver and have problems rebooting, you can use the LastKnownGood process to recover your working configuration.

- Pressing F8 during the operating system selection phase displays a screen with the Windows Advanced Options menu that provides the following options: Safe Mode, Safe Mode With Networking, Safe Mode With Command Prompt, Enable Boot Logging, Enable VGA Mode, LastKnownGood Configuration, Directory Services Restore Mode, and Debugging Mode.

- The Windows XP Professional Recovery Console is a command-line interface that you can use to perform a variety of troubleshooting and recovery tasks.

CHAPTER 19

Deploying Windows XP Professional

About This Chapter

This chapter prepares you to automate the process of installing Microsoft Windows XP Professional. Automated deployments can be done in three ways. The decision to use a specific method over another is usually determined by the resources, infrastructure, and deployment time required. Small deployments or situations involving many different hardware configurations often use an unattended file created with Windows Setup Manager. Many larger enterprise deployments use disk duplication to deploy systems, but using disk duplication usually requires third-party software. Microsoft provides Remote Installation Services (RIS) for use in environments where Active Directory service is available. This chapter will also look at some tools in Windows XP Professional that help make your deployment of Windows XP Professional easier. These tools include the File and Transfer Wizard, the Disk Management snap-in, and Windows Installer.

Before You Begin

To complete this chapter, you must have

- A computer that meets or exceeds the minimum hardware requirements listed in the preface, "About This Book"

Lesson 1: Automating Installations Using Windows Setup Manager

This lesson presents methods that will help you automate Windows XP Professional installations. When you must install Windows XP Professional on computers with varying configurations, scripting provides automation with increased flexibility. You will learn how the Windows Setup Manager makes it easy to create the UNATTEND.TXT files that are necessary for scripted installations.

After this lesson, you will be able to

- Install the Windows XP Professional Deployment Tools
- Automate installations of Windows XP Professional using the Windows Setup Manager
- Describe how to apply application upgrades or update packs while upgrading previous versions of Windows

Estimated lesson time: 45 minutes

Automating Installations Using the Windows Setup Manager

The computers in most networks are not identical, but they still have many similarities. It is possible to use installation scripts to specify the variations in the hardware configurations of the computers that are to receive installations.

The Windows Setup Manager allows you to quickly create a script for a customized installation of Windows XP Professional without concern for cryptic text file syntax. The Windows Setup Manager enables you to create scripts to perform customized installations on workstations and servers that meet the specific hardware and network requirements of your organization (see Figure 19.1).

Figure 19.1   The Welcome To The Windows Setup Manager Wizard page

You can create or modify an answer file, typically named UNATTEND.TXT, by using the Windows Setup Manager. You can also create UNATTEND.TXT files with a simple text editor, such as Notepad, but using the Windows Setup Manager reduces errors in syntax. The Windows Setup Manager is copied to your hard drive by extracting the files in DEPLOY.CAB located on your Windows XP Professional CD-ROM in the \Support\Tools folder. To extract the files, double-click the .cab file to display the files, select the files you want to extract, right-click the files, and then select Extract on the menu that appears.

Note For detailed steps on how to install the Windows Setup Manager, see the next practice, "Installing the Windows XP Deployment Tools," in this chapter.

Windows Setup Manager does the following:

- Provides a wizard with an easy-to-use graphical interface with which you can create and modify answer files (UNATTEND.TXT).
- Makes it easy to create Uniqueness Database Files (UNATTEND.UDB).

Note A Uniqueness Database File (UDB) provides the ability to specify per-computer parameters. The UDB modifies an answer file by overriding values in the answer file. When you run Setup with WINNT32.EXE you use the /udf:id[,UDB_file] switch. The UDB overrides values in the answer file, and the identifier (id) determines which values in the .udb file are used.

- Makes it easy to specify computer-specific or user-specific information.
- Simplifies the inclusion of application setup scripts in the answer file.
- Creates the distribution folder that you use for the installation files.

Note If you are upgrading systems to Windows XP Professional, you can add any application upgrades or update packs to the distribution folder and enter the appropriate commands in the Additional Commands page of the Windows Setup Manager Wizard so that these upgrades or update packs are applied to the application as part of the upgrade.

When you start the Windows Setup Manager, it displays the Welcome To The Windows Setup Manager Wizard page. When you click Next, you are presented with two options:

- Create A New Answer File
- Modify An Existing Answer File

If you select Create A New Answer File, you then need to choose the type of answer file you want to create. Windows Setup Manager can create the following types of answer files:

- Windows Unattended Installation
- Sysprep Install
- Remote Installation Services (RIS)

Note RIS is discussed later in this chapter in Lesson 3, "Performing Remote Installations."

The remainder of the Windows Setup Manager Wizard allows you to specify the level of user interaction with the Setup program and to enter all the information required to complete the setup.

Note The SYSDIFF.EXE program is often used in conjunction with Windows Setup Manager to install Windows using difference files.

Practice: Installing the Windows XP Professional Deployment Tools

In this practice, you extract the Windows XP Professional Deployment Tools from the Windows XP Professional CD-ROM you used for program installation, and then you use the Windows System Manager to create an unattended setup script.

Exercise 1: Extracting the Windows XP Deployment Tools

In this exercise, you extract the Windows Deployment Tools from the CD-ROM you used to install Windows XP Professional and copy them to your hard drive.

▶ **To install the System Preparation Tools**

1. Log on as Administrator and insert the Windows XP Professional CD-ROM in the CD-ROM drive.

2. Click Exit to close the Welcome To Microsoft Windows XP screen that was launched by inserting the CD-ROM.

3. Start Explorer and create the folder C:\Deploy.

   The C:\Deploy folder is used to contain the files extracted from DEPLOY.CAB on the Windows XP Professional CD-ROM.

4. Double-click D:\Support\Tools\Deploy.

Note If D is not the correct drive letter for your CD-ROM drive, replace the D with the letter representing your CD-ROM drive.

Windows XP Professional displays the contents of DEPLOY.CAB.

5. Select all of the files listed in DEPLOY.CAB.

Note To select all the files in DEPLOY.CAB, hold down the CTRL key, and then click each of the files listed.

6. Hold down the CTRL key and right-click any of the files listed in DEPLOY.CAB.

7. Click Extract on the shortcut menu.

Windows XP Professional displays the Select A Destination dialog box.

8. Click My Computer, click Local Disk (C:), click Deploy, and then click Extract.

9. Click C:\Deploy to view its contents.

The files in C:\Deploy include the following:

- **Deploy.** Compiled Hypertext Markup Language (HTML) help file
- **Readme.** Text document
- **Ref.** Compiled HTML help file
- **Setupmgr.** Compiled HTML help file
- **Setupmgr.** Microsoft Setup Manager Wizard
- **Sysprep.** Sysprep tool

10. Double-click Readme.

11. Take a moment to view the topics covered in the README.TXT file and then close Notepad.

Exercise 2: Creating an Unattended Setup Script Using Windows Setup Manager

In this exercise, you use the Windows Setup Manager to create an unattended setup script. At the same time, the Windows Setup Manager Wizard creates a distribution folder and a .udb file.

▶ **To create an unattended setup script using Setup Manager Wizard**

1. Double-click C:\Deploy\Setupmgr

Important By default, Windows XP Professional does not show common file extensions, so there are two Setupmgr files in the Deploy folder. You need to double-click the Microsoft Setup Manager Wizard.

Windows XP Professional starts the Windows Setup Manager Wizard.

2. Click Next.

   The New Or Existing Answer File page appears.

3. Ensure that Create A New Answer File is selected, and then click Next.

   The Windows Setup Manager Wizard displays the Product To Install page, which provides the following three options:

   - Windows Unattended Installation
   - Sysprep Install
   - Remote Installation Services

4. Ensure that Windows Unattended Installation is selected, and then click Next.

   The Windows Setup Manager Wizard displays the Platform page.

5. Ensure that Windows XP Professional is selected, and then click Next.

   The Windows Setup Manager Wizard displays the User Interaction Level page, which has the following five options:

   - **Provide Defaults.**   The answers you provide in the answer file are the default answers that the user sees. The user can accept the default answers or change any of the answers supplied by the script.

   - **Fully Automated.**   The installation is fully automated. The user does not have the chance to review or change the answers supplied by the script.

   - **Hide Pages.**   The answers provided by the script are supplied during the installation. Any page for which the script supplies all answers is hidden from the user, so the user cannot review or change the answers supplied by the script.

   - **Read Only.**   The script provides the answers, and the user can view the answers on any page that is not hidden, but the user cannot change the answers.

   - **GUI Attended.**   The text-mode portion of the installation is automated, but the user must supply the answers for the GUI-mode portion of the installation.

6. Select Fully Automated, and then click Next.

   The Windows Setup Manager Wizard displays the Distribution Folder page. The Setup Manager Wizard can create a distribution folder on your computer or network containing the required source files. You can add files to this distribution folder to further customize your installation.

7. Select No, This Answer File Will Be Used To Install From A CD, and then click Next.

   The Windows Setup Manager Wizard displays the License Agreement page.

8. Click I Accept The Terms Of The License Agreement, and then click Next.

   The Windows Setup Manager Wizard displays the Customize The Software page.

9. Enter your name in the Name text box and your organization in the Organization text box, and then click Next.

   The Windows Setup Manager Wizard displays the Display Settings page.

10. Leave the default settings on the Display Settings page, and then click Next.

    The Windows Setup Manager displays the Time Zone page.

11. Select the appropriate time zone and then click Next.

    The Windows Setup Manager Wizard displays the Providing The Product Key page.

12. Type in the appropriate product key.

Note   The product key identifies your copy of Windows XP Professional, so you need a separate license for each copy that you install.

---

13. Click Next.

    The Windows Setup Manager Wizard displays the Computer Names page. Notice that you have three choices:

    - Enter a series of names to be used during the various iterations of the script.

    - Click Inport and provide the name of a text file that has one computer name per line listed. Setup imports and uses these names as the computer names in the various iterations of the script.

    - Select Automatically Generate Computer Names Based On Organization Name to allow the system to automatically generate the computer names to be used.

14. In the Computer Name text box, type **PRO2**, and then click Add. Repeat this step to add PRO3 and PRO4 to the list of names.

    Notice that the names PRO2, PRO3, and PRO4 appear in the Computers To Be Installed text box.

15. Click Next.

    The Windows Setup Manager Wizard displays the Administrator Password page, which appears with the following two options:

    - Prompt The User For An Administrative Password

    - Use The Following Administrative Password (127 Characters Maximum)

Note   You selected the User Interaction level of Fully Automated, so the Prompt The User For An Administrative Password option is unavailable.

Notice that you have the option to encrypt the Administrator's password in the answer file. You also have the option to have the Administrator log on automatically and you can set the number of times you want the Administrator to log on automatically when the computer is restarted.

16. Ensure that Use The Following Administrative Password (127 Characters Maximum) is selected, and then type **password** in the Password text box and the Confirm Password text box.

17. Select Encrypt Administrator Password In Answer File and then click Next.

    The Windows Setup Manager Wizard displays the Networking Components page with the following two options:

    - **Typical Settings.** Installs Transmission Control Protocol/Internet Protocol (TCP/IP), enables Dynamic Host Configuration Protocol (DHCP), installs the Client for Microsoft Networks protocol, and installs File and Printer Sharing for Microsoft Networks for each destination computer.

    - **Custom Settings.** Allows you to select and configure the networking components to be installed.

18. Ensure Typical Settings is selected, and then click Next.

    The Windows Setup Manager Wizard displays the Workgroup Or Domain page.

19. Click Next to accept the default of the computers joining a workgroup named WORKGROUP.

    The Windows Setup Manager Wizard displays the Telephony page.

20. Select the appropriate setting for What Country/Region Are You In.

21. Select the appropriate setting for What Area (Or City) Code Are You In.

22. Select the appropriate setting for If You Dial A Number To Access An Outside Line, What Is It.

23. Select the appropriate setting for The Phone System At This Location Uses, and then click Next.

    The Windows Setup Manager Wizard displays the Regional Settings page. The default selection is Use The Default Regional Settings For The Windows Version You Are Installing.

24. Click Next to accept the default.

    The Windows Setup Manager Wizard displays the Languages page, which allows you to add support for additional languages.

25. Click Next to accept the default.

    The Windows Setup Manager Wizard displays the Browser And Shell Settings page with the following three options:

    - Use Default Internet Explorer Settings

    - Use An Autoconfiguration Script Created By The Internet Explorer Administration Kit To Configure Your Browser

    - Individually Specify Proxy And Default Home Page Settings

26. Click Next to accept the default of Use Default Internet Explorer Settings.

    The Windows Setup Manager Wizard displays the Installation Folder page with the following three options:

    ■ **A Folder Named Windows.**   This is the default selection.

    ■ **A Uniquely Named Folder Generated By Setup.**   Setup generates a unique folder name so that the installation folder will be less obvious. This folder name is recorded in the registry, so programs and program installations can easily access the Windows XP Professional system files and folders.

    ■ **This Folder.**   If you select this option you must specify a path and folder name.

27. Select This Folder. In the This Folder text box, type **WINXPPro**, and then click Next.

    The Windows Setup Manager Wizard displays the Install Printers page, which allows you to specify a network printer to be installed the first time a user logs on after Setup.

28. Click Next to continue without having the script install any network printers.

    The Windows Setup Manager Wizard displays the Run Once page. This page allows you to configure Windows to run one or more commands the first time a user logs on.

29. Click Next to continue without having the script run any additional commands.

    The Windows Setup Manager Wizard displays the Additional Commands page. This page allows you to specify additional commands to be run at the end of the unattended setup.

30. Click Finish to complete the script without having the script run any additional commands.

    The Windows Setup Manager Wizard displays a dialog box indicating that the Windows Setup Manager has successfully created an answer file. It also prompts you for a location and a name for the script. The default is C:\Deploy\UNATTEND.TXT

Note   If multiple computer names were specified, the wizard also creates a UDB file.

---

31. Click OK to accept the default filename and location.

    The Windows Setup Manager Wizard displays the Setup Manager Complete page, indicating that three new files were created in C:\Deploy: UNATTEND.TXT, UNATTEND.UDB, and UNATTEND.BAT.

32. On the File menu, click Exit.

Lesson Review

The following questions will help you determine whether you have learned enough to move on to the next lesson. If you have difficulty answering these questions, review the material in this lesson before beginning the next lesson. The answers are in Appendix A, "Questions and Answers."

1. What is the purpose of the Windows Setup Manager?

2. How could you apply an application update pack as part of the Windows XP Professional installation?

3. What type of answer files does the Windows Setup Manager allow you to create?

4. Why would you use a UDB?

Lesson Summary

- The Windows Setup Manager Wizard makes it easy to create the UNATTEND.TXT files that are necessary for scripted installations.

- The Windows Setup Manager provides a wizard with an easy-to-use graphical interface with which you can create and modify answer files and UDBs.

- To use the Windows Setup Manager, you must extract the files located in the \Support\Tools\DEPLOY.CAB file on the Windows XP Professional CD-ROM.

- The Windows Setup Manager makes it easy to specify computer-specific or user-specific information and to include application setup scripts in the answer file.

- The Windows Setup Manager can also create the distribution folder and copy the installation files to it.

Lesson 2:   Using Disk Duplication to Deploy Windows XP Professional

When you install Windows XP Professional on several computers with identical hardware configurations, the most efficient installation method to use is disk duplication. By creating a disk image of a Windows XP Professional installation and copying that image onto multiple destination computers, you save time in the rollout of Windows XP Professional. This method also creates a convenient baseline that you can easily recopy onto a computer that is experiencing significant problems.

One of the tools that you will use for disk duplication is the System Preparation tool (SYSPREP.EXE) that ships with Windows XP Professional. Knowing how to use the System Preparation tool can help you prepare master disk images for efficient mass installations. There are a number of third-party disk-imaging tools that you can use to copy the image to other computers. This lesson explains how to use the System Preparation tool to prepare the master image.

After this lesson, you will be able to

- Install and use the Windows XP Professional System Preparation tool to deploy Windows XP Professional

Estimated lesson time: 40 minutes

Examining the Disk Duplication Process

To install Windows XP Professional using disk duplication, you first need to install and configure Windows XP Professional on a test computer. You then need to install and configure any applications and application update packs on the test computer. Next, run SYSPREP.EXE on the test computer to prepare it for duplication.

Extracting the Windows System Preparation Tool

Before you can use the Windows System Preparation tool, you must copy the necessary files onto the computer you are using to create the master image. To copy the System Preparation tool, you must extract the files from \Support\ Tools\DEPLOY.CAB on the Windows XP Professional CD-ROM. For the steps to do this, see Exercise 1, "Extracting the Windows XP Professional Deployment Tools," in Lesson 1 of this chapter.

Using the System Preparation Tool to Prepare the Master Image

The System Preparation tool was developed to eliminate problems encountered in disk copying. First of all, every computer must have a unique security identifer (SID). If you copied an existing disk image to other computers, every computer on which the image was copied would have the same SID. To prevent this problem, the System Preparation tool adds a system service to the master image that creates a unique local domain SID the first time the computer to which the master image is copied is started.

The System Preparation tool also allows you to add a Mini-Setup Wizard to the master copy. This Mini-Setup Wizard runs the first time the computer to which the master image is copied is started. The Mini-Setup Wizard guides the user through entering the user-specific information such as the following:

- End-user license agreement
- Product ID
- Regional settings
- User name
- Company name
- Network configuration
- Whether the computer is joining a workgroup or domain
- Time zone selection

Note   The Mini-Setup Wizard can be scripted so that this user-specific information can be entered automatically.

The System Preparation tool causes the master image to force the computer on which the master image is copied to run a full Plug and Play device detection. The hard drive controller device driver and the hardware abstraction layer (HAL) on the computer on which the disk image was generated and on the computer to which the disk image was copied must be identical. The other peripherals, such as the network adapter, the video adapter, and sound cards on the computer on which the disk image was copied need not be identical to the ones on the computer on which the image was generated.

The System Preparation tool can also be customized. Table 19.1 describes some of the switches you can use to customize SYSPREP.EXE.

Table 19.1   Switches for SYSPREP.EXE

Switch	Description
/quiet	Runs with no user interaction because it does not show the user confirmation dialog boxes
/nosidgen	Does not regenerate SID on reboot
/pnp	Forces Setup to detect Plug and Play devices on the destination computers on the next reboot
/reboot	Restarts the source computer after SYSPREP.EXE has completed
/noreboot	Shuts down without a reboot
/forceshutdown	Forces a shutdown instead of powering off

Note   For a complete list of the switches for SYSPREP.EXE, start a command prompt, change to the Deploy folder or the folder where you installed SYSPREP.EXE, type **sysprep.exe /?** and press ENTER.

Practice: Using the Windows XP Professional System Preparation Tool to Prepare a Master Image

In this practice, you use the Windows System Preparation tool to prepare a master image for disk duplication.

Note   If you haven't completed Exercise 1 of Lesson 1 in this chapter, you must complete that exercise and extract the System Preparation tool from the Windows XP Professional CD-ROM before you can complete the following exercise.

Caution   If you complete the following exercise, you will have to reinstall Windows XP Professional on your computer.

▶   **To use the System Preparation tool**

1. Log on as Administrator.
2. Double-click C:\Deploy\Sysprep.

Note   If you did not extract the deployment tools to C:\Deploy, use the correct path to Sysprep.

A Windows System Preparation Tool dialog box appears, warning you that running Sysprep version 2.0 might modify some of the security parameters of this system.

Note   You should run Sysprep only if you are preparing your computer for duplication.

3. If you are certain that you do not mind having to reinstall Windows XP Professional, click OK to continue.

    Sysprep displays a System Preparation Tool dialog box allowing you to configure Sysprep.

Note   To quit Sysprep, in the Flags box, click the down-pointing arrow in the Shutdown box, select Quit, and then click Reseal to stop System Preparation from running on your computer.

4. In the Flags box, select Mini-Setup and then click Reseal.

    Sysprep displays a Windows System Preparation Tool message box, telling you that you have chosen to regenerate the SIDs on the next reboot. You only need to regenerate SIDs if you plan on imaging after shutdown.

Note   If you did not want to regenerate SIDs, you would click Cancel, select the NoSIDGEN check box in the Flags box, and then click Reseal.

5. Click OK.

    Sysprep displays a Sysprep Is Working message box telling you that the tool is removing the system-specific data on your computer.

6. Your computer shuts down and prompts you that it is now safe to turn off the computer.

7. Turn your computer off.

Note   You can run Setup Manager to create a SYSPREP.INF file, which provides answers to the Mini-Setup program on the destination computers. You can also use this file to specify customized drivers. Setup Manager creates a Sysprep folder at the root of the drive image and places SYSPREP.INF in this folder. The Mini-Setup program checks for SYSPREP.INF in the Sysprep folder at the root of the drive in which Windows XP Professional is being installed.

Installing Windows XP Professional from a Master Disk Image

After running Sysprep on your test computer, you are ready to run a third-party disk image copying tool to create a master disk image. Save the new disk image on a shared folder or CD-ROM and then copy this image to the multiple destination computers.

End users can then start the destination computers. The Mini-Setup Wizard prompts the user for computer-specific variables, such as the administrator password for the computer and the computer name. If a SYSPREP.INF file was provided, the Mini-Setup Wizard is bypassed and the system loads Windows XP Professional without user intervention. You can also automate the completion of the Mini-Setup Wizard further by creating a SYSPREP.INF file.

Note   When you use disk duplication, the mass storage controllers and HALs for the test computer and all destination computers must be identical.

Practice: Installing Windows XP Professional from a Master Image

In this practice, you use a master disk image, which you created earlier, to install Windows XP Professional. Normally you would use a third-party tool to copy this disk image to another computer. For the purposes of this practice, you reinstall using the master disk image as if it were a computer that had the disk image copied to it.

▶   **To install Windows XP Professional from a master disk image**

1. Power on your computer.

    Setup displays the following message: Please Wait While Windows Prepares To Start.

    After a few minutes, Setup displays the Welcome To The Windows XP Setup Wizard page.

2. Click Next to continue with Setup.

    The Windows XP Professional Setup Wizard displays the License Agreement page.

3. Read through the license agreement, click I Accept This Agreement, and then click Next.

    The Windows XP Professional Setup Wizard displays the Regional And Language Options page.

4. Ensure the Regional And Language Options and Text Input Languages settings are correct, and then click Next.

    The Windows XP Professional Setup Wizard displays the Personalize Your Software page.

5. In the Name text box, type your name. In the Organization text box, type your organization name, and then click Next.

    The Windows XP Professional Setup Wizard displays the Your Product Key page.

6. Enter your product key, and then click Next.

The Windows XP Professional Setup Wizard displays the Computer Name And Administrator Password page.

7. In the Computer Name text box, type **PRO1**.

8. In the Password and Confirm Password text boxes, type **password**, and then click Next.

The Windows XP Professional Setup Wizard displays the Modem Dialing Information page.

Note If you don't have a modem, you might not get this page. If you do not get the Modem Dialing Information page, skip to step 13.

---

9. Select the appropriate setting for What Country/Region Are You In.

10. Select the appropriate setting for What Area Or City Code Are You In.

11. Select the appropriate setting for If You Dial A Number To Access An Outside Line, What Is It.

12. Select the appropriate setting for The Phone System At This Location Uses, and then click Next.

The Windows XP Professional Setup Wizard displays the Date And Time Settings page.

13. Ensure the settings for Date, Time, Time Zone, and Daylight Saving Changes are correct and then click Next.

The Windows XP Professional Setup Wizard displays the Networking Settings page.

14. Ensure the default setting of Typical Settings is selected and then click Next.

The Windows XP Professional Setup Wizard displays the Workgroup Or Computer Domain page.

15. Ensure that No, This Computer Is Not On A Network Or Is On A Network Without A Domain is selected.

16. Ensure that WORKGROUP appears in the Workgroup Or Computer Domain Box, and then click Next.

The Windows XP Professional Setup Wizard displays the Performing Final Tasks page and then it displays the Completing The Windows XP Setup Wizard page.

17. Click Finish.

The system will reboot and the Welcome screen appears.

18. Log on as you normally would.

Lesson Review

The following questions will help you determine whether you have learned enough to move on to the next lesson. If you have difficulty answering these questions, review the material in this lesson before beginning the next lesson. The answers are in Appendix A, "Questions and Answers."

1. What is disk duplication?

2. What is the purpose of the System Preparation tool?

3. What does the /quiet switch do when you run SYSPREP.EXE?

Lesson Summary

- The System Preparation tool (SYSPREP.EXE) prepares the master computer to be duplicated.
- One of the primary functions of the System Preparation tool is to delete security identifiers (SIDs) and all other user-specific or computer-specific information.
- After you run SYSPREP.EXE on the master computer, you can use a third-party tool to capture the image and copy it to the destination computers.
- When the user restarts the destination computer, the Windows Setup Wizard appears but requires very little input to complete. You can automate the completion of the Windows Setup Wizard by creating a SYSPREP.INF file.

Lesson 3: Performing Remote Installations

The most efficient method of deploying Windows XP Professional is to use remote installation. You can perform remote installations of Windows XP Professional if you have a Microsoft Windows 2000 Server infrastructure in place and the computers in your network support remote boot.

After this lesson, you will be able to

- Describe how to deploy Windows XP Professional using RIS
- Install RIS
- Create a boot floppy

Estimated lesson time: 60 minutes

Note   To install RIS and create a boot floppy for network interface cards that are not equipped with a Pre-Boot Execution Environment (PXE) boot ROM, or for systems with basic input/output systems (BIOS) that don't support starting from the PXE boot ROM, you must have a computer running one of the Windows 2000 Server family of products. You also must have either the CD-ROM or access to a network source of files used to install the Server product and Windows XP Professional.

Understanding Remote Installation

Remote installation is the process of connecting to a server running RIS, called the RIS server, and then starting an automated installation of Windows XP Professional on a local computer. Remote installation enables administrators to install Windows XP Professional on client computers throughout a network from a central location. This reduces the time spent by administrators visiting all the computers in a network, thereby reducing the cost of deploying Windows XP Professional.

RIS provides the following benefits:

- It enables remote installation of Windows XP Professional.
- It simplifies server image management by eliminating hardware-specific images and by detecting Plug and Play hardware during setup.
- It supports recovery of the operating system and computer in the event of computer failure.
- It retains security settings after restarting the destination computer.
- It reduces total cost of ownership (TCO) by allowing either users or technical staff to install the operating system on individual computers.

Installing and Configuring RIS

Before beginning a rollout of Windows XP Professional using RIS, you should become familiar with the prerequisites for the service and you must install the service using the Remote Installation Services Setup Wizard.

Examining the Prerequisites

RIS is only available on computers running one of the Windows 2000 Server family of products. The RIS server can be a domain controller or a member server. Table 19.2 lists the network services required for RIS and their RIS function. These network services do not have to be installed on the same computer as RIS, but they must be available somewhere on the network.

Table 19.2   Network Services Requirements for RIS

Network service	RIS function
DNS Service	RIS relies on the DNS server for locating both the directory service and client computer accounts.
DHCP service	Client computers that can perform a network boot receive an IP address from the DHCP server.
Active Directory	RIS relies on the Active Directory service in Windows XP Professional for locating existing client computers as well as existing RIS servers.

Remote installation requires that RIS (included on the Windows 2000 Server CD-ROM) be installed on a volume that is shared over the network. This shared volume must meet the following criteria:

- The shared volume cannot be on the same drive that is running Windows 2000 Server.
- The shared volume must be large enough to hold the RIS software and the various Windows XP Professional images.
- The shared volume must be formatted with the Windows 2000 NTFS file system version 5 or later.

Using the Remote Installation Services Setup Wizard

When your network meets the prerequisites for RIS, you can run the Remote Installation Services Setup Wizard, which does the following:

- It installs the RIS software.
- It creates the remote installation folder and copies the Windows XP Professional installation files to the server.
- It adds .sif files, which are a variation of an UNATTEND.TXT file.
- It configures the Client Installation Wizard screens that appear during a remote installation.

- It updates the registry.
- It creates the Single-Instance Store volume.
- It starts the required RIS.

When installation of RIS is complete, you can configure RIS using the server's computer object in the Active Directory Users and Computers console. For more information on the management of Active Directory objects, see Chapter 5, "Using the DNS Service and Active Directory Service."

The RIS server stores the RIS images used to automatically install Windows XP Professional on client computers that are enabled for remote boot. The RIS server can be a domain controller or a stand-alone server that is a member of a domain containing Active Directory.

Practice: Installing and Configuring RIS

In this practice, you install Windows 2000 RIS from a Windows 2000 Server CD-ROM and then configure RIS.

Note To complete this exercise you need to have a Windows XP Professional CD-ROM or access to a shared folder that contains the Windows XP Professional installation files. You must also have a drive on a computer running one of the Windows 2000 Server family of products on which you installed RIS, formatted with NTFS version 5 or later and containing enough room to hold the Windows XP Professional installation files. There must be a DHCP server available on your network, a DNS server on your network, and a domain.

Exercise 1: Installing RIS

In this exercise, you install RIS on a computer running Windows 2000 Server.

▶ **To install RIS**

1. Log on as Administrator, and insert the Windows 2000 Server CD-ROM into your CD-ROM drive.
2. Click Start, point to Settings, and then click Control Panel.
3. Double-click Add/Remove Programs.

   Control Panel displays the Add/Remove Programs window.
4. Click Add/Remove Windows Components.
5. In the Add/Remove Windows Components window, in the Components box, select Remote Installation Services.

   Do not change the other items that are currently selected.

6. Click Next.

Setup installs and configures RIS.

The Completing The Windows Components Wizard page appears.

7. Click Finish.

A System Settings Change dialog box appears, indicating that you must reboot before the new settings will take effect.

8. Remove the Windows 2000 Server CD-ROM from your CD-ROM drive and click Yes.

Exercise 2: Configuring RIS

In this exercise, you configure RIS.

▶ **To configure RIS**

1. Log on as administrator.

The Microsoft Windows 2000 Configure Your Server screen appears, indicating that you have selected components that require additional configuration.

2. Click Finish Setup.

The Add/Remove Programs window appears, indicating that you now need to configure RIS.

3. Click Configure.

Windows 2000 Server displays the Welcome To The Remote Installation Services Setup Wizard page.

4. Read the information in the Welcome page and then click Next.

The Remote Installation Services Setup Wizard displays the Remote Installation Folder Location page.

Notice the drive on which you create the Remote Installation folder cannot be the system drive and must be formatted with NTFS version 5 or later.

5. Enter **E:\RemoteInst** in the Path text box.

Note Enter an appropriate path for your system. The folder should not exist; it is created as part of the configuration process. Remember that the drive must be on the computer on which you installed RIS, must be formatted with NTFS version 5 or later, and must have about 300 MB of space available to hold the Windows XP Professional installation files.

---

6. Click Next to accept the default settings.

Note By default, the RIS server does not support client computers until you configure it to do so.

The Remote Installation Services Setup Wizard displays the Initial Settings page.

7. Select the Respond To Client Computers Requesting Service check box and then click Next.

The Remote Installation Services Setup Wizard displays the Installation Sources Files Location page.

8. Enter the path to the installation source files and then click Next.

Note If you were using a Windows XP Professional CD-ROM in the CD-ROM drive of the server on which you were configuring RIS, you would enter $X:\backslash$i386, where X is the drive letter for the CD-ROM drive.

The Remote Installation Services Setup Wizard displays the Windows Installation Image Folder Name page.

9. In the Folder Name text box, type **WINXP.PRO** and then click Next.

The Remote Installation Services Setup Wizard displays the Friendly Description And Help Text page.

10. Click Next to accept the default friendly description and help text.

Note The default description is Microsoft Windows XP Professional. The help text is "Automatically installs Windows Professional without prompting the user for input."

The Remote Installation Services Setup Wizard displays the Review Settings page.

11. Review the information and then click Finish.

It takes several minutes for the following steps to complete:

- The remote installation folder is created.
- The files needed by the services are copied.
- The Windows installation files are copied.
- The client installation wizard screen files are updated.
- A new unattended Setup answer file is created.
- RIS is created.
- The registry is updated.
- The Single-Instance-Store volume is created.
- The required RIS are started.

12. When all the tasks are completed, click Done and close any open windows.

Understanding Client Requirements for Remote Installation

Client computers that support remote installation must have one of the following configurations:

- A configuration meeting the Net PC specification.
- A network adapter card with a PXE boot ROM and BIOS support for starting from the PXE boot ROM.
- A supported network adapter card and a remote installation boot disk.

Net PCs

The Net PC is a highly manageable platform with the ability to perform a network boot, manage upgrades, and prevent users from changing the hardware or operating system configuration. Additional requirements for the Net PC are as follows:

- The network adapter must be set as the primary boot device within the system BIOS.
- The user account that will be used to perform the installation must be assigned the user right Log On as a Batch Job. For more information on assigning user rights, see Chapter 13, "Configuring Security Settings and Internet Options."

Note   The Administrator group does not have the right to log on to a batch job by default and thus will need to be assigned this right prior to attempting a remote installation.

- Users must be assigned permission to create computer accounts in the domain they are joining. The domain is specified in the Advanced Settings on the RIS server.

Computers Not Meeting the Net PC Specification

Computers that do not directly meet the Net PC specification can still interact with the RIS server. To enable remote installation on a computer that does not meet the Net PC specification, perform the following steps:

1. Install a network adapter card with a PXE boot ROM.
2. Set the BIOS to start from the PXE boot ROM.
3. The user account that will be used to perform the installation must be assigned the user right Log On as a Batch Job.
4. Users must be assigned permission to create computer accounts in the domain they are joining. The domain is specified in the Advanced Settings on the RIS server.

Creating Boot Floppies

If the network adapter card in a client is not equipped with a PXE boot ROM or the BIOS does not allow starting from the network adapter card, create a remote installation boot disk. The boot disk simulates the PXE boot process. Windows 2000 ships with the Windows 2000 Remote Boot Disk Generator (see Figure 19.2), which allows you to easily create a boot disk.

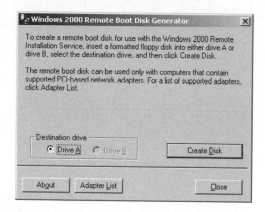

Figure 19.2   Windows 2000 Remote Boot Disk Generator

Run RBFG.EXE to start the Windows 2000 Remote Boot Disk Generator. The RBFG.EXE file is located in the \RemoteInstall\Admin\i386 folder on the Remote Installation server. These boot floppies only support the Peripheral Component Interconnect (PCI)-based network adapters listed in the Adapters List. To see the list of the supported network adapters, click Adapter List, as shown in Figure 19.2. A partial listing of the supported network adapter cards is shown in Figure 19.3.

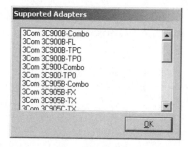

Figure 19.3   Network adapters supported by boot floppies

You also need to set the user rights and permissions. The user account that will be used to perform the installation must be assigned the user right Log On as a Batch Job. The users must be assigned permission to create computer accounts in the domain they are joining. The domain is specified in the Advanced Settings on the RIS server.

Practice: Creating a Remote Boot Disk

In this practice, you create a remote boot disk.

▶ **To create a remote boot disk**

1. Log on as administrator.
2. Click Start and then click Run.

   The Run dialog box appears.
3. Type **E:\RemoteInst\Admin\i386\rbfg** in the Open text box.

Note   Your path for RBFG.EXE may vary. See Step 5 under the procedure to install RIS in the previous practice.

4. Click OK.

   The Windows 2000 Remote Boot Disk Generator window appears.
5. Read the information in the Windows 2000 Remote Boot Disk Generator window and then click Adapter List.
6. Scroll through the list of supported adapters, and then click OK to return to the Windows 2000 Remote Boot Disk Generator.
7. Insert a formatted 3.5-inch floppy into your floppy disk drive.

Note   If you have more than one floppy disk drive in your computer, make sure you select the appropriate floppy disk drive in the Windows 2000 Remote Boot Disk Generator.

8. Click Create Disk.

   A Windows 2000 Remote Boot Disk Generator dialog box appears, prompting you to create another boot floppy.
9. Click No.
10. Click Close to close the Windows 2000 Remote Boot Disk Generator window.

Lesson Review

The following questions will help you determine whether you have learned enough to move on to the next lesson. If you have difficulty answering these questions, review the material in this lesson before beginning the next lesson. The answers are in Appendix A, "Questions and Answers."

1. What is a RIS server and what is it used for?

2. What network services are required for RIS?

3. What can you do if the network adapter card in a client is not equipped with a PXE boot ROM? Does this solution work for all network adapter cards? Why or why not?

4. What user rights must be assigned to the user account that will be used to perform the remote installation?

Lesson Summary

- If you have a Windows 2000 Server infrastructure in place and the computers in your network support remote boot, the most efficient method of deploying Windows XP Professional is to use remote installation.

- Remote installation is the process of connecting to a Remote Installation Services (RIS) server and starting an automated installation of Windows XP Professional on a local computer.

- Remote installation enables administrators to install Windows XP Professional on client computers throughout a network from a central location.

- Client computers that support remote installation must have one of the following configurations:

    - A configuration meeting the Net PC specification, and the network adapter must be set as the primary boot device within the system BIOS

    - A network adapter card with a Pre-Boot Execution Environment (PXE) boot ROM and BIOS support for starting from the PXE boot ROM

    - A supported network adapter card and a remote installation boot disk

- The user account that will be used to perform the installation must be assigned the user right Log On as a Batch Job and must be assigned permission to create computer accounts in the domain they are joining.

Lesson 4: Using Tools to Simplify Deployment

There are some additional tools in Windows XP Professional that will help make your deployment of the operating system easier. These tools include the File and Transfer Wizard, the Disk Management snap-in, and Windows Installer and the .msi package file format.

After this lesson, you will be able to

- Use the Files and Settings Transfer Wizard
- Use the Disk Management snap-in
- Understand how to manage applications using Windows Installer

Estimated lesson time: 60 minutes

Using the Files and Settings Transfer Wizard

Windows XP Professional provides the Files and Settings Transfer Wizard to simplify the task of moving data files and personal settings from your old computer to your new one. You don't have to configure all of your personal settings on your new computer because you can move your old settings, including display settings, Microsoft Internet Explorer and Microsoft Outlook Express options, dial-up connections, and your folder and taskbar options, to your new computer. The wizard also helps you move specific files and folders to your new computer as well.

Connecting Your Old and New Computers

The best way to connect your old computer to your new computer is to use a direct cable connection or a network.

To directly connect your computers using a cable, you must have the following items:

- An available COM port (serial port) on both computers
- A null modem cable long enough to connect the two computers

Tip Null modem cables are sometimes called serial file transfer cables. The null modem cable must be serial. You cannot use parallel cables for file transfers using the Direct cable option. Most older computers have 25-pin COM ports and most newer ones have 9-pin COM ports. Before you purchase your cable, check what type of COM ports are on your computers.

When you have connected your computers with a null modem cable, you are ready to run the Files and Settings Transfer Wizard.

The best way to connect your old and new computers is with a network. To connect your computers and use a network, you must have the following items:

- A network interface card (NIC) or a universal serial bus (USB) network interface installed in both computers
- Network cables, and in most cases a hub, to connect the two computers

When you have connected your two computers with cables and a hub, you can use the Network Setup Wizard to set up your network.

Note   For information about running the Network Setup Wizard, see Chapter 6, "Setting Up, Configuring, and Troubleshooting Common Setup and Configuration Problems for Network Printers."

After you have set up your network by running the Network Setup Wizard, or if both of your computers are part of a larger network, you are ready to run the Files and Settings Transfer Wizard.

To open the Files and Settings Transfer Wizard, do the following:

1. Click Start, point to All Programs, point to Accessories, and point to System Tools.
2. Click Files And Settings Transfer Wizard.

    Windows XP Professional starts the Files and Settings Transfer Wizard.
3. In the Welcome To The Files And Settings Transfer Wizard page, click Next.

    The Files and Settings Transfer Wizard displays the What Computer Is This page, which has the following two options:

    - **New Computer.**   Select this option if you want to transfer your files and settings to this computer.

    - **Old Computer.**   Select this option if you want to transfer the files and settings on this computer to your new computer.

Note   The old computer can be running Microsoft Windows 95, Microsoft Windows 98, Microsoft Windows 98SE, Microsoft Windows Me, Microsoft Windows NT 4, Windows 2000, or Windows XP (32-bit).

---

4. Select the Old Computer option and click Next.

The Files and Settings Transfer Wizard displays the Select The Transfer Method page, which has the following three options:

- **Direct Cable.**   A cable that connects your computer's serial ports.
- **Floppy Drive Or Other Removable Media.**   Both computers must have the same type of drive.
- **Other.**   You can save files and settings to any disk drive or folder on your computer.

Note   If you are saving the files and settings to your computer, you can click Browse to locate or create a new folder to hold the files and settings.

5. Select the appropriate option and click Next.

The Files and Settings Transfer Wizard displays the What Do You Want To Transfer page, which has the following three options:

- Settings Only

Note   The following settings are transferred: Accessibility, Command Prompt Settings, Display Properties, Internet Explorer Settings, Microsoft Messenger, Microsoft NetMeeting, Mouse And Keyboard, MSN Explorer, Network Printer And Drives, Outlook Express, Regional Settings, Sounds And Multimedia, Taskbar Options, Windows Media Player, and Windows Movie Maker.

- Files Only

Note   The following folders are transferred: Desktop, Fonts, My Documents, My Pictures, Shared Desktop, and Shared Documents. The following files types are transferred: *.asf (Windows Media Audio/Video file), *.asx (Windows Media Audio/Video shortcut), *.AU (AU format sound), *.avi (video clip), *.cov (fax cover page file), *.cpe (fax cover page file), *.doc (WordPad document), *.eml (Internet e-mail message), *.m3u (M3U file), *.mid (MIDI sequence), *.midi (MIDI sequence), *.mp2 (Movie File MPEG), *.mp3 (MP3 Format Sound), *.mpa (Movie File MPEG), *.mpeg (Movie File MPEG), *.MSWMM (Windows Movie Maker Project), *.nws (Internet News Message), *.rft (Rich Text Format), *.snd (AU Sound Format), *.wav (Wave Sound), *.wm (Windows Media Audio/Video file), *.wma (Windows Media Audio file), *.wri (Write document).

- Both Files And Settings

Tip   You can select the Let Me Select A Custom List Of Files And Settings When I Click Next check box if you don't want all the default folders, file types, and settings to be transferred.

6. Select the appropriate option and click Next.

   Unless you select the Let Me Select A Custom List Of Files And Settings When I Click Next check box, the Files and Settings Transfer Wizard displays the Collection In Progress page.

   The Files and Settings Transfer Wizard displays the Completing The Collection Phase page.

Caution   This page indicates any files and settings that the wizard could not collect. You must manually transfer these files and settings or they will not be transferred to your new computer.

7. Click Finish to complete the wizard on your old computer.

8. Move to your new computer and run the Files and Settings Transfer Wizard on it to complete the transfer of files and settings.

Using Disk Management

The Disk Management snap-in provides a central location for disk information and management tasks, such as creating and deleting partitions and volumes, formatting them with the file allocation table (FAT), FAT32, or NTFS file systems, and assigning drive letters to them. With the proper permissions you can manage disks locally and on remote computers. In addition to monitoring disk information, some of the other disk management tasks that you might need to perform include adding and removing hard disks and changing the disk storage type.

Note   For a review of the FAT, FAT32, and NTFS file systems, see Chapter 2, "Installing Windows XP Professional."

Setting Up a Hard Disk

Whether you are setting up the remaining free space on a hard disk on which you installed Windows XP Professional or setting up a new hard disk, you need to be aware of the tasks involved. Before you can store data on a new hard disk, you must perform the following tasks to prepare the disk:

1. Initialize the disk with a storage type.

   Initialization defines the fundamental structure of a hard disk. Windows XP Professional supports basic storage and dynamic storage. A physical disk can be either basic or dynamic; you can't use both storage types on one disk.

2. Create partitions on a basic disk or create volumes on a dynamic disk.

3. Format the disk. After you create a partition or volume, you must format it with the FAT, FAT32, or NTFS file system.

Understanding Basic Storage

The traditional industry standard is basic storage. It dictates the division of a hard disk into partitions. A partition is a portion of the disk that functions as a physically separate unit of storage. Windows XP Professional recognizes primary and extended partitions. A disk that is initialized for basic storage is called a *basic disk*. A basic disk can contain primary partitions, extended partitions, and logical drives (see Figure 19.4).

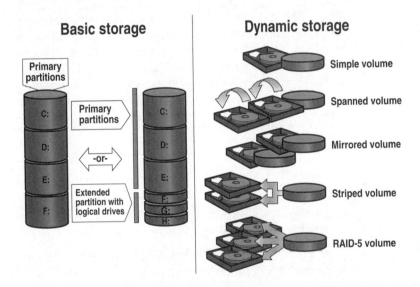

Figure 19.4   Basic and dynamic storage types

Because basic storage is the traditional industry standard, all versions of Microsoft Windows, Microsoft MS-DOS, Windows NT, Windows 2000, and Windows XP support basic storage. For Windows XP Professional, basic storage is the default.

You can divide a basic disk into primary and extended partitions. Partitions function as physically separate storage units. Table 19.3 describes some of the characteristics of primary partitions and extended partitions.

Table 19.3   Primary and Extended Partitions

Primary partitions	Extended partitions
A basic disk can contain up to four primary partitions, or up to three primary partitions if there is an extended partition.	A basic disk can contain only one extended partition.
Can be marked as the active partition, where the hardware looks for the boot files to start the operating system (only one active partition per hard disk).	Can't be marked as the active partition.
Formatted and assigned a drive letter.	Divided into logical drives, each of which is formatted and assigned a drive letter.

Note   The Windows XP Professional *system partition* is the active partition that contains the hardware-specific files required to load the operating system. The Windows XP Professional *boot partition* is the primary partition or logical drive where the operating system files are installed. The boot partition and the system partition can be the same partition. However, the system partition must be on the active partition, typically drive C, whereas the boot partition could be on another primary partition or an extended partition.

You create a partition by following these steps:

1. Select Disk Management in the Storage section of the Computer Management snap-in.
2. On the basic disk where you want to create the partition, right-click the unallocated space, then click New Partition.

   Disk Management starts the New Partition Wizard.
3. In the New Partition Wizard, click Next.
4. Select Primary Partition or Extended Partition.
5. Specify the size of the partition you want to create.
6. Assign a drive letter, assign a path, or select Do Not Assign A Drive Letter Or Drive Path and then click Next.
7. Select a file system to format the partition or select Do Not Format The Partition and then click Next.
8. Review the information displayed in the Completing The New Partition Wizard page and, if it is correct, click Finish to create the partition.

Tip If any of the information in the Completing The New Partition Wizard page is incorrect, click Back to back up and correct it.

Understanding Dynamic Storage

Windows 2000 and Windows XP Professional support *dynamic storage*, which is a standard that creates a single partition including the entire disk. A disk that you initialize for dynamic storage is a *dynamic disk*. You divide dynamic disks into volumes, which can consist of a portion, or portions, of one or more physical disks.

When you have converted a basic disk to dynamic storage, you can create Windows XP Professional volumes. Consider which among the following volume types best suit your needs for efficient use of disk space and performance.

- **Simple volume.** Contains disk space from a single disk and is not fault tolerant.

- **Spanned volume.** Includes disk space from multiple disks (up to 32). Windows XP Professional writes data to a spanned volume on the first disk, completely filling the space, and continues in this manner through each disk that you include in the spanned volume. These volumes are not fault tolerant. If any disk in a spanned volume fails, the data in the entire volume is lost.

- **Striped volume.** Combines areas of free space from multiple hard disks (up to 32) into one logical volume. In a striped volume, Windows XP Professional optimizes performance by adding data to all disks at the same rate. If a disk in a striped volume fails, the data in the entire volume is lost.

Note Windows 2000 Server products provide fault tolerance on dynamic disks. Fault tolerance is the ability of a computer or operating system to respond to some catastrophic events without loss of data. The Windows 2000 Server products provide striped volumes and RAID-5 volumes that are fault tolerant. Windows XP Professional does not provide fault tolerance.

Creating multiple partitions or volumes on a single hard disk allows you to efficiently organize data for tasks such as backing up. For example, create a partition for the operating system, one for applications, and one for data. When you back up your data, you can back up the entire data partition on a daily basis and only back up the application and operating system partitions on a monthly or quarterly basis.

Note Removable storage devices contain primary partitions only. You can't create extended partitions, logical drives, or dynamic volumes on a removable storage device. You can't mark a primary partition on a removable storage device as active.

Working with Simple Volumes

A simple volume contains disk space from a single disk. You can extend a simple volume to include unallocated space on the same disk. You can create a simple volume and format it with NTFS, FAT, or FAT32. You can extend a simple volume only if it is formatted with NTFS.

You can create a simple volume by following these steps:

1. Select Disk Management in the Storage section of the Computer Management snap-in.

2. On the dynamic disk where you want to create the volume, right-click the unallocated space, and then click New Volume.

   Disk Management starts the New Volume Wizard.

3. In the New Volume Wizard, click Next.

4. Click Simple Volume, and then follow the instructions on your screen.

To extend an NTFS simple volume, right-click the simple volume that you want to extend, click Extend Volume, and then follow the instructions on your screen. When you extend a simple volume to another disk, it becomes a spanned volume.

Working with Spanned Volumes

A spanned volume consists of disk space from multiple dynamic disks; spanned volumes enable you to combine the available free space on these disks. Spanned volumes can't be part of a striped volume and are not fault tolerant. Only NTFS-spanned volumes can be extended, and deleting any part of a spanned volume deletes the entire volume.

You can combine various-sized areas of free space from 2 to 32 dynamic disks into one large logical volume. Windows XP Professional organizes spanned volumes so that data is stored in the space on one disk until it is full, and then, starting at the beginning of the next disk, data is stored in the space on the second disk, and so forth.

You can extend existing spanned volumes formatted with NTFS by adding free space. Disk Management formats the new area without affecting any existing files on the original volume. You can't extend volumes formatted with FAT or FAT32 and you can't extend the system volume or a boot volume.

Working with Striped Volumes

Striped volumes offer the best performance of all the Windows XP Professional disk management strategies. In a striped volume, data is written evenly across all physical disks in 64-KB units. Because all the hard disks that belong to the striped volume perform the same functions as a single hard disk, Windows XP can issue and process concurrent I/O commands simultaneously on all hard disks. In this way, striped volumes can increase system I/O speed.

You create striped volumes by combining areas of free space from multiple disks (from 2 to 32) into one logical volume. With a striped volume, Windows writes data to multiple disks, similar to spanned volumes. However, on a striped volume, Windows XP writes files across all disks so that data is added to all disks at the same rate. Like spanned volumes, striped volumes don't provide fault tolerance. If a disk in a striped volume fails, the data in the entire volume is lost. You cannot extend striped volumes.

To create a striped volume, follow these steps:

1. In Disk Management, on the dynamic disk where you want to create the striped volume, right-click the unallocated space, and then click New Volume.

   Disk Management launches the New Volume Wizard.

2. In the New Volume Wizard, click Next.

3. Click Striped Volume, and then follow the instructions on your screen.

Adding Disks

When you install new disks in a computer running Windows XP Professional, they are added as basic storage. To add a new disk, install or attach the new physical disk (or disks), and then click Rescan Disks on the Action menu of the Disk Management snap-in. You must use Rescan Disks every time you remove or add a disk to a computer. You shouldn't need to restart the computer when you add a new disk. However, you might need to restart the computer if Disk Management doesn't detect the new disk after you run Rescan Disks.

Disk Management makes all aspects of managing disks easier. For example, once you have installed your new disk, on the Action menu, point to All Tasks to select the following options: Mark Partition As Active and Change Drive Letter And Paths, Format, or Properties. Table 19.4 describes the information displayed in the Properties dialog box for a disk.

Table 19.4 Tabs of the Properties Dialog Box for a Disk

Tab	Description
General	Lists the device type, manufacturer, and physical location of the device, including the bus number or the Small Computer System Interface (SCSI) identifier; lists the device status and provides access to the Troubleshooter for the device
Policies	Allows you to set the following options for Write Caching and Safe Removal: **Optimize For Quick Removal.** Disables write caching on the disk and in Windows **Optimize For Performance.** Enables write caching in Windows to improve disk performance **Enable Write Caching On This Disk.** Enables write caching to improve disk performance, but a power outage or equipment failure might result in data loss or corruption

(continued)

Table 19.4   *(continued)*

Tab	Description
Volumes	Lists the volumes contained in this disk
Driver	Allows you to get detailed information about the driver, to update the driver, to roll back the driver, and to uninstall the driver

Table 19.5 describes the information displayed in the Properties dialog box for a partition or volume.

Table 19.5   Tabs of the Properties Dialog Box for a Partition or Volume

Tab	Description
General	Lists the volume label, type, file system, the used space, the free space, and the total disk capacity. It also allows you to run Disk Cleanup, and on NTFS volumes it allows you to compress the drive and to allow the Indexing Service to index the disk for fast file searching.
Tools	Allows you to check the partition or volume for errors, to defragment it, and to back it up.
Hardware	Shows you all drives on the computer and allows you to view the properties of each device including the manufacturer, the location, and the status of the device. It also allows you to access the troubleshooter for the device.
Sharing	Allows you to share the drive, to set permissions on the share, and to determine the type of caching for the share.
Security	Allows you to set the NTFS permissions. This tab is available only if it is formatted with the NTFS file system.
Quota	Allows you to enable and configure quota management. This tab is available only if it is formatted with the NTFS file system.

Note   You can also add disks that you remove from another computer and move them to your computer. When you move a dynamic disk to your computer from another computer, you can see and use any existing volumes on that disk, unless a volume on the disk extends to multiple disks and you don't move all the disks for that volume.

Changing Storage Type

You can upgrade a disk from basic storage to dynamic storage at any time without loss of data. However, any disk to be upgraded must contain at least 1 MB of unallocated space for the upgrade to succeed. Before you upgrade disks, close any programs that are running on those disks.

Caution   Always back up the data on a disk before converting the storage type.

Table 19.6 shows the results of converting a disk from basic storage to dynamic storage.

Table 19.6 Basic Disk and Dynamic Disk Organization

Basic disk organization	Dynamic disk organization
System partition	Simple volume
Boot partition	Simple volume
Primary partition	Simple volume
Extended partition	Simple volume for each logical drive and any remaining unallocated space
Logical drive	Simple volume
Volume set	Spanned volume
Stripe set	Striped volume

To upgrade a basic disk to a dynamic disk, in the Disk Management snap-in, right-click the basic disk that you want to upgrade, and then click Upgrade To Dynamic Disk. A wizard provides on-screen instructions. The upgrade process requires that you restart your computer when complete.

If you find it necessary to convert a dynamic disk to a basic disk, you must remove all volumes from the dynamic disk before you can change it to a basic disk. To convert a dynamic disk to a basic disk, right-click the dynamic disk, and then click Revert To Basic Disk.

Caution All data on a dynamic disk will be lost when you convert it to a basic disk.

Using Refresh and Rescan Disks

If you need to update the information displayed in Disk Management, you can use the Refresh and Rescan commands. The Refresh command updates the drive letter, file system, volume, and removable media information, and determines whether unreadable volumes are now readable. To update disk information, on the Action menu, click Refresh.

Rescan Disks updates hardware information. When Disk Management rescans disks, it scans all attached disks for disk configuration changes. It also updates information on removable media, CD-ROM drives, basic volumes, file systems, and drive letters. Rescanning disks can take several minutes, depending on the number of hardware devices installed. To update disk information, click the Action menu, and then click Rescan Disks.

Managing Disks on a Remote Computer

In a workgroup environment, you can manage disks on a remote computer running Windows XP Professional if you have the same account with the exact same password set up on both the local and remote computer.

Note   In a domain environment, members of the Domain Admins group or the Server Operators group can manage disks on remote computers.

To manage disks on a remote computer, open an empty Microsoft Management Console (MMC) console, add the Computer Management snap-in, and focus it on the remote computer.

Using Windows Installer

Windows Installer and the .msi package file format simplify the installation and removal of software applications. If there is a problem during the installation of a software application or the installation fails, Windows Installer can restore or roll back the operating system to its original state. Windows Installer also reduces conflicts between applications by preventing the installation of an application from overwriting a dynamic-link library (DLL) used by another application. Windows Installer can determine if an application you installed using it has any missing or corrupted files and then can replace them to resolve the problem.

To preserve users' disk space, Windows Installer allows you to install only the essential files required to run an application. It supports the installation of application features on demand, which means that the first time a user accesses any feature not included in the minimal installation, the necessary files are automatically installed. Windows Installer allows you to configure unattended application installations and it supports both 32-bit and 64-bit applications.

Windows Installer supports Microsoft's new .NET technology. The .NET framework and the common language runtime allow developers to create write-once, compile-once, run anywhere applications. The .NET framework delivers code reuse, code specialization, resource management, multilanguage development, security, deployment, and administration. Windows Installer also provides software restriction policies that provide virus protection, including protection from Trojan horse viruses and worms propagated through e-mail and the Web.

Windows Installer is a core part of Intellimirror and a core component of the Windows Group Policy-based change and configuration management technology. Windows Installer has a client-side installer service, MSIEXEC.EXE, and a package .msi file. The installer service is an operating system service that allows the operating system to control the installation. Windows Installer uses the information stored in the package file to install the application.

This feature is used in a domain environment but it can also be configured for a workgroup environment. You can view how to configure Windows Installer

Group Policy options for users in a workgroup environment if you click Start, point to All Programs, point to Administrative Tools, and click Local Group Policy. In the Local Group Policy snap-in (see Figure 19.5), click Local Computer Policy\User Configuration\Administrative Templates\Windows Components\Windows Installer.

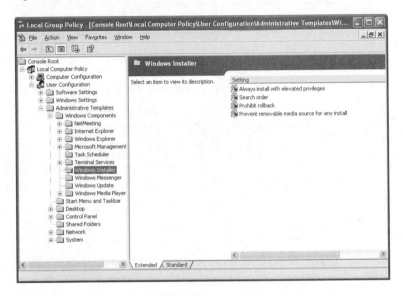

Figure 19.5   Group Policy Windows Installer options for users

To configure Windows Installer Group Policy options for computers, in the Local Group Policy snap-in, click Local Computer Policy\Computer Configuration\ Administrative Templates\Windows Components\Windows Installer.

Note   For detailed steps on how to configure Group Policy, see Chapter 13, "Configuring Security Settings and Internet Options."

To add, modify, or remove categories for applications to be managed, you must be a domain administrator or have equivalent rights.

Troubleshooting Windows Installer Packages

How you troubleshoot a Windows Installer package depends on the problem you are having. If a Windows Installer package doesn't install correctly, you need to determine if the package has become corrupted. To repair a corrupted Windows Installer package, use the Windows Installer repair option. Open a command prompt and type the following command:

```
msiexec /f[p][o][e][d][c[][a][u][m][s][v] {package|ProductCode}
```

For an explanation of the parameters used with the /f switch in the MSIEXEC.EXE command, see Table 19.7.

Table 19.7   Parameters for the /f Switch for MSIEXEC.EXE

Parameters	Description
P	Reinstall only if the file is missing
O	Reinstall if the file is missing or if an older version is installed
E	Reinstall if the file is missing or if an equal or older version is installed
D	Reinstall if the file is missing or if a different version is installed
C	Reinstall if the file is missing or if the stored checksum does not match the calculated value
A	Force all the files to be reinstalled
U	Rewrite all the required user-specific registry entries
M	Rewrite all the required computer-specific registry entries
S	Overwrite all the existing shortcuts
V	Run from source and recache the local package

There are several additional switches for the MSIEXEC.EXE command. These switches include the ones explained in Table 19.8. In this table, package is the name of the Windows Installer Package file and *ProductCode* is the globally unique identifier (GUID) of the Windows Installer package. For a complete listing of switches, see Help and Support Center.

Table 19.8   Switches for MSIEXEC.EXE

Switch	Parameter	Description
/I	{package|*ProductCode*}	Installs or configures a product For example: msiexec /i a:\sample.msi
/a	package	Administrative installation option For example: msiexec /a a:\sample.msi
/x	{package|*ProductCode*}	Uninstalls a product For example: msiexec /x sample.msi
/j	[u|m]package]	Advertises a product, as follows: **u** Advertises to the current user **m** Advertises to all users For example: msiexec /jm sample.msi
/L	[i][w][e][a][r][u] [c][m][p][v][+][!]logfile	The path to the log file. The parameters specify what to log, as follows: **i** Log status messages **w** Log nonfatal warnings **e** Log all error messages

Table 19.8   *(continued)*

Switch	Parameter	Description
	a	Log all startup actions
	r	Log action-specific records
	u	Log user requests
	c	Log initial user interface parameters
	m	Log out of memory
	p	Log terminal properties
	v	Log verbose output
	+	Append to existing file
	!	Flush each line to the log
	*	Log all information except the v option (wildcard)
		To include the v options, specify /L*v

If the installation process stops before completing, either Windows Installer was unable to read the package or conditions on your computer prevented it from installing the application. Open Event Viewer and review the Application log.

Note   For more information about how to use Event Viewer, see Chapter 12, "Auditing Resources and Events."

Publishing and Installing Applications

Publishing an application does not install the application on users' computers and it does not place any shortcuts on users' desktops or Start menus. Published applications are stored in Active Directory and the application is available to users to install using Add or Remove Programs in Control Panel.

Important   Applications can only be published to users, not to computers.

Practice: Upgrading a Basic Disk to a Dynamic Disk

In this practice, you upgrade a basic disk to a dynamic disk and then use Disk Management to verify that the disk is now using dynamic storage.

▶ **To upgrade a basic disk to a dynamic disk**

1. Log on as Fred or with a user account that is a member of the Administrators group.
2. Click Start, right-click My Computer, and then click Manage.

   The Computer Management window appears.

3. In the console tree, if necessary, double-click Storage to expand it, and then click Disk Management.

   Notice that Disk 0's type is Basic.

4. In the lower right pane of the Computer Management window, right-click Disk 0, and then click Convert To Dynamic Disk.

   Disk Management displays the Convert To Dynamic Disk dialog box.

5. Ensure that Disk 0 is the only disk selected for upgrade, and then click OK.

   Disk Management displays the Disks To Convert dialog box.

6. Click Convert.

   Disk Management displays a Disk Management message box, indicating that after the upgrade, you will not be able to start other installed operating systems from any volume on these disks.

7. Click Yes to continue.

   Disk Management displays a Convert Disk To Dynamic message box, notifying you that any file systems on any of the disks to be upgraded will be dismounted.

8. Click Yes to continue.

   Disk Management displays a Caution message box, notifying you that the system will now restart.

9. Click OK.

   Your computer restarts.

▶ **To verify the conversion to a dynamic disk**

1. Log on as Fred or with a user account that is a member of the Administrators group.

2. Click Start, right-click My Computer, and then click Manage.

3. In the console tree, if necessary, double-click Storage to expand it, and then click Disk Management.

   Notice that the storage type of Disk 0 is Dynamic.

4. Close Disk Management and do not save the console settings.

Lesson Review

The following questions will help you determine whether you have learned the material presented in this lesson. If you have difficulty answering these questions, review the material in this lesson before moving on. The answers are in Appendix A, "Questions and Answers."

1. When do you use the Files and Settings Transfer Wizard?

2. Which of the following statements are true for the Files and Settings Transfer Wizard? (Choose all answers that are correct.)

    a. You run the Files and Settings Transfer Wizard only on your old computer.

    b. You must run the Files and Settings Transfer Wizard on both your old and your new computers.

    c. You can use a standard 25-pin cable to connect the parallel ports on your old and new computers to run the Files and Settings Transfer Wizard.

    d. You can use serial ports to directly connect your old and new computers to run the Files and Settings Transfer Wizard.

3. Which of the following statements are true for a disk that uses dynamic storage? (Choose all answers that are correct.)

    a. The system partition for Windows NT is never on a dynamic disk.

    b. A dynamic disk can be partitioned into four primary partitions or three primary partitions and one extended partition.

    c. The convert command allows you to convert a basic disk into a dynamic disk.

    d. A dynamic disk has a single partition that includes the entire disk.

4. How can Windows Installer help you minimize the amount of disk space taken up on a user's disk when you install a new application on that user's disk?

5. Which of the following statements about publishing and installing applications are correct? (Choose all answers that are correct.)

    a. Applications can be published to users or to computers.

    b. Publishing an application installs the application on the users' computers, but it does not place any shortcuts on the users' desktops or Start menus.

    c. Publishing an application does not install the application on the users' computers.

    d. Published applications are stored in Active Directory and the application is available to users to install using Add or Remove Programs in Control Panel.

Lesson Summary

- The Files and Settings Transfer Wizard simplifies the task of moving data files and personal settings from your old computer to your new one.

- The Files and Settings Transfer Wizard can move your display settings, Internet Explorer and Outlook Express options, dial-up connections, and your folder and taskbar options to your new computer.

- The Files and Settings Transfer Wizard allows you to connect your computers using a null modem cable connected to a serial port on each computer or with a network.

- The Disk Management snap-in provides a central location for disk information and management tasks, such as creating and deleting partitions and volumes; formatting them with the FAT, FAT32, or NTFS file systems; and assigning drive letters to them.

- The Disk Management snap-in provides a way to manage disks locally and on remote computers.

- A disk that is initialized for basic storage is called a basic disk and can contain primary partitions, extended partitions, and logical drives.

- A disk that is initialized for dynamic storage is a dynamic disk and can be divided into volumes, which can consist of a portion, or portions, of one or more physical disks.

- Windows Installer is a core part of Intellimirror and a core component of the Windows Group Policy-based change and configuration management technology.

- Windows Installer has a client-side installer service, MSIEXEC.EXE, which allows the operating system to control the installation.

- Windows Installer uses the information stored in the package file, an .msi file, to install the application.

APPENDIX A

Questions and Answers

Chapter 1: Introduction to Windows XP Professional

Lesson 1: Exploring New Features and Improvements

Page 12

Lesson Review

1. Which of the following statements about Automatic Updates (AU) are correct? (Choose all that apply.)

    a. AU is a proactive service that runs in the background and automatically detects, downloads, and installs Windows updates on a computer.

    b. AU allows multiple administrative users to run the AU client concurrently.

    c. AU allows users with administrative privileges to automatically download and install Windows updates on a computer.

    d. AU uses only idle bandwidth so that downloads do not interrupt or slow down other network activity.

    c and d

2. What is ClearType support?

    Windows XP Professional supports ClearType, a new text display technology that triples the horizontal resolution available for rendering text through software. This feature provides a clearer text display on an LCD screen with digital interface.

3. The Desktop Cleanup Wizard helps you keep your desktop free of _____ that you don't use regularly. By default, it runs every _____ days.

    Shortcuts, 60 days

4. What does the Fast User Switching for Multiple Users of a Computer feature provide on computers running Windows XP Professional?

The Fast User Switching feature allows multiple users to share a computer without requiring each user to close all running applications and log off before another user can log on to the computer.

5. Internet Explorer version _____ comes included with Windows XP Professional.

6.0

Lesson 2: Troubleshooting Using Help and Support Center

Page 21

Lesson Review

1. How can Windows XP Professional help you in making a recommendation about how to upgrade the equipment in your office?

The Compatible Hardware and Software feature provides you with current and comprehensive hardware and software compatibility information so that you can feel confident that your upgrade recommendation will be correct.

2. If you are talking with a support engineer about a problem you are having with your computer and the engineer asks you for the BIOS level on your computer, how can you use Help and Support Center to find this information?

Use My Computer Properties. Click Start, and then click Help And Support. In the Help And Support Center window, under Pick A Task, click Use Tools To View Your Computer Information And Diagnose Problems. Under Tools, click My Computer Information, and then click View General System Information About This Computer. Under Specifications the BIOS version is listed.

The Windows Help system uses HTML to format and display information, so with an Internet connection, you can search for every occurrence of a word or phrase across all Windows compiled HTML Help files.

3. If you have administrative responsibility for your company's workgroup and have administrative control over all computers in the workgroup, how can you easily determine the model and driver for each network adapter in the workgroup?

In the Help And Support Center window, under Pick A Task, click Use Tools To View Your Computer Information And Diagnose Problems. Under Tools, click My Computer Information, and then click View Advanced System Information. Under What Do You Want To Do, click View Computer Information For Another Computer. The View Remote Computer – Web Page dialog box appears, which allows you

to specify the path to the remote computer for which you want to view information. When you are viewing the information on the remote computer, click Find Information About The Hardware Installed On This Computer to determine the model and driver for the network adapter. Repeat this process for all computers in the workgroup.

Lesson 3: Understanding Workgroups and Domains

Page 25

Lesson Review

1. Which of the following statements about a Windows XP Professional workgroup are correct? (Choose all that apply.)

    a. A workgroup is also called a peer-to-peer network.

    b. A workgroup is a logical grouping of network computers that share a central directory database.

    c. A workgroup becomes impractical in environments with more than 100 computers.

    d. A workgroup can contain computers running Microsoft Windows 2000 Server as long as the server is not configured as a domain controller.

    a and d

2. What is a domain controller?

    A domain controller is a computer running Windows 2000 Server that is configured as a domain controller so that it can manage all security-related aspects of user and domain interactions.

3. A directory database contains user accounts and security information for the domain and is known as the _____. This directory database is the database portion of _____, which is the Windows 2000 directory service.

    Directory, Active Directory service

4. A _____ provides a single logon for users to gain access to network resources that they have permissions to access, such as file, print, and application resources.

    Domain

Lesson 4: Logging On and Off Windows XP Professional

Page 32

Lesson Review

1. What can you do when you log on locally to a computer, and what determines what you can do when you log on locally to a computer?

    When you log on locally to a computer, you can access the appropriate resources on that computer and you can perform specific system tasks. What you can do when logged on locally to a computer is determined by

the access token assigned to the user account you used to log on. The access token is your identification for that local computer; it contains your security settings. These security settings allow you to access specific resources on that computer and to perform specific system tasks.

2. What is the main difference in the authentication process for logging on locally to a computer and logging on to a domain?

When you log on locally to a computer, its security subsystem uses the local security database to authenticate the user name and password you entered. When you log on to a domain, a domain controller uses the directory to authenticate the user name and password you entered.

3. How can you configure Windows XP Professional to use the Log On To Windows dialog box instead of the Welcome screen to allow users to log on locally to the computer?

You use the User Accounts program located in Control Panel to configure Windows XP Professional to display the Log On To Windows dialog box. The User Accounts program contains the Change The Way Users Log On Or Off task that you use.

4. Which of the following computers can a user log on to locally? (Choose all that apply.)

   a. A computer running Windows XP Professional that is in a workgroup

   b. A computer running Windows XP Professional that is in a domain

   c. A computer running Windows 2000 Server that is configured as a domain controller

   d. A computer running Windows 2000 Server that is a member server in a domain

   a, b, and d

5. Which of the following statements about the Windows Security dialog box are correct? (Choose all that apply.)

   a. It is accessed by pressing CTRL+ALT+DELETE.

   b. It tells how long the current user has been logged on.

   c. It allows you to log off the computer or domain.

   d. It allows a user with administrative permissions to change other users' passwords.

   a and c

Chapter 2: Installing Windows XP Professional

Lesson 1: Getting Started

Page 43

Lesson Review

1. What are the minimum and recommended memory requirements for installing Windows XP Professional?

   The minimum amount of memory required to install Windows XP Professional is 64 MB, and the recommended amount of memory is 128 MB.

2. The minimum hard disk space required for installing Windows XP Professional is

   a. 1.5 GB on a 2-GB hard disk

   b. 1 GB on a 2-GB hard disk

   c. 500 MB on a 1-GB hard disk

   d. 750 MB on a 2-GB hard disk

   a

3. Where can you find the most recent versions of the HCL for released operating systems?

   On the Microsoft Web site at *http://www.microsoft.com/hcl/*

4. Joining a domain during Windows XP Professional installation requires which of the following? (Choose all that apply.)

   a. You must know the DNS name for the domain the computer will join.

   b. You must have a user account in the domain.

   c. At least one domain controller in the domain must be online when you install a computer in the domain.

   d. At least one DNS server must be online when you install a computer in the domain.

   a, c, and d

5. Which of the following statements about file systems are correct? (Choose all that apply.)

   a. File- and folder-level security are available only with NTFS.

   b. Disk compression is available with FAT, FAT32, and NTFS.

   c. Dual booting between Microsoft Windows 98 and Windows XP Professional is available only with NTFS.

   d. Encryption is available only with NTFS.

   a and d

Lesson 2: Installing Windows XP Professional from a CD-ROM

Lesson Review

1. If TCP/IP is installed on your computer, what is the maximum length for the computer name you specify during installation?

   63 characters

2. Can you change the computer name after installation without having to reinstall Windows XP Professional? If you can change the name, how do you do it? If you cannot change the name, why not?

   Yes. To change the computer name after installation is complete, click Start, click My Computer, click View System Information, click the Computer Name tab, and then click Change.

3. Which of the following statements about joining a workgroup or a domain are correct? (Choose all that apply.)

   a. You cannot add your computer to a workgroup or a domain during installation.

   b. If you add your computer to a workgroup during installation, you can join the computer to a domain later.

   c. If you add your computer to a domain during installation, you can join the computer to a workgroup later.

   d. You cannot add your computer to a workgroup or a domain during installation.

   b and c

4. Which of the following configurations can you change after installing Windows XP Professional? (Choose all that apply.)

   a. Language

   b. Locale

   c. Keyboard settings

   d. Network protocol

   a, b, c, and d

5. When you install networking components with typical settings, what components are installed? What does each component do?

   There are four components. The Client for Microsoft Networks allows your computer to access network resources. File and Printer Sharing for Microsoft Networks allows other computers to access file and print resources on your computer. The QoS Packet Scheduler helps provide a guaranteed delivery system for network traffic, such as TCP/IP packets. The TCP/IP is the default networking protocol that allows your computer to communicate over LANs and WANs.

Lesson 3: Installing Windows XP Professional over the Network

Page 69   ## Lesson Review

1. On which of the following operating systems running on the client computer do you use WINNT32.EXE to install Windows XP Professional? (Choose all that apply.)

   a. Windows 3.0 or later

   b. Windows 95

   c. Windows 98

   d. Windows NT 4

   b, c, and d

2. On which of the following operating systems running on the client computer do you use WINNT.EXE to install Windows XP Professional? (Choose all that apply.)

   a. Windows 3.0 or later

   b. Windows 95

   c. Windows Me

   d. Windows NT 4

   a

3. What Windows XP Professional command allows you to verify that your computer is compatible with Windows XP Professional before you begin installing it?

   WINNT32.EXE with the /checkupgradeonly switch

4. You use the _____ switch with WINNT32.EXE to prevent Setup from restarting the computer after completing the file-copy phase.

   /noreboot

5. You use the _____ switch with WINNT32.EXE to tell Setup to copy all installation source files to your local hard disk.

   /makelocalsource

Lesson 4: Upgrading Earlier Versions of Windows to Windows XP Professional

Page 75   ### Lesson Review

1. Which of the following operating systems can be upgraded directly to Windows XP Professional? (Choose all that apply.)

    a. Windows NT Workstation 4.0

    b. Windows NT 3.51

    c. Windows 2000 Professional

    d. Windows NT Server 4.0

    a and c

2. How can you upgrade a computer running Windows 95 to Windows XP Professional?

    Upgrade your computer to Windows 98 first, and then upgrade to Windows XP Professional.

3. Before you upgrade a computer running Windows NT 4, which of the following actions should you perform? (Choose all that apply.)

    a. Create a 2-GB partition on which to install Windows XP Professional.

    b. Verify that the computer meets the minimum hardware requirements.

    c. Generate a hardware and software compatibility report.

    d. Format the partition containing Windows NT 4 so that you can install Windows XP Professional.

    b and c

4. How can you verify that your computer is compatible with Windows XP Professional and therefore can be upgraded?

    Use the Windows XP Professional Compatibility tool.

Lesson 5: Troubleshooting Windows XP Professional Setup

Page 78   ### Lesson Review

1. If you encounter an error during setup, which of the following log files should you check? (Choose all that apply.)

    a. SETUPERR.LOG

    b. NETSETUP.LOG

    c. SETUP.LOG

    d. SETUPACT.LOG

    a and d

2. If your computer cannot connect to the domain controller during installation, what should you do?

   First, verify that a domain controller is running and online, and then verify that the server running the DNS service is running and online. If both servers are online, verify that the network adapter card and protocol settings are correctly set and that the network cable is plugged into the network adapter card.

3. If your computer cannot connect to read the CD-ROM during installation, what should you do?

   Use a different CD-ROM. (To request a replacement CD-ROM, contact Microsoft or your vendor.) You can also try using a different computer and CD-ROM drive. If you can read the CD-ROM on a different computer, you can do an over-the-network installation.

Chapter 3: Setting Up and Managing User Accounts

Lesson 1: Understanding User Accounts

Page 87

Lesson Review

1. Where do local user accounts allow users to log on and gain access to resources?

   Only on the computer on which the local user account is created.

2. Where should you create user accounts for computers running Windows XP Professional that are part of a domain?

   You should create it on one of the domain controllers. You should not use local user accounts on Windows XP Professional computers that are part of a domain.

3. Which of the following statements about domain user accounts are correct? (Choose all that apply.)

   a. Domain user accounts allow users to log on to the domain and gain access to resources anywhere on the network, as long as the users have the required access permissions.

   b. If at least one computer running one of the Windows 2000 Server products is configured as a domain controller, you should use domain user accounts only.

   c. The domain controller replicates the new user account information to all other computers in the domain.

   d. A new domain user account is established in the local security database on the domain controller on which you created the account.

   a and b

4. Which of the following statements about built-in accounts are correct? (Choose all that apply.)

   a. You can delete the Guest account.

   b. You cannot delete the Administrator account.

   c. You cannot rename the Guest account.

   d. You can rename the Administrator account.

   b and d

5. How do you disable the Guest account?

   Click Start, click Control Panel, and then click User Accounts. In the User Accounts window, click the Guest icon. In the What Do You Want To Change About The Guest Account window, click Turn Off The Guest Account. The Guest Account is now disabled.

Lesson 2: Planning New User Accounts

Page 90   **Lesson Review**

1. The maximum number of characters that Windows XP Professional recognizes in a local user account name is _____.

   20

2. When are duplicate local user accounts valid in a network of computers running Windows XP Professional?

   They are valid as long as they are not on the same computer. In fact, in a workgroup, you must create the same user account on each computer in the workgroup that you want the user to be able to access.

3. Passwords can be up to _____ characters long with a minimum length of _____ characters recommended.

   128, 8

4. Which of the following sets of characters are valid to use in a local user account name on a computer running Windows XP Professional? (Choose all that apply.)

   a. 0 ( ) 9

   b. - + = >

   c. A through Z; a through z

   d. [ ] _ |

   a and c

5. When users create their own passwords, which of the following guidelines should they observe? (Choose all that apply.)

    a. Use the maximum number of characters allowed in a password.

    b. Use a password that is hard for others to guess.

    c. Use at least one uppercase letter, one lowercase letter, one numeral, and one valid nonalphanumeric character.

    d. Use the name of your spouse, child, cat, or dog so that you can easily remember it.

    b and c

Lesson 3: Creating, Modifying, and Deleting User Accounts

Practice: Creating, Modifying, and Deleting Local User Accounts

Page 104

Exercise 4: Creating a New Local User Account Using the Computer Management Snap-In

▶ **To create a local user account using the Computer Management snap-in**

8. Click Start, click Control Panel, and then click User Accounts.

    The User Accounts window appears.

    What type of account is User3?

    The account type for User3 is Limited Account.

13. In the Password and Confirm Password text boxes, type User4.

    How does the password appear on the screen? Why?

    The password is displayed as asterisks as you type. This prevents others from viewing the password as you enter it.

Page 105

Exercise 5: Testing a New Local User Account

▶ **To test a local user account**

3. On the Welcome screen, click User3.

    What happens?

    A Logon Message dialog box appears, informing you that you are required to change your password at first logon.

Page 107

Lesson Review

1. Which of the following statements about the Windows XP Professional User Accounts tool are correct? (Choose all that apply.)

   a. The User Accounts tool allows you to remotely create, modify, and delete user accounts on all computers in the network running Windows XP Professional.

   b. The User Accounts tool allows you to view and modify all accounts on the computer.

   c. The tasks you can perform with the User Accounts tool depend on the type of account you use to log on to the local computer.

   d. The User Accounts tool allows users to delete, create, or remove their individual passwords.

   c and d

2. Which of the following tasks can both account types perform? (Choose all that apply.)

   a. Change your picture

   b. Change your account type

   c. Create, change, or remove your password

   d. Change your account name

   a and c

3. Which of the following statements about logging on or logging off a computer running Windows XP Professional are true? (Choose all that apply.)

   a. You can quickly switch to another user account without logging off and closing all programs that you are running.

   b. The User Accounts tool allows you to disable a local user account to prevent users from using the disabled account to log on.

   c. When you use the Welcome screen to log on to the local computer, you can only log on using one of the accounts displayed on the Welcome screen.

   d. The User Accounts tool allows you to replace the Welcome screen with a logon prompt that requires users to type their individual user names and passwords.

   a and d

4. When you use the Computer Management snap-in to create a new user account, which check box do you select to prevent a new employee from using the new account until the employee starts working for the company?

   Account Disabled

Lesson 4: Setting Properties for User Accounts

Practice: Modifying User Account Properties

Page 114

Exercise 2: Testing User Account Properties

▶ **To test User Account properties**

8. Click Change Password.

What happens? Why?

A User Accounts dialog box appears with the message Windows Cannot Change The Password. You set the User Cannot Change Password option for User1.

Page 114

Lesson Review

1. When can you select the Account Is Locked Out check box for a user and why?

Never, because the Account Is Locked Out check box is unavailable when the account is active and is not locked out of the system. The system locks out a user if the user exceeds the limit for the number of failed logon attempts.

2. Which of the following statements about local user account properties are correct? (Choose all that apply.)

a. You can configure all of the default properties associated with each local user account using the User Accounts tool located in the Control Panel.

b. In Computer Management, the General tab in the *account-name* Properties dialog box for a user account allows you to disable the account.

c. In Computer Management, the General tab in the *account-name* Properties dialog box for a user account allows you to select the Account Is Locked Out check box to prevent the user from logging on to the computer.

d. You can use the Computer Management snap-in to configure all of the default properties associated with each local user account.

b and d

3. Which of the following statements about user profiles are correct? (Choose all that apply.)

a. A user profile is a collection of folders and data that stores the user's current desktop environment, application settings, and personal data.

b. A user profile contains all the network connections that are established when a user logs on to a computer.

c. Windows XP Professional creates a user profile when you create a new local user account.

d. You must create each user profile by copying and modifying an existing user profile.

a and b

4. Which of the following statements about user profiles are correct? (Choose all that apply.)

   a. Users should store their documents in home directories rather than in their My Documents folders.

   b. The Profile tab in the *account-name* Properties dialog box for a user account allows you to set a path for the user profile, logon script, and home folder.

   c. A user profile contains the My Documents folder, which provides a place for users to store personal files.

   d. When users change their desktop settings, the changes are reflected in their user profiles.

   b, c and d

5. What three tasks must you perform to create a home folder on a network server?

   First, you must create and share a folder in which to store all home folders on a network server. Second, for the shared folder, remove the default Full Control permission from the Everyone group and assign Full Control to the Users group for users that will reside in this shared folder. Third, provide the path to the user's home folder in the shared home directory folder in the Profile tab of the Properties dialog box for the user account.

Lesson 5: Implementing Groups

Page 125

Lesson Review

1. What are groups, and why do you use them?

   A group is a collection of user accounts. A group simplifies administration by allowing you to assign permissions and rights to a group of users rather than to each individual user account.

2. An administrator or owner of a resource uses _____ to control what users can do with a resource such as a folder, file, or printer.

   Permissions

3. You use local groups to assign permissions to resources residing _____.

   On the computer on which the local group is created

4. Which of the following statements about local groups are correct? (Choose all that apply.)

   a. If a computer running Windows XP Professional is part of a domain, the local groups for that computer are stored in the Directory rather than in the local security database on that computer.

   b. Local groups allow you to grant permission to the group to perform system tasks, such as changing the time on a computer and backing up or restoring files.

c. A local group is a collection of user accounts on a computer that you can use to control access to resources residing on that computer.

d. You can use the Computer Management snap-in to create groups, to add members to existing groups, and to delete groups from a computer running Windows XP Professional.

c and d

5. Which of the following statements about local groups are correct? (Choose all that apply.)

a. You can use local groups only on the computer on which you create them.

b. Local groups are available on member servers and domain computers running Windows 2000 Server.

c. Local groups appear in Active Directory so you can administer them centrally.

d. You must create each user profile by copying and modifying an existing user profile.

a and b

6. Which of the following statements about deleting local groups are correct? (Choose all that apply.)

a. Each group that you create has a unique identifier that cannot be reused.

b. You can restore access to resources by recreating the group.

c. When you delete a group, you also remove the permissions and rights associated with it.

d. Deleting a group deletes the user accounts that are members of the group.

a and c

7. What is the difference between built-in system groups and built-in local groups found on computers running Windows XP Professional? Give at least two examples of each type of group.

Built-in local groups give rights to perform system tasks on a single computer, such as backing up and restoring files, changing the system time, and administering system resources. Some examples of built-in local groups are Administrators, Backup Operators, Guests, Power Users, Replicator, and Users.

Built-in system groups do not have specific memberships that you can modify, but they can represent different users at different times, depending on how a user gains access to a computer or resource. You do not see system groups when you administer groups, but they are available for use when you assign rights and permissions to resources. Some examples of built-in system groups are Everyone, Authenticated Users, Creator Owner, Network, Interactive, Anonymous Logon, and Dialup.

Chapter 4: Installing, Configuring, and Troubleshooting Network Protocols

Lesson 1: Understanding the TCP/IP Protocol Suite

Page 131   ### Lesson Review

1. What are the four layers to which the TCP/IP suite of protocols maps? What are the functions of the protocols that map to each layer?

   Application, transport, Internet, and network interface. The protocols that map to the application layer allow applications to gain access to the network. The protocols that map to the transport layer provide communication sessions between computers. The protocols that map to the Internet layer encapsulate packets into Internet datagrams and run all the necessary routing algorithms. The protocols that map to the network interface layer put frames on the wire and pull frames off the wire.

2. Which of the following statements correctly describes IP? (Choose all answers that are correct.)

   a. IP guarantees packet arrival and correct packet sequence.

   b. IP provides connection-oriented, reliable communications for applications that typically transfer large amounts of data at one time.

   c. IP is primarily responsible for addressing and routing packets between hosts.

   d. IP provides connectionless packet delivery for all other protocols in the suite.

   c and d

3. Which of the following statements correctly describes TCP? (Choose all answers that are correct.)

   a. TCP provides connectionless communications but does not guarantee that packets will be delivered.

   b. TCP provides connection-oriented, reliable communications for applications that typically transfer large amounts of data at one time.

   c. TCP provides services that allow the application to bind to a particular port and IP address on a host.

   d. TCP provides and assigns a sequence number to each segment of data that is transmitted.

   b and d

4. Which of the four layers to which the TCP/IP suite of protocols maps does IGMP map to and what is IGMP used for?

   IGMP maps to the Internet layer and provides multicasting.

5. What is multicasting?

   Multicasting is the process of sending a message simultaneously to more than one destination. IP multicast traffic is sent to a single MAC address but is processed by multiple hosts.

6. The two transport layer protocols are _____ and _____.

   TCP and UDP

7. Which of the following statements correctly describes ARP? (Choose all answers that are correct.)

   a. ARP is a protocol included in the Internet layer.

   b. ARP is a protocol included in the transport layer.

   c. ARP provides IP address mapping to the MAC sublayer address to acquire the physical MAC control address of the destination.

   d. ARP is primarily responsible for addressing and routing packets between hosts.

   a and c

Lesson 2: Configuring and Troubleshooting TCP/IP

Practice: Configuring TCP/IP

Exercise 4: Obtaining an IP Address Using Automatic Private IP Addressing

Page 148

▶ **To obtain an IP address by using Automatic Private IP Addressing**

2. At the command prompt, type **ipconfig /renew** and then press ENTER.

   There is a pause while Windows XP Professional attempts to locate a DHCP server on the network.

   What message appears, and what does it indicate?

   The message is as follows: An error occurred while renewing interface Local Area Connection: The semaphore timeout period has expired. This error message indicates that Windows XP Professional could not renew the TCP/IP configuration.

▶ **To test the TCP/IP configuration**

2. Pressing SPACEBAR as necessary, record the current TCP/IP settings for your local area connection in the following table.

Setting	Value
IP address	
Subnet mask	
Default gateway	

Is this the same IP address assigned to your computer in Exercise 3? Why or why not?

No, this is not the same IP address assigned to the computer in Exercise 3. It is not the same address because this address is assigned by the Windows XP Professional Automatic Private IP Addressing.

5. If you have a computer to test TCP/IP connectivity with your computer, type **ping** *ip_address* (where *ip_address* is the IP address of the computer that you are using to test connectivity) and then press ENTER. If you do not have a computer to test connectivity, skip this step and proceed to Exercise 5.

Were you successful? Why or why not?

No, you would not be successful. Your computer has an address assigned by Automatic Private IP Addressing and the test computer is on a different subnet.

Page 150
Lesson Review

1. Why would you assign a computer a static IP address?

You can assign static IP addresses if there are no DHCP servers on the network, or you can use the Automatic Private IP Addressing feature. You should assign a static IP address to selected network computers, such as the computer running the DHCP Service. The computer running the DHCP Service cannot be a DHCP client, so it must have a static IP address.

2. Which of the following statements correctly describe IP addresses? (Choose all answers that are correct.)

a. Logical 64-bit addresses that identify a TCP/IP host.

b. Each network adapter card in a computer running TCP/IP requires a unique IP address.

c. 192.168.0.108 is an example of a class C IP address.

d. The host ID in an IP address is always the last two octets in the address.

b and c

3. What is the purpose of a subnet mask?

A subnet mask blocks out part of the IP address so that TCP/IP can distinguish the network ID from the host ID.

4. By default, client computers running Windows XP Professional, Windows 95, or Windows 98 obtain TCP/IP configuration information automatically from the DHCP Service: True or false?

True

5. Which of the following statements about obtaining an IP address automatically are true? (Choose all answers that are correct.)

   a. Windows XP Professional includes the DHCP Service.

   b. Windows XP Professional includes an Automatic Private IP Addressing feature, which provides DHCP clients with limited network functionality if a DHCP server is unavailable during startup.

   c. The Internet Assigned Numbers Authority (IANA) has reserved 169.254.0.0 through 169.254.255.255 for Automatic Private IP Addressing.

   d. You should always disable Automatic Private IP Addressing in small workgroups.

   b and c

6. Your computer running Windows XP Professional was configured manually for TCP/IP. You can connect to any host on your own subnet, but you cannot connect to or even ping any host on a remote subnet. What is the likely cause of the problem and how would you fix it?

   The default gateway might be missing or incorrect. You specify the default gateway in the Internet Protocol (TCP/IP) Properties dialog box (in the Network And Internet Connections dialog box under Network Connections). Other possibilities are that the default gateway is offline or the subnet mask is incorrect.

7. Your computer's Computer Name is Pro1 and you ping Pro1. The local address for Pro1 is returned as 169.254.x.y. What does this tell you?

   Automatic Private IP Addressing of Windows XP Professional has assigned your computer Pro1. This means that the local DHCP server is not configured properly or cannot be reached from your computer.

Lesson 3: Installing, Configuring, and Troubleshooting NWLink

Page 159

Practice: Installing and Configuring NWLink

▶   **To install and configure NWLink**

5. Click Protocol, and then click Add.

Windows XP Professional displays the Select Network Protocol dialog box.

What protocols can you install?

   Network Monitor Driver and NWLink IPX/SPX/NetBIOS Compatible Transport Protocol. Network Monitor Driver enables Network Monitor to receive frames (also called packets) from the local network adapter. You can use the frames to detect and troubleshoot problems on LANs.

7. Select NWLink IPX/SPX/NetBIOS Compatible Transport Protocol, and then click Properties.

What type of frame detection is selected by default?

Auto Detect

8. Click the arrow to view the Frame Type drop-down menu selections.

What other frame types are listed?

Ethernet 802.2, Ethernet 802.3, Ethernet II, and Ethernet SNAP

9. Select one of the frame types listed, other than Auto Detect.

Why is the Network Number option now active?

Each frame type configured on a network adapter card requires a network number.

▶   **To determine the installed network number and frame type on the client**

3. At the command prompt, type **ipxroute config** and press ENTER.

What is the network number and frame type for the LAN?

The network number is 00000000 and the frame type is 802.2. Answers may vary.

Page 160   ## Lesson Review

1. Your computer running Windows XP Professional can communicate with some but not all of the NetWare servers on your network. Some of the NetWare servers are running frame type 802.2 and some are running 802.3. What is the likely cause of the problem?

Although the NWLink implementation in Windows XP Professional can automatically select a frame type for IPX/SPX-compatible protocols, it can automatically detect only one frame type. This network uses two frame types. To resolve the problem, you must manually configure the additional frame type (802.3).

2. How can you verify that the network number and frame type are correct for your client computer running Windows XP Professional and attempting to access a NetWare server?

On the client, start a command prompt. At the command prompt, type command and then click OK to open a command prompt. In the Run dialog box, type ipxroute config and then press ENTER. Verify that the network number and frame type in the Network and Frame columns are correct for your installation.

3. Which of the following statements about NWLink are true? (Choose all answers that are correct.)

    a. NWLink allows computers running Windows XP Professional to communicate with other network devices that are using IPX/SPX.

    b. NWLink provides NetWare clients with access to Microsoft SQL Server.

    c. NWLink provides NetWare clients access to file and print resources on a computer running Windows 2000 Server.

    d. NWLink provides NetWare clients with access to Microsoft SNA Server.

a, b, and d

4. Which of the following commands or tools do you type in a command prompt to determine information about the stack, including the current IPX status, network number, MAC address, interface name, and frame type?

    a. Ipconfig

    b. Iproute config

    c. Ipxroute config

    d. Ipxroute ripout

c

Lesson 4: Network Bindings

Practice: Working with Network Bindings

Page 166

Exercise 1: Changing the Binding Order for a Protocol

▶ **To change the protocol binding order**

4. In the Network Connections window, on the Advanced menu, click Advanced Settings.

The Advanced Settings dialog box appears.

What is the order of the protocols listed under Client For Microsoft Networks?

The NWLink IPX/SPX/NetBIOS Compatible Transport Protocol was the last protocol installed, so it is the first one listed. Internet Protocol (TCP/IP) is listed second.

Page 168

Lesson Review

1. What is binding?

Binding is the process of linking network components on different levels to enable communication between those components.

2. What is the significance of the binding order of network protocols?

You specify the binding order to optimize network performance. For example, a computer running Windows XP Professional has both TCP/IP and NWLink IPX/SPX installed. However, most of the servers to which this computer connects are running only TCP/IP. You would adjust the binding order so that the workstation binding to TCP/IP is listed before the workstation bindings for NWLink IPX/SPX. In this way, when a user attempts to connect to a server, Client for Microsoft Networks first attempts to establish the connection using TCP/IP.

3. Can a network component bind to more than one component above or below it? Why is that important?

A network component can be bound to one or more network components above or below it. This is important because the services that each component provides can be shared by all other components that are bound to it. For example, a network adapter card can be bound to more than one network protocol at a time.

4. What function does NDIS provide and what version is in Windows XP Professional?

NDIS provides the capability to bind multiple protocols to multiple network adapter card drivers. The version in Windows XP Professional is 5.1.

Chapter 5: Using the DNS Service and Active Directory Service

Lesson 1: Understanding DNS

Page 176   **Lesson Review**

1. What is DNS and what is it used for?

DNS is a naming system that is used in TCP/IP networks to translate computer names to IP addresses. DNS makes it easy to locate computers and other resources on IP-based networks.

2. Which of the following statements correctly describes DNS root domains? (Choose all answers that are correct.)

a. The root domain is at the top of the hierarchy.

b. The root domain is at the bottom of the hierarchy.

c. The root domain is represented by a two- or three-character name code.

d. The root domain is represented by a period (.).

a and d

3. Which of the following are second-level domain names? (Choose all answers that are correct.)

   a. gov

   b. Microsoft.com

   c. au

   d. ed.gov

   b and d

4. _____ provide a way to partition the domain namespace into manageable sections and each _____ represents a discrete portion of the domain namespace.

   Zones; zone

Lesson 2: Understanding Name Resolution

Page 182

Lesson Review

1. What is a forward lookup query and how is it resolved?

   A forward lookup query is the resolving of a user-friendly DNS domain name to an IP address. To resolve a forward lookup query, a client passes a lookup query to its local name server. If the local name server can resolve the query, it returns the IP address for the name so the client can contact it. If the local name server cannot resolve the query, it passes the query on to one of the DNS root servers. The DNS root server sends back a referral to a name server that can resolve the request. The local name server sends the request to the name server it was referred to by the DNS root server. An IP address is returned to the local name server and the local name server sends the IP address to the client.

2. In DNS name resolution, which of the following statements about Time to Live (TTL) are correct? (Choose all answers that are correct.)

   a. TTL is the length of time a query can exist before it is resolved or discarded.

   b. Shorter TTL values help ensure that data about the domain namespace is more current across the network.

   c. Longer TTL values increase the amount of DNS traffic.

   d. Longer TTL values cause the cached values to be retained longer.

   b and d

3. Which of the following statements about DNS name and address resolution are correct? (Choose all answers that are correct.)

a. The DNS distributed database is indexed by both names and IP addresses.

b. The top-level domain in-addr.arpa is used for both forward and reverse queries.

c. In the in-addr.arpa domain, the order of the IP address octets is reversed.

d. Troubleshooting tools, such as the nslookup command-line tool, use reverse lookup queries to report back host names.

c and d

Lesson 3: Configuring a DNS Client

Page 188

Lesson Review

1. What is a HOSTS file and when would you create one?

A HOSTS file is a manually maintained local file that contains host-to-IP address and NetBIOS-to-IP name resolution. You use a HOSTS file for networks without access to a DNS name server to provide host-to-IP address and NetBIOS-to-IP name resolution for applications and services.

2. Which of the following statements about configuring a DNS client are correct? (Choose all answers that are correct.)

a. If you select the Obtain DNS Server Address Automatically option, at least one of the available DNS servers must be configured to broadcast its IP address.

b. If you select the Use The Following DNS Server Addresses, you are limiting your DNS client to being able to use only two DNS servers, the preferred DNS server and the alternate DNS server.

c. To use the Obtain DNS Server Address Automatically option, you must have a DHCP server available on your network.

d. To configure a DNS client, you use Network and Internet Connections, which is located in Control Panel.

c and d

3. Which of the following functions do you perform using the Advanced TCP/IP Settings dialog box? (Choose all answers that are correct.)

a. Edit the IP address of a DNS server.

b. Delete the IP address of a DNS server.

c. Enter additional IP addresses for other available DNS servers.

d. Edit the IP addresses of the DHCP servers on the network.

a, b, and c

4. What does selecting the Append These DNS Suffixes (In Order) option do?

This option allows you to specify a list of domains to try when there is a query for an unqualified name. Queries are limited to the domains that you listed.

Lesson 4: Understanding Active Directory

Page 192

Lesson Review

1. _____ is the directory service included in the Windows 2000 Server products.

Active Directory

2. What is a directory service?

A directory service is a network service that identifies all resources on a network and makes them accessible to users and applications.

3. What are two ways that Active Directory simplifies administration?

Active Directory organizes resources hierarchically in domains. The domain is the basic unit of replication and security in a Windows 2000 network. All domain controllers in a domain are peers, so you can make changes to any domain controller, and the updates are replicated to all other domain controllers in the domain.

Active Directory simplifies administration by providing a single point of administration for all objects on the network, so an administrator can log on to one computer and administer objects on any computer in the network.

4. Active Directory uses _____ as its domain naming and location service.

DNS

Lesson 5: Understanding Active Directory Structure and Replication

Page 200

Lesson Review

1. In Active Directory, you organize resources in a logical structure. What advantage does this provide?

Grouping resources logically enables you to find a resource by its name rather than its physical location. Because you group resources logically, Active Directory makes the network's physical structure transparent to users.

2. A(n) _____ is a distinct, named set of attributes that represents a network resource.

object

3. What component do you use to organize objects into logical administrative groups?

    a. Site

    b. Tree

    c. Domain

    d. OU

    d

4. A(n) _____ is a grouping or hierarchical arrangement of one or more _____ that form a disjointed namespace.

    Forest; domain trees

5. A site is a combination of one or more IP subnets connected by a highly reliable and fast link to localize as much network traffic as possible. Fast network connections are at least _____ and an available bandwidth of _____ is sufficient.

    a. 256 Kbps, 128 Kbps and higher

    b. 512 Kbps, 128 Kbps and higher

    c. 512 Kbps, 256 Kbps and higher

    d. 1024 Kbps, 512 Kbps and higher

    b

6. The physical components of Active Directory are _____ and _____.

    Domain controllers; sites

Lesson 6: Understanding Active Directory Concepts

Page 208

Lesson Review

1. What is the Active Directory schema?

    The Active Directory schema defines objects that can be stored in Active Directory. The schema is a list of definitions that determines the kinds of objects and the type of information about those objects that can be stored in Active Directory.

2. Which of the following statements are correct for Active Directory Global Catalogs?

    a. The Global Catalog is the central repository of information about objects in a tree or forest.

    b. By default, a Global Catalog is created automatically on the first domain controller in the first domain in the forest.

    c. The Global Catalog is a list of definitions that determines the kinds of objects and the type of information about those objects that can be stored in Active Directory.

    d. Only experienced developers or network administrators should dynamically extend the Global Catalog.

a and b

3. Every object in Active Directory has a _____ that uniquely identifies an object and contains sufficient information for a client to retrieve the object from the Directory.

DN

4. A _____ is a 128-bit number that is assigned to an object when it is created and is guaranteed to be unique.

GUID

5. What is the difference between a contiguous namespace and a disjointed namespace? Give an example of each type of namespace.

In a contiguous namespace, the name of the child object in an object hierarchy always contains the name of the parent domain. A tree is a contiguous namespace. In a disjointed namespace, the names of a parent object and of a child of the same parent object are not directly related to one another. A forest is a disjointed namespace.

Chapter 6: Setting Up, Configuring, and Troubleshooting Common Setup and Configuration Problems for Network Printers

Lesson 1: Introduction to Windows XP Professional Printing

Page 215

Lesson Review

1. _____ are connected to a physical port on the print server.

Local printers

2. Do you have to have a computer running one of the Windows Server products to have a print server on your network? Why?

No. A print server is a computer that manages one or more printers on a network. The print server receives and processes documents from client computers. If you have a computer running Windows XP Professional and it has a shared printer attached to it, it is by definition a print server. However, if the print server will manage many heavily used printers, Microsoft recommends a dedicated print server and most dedicated print servers run one of the Windows Server products.

3. Windows XP Professional can provide _____ concurrent connections from other computers for file and print services.

   a. 20

   b. 10

   c. unlimited

   d. 30

   b

4. A _____ is one file or a set of files containing information that Windows XP Professional requires to convert print commands into a specific printer language, such as PostScript.

   Printer driver

5. Windows XP Professional printing supports which of the following software interfaces or printer ports? (Choose all answers that are correct.)

   a. LPT

   b. COM

   c. USB

   d. HP JetDirect

   a, b, c, and d

6. Windows XP Professional printing supports which of the following types of computers? (Choose all answers that are correct.)

   a. Macintosh computers

   b. UNIX computers

   c. NetWare clients

   d. Windows 98 computers

   b and d

Lesson 2: Setting Up Network Printers

Page 234

Lesson Review

1. Which of the following tasks are done with the Add Printer Wizard? (Choose all answers that are correct.)

   a. Taking a local printer offline

   b. Printing multiple copies of a document

   c. Adding an LPR port

   d. Making a printer that is connected to your computer available to other network users

   c and d

2. What is the default printer in Windows XP Professional?

The default printer is the printer used for all Windows-based applications. You would select this option so that you do not have to set a printer for each application. The first time that you add a printer to the print server, this option does not appear because the printer is automatically selected as the default printer.

3. After you get home from the store, you unpack your new computer and printer. You install Windows XP Professional, and you want to install your printer. You want to set up the printer as your default printer. During the installation you are not prompted to use the printer as your default printer for all Windows-based applications. You know you have seen this option at work when you install local printers. Why aren't you seeing it on your home computer?

The first time that you add a printer to a computer, this option does not appear. The printer is automatically selected as the default printer.

4. Which of the following statements about adding and using an LPR port are correct? (Choose all answers that are correct.)

   a. The LPR port is designed for computers that need to communicate with Macintosh computers in accordance with RFC 1179.

   b. A network-connected printer must have a card that supports the LPD for TCP/IP printing to work properly.

   c. When you are trying to add an LPR port, if the LPR Port option is not available, install the optional networking component, Print Services for UNIX.

   d. LPD is a service on the client computer that sends documents (print jobs) out the LPR port.

   b and c

5. After you add and share a printer on a computer running Windows XP Professional, the tasks to set up client computers vary depending on which operating systems are running on the client computers. Which of the following operating systems running on client computers would require additional software or services to be installed before users on these computers can connect to the shared printer? (Choose all answers that are correct.)

   a. Windows 98

   b. NetWare

   c. Windows 2000 Professional

   d. UNIX

   b and d

Lesson 3: Connecting to Network Printers

Page 240

Lesson Review

1. When you add and share a printer, by default, who can connect to that printer?

   By default, all users can connect to that printer.

2. Which of the following operating systems running on a client computer allow you to use the Net Use command to connect to a network printer? (Choose all answers that are correct.)

   a. Windows 2000

   b. Windows Me

   c. Windows NT 4

   d. Windows XP Professional

   a, b, c, and d

3. Which of the following operating systems running on a client computer allow you to connect to a network printer by using Active Directory search capabilities? (Choose all answers that are correct.)

   a. Windows 2000

   b. Windows Me

   c. Windows NT 4

   d. Windows XP Professional

   a and d

4. Which of the following operating systems running on a client computer allow you to use a Web browser to connect to a network printer? (Choose all answers that are correct.)

   a. Windows 2000

   b. Windows ME

   c. Windows NT 4

   d. Windows XP Professional

   a and d

5. You have a small workgroup consisting of five computers running Windows XP Professional at your house. You are giving your friend, who has never seen Windows XP Professional, a tour around the new operating system. You are demonstrating how the Search Assistant works, but the Find Printers feature is missing. Why?

   The Find Printers feature is not available in the Search Assistant unless you are logged on to a Windows 2000 domain. If you are using a stand-alone computer or one that is in a workgroup, the Find Printers component is not available.

Lesson 4: Configuring Network Printers

Page 247

Lesson Review

1. What are some advantages to sharing a printer?

   Sharing a printer allows other users on the network to use the printer. It simplifies administration because you can administer multiple printers simultaneously.

2. How do you share a printer?

   In the Properties dialog box for the printer, in the Sharing tab, click Share Name and type in a share name.

3. Which of the following statements about a printing pool in Windows XP Professional are correct? (Choose all answers that are correct.)

   a. All printers in a printing pool must be network interface printers.

   b. A printing pool consists of two or more identical printers that are connected to one print server and act as a single printer.

   c. If you use printers that are not identical, they must use the same printer driver.

   d. If you use printers that are not identical, you must install all the required printer drivers on the print server.

   b and c

4. Why would you create virtual printers and vary the priorities on them?

   Creating virtual printers that print to the same physical printer and varying the printer priority allows you to set priorities among groups of documents that all print on the same physical printer. Users can send critical documents to a high-priority virtual printer and noncritical documents to a lower priority virtual printer. The critical documents always print first, even though there is only one physical printer.

Lesson 5: Troubleshooting Setup and Configuration Problems

Page 251

Lesson Review

1. How do you access and use the printing troubleshooter?

   Click Start, click Control Panel, and click Printers And Other Hardware. In the Printers And Other Hardware window, under Troubleshooters, click Printers. The Help And Support Services window appears with the printing troubleshooter displayed.

2. What should you check if documents print correctly on some printers in a printing pool but not all of them?

Verify that all print devices in the printer pool are identical or that they use the same printer driver.

3. What should you check if printing is slow because the print server is taking a long time to render the job?

Try defragmenting the print server's disk and check that there is adequate space for temporary files on the hard disk.

4. What should you check if pages are only partially printing?

There might not be enough memory to print the document, so consider adding memory to the print server. The printer might not have enough toner, so try replacing the printer's toner cartridge.

Chapter 7: Administering and Troubleshooting Common Administrative Problems for Network Printers

Lesson 1: Understanding Printer Administration

Page 259

Lesson Review

1. What are the four major types of tasks involved with administering network printers?

Managing printers, managing documents, troubleshooting printers, and performing tasks that require the Manage Printers permission

2. Microsoft Windows XP Professional allows you to control printer usage and administration by assigning _____.

Permissions

3. Which level of printer permissions provided by Windows XP Professional grants users the ability to perform the most printing tasks?

a. Manage Printers

b. Manage Documents

c. Print

d. Full Control

a

4. Which of the following tabs do you use to assign printer permissions to users and groups?

   a. Security tab of the Properties dialog box for the printer

   b. Security tab of the Properties dialog box for the user or group

   c. Permissions tab of the Properties dialog box for the printer

   d. Permissions tab of the Properties dialog box for the user or group

   a

5. Which Windows XP Professional printer permission allows users to pause, resume, restart, and cancel all other users' documents? (Choose all answers that are correct.)

   a. Print

   b. Manage Printers

   c. Full Control

   d. Manage Documents

   b and d

Lesson 2: Managing Printers

Page 268

Lesson Review

1. If a printer has multiple trays that regularly hold different paper sizes, you can assign a form to a specific tray. How do you assign a form to a paper tray?

   In the Properties dialog box for the printer, click the Device Settings tab. In the box next to each paper tray, select the form for the paper type you want to assign to that tray.

2. A _____ is a file that contains print device commands that identify and separate printed documents.

   Separator page

3. Which of the following tabs do you use to redirect documents to a different printer?

   a. Advanced tab of the Properties dialog box for the printer

   b. Security tab of the Properties dialog box for the printer

   c. Ports tab of the Properties dialog box for the printer

   d. Device Settings tab of the Properties dialog box for the printer

   c

4. Which of the following tabs do you use to take ownership of a printer?

a. Advanced tab of the Properties dialog box for the printer

b. Security tab of the Properties dialog box for the printer

c. Ports tab of the Properties dialog box for the printer

d. Permissions tab of the Properties dialog box for the printer

b

5. Which of the following tabs do you use to set up a separator page?

a. Advanced tab of the Properties dialog box for the printer

b. Security tab of the Properties dialog box for the printer

c. Ports tab of the Properties dialog box for the printer

d. Permissions tab of the Properties dialog box for the printer

a

Lesson 3: Managing Documents

Page 273

Practice: Managing Documents

▶ **To set a notification**

3. In the Printer window, select BIG, and then, on the Document menu, click Properties.

Windows XP Professional displays the BIG Document Properties dialog box with the General tab active.

Which user is specified in the Notify text box? Why?

The user account that you are logged on with is specified because that is who created the print job.

▶ **To increase the priority of a document**

1. In the BIG Document Properties dialog box, in the General tab, notice the default priority.

What is the current priority? Is it the lowest or highest priority?

The current priority is 1, which is the lowest priority.

Page 274

Lesson Review

1. What is the difference between resuming printing of a document and restarting printing of a document?

When you restart a document, it begins printing again from the beginning of the document. When you resume printing a document, it continues from where it left off printing.

2. Which of the following statements about the range of priorities for a document to be printed is correct?

   a. Priorities for a document range from 1 to 10, with 1 being the highest priority.

   b. Priorities for a document range from 1 to 10, with 10 being the highest priority.

   c. Priorities for a document range from 1 to 99, with 1 being the highest priority.

   d. Priorities for a document range from 1 to 99, with 99 being the highest priority.

   d

3. You set the notification, priority, and printing time for a document in the _____ tab of the Properties dialog box for the document.

   General

4. By default, Windows XP Professional enters the _____ logon name in the Notify text box of a document.

   a. Administrator's

   b. Owner of the printer's

   c. Owner of the document's

   d. Person who printed the document's

   d

Lesson 4: Administering Printers Using a Web Browser

Page 277

Lesson Review

1. If you are using a computer running Windows XP Professional as your print server, users can gain access to the printers on it by using a Web browser only if the print server has _____ installed.

   Internet Information Services (IIS)

2. How can you gain access to all printers on a print server?

   In a Web browser or any of the windows or folders within the Windows XP Professional interface that has an address bar, type *http://print_server_name/printers*

3. Can you pause and resume operation of a printer that you have used Internet Explorer to connect to?

   Yes, if you have the Manage Printers permission for the printer, you can also pause or resume operation of a printer that you used Internet Explorer to connect to.

Lesson 5: Troubleshooting Common Printing Problems

Page 282   **Lesson Review**

1. When you detect a printing problem, what three things should you always check before you start troubleshooting the problem?

   Always verify that the printer is plugged in, turned on, and connected to the print server.

2. If a user reports to you that he or she cannot print, what are some of the areas you should check?

   Answers may vary. Suggested areas you should check include the following: Can other users print normally? Is the print server operational and is there enough disk space for spooling? Does the client computer have the correct printer driver?

3. The _____ feature included in Windows XP Professional allows you to invite an expert to take full control of your computer over the Internet to resolve printing problems on your computer.

   Remote Assistance

Chapter 8: Securing Resources with NTFS Permissions

Lesson 1: Understanding and Applying NTFS Permissions

Page 289   **Lesson Review**

1. Which of the following statements correctly describe NTFS file and folder permissions? (Choose all answers that are correct.)

   a. NTFS security is effective only when a user gains access to the file or folder over the network.

   b. NTFS security is effective when a user gains access to the file or folder on the local computer.

   c. NTFS permissions specify which users and groups can gain access to files and folders and what they can do with the contents of the file or folder.

   d. NTFS permissions can be used on all file systems available with Windows XP Professional.

   b and c

2. Which of the following NTFS folder permissions allow you to delete the folder?

   a. Read

   b. Read & Execute

   c. Modify

   d. Administer

   c

3. Which of the NTFS file permissions should you assign to a file if you want to allow users to delete the file but do not want to allow users to take ownership of a file?

   Modify

4. What is an access control list (ACL) and what is the difference between an ACL and an access control entry (ACE)?

   An ACL is stored with every file and folder on an NTFS volume and contains a list of all user accounts or groups that have been assigned permissions to that file or folder. An ACE is an entry in an ACL that contains the operations that a user or group is allowed or specifically denied to perform on that file or folder.

5. What are a user's effective permissions for a resource?

   A user's effective permissions for a resource are the sum of the NTFS permissions assigned to the individual user account and to all of the groups to which the user belongs. If there are any Deny permissions set, they override all instances in which that permission is allowed and must be removed from the user's effective permissions.

6. By default, what inherits the permissions that you assign to the parent folder?

   By default, the permissions that you assign to the parent folder are inherited by and propagated to the subfolders and files that are contained in the parent folder.

Lesson 2: Assigning NTFS Permissions and Special Permissions

Practice: Planning and Assigning NTFS Permissions

Page 298

Exercise 1: Determining the Default NTFS Permissions for a Folder

▶ **To determine the default permissions on a folder**

4. Click the Security tab to display the permissions for the Public folder.

   If any of the users or groups have special permissions, click the user or group and then click Advanced to see which special permissions are set.

   Windows XP Professional displays the Public Properties dialog box with the Security tab active.

   What are the existing folder permissions?

   The Administrators group has Full Control. The CREATOR OWNER has special permissions, Full Control. The account that created the folder has special permissions, Full Control. SYSTEM has Full Control. The Users group has Read & Execute, List Folder Contents, Read, and special permissions of Create Files/Write Data and Create Folders/Append Data.

▶ **To test the folder permissions for the Public folder**

3. In the Public folder, create a text document named USER81 and type in the following text: **The first four letters in the alphabet are a, b, c, and d.**

   Were you successful? Why or why not?

   Yes, because the Users group is assigned the special permissions of Create Files/Write Data and Create Folders/Append Data for the Public folder.

4. Attempt to perform the following tasks for the file that you just created:

   - Open the file
   - Modify the file
   - Delete the file

   Which tasks were you able to complete and why?

   You can open, modify, and delete the file because you created the file and are therefore the CREATOR OWNER. CREATOR OWNER has been assigned the NTFS Full Control permission for the Public folder.

8. Attempt to perform the following tasks on the USER81 text document:

   - Open the file
   - Modify the file
   - Delete the file

   Which tasks were you able to complete and why?

   You can open the file because the Users group has Read permission in the Public folder.

When you attempt to modify the file, you get an error message. You cannot modify the file because the Users group does not have either Full Control or Modify permissions for the Public folder. Users can create files and folders in the Public folders and they have Full Control permission for the file and folders that they created, but they cannot modify files and folders for which they are not the creator or owner.

You cannot delete the file. You can only read files and folders for which you are not the owner.

Page 300

Exercise 2: Assigning NTFS Permissions

Based on what you learned in Exercise 1, what changes in permission assignments do you need to make to meet each of these four criteria? Why?

The first three criteria are met by the default permission assignments. To allow User82 the ability to modify or delete all files in the Public folder. you could change the special permission assigned to User82 to Full Control.

You are currently logged on as User82. Can you change the permissions assigned to User82 while logged on as User82? Why or why not?

No, you cannot change the permissions assigned User82 while logged on as User82 because User82 is not a member of the Administrators group, is not the owner of the Public folder, and does not have the Full Control permission for the Public folder. Only Administrators, the owners of files or folders, and users with Full Control permission can assign NTFS permissions to users and groups to control access to files and folders.

▶ **To assign NTFS permissions for a folder**

7. Click OK to close the Select Users Or Groups dialog box.

   User82 now appears in the Group Or User Name box in the Public Properties dialog box.

   What permissions are assigned to User82?

   Read & Execute, List Folder Contents, and Read

▶ **To test NTFS permissions for a folder**

4. Attempt to perform the following tasks on the USER81 text document:

   ▪ Open the file
   ▪ Modify the file
   ▪ Delete the file

   Which tasks were you able to record and why?

   User82 can open, modify, and delete the file because User82 has been assigned the Full Control permission for the Public folder.

Page 302

Exercise 3: Testing NTFS Permissions

▶   **To test permissions for the Library folder while logged on as User82**

3. Attempt to perform the following tasks on USER81:

   ▪ Open the file

   ▪ Modify the file

   ▪ Delete the file

   Which tasks were you able to record and why?

   User82 can open, modify, and delete the file because User82 has been assigned the Full Control permission for the Library folder. The Inherit From Parent The Permission Entries That Apply To Child Objects check box is selected by default. Therefore the Full Control permission was inherited by the Library folder from the Public folder.

Page 303

Lesson Review

1. By default, when you format a volume with NTFS, the
   _____ permission is assigned to the Everyone group.

   Full Control

2. When you assign permissions for public data folders, it is recommended that
   you assign the _____ permission and the
   _____ permission to the Users group and the
   _____ permission to the CREATOR OWNER user.

   Read & Execute; Write; Full Control

3. Which of the following users can assign permissions to user accounts and
   groups? (Choose all answers that are correct.)

   a. Administrators

   b. Power users

   c. Users with the Full Control permission

   d. Owners of files and folders

   a, c, and d

4. Which of the following tabs in the Properties dialog box for the file or folder do
   you use to assign or modify NTFS permissions for a file or a folder?

   a. Advanced

   b. Permissions

   c. Security

   d. General

   c

5. What is the purpose of the Traverse Folder/Execute File special permission?

Traverse Folder allows or denies moving through folders to access other files or folders, even when the user has no permissions for the traversed folder. Execute File allows or denies running executable files (application files).

6. What is the difference between the Delete permission and Delete Subfolder and Files permission?

Delete allows or denies the deleting of a file or folder. Even if a user does not have the Delete permission for a file or folder, the user can still delete the file or folder if the Delete Subfolder and Files permission has been granted to the user on the parent folder.

Lesson 3: Solving Permissions Problems

Practice: Managing NTFS Permissions

Page 309

Exercise 1: Taking Ownership of a File

▶   **To determine the permissions for a file**

6. Click the Owner tab.

Who is the current owner of the OWNER file?

The Administrators group

▶   **To take ownership of a file**

6. Under Change Owner To, select User81, and then click Apply.

Who is now the owner of the OWNER file?

User81

Page 311

Exercise 2: Copying and Moving Folders

▶   **To create a folder while logged on as a user**

1. While you are logged on as User81, in Windows Explorer, in the root folder of drive C, create a folder named Temp1.

What are the permissions that are assigned to the folder?

User or group	Permissions
Administrators (PRO1\Administrators)	Full Control
Creator and owner	Full Control
System	Full Control
User81	Full Control
Users (PRO1\Users)	Read & Execute, List Folder Contents, Read Special permissions – Create Files/ Write Data and Create Folders/ Append Data

Who is the owner? Why?

User81 is the owner because the person who creates a folder or file is the owner.

▶ **To create a folder while logged on as a member of the Administrators group**

2. In the root folder of drive C, create the folders Temp2 and Temp3.

What are the permissions for the Temp2 and Temp3 folders that you just created?

User or group	Permissions
Administrators (PRO1\Administrators)	Full Control
Creator and owner	Full Control
System	Full Control
Fred or the name of the user account you used to create Temp2	Full Control
Users (PRO1\Users)	Read & Execute, List Folder Contents, Read Special permissions – Create Files/ Write Data and Create Folders/ Append Data

Who is the owner of the Temp2 and Temp3 folders? Why?

The Administrators group or Fred (the name of the user account you used to create Temp2 if you did not log on as Administrator) is the owner because the person who creates a folder or file is the owner. If the person is a member of the Administrators group, the Administrators group is the owner.

▶ **To copy a folder to another folder within a Windows XP Professional NTFS volume**

2. Select C:\Temp1\Temp2, and then compare the permissions and ownership with C:\Temp2.

Who is the owner of C:\Temp1\Temp2 and what are the permissions? Why?

The owner of C:\Temp1\Temp2 is the user account that performed the copy. The permissions for C:\Temp1\Temp2 are now the same as the permissions of Temp1. When you copy a folder or file into another folder, the permissions assigned to it are always the same as the permissions on the destination folder.

▶ **To move a folder within the same NTFS volume**

2. In Windows Explorer, select C:\Temp3, and then move it to C:\Temp1.

What happens to the permissions and ownership for C:\Temp1\Temp3? Why?

Nothing; they do not change.

Page 313

Exercise 3: Deleting a File with All Permissions Denied

▶ **To view the result of the Full Control permission being denied for a folder**

1. In Windows Explorer, double-click the NOACCESS text document in the Temp3 folder to open it.

Were you successful? Why or why not?

No. The Users group has Full Control denied.

5. Type **Del NOACCESS.TXT** and press ENTER.

Were you successful? Why or why not?

Yes, because Full Control includes the Delete Subfolders and Files special permission for POSIX compliance. This special permission allows a user to delete files in the root of a folder to which the user has been assigned Full Control permission. This permission overrides the file permissions.

How would you prevent users with Full Control permission for a folder from deleting a file in that folder for which they have been denied the Full Control permission?

Allow users all of the individual permissions, and then deny users the Delete Subfolders and Files special permission.

Page 314

Lesson Review

1. Which of the following statements about copying a file or folder are correct? (Choose all answers that are correct.)

a. When you copy a file from one folder to another folder on the same volume, the permissions on the file do not change.

b. When you copy a file from a folder on an NTFS volume to a folder on a FAT volume, the permissions on the file do not change.

c. When you copy a file from a folder on an NTFS volume to a folder on another NTFS volume, the permissions on the file match those of the destination folder.

d. When you copy a file from a folder on an NTFS volume to a folder on a FAT volume, the permissions are lost.

c and d

2. Which of the following statements about moving a file or folder are correct? (Choose all answers that are correct.)

   a. When you move a file from one folder to another folder on the same volume, the permissions on the file do not change.

   b. When you move a file from a folder on an NTFS volume to a folder on a FAT volume, the permissions on the file do not change.

   c. When you move a file from a folder on an NTFS volume to a folder on another NTFS volume, the permissions on the file match those of the destination folder.

   d. When you move a file from a folder on an NTFS volume to a folder on the same volume, the permissions on thc filc match those of the destination folder.

   a and c

3. When you assign NTFS permissions you should assign the _____ (least/most) restrictive permissions.

   Most

4. If you don't want a user or group to gain access to a particular folder or file, should you deny access permissions to that folder or file?

   You should not assign permissions to the folder or file rather than deny permission to access the folder or file. Denying permissions should be an exception, not common practice.

Chapter 9: Administering Shared Folders

Lesson 1: Understanding Shared Folders

Page 321

Practice: Applied Permissions

1. User101 is a member of Group1, Group2, and Group3. Group1 has Read permission. Group2 has Full Control permission for FolderA, and Group3 has change permissions assigned for FolderA. What are User101's effective permissions for FolderA?

   Because User101 is a member of Group1, Group2, and Group3, User101's effective permission is Full Control, which includes all capabilities of the Read permission and the Change permission.

2. User102 has been granted the Full Control shared folder permission for FolderB as an individual user. User102 is a member of the Managers group, which has been granted Change permission for FolderB, and a member of the Sales group, which has been denied all access to FolderB. What are User102's effective permissions for FolderB?

   User102 has been granted Full Control to FolderB, but because User102 is a member of the Managers group and the Sales group, User102's effective permission is denied Full Control access to FolderB. Denied permission overrides all other permissions.

Page 322

Lesson Review

1. Because you use NTFS permissions to specify which users and groups can access files and folders and what these permissions allow users to do with the contents of the file or folder, why do you need to share a folder or use shared folder permissions?

   Although NTFS security is effective whether a user gains access to the file or folder at the computer or over the network, NTFS permissions do not make folders available over the network. Sharing folders is the only way to make folders and their contents available over the network. Shared folder permissions also provide another way to secure file resources. They can be used on FAT or FAT32 partitions, as well as NTFS partitions, whereas NTFS permissions are available only on NTFS volumes.

2. Which of the following permissions are shared folder permissions? (Choose all answers that are correct.)

   a. Read

   b. Write

   c. Modify

   d. Full Control

   a and d

3. _____ (Denied /Allowed) permissions take precedence over _____ (denied /allowed) permissions on a shared folder.

   Denied permissions take precedence over allowed permissions on a shared folder.

4. When you copy a shared folder, the original folder is _____ (no longer shared /still shared) and the copy is _____ (not shared /shared).

   When you copy a folder, the original folder is still shared and the copy is not shared.

5. When you move a shared folder, the folder is _____ (no longer shared /still shared).

   When you move a shared folder, the folder is no longer shared.

6. When you rename a shared folder, the folder is _____ (no longer shared /still shared).

   When you rename a shared folder, the folder is no longer shared.

Lesson 2: Planning, Sharing, and Connecting to Shared Folders

Page 335

Lesson Review

1. What is a shared application folder? What is the main advantage of using shared applications?

   Shared application folders are used for applications that are installed on a network server and can be used from client computers. The main advantage of shared applications is that you don't need to install and maintain most components of the applications on each computer.

2. In a Windows workgroup, the _____ group and the _____ group can share folders on the Windows 2000 stand-alone server or the computer running Windows XP Professional on which the group exists.

   Administrators group and Power Users group

3. Windows XP Professional automatically shares folders for administrative purposes. These shares are marked with a _____, which hides them from users who browse the computer.

   Dollar sign ($)

4. The system root folder, which is C:\Windows by default, is shared as _____. Administrators can access this shared folder to administer Windows XP Professional without knowing in which folder it is installed. Only members of the Administrators group have access to this share. Windows XP Professional assigns the Full Control permission to the Administrators group.

   Admin$

5. To assign permissions to user accounts and groups for a shared folder, which of the following tabs do you use?

   a. The Permissions tab of the Properties dialog box of the shared folder

   b. The Sharing tab of the Properties dialog box of the shared folder

   c. The General tab of the Properties dialog box of the shared folder

   d. The Security tab of the Properties dialog box of the shared folder

   b

6. Which of the following statements about size of the cache for making shared folders available offline is correct?

   a. By default, the cache size is set to 20 percent of the available disk space.

   b. By default, the cache size is set to 15 percent of the available disk space.

   c. By default, the cache size is set to 10 percent of the available disk space.

   d. By default, the cache size is set to 5 percent of the available disk space.

   c

Lesson 3: Combining Shared Folder Permissions and NTFS Permissions

Practice: Managing Shared Folders

Page 338

Exercise 1: Combining Permissions

Figure 9.11 shows examples of shared folders on NTFS volumes. These shared folders contain subfolders that have also been assigned NTFS permissions. Determine a user's effective permissions for each example.

1. In the first example, the Data folder is shared. The Sales group has the shared folder Read permission for the Data folder and the NTFS Full Control permission for the Sales subfolder.

   What are the Sales group's effective permissions for the Sales subfolder when they gain access to the Sales subfolder by making a connection to the Data shared folder?

   The Sales group has the Read permission for the Sales subfolder because when shared folder permissions are combined with NTFS permissions, the more restrictive permission applies.

2. In the second example, the Users folder contains user home folders. Each user home folder contains data accessible only to the user for whom the folder is named. The Users folder has been shared, and the Users group has the shared folder Full Control permission for the Users folder. User1 and User2 have the NTFS Full Control permission for their home folder only and no NTFS permissions for other folders. These users are all members of the Users group.

   What permissions does User1 have when he or she accesses the User1 subfolder by making a connection to the Users shared folder? What are User1's permissions for the User2 subfolder?

   User1 has the Full Control permission for the User1 subfolder because both the shared folder permission and the NTFS permission allow Full Control. User1 can't access the User2 subfolder because she or he has no NTFS permission to gain access to it.

Page 340

Exercise 2: Planning Shared Folders

In this exercise, you plan how to share resources on servers in the main office of a manufacturing company. Record your decisions in the table at the end of this exercise.

You have two choices for permissions: you can rely entirely on NTFS permissions and assign Full Control for all shared folders to the Everyone group, or you can use shared folder permissions according to resource needs. The following suggested shared folders include required permissions if you decide to assign shared folder permissions.

Share Management Guidelines as MgmtGd. Assign the Full Control permission to the Managers group.

Share Data as Data. Assign the Full Control permission to the Administrators built-in group.

Share Data\Customer Service as CustServ. Assign the Change permission to the Customer Service group.

Share Data\Public as Public. Assign the Change permission to the Users built-in group.

Share Applications as Apps. Assign the Read permission to the Users built-in group and the Full Control permission to the Administrators built-in group.

Share Project Management as ProjMan. Assign the Change permission to the Managers group and the Full Control permission to the Administrators built-in group.

Share Database\Customers as CustDB. Assign the Change permission to the CustomerDBFull group, the Read permission to the CustomerDBRead group, and the Full Control permission to the Administrators built-in group.

Share Users as Users. Create a folder for every employee below this folder. Assign the Full Control permission to each employee for his or her own folder. Preferably, have Windows XP Professional create the folder and assign permission automatically when you create each user account.

Page 342

Exercise 4: Assigning Shared Folder Permissions

▶   To assign permissions to a group

2. In the Name text box, type **administrators** and then click OK.

   Windows XP Professional adds Administrators to the list of names with permissions.

   Which type of access does Windows XP Professional assign to the Administrators group by default?

   The Read permission

3. In the Permissions For Administrators dialog box, under Allow, select the Full Control check box.

   Why did Windows Explorer also select the Change permission for you?

   Full Control includes both the Change permission and the Read permission.

Page 345

Exercise 8 (Optional): Testing NTFS and Shared Folder Permissions

In this exercise, you use different user accounts to test how NTFS permissions and shared folder permissions combine. To answer the questions in this exercise, refer to the tables in Exercise 7.

▶ **To test permissions for the Manuals folder when a user logs on locally**

3. In the Manuals folder, attempt to create a test document.

Were you successful? Why or why not?

No, Windows XP Professional displays an Unable To Create Folder dialog box. Only Administrators have the NTFS permission to create and modify files in the Manuals folder.

▶ **To test permissions for the Manuals folder when a user makes a connection over the network**

7. In the Manuals window, attempt to create a file.

Were you successful? Why or why not?

No. Although the Users group has the Full Control shared folder permission for \\PRO1\MktApps, only Administrators have the NTFS permission to create and modify files in the Manuals folder.

▶ **To test permissions for the Manuals folder when a user logs on over the network as Administrator**

4. In the Manuals window, attempt to create a file.

Were you successful? Why or why not?

Yes. The Administrators group has the Full Control NTFS permission and Full Control shared folder permission for \\PRO1\MktApps\Manuals.

▶ **To test permissions for the Public folder when a user makes a connection over the network**

5. In the Public window, attempt to create a file.

Were you successful? Why or why not?

Yes. User1 has the Full Control NTFS permission for the folder and Full Control shared folder permission for \\PRO1\MktApps\Public.

Page 347

Lesson Review

1. If you are using both shared folder and NTFS permissions, the _____ (least/most) restrictive permission is always the overriding permission.

Most

2. Which of the following statements about combining shared folder permissions and NTFS permissions are true? (Choose all answers that are correct.)

   a. You can use shared folder permissions on all shared folders.

   b. The Change shared folder permission is more restrictive than the Read NTFS permission.

   c. You can use NTFS permissions on all shared folders.

   d. The Read NTFS permission is more restrictive than the Change shared folder permission.

   a and d

3. Which of the following statements about shared folder permissions and NTFS permissions are true? (Choose all answers that are correct.)

   a. NTFS permissions apply only when the resource is accessed over the network.

   b. NTFS permissions apply whether the resource is accessed locally or over the network.

   c. Shared folder permissions apply only when the resource is accessed over the network.

   d. Shared folder permissions apply whether the resource is accessed locally or over the network.

   b and c

4. If needed, you can apply different _____ permissions to each folder, file, and subfolder.

   NTFS

Chapter 10: Configuring Windows XP Professional

Lesson 1: Configuring and Troubleshooting the Display

Page 358

Lesson Review

1. You can enable _____ to restrict access to Display options.

   Group Policy settings

2. Which of the following items does the Desktop Items dialog box allow you to choose to include or exclude an icon on your desktop? (Choose all answers that are correct.)

   a. My Documents

   b. Control Panel

   c. My Network Places

   d. Recycle Bin

   a and c

3. Windows XP Professional supports extension of your display across a maximum of _____ monitors.

10

4. You must use _____ or _____ video adapters when configuring multiple displays.

PCI or AGP video adapters

5. If one of the display adapters is built into the motherboard, the motherboard adapter always becomes the _____ (primary/secondary) adapter.

Secondary

Lesson 2: Configuring Power Management

Page 366

Lesson Review

1. What is a power scheme and why would you use one?

Power schemes allow you to configure Windows XP Professional to turn off the power to your monitor and your hard disk to conserve energy.

2. Which of the following statements about Windows XP Professional power schemes are true? (Choose all answers that are correct.)

a. Windows XP Professional ships with six built-in power schemes.

b. Windows XP Professional allows you to create you own power schemes.

c. Windows XP Professional allows you to modify existing power schemes, but you cannot create new ones.

d. Windows XP Professional does not ship with any built-in power schemes.

a and b

3. A _____ is a device that connects between a computer and a power source to ensure that the electrical flow to the computer is not abruptly stopped because of a blackout.

UPS

4. What does hibernate mode do?

When your computer hibernates, it saves the current system state to your hard disk, and then your computer shuts down. When you start the computer after it has been hibernating, it returns to its previous state, restarts any programs that were running, and restores any active network connections.

5. _____ means that you can remove or exchange devices such as floppy drives, DVD/CD drives, and hard drives without shutting down your system or restarting your system. Windows XP Professional automatically detects and configures these devices.

Hot swapping

Lesson 3: Configuring Operating System Settings

Page 386

Lesson Review

1. What performance options can you control with the tabs of the Performance Options dialog box?

   The Visual Effects tab of the Performance Options dialog box provides a number of options that allow you to manually control the visual effects on your computer. The Advanced tab of the Performance Options dialog box allows you to adjust the application response, which is the priority of foreground applications versus background applications, and virtual memory.

2. Which of the following statements about the use of virtual memory in Windows XP Professional are correct? (Choose all answers that are correct.)

   a. When you install Windows XP Professional, Setup creates a virtual memory paging file, PAGEFILE.SYS, on the partition where you installed Windows XP Professional.

   b. In some environments, you might find it advantageous to use multiple paging files.

   c. If the entire paging file is not in use, it can decrease below the initial size that was set during installation.

   d. Unused space in the paging file remains unavailable to all programs, even the internal Windows XP Professional VMM.

   a and b

3. When you first turn on the computer, the system displays a Please Select The Operating System To Start screen, which lists the available operating systems. What happens if a user does not select an operating system before the countdown timer reaches zero?

   If a user doesn't choose an operating system, the system starts the preselected operating system when the countdown timer reaches zero.

4. What requirements must be met for the Write Debugging Information recovery option to work?

   A paging file must be on the system partition (the partition that contains the %systemroot% folder). You must have enough disk space to write the file to the location you specify. A small memory dump requires a paging

file of at least 2 MB on the boot volume. A kernel memory dump requires 50 MB to 800 MB available in the paging file on the boot volume. A complete memory dump requires a paging file on the boot volume large enough to hold all the RAM on your computer plus 1 MB. With a small memory dump, a new dump file will be created every time the system stops unexpectedly. For a complete memory dump or kernel memory dump, if you want the new dump file to overwrite an existing file, select the Overwrite Any Existing File check box.

5. What is the Windows XP Professional Remote Assistance feature?

   If you have a computer problem, the Remote Assistance feature allows you to invite a remote assistant to help you over the Internet. The remote assistant can chat with you about the problem and view your desktop. He or she can also transfer any files required to fix the problem. With your permission, the remote assistant can get full control of your computer to perform any complex steps needed to fix the problem.

6. To join a domain, you use the _____ tab of the _____ dialog box.

   Computer Name; System Properties.

Lesson 4: Configuring and Troubleshooting the Desktop Environment

Page 397

Lesson Review

1. How can you configure Windows XP Professional to use multiple languages?

   To configure multiple languages, in Control Panel, click Date, Time, Language, And Regional Options. In the Date, Time, Language, And Regional Options window, click Regional And Language Options to open the Regional And Language Options dialog box. In the Languages tab of the Regional And Languages Options dialog box, click Details. Windows XP Professional displays the Text Services And Input Languages dialog box. Click Add. Click the down-pointing arrow at the end of the Input Language list box. Scroll through the list of languages and select the ones you want to add. If you added at least one language to the one already installed on your computer, your computer is now supporting multiple languages.

2. Turning on _____ allows you to press a multiple key combination, like CTRL+ALT+DELETE, one key at a time. (Choose all answers that are correct.)

   a. FilterKeys

   b. StickyKeys

   c. ToggleKeys

   d. MultiKeys

   b

3. Turning on _____ causes the keyboard to ignore brief or repeated keystrokes. This option also allows you to configure the keyboard repeat rate, which is the rate at which a key continuously held down repeats the keystroke.

FilterKeys

4. When using MouseKeys, to speed up the mouse pointer movement, hold down the _____ key while you press the numeric keypad directional keys. To slow down the mouse pointer movement, hold down the _____ key while you press the numeric keypad directional keys.

CTRL; SHIFT

5. The _____ tab in the Accessibility Options dialog box includes the Notification feature, which allows you to configure Windows XP Professional to give a warning message when a feature is activated and to make a sound when turning a feature on or off.

General tab

Lesson 5: Managing Windows Components

Page 402

Lesson Review

1. How do you add Windows components to your Windows XP Professional installation?

   In Control Panel, click Add Or Remove Programs. In the Add or Remove Windows Programs window, click Add/Remove Windows Components to start the Windows Components Wizard. You use the Windows Components Wizard to select the Windows components that you want to add to or remove from your Windows XP Professional installation.

2. What service does Internet Information Services (IIS) provide?

   Internet Information Services (IIS) allows you to publish information on the Internet or on your intranet. You place your files in directories on your server and IIS allows users to establish HTTP connections and view the files with their Web browsers.

3. How many simultaneous client connections can you have using Internet Information Services for Windows XP Professional?

   a. 8

   b. 10

   c. 20

   d. 32

   b

4. How do you administer Internet Information Services (IIS) for Windows XP Professional?

You use the Internet Information Services snap-in to manage IIS and the content of and access to your Web and FTP sites.

Chapter 11: Installing, Managing, and Troubleshooting Hardware Devices and Drivers

Lesson 1: Understanding Automatic and Manual Hardware Installation

Page 412

Lesson Review

1. When you initiate automatic hardware installation by starting the Add Hardware Wizard, what does Windows XP Professional query the hardware about?

The resources the hardware requires and the settings for those resources.

2. _____ are channels that allow a hardware device, such as a floppy disk drive, to access memory directly, without interrupting the microprocessor.

DMAs

3. Why would you install a hardware device manually?

If Windows XP Professional fails to automatically detect a hardware device.

Lesson 2: Configuring and Troubleshooting Hardware Devices

Page 426

Lesson Review

1. Windows XP Professional automatically identifies Plug and Play devices and arbitrates their resource requests; the resource allocation among these devices is _____ (permanent/not permanent).

Not permanent

2. How can you free any resource settings that you manually assigned to a Plug and Play device?

To free the resource settings you manually assigned and allow Windows XP Professional to again arbitrate the resources, in Device Manager select the Use Automatic Settings check box in the Resources tab of the Properties dialog box for the device.

3. Which of the following devices are not shown by default in Device Manager? (Choose all that apply.)

    a. Devices sharing an IRQ

    b. Phantom devices

    c. Plug and Play devices

    d. Non–Plug and Play devices

b and d

4. You get a call on the help desk from a user upset because he cannot send faxes from Outlook Express. What should you tell the user?

Tell the user that Outlook Express is not compliant with a MAPI client interface and cannot be used to send faxes. Tell him to use Outlook 2000 to send faxes.

5. You get a call on the help desk from a user wondering why there is no Wireless Link icon in Control Panel on her desktop computer like the one on her laptop computer. What should you tell the user?

Tell the user that the Wireless Link icon appears in Control Panel only if she has already installed an infrared device on her computer. Apparently, infrared devices are not installed on her desktop computer.

Lesson 3: Viewing and Configuring Hardware Profiles

Page 429

Lesson Review

1. What is the minimum number of hardware profiles you can have on your computer?

Windows XP Professional creates an initial profile during installation, which is listed as Profile 1 (Current), so one is the minimum number of hardware profiles you can have on a computer.

2. Computer hardware profiles are an especially important feature for what type of computers?

    a. Computers in a network environment

    b. Computers in a domain

    c. Stand-alone computers

    d. Portable computers

    d

3. Windows XP Professional creates an initial profile during installation and assigns it the name of _____ in the list of hardware profiles available on the computer.

    Profile 1 (Current)

4. Which of the following statements are true about hardware profiles in Windows XP Professional? (Choose all that apply.)

    a. Windows XP Professional only prompts the user to select a hardware profile during startup if there are two or more profiles in the Available Hardware Profiles list.

    b. It is a good idea to delete the default profile when you create a new profile to avoid confusion.

c. You can configure Windows XP Professional to always start the default profile by selecting the Do Not Display The Select Hardware Profile check box.

d. You can select the Wait Until I Select A Hardware Profile option to have Windows XP Professional wait for you to select a profile at startup.

a and d

Lesson 4: Configuring, Monitoring, and Troubleshooting Driver Signing

Page 435

Lesson Review

1. Why does Microsoft digitally sign the files in Windows XP Professional?

Windows XP Professional drivers and operating system files have been digitally signed by Microsoft to ensure their quality and to simplify troubleshooting of altered files. Some applications overwrite existing operating files as part of their installation process, which might cause system errors that are difficult to troubleshoot.

2. Which of the following tools would you use to block the installation of unsigned files?

a. File Signature Verification

b. Driver Signing Options in the System Control Panel

c. System File Checker

d. Sigverif

b

3. How can you view the file signature verification log file?

By default, the Windows File Signature Verification tool saves the file signature verification to a log file. To view the log file, click Start, click Run, type sigverif, and then press ENTER. Click Advanced, click the Logging tab, and then click View Log.

Lesson 5: Configuring Computers with Multiple Processors

Page 437

Lesson Review

1. Adding processors to your system to improve performance is called

_____.

Scaling

2. How can you manually update a driver on your computer?

You open Device Manager, right-click the appropriate device, and then click Properties. In the Driver tab, click Update Driver. The Welcome To The Hardware Update Wizard page appears and guides you through the rest of the update process.

Chapter 12: Auditing Resources and Events

Lesson 1: Planning an Audit Policy

Page 442

Lesson Review

1. What is auditing?

   Auditing is a process that tracks both user activities and Windows XP Professional activities on a computer and records these events in the security log.

2. What is an audit policy?

   An audit policy defines the types of security events that Windows XP Professional records in the security log on each computer.

3. On a computer running Windows XP Professional, auditing is turned _____ (on/off) by default.

   Off

4. When you are auditing events on a computer running Windows XP Professional, where are the audited events being recorded?

   Windows XP Professional writes events to the security log on the computer on which the event occurs.

5. When you are auditing events on a computer running Windows XP Professional, why would you track failed events?

   Tracking failed events can alert you to potential security breaches.

Lesson 2: Implementing an Audit Policy

Page 450

Lesson Review

1. What are the requirements to set up and administer auditing?

   You must have the Manage Auditing And Security Log user right for the computer for which you want to configure an audit policy or review an audit log. The files and folders you want to audit must be on an NTFS volume.

2. What are the two steps in setting up auditing?

   Setting the audit policy and enabling auditing of specific resources

3. How do you set audit policies for a local computer?

   In the console pane of an MMC console containing the Group Policy snap-in that is pointed at the Local Computer, click Local Computer Policy\Computer Configuration\Windows Settings\Security Settings\Local Policies\Audit Policy. Next, in the details pane, select the event to audit. On the Action menu, click Properties. In the Properties dialog box for the event, select the Success check box or the Failure check

box, or both, depending on whether you want to set the audit policy to track successful attempts, failed attempts, or both.

4. What are some reasons for auditing system events?

Auditing system events allows you to determine if a user restarted or shut down the computer or if any event occurred that affects Windows XP Professional security or the security log. Auditing system events allows you to detect if the audit log is full and Windows XP Professional is discarding entries.

5. By default, any auditing changes that you make to a parent folder _____ (are inherited/are not inherited) by all child folders and all files in the parent and child folders.

Are inherited

Lesson 3: Using Event Viewer

Practice: Auditing Resources and Events

Page 456

Exercise 1: Planning an Audit Policy

In this exercise, you plan an audit policy for your computer. You need to determine the following:

- Which types of events to audit
- Whether to audit the success or failure of an event, or both

Record your decisions to audit successful events, failed events, or both for the actions listed in the following table:

Record unsuccessful attempts to gain access to the computer: Audit Failed Logon Events

Record unauthorized access to the files that make up the customer database: Audit Successful Object Access

For billing purposes, track color printer use: Audit Successful Object Access

Track whenever someone tries to tamper with the computer's hardware: Audit Failed System Events

Keep a record of actions that an administrator performs to track unauthorized changes: Audit Successful System Events

Track backup procedures to prevent data theft: Audit Successful Privilege Use

Track unauthorized access to sensitive Active Directory objects: Audit Successful and Failed Directory Service Access

Action to audit	Successful	Failed
Account Logon Events		
Account Management		
Directory Service Access	X	X
Logon Events		X
Object Access	X	
Policy Change		
Privilege Use	X	
Process Tracking		
System Events	X	X

Page 460

Exercise 5: Testing the Auditing Policy Set Up on the AUDIT File

▶   **To test the auditing policy**

8. Save the file.

   Were you able to save the file? Why or why not?

   No, because User2 is a member of the Users group and only has permission to read the file.

Page 462

Lesson Review

1. What are the three Windows XP Professional logs you can view with Event Viewer and what is the purpose of each log?

   The application log contains errors, warnings, or information that programs, such as a database program or an e-mail program, generate. The program developer presets which events to record.

   The security log contains information about the success or failure of audited events. The events that Windows XP Professional records are a result of your audit policy.

   The system log contains errors, warnings, and information that Windows XP Professional generates. Windows XP Professional presets which events to record.

2. How can you view the security log on a remote computer?

   You can view the security log on a remote computer by opening the MMC console and pointing Event Viewer to the remote computer. You must also have administrative privileges for the computer at which the events occurred.

3. The two ways that Event Viewer provides for locating specific events are the _____ command and the _____ command. What do each of the commands allow you to do?

Filter; Find

The Filter command allows you to change what appears in the log.

The Find command allows you to search for specific events.

4. The size of each log can be from _____ KB to _____ GB, and the default size is _____ KB.

64 KB, 4 GB, 512 KB

5. If you select the Do Not Overwrite Events option, what happens when the log becomes full?

If you select the Do Not Overwrite Events option, you must clear the log manually. When the log becomes full, Windows XP Professional stops. However, no security log entries are overwritten.

Chapter 13: Configuring Security Settings and Internet Options

Lesson 1: Configuring Account Policies

Practice: Configuring Account Policy

Page 470

Exercise 2: Configuring and Testing Additional Account Policy Settings

▶   **To configure Account Policy settings**

1. Use the Local Group Policy custom MMC console you created to configure the following Account Policy settings:

   ■ A user should have at least five different passwords before using a previously used password.

   ■ After changing a password, a user must wait 24 hours before he or she can change it again.

   ■ A user should change his or her password every 3 weeks.

   What settings did you use for each of the three listed items?

   Set Enforce Password History to 5 so that users must have at least five different passwords before they use a previously used password.

   Set Minimum Password Age to 1 day so that a user must wait 24 hours before he or she can change it again.

   Set Maximum Password Age to 21 days so that a user must change his or her password every three weeks.

▶   **To test Account Policy settings**

10. Click Change Password.

Were you successful? Why or why not?

No, because you must wait 24 hours (one day) before you can change your password a second time. A Change Password dialog box appears, indicating that you cannot change the password at this time.

Page 471

Exercise 3: Configuring Account Lockout Policy

▶   **To configure Account Lockout Policy settings**

7. Use Account Lockout Policy settings to do the following:

   ▪ Lock out a user account after four failed logon attempts.

   ▪ Lock out user accounts until an administrator unlocks the user account.

   What Account Lockout Policy settings did you use for each of the two conditions?

   Set the account lockout threshold to 4 to lock out a user account after four failed logon attempts. When you set one of the three Account Lockout options and the other two options have not been set, a dialog box appears indicating that the other two options will be set to default values.

   Set the account lockout duration to 0 to ensure that locked accounts remain locked until an administrator unlocks them.

Page 471

Lesson Review

1. What tool does Microsoft Windows XP Professional provide for you to configure Password Policy?

   The Microsoft Windows XP Professional Group Policy snap-in.

2. What is the range of values Windows XP Professional allows you to set for the Enforce Password History setting and what do those values mean?

   You can set the value from 0 to 24. A value of 0 indicates that no password history is being kept. All values indicate the number of new passwords that a user must use before he or she can reuse an old password.

3. The range of values Windows XP Professional allows you to set for the Maximum Password Age setting is _____ to _____ days. The default value is _____ days.

   0 to 999 days; 42 days

4. Which of the following selections are requirements for a password if the Passwords Must Meet Complexity Requirements setting is enabled? (Choose all that apply.)

   a. All passwords must exceed the specified minimum password length.

   b. All passwords must comply with the password history settings.

   c. No passwords can contain capitals or punctuation.

   d. No passwords can contain the user's account or full name.

   b and d

5. What is Account Lockout Duration and what is the range of values?

   This value indicates the number of minutes that the system will prevent the user account from logging on to Windows XP Professional. You can set the value from 0 to 99,999 minutes.

Lesson 2: Configuring User Rights

Page 479

Lesson Review

1. Which of the following statements about user rights are correct? (Choose all that apply.)

   a. Microsoft recommends that you assign user rights to individual user accounts.

   b. Microsoft recommends that you assign user rights to groups rather than individual user accounts.

   c. User rights allow users assigned the right to perform a specific action, such as backing up files and directories.

   d. There are two types of user rights: privileges and logon rights.

   b, c, and d

2. If your computer running Windows XP Professional is part of a Windows 2000 domain environment and you configure the Local Security Policies on your computer so that you assign yourself the Add Workstation To A Domain user right, can you add additional workstations to the domain? Why or why not?

   For the Add Workstation To A Domain privilege to be effective, it must be assigned as part of the default domain controller policy for the domain, not the Local Security Policy on your computer running Windows XP Professional.

3. What benefit does the Back Up Files And Directories user right provide?

   The Back Up Files And Directories user right improves the security on your system. It allows a user to back up the system without being assigned file and folder permissions to access all files and folders on the system. In other words, the person backing up the files can back up secure files without being able to read them.

4. What are logon rights and what do they do?

A logon right is a user right assigned to a group or individual user account. Logon rights control the way users can log on to a system.

Lesson 3: Configuring Security Options

Page 486

Lesson Review

1. How can you require a user to be logged on to the computer to shut it down? (Discuss using the Welcome screen and using CTRL+ALT+DELETE to log on.)

If Windows XP Professional is configured to use the Welcome screen or CTRL+ALT+DELETE to log on, by default you do not have to log on to shut down the computer. In the Group Policy snap-in's console tree, click Local Computer Policy, Computer Configuration, Windows Settings, Security Settings, Local Policies, and Security Options. In the details pane, right-click Shutdown: Allow System To Be Shut Down Without Having To Log On, and then click Properties and click Disabled.

2. By default Windows XP Professional does not clear the virtual memory pagefile when the system is shut down. Why can this be considered a security breach and what can you do to resolve it?

The data in the pagefile might be accessible to users who are not authorized to view that information. To clear the pagefile each time the system is shut down, start the Group Policy snap-in, expand Local Policies, and select Security Options. Right-click Shutdown: Clear Virtual Memory Pagefile and then click Properties. Select Enabled.

3. Why does forcing users to press CTRL+ALT+DELETE improve security on your computer?

Requiring users to press CTRL+ALT+DELETE to log on to the computer increases security on your computer because you are forcing users to use a key combination recognized only by Windows. Using this key combination ensures that users are giving the password only to Windows and not to a program waiting to capture user passwords.

4. By default, Windows XP Professional displays the last user name to log on to the computer in the Windows Security dialog box. Why is this considered a security risk and what can you do to resolve it?

In some situations this is considered a security risk because an unauthorized user can see a valid user account displayed on the screen. This makes it much easier to break into the computer. To resolve this security problem, in the Group Policy snap-in, click the Local Policies node in the console pane, and then click Security Options. In the details pane, right-click Interactive Logon: Do Not Display Last User Name, click Properties, and select Enabled.

5. How can you disable the Welcome screen in Windows XP Professional?

In the User Accounts tool, click Change The Way Users Log On Or Off and then clear the Use The Welcome Screen check box.

Lesson 4: Configuring Internet Explorer Security Options

Page 496

Lesson Review

1. What is a cookie? How can you delete all the cookies that are stored on your computer?

A cookie is a file created by a Web site; the cookie stores information about you on your computer. In the Temporary Internet Files section in the General tab, click Delete Cookies to delete all cookies now.

2. How can you control which cookies are stored on your computer?

The Privacy tab of the Internet Properties dialog box allows you to determine how cookies will be handled on your computer.

3. As a concerned parent, how can you help protect your children from adult material found on the Internet?

The Content tab gives you access to the Content Advisor, which allows you to control what can be viewed on the Internet. You can control access to Web sites based on language, nudity, sex, and violence. You can also create a list of Web sites that are never viewable, no matter how they are rated.

4. How can you speed up the downloading of pages?

In the Multimedia section of the Advanced tab in the Internet Properties dialog box, you can clear the Play Animations In Web Pages, Play Sounds In Web Pages, and Show Pictures check boxes to speed up the downloading of pages containing animations, sounds, and graphical images.

5. How can you have the Internet Temporary Files folder emptied each time you close your browser?

In the Security section of the Advanced tab in the Internet Properties dialog box, you can select the Empty Internet Temporary Files Folder When Browser Is Closed check box. Selecting this check box specifies that you want to empty the Internet Temporary Files folder when the browser is closed. This option is not selected by default.

Chapter 14: Managing Data Storage

Lesson 1: Managing Compression

Practice: Managing Compression

Page 507

Exercise 1: Compressing Files in an NTFS Partition

▶ **To view the capacity and free space for drive C**

3. Right-click drive C, and then click Properties.

   Windows XP Professional displays the Local Disk (C:) Properties dialog box with the General tab active.

   What is the capacity of drive C?

   Answers will vary.

   What is the free space on drive C?

   Answers will vary.

▶ **To uncompress a folder**

5. Click OK to close the Compressed2 Properties dialog box.

   Because the Compressed2 folder is empty, Windows XP Professional does not display the Confirm Attributes Changes dialog box asking you to specify whether to uncompress only this folder or this folder and all subfolders.

   What indication do you have that the Compressed2 folder is no longer compressed?

   The folder name is now displayed in the original color (typically black).

Page 509

Exercise 2: Copying and Moving Files

▶ **To create a compressed file**

3. Type **Text1** and then press ENTER.

   How can you verify that Text1 is compressed?

   The folder name is displayed in the alternate color (typically blue).

▶ **To copy a compressed file to an uncompressed folder**

2. Examine the properties for Text1 in the Compressed2 folder.

   Is the Text1 file in the Compressed\Compressed2 folder compressed or uncompressed? Why?

   Uncompressed. A new file inherits the compression attribute of the folder in which it is created.

► **To move a compressed file to an uncompressed folder**

1. Examine the properties of the Text1 file in the Compressed folder.

   Is Text1 compressed or uncompressed?

   Compressed.

3. Examine the properties of Text1 in the Compressed2 folder.

   Is Text1 compressed or uncompressed? Why?

   Compressed. When a file is moved to a new folder on the same partition its compression attribute doesn't change.

Page 510

Lesson Review

1. When Bob tried to copy a compressed file from one NTFS volume to another, the file was not copied and he got an error message stating that there was not enough disk space for the file. Before he attempted to copy the file, Bob verified that there was enough room for the compressed bitmap on the destination volume. Why did he get the error message?

   If you copy a compressed file to an NTFS volume with enough space for the compressed file, but not enough space for the uncompressed file, you might get an error message stating that there is not enough disk space for the file. The file will not be copied to the volume.

2. Which of the following will Windows XP Professional allow you to compress using NTFS compression? (Choose all answers that are correct.)

   a. A FAT volume

   b. An NTFS volume

   c. A bitmap stored on a floppy

   d. A folder on an NTFS volume

   b and d

3. When you move a file between NTFS volumes, does the file retain the compression state of the source folder or does the file inherit the compression state of the target folder? Why?

   When you move a file or folder between NTFS volumes, the file or folder inherits the compression state of the target folder. Windows XP Professional treats a move as a copy and then a delete, so the files inherit the compression state of the target folder.

4. What does Windows XP Professional do when you try to copy a compressed file to a floppy disk? Why?

   When you copy a compressed file to a floppy disk, Windows XP Professional automatically uncompresses the file because floppy disks cannot be formatted with NTFS and cannot use NTFS compression.

5. Which of the following types of files or data are good candidates for NTFS compression? (Choose all statements that are correct.)

a. Encrypted data

b. Frequently updated data

c. Bitmaps

d. Static data

c and d

Lesson 2: Managing Disk Quotas

Practice: Enabling and Disabling Disk Quotas

Page 518

Exercise 1: Configuring Quota Management Settings

▶ **To configure default quota management settings**

6. Click Limit Disk Usage To.

What is the default disk space limit for new users?

1 KB

▶ **To configure quota management settings for a user**

1. In the Quota tab of the Local Disk (C:) Properties dialog box, click Quota Entries.

Windows XP Professional displays the Quota Entries For Local Disk (C:) dialog box.

Are any user accounts listed? Why or why not?

Yes. The accounts listed are those that have logged on and gained access to drive C.

4. In the Name text box, type **User5**, and then click OK.

Windows XP Professional displays the Add New Quota Entry dialog box.

What are the default settings for the user you just set a quota limit for?

Limit Disk Space To 1 KB and Set The Warning Level To 1 KB are the default settings that are set for drive C.

▶   **To test quota management settings**

5. Copy the i386 folder from your CD-ROM to the User5 folder.

   Windows XP Professional begins copying files from the i386 folder on the CD-ROM to a new i386 folder in the User5 folder on drive C. After copying some files, Windows XP Professional displays the Error Copying File Or Folder dialog box indicating that there is not enough room on the disk.

   Why did you get this error message?

   You have exceeded your quota limit and because the Deny Disk Space To Users Exceeding Quota Limit check box is selected, once you exceed your quota limit, you can't use more disk space.

Page 520

Lesson Review

1. What is the purpose of disk quotas?

   Disk quotas allow you to allocate disk space to users and monitor the amount of hard disk space that users have used and the amount that they have left against their quota.

2. Which of the following statements about disk quotas in Windows XP Professional is correct?

   a. Disk quotas track and control disk usage on a per-user, per-disk basis.

   b. Disk quotas track and control disk usage on a per-group, per-volume basis.

   c. Disk quotas track and control disk usage on a per-user, per-volume basis.

   d. Disk quotas track and control disk usage on a per-group, per-disk basis.

   c

3. Which of the following statements about disk quotas in Windows XP Professional is correct? (Choose all answers that are correct.)

   a. Disk quotas can only be applied to Windows XP Professional NTFS volumes.

   b. Disk quotas can be applied to any Windows XP Professional volume.

   c. You must be logged on with the Administrator user account to configure default quota management settings.

   d. Members of the Administrators and Power Users groups can configure default quota management settings.

   a and c

4. You get a call from an administrator who cannot delete a quota entry for a user account. What would you tell the administrator to check?

   Tell the administrator to verify that all files owned by the user are removed or that another user has taken ownership of the files. You cannot delete a quota entry for a user account if there are files owned by that user on the volume.

Lesson 3: Increasing Security with EFS

Practice: Encrypting Files

Page 528

Exercise 2: Testing the Encrypted Files

▶   **To test an encrypted file**

2. Start Windows Explorer and open C:\Secret\File1.

What happens?

A Notepad dialog box appears indicating that access is denied.

Page 529

Lesson Review

1. What is encryption and what is the Microsoft EFS?

Encryption makes information indecipherable to protect it from unauthorized viewing or use. Microsoft EFS provides encryption for data in NTFS files stored on disk. This encryption is public key–based and runs as an integrated system service, making it easy to manage, difficult to attack, and transparent to the file owner.

2. Which of the following files and folders will Windows XP Professional allow you to encrypt? (Choose all answers that are correct.)

a. A file on an NTFS volume

b. A folder on a FAT volume

c. A file stored on a floppy

d. A folder on an NTFS volume

a and d

3. How do you encrypt a folder? Is the folder actually encrypted?

To encrypt a folder, in the Properties dialog box for the folder, click the General tab. In the General tab, click Advanced, and then select the Encrypt Contents To Secure Data check box. All files placed in the folder are encrypted and the folder is now marked for encryption. Folders that are marked for encryption are not actually encrypted; only the files within the folder are encrypted.

4. If the private key belonging to the owner of an encrypted file is not available, how can you decrypt the file?

If the owner's private key is unavailable, a recovery agent can open the file using his or her own private key.

5. By default, the recovery agent for a computer running Windows XP Professional in a workgroup is _____ and the recovery agent for a computer running Windows XP Professional in a domain environment is _____.

The administrator of the local computer; the domain administrator

Page 542

Lesson 4: Using Disk Defragmenter, Check Disk, and Disk Cleanup

Practice: Managing NTFS Compression

Exercise 3: Running Disk Cleanup

▶ **To use Disk Cleanup on a hard drive**

3. Click the More Options tab.

    When would you use the options available in the More Options tab?

    When running Disk Cleanup did not free up enough space on your hard drive and you need to find some additional space. The More Options tab allows you to delete Windows components, installed programs, and saved system restore points to free up additional space.

Page 543

Lesson Review

1. What is fragmentation and what problems does it cause?

    Fragmentation is the scattering of the parts of a file over the disk rather than having all parts of the file located in contiguous space. Over time a hard disk will contain fragmented files and folders that cause Windows XP Professional to take longer to access the files. Creating new files and folders also takes longer because the available free space on the hard disk is scattered.

2. The process of finding and consolidating fragmented files and folders is called _____. The Windows XP Professional system tool that locates fragmented files and folders and arranges them in contiguous space is

    _____.

    Defragmenting or defragmentation; Disk Defragmenter

3. Windows XP Professional provides a tool to locate fragmented files and folders and arrange them in contiguous space on volumes formatted with which file systems?

    NTFS, FAT, and FAT32

4. Which of the following functions does Check Disk perform? (Choose all answers that are correct.)

    a. Locate fragmented files and folders and arrange contiguously

    b. Locate and attempt to repair file system errors

    c. Locate bad sectors and recover readable information from those bad sectors

    d. Delete temporary files and offline files

    b and c

5. Why do you need to empty the Recycle Bin?

When you delete a file from a computer, it is not permanently removed from the computer until you empty the Recycle Bin (by deleting the files contained in the Recycle Bin).

Chapter 15: Monitoring, Managing, and Maintaining Network Resources

Lesson 1: Monitoring Access to Shared Folders

Page 550

Lesson Review

1. Why is it important to manage network resources?

You need to know which users access a network resource so that you can notify them if a resource becomes temporarily or permanently unavailable. You monitor confidential resources to verify that only authorized users are accessing them. You determine how much all resources are being used to help you plan for future system growth.

2. On a computer running Windows XP Professional, members of the _____ and _____ groups can use the Shared Folders snap-in to monitor network resources.

Administrators and Power Users

3. How can you determine what files are open on a computer running Windows XP Professional?

Use the Open Files folder in the Shared Folders snap-in to view a list of open files and the users who have a current connection to each file.

4. Which of the following statements about monitoring network resources are correct? (Choose all answers that are correct.)

a. You can use the Shared Folders snap-in to disconnect all users from all open files.

b. You can use the Shared Folders snap-in to disconnect one user from one file.

c. If you change the NTFS permissions for an open file, the changes affect all users who have the file open immediately.

d. If you make changes to the NTFS permissions for an open file, the changes do not affect the user who has that file opened until he or she closes and reopens the file.

a and d

Lesson 2: Creating and Sharing Local and Remote Folders

Page 555

Lesson Review

1. Which of the following tools can you use to create a shared folder on a remote computer? (Choose all answers that are correct.)

    a. Windows Explorer

    b. Computer Management snap-in

    c. Domain Management snap-in

    d. Shared Folders snap-in

    b and d

2. How can you create and share a folder on a remote computer?

    You can create and share a folder on a remote computer by creating a custom MMC console, adding either the Computer Management snap-in or the Shared Folders snap-in, and pointing it to the remote computer that you want to manage shares on.

3. Can you create a custom tool that will allow you to administer more than one specific remote computer? How?

    Yes. When you add the Computer Management snap-in or Shared Folders snap-in to a custom MMC console, select the Allow The Selected Computer To Be Changed When Launching From The Command Line check box. You can then specify the remote computer that you want to administer when you launch the command.

Lesson 3: Monitoring Network Users

Page 560

Lesson Review

1. How can you determine which users have a connection to open files on a computer and the files to which they have a connection?

    The Sessions folder in the Computer Management snap-in or Shared Folders snap-in shows you a list of all users with a connection to an open file and the files to which they have a connection.

2. How can you disconnect a specific user from a file?

    In the Computer Management console or Shared Folders console, click Sessions. Select the user that you want to disconnect in the details pane. On the Action menu, click Close Session.

3. Why would you send an administrative message to users with current connections?

    To inform the users that you are about to disconnect them from the resource they are connected to so that you can perform a backup or restore operation, upgrade software or hardware, or shut down the computer.

4. What can you do to prevent a user from reestablishing a network connection after you have disconnected that user from a shared folder?

To prevent all users from reconnecting, stop sharing the folder. To prevent only one user from reestablishing a connection, change the permissions for the folder so that the user no longer has access, and then disconnect the user from the shared folder.

Lesson 4: Using Offline Folders and Files

Page 568

Lesson Review

1. How do you configure your computer to use offline folders and files?

To configure your computer to use offline folders and files, on the Tools menu of My Computer, click Folder Options. In the Offline Files tab of Folder Options, you enable the Enable Offline Files and the Synchronize All Offline Files Before Logging Off check boxes.

2. What tools does Windows XP Professional provide for you to configure your computer to provide offline files? What must you do to allow others to access files on your computer?

Windows Explorer and My Computer. You must share the folder containing the file.

3. What does Synchronization Manager do?

Synchronization Manager allows you to manually synchronize or schedule the synchronization of the files on your computer with the ones on the network resource.

Lesson 5: Using Scheduled Tasks

Page 573

Lesson Review

1. How can Scheduled Tasks help you monitor, manage, and maintain network resources?

Scheduled Tasks can be used to automatically launch any script, program, or document to start at a specified time and interval or when certain operating system events occur. You can use Scheduled Tasks to complete many administrative tasks for you, run maintenance programs at specific intervals on the local or remote computers, and run programs when there is less demand for computer resources.

2. Which of the following are valid choices for the frequency with which Scheduled Tasks schedules programs to run? (Choose all answers that are correct.)

a. Daily

b. One time only

c. When the computer shuts down

d. When a user logs off

a and b

3. Why do you have to assign a user account and password for each task that you schedule using the Scheduled Task Wizard?

You enter a user name and password to have the task run under the security settings for that user account. For example, you can run a scheduled backup by using a user account that has the required rights to back up data but does not have other administrative privileges. The default is to use the user name of the person scheduling the task.

4. If none of your scheduled tasks are starting, what is one thing that you need to check?

If none of your scheduled tasks are starting, open the Task Scheduler and click Advanced to make sure that the Task Scheduler Service is running. If it is not running, you can use the Advanced menu to start it.

Lesson 6: Using Task Manager

Page 580

Practice: Using Task Manager

▶ **To monitor programs, processes, and system performance**

2. Press CTRL+SHIFT+ESC to launch Task Manager.

What programs are currently running on your system?

Answers will vary, but there might not be any programs running.

5. Click the Processes tab.

How many processes are running?

Answers will vary.

8. Click the Performance tab.

What percentage of your CPU's capacity is being used?

Answers will vary, but should be low.

Do you think that your CPU could be slowing down the performance on your system?

Answers could vary, but if the CPU is barely being utilized then the CPU would not be slowing down the performance of the computer.

Page 581

Lesson Review

1. Which of the following methods can you use to start Task Manager? (Choose all answers that are correct.)

   a. Press CTRL+ALT+ESC

   b. Right-click the Desktop and click Task Manager

   c. Press CTRL+SHIFT+ESC

   d. Press CTRL+ALT+DELETE and, if necessary, click Task Manager

   c and d

2. Which of the following tabs can be found in Task Manager? (Choose all answers that are correct.)

   a. Networking tab

   b. Programs tab

   c. Processes tab

   d. General tab

   a and c

3. What are page faults? Do you think a larger or smaller number of page faults indicate better system performance? Why?

   Each time data has to be retrieved from the pagefile on the hard disk for a process, the data has been paged out of physical memory. This is known as a page fault. A smaller number of page faults indicates better system performance because it is faster to retrieve data from RAM than from a paging file on the hard drive.

4. What does CPU usage represent? In general, is system performance better with a high CPU usage value or a low value?

   CPU usage is the percentage of time that the processor is running a thread other than the idle thread. You don't want the CPU to be a bottleneck to the system. If the CPU usage is too high, it could indicate that the CPU is slowing down system performance.

Lesson 7: Using Performance Console

Page 587

Practice: Using System Monitor

▶ **To monitor system resources**

3. Click Administrative Tools, and then double-click the Performance shortcut.

   Windows XP Professional starts the Performance console with the System Monitor selected.

   What objects and counters are selected by default?

   Memory with the Pages/Sec counter

   PhysicalDisk with the Average Disk Queue Length counter

   Processor with the Processor Time counter

4. Under the graph, right-click Counter and then click Add Counters.

   Windows XP Professional displays the Add Counters dialog box.

   What performance object is selected by default?

   Processor

Page 588

Lesson Review

1. Which of the following monitoring tools are included in the Performance console? (Choose all answers that are correct.)

   a. System Monitor snap-in

   b. Task Manager snap-in

   c. Performance Logs and Alerts snap-in

   d. Task Scheduler

   a and c

2. Why should you monitor resources and overall system performance?

   Monitoring resources and overall system performance helps you determine how well your system is currently performing, detect and eliminate bottlenecks, recognize trends so that you can plan for future growth and upgrades, and evaluate the effects of tuning and configuration changes on your system.

3. What is a baseline and what is a bottleneck?

   A baseline is a measurement derived from collecting data over an extended period of time that represents resource usage under normal conditions. A bottleneck is any component that slows down the performance of the entire system.

4. Why do you need to determine a baseline when you monitor system resources and system performance?

When you monitor system performance, you compare the current performance of the system to the baseline. If the current system performance is worse than the baseline, then you need to check for bottlenecks. After you have resolved the problem, you again monitor system performance so that you can verify that the action you took actually resolved the bottleneck and improved system performance.

Chapter 16: Backing Up and Restoring Data

Lesson 1: Using the Backup Utility

Page 599

Lesson Review

1. How do you access the Backup or Restore Wizard?

To access the Backup or Restore Wizard, on the Start menu, point to All Programs, point to Accessories, point to System Tools, and then click Backup; or, on the Start menu, click Run, type ntbackup, and then click OK.

2. What two operations can you perform using the Backup or Restore Wizard?

You use the Backup or Restore Wizard to back up all or a portion of the files on your computer or network (using the Back Up Files And Settings option) and to restore data that you have backed up (using the Restore Files And Settings option).

3. What is the primary goal of backing up data?

The primary goal of backing up data is to be able to restore that data if necessary.

4. If you want to perform a backup but do not want to clear markers or affect other backup types, you should perform a _____ backup.

Copy

5. During a _____ backup, only selected files and folders that have a marker are backed up, but the backup does not clear markers. If you performed two of these backups in a row on a file and nothing changed in the file, the entire file would be backed up each time.

Differential

6. How can you change the default settings for backup and restores for all backup and restore operations using the Backup Utility?

You can change the default settings for the Backup Utility for all backup and restore jobs by changing the settings in the tabs in the Options dialog box. To access the Options dialog box, in the Welcome To The Backup Or Restore Wizard page, click Advanced Mode. On the Tools menu, click Options.

7. You performed a normal backup on Monday. For the remaining days of the week, you only want to back up files and folders that have changed since the previous day. What backup type do you select? Why?

   Incremental. The incremental backup type backs up changes since the last markers were set and then clears the markers. Thus, for Tuesday through Friday, you back up only changes since the previous day.

Lesson 2: Backing Up Data

Page 610

Lesson Review

1. What are the four choices in the What To Back Up page of the Backup or Restore Wizard and what does each choice allow you to do?

   The first choice is My Documents And Settings. Selecting this option backs up certain areas that pertain to the currently logged on user. All of the files located in the My Documents folder, your Favorites folder, desktop items, and cookies are backed up in this option.

   The second choice is Everyone's Documents And Settings. Selecting this option backs up each user's My Documents folder, Favorites folder, desktop items, and cookies.

   The third choice is All Information On This Computer. Selecting this option backs up all files on the computer, except those files that the Backup Utility excludes by default, such as certain power management files.

   The fourth choice is Let Me Choose What To Back Up. Selecting this option allows you to select the files and folders you want to back up, including files and folders on the computer where you run the Backup Utility and any shared file or folder on the network.

2. When should you select the Allow Only The Owner And The Administrator Access To The Backup Data And Any Backups Appended To This Media check box?

   You should select this check box when you want to minimize the risk of unauthorized access to your data.

3. If your boss wants daily backups to occur at 1:00 A.M., what could you do to save yourself the trouble of having to go to the office each morning at 1:00 A.M. to do the backups?

   You can use the Backup or Restore Wizard to schedule the backup to occur automatically by clicking Later on the When To Back Up page of the Backup or Restore Wizard and specifying that the backup should occur daily at 1:00 A.M.

4. If you don't have a tape drive, can you still perform backups? How?

Yes. You can use a tape or file as the target medium for the backup and a file can be located on any disk-based media, including a hard disk, a shared network folder, or a removable disk, such as an Iomega Zip drive.

5. Why should you e-mail or send a console message to users before you begin a backup?

You should notify users to close files before you begin backing up data because the backup will not contain the correct data if users are still editing files while you perform the backup. Rather than skip the files that are being written to, the Backup Utility will back up these files unless you select the Disable Volume Shadow Copy check box. It is best to have all users log off before doing a backup.

Lesson 3: Restoring Data

Page 616

Lesson Review

1. What is a trial restore and why is it important that you perform it?

A trial restore involves restoring a backup to an alternate location and comparing the restored data to the data on the original hard disk. You should perform trial restores to verify that the Backup Utility is backing up your files correctly and that any hardware problems show up with software verifications.

2. A _____ is an index of the files and folders from a backup job that Windows XP Professional automatically creates and stores with the backup job and on the computer running the Backup Utility.

Catalog

3. What is a backup set?

A backup set is a collection of files or folders from one volume that you back up during a backup job.

4. If you back up two volumes on a hard disk during a backup job, how many backup sets are created for the job?

Two

5. What are the three Advanced restore settings that allow you to specify how to restore files that already exist?

Leave Existing Files (Recommended), Replace Existing Files If They Are Older Than The Backup Files, and Replace Existing Files

6. When do you use the Advanced restore setting Restore Security and when is it available?

The Restore Security setting applies the original permissions including access permissions, audit entries, and ownership, to files that you are restoring to an NTFS volume. The Restore Security option is only available if you have backed up data from an NTFS volume and are restoring to an NTFS volume.

Lesson 4: Using the Automated System Recovery Wizard

Page 619

Lesson Review

1. What four wizards does the Backup Utility provide access to?

The Backup Utility provides access to the Backup And Restore Wizard, the Backup Wizard (Advanced), the Restore Wizard (Advanced), and the Automated System Recovery Wizard.

2. What two things does the Automated System Recovery Wizard create during a backup?

The Automated System Recovery Wizard creates a floppy disk containing your system settings and a backup of your local system partition.

3. What two pieces of information do you have to supply to the Automated System Recovery Wizard?

The appropriate media type and the backup media or filename

Chapter 17: Configuring Network and Internet Connections

Lesson 1: Configuring Inbound Connections

Page 626

Lesson Review

1. The Network Connection Type page of the New Connection Wizard has four selections. What are the four selections and which selection do you use to allow inbound dial-up connections?

The four selections in the Network Connection Type page are Connect To The Internet, Connect To The Network At My Workplace, Set Up A Home Or Small Office Network, and Set Up An Advanced Connection.

You use the Set Up An Advanced Connection option to configure an inbound connection.

2. Other than allowing VPN connections, what does Windows XP Professional do when you configure a new connection to allow virtual private connections?

If you choose to allow VPN connections, Windows XP Professional modifies the ICF so that your computer can send and receive VPN packets.

3. What is callback and why would you enable it?

Callback forces the remote server, in this case your computer, to disconnect from the client calling in, and then call the client computer back.

You would use callback to have the bill for a phone call charged to your phone number rather than to the phone number of the user who called in. You could also use callback to increase security because you can specify the number that the system calls back. If an unauthorized user calls in, this prevents the unauthorized user from accessing the system.

Lesson 2: Configuring Outbound Connections

Page 634

Lesson Review

1. What are the three outbound connection selections that you can configure using the New Connection Wizard and what does each allow you to do?

The first choice is Connect To The Internet. Selecting this option allows you to choose an ISP to establish a connection to the Internet, manually configure a connection to the Internet, or use a CD-ROM provided by an ISP to establish a connection to the Internet.

The second choice is Connect To The Network At My Workplace. Selecting this option allows you to establish a connection to a private network either by using a dial-up modem and regular or ISDN phone line or by using a VPN connection.

The third choice is Set Up An Advanced Connection. Selecting this option allows you to establish a connection directly to another computer using a serial, parallel, or infrared port or to set up this computer so that other computers can connect to it.

2. How can you configure a direct connection to another computer?

Use the New Connection Wizard. Click Start, click My Computer, click My Network Places, click View Network Connections, and then click Create A New Connection. In the Welcome To The New Connection Wizard page, click Next and, in the Network Connection Type page, click Set Up An Advanced Connection. In the Advanced Connections Options page, click Connect Directly To Another Computer.

3. Using the New Connection Wizard to create an outgoing connection to the network at your office, how can you have a shortcut appear on your desktop for easy access to the connection?

   In the Completing The New Connection Wizard page, select the Add A Shortcut To The Connection To My Desktop check box.

Lesson 3: Enabling and Configuring Home and Small Business Components

Page 643

Lesson Review

1. What is ICF?

   Internet Connection Firewall (ICF) is firewall software that is used to set restrictions on what information is communicated from your home or small business network to and from the Internet.

2. What happens if you configure ICF and enable any one of the ICMP options?

   If you enable any of the ICMP options, your network can become visible to the Internet and vulnerable to attack.

3. By default the ICF Security Log file is named _____ and has a size limit of _____.

   PFIREWALL.LOG; 4096 KB

4. Which of the following statements about ICF are correct? (Choose all answers that are correct.)

   a. ICF is available in the Windows XP Professional 64-bit edition.

   b. ICF should not be enabled on VPN connections.

   c. ICF should be enabled on your shared Internet connection.

   d. ICF must be purchased as an add-on package and is not included in Windows XP Professional.

   b and c

5. When do you use ICS?

   You use Internet Connection Sharing (ICS) so that only one of the computers on your network needs to be connected to the Internet. ICS allows the other computers on your network to connect to the Internet through this connection.

6. How do you enable on-demand dialing for a shared ICS connection?

   Enable ICS by selecting the Establish A Dial-Up Connection Whenever A Computer On My Network Attempts To Access The Internet check box in the Advanced tab. This check box enables on-demand dialing for the shared connection.

7. What is Network Bridge and what algorithm does it use?

Network Bridge allows you to connect LAN segments, even if they are using different types of network media, without having to use routers to connect them. It uses the IEEE Spanning Tree Algorithm (STA) to ensure that there are no bridge loops.

8. Which of the following types of adapters can you use in a Network Bridge? (Choose all answers that are correct.)

a. Ethernet adapters

b. IEEE-1394 adapters

c. Token Ring adapters

d. Adapters that have ICF or ICS enabled

a and b

Chapter 18: Modifying and Troubleshooting the Boot Process
Lesson 1: Understanding the Boot Process

Page 655   **Lesson Review**

1. Windows XP Professional modifies the boot sector during installation so that _____ loads during system startup.

NTLDR

2. What is the purpose of the BOOT.INI file and what happens if it is not present?

NTLDR reads BOOT.INI to determine the operating system selections to be loaded. If BOOT.INI is missing, NTLDR attempts to load Windows XP Professional from the Windows folder on the first partition of the first disk, typically C:\Windows.

3. What does the BOOTSECT.DOS file contain and when it is used?

BOOTSECT.DOS is a copy of the boot sector that was on the system partition at the time that Windows XP Professional was installed. BOOTSECT.DOS is used if you are booting more than one operating system and you choose to load an operating system other than Windows XP Professional.

4. A user calls you and tells you that Windows XP Professional does not appear to be loading correctly. The Hardware Profile/Configuration Recovery menu does not appear when the computer is restarted, but it does appear on the computer of the person sitting in the next cubicle when that computer is restarted. What would you tell the user?

The user probably has only one hardware profile. If there is a single hardware profile, NTLDR does not display the Hardware Profile/Configuration Recovery menu and instead loads Windows XP Professional using the default hardware profile configuration.

Lesson 2: Editing the Registry

Practice: Using the Registry Editor

Page 664

Exercise 1: Exploring the Registry

▶ **To view information in the registry**

6. Expand DESCRIPTION and then double-click the System subkey.

What are the SystemBIOSDate and SystemBIOSVersion of your computer?

Answers will vary.

What is the computer type of your local machine according to the Identifier entry?

Answers will vary.

Page 665

Exercise 3: Modifying the Registry

▶ **To verify the new registry value**

2. Click the Advanced tab, and then click Environment Variables.

The Environment Variables dialog box appears.

Does the test variable appear in the User Variables For Administrator list?

Yes. You successfully edited the registry and added a User Environment variable.

Page 666

Lesson Review

1. What is the registry and what does it do?

The registry is a hierarchical database in which Windows XP Professional stores hardware and software settings. The registry provides the appropriate initialization information to boot Windows XP Professional, to start applications, and to load components, such as device drivers and network protocols.

2. What is the purpose of the BOOTSECT.DOS file and what happens if it is not present?

BOOTSECT.DOS is a copy of the boot sector that was on the system partition at the time that Windows XP Professional was installed. BOOTSECT.DOS is only used if you are booting more than one operating system and you choose to load an operating system other than Windows XP Professional. If you do not have more than one operating system, you will not have a BOOTSECT.DOS file and Windows XP Professional will boot normally.

3. What are some of the Windows XP Professional components that use the registry?

Windows NT kernel, device drivers, user profiles, setup programs, hardware profiles, and NTDETECT.COM

4. How do you access the Registry Editor?

On the Start menu, click Run, type regedt32, and then click OK.

5. Why should you make most of your configuration changes through either Control Panel or Administrative Tools rather than by editing the registry directly with the Registry Editor?

Using the Registry Editor to modify the registry is dangerous because the Registry Editor saves data automatically as you make entries or corrections, so new registry data takes effect immediately. If you incorrectly edit the registry it can cause serious, system-wide problems that could require you to reinstall Windows XP Professional.

Lesson 3: Using Startup and Recovery Tools

Practice: Using the Windows XP Professional Recovery Console

Page 675

Optional Exercise 1: Troubleshooting a Windows XP Professional Installation

▶   **To create a system boot failure**

6. Restart the computer.

What error do you receive when attempting to restart the computer?

NTLDR is missing.

Press CTRL+ALT+DEL to restart.

Page 678

Lesson Review

1. What is safe mode and why do you use it?

   Starting Windows XP Professional in safe mode uses limited device drivers and system services and no network connections. Safe mode also ignores programs that automatically start up, user profiles, programs listed in the registry to automatically run, and all local group policies.

   You use safe mode because it provides access to Windows XP Professional configuration files so you can make configuration changes. You can disable or delete a system service, a device driver, or application that automatically starts that prevents the computer from starting normally.

2. How do you start Windows XP Professional in safe mode?

   To start Windows XP Professional in safe mode, restart or boot the computer and press F8 during the operating system selection phase.

3. When is the LastKnownGood configuration created?

   After you reboot the computer, the kernel copies the information in the Current control set to the Clone control set during the kernel initialization phase. When you successfully log on to Windows XP Professional, the information in the Clone control set is copied to the LastKnownGood control set.

4. When do you use the LastKnownGood configuration?

   If you change the Windows XP Professional configuration to load a driver and have problems rebooting, you use the LastKnownGood process to recover your working configuration.

5. How can you install the Windows XP Professional Recovery Console on your computer?

   To install the Recovery Console, insert the Microsoft Windows XP Professional CD-ROM into your CD-ROM drive. Open a Command Prompt window, change to the i386 folder on the Windows XP Professional CD, and then run the winnt32 command with the /cmdcoms switch.

Chapter 19: Deploying Windows XP Professional

Lesson 1: Automating Installations Using Windows Setup Manager

Page 690   **Lesson Review**

1. What is the purpose of the Windows Setup Manager?

   The Windows Setup Manager makes it easy to create the UNATTEND.TXT files and .udb files that you use to run unattended (scripted) installations.

2. How could you apply an application update pack as part of the Windows XP Professional installation?

   If you were upgrading systems to Windows XP Professional, you would add the application update pack to the distribution folder so the necessary files are available. You would also need to add the commands to execute in the Additional Commands page of the Windows Setup Manager Wizard so that the update packs will be applied to the application as part of the Windows XP Professional installation (upgrade).

3. What type of answer files does the Windows Setup Manager allow you to create?

   Windows Unattended Installation, Sysprep Install, and RIS

4. Why would you use a UDB?

   A UDB allows you to specify per-computer parameters for an unattended installation. This file overrides values in the answer file.

Lesson 2: Using Disk Duplication to Deploy Windows XP Professional

Page 697   **Lesson Review**

1. What is disk duplication?

   Creating a disk image of a Windows XP Professional installation and copying that image to multiple computers with identical hardware configurations.

2. What is the purpose of the System Preparation tool?

   The System Preparation tool was developed to prepare a master image for disk copying. Every computer must have a unique SID. The System Preparation tool adds a system service to the master image that will create a unique local domain SID the first time the computer to which the master image is copied is started. The System Preparation tool also adds a Mini-Setup Wizard to the master copy that runs the first time the computer to which the master image is copied is started and guides you through entering user-specific information.

3. What does the /quiet switch do when you run SYSPREP.EXE?

The /quiet switch causes SYSPREP.EXE to run without any user intervention.

Lesson 3: Performing Remote Installations

Page 706

Lesson Review

1. What is a RIS server and what is it used for?

A RIS server is a computer running Windows 2000 Server and running the RIS. The RIS server is used to perform remote installations of Windows XP Professional. Remote installation enables administrators to install Windows XP Professional on client computers throughout a network from a central location.

2. What network services are required for RIS?

DNS Service, DHCP, and Active Directory

3. What can you do if the network adapter card in a client is not equipped with a PXE boot ROM? Does this solution work for all network adapter cards? Why or why not?

If the network adapter card in a client is not equipped with a PXE boot ROM, you can create a remote installation boot disk that simulates the PXE boot process.

A remote installation boot disk will not work for all network adapter cards; it only works for those cards supported by the Windows 2000 Remote Boot Disk Generator.

4. What user rights must be assigned to the user account that will be used to perform the remote installation?

The user account that will be used to perform the installation must be assigned the user right Log On as a Batch Job.

Lesson 4: Using Tools to Simplify Deployment

Page 722

Lesson Review

1. When do you use the Files and Settings Transfer Wizard?

The Files and Settings Transfer Wizard helps you move data files and personal settings when you upgrade your hardware. The settings you can move include display settings, Internet Explorer and Outlook Express options, dial-up connections, and your folder and taskbar options. The wizard also helps you move specific files and folders to your new computer as well.

2. Which of the following statements are true for the Files and Settings Transfer Wizard? (Choose all answers that are correct.)

   a. You run the Files and Settings Transfer Wizard only on your old computer.

   b. You must run the Files and Settings Transfer Wizard on both your old and your new computers.

   c. You can use a standard 25-pin cable to connect the parallel ports on your old and new computers to run the Files and Settings Transfer Wizard.

   d. You can use serial ports to directly connect your old and new computers to run the Files and Settings Transfer Wizard.

   b and d

3. Which of the following statements are true for a disk that uses dynamic storage? (Choose all answers that are correct.)

   a. The system partition for Windows NT is never on a dynamic disk.

   b. A dynamic disk can be partitioned into four primary partitions or three primary partitions and one extended partition.

   c. The convert command allows you to convert a basic disk into a dynamic disk.

   d. A dynamic disk has a single partition that includes the entire disk.

   a and d

4. How can Windows Installer help you minimize the amount of disk space taken up on a user's disk when you install a new application on that user's disk?

   Windows Installer allows you to install only the essential files required to run an application to reduce the amount of space used on a user's hard disk. The first time a user accesses any feature not included in the minimal installation, the necessary files are automatically installed.

5. Which of the following statements about publishing and installing applications are correct? (Choose all answers that are correct.)

   a. Applications can be published to users or to computers.

   b. Publishing an application installs the application on the users' computers, but it does not place any shortcuts on the users' desktops or Start menus.

   c. Publishing an application does not install the application on the users' computers.

   d. Published applications are stored in Active Directory and the application is available to users to install using Add or Remove Programs in Control Panel.

   c and d

Glossary

A

AC-3 The coding system used by Dolby Digital. A standard for high-quality digital audio that is used for the sound portion of video stored in digital format.

Accelerated Graphics Port (AGP) A type of expansion slot that is solely for video cards. Designed by Intel and supported by Windows XP Professional, AGP is a dedicated bus that provides fast, high-quality video and graphics performance.

access control entry (ACE) The entries on the access control list (ACL) that control user account or group access to a resource. The entry must allow the type of access that is requested (for example, Read access) for the user to gain access. If no ACE exists in the ACL, the user cannot gain access to the resource or folder on an NTFS partition. *See also* access control list (ACL).

access control list (ACL) A list of all user accounts and groups that have been granted access for the file or folder on an NTFS partition or volume, as well as the type of access they have been granted. When a user attempts to gain access to a resource, the ACL must contain an entry, called an access control entry (ACE), for the user account or group to which the user belongs. *See also* access control entry (ACE).

access permissions Features that control access to shared resources in Windows XP Professional.

access token A data structure containing security information that identifies a user to the security subsystem on a computer running Windows XP Professional, Windows 2000, or Windows NT. An access token contains a user's security ID, the security IDs for groups that the user is a member of, and a list of the user's privileges on the local computer.

account *See* user account.

account lockout A Windows XP Professional security feature that locks a user account if a number of failed logon attempts occur within a specified amount of time, based on account policy lockout settings. Locked accounts cannot log on.

account policy Controls how passwords must be used by all user accounts on an individual computer or in a domain.

ACE *See* access control entry (ACE).

ACL *See* access control list (ACL).

ACPI *See* Advanced Configuration and Power Interface (ACPI).

Active Directory service The directory service included in Windows 2000 Server products. It identifies all resources on a network and makes them accessible to users and applications.

Address Resolution Protocol (ARP) Determines hardware addresses (MAC addresses) that correspond to an Internet Protocol (IP) address.

ADSL *See* Asymmetric Digital Subscriber Line (ADSL).

Advanced Configuration and Power Interface (ACPI) An open industry specification that defines power management on a wide range of mobile, desktop, and server components and peripherals. ACPI is the foundation for the OnNow industry initiative that allows system manufacturers to deliver computers that will start at the touch of a keyboard. ACPI design is essential to take full advantage of power management and Plug and Play in Windows XP Professional. Check the manufacturer's documentation to verify that a computer is ACPI-compliant.

Advanced Power Management (APM) A software interface designed by Microsoft and Intel used between hardware-specific power management software, such as that located in a system BIOS, and an operating system power management driver.

agent A program that performs a background task for a user and reports to the user when the task is done or when some expected event has taken place.

American National Standards Institute (ANSI) An organization of American industry and business groups dedicated to the development of trade and communication standards. ANSI is the American representative to the International Organization for Standardization (ISO). *See also* International Organization for Standardization (ISO).

analog A system that encodes information using frequency modulation in a nonbinary context. Modems use analog encoding to transmit data through a phone line. An analog signal can be any frequency, allowing many possibilities. Because of this, a device has to interpret the signal, often finding errors. *See also* digital, modem.

analog line A communication line that carries information using frequency modulation. *See also* digital line.

API *See* application programming interface (API).

APM *See* Advanced Power Management (APM).

application layer The top (seventh) layer of the OSI reference model. This layer serves as the window that application processes use to access network services. It represents the services that directly support user applications, such as software for file transfers, database access, and e-mail.

application programming interface (API) A set of routines that an application program uses to request and carry out lower level services performed by the operating system.

application protocols Protocols that work at the higher end of the OSI reference model, providing application-to-application interaction and data exchange. Popular application protocols include File Transfer Access and Management (FTAM), a file access protocol; Simple Mail Transfer Protocol (SMTP), a TCP/IP protocol for transferring e-mail; Telnet, a TCP/IP protocol for logging on to remote hosts and processing data locally; NetWare Core Protocol (NCP), the primary protocol used to transmit information between a NetWare server and its clients.

ARP *See* Address Resolution Protocol (ARP).

ASCII (American Standard Code for Information Interchange) A coding scheme that assigns numeric values to letters, numbers, punctuation marks, and certain other characters. By standardizing the values used for these characters, ASCII enables computers and programs to exchange information.

Asymmetric Digital Subscriber Line (ADSL) A recent modem technology that converts existing twisted-pair telephone lines into access paths for multimedia and high-speed data communications. These new connections can transmit more than 8 Mbps to the subscriber and up to 1 Mbps from the subscriber. ADSL is recognized as a physical layer transmission protocol for unshielded twisted-pair media.

asynchronous transfer mode (ATM) An advanced implementation of packet switching that provides high-speed data transmission rates to send fixed-size cells over local area networks (LANs) or wide area networks (WANs). Cells are 53 bytes— 48 bytes of data with 5 additional bytes of address. ATM accommodates voice, data, fax, real-time video, CD-quality audio, imaging, and multimegabit data transmission. ATM uses switches as multiplexers to permit several computers to put data on a network simultaneously. Most commercial ATM boards transmit data at about 155 Mbps, but theoretically a rate of 1.2 Gbps is possible.

asynchronous transmission A form of data transmission in which information is sent one character at a time, with variable time intervals between characters. Asynchronous transmission does not rely on a shared timer that allows the sending and receiving units to separate characters by specific time periods. Therefore, each transmitted character consists of a number of data bits (which compose the character itself) preceded by a start bit and ending in an optional parity bit followed by a 1-, 1.5-, or 2-stop bit.

ATM *See* asynchronous transfer mode (ATM).

auditing A process that tracks network activities by user accounts and a routine element of network security. Auditing can produce records of users who have accessed—or attempted to access—specific resources; help administrators identify unauthorized activity; and track activities such as logon attempts, connection and disconnection from designated resources, changes made to files and directories, server events and modifications, password changes, and logon parameter changes.

audit policy Defines the types of security events that Windows XP Professional records in the security log on each computer.

authentication Verification based on user name, passwords, and time and account restrictions.

automated installation An unattended setup using one or more of several methods such as Remote Installation Services, bootable CD, and Sysprep.

Automatic Private IP Addressing (APIPA) A feature of Windows XP Professional that automatically configures a unique Internet Protocol (IP) address from 169.254.0.1 to 169.254.255.255 and a subnet mask of 255.255.0.0 when the Transmission Control Protocol/Internet Protocol (TCP/IP) is configured for dynamic addressing and a Dynamic Host Configuration Protocol (DHCP) server is not available.

B

back end In a client/server application, the part of the program that runs on the server.

backup A duplicate copy of a program, a disk, or data made to secure valuable files from loss.

backup job A single process of backing up data.

bandwidth In analog communication, the difference between the highest and lowest frequencies in a given range.

Bandwidth Allocation Protocol (BAP) A Point-to-Point Protocol (PPP) control protocol that helps provide bandwidth on demand. BAP dynamically controls the use of multilinked lines and is a very efficient mechanism for controlling connection costs while dynamically providing optimum bandwidth.

BAP *See* Bandwidth Allocation Protocol (BAP).

base I/O port Specifies a channel through which information is transferred between a computer's hardware, such as the network interface card (NIC) and its CPU.

baseline A measurement derived from the collection of data over an extended period of time. The data should reflect varying but typical types of workloads and user connections. The baseline is an indicator of how individual system resources or a group of resources are used during periods of normal activity.

base memory address Defines the address of the location in a computer's memory (RAM) that is used by the network interface card (NIC). This setting is sometimes called the RAM start address.

basic disk A physical disk that contains primary partitions or extended partitions with logical drives used by Windows XP Professional, Windows 2000, and all versions of Windows NT. Basic disks can also contain volume, striped, mirror, or RAID-5 sets that were created using Windows NT 4.0 or earlier versions. As long as a compatible file format is used, basic disks can be accessed by MS-DOS, Windows 95, Windows 98, and all versions of Windows NT.

basic input/output system (BIOS) The set of essential software routines that tests hardware at startup, assists with starting the operating system, and supports the transfer of data among hardware devices. The BIOS is stored in read-only memory (ROM) so that it can be executed when the computer is started. Although critical to performance, the BIOS is usually invisible to computer users.

baud A measure of data-transmission speed named after the French engineer and telegrapher Jean-Maurice-Emile Baudot. It is a measure of the speed of oscillation of the sound wave on which a bit of data is carried over telephone lines. Because baud was originally used to measure the transmission speed of telegraph equipment, the term sometimes refers to the data-transmission speed of a modem. However, current modems can send at a speed higher than one bit per oscillation, so baud is being replaced by the more accurate bps (bits per second) as a measure of modem speed.

baud rate Refers to the speed at which a modem can transmit data. Often confused with bps (the number of bits per second transmitted), baud rate actually measures the number of events, or signal changes, that occur in one second. Because one event can actually encode more than one bit in high-speed digital communication, baud rate and bps are not always synonymous, and the latter is the more accurate term to apply to modems. For example, the 9600-baud modem that encodes four bits per event actually operates at 2400 baud but transmits at 9600 bps (2400 events times 4 bits per event), and thus it should be called a 9600-bps modem.

bind To associate two pieces of information with one another.

binding A process that establishes the communication channel between network components on different levels to enable communication between those components—for example, the binding of a protocol driver (such as TCP/IP) and a network adapter.

bisync (binary synchronous communications protocol) A communications protocol developed by IBM. Bisync transmissions are encoded in either ASCII or EBCDIC. Messages can be of any length and are sent in units called frames, optionally preceded by a message header. Because bisync uses synchronous transmission, in which message elements are separated by a specific time interval, each frame is preceded and followed by special characters that enable the sending and receiving machines to synchronize their clocks.

bit Short for binary digit: either 1 or 0 in the binary number system. In processing and storage, a bit is the smallest unit of information handled by a computer. It is represented physically by an element such as a single pulse sent through a circuit or small spot on a magnetic disk capable of storing either a 1 or 0. Eight bits make a byte.

bits per second (bps) A measure of the speed at which a device can transfer data. *See also* baud rate.

bit time The time it takes for each station to receive and store a bit.

bootable CD An automated installation method that runs Setup from a CD-ROM. This method is useful for computers at remote sites with slow links and no local IT department.

boot sector A critical disk structure for starting your computer, located at sector 1 of each volume or floppy. It contains executable code and data that is required by the code, including information used by the file system to access the volume. The boot sector is created when you format the volume.

boot-sector virus A type of virus that resides in the first sector of a floppy disk or hard drive. When the computer is booted, the virus executes. In this common method of transmitting viruses from one floppy disk to another, the virus replicates itself onto the new drive each time a new disk is inserted and accessed.

bottleneck A device or program that significantly degrades network performance. Poor network performance results when a device uses noticeably more CPU time than it should, consumes too much of a resource, or lacks the capacity to handle the load. Potential bottlenecks can be found in the CPU, memory, network interface card (NIC), and other components.

bps *See* bits per second (bps).

broadcast A transmission sent simultaneously to more than one recipient. In communication and on networks, a broadcast message is one distributed to all stations or computers on the network.

broadcast storm An event that occurs when there are so many broadcast messages on the network that they approach or surpass the capacity of the network bandwidth. This can happen when one computer on the network transmits a flood of frames, saturating the network with traffic so it can no longer carry messages from any other computer. Such a broadcast storm can shut down a network.

buffer A reserved portion of RAM in which data is held temporarily, pending an opportunity to complete its transfer to or from a storage device or another location in memory.

built-in groups One type of group account used by Windows XP Professional. Built-in groups, as the name implies, are included with the operating system. Built-in groups have been granted useful collections of rights and built-in abilities. In most cases, a built-in group provides all the capabilities needed by a particular user. For example, if a user

account belongs to the built-in Administrators group, logging on with that account gives the user administrative capabilities. *See also* user account.

bus Parallel wires or cabling that connect components in a computer.

byte A unit of information consisting of 8 bits. In computer processing or storage, a byte is often equivalent to a single character, such as a letter, numeral, or punctuation mark. Because a byte represents only a small amount of information, amounts of computer memory are usually given in kilobytes (1024 bytes or 2 raised to the 10th power), megabytes (1,048,576 bytes or 2 raised to the 20th power), gigabytes (1024 megabytes), terabytes (1024 gigabytes), petabytes (1024 terabytes), or exabytes (1024 petabytes).

C

cache A special memory subsystem or part of RAM in which frequently used data values are duplicated for quick access. A memory cache stores the contents of frequently accessed RAM locations and the addresses where these data items are stored. When the processor references an address in memory, the cache checks to see whether it holds that address. If it does hold the address, the data is returned to the processor; if it does not, regular memory access occurs. A cache is useful when RAM accesses are slow compared with the microprocessor speed.

CAL *See* client access license (CAL).

callback A feature on Windows XP Professional that you can set that causes the remote server to disconnect and call back the client attempting to access the remote server. This reduces the client's phone bill by having the call charged to the remote server's phone number. The callback feature can also improve security by calling back the phone number that you specified.

central processing unit (CPU) The computational and control unit of a computer; the device that interprets and carries out instructions. Single-chip CPUs, called microprocessors, made personal computers possible. Examples include the 80286, 80386, 80486, and Pentium processors.

client A computer that accesses shared network resources provided by another computer, called a server.

client access license (CAL) A CAL gives client computers the right to connect to computers running one of the Windows Server family of products.

client/server A network architecture designed around the concept of distributed processing in which a task is divided between a back end (server) that stores and distributes data, and a front end (client) that requests specific data from the server.

codec (compression/decompression) Compression/decompression technology for digital video and stereo audio.

companion virus A virus that uses the name of a real program but has a different file extension from that of the program. The virus is activated when its companion program is opened. The companion virus uses a .com file extension, which overrides the .exe file extension and activates the virus.

compression state Each file and folder on an NTFS volume has a compression state, either compressed or uncompressed.

control set A Windows XP Professional installation contains control sets stored as subkeys in the registry. The control sets contain configuration data used to control the system, such as a list of which device drivers and services to load and start.

CPU *See* central processing unit (CPU).

D

database management system (DBMS) A layer of software between the physical database and the user. The DBMS manages all requests for database action from the user, including keeping track of the physical details of file locations and formats, indexing schemes, and so on. In addition, a DBMS permits centralized control of security and data integrity requirements.

data encryption *See* encryption.

data encryption standard (DES) A commonly used, highly sophisticated algorithm developed by the U.S. National Bureau of Standards for encrypting and decoding data. This encryption algorithm uses a 56-bit key, and maps a 64-bit input block to a 64-bit output block. The key appears to be a 64-bit key, but one bit in each of the 8 bytes is used for odd parity, resulting in 56 bits of usable key. *See also* encryption.

data frames Logical, structured packages in which data can be placed. Data being transmitted is segmented into small units and combined with control information such as message start and message end indicators. Each package of information is transmitted as a single unit, called a frame. The data-link layer packages raw bits from the physical layer into data frames. The exact format of the frame used by the network depends on the topology. *See also* frame.

data-link layer The second layer in the OSI reference model. This layer packages raw bits from the physical layer into data frames. *See also* Open Systems Interconnection (OSI) reference model.

data stream An undifferentiated, byte-by-byte flow of data.

DBMS *See* database management system (DBMS).

defragmenting The process of finding and consolidating fragmented files and folders.

Defragmenting involves moving the pieces of each file or folder to one location so that each occupies a single, contiguous space on the hard disk. The system can then access and save files and folders more efficiently.

DES *See* data encryption standard (DES).

device A generic term for a computer subsystem. Printers, serial ports, and disk drives are referred to as devices.

DHCP *See* Dynamic Host Configuration Protocol (DHCP).

digital A system that encodes information numerically, such as 0 and 1, in a binary context. Computers use digital encoding to process data. A digital signal is a discrete binary state, either on or off. *See also* analog, modem.

digital line A communication line that carries information only in binary-encoded (digital) form. To minimize distortion and noise interference, a digital line uses repeaters to regenerate the signal periodically during transmission. *See also* analog line.

digital video disc (DVD) An optical storage medium with higher capacity and bandwidth than a compact disc. A DVD can hold a full-length film with up to 133 minutes of high-quality video, in MPEG-2 format, and audio. Also known as digital versatile disc.

DIP (dual inline package) switch One or more small rocker or sliding switches that can be set to one of two states—closed or open—to control options on a circuit board.

direct memory access (DMA) Memory access that does not involve the microprocessor; frequently employed for data transfer directly between memory and an "intelligent" peripheral device such as a disk drive.

direct memory access (DMA) channel A channel for direct memory access that does not involve the microprocessor, providing data transfer directly between memory and a disk drive.

directory Stores information about network resources, as well as all the services that make the information available and useful. The resources stored in the directory, such as user data, printers, servers, databases, groups, computers, and security policies, are known as objects. The directory is part of Active Directory.

directory service A network service that identifies all resources on a network and makes them accessible to users and applications.

disk duplexing *See* disk mirroring, fault tolerance.

diskless computers Computers that have neither a floppy disk nor a hard disk. Diskless computers depend on special ROM to provide users with an interface through which they can log on to the network.

disk mirroring A technique, also known as disk duplicating, in which all or part of a hard disk is duplicated onto one or more hard disks, each of which ideally is attached to its own controller. With disk mirroring, any change made to the original disk is simultaneously made to the other disk or disks. Disk mirroring is used in situations in which a backup copy of current data must be maintained at all times. *See also* disk striping, fault tolerance.

disk striping Divides data into 64K blocks and spreads it equally at a fixed rate and in a fixed order among all disks in an array. However, disk striping does not provide any fault tolerance because there is no data redundancy. If any partition in the set fails, all data is lost. *See also* disk mirroring, fault tolerance.

distribution server *S*tores the distribution folder structure, which contains the files needed to install a product, for example Windows XP Professional.

DMA *See* direct memory access (DMA).

DMA channel *See* direct memory access (DMA) channel.

DNS *See* Domain Name System (DNS).

domain For Microsoft networking, a collection of computers and users that share a common database and security policy that are stored on a computer running Windows 2000 Server and configured as a domain controller. Each domain has a unique name. *See also* workgroup.

domain controller For Microsoft networking, the Windows 2000 Server–based computer that authenticates domain logons and maintains the security policy and master database for a domain.

domain namespace The naming scheme that provides the hierarchical structure for the DNS database.

Domain Name System (DNS) A general-purpose, distributed, replicated, data-query service used primarily on the Internet and on private Transmission Control Protocol/Internet Protocol (TCP/IP) networks for translating host names into Internet addresses.

downtime The amount of time a computer system or associated hardware remains nonfunctioning. Although downtime can occur because hardware fails unexpectedly, it can also be a scheduled event, such as when a network is shut down to allow time for maintaining the system, changing hardware, or archiving files.

driver A software component that permits a computer system to communicate with a device. For example, a printer driver is a device driver that translates computer data into a form understood by the target printer. In most cases, the driver also

manipulates the hardware to transmit the data to the device.

duplex transmission Also called full-duplex transmission. Communication that takes place simultaneously, in both directions. *See also* full-duplex transmission.

DVD *See* digital video disc (DVD).

dynamic disk A physical disk that is managed by Disk Management. Dynamic disks can contain only dynamic volumes, which are created by using Disk Management. Dynamic disks cannot contain partitions or logical drives, nor can they be accessed by MS-DOS.

Dynamic Host Configuration Protocol (DHCP) A protocol for automatic TCP/IP configuration that provides static and dynamic address allocation and management. *See also* Transmission Control Protocol/Internet Protocol (TCP/IP).

dynamic-link library (DLL) A feature of the Microsoft Windows family of operating systems and the OS/2 operating system. DLLs allow executable routines, generally serving a specific function or set of functions, to be stored separately as files with .dll extensions and to be loaded only when needed by the program that calls them.

E

EAP *See* Extensible Authentication Protocol (EAP).

EBCDIC *See* Extended Binary Coded Decimal Interchange Code (EBCDIC).

effective permissions The sum of the NTFS permissions assigned to the user account and to all of the groups to which the user belongs. If a user has Read permission for a folder and is a member of a group with Write permission for the same folder, then the user has both Read and Write permission for the folder.

EISA *See* Extended Industry Standard Architecture (EISA).

Encrypting File System (EFS) A feature of Windows 2000 and Windows XP Professional that protects sensitive data in files that are stored on disk using the NTFS file system. It uses symmetric key encryption in conjunction with public key technology to provide confidentiality for files. It runs as an integrated system service, which makes it easy to manage, difficult to attack, and transparent to the file owner and applications.

encryption The process of making information indecipherable to protect it from unauthorized viewing or use, especially during transmission or when the data is stored on a transportable magnetic medium. A key is required to decode the information. *See also* data encryption standard (DES).

Enhanced Small Device Interface (ESDI) A standard that can be used with high-capacity hard disks and tape drives to enable high-speed communication with a computer. ESDI drivers typically transfer data at about 10 Mbps.

ESDI *See* Enhanced Small Device Interface (ESDI).

event An action or occurrence to which a program might respond. Examples of events are mouse clicks, key presses, and mouse movements. Also, any significant occurrence in the system or in a program that requires users to be notified or an entry to be added to a log.

exabyte *See* byte.

Extended Binary Coded Decimal Interchange Code (EBCDIC) A coding scheme developed by IBM for use with IBM mainframe and personal computers as a standard method of assigning binary (numeric) values to alphabetic, numeric, punctuation, and transmission-control characters.

Extended Industry Standard Architecture (EISA) A 32-bit bus design for x86-based computers introduced in 1988. EISA was specified by an industry consortium of nine computer companies (AST Research, Compaq, Epson, Hewlett-Packard, NEC, Olivetti, Tandy, Wyse, and Zenith). An EISA device uses cards that are upwardly compatible from ISA. *See also* Industry Standard Architecture (ISA).

Extensible Authentication Protocol (EAP) An extension to the Point-to-Point Protocol (PPP) that works with dial-up, PPTP, and L2TP clients. EAP allows for an arbitrary authentication mechanism to validate a dial-up connection. The exact authentication method to be used is negotiated by the dial-up client and the remote access server.

F

FAT *See* file allocation table (FAT).

FAT32 A derivative of the file allocation table file system. FAT32 supports smaller cluster sizes than FAT in the same given disk space, which results in more efficient space allocation on FAT32 drives. *See also* file allocation table (FAT).

fault tolerance The ability of a computer or an operating system to respond to an event such as a power outage or a hardware failure in such a way that no data is lost and any work in progress is not corrupted.

Fiber Distributed Data Interface (FDDI) A standard developed by the ANSI for high-speed, fiber-optic local area networks. FDDI provides specifications for transmission rates of 100 Mbps on networks based on the Token Ring standard.

file allocation table (FAT) A file system based on a file allocation table (FAT) maintained by some operating systems, including Windows NT, Windows 2000, and Windows XP Professional, to keep track of the status of various segments of disk space used for file storage.

file infector A type of virus that attaches itself to a file or program and activates any time the file is used. Many subcategories of file infectors exist. *See also* companion virus, macro virus, polymorphic virus, stealth virus.

File Transfer Protocol (FTP) A process that provides file transfers between local and remote computers. FTP supports several commands that allow bidirectional transfer of binary and ASCII files between computers. The FTP client is installed with the TCP/IP connectivity utilities. *See also* ASCII (American Standard Code for Information Interchange), Transmission Control Protocol/Internet Protocol (TCP/IP).

firewall A security system, usually a combination of hardware and software, intended to protect a network against external threats coming from another network, including the Internet. Firewalls prevent an organization's networked computers from communicating directly with computers that are external to the network, and vice versa. Instead, all incoming and outgoing communication is routed through a proxy server outside the organization's network. Firewalls also audit network activity, recording the volume of traffic and information about unauthorized attempts to gain access. *See also* proxy server.

firmware Software routines stored in read-only memory (ROM). Unlike random access memory (RAM), ROM stays intact even in the absence of electrical power. Startup routines and low-level input/output (I/O) instructions are stored in firmware.

flow control Regulating the flow of data through routers to ensure that no segment becomes overloaded with transmissions.

forest A grouping or hierarchical arrangement of one or more domain trees that form a disjointed namespace.

fragmentation The scattering of the parts of a file over different parts of the disk rather than having all parts of the file located in contiguous space. When a hard disk contains numerous fragmented files and folders, the computer takes longer to gain access to files and folders because it requires several additional reads to collect the various pieces. Creating new files and folders also takes longer because the available free space on the hard disk is scattered.

frame A package of information transmitted on a network as a single unit. Frame is a term most often used with Ethernet networks. A frame is similar to the packet used in other networks. *See also* data frames, packet.

frame preamble Header information added to the beginning of a data frame in the physical layer of the OSI reference model.

frame relay An advanced, fast-packet, variable-length, digital, packet-switching technology. It is a point-to-point system that uses a private virtual circuit (PVC) to transmit variable-length frames at the data-link layer of the OSI reference model. Frame relay networks can also provide subscribers with bandwidth, as needed, that allows users to make nearly any type of transmission.

front end In a client/server application, the part of the program carried out on the client computer.

FTP *See* File Transfer Protocol (FTP).

full-duplex transmission Also called duplex transmission. Communication that takes place simultaneously, in both directions. *See also* duplex transmission.

G

gateway A device used to connect networks using different protocols so that information can be passed from one system to the other. Gateways function at the network layer of the OSI reference model.

Gb *See* gigabit (Gb).

GB *See* gigabyte (GB).

gigabit (Gb) 1,073,741,824 bits. Also referred to as 1 billion bits.

gigabyte (GB) Commonly, 1000 megabytes. However, the precise meaning often varies with the context. A gigabyte is 1 billion bytes. In the context of computing, bytes are often expressed in multiples of powers of two. Therefore, a gigabyte can also be either 1000 megabytes or 1024 megabytes, where a megabyte is considered to be 1,048,576 bytes (2 raised to the 20th power).

Global Catalog A service and a physical storage location that contains a replica of selected attributes for every object in Active Directory.

global group One type of group account used by Windows 2000 Server. Used across an entire domain, global groups are created on domain controllers in the domain in which the user accounts reside. Global groups can contain only user accounts from the domain in which the global group is created. Members of global groups obtain resource permissions when the global group is added to a local group. *See also* group.

group In networking, an account containing other accounts that are called members. The permissions and rights granted to a group are also provided to its members; thus, groups offer a convenient way to grant common capabilities to collections of user accounts. For Windows XP Professional, groups are managed with the Computer Management snap-in. For Windows 2000 Server, groups are managed with the Active Directory Users and Computers snap-in.

Group Policy An administrator's tool for defining and controlling how programs, network resources, and the operating system operate for users and computers in an organization. In an Active Directory environment, Group Policy is applied to users or components on the basis of their membership in sites, domains, or organizational units.

H

handshaking A term applied to modem-to-modem communication. Refers to the process by which information is transmitted between the sending and receiving devices to maintain and coordinate data flow between them. Proper handshaking ensures that the receiving device will be ready to accept data before the sending device transmits it.

hard disk One or more inflexible platters coated with material that allows the magnetic recording of computer data. A typical hard disk rotates at up to 7200 revolutions per minute (RPM), and the read/write heads ride over the surface of the disk on a cushion of air 10 to 25 millionths of an inch deep. A hard disk is sealed to prevent contaminants from interfering with the close head-to-disk tolerances. Hard disks provide faster access to data than floppy disks and are capable of storing much more information. Because platters are rigid, they can be stacked so that one hard-disk drive can access more than one platter. Most hard disks have between two and eight platters.

hardware The physical components of a computer system, including any peripheral equipment such as printers, modems, and mouse devices.

Hardware Compatibility List (HCL) A list of computers and peripherals that have been tested and have passed compatibility testing with the product for which the HCL is being developed. For example, the Windows XP HCL lists products that have been tested and found to be compatible with Windows XP.

hardware loopback A connector on a computer that is useful for troubleshooting hardware problems, allowing data to be transmitted to a line, then returned as received data. If the transmitted data does not return, the hardware loopback detects a hardware malfunction.

HCL *See* Hardware Compatibility List (HCL).

HDLC *See* High-Level Data Link Control (HDLC).

header In network data transmission, one of the three sections of a packet component. It includes an alert signal to indicate that the packet is being transmitted, the source address, the destination address, and clock information to synchronize transmission.

hertz (Hz) The unit of frequency measurement. Frequency measures how often a periodic event occurs, such as the manner in which a wave's amplitude changes with time. One hertz equals one cycle per second. Frequency is often measured in kilohertz (KHz, 1000 Hz), megahertz (MHz), gigahertz (GHz, 1000 MHz), or terahertz (THz, 10,000 GHz).

High-Level Data Link Control (HDLC) A widely accepted international protocol, developed by the International Organization for Standardization (ISO), that governs information transfer. HDLC is a bit-oriented, synchronous protocol that applies to the data-link (message packaging) layer of the OSI reference model. Under the HDLC protocol, data is transmitted in frames, each of which can contain a variable amount of data that must be organized in a particular way. *See also* data frames, frame.

histogram A chart consisting of horizontal or vertical bars. The widths or heights of these bars represent the values of certain data.

host *See* server.

hot fixing *See* sector sparing.

HTML *See* Hypertext Markup Language (HTML).

Human Interface Device (HID) A firmware specification standard for input and output devices such as drawing tablets, keyboards, universal serial bus (USB) speakers, and other specialized devices designed to improve accessibility.

Hypertext Markup Language (HTML) A language developed for writing pages for the World Wide Web. HTML allows text to include codes that define fonts, layout, embedded graphics, and hypertext links. Hypertext provides a method for presenting text, images, sound, and videos that are linked together in a nonsequential web of associations.

Hypertext Transfer Protocol (HTTP) The method by which World Wide Web pages are transferred over the network.

I

ICM *See* Image Color Management (ICM) 2.0.

ICMP *See* Internet Control Message Protocol (ICMP).

IDE *See* Integrated Device Electronics (IDE).

IEEE *See* Institute of Electrical and Electronics Engineers (IEEE).

IEEE 1394 Firewire A standard for high-speed serial devices such as digital video and digital audio editing equipment.

IEEE Project 802 A networking model developed by the IEEE. Named for the year and month it began (February 1980), Project 802 defines local area network (LAN) standards for the physical and data-link layers of the OSI reference model. Project 802 divides the data-link layer into two sublayers: media access control (MAC) and logical link control (LLC).

Image Color Management (ICM) 2.0 An operating system application programming interface (API) that helps ensure that colors you see on your monitor match those on your scanner and printer.

Industry Standard Architecture (ISA) An unofficial designation for the bus design of the IBM Personal Computer (PC) PC/XT. It allows various adapters to be added to the system by inserting plug-in cards into expansion slots. Commonly, ISA refers to the expansion slots themselves; such slots are called 8-bit slots or 16-bit slots. *See also* Extended Industry Standard Architecture (EISA), Micro Channel Architecture.

infrared transmission Electromagnetic radiation with frequencies in the electromagnetic spectrum in the range just below that of visible red light. In network communications, infrared technology offers extremely high transmission rates and wide bandwidth in line-of-sight communications.

Institute of Electrical and Electronics Engineers (IEEE) An organization of engineering and electronics professionals; noted in networking for developing the IEEE 802.x standards for the physical and data-link layers of the OSI reference model, applied in a variety of network configurations.

Integrated Device Electronics (IDE) A type of disk drive interface in which the controller electronics reside on the drive itself, eliminating the need for a separate network interface card. The IDE interface is compatible with the Western Digital ST-506 controller.

Integrated Services Digital Network (ISDN) A worldwide digital communication network that evolved from existing telephone services. The goal of the ISDN is to replace current telephone lines, which require digital-to-analog conversions, with completely digital switching and transmission facilities capable of carrying data ranging from voice to computer transmissions, music, and video. The ISDN is built on two main types of communications channels: B channels, which carry voice, data, or images at a rate of 64 Kbps (kilobits per second); and a D channel, which carries control information, signaling, and link management data at 16 Kbps. Standard ISDN Basic Rate desktop service is called 2B+D. Computers and other devices connect to ISDN lines through simple, standardized interfaces.

interfaces Boundaries that separate layers from each other. For example, in the OSI reference model, each layer provides some service or action that prepares the data for delivery over the network to another computer.

International Organization for Standardization (ISO) An organization made up of standards-setting groups from various countries. For example, the United States member is the American National Standards Institute (ANSI). The ISO works to establish global standards for communications and information exchange. Primary among its accomplishments is development of the widely accepted OSI reference model. Note that the ISO is often wrongly identified as the International Standards Organization, probably because of the acronym *ISO*; however, ISO is derived from *isos,* which means *equal* in Greek, rather than an acronym.

Internet Control Message Protocol (ICMP) Used by Internet Protocol (IP) and higher level protocols to send and receive status reports about information being transmitted.

Internet Protocol (IP) The TCP/IP protocol for packet forwarding. *See also* Transmission Control Protocol/Internet Protocol (TCP/IP).

Internet Protocol Security (IPSec) A framework of open standards for ensuring secure private communications over IP networks by using cryptographic security services.

Internet service provider (ISP) A company that provides individuals or companies access to the Internet and the World Wide Web. An ISP provides a telephone number, a user name, a password, and other connection information, so users can connect their computer to the ISP's computers. An ISP typically charges a monthly or hourly connection fee.

internetworking The intercommunication in a network that is made up of smaller networks.

Internetwork Packet Exchange/Sequenced Packet Exchange (IPX/SPX) A protocol stack that is used in Novell networks. IPX is the NetWare protocol for packet forwarding and routing. It is a relatively small and fast protocol on a local area network (LAN), is a derivative of Xerox Network System (XNS), and supports routing. SPX is a connection-oriented protocol used to guarantee the delivery of the data being sent. NWLink is the Microsoft implementation of the IPX/SPX protocol.

interoperability The ability of components in one system to work with components in other systems.

interrupt request (IRQ) An electronic signal sent to a computer's CPU to indicate that an event has taken place that requires the processor's attention.

intranet A network within an organization that uses Internet technologies and protocols but is available only to certain people, such as employees of a company. An intranet is also called a private network.

IP *See* Internet Protocol (IP). *See also* Transmission Control Protocol/Internet Protocol (TCP/IP).

IP address A 32-bit address used to identify a node on an Internet Protocol (IP) internetwork. Each node on the IP internetwork must be assigned a unique IP address, which is made up of the network ID plus a unique host ID. This address is typically represented with the decimal value of each octet separated by a period (for example, 192.168.7.23). In Windows XP Professional, the IP addresses can be configured manu-

ally, or if you have a computer running Windows 2000 Server and DHCP, the IP addresses can be configured dynamically. *See also* Dynamic Host Configuration Protocol (DHCP).

ipconfig A diagnostic command that displays all current TCP/IP network configuration values. It is of particular use on systems running DHCP because it allows users to determine which TCP/IP configuration values have been configured by the DHCP server.

IPSec *See* Internet Protocol Security (IPSec).

IPX/SPX *See* Internetwork Packet Exchange/Sequenced Packet Exchange (IPX/SPX).

IRQ *See* interrupt request (IRQ).

ISA *See* Industry Standard Architecture (ISA).

ISDN *See* Integrated Services Digital Network (ISDN).

ISO *See* International Organization for Standardization (ISO).

J

jumper A small plastic-and-metal plug or wire for connecting different points in an electronic circuit. Jumpers are used to select a particular circuit or option from several possible configurations. Jumpers can be used on network interface cards to select the type of connection through which the card will transmit, either DIX or BNC.

K

Kerberos authentication protocol An authentication mechanism used to verify user or host identity. The Kerberos v5 authentication protocol is the default authentication service for Windows XP Professional. Internet Protocol security and the QoS Admission Control Service use the Kerberos protocol for authentication.

key In database management, an identifier for a record or group of records in a data file. Most often, the key is defined as the contents of a single field, called the key field in some database management programs and the index field in others. Keys are maintained in tables and are indexed to speed record retrieval. Keys also refer to code that deciphers encrypted data.

kilo (K) Refers to 1000 in the metric system. In computing terminology, because computing is based on powers of 2, kilo is most often used to mean 1024 (2 raised to the 10th power). To distinguish between the two contexts, a lowercase k is often used to indicate 1000 and an uppercase K for 1024. A kilobyte is 1024 bytes.

kilobit (Kbit) 1024 bits. *See also* bit, kilo (K).

kilobyte (KB) 1024 bytes. *See also* byte, kilo (K).

L

L2TP *See* Layer Two Tunneling Protocol (L2TP).

LAN *See* local area network (LAN).

LAN requester *See* requester (LAN requester).

laser transmission Wireless network that uses a laser beam to carry data between devices.

LAT *See* local area transport (LAT).

layering The coordination of various protocols in a specific architecture that allows the protocols to work together to ensure that the data is prepared, transferred, received, and acted on as intended.

Layer Two Tunneling Protocol (L2TP) Its primary purpose is to create an encrypted tunnel through an untrusted network. L2TP is similar to Point-to-Point Tunneling Protocol (PPTP) in that it provides tunneling but not encryption. L2TP provides a secure tunnel by cooperating with other encryption technologies such as IPSec. L2TP functions with IPSec to provide a secure virtual private network solution.

line printer A connectivity tool that runs on client systems and is used to print files to a computer running an LPD server.

line printer daemon (LPD) A service on the print server that receives documents (print jobs) from line printer remote (LPR) tools running on client systems.

link The communication system that connects two local area networks (LANs). Equipment that provides the link, including bridges, routers, and gateways.

local area network (LAN) Computers connected in a geographically confined network, such as in the same building, campus, or office park.

local area transport (LAT) A nonroutable protocol from Digital Equipment Corporation.

local computer A computer that can be accessed directly without using a communications line or a communications device, such as a network adapter or a modem.

local group One type of group account used by Windows XP. Implemented in each local computer's account database, local groups contain user accounts and other global groups that need to have access, rights, and permissions assigned to a resource on a local computer. Local groups cannot contain other local groups.

local user The user at the computer.

logical drive A volume created within an extended partition on a basic disk. You can format and assign a drive letter to a logical drive. Only basic disks can contain logical drives. A logical drive cannot span multiple disks.

logical link control (LLC) sublayer One of two sublayers created by the IEEE 802 project out of the data-link layer of the OSI reference model. The LLC is the upper sublayer that manages data-link communication and defines the use of logical interface points, called service access points (SAPs), used by computers to transfer information from the LLC sublayer to the upper OSI layers. *See also* media access control (MAC) sublayer, service access point (SAP).

logon script Files that can be assigned to user accounts. Typically a batch file, a logon script runs automatically every time the user logs on. It can be used to configure a user's working environment at every logon, and it allows an administrator to influence a user's environment without managing all aspects of it. A logon script can be assigned to one or more user accounts.

M

macro virus A virus written in the internal macro language of applications. In many cases macro viruses cause no damage to data, but in some cases malicious macros have been written that can damage your work. *See also* companion virus, file infector, polymorphic virus, stealth virus.

master boot record (MBR) The first sector on a hard disk, this data structure starts the process of booting the computer. The MBR contains the partition table for the disk and a small amount of executable code called the master boot code.

Mb *See* megabit (Mb).

MB *See* megabyte (MB).

Mbps *See* millions of bits per second (Mbps).

media The vast majority of local area networks (LANs) today are connected by some sort of wire or cabling that acts as the LAN transmission medium, carrying data between computers. The cabling is often referred to as the media.

media access control (MAC) driver The device driver located at the media access control sublayer of the OSI reference model. This driver is also known as the NIC driver. It provides low-level access to network interface cards (NICs) by providing data-transmission support and some basic NIC management functions. These drivers also pass data from the physical layer to transport protocols at the network and transport layers.

media access control (MAC) sublayer One of two sublayers created by the IEEE 802 project out of the data-link layer of the OSI reference model. The MAC sublayer communicates directly with the network interface card and is responsible for delivering error-free data between two computers on the network. *See also* logical link control (LLC) sublayer.

megabit (Mb) Usually, 1,048,576 bits; sometimes interpreted as 1 million bits. *See also* bit.

megabyte (MB) 1,048,576 bytes (2 raised to the 20th power); sometimes interpreted as 1 million bytes. *See also* byte.

Micro Channel Architecture The design of the bus in IBM PS/2 computers (except Models 25 and 30). The Micro Channel is electrically and physically incompatible with the IBM PC/AT bus. Unlike the PC/AT bus, the Micro Channel functions as either a 16-bit or 32-bit bus. The Micro Channel also can be driven independently by multiple bus master processors. *See also* Extended Industry Standard Architecture (EISA), Industry Standard Architecture (ISA).

Microcom Network Protocol (MNP) The standard for asynchronous data-error control developed by Microcom Systems. The method works so well that other companies have adopted not only the initial version of the protocol, but later versions as well. Currently, several modem vendors incorporate MNP Classes 2, 3, 4, and 5.

Microsoft Technical Information Network (TechNet) Provides informational support for all aspects of networking, with an emphasis on Microsoft products.

millions of bits per second (Mbps) The unit of measure of supported transmission rates on the following physical media: coaxial cable, twisted-pair cable, and fiber-optic cable. *See also* bit.

MNP *See* Microcom Network Protocol (MNP).

mobile computing Incorporates wireless adapters using cellular telephone technology to connect portable computers with the cabled network.

modem A communications device that enables a computer to transmit information over a standard telephone line. Because a computer is digital, it works with discrete electrical signals representing binary 1 and binary 0. A telephone is analog and carries a signal that can have many variations. Modems are needed to convert digital signals to analog and back. When transmitting, modems impose (modulate) a computer's digital signals onto a continuous carrier frequency on the telephone line. When receiving, modems sift out (demodulate) the information from the carrier and transfer it in digital form to the computer.

multitasking A mode of operation offered by an operating system in which a computer works on more than one task at a time. There are two primary types of multitasking: preemptive and nonpreemptive. In preemptive multitasking, the operating system can take control of the processor without the task's cooperation. In nonpreemptive multitasking, the processor is never taken from a task. The task itself decides when to give up the processor. A true multitasking operating system can run as many tasks as it has processors. When there are more tasks than processors, the computer must "time slice" so that the available processors devote a certain amount of time to one task and then move on to the next task, alternating between tasks until all are completed.

N

Name Binding Protocol (NBP) An Apple protocol responsible for keeping track of entities on the network and matching names with Internet addresses. It works at the transport layer of the OSI reference model.

namespace Any bounded area in which a name can be resolved. Name resolution is the process of translating a name into some object or information that the name represents. The Active Directory namespace is based on the Domain Name System (DNS) naming scheme, which allows for interoperability with Internet technologies.

NBP *See* Name Binding Protocol (NBP).

nbtstat A diagnostic command that displays protocol statistics and current Transmission Control Protocol/Internet Protocol (TCP/IP) connections using NBT (NetBIOS over TCP/IP). This command is available only if the TCP/IP protocol has been installed. *See also* netstat.

NDIS *See* Network Device Interface Specification (NDIS).

NetBEUI (NetBIOS Extended User Interface) A protocol supplied with all Microsoft network products. NetBEUI advantages include small stack size (important for MS-DOS–based computers), speed of data transfer on the network medium, and compatibility with all Microsoft-based networks. The major drawback of NetBEUI is that it is a local area network (LAN) transport protocol and therefore does not support routing. It is also limited to Microsoft-based networks.

NetBIOS (network basic input/output system) An application programming interface (API) that can be used by application programs on a local area network (LAN) consisting of IBM-compatible microcomputers running MS-DOS, OS/2, or some version of UNIX. Primarily of interest to programmers, NetBIOS provides application programs with a uniform set of commands for requesting the lower level network services required to conduct sessions between nodes on a network and transmit information between them.

netstat A diagnostic command that displays protocol statistics and current Transmission Control Protocol/Internet Protocol (TCP/IP) network connections. This command is available only if the TCP/IP protocol has been installed. *See also* nbtstat.

NetWare Core Protocol (NCP) Defines the connection control and service-request encoding that make it possible for clients and servers to interact. This is the protocol that provides transport and session services. NetWare security is also provided within this protocol.

network In the context of computers, a system in which a number of independent computers are linked together to share data and peripherals, such as hard disks and printers.

network adapter card *See* network interface card (NIC).

Network Device Interface Specification (NDIS) A standard that defines an interface for communication between the media access control (MAC) sublayer and protocol drivers. NDIS allows for a flexible environment of data exchange. It defines the software interface, called the NDIS interface, which is used by protocol drivers to communicate with the network interface card. The advantage of NDIS is that it offers protocol multiplexing so that multiple protocol stacks can be used at the same time. *See also* Open Data-Link Interface (ODI).

network interface card (NIC) An expansion card installed in each computer and server on the network. The NIC acts as the physical interface or connection between the computer and the network cable.

network layer The third layer in the OSI reference model. This layer is responsible for addressing messages and translating logical addresses and names into physical addresses. This layer also determines the route from the source to the destination computer. It determines which path the data should take based on network conditions, priority of service, and other factors. It also manages traffic problems such as switching, routing, and controlling the congestion of data packets on the network. *See also* Open Systems Interconnection (OSI) reference model.

network monitors Monitors that track all or a selected part of network traffic. They examine frame-level packets and gather information about packet types, errors, and packet traffic to and from each computer.

NIC *See* network interface card (NIC).

node On a local area network (LAN), a device that is connected to the network and is capable of communicating with other network devices. For example, clients, servers, and repeaters are called nodes.

nonpreemptive multitasking A form of multitasking in which the processor is never taken from a task. The task itself decides when to give up the processor. Programs written for nonpreemptive multitasking systems must include provisions for yielding control of the processor. No other program can run until the nonpreemptive program gives up control of the processor. *See also* multitasking, preemptive multitasking.

Novell NetWare One of the leading network architectures.

O

object A distinct, named set of attributes that represent a network resource. Object attributes are characteristics of objects in the Active Directory

directory. For example, the attributes of a user account might include the user's first and last names, department, and e-mail address.

ODI *See* Open Data-Link Interface (ODI).

ohm The unit of measure for electrical resistance. A resistance of 1 ohm will pass 1 ampere of current when a voltage of 1 volt is applied. A 100-watt incandescent bulb has a resistance of approximately 130 ohms.

Open Data-Link Interface (ODI) A specification defined by Novell and Apple to simplify driver development and to provide support for multiple protocols on a single network interface card. Similar to Network Device Interface Specification (NDIS) in many respects, ODI allows Novell NetWare drivers to be written without concern for the protocol that will be used on top of them.

Open Shortest Path First (OSPF) A routing protocol for IP networks, such as the Internet, that allows a router to calculate the shortest path to each node for sending messages.

Open Systems Interconnection (OSI) reference model A seven-layer architecture that standardizes levels of service and types of interaction for computers exchanging information through a network. It is used to describe the flow of data between the physical connection to the network and the end-user application. This model is the best known and most widely used model for describing networking environments.

organizational unit (OU) A container used to organize objects within a domain into logical administrative groups. An OU can contain objects such as user accounts, groups, computers, printers, applications, file shares, and other OUs.

OSI *See* Open Systems Interconnection (OSI) reference model.

OSPF *See* Open Shortest Path First (OSPF).

P

packet A unit of information transmitted as a whole from one device to another on a network. In packet-switching networks, a packet is defined more specifically as a transmission unit of fixed maximum size that consists of binary digits representing data; a header containing an identification number, source, and destination addresses; and sometimes error-control data. *See also* frame.

packet assembler/disassembler (PAD) A device that breaks large chunks of data into packets, usually for transmission over an X.25 network, and reassembles them at the other end. *See also* packet switching.

Packet Internet Groper (ping) A simple tool that tests if a network connection is complete, from the server to the workstation, by sending a message to the remote computer. If the remote computer receives the message, it responds with a reply message. The reply consists of the remote workstation's Internet Protocol (IP) address, the number of bytes in the message, how long it took to reply—given in milliseconds (ms)—and the length of time-to-live (TTL) in seconds. Ping works at the IP level and will often respond even when higher level TCP-based services cannot.

packet switching A message delivery technique in which small units of information (packets) are relayed through stations in a computer network along the best route available between the source and the destination. Data is broken into smaller units and then repacked in a process called packet assembly/disassembly (PAD). Although each packet can travel along a different path, and the packets composing a message can arrive at different times or out of sequence, the receiving computer reassembles the original message. Packet-switching networks are considered fast and efficient. Standards for packet switching on networks are documented in the CCITT recommendation X.25.

PAD *See* packet assembler/disassembler (PAD).

page-description language (PDL) A language that communicates to a printer how printed output should appear. The printer uses the PDL to construct text and graphics to create the page image. PDLs are like blueprints in that they set parameters and features such as type sizes and fonts, but leave the drawing to the printer.

page fault An error that occurs when the requested code or data cannot be located in the physical memory that is available to the requesting process.

paging The process of moving virtual memory back and forth between physical memory (RAM) and the disk. Paging occurs when physical memory becomes full.

paging file A special file on one or more of the hard disks of a computer running Windows XP Professional. Windows XP Professional uses virtual memory to store some of the program code and other information in RAM and to temporarily store some of the program code and other information on the computer's hard disks. This increases the amount of available memory on the computer.

parity An error-checking procedure in which the number of 1s must always be the same—either odd or even—for each group of bits transmitted without error. Parity is used for checking data transferred within a computer or between computers.

partition A logical division of a hard disk that functions as if it were a physically separate unit. Each partition can be formatted for a different file system.

password-protected share Access to a shared resource that is granted when a user enters the appropriate password.

PBX (Private Branch Exchange) A switching telephone network that allows callers within an organization to place intraorganizational calls without going through the public telephone system.

PDA *See* personal digital assistant (PDA).

PDL *See* page-description language (PDL).

PDN *See* public data network (PDN).

peer-to-peer network A network in which there are no dedicated servers or hierarchy among the computers. All computers are equal and therefore known as peers. Generally, each computer functions as both client and server.

peripheral A term used for devices such as disk drives, printers, modems, mouse devices, and joysticks that are connected to a computer and controlled by its microprocessor.

Peripheral Component Interconnect (PCI) 32-bit local bus used in most Pentium computers and in the Apple Power Macintosh. Meets most of the requirements for providing Plug and Play functionality.

permanent virtual circuit (PVC) A permanent logical connection between two nodes on a packet-switching network; similar to leased lines that are permanent and virtual, except that with PVC the customer pays only for the time the line is used. This type of connection service is gaining importance because both frame relay and ATM use it. *See also* packet switching, virtual circuit.

permissions *See* access permissions.

personal digital assistant (PDA) A type of handheld computer that provides functions including personal organization features—like a calendar, note taking device, database manipulation, calculator, and communications functions. For communication, a PDA uses cellular or wireless technology that is often built into the system but can be supplemented or enhanced by means of a PC card.

petabyte *See* byte.

phase change rewritable (PCR) A type of rewritable optical technology in which the optical devices come from one manufacturer (Matsushita/Panasonic) and the media come from two (Panasonic and Plasmon).

physical layer The first (bottom) layer of the OSI reference model. This layer addresses the transmission of the unstructured raw bitstream over a physical medium (the networking cable). The physical layer relates the electrical/optical, mechanical, and functional interfaces to the cable and also carries the signals that transmit data generated by all of the higher OSI layers. *See also* Open Systems Interconnection (OSI) reference model.

ping *See* Packet Internet Groper (ping).

Plug and Play A set of specifications developed by Intel that allows a computer to automatically detect and configure a device and install the appropriate device drivers.

Point of Presence (POP) The local access point for a network provider. Each POP provides a telephone number that allows users to make a local call for access to online services.

point-to-point configuration Dedicated circuits that are also known as private, or leased, lines. They are the most popular wide area network (WAN) communication circuits in use today. The carrier guarantees full-duplex bandwidth by setting up a permanent link from each end point, using bridges and routers to connect local area networks (LANs) through the circuits. *See also* Point-to-Point Protocol (PPP), Point-to-Point Tunneling Protocol (PPTP), duplex transmission.

Point-to-Point Protocol (PPP) A data-link protocol for transmitting Transmission Control Protocol/Internet Protocol (TCP/IP) packets over dial-up telephone connections, such as between a computer and the Internet. PPP was developed by the Internet Engineering Task Force in 1991.

Point-to-Point Tunneling Protocol (PPTP) An extension of the Point-to-Point Protocol (PPP) used for communications on the Internet. It was developed by Microsoft to support virtual private networks (VPNs), which allow individuals and organizations to use the Internet as a secure means of communication. PPTP supports encapsulation of encrypted packets in secure wrappers that can be transmitted over a Transmission Control Protocol/Internet Protocol (TCP/IP) connection. *See also* virtual private network (VPN).

polymorphic virus A virus that produces varied but operational copies of itself. Polymorphic viruses change their structure to prevent virus scanners from detecting all instances of the virus. *See also* companion virus, file infector, macro virus, stealth virus.

preemptive multitasking A form of multitasking (the ability of a computer's operating system to work on more than one task at a time). With preemptive multitasking—as opposed to nonpreemptive multitasking—the operating system can take control of the processor without the task's cooperation. *See also* nonpreemptive multitasking.

presentation layer The sixth layer of the OSI reference model. This layer determines the form used to exchange data between networked computers. At the sending computer, this layer translates data from a format sent down from the application layer into a commonly recognized, intermediary format. At the receiving end, this layer translates the intermediary format into a format useful to that computer's application layer. The presentation layer manages network security issues by providing services such as data encryption, provides rules for data transfer, and performs data compression to reduce the number of bits that need to be transmitted. *See also* Open Systems Interconnection (OSI) reference model.

printer driver One or more files containing information that Windows XP Professional requires to convert print commands into a specific printer language, such as PostScript. A printer driver is specific to each print device model.

printer port The software interface through which a computer communicates with a print device by means of a locally attached interface. These supported interfaces include LPT, COM, USB, and network-attached devices such as the HP JetDirect and Intel NetPort.

print queue A buffer in which a print job is held until the printer is ready to print it.

print server The computer on which the printers reside. The print server receives and processes documents from client computers. You set up and share network printers on print servers.

private key The secret half of a cryptographic key pair that is used with a public key algorithm. Private keys are typically used to digitally sign data and to decrypt data that has been encrypted with the corresponding public key.

protocol The system of rules and procedures that govern communication between two or more devices. Many varieties of protocols exist, and not all are compatible, but as long as two devices are using the same protocol, they can exchange data. Networking software usually implements multiple levels of protocols layered one on top of another. Windows XP Professional includes TCP/IP- and IPX/SPX-compatible protocols.

protocol driver The driver responsible for offering four or five basic services to other layers in the network, while "hiding" the details of how the services are actually implemented. Services performed include session management, datagram service, data segmentation and sequencing, acknowledgment, and possibly routing across a wide area network (WAN).

protocol stack A layered set of protocols that work together to provide a set of network functions.

proxy server A firewall component that manages Internet traffic to and from a local area network (LAN). The proxy server decides whether it is safe to let a particular message or file pass through to the organization's network, provides access control to the network, and filters and discards requests as specified by the owner, including requests for unauthorized access to proprietary data. *See also* firewall.

public data network (PDN) A commercial packet-switching or circuit-switching wide area network (WAN) service provided by local and long-distance telephone carriers.

public key The nonsecret half of a cryptographic key pair that is used with a public algorithm. Public keys are typically used to verify digital signatures or decrypt data that has been encrypted with the corresponding private key.

PVC *See* permanent virtual circuit (PVC).

Q

QoS *See* quality of service.

quality of service (QoS) A set of quality assurance standards and mechanisms for data transmission.

R

RADIUS *See* Remote Authentication Dial-In User Service (RADIUS).

RAID *See* redundant array of independent disks (RAID).

random access memory (RAM) Semiconductor-based memory that can be read and written to by the microprocessor or other hardware devices. The storage locations can be accessed in any order. Note that the various types of read-only memory (ROM) are also capable of random access. However, RAM is generally understood to refer to volatile memory, which can be written as well as read. *See also* read-only memory (ROM).

read-only memory (ROM) Semiconductor-based memory that contains instructions or data that can be read but not modified. *See also* random access memory (RAM).

redirector Networking software that accepts input/output (I/O) requests for remote files, named pipes, or mail slots and sends (redirects) the requests to a network service on another computer.

Reduced Instruction Set Computing (RISC) A type of microprocessor design that focuses on rapid and efficient processing of a relatively small set of instructions. RISC architecture limits the number of instructions that are built into the microprocessor, but it optimizes each so it can be carried out very rapidly, usually within a single clock cycle.

redundancy system A fault-tolerant system that protects data by duplicating it in different physical sources. Data redundancy allows access to data even if part of the data system fails. *See also* fault tolerance.

redundant array of independent disks (RAID) A standardization of fault-tolerant options in five levels. The levels offer various combinations of performance, reliability, and cost. Formerly known as redundant array of inexpensive disks.

redundant array of inexpensive disks (RAID) *See* redundant array of independent disks (RAID).

registry In Windows XP Professional, Windows 2000, Windows NT, Windows 98, and Windows 95, a database of information about a computer's configuration. The registry is organized in a hierarchical structure and consists of subtrees and their keys, hives, and entries.

Remote Authentication Dial-In User Service (RADIUS) A security authentication protocol widely used by Internet service providers (ISPs). RADIUS provides authentication and accounting services for distributed dial-up networking.

remote-boot PROM (programmable read-only memory) A special chip in the network interface card that contains the hardwired code that starts the computer and connects the user to the network, used in computers for which there are no hard disk or floppy drives. *See also* diskless computers.

remote installation The process of connecting to a server running Remote Installation Services (RIS), called the RIS server, and then starting an automated installation of Windows XP Professional on a local computer.

remote user A user who dials in to the server over modems and telephone lines from a remote location.

requester (LAN requester) Software that resides in a computer and forwards requests for network services from the computer's application programs to the appropriate server. *See also* redirector.

Request for Comment (RFC) A document that defines a standard. RFCs are published by the Internet Engineering Task Force (IETF) and other working groups.

resource publishing The process of making an object visible and accessible to users in a Windows 2000 domain.

resources Any part of a computer system. Users on a network can share computer resources, such as hard disks, printers, modems, CD-ROM drives, and even the processor.

RFC *See* Request for Comment (RFC).

rights Authorization with which a user is entitled to perform certain actions on a computer network. Rights apply to the system as a whole, whereas permissions apply to specific objects. For example, a user might have the right to back up an entire computer system, including the files that the user does not have permission to access. *See also* access permissions.

RIS *See* remote installation.

RISC *See* Reduced Instruction Set Computing (RISC).

ROM *See* read-only memory (ROM).

routable protocols The protocols that support multipath LAN-to-LAN communications. *See also* protocol.

router A device used to connect networks of different types, such as those using different architectures and protocols. Routers work at the network layer of the OSI reference model. This means they can switch and route packets across multiple networks, which they do by exchanging protocol-specific information between separate networks. Routers determine the best path for sending data and filter broadcast traffic to the local segment.

Routing Information Protocol (RIP) A protocol that uses distance-vector algorithms to determine routes. With RIP, routers transfer information among other routers to update their internal routing tables and use that information to determine the best routes based on hop counts between routers. TCP/IP and IPX support RIP.

RS-232 standard An industry standard for serial communication connections. Adopted by the Electrical Industries Association (EIA), this recommended standard defines the specific lines and signal characteristics used by serial communications controllers to standardize the transmission of serial data between devices.

S

safe mode A method of starting Windows XP Professional using basic files and drivers only, without networking. Safe mode is available by pressing the F8 key when prompted during startup. This allows the computer to start when a problem prevents it from starting normally.

SAP (service access point) *See* service access point (SAP).

SAP (Service Advertising Protocol) *See* Service Advertising Protocol (SAP).

schema Contains a formal definition of the contents and structure of Active Directory, including all attributes, classes, and class properties. For each object class, the schema defines what attributes an instance of the class must have, what additional attributes it can have, and what object class can be a parent of the current object class.

SCSI *See* Small Computer System Interface (SCSI).

SDLC *See* Synchronous Data Link Control (SDLC).

sector A portion of the data-storage area on a disk. A disk is divided into sides (top and bottom), tracks (rings on each surface), and sectors (sections of each ring). Sectors are the smallest physical storage units on a disk and are of fixed size—typically capable of holding 512 bytes of information each.

sector sparing A fault-tolerant system also called hot fixing. It automatically adds sector-recovery capabilities to the file system during operation. If bad sectors are found during disk I/O, the fault-tolerant driver will attempt to move the data to a good sector and map out the bad sector. If the mapping is successful, the file system is not alerted. It is possible for SCSI devices to perform sector sparing, but AT devices (ESDI and IDE) cannot.

security Making computers and data stored on them safe from harm or unauthorized access.

security identifier (SID) A data structure of variable length that uniquely identifies user, group, service, and computer accounts within an enterprise. Every account is issued a SID when the account is first created. Access control mechanisms in Windows XP Professional and Windows 2000 identify security principals by SID rather than by name.

security log Records security events, such as valid and invalid logon attempts and events relating to creating, opening, or deleting files or other objects.

segment The length of cable on a network between two terminators. A segment can also refer to messages that have been broken up into smaller units by the protocol driver.

Sequenced Packet Exchange (SPX) Part of Novell's IPX/SPX protocol suite for sequenced data. *See also* Internetwork Packet Exchange/ Sequenced Packet Exchange (IPX/SPX).

serial transmission One-way data transfer. The data travels on a network cable with one bit following another.

server A computer that provides shared resources to network users. *See also* client.

server-based network A network in which resource security and most other network functions are provided by dedicated servers. Server-based networks have become the standard model for networks serving more than 10 users. *See also* peer-to-peer network.

server message block (SMB) The protocol developed by Microsoft, Intel, and IBM that defines a series of commands used to pass information between network computers. The redirector packages SMB requests into a network control block (NCB) structure that can be sent over the network to a remote device. The network provider listens for SMB messages destined for it and removes the data portion of the SMB request so that it can be processed by a local device.

service access point (SAP) The interface between each of the seven layers in the OSI protocol stack that has connection points, similar to addresses, used for communication between layers. Any protocol layer can have multiple SAPs active at one time.

Service Advertising Protocol (SAP) Allows service-providing nodes (including file, printer, gateway, and application servers) to advertise their services and addresses.

service pack A software upgrade to an existing software distribution that contains updated files consisting of patches and fixes.

session A connection or link between stations on a network.

session layer The fifth layer of the OSI reference model. This layer allows two applications on different computers to establish, use, and end a connection called a session. This layer performs name recognition and functions, such as security, needed to allow two applications to communicate over the network. The session layer provides synchronization between user tasks. This layer also implements dialog control between communicating processes, regulating which side transmits, when, for how long, and so on. *See also* Open Systems Interconnection (OSI) reference model.

session management Establishing, maintaining, and terminating connections between stations on the network.

sharing Means by which files of folders are publicly posted on a network for access by anyone on the network.

shell A piece of software, usually a separate program, that provides direct communication between the user and the operating system. This usually, but not always, takes the form of a command-line interface. Examples of shells are Macintosh Finder and the MS-DOS command interface program COMMAND.COM.

Simple Mail Transfer Protocol (SMTP) A TCP/IP protocol for transferring e-mail. *See also* application protocols, Transmission Control Protocol/Internet Protocol (TCP/IP).

Simple Network Management Protocol (SNMP) A network management protocol installed with TCP/IP and widely used on TCP/IP and IPX networks. SNMP transports management information and commands between a management program run by an administrator and the network management agent running on a host. The SNMP agent sends status information to one or more hosts when the host requests it or when a significant event occurs.

simultaneous peripheral operation on line (spool) Facilitates the process of moving a print job from the network into a printer.

site A combination of one or more Internet Protocol (IP) subnets, typically connected by a high-speed link.

Small Computer System Interface (SCSI) A standard, high-speed parallel interface defined by the ANSI. A SCSI interface is used for connecting microcomputers to peripheral devices, such as hard disks and printers, and to other computers and LANs. Pronounced "scuzzy."

smart card A credit card-sized device that is used with a PIN number to enable certificate-based authentication and single sign-on to the enterprise. Smart cards securely store certificates, public and private keys, passwords, and other types of personal information. A smart card reader attached to the computer reads the smart card.

SMB *See* server message block (SMB).

SMP *See* symmetric multiprocessing (SMP).

SMTP *See* Simple Mail Transfer Protocol (SMTP).

SNMP *See* Simple Network Management Protocol (SNMP).

software Computer programs or sets of instructions that allow the hardware to work. Software can be grouped into four categories: system software, such as operating systems, that control the workings of the computer; application software, such as word processing programs, spreadsheets, and databases, which perform the tasks for which people use computers; network software, which enables groups of computers to communicate; and language software, which provides programmers with the tools they need to write programs.

SONET *See* Synchronous Optical Network (SONET).

spanning tree algorithm (STA) An algorithm (mathematical procedure) implemented to eliminate redundant routes and avoid situations in which multiple local area networks (LANs) are joined by more than one path by the IEEE 802.1 Network Management Committee. Under STA, bridges exchange certain control information in an attempt to find redundant routes. The bridges determine which would be the most efficient route, and then use that one and disable the others. Any of the disabled routes can be reactivated if the primary route becomes unavailable.

SQL *See* structured query language (SQL).

STA *See* spanning tree algorithm (STA).

stand-alone computer A computer that is not connected to any other computers and is not part of a network.

stand-alone environment A work environment in which each user has a personal computer but works independently, unable to share files and other important information that would be readily available through server access in a networking environment.

stealth virus A variant of file-infector virus. This virus is so named because it attempts to hide from detection. When an antivirus program attempts to find it, the stealth virus tries to intercept the probe and return false information indicating that it does not exist.

stripe set A form of fault tolerance that combines multiple areas of unformatted free space into one large logical drive, distributing data storage across all drives simultaneously. In Windows 2000, a stripe set requires at least two physical drives and can use up to 32 physical drives. Stripe sets can combine areas on different types of drives, such as Small Computer System Interface (SCSI), Enhanced Small Device Interface (ESDI), and Integrated Device Electronics (IDE) drives.

Structured Query Language A widely accepted standard database sublanguage used in querying, updating, and managing relational databases.

subnet A subdivision of an Internet Protocol (IP) network. Each subnet has its own unique subnetted network ID.

subnet mask A 32-bit value expressed as four decimal numbers from 0 to 255, separated by periods (for example, 255.255.255.0). This number allows TCP/IP to determine the network ID portion of an IP address.

Switched Multimegabit Data Services (SMDS) A high-speed, switched-packet service that can provide speeds of up to 34 Mbps.

switched virtual circuit (SVC) A logical connection between end computers that uses a specific route across the network. Network resources are dedicated to the circuit, and the route is maintained until the connection is terminated. These are also known as point-to-multipoint connections. *See also* virtual circuit.

symmetric multiprocessing (SMP) SMP systems, such as Windows 2000, use any available processor on an as-needed basis. With this approach, the system load and application needs can be distributed evenly across all available processors.

Synchronization Manager In Windows XP Professional, the tool used to ensure that a file or folder on a client computer contains the same data as a matching file or folder on a server.

Synchronous Data Link Control (SDLC) The data link (data transmission) protocol most widely used in networks conforming to IBM's Systems Network Architecture (SNA). SDLC is a communications guideline that defines the format in which information is transmitted. As its name implies, SDLC applies to synchronous transmissions. SDLC is also a bit-oriented protocol and organizes information in structured units called frames.

Synchronous Optical Network (SONET) A fiber-optic technology that can transmit data at more than one gigabit per second. Networks based on this technology are capable of delivering voice, data, and video. SONET is a standard for optical transport formulated by the Exchange Carriers Standards Association (ECSA) for the ANSI.

systemroot The path and folder name where the Windows XP Professional system files are located. Typically, this is C:\Windows, although a different drive or folder can be designated when Windows XP Professional is installed. The value of %systemroot% can be used to replace the actual location of the folder that contains the Windows XP Professional system files. To identify your systemroot folder, click Start, click Run, type **%systemroot%** and click OK.

T

TCO *See* total cost of ownership (TCO).

TCP *See* Transmission Control Protocol (TCP).

TCP/IP *See* Transmission Control Protocol/ Internet Protocol (TCP/IP).

TDI *See* transport driver interface (TDI).

Technet *See* Microsoft Technical Information Network (TechNet).

Telnet The command and program used to log on from one Internet site to another. The Telnet command and program brings the user to the logon prompt of another host.

terabyte *See* byte.

thread A type of object within a process that runs program instructions. Using multiple threads allows concurrent operations within a process and enables one process to run different parts of its program on different processors simultaneously.

throughput A measure of the data transfer rate through a component, connection, or system. In networking, throughput is a good indicator of the system's total performance because it defines how well the components work together to transfer data from one computer to another. In this case, the throughput would indicate how many bytes or packets the network could process per second.

topology The arrangement or layout of computers, cables, and other components on a network. Topology is the standard term that most network professionals use when referring to the network's basic design.

total cost of ownership (TCO) The total amount of money and time associated with purchasing computer hardware and software, and deploying, configuring, and maintaining the hardware and software. It includes hardware and software updates, training, maintenance and administration, and technical support. One other major factor is lost productivity caused by user errors, hardware problems, software upgrades, and retraining.

tracert A Trace Route command-line tool that shows every router interface through which a TCP/IP packet passes on its way to a destination.

trailer One of the three sections of a packet component. The exact content of the trailer varies depending on the protocol, but it usually includes an error-checking component (CRC).

Transmission Control Protocol (TCP) The TCP/IP protocol for sequenced data. *See also* Transmission Control Protocol/Internet Protocol (TCP/IP).

Transmission Control Protocol/Internet Protocol (TCP/IP) An industry standard suite of protocols providing communications in a heterogeneous environment. In addition, TCP/IP provides a routable, enterprise networking protocol and access to the Internet and its resources. It is a transport layer protocol that actually consists of several other protocols in a stack that operates at the session layer. Most networks support TCP/IP as a protocol.

transport driver interface (TDI) An interface that works between the file-system driver and the transport protocols, allowing any protocol written to TDI to communicate with the file-system drivers.

transport layer The fourth layer of the OSI reference model. It ensures that messages are delivered error free, in sequence, and without losses or duplications. This layer repackages messages for efficient transmission over the network. At the receiving end, the transport layer unpacks the messages, reassembles the original messages, and sends an acknowledgment of receipt. *See also* Open Systems Interconnection (OSI) reference model.

transport protocols Protocols that provide for communication sessions between computers and ensure that data is able to move reliably between computers.

tree A grouping of hierarchical arrangements of one or more Windows 2000 domains that share a contiguous namespace.

Trojan horse virus A type of virus that appears to be a legitimate program that might be found on any system. A Trojan horse virus can destroy files and cause physical damage to disks.

trust relationship Trust relationships are links between domains that enable pass-through authentication, in which a user has only one user account in one domain but can access the entire network. User accounts and global groups defined in a trusted domain can be given rights and resource permissions in a trusting domain even though those accounts do not exist in the trusting domain's database. A trusting domain honors the logon authentication of a trusted domain.

U

UDP *See* User Datagram Protocol (UDP).

Uniform Resource Locator (URL) Provides the hypertext links between documents on the World Wide Web (WWW). Every resource on the Internet has its own URL that specifies the server to access as well as the access method and the location. URLs can use various protocols including File Transfer Protocol (FTP) and Hypertext Transfer Protocol (HTTP).

uninterruptible power supply (UPS) A device connected between a computer or another piece of electronic equipment and a power source, such as an electrical outlet. The UPS ensures that the electrical flow to the computer is not interrupted because of a blackout and, in most cases, protects the computer against potentially damaging events such as power surges and brownouts. All UPS units are equipped with a battery and loss-of-power sensor. If the sensor detects a loss of power, it immediately switches to the battery so that users have time to save their work and shut off the computer. Most higher end models have features such as power filtering, sophisticated surge protection, and a serial port so that an operating system capable of communicating with a

UPS (such as Windows XP Professional) can work with the UPS to facilitate automatic system shutdown.

Universal Naming Convention (UNC) A convention for naming files and other resources beginning with two backslashes (\\), indicating that the resource exists on a network computer. UNC names conform to the \\Servername\Sharename syntax.

universal serial bus (USB) A serial bus with a data transfer rate of 12 megabits per second (Mbps) for connecting peripherals to a microcomputer. USB can connect up to 127 peripheral devices to the system through a single, general-purpose port. This is accomplished by daisy chaining peripherals together. USB is designed to support the ability to automatically add and configure new devices as well as the ability to add such devices without having to shut down and restart the system.

UPS *See* uninterruptible power supply (UPS).

URL *See* Uniform Resource Locator (URL).

USB *See* universal serial bus (USB).

user account Consists of all of the information that defines a user on a network. This includes the user name and password required for the user to log on, the groups in which the user account has membership, and the rights and permissions the user has for using the system and accessing its resources.

User Datagram Protocol (UDP) A connectionless protocol, responsible for end-to-end data transmission.

user groups Groups of users who meet online or in person to discuss installation, administration, and other network challenges for the purpose of sharing and drawing on each other's expertise in developing ideas and solutions.

V

virtual circuit A logical connection between two nodes on a packet-switching network; similar to leased lines that are permanent and virtual, except that with a virtual circuit, the customer pays only for the time the line is used. This type of connection service is gaining importance because both frame relay and ATM use it. *See also* packet switching, permanent virtual circuit.

virtual memory The space on one or more of a computer's hard drives used by Windows XP Professional as if it were random access memory (RAM). This space on the hard drives is known as a paging file. The benefit of virtual memory is being able to run more applications at one time than you would be able to using just the RAM (physical memory) on the computer.

virtual private network (VPN) A set of computers on a public network such as the Internet that communicate among themselves using encryption technology. In this way their messages are safe from being intercepted and understood by unauthorized users. VPNs operate as if the computers were connected by private lines.

virus Computer programming, or code, that hides in computer programs or on the boot sector of storage devices such as hard disk drives and floppy disk drives. The primary purpose of a virus is to reproduce itself as often as possible; a secondary purpose is to disrupt the operation of the computer or the program.

volume set A collection of hard-disk partitions that are treated as a single partition, thus increasing the disk space available in a single drive letter. Volume sets are created by combining between 2 and 32 areas of unformatted free space on one or more physical drives. These spaces form one large logical volume set that is treated like a single partition.

VPN *See* virtual private network (VPN).

W

wide area network (WAN) A computer network that uses long-range telecommunication links to connect networked computers across long distances.

workgroup A collection of computers grouped for sharing resources such as data and peripherals over a local area network (LAN). Each workgroup is identified by a unique name. *See also* domain, peer-to-peer network.

World Wide Web (the Web, WWW) The Internet multimedia service that contains a vast storehouse of hypertext documents written in Hypertext Markup Language (HTML). *See also* Hypertext Markup Language (HTML).

WORM *See* Write-Once Read-Many (WORM).

Write-Once Read-Many (WORM) Any type of storage medium to which data can be written only once but can be read any number of times. Typically, this is an optical disc whose surface is permanently etched using a laser to record information.

Z

zones A zone represents a discrete portion of the domain namespace. Zones provide a way to partition the domain namespace into discrete manageable sections.

Index

For the skills you need on the job. And on the MCP exam.

Learn by doing—learn for the job—with official MCSE TRAINING KITS. Whether you choose a book-and-CD Training Kit or the all-multimedia learning experience of an Online Training Kit, you'll gain hands-on experience building essential systems support skills—as you prepare for the corresponding MCP exam. It's official Microsoft self-paced training—how, when, and where you study best.

Readiness Reviews

Test your readiness for the MCSE exams

Ready
solutions
for the
IT administrator

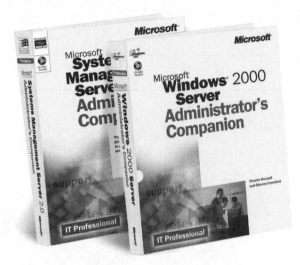

Keep your IT systems up and running with the ADMINISTRATOR'S COMPANION series from Microsoft. These expert guides serve as both tutorials and references for critical deployment and maintenance of Microsoft products and technologies. Packed with real-world expertise, hands-on numbered procedures, and handy workarounds, ADMINISTRATOR'S COMPANIONS deliver ready answers for on-the-job results.

Microsoft® SQL Server™ 2000 Administrator's Companion

U.S.A. $59.99
Canada $86.99
ISBN 0-7356-1051-7

Microsoft Exchange 2000 Server Administrator's Companion

U.S.A. $59.99
Canada $86.99
ISBN 0-7356-0938-1

Microsoft Windows® 2000 Server Administrator's Companion

U.S.A. $ 69.99
Canada $ 107.99
ISBN 1-57231-819-8

Microsoft Systems Management Server 2.0 Administrator's Companion

U.S.A. $59.99
Canada $92.99
ISBN 0-7356-0834-2

Microsoft Press® products are available worldwide wherever quality computer books are sold. For more information, contact your book or computer retailer, software reseller, or local Microsoft Sales Office, or visit our Web site at mspress.microsoft.com. To locate your nearest source for Microsoft Press products, or to order directly, call 1-800-MSPRESS in the United States (in Canada, call 1-800-268-2222).

Prices and availability dates are subject to change.

Microsoft®

mspress.microsoft.com

Practical, *portable* *guides for* **IT administrators**

For immediate answers that will help you administer Microsoft products efficiently, get ADMINISTRATOR'S POCKET CONSULTANTS. Ideal at the desk or on the go from workstation to workstation, these hands-on, fast-answers reference guides focus on what needs to be done in specific scenarios to support and manage mission-critical products.

Microsoft® Windows® 2000 Administrator's Pocket Consultant
ISBN 0-7356-0831-8

Microsoft Windows NT® Server 4.0 Administrator's Pocket Consultant
ISBN 0-7356-0574-2

Microsoft SQL Server™ 2000 Administrator's Pocket Consultant
ISBN 0-7356-1129-7

Microsoft Exchange 2000 Server Administrator's Pocket Consultant
ISBN 0-7356-0962-4

Microsoft Windows 2000 and IIS 5.0 Administrator's Pocket Consultant
ISBN 0-7356-1024-X

Microsoft Press® products are available worldwide wherever quality computer books are sold. For more information, contact your book or computer retailer, software reseller, or local Microsoft Sales Office, or visit our Web site at mspress.microsoft.com. To locate your nearest source for Microsoft Press products, or to order directly, call 1-800-MSPRESS in the United States (in Canada, call 1-800-268-2222).

Prices and availability dates are subject to change.

Microsoft®
mspress.microsoft.com

MICROSOFT LICENSE AGREEMENT
Book Companion CD

IMPORTANT—READ CAREFULLY: This Microsoft End-User License Agreement ("EULA") is a legal agreement between you (either an individual or an entity) and Microsoft Corporation for the Microsoft product identified above, which includes computer software and may include associated media, printed materials, and "online" or electronic documentation ("SOFTWARE PRODUCT"). Any component included within the SOFTWARE PRODUCT that is accompanied by a separate End-User License Agreement shall be governed by such agreement and not the terms set forth below. By installing, copying, or otherwise using the SOFTWARE PRODUCT, you agree to be bound by the terms of this EULA. If you do not agree to the terms of this EULA, you are not authorized to install, copy, or otherwise use the SOFTWARE PRODUCT; you may, however, return the SOFTWARE PRODUCT, along with all printed materials and other items that form a part of the Microsoft product that includes the SOFTWARE PRODUCT, to the place you obtained them for a full refund.

SOFTWARE PRODUCT LICENSE

The SOFTWARE PRODUCT is protected by United States copyright laws and international copyright treaties, as well as other intellectual property laws and treaties. The SOFTWARE PRODUCT is licensed, not sold.

1. **GRANT OF LICENSE.** This EULA grants you the following rights:

    a. **Software Product.** You may install and use one copy of the SOFTWARE PRODUCT on a single computer. The primary user of the computer on which the SOFTWARE PRODUCT is installed may make a second copy for his or her exclusive use on a portable computer.

    b. **Storage/Network Use.** You may also store or install a copy of the SOFTWARE PRODUCT on a storage device, such as a network server, used only to install or run the SOFTWARE PRODUCT on your other computers over an internal network; however, you must acquire and dedicate a license for each separate computer on which the SOFTWARE PRODUCT is installed or run from the storage device. A license for the SOFTWARE PRODUCT may not be shared or used concurrently on different computers.

    c. **License Pak.** If you have acquired this EULA in a Microsoft License Pak, you may make the number of additional copies of the computer software portion of the SOFTWARE PRODUCT authorized on the printed copy of this EULA, and you may use each copy in the manner specified above. You are also entitled to make a corresponding number of secondary copies for portable computer use as specified above.

    d. **Sample Code.** Solely with respect to portions, if any, of the SOFTWARE PRODUCT that are identified within the SOFTWARE PRODUCT as sample code (the "SAMPLE CODE"):

        i. **Use and Modification.** Microsoft grants you the right to use and modify the source code version of the SAMPLE CODE, *provided* you comply with subsection (d)(iii) below. You may not distribute the SAMPLE CODE, or any modified version of the SAMPLE CODE, in source code form.

        ii. **Redistributable Files.** Provided you comply with subsection (d)(iii) below, Microsoft grants you a nonexclusive, royalty-free right to reproduce and distribute the object code version of the SAMPLE CODE and of any modified SAMPLE CODE, other than SAMPLE CODE, or any modified version thereof, designated as not redistributable in the Readme file that forms a part of the SOFTWARE PRODUCT (the "Non-Redistributable Sample Code"). All SAMPLE CODE other than the Non-Redistributable Sample Code is collectively referred to as the "REDISTRIBUTABLES."

        iii. **Redistribution Requirements.** If you redistribute the REDISTRIBUTABLES, you agree to: (i) distribute the REDISTRIBUTABLES in object code form only in conjunction with and as a part of your software application product; (ii) not use Microsoft's name, logo, or trademarks to market your software application product; (iii) include a valid copyright notice on your software application product; (iv) indemnify, hold harmless, and defend Microsoft from and against any claims or lawsuits, including attorney's fees, that arise or result from the use or distribution of your software application product; and (v) not permit further distribution of the REDISTRIBUTABLES by your end user. Contact Microsoft for the applicable royalties due and other licensing terms for all other uses and/or distribution of the REDISTRIBUTABLES.

2. **DESCRIPTION OF OTHER RIGHTS AND LIMITATIONS.**

    - **Limitations on Reverse Engineering, Decompilation, and Disassembly.** You may not reverse engineer, decompile, or disassemble the SOFTWARE PRODUCT, except and only to the extent that such activity is expressly permitted by applicable law notwithstanding this limitation.

    - **Separation of Components.** The SOFTWARE PRODUCT is licensed as a single product. Its component parts may not be separated for use on more than one computer.

    - **Rental.** You may not rent, lease, or lend the SOFTWARE PRODUCT.

- **Support Services.** Microsoft may, but is not obligated to, provide you with support services related to the SOFTWARE PRODUCT ("Support Services"). Use of Support Services is governed by the Microsoft policies and programs described in the user manual, in "online" documentation, and/or in other Microsoft-provided materials. Any supplemental software code provided to you as part of the Support Services shall be considered part of the SOFTWARE PRODUCT and subject to the terms and conditions of this EULA. With respect to technical information you provide to Microsoft as part of the Support Services, Microsoft may use such information for its business purposes, including for product support and development. Microsoft will not utilize such technical information in a form that personally identifies you.

- **Software Transfer.** You may permanently transfer all of your rights under this EULA, provided you retain no copies, you transfer all of the SOFTWARE PRODUCT (including all component parts, the media and printed materials, any upgrades, this EULA, and, if applicable, the Certificate of Authenticity), **and** the recipient agrees to the terms of this EULA.

- **Termination.** Without prejudice to any other rights, Microsoft may terminate this EULA if you fail to comply with the terms and conditions of this EULA. In such event, you must destroy all copies of the SOFTWARE PRODUCT and all of its component parts.

3. **COPYRIGHT.** All title and copyrights in and to the SOFTWARE PRODUCT (including but not limited to any images, photographs, animations, video, audio, music, text, SAMPLE CODE, REDISTRIBUTABLES, and "applets" incorporated into the SOFTWARE PRODUCT) and any copies of the SOFTWARE PRODUCT are owned by Microsoft or its suppliers. The SOFT-WARE PRODUCT is protected by copyright laws and international treaty provisions. Therefore, you must treat the SOFTWARE PRODUCT like any other copyrighted material **except** that you may install the SOFTWARE PRODUCT on a single computer provided you keep the original solely for backup or archival purposes. You may not copy the printed materials accompanying the SOFTWARE PRODUCT.

4. **U.S. GOVERNMENT RESTRICTED RIGHTS.** The SOFTWARE PRODUCT and documentation are provided with RESTRICTED RIGHTS. Use, duplication, or disclosure by the Government is subject to restrictions as set forth in subparagraph (c)(1)(ii) of the Rights in Technical Data and Computer Software clause at DFARS 252.227-7013 or subparagraphs (c)(1) and (2) of the Commercial Computer Software—Restricted Rights at 48 CFR 52.227-19, as applicable. Manufacturer is Microsoft Corporation/One Microsoft Way/Redmond, WA 98052-6399.

5. **EXPORT RESTRICTIONS.** You agree that you will not export or re-export the SOFTWARE PRODUCT, any part thereof, or any process or service that is the direct product of the SOFTWARE PRODUCT (the foregoing collectively referred to as the "Restricted Components"), to any country, person, entity, or end user subject to U.S. export restrictions. You specifically agree not to export or re-export any of the Restricted Components (i) to any country to which the U.S. has embargoed or restricted the export of goods or services, which currently include, but are not necessarily limited to, Cuba, Iran, Iraq, Libya, North Korea, Sudan, and Syria, or to any national of any such country, wherever located, who intends to transmit or transport the Restricted Components back to such country; (ii) to any end user who you know or have reason to know will utilize the Restricted Components in the design, development, or production of nuclear, chemical, or biological weapons; or (iii) to any end user who has been prohibited from participating in U.S. export transactions by any federal agency of the U.S. government. You warrant and represent that neither the BXA nor any other U.S. federal agency has suspended, revoked, or denied your export privileges.

DISCLAIMER OF WARRANTY

NO WARRANTIES OR CONDITIONS. MICROSOFT EXPRESSLY DISCLAIMS ANY WARRANTY OR CONDITION FOR THE SOFTWARE PRODUCT. THE SOFTWARE PRODUCT AND ANY RELATED DOCUMENTATION ARE PROVIDED "AS IS" WITHOUT WARRANTY OR CONDITION OF ANY KIND, EITHER EXPRESS OR IMPLIED, INCLUDING, WITHOUT LIMITA-TION, THE IMPLIED WARRANTIES OF MERCHANTABILITY, FITNESS FOR A PARTICULAR PURPOSE, OR NONINFRINGEMENT. THE ENTIRE RISK ARISING OUT OF USE OR PERFORMANCE OF THE SOFTWARE PRODUCT REMAINS WITH YOU.

LIMITATION OF LIABILITY. TO THE MAXIMUM EXTENT PERMITTED BY APPLICABLE LAW, IN NO EVENT SHALL MICROSOFT OR ITS SUPPLIERS BE LIABLE FOR ANY SPECIAL, INCIDENTAL, INDIRECT, OR CONSEQUENTIAL DAM-AGES WHATSOEVER (INCLUDING, WITHOUT LIMITATION, DAMAGES FOR LOSS OF BUSINESS PROFITS, BUSINESS INTERRUPTION, LOSS OF BUSINESS INFORMATION, OR ANY OTHER PECUNIARY LOSS) ARISING OUT OF THE USE OF OR INABILITY TO USE THE SOFTWARE PRODUCT OR THE PROVISION OF OR FAILURE TO PROVIDE SUPPORT SERVICES, EVEN IF MICROSOFT HAS BEEN ADVISED OF THE POSSIBILITY OF SUCH DAMAGES. IN ANY CASE, MICROSOFT'S ENTIRE LIABILITY UNDER ANY PROVISION OF THIS EULA SHALL BE LIMITED TO THE GREATER OF THE AMOUNT ACTUALLY PAID BY YOU FOR THE SOFTWARE PRODUCT OR US$5.00; PROVIDED, HOWEVER, IF YOU HAVE ENTERED INTO A MICROSOFT SUPPORT SERVICES AGREEMENT, MICROSOFT'S ENTIRE LIABILITY REGARDING SUPPORT SERVICES SHALL BE GOVERNED BY THE TERMS OF THAT AGREEMENT. BECAUSE SOME STATES AND JURISDICTIONS DO NOT ALLOW THE EXCLUSION OR LIMITATION OF LIABILITY, THE ABOVE LIMITATION MAY NOT APPLY TO YOU.

MISCELLANEOUS

This EULA is governed by the laws of the State of Washington USA, except and only to the extent that applicable law mandates governing law of a different jurisdiction.

Should you have any questions concerning this EULA, or if you desire to contact Microsoft for any reason, please contact the Microsoft subsidiary serving your country, or write: Microsoft Sales Information Center/One Microsoft Way/Redmond, WA 98052-6399.

Get a **Free**
e-mail newsletter, updates,
special offers, links to related books,
and more when you

register on line!

Register your Microsoft Press® title on our Web site and you'll get a FREE subscription to our e-mail newsletter, *Microsoft Press Book Connections.* You'll find out about newly released and upcoming books and learning tools, online events, software downloads, special offers and coupons for Microsoft Press customers, and information about major Microsoft® product releases. You can also read useful additional information about all the titles we publish, such as detailed book descriptions, tables of contents and indexes, sample chapters, links to related books and book series, author biographies, and reviews by other customers.

Registration is easy. Just visit this Web page and fill in your information:

http://www.microsoft.com/mspress/register

Microsoft®

System Requirements

To get the most out of the *MCSE Training Kit—Microsoft Windows XP Professional* and the Supplemental Course Materials CD-ROM, you will need a computer equipped with the following minimum configuration:

- 233 megahertz (MHz) or equivalent Intel Pentium-compatible CPU

- 64 megabytes (MB) minimum memory (128 MB recommended)

- 1.5 GB hard disk space on a 2-GB hard disk minimum

- Microsoft Windows XP Professional on either a CD-ROM or a network share (a computer running Windows 2000 Server and configured as a domain controller is required for the optional practices)

- Network adapter card and related cable (hub or connection to an existing network is required for the optional practices)

- Video display adapter and monitor with Video Graphics Adapter (VGA) resolution or higher

- CD-ROM drive, 12× or faster recommended, (not required for installing Windows XP Professional over a network) or DVD drive

- Keyboard

- Microsoft Mouse or compatible pointing device